AMERICAN CATHOLICS
AND THE QUEST FOR EQUALITY
IN THE CIVIL WAR ERA

AMERICAN CATHOLICS

AND THE QUEST FOR

EQUALITY

+ IN THE +

CIVIL WAR ERA

Robert Emmett Curran

LOUISIANA STATE UNIVERSITY PRESS

BATON ROUGE

Published with the assistance of the V. Ray Cardozier Fund

Published by Louisiana State University Press
lsupress.org

Manufactured in the United States of America
First printing

DESIGNER: Barbara Neely Bourgoyne
TYPEFACE: Adobe Text Pro
PRINTER AND BINDER: Sheridan Books

JACKET PHOTOGRAPH: Roman Catholic Cathedral of St. John and St. Finbar,
Charleston, SC, destroyed in December 1861. *Library of Congress.*

Cataloging-in-Publication Data are available from the Library of Congress.

ISBN 978-0-8071-7930-7 (cloth: alk. paper)
ISBN 978-0-8071-7966-6 (pdf)
ISBN 978-0-8071-7965-9 (epub)

For Cyprian Davis, OSB, and all those
who have heeded Lincoln's call

CONTENTS

ACKNOWLEDGMENTS

This book has been more than a decade in the making. Over that span I have become indebted to many people who have abetted my research: Tricia Pyne, director of the Associated Archives of St. Mary's University and Seminary, and Alison Foley, associate archivist; Edward Papenfuse, director of the Baltimore City Archives; Connie Fitzgerald, OCD, archivist of the Baltimore Carmel; William Kevin Cawley, senior archivist, and his assistant, Joseph Smith, of the University of Notre Dame Archives; George Rugg, curator of the University of Notre Dame Special Collections; Timothy Meagher, director, and W. John Shepherd of the Catholic University of America Archives; Brendan Fahey, archivist of the Catholic Diocese of Charleston Archives, and his associate, Melissa Bronheim; Edie Jeter of the Diocese of Richmond Archives; Gillian M. Brown of the Catholic Diocese of Savannah Archives; Stephanie Brooks, Library Express leader, Eastern Kentucky University; Martha Jacob, OSU, of the Ursuline Sisters of Louisville Archives; Lynn Conway, archivist of Georgetown University; J. Leon Hooper, SJ, of the Woodstock Theological Library at Georgetown University. Grants from the Graduate School of Arts and Sciences of Georgetown University enabled me to take full advantage, on-site, of these key archives containing the records of the Catholic experience.

Special thanks to Robert Worden, William Kurtz, Connor Donnan, and James Johnston for making available important unpublished materials. Hugh Cloke, Drew Denton, Don H. Doyle, John Hirsh, Ronald Johnson, Michael Kazin, Joseph Mannard, Elizabeth McKeown, Suzanne Krebsack, James Scanlon, and Janice Sumner-Lewis all read portions of the manuscript and provided invaluable advice that made this a far better volume. The final draft benefited greatly from the critiques of the two anonymous readers at Louisiana State University Press. And Rand Dotson and Stan Ivester proved indispensable in shaping the manuscript for publication. One can only count one's blessings in having such an editor and copyeditor respectively.

But to no one do I owe more than to my wife, Eileen, who, for too many years, has borne the brunt of my concentration on this project. That debt one can never acknowledge sufficiently.

AMERICAN CATHOLICS
AND THE QUEST FOR EQUALITY
IN THE CIVIL WAR ERA

All Should Have an Equal Chance

On Washington's Birthday, 1861, Abraham Lincoln was nearing the end of his celebratory tour of northern cities on his way to Washington to become the nation's sixteenth president. Fittingly, he chose this date to make his appearance at Philadelphia's Independence Hall, the birthplace of the republic that was rapidly unraveling even as the president-elect prepared to take office. In remarks meant to be worthy of the unique venue in which he was speaking, Lincoln told the assemblage: "I have often inquired of myself, what great principle or idea it was that kept this Confederacy so long together. It was ... something in that Declaration giving liberty, not alone to the people of this country, but hope to the world for all future time. It was that which gave promise that in due time the weights should be lifted from the shoulders of all men, and that *all* should have an equal chance. This is the sentiment embodied in that Declaration of Independence."[1]

The nation to which the Declaration gave birth, Lincoln knew all too well, still fell well short of fulfilling its promise. The United States from its conception was a post-Edenic republic. When the Continental Congress had presented the Declaration of Independence to the world as its justification for rebellion, the British writer Samuel Johnson remarked that a bunch of slave drivers should be the last to yelp about freedom. Slavery was the nation's original sin, leaving its mark upon North and South, on slaveholder and non-slaveholder alike. Equality and freedom were, for far too many, observed in the breach.

By far, the worst lot was that of the bonded African Americans. But others fell far short of the American promise of the basic freedom and opportunity to achieve success, to know prosperity, to participate fully in the republican experiment. Jews and Catholics were two such groups. Even after the adoption of a federal constitution that barred religious tests, for many years they were still unable to exercise the full rights of citizenship in many of the new states.

They still carried the stigma of being outsiders in a country that, despite its Constitution, tended to equate nationality with Anglo-Saxon Protestant Christianity. Then there were the non-European newcomers to the country. The very first US Congress, in 1790, enacted a law that restricted naturalization to Caucasian immigrants. Asians, Africans, and all other peoples of color could have no thought of becoming citizens by coming to America. And then there were the indigenous peoples, with whom the government made treaties but treated as permanent wards to whom it had no binding obligations. Finally, there was the female half of the nation. Despite Abigail Adams's plea to her husband, John, to "remember the Ladies," the Founding Fathers had found no formal place for them in the republic they were creating. Whatever their status, the country's women had no more claim to being fully American than did the others outside the pale of full citizenship.

Six weeks after Lincoln's remarks at Independence Hall, the outbreak of war provided the president, and the nation, the opportunity, indeed the necessity, of advancing that promise of equal opportunity in a fundamental way. This book is the story of how one such marginal group, all too aware of its status in American society, grappled with momentous developments over three decades (1846–77) in pursuit of a promised equality that had never fully included its members.

Introduction

The triumph of the Protestant Reformation in England at the very beginning of the colonization of America by the island kingdom had dire consequences for English Catholics both at home and in British America. Protestant England's two great imperial rivals in the New World were the Catholic powers Spain and France. That reality made it all the more logical to consider English Catholics as internal aliens, especially since Catholics pledged religious allegiance to a pope who was not merely a spiritual leader but also the ruler of a state. That bred a chronic suspicion that Catholics could not become full citizens inasmuch as faith trumped nationality in determining their ultimate loyalty. Thus, most colonies, by law and/or practice, banned Catholics. In the few provinces that they were tolerated—Maryland, Pennsylvania, Rhode Island—law or custom relegated them to sub-citizenship status during most of the century and a half of the colonial era.[1]

That suspicion survived, even after Catholics gained citizenship in the new republic. Until the 1830s, Roman Catholics had had an insignificant presence in the United States, confined principally to the border states of Maryland, Kentucky, and Missouri. Within two decades, conversions and immigration from Catholic portions of Ireland and Germany had made Roman Catholicism the largest Christian denomination in the land, its adherents now concentrated in urban areas in the North.[2] That startling demographic change, plus a highly touted tour of the United States by a papal emissary, revitalized a Protestant-based nativism that became a major political force, in large part by depicting Catholics, with their conflicted loyalties, as clear and present dangers to the republic. In the political realignment that took place in the 1850s, Catholics became the backbone of the northern wing of a Democratic Party committed to immigration and slavery.

When the country's polarization over the slavery issue drove eleven southern states to secede from the Union, most Catholics opposed coercion as a means to preserve the nation, in part because of the conciliar tradition which privileged local over centralized rule. Nonetheless, by and large, Catholics aligned with their respective sections, seeing the war as an opportunity to prove their loyalty and to make progress toward the equality which had historically eluded them. Critical exceptions were those Catholics in the historic Catholic heartland in the border states. In Maryland, Kentucky, and Missouri, where the majority of its citizens remained, if somewhat reluctantly, loyal to the Union, the Catholic minority was overwhelmingly sympathetic toward, if not supportive of, the Confederacy. What united most white Catholics, both in the North and the South, was a commitment to slavery and the racial order it guaranteed.

For many northern Catholics, Abraham Lincoln's Emancipation Proclamation, in violating the property protections that the Constitution provided, delegitimized the war. It perverted the order that nature had established and Church teaching sanctioned. Within the Catholic community, descendants of refugees from the slave insurrection of the 1790s in Saint-Domingue fed fears of Lincoln's executive order leading to a new Haiti, but on a terrifyingly larger scale. Such anticipations reinforced a racism which regarded Blacks as threats to Catholics' economic, social, and political status. The few Catholic bishops and laity who defended emancipation tended to be ostracized, their publications boycotted.

Both defenders and opponents of emancipation sought to gain papal support for their positions. Bishop Martin Spalding's critique of Lincoln's proclamation made Roman authorities take a more sympathetic view toward the Confederacy but brought no gag order for American prelates, like John Purcell of Cincinnati, who had become advocates of emancipation. In late 1864, the Holy See, under pressure from certain American Catholics to take a stand on the issue of slavery, condemned chattel slavery as being incompatible with Christianity, but the finding was not made public.

Over the latter half of the war, Catholics increasingly denounced the tyrannical centralization of power and suppression of civil liberties to which the Lincoln administration resorted in its prosecution of the war, particularly through its emancipation policy. Resistance to the war by Catholics became more and more violent, culminating in the New York City riot of July 1863. Catholics became key members of the Sons of Liberty and other organizations which sought to force a peace settlement by whatever means necessary. Catholics, unsurprisingly, were an integral part of the conspiracy to kidnap President Lincoln, which morphed into the president's assassination. That complicity exacerbated charges of Catholic disloyalty from traditional critics. Despite that scar, northern Catholics felt that their overall war service which had cost them so dearly had very much burnished their image. The stage seemed set for a revival, with a much broader reach, of the conversions to Roman Catholicism that had marked the early decades of the nineteenth century in America.

Beyond that, from the sacrifices they had made on countless battlefields, Catholics could hope to have earned an unprecedented equality of place among their fellow citizens, which would enable them, at last, to consider America, as their first bishop, John Carroll, put it, a country they could "call their own." They were sharing in the liberating experience that victory had meant for the formerly bonded, and theoretically for all minorities, the new birth of freedom that Lincoln had promised at Gettysburg, the inclusion within the mainstream of American society of the many who, before the war, had been on its periphery or beyond.

With victory by the North there did come a certain remaking of the nation, or its "Reconstruction," as the national government's experiment in political, economic, and social revolution that began during the war itself came to be known. Three amendments to the Constitution spelled out the enlargement of the citizenry, a result of the expanded dimensions of freedom that the war had brought. This concluding phase of the Civil War that we know as Reconstruction settled how real and lasting the expansion of liberty and equality would be for anyone who previously had been on the underside of American life. Catholics were a vital part of this settlement, just as they had been central players in the war. White Catholics, particularly in the South, found a new acceptance, borne of their contributions toward the restoration of a variant of the old order in that region.

Meanwhile, Rome-centric forces within the American church were key to the creation of a web of institutions parallel to the larger society which increasingly set Catholics apart in the postwar era, even as they became major political players in both North and South—a kind of *Plessy v. Ferguson* arrangement for white Catholics.

When I began this study more than a decade ago, the only general works focusing on Catholics and the Civil War era were Benjamin J. Blied's path-setting *Catholics and the Civil War* (1945) and John McGreevy's magisterial *Catholicism and American Freedom: A History* (2003). Studies of the war involvement of various ethnic groups, particularly that of the Germans and the Irish, provided windows into the Catholic experience.[3] Over the past five years two books have changed the shape of the field in a major way: William B. Kurtz's *Excommunicated from the Union: How the Civil War Cre-*

ated a *Separate Catholic America* (2016); and Gracjan Kraszewski's *Catholic Confederates: Faith and Duty in the Civil War South* (2020). Kurtz limits his focus to Catholics in the North, including the border states. He argues that Catholics, failing in their attempts to use the war to prove their patriotism, found it and its aftermath to be a profoundly alienating experience that led to the establishment of the Catholic ghetto in America. Kraszewski's volume represents the first scholarly study of the overwhelming majority of white Catholics who found in the Confederacy a propitious opportunity to become full citizens. Neither deals directly with Reconstruction, but I have benefited greatly from both monographs.

This book, for the first time, provides a comprehensive history of the impact the developments from the Mexican-American War to the end of Reconstruction had upon the entire Catholic community, including Blacks and indigenous Americans. It explores the ways in which Catholics contributed to the testing of that fundamental proposition of equality set down by those who had created the republic. In the end the revolution that the war touched off remained unfinished, indeed was turned backward, in no small part by Catholics whose pursuit of equality was marred by a truncated vision of who deserved to share in its realization.

†

CHAPTER 1

The Mexican-American War
and Catholic Loyalty

*It will serve to destroy those calumnies of the enemies of
our Religion who for so long have been charging that Catholics . . .
are opposed to our form of government, that they are not faithful
subjects, that they always take the part of the enemy.*
—PETER VERHAEGEN, SJ, JUNE 1846

A CALL TO ARMS

"I wish to God it were in my power to make my voice heard in this vast assembly,"
James T. Brady, a local Democratic politician, shouted into the sea of humanity that was overflowing the park across from City Hall in lower Manhattan in
late May of 1846. Democratic mayor Andrew Mickle had called the meeting to
demonstrate support for the war with Mexico that President James Polk had
declared on May 11. By the time Brady, the fourth speaker on the program,
ascended the podium, war fever had totally possessed the estimated crowd of
fifty thousand. Brady immediately parlayed their raw emotion into unbridled
patriotism: "I came here, not to argue the question of war. It is enough for
me to know that war exists, and . . . American honor is to be vindicated. . . .
In this struggle there will be no distinction of class or country. The natives
of Ireland, and of Scotland, and of America, will go to battle together, and
fight shoulder to shoulder in defence of the honor of our common country."[1]

BISHOPS HEEDING
THE GOVERNMENT'S CALL

That very hour in which Brady was urging the New York crowd to take up
arms, whatever their ethnic origin, two hundred miles south, in Washington,
DC, Catholic bishops, including John Hughes of New York, were demon-

strating their patriotism in an unprecedented manner. For the first time in the history of the republic, American officials had summoned prelates of the Roman Catholic Church to the nation's capital. The occasion for the call was the same as that for the mass meeting in Manhattan: the war with Mexico.

President Polk had invited Hughes and two others who had gathered in Baltimore for the prelates' triennial council to come to Washington to discuss "some public affairs of importance." Hughes almost surely knew what "public affairs" the president had in mind. The war that the United States had just declared against a country whose official religion was Catholicism had become a topic of discussion during the council, and indeed had made its way, if obliquely, into the pastoral letter that the bishops released at the conclusion of their meeting. The prelates had reminded American Catholics that their obedience to the pope "is in no way inconsistent with your civil allegiance.... We have always taught you to render to Caesar the things that are Caesar's, to God the things that are God's." Allegiance to the Catholic faith was perfectly compatible with being faithful citizens.[2]

By the 1840s Catholics made up at least a third of the American Army, the vast majority of them Irish immigrants.[3] The Polk administration was seeking, for the first time, to appoint Catholic priests as chaplains for Catholic soldiers who often complained of facing religious discrimination. But Polk had more in mind than boosting the morale of the Catholics in the ranks of the regular army. He wanted priests, Spanish-speakers preferably, who could serve as good-will agents sending clear signals to the Mexicans that the United States was not promoting any kind of crusade against the religion of the Mexican people. The following day, Peter Verhaegen, the Jesuit regional superior, agreed to make two of his priests, John McElroy and Anthony Rey, available for government service.[4] Neither spoke Spanish, but Rey, a French immigrant, was fluent in several other languages. Verhaegen welcomed the unexpected appointments as providential. They would "destroy those calumnies of the enemies of our Religion," he wrote the superior general in Rome, "who for so long have been charging that Catholics and especially the Catholic clergy of the United States, are opposed to our form of government, that they are not faithful subjects."[5]

The government's reaching out to the Roman Catholic hierarchy for the appointment of chaplains for the American expeditionary force to Mexico predictably produced a widespread backlash. The schismatic priest, William Hogan, in a book he published in the following year, asked: "Does President Polk understand ... that each of those chaplains as well as each and every individual R.C. priest and Bishop in the US and elsewhere is bound by a solemn oath to hold no faith or give any allegiance to him as President of the United States; or to any president, king executive magistrate or otherwise who is not a Roman Catholic."[6] Nativists accused the Polk administration of cow-towing to papists to win their support, of giving them a recognition that amounted to state approval. The *Philadelphia Daily Sun* judged that, "If the President can recognize the Romish religion, he can *establish it.*"[7]

VOLUNTEERING AS A
DEMONSTRATION OF PATRIOTISM

President Polk, in his message to Congress, had called for 50,000 volunteers. All in all, the more than 112,000 who responded were overwhelmingly southern, native-born, and rural.[8] But among the urban volunteer companies, German and Irish Catholic immigrants dominated.[9] In Savannah the Irish company of Jasper Greens won the lottery to represent the city in the expeditionary force. As one of its members pleaded in a local paper before shipping out to Mexico: "When we return from the war . . . please God, would it be asking too much . . . to give up that old joke of the Catholic being opposed to liberty? . . . Nativism! Nativism . . . Hide thy head!"[10]

Catholic newspapers consistently pointed to the hundreds of Catholic immigrants serving among the volunteers as conclusive demonstrations of their patriotism. Tracking the war's development, the Catholic press lost no opportunity to highlight individual Catholic soldiers as well as Catholic units, distinguishing themselves by their service, which confirmed not only their loyalty, but a military competence that was equal to that of the native-born.

MONTERREY

In late August an American expeditionary force under General Zachary Taylor of fewer than seven thousand men marched out of Matamoros and headed 180 miles west to Monterrey, a city of ten thousand. In mid-September they reached the city, where they were joined by approximately one thousand volunteers from five states, including Kentucky, Maryland, and Ohio. Anthony Rey was with the army. John McElroy had remained behind to minister to the American garrison and the hospitalized.[11] On September 21 the Americans initiated their assault on Monterrey, a two-pronged attack on the lower town and the heights to the town's rear, where Colonel Thomas Childs had led infantry and artillery units, in a driving rainstorm, up the rocky hillside to Loma de Independencia, some seven hundred to eight hundred feet above the city.[12] Two days later, the Americans launched a two-front attack upon the city, from the heights to the northwest, and from the city's northeast section. House-to-house fighting ensued. Rey was in the midst of the action, ministering to the wounded and dying, as he made his way through the streets of Monterrey while the missiles crisscrossed the town.[13] The Mexican commander, General Pedro de Ampudia, fearing that the American artillery overlooking the city would explode the stockpile of ammunition he had had stored in the cathedral, proposed an armistice. The Americans would allow the Mexican Army to withdraw from the city with their small arms, six artillery pieces, two weeks' provisions, and an American promise to respect private property. Taylor, calculating that securing Monterrey by negotiation was far better than by further fighting, agreed.[14]

The peace that Taylor expected the armistice to produce did not materialize, as the Mexicans utilized the lull in the fighting, not to negotiate but to strengthen their forces to contest any further advance by the Americans. President Polk, furious with Taylor for agreeing to the armistice, stripped him of his command of the expeditionary force. In his place he named Winfield Scott and transferred four-fifths of Taylor's army to the new commander. With a new commander arriving, and the war continuing, Anthony Rey thought that these developments warranted a change in the chaplains' strategy as well. If Matamoros became more and more peripheral to the war effort, as the US expeditionary force drove deeper into Mexico, didn't it make sense for John McElroy to relocate to Monterrey, which was becoming more and more the center of the American operation? As for Rey, he was prepared to go with the army, wherever that might be. The younger Jesuit had not forgotten the president's concern that they serve as good-will ambassadors for the United States. He informed McElroy that his Spanish was improving substantially. "I can now make myself understood tolerably well in Spanish, and can understand nearly everything said to me. . . . I find this a great advantage."[15]

A CHANGING MISSION
AND AN ABORTED JOURNEY

As the war fronts multiplied with General Winfield Scott's arrival, it became clearer to Rey that they needed more priests. The Jesuits' efforts to secure Spanish-speaking priests from southern dioceses proved fruitless. With no hope of additional assistance, Rey repeated his proposal that they become itinerants in their ministry to meet the increasingly dispersed military population. Rey still saw himself bound to the president's directive that they do all they could to convey the impression that the United States was not at war with the Catholic Church. His experience in dealing with the local Church had bolstered his confidence about fulfilling their charge. When he had gone to present himself to the local pastor in Saltillo, the pastor had cordially invited him to make Saltillo his base and had promised to minister to the hospitalized Americans in Rey's absence. The swelling congregation of American soldiers and local Mexicans at the high Mass which Rey celebrated, with the pastor and his curate participating, was a testament to the possibilities for peace and reconciliation.[16]

With an effective monopoly on ministry, at least in Taylor's army, the two priests found a harvest of converts, especially among the unchurched. Given the youth and southern origins of so large a portion of the volunteers, most of those growing up in evangelical circles would by doctrine or custom not have been baptized. The near certainty of death for the perilously infected or gravely wounded was a strong incentive to take advantage of all the spiritual aid the Church could render in one's final hours, even if the ministers were dreaded papists. Over his ten months at Matamoros, McElroy instructed and baptized eighty-four soldiers, almost all of whom were on their deathbeds.

Ultimately, for John McElroy, loyalty to country did not compel one to put himself in harm's way to promote, however indirectly, the notion that the American expeditionary force was one that the Mexican people had no reason to fear, much less resist. Even in Matamoros, the town-bound Jesuit could sense the growing opposition of the natives. As the guerrilla insurgency spread in the winter of 1846–47, McElroy had a better grasp of the broader ethno-social developments than did the more mobile but less experienced Rey. McElroy wrote to Anthony Rey in mid-December 1846: "they seem to increase in hostility, day by day, towards all Americans," including chaplains. "Our Lord," he had concluded, "had other views than those of the President in sending us here." Everything indicated that Matamoros would continue to be a staging area and medical hub for the army. There were the fifty Catholics among the garrison troops; there were the sixty Catholic wives of soldiers; there was the hundred English-speaking local Catholics; the hospital population was at three hundred and growing by the day: Clearly here he could better achieve the greater good than anywhere else he could station himself.[17]

In mid-January, Rey wrote McElroy that he intended to get to Matamoras by January 24, at the latest, in order to consult with him. For the rest of the month, McElroy awaited Rey's arrival. When January passed into February with no further word from Rey, McElroy began to make inquiries. He learned that Mexican guerrillas had attacked several army wagon-trains, including one in which Rey reportedly had been. Then came the confirmation of his worst fear: that Rey, apparently confident, from his many contacts with the locals, of his safety in hostile territory, had ignored warnings and started out with only his orderly on their way toward Matamoros. Near Marine, some twenty-five miles from Monterrey, a band of irregulars had taken them prisoner and proceeded to kill Rey's army companion. Rey they immediately recognized as a priest and hesitated to kill him as well. They put the decision to one of their party who happened to be the sacristan of the local church. He feared that, if they let the priest survive, Rey would be able to identify them as the killers of the American soldier. That fear cost Rey his life.[18] In early May 1847 John McElroy returned to Washington.

THE RISE OF
MEXICAN PATRIOTISM

The growing Mexican hostility, which had cost Rey his life, reflected an emerging patriotism that regarded American expansionism, beginning with the annexation of Texas and culminating in Taylor's invasion, as a mortal threat to national sovereignty and the national religion.[19] Observers of the Catholic Church in Mexico may have lamented the spiritual ennui which characterized much of the hierarchy and clergy, but they still were a powerful influence upon the people. As Peter Guardino makes clear in his comprehensive study of the war, the church pervaded Mexican culture, from its feast days dominating the calendar to its spires and bell towers shaping the sky- and sound-lines of cities and villages. Catholicism, in all its ancient ways, cast a sacred ambiance over the Mexican landscape. The Mexican clergy were divided between those urging resistance to the invaders and those seeking a peaceful settlement to the conflict. But the militant faction prevailed in shaping opinion. Our Lady of Guadalupe, being at the center of Mexican devotional life, became the perfect patron of the country's religious-fueled patriotism. Promoters of resistance were quick to utilize her image on banners in rallying the nation behind the war effort.[20]

In mid-February, the Mexican commander, Santa Anna, decided to attack Taylor's depleted army before it could link up with Scott's on the coast. On February 22, near a hacienda named Buena Vista, the Mexicans struck. The Americans, outnumbered three to one, managed barely to hold their line throughout a day of assaults. John Paul Jones O'Brien, the Philadelphia native of immigrant parents, commanded a battery of artillery that kept the Mexicans from achieving a fatal breakthrough.[21] Despite O'Brien's heroics, few thought that Taylor's army could survive a second day of such assaults. They were saved by the unprecedentedly severe winter and the lack of food which forced Santa to order a retreat, despite being on the brink of victory. That decision not only allowed the Americans to escape what many expected to be a crushing defeat, but the Mexicans' subsequent retreat to San Luis Potosi proved to be disastrous, as the unforgiving winter weather stripped the army, through deaths and desertions, of more men than they had lost at Buena Vista.[22]

WINFIELD SCOTT
AND A SECOND FRONT

Having occupied Veracruz, after a massive three-day land-sea bombardment that reduced much of the port city of sixty-five hundred to rubble and killed hundreds, mostly civilians, Winfield Scott, in April 1847, set his army westward toward Mexico City. Fifty miles out of Veracruz, they encountered Santa Anna's army, occupying the hills of Cerro Gordo, which commanded the ravine through which the National Road to the capital passed. Captain Pierre Gustave Toutant Beauregard, a West Point graduate, led a reconnaissance around the Mexican Army's position between high ridges and a river that brought the team well behind Santa Anna's line. Beauregard subsequently fell ill, which forced General Scott to have another West Point graduate, Robert E. Lee, follow up on the scouting that Beauregard had begun. Lee found a path through which the Americans could flank the Mexicans and block their retreat.

With Beauregard and Lee's information, Scott conceived a three-pronged attack, combining flanking moves and a direct assault, to be executed simultaneously. Catholics William Harney and James Shields led two of the three divisions. When the division leaders failed to coordinate their attacks, the enemy's lines held. Then Lieutenant Colonel Harney's attacking troops, aided by artillery, managed to make their way under fire up the steep slope commanding a side of the ravine to overrun the Mexican breastworks on the summit. Shields's division, following the flanking path discovered by Lee, turned the tide, getting in the Mexicans' rear to obstruct any Mexican retreat. Shields led the chase of a Mexican battery, when suddenly the battery wheeled to level a grapeshot volley, some of which found Shields's right lung. After three hours, the Mexicans were in full flight. Mexican casualties (twelve hundred) were triple that which the Americans suffered. About six thousand demoralized and scattered Mexicans eluded Shields's trap to fight another day.[23]

Surgeons pronounced James Shields a "goner," with his badly pierced lung. It fell to a French doctor in the employ of the Mexican government to mount a handkerchief on a ramrod and force it into the wound, thereby providing some primitive sterilization that allowed Shields not only to recover, but to play a highly active role in the remainder of the campaign.[24] Among those breveted to brigadier general for bravery at Cerro Gordo was Colonel Bennet Riley, a native of St. Mary's County in Maryland, the ancient seat of Catholic America.

DESERTION AND
THE SAN PATRICIOS

Some ninety-two hundred Americans deserted during the war, regulars accounting for most of them.[25] Early in the war the Philadelphia *Sun* warned that foreign-born soldiers, especially the Irish Catholics, would take the first opportunity to go over to the Mexicans. Catholic newspapers were quick to deny such a claim. The *Pilot* even printed statistics showing that the typical deserter was a native-born Protestant.[26] John C. Pinheiro found that the native-born constituted the majority of deserters; religion played no part in their decisions to abandon the army. They likely were not Catholic.[27] The hundreds who deserted typically turned themselves over to Mexican authorities, who were offering 320 acres to all American soldiers who became Mexican citizens.[28] Some gave as their reason their repugnance at fighting fellow Catholics.[29]

The most notorious group of deserters became part of the San Patricio Battalion, organized by a native Irelander, John Riley. Riley was a two-time deserter, first from the British Army in Canada somewhere around 1843, then from the US Army, which he joined in 1845 only to defect seven months later, in April 1846, from Taylor's force on the Rio Grande. Riley justified his leave-taking by comparing the United States' occupation of Mexico with England's occupation of Ireland. In both instances, Anglo-Saxon Protestants were subjugating Catholics they considered inferior.[30] Riley subsequently organized the San Patricios and personally recruited more than 150 others, mostly fellow Irish in the US Army.[31] By July of 1847, the San Patricios counted more than 200 in their ranks. They continued to add deserters to their battalion throughout the war.

Riley's second-in-command was another Irish deserter, Patrick Dalton. In all, the Irish or Irish Americans accounted for more than 60 percent of the

Patricios. All were privates in the US Army. According to the battalion's biographer, few of the San Patricios shared Riley's linkage of the United States' invasion with the British occupation of Ireland. Robert Miller found that they defected for a grab bag of reasons: liquor, dalliances, escape from brutal discipline, poor health, the promise of land for a year's service in the Mexican Army, and the availability of Catholic ministry in an American Army that, except for McElroy and Rey's relatively brief interlude, largely lacked it.[32] Another historian, Kerby Miller, argues that the deserters saw a continuum between their brutal treatment by the British in Ireland and the discrimination they experienced at the hands of nativist officers in the army. He also sees in their desertions a protest against the injustice of the war being waged against a Catholic country.[33] Whatever their motivation, the San Patricios became one of Mexico's ablest units throughout the war.

INSURGENCY

To prevent the conflict from morphing into a religious war, Polk had not only secured Catholic chaplains, but also had the War Department order US soldiers to strictly respect the state religion's holy places. That, however, required an expeditionary force that was disciplined. US volunteers were notoriously undisciplined, as they displayed from their first days at Matamoros, despite Zachary Taylor's threats to court-martial and dishonorably discharge those abusing Mexicans and their sacred places.[34] The anti-Catholic animus that so many US volunteers carried with them into Mexico, abetted by recruiters' promises of plunder to be garnered from churches and other Catholic institutions, led to vandalism and outrages against the Mexican Church and populace. Two weeks after the first volunteers arrived, Lieutenant George Meade reported that they were behaving "more like a body of hostile Indians than of civilized whites. . . . The consequence is that they are exciting a feeling among the people which will induce them to rise up en masse."[35]

Meade was spot on in both of his observations. The American volunteers were displaying the same criminal behavior that the Comanches had become notorious for in their chronic terrorizing of the region. Mexicans had engaged in guerrilla warfare in response to their Indian abusers. And so they turned, as early as the summer of 1846, to the same tactics of targeted retaliation against these "Comanches of the North" (as they called the Americans). Anthony Rey had been one of their victims. By the late winter of 1847 guerrilla warfare was peaking, now strengthened by army cavalry units who assisted the guerrillas in cutting American supply lines. That resistance led President Polk to reiterate, in his December 1847 annual message to Congress, that the war had nothing to do with the religion of the Mexican people, pointing out that he had taken every step to ensure that Church property and all things Catholic would be respected by the occupying troops.[36] No general worked harder to prevent atrocities from feeding guerrilla resistance than did Winfield Scott, who went out of his way to punish those responsible for atrocities, to scrupulously pay for damages, to do everything possible to respect the Catholic religion, including attending Catholic Masses and other liturgical events.[37] Also notable in attempting to thwart American atrocities was Colonel Thomas Childs, whom the City Council of Puebla cited for his efforts.[38]

Nonetheless, by the summer of 1847, atrocities persisted, as did guerrilla resistance. Guerrillas were so effective in disrupting supply lines and harassing Scott's troops that many Mexicans began to think that the war was indeed winnable. But the more success that the guerrillas enjoyed, the more the larger community paid the price for that success.[39] Scott issued orders for the implementation of a guerrilla policy that established military commissions to try Mexicans suspected of guerrilla involvement, fined or seized the property of those found to support guerrillas, and held entire villages responsible for the depredations carried out by individuals.[40]

Despite American victories at Veracruz and Cerra Gordo, opposition to the war grew steadily back in the states. The US press began to report the crimes and outrages committed by volunteers against civilians. With many American reporters traveling with Scott's army, the bombardment of Veracruz became the most publicized battle of the war, bringing to the American public the terrible carnage inflicted on Mexican civilians. News of fresh American atrocities as well as of the persistent guerrilla activity ate away at any unified support for Mr. Polk's war.[41] Opponents of the war, citing the anti-Catholicism that it had festered, appealed to American Catholics to put church over the Democratic Party which so many Catholics traditionally supported. Even the Catholic press, which had largely welcomed the war as a golden opportunity for Catholics to prove their bona fides as Americans, wearied of a war that had lasted so much longer than had been promised in the spring of 1846 and had brought so much destruction to Catholic Mexico. The *Freeman's Journal* spoke for Catholic editors when it complained in late June 1847 that the war had become little more than an exercise in Protestant propaganda "at the point of the bayonet."[42] The report in May 1847 that the US government was considering confiscating church property in Mexico brought swift condemnation from the Catholic press.[43] The *Freeman's Journal* accused the Trinity Land Company, which had claimed Mexico owed it more than $42.5 million, of being behind the expropriation push.[44]

ON TO MEXICO CITY

On May 15, 1847, Winfield Scott marched his six-thousand-strong army into Puebla, the second largest city in Mexico, with its eighty thousand inhabitants. The level of guerrilla activity as well as the lack of troops kept Scott's army in Pueblo for several months in the late spring and summer of 1847. With reinforcements bringing his effectives to more than ten thousand, Winfield Scott marched his army out of Pueblo on August 7, 1847. It would live off of the country until it reached Mexico City, ninety-three miles to the west.[45] As Scott's army approached the capital, Mexican propagandists reinforced the popular will to resist by planting the fear that any American occupation of the city would bring on a massive scale the looting, rape, and other forms of blood lust that they had come to know all too well in encountering the Americans.[46] Propaganda, in the name of the Irish deserters, was also targeting the Irish Catholics in Scott's army. "My countrymen, Irishmen! . . . for that love of liberty for which our common country is so long contending, for the sake of that holy religion which we have for ages professed, . . . abandon a slavish hireling's life with a nation who . . . treats you with contumely & disgrace."[47] In place of the discrimination Catholic Americans experienced within the US Army as a despised religious and ethnic minority, Mexico was offering equality and no unfair slave-labor competition.

On August 20, at Churubusco, near the Franciscan monastery of San Mateo, the Mexican rear guard held off the Americans for several hours, allowing the main portion of Santa Ana's army to reach Mexico City safely. Futile assaults were the price the Americans paid. Riley's brigade joined the attack on the American right but lost its momentum when his men got swallowed up in the cornfields. The Americans were encountering something they had rarely, if ever seen: a Mexican force in a superb position putting up a tenacious defense. For once the Mexican artillery outperformed their American counterpart. Shields's brigade lost a third of its effectives in the battle. Hand-to-hand combat marked the fierce struggle around and within the monastery walls. Among the most intrepid defenders were some two hundred and sixty San Patricios, barricaded in the steeple of the monastery. Knowing that their capture almost surely was their death sentence, the battalion of deserters persisted in extending the fighting, long after their Mexican fellow soldiers were ready to raise the white flag.

Finally, the Americans found a soft spot in the defense on the southern end of the monastery. A regiment scaled the parapet, forcing the defenders in that area, including the San Patricios, to the interior of the building. The battle raged on until, at last, one of the Patricios raised a white handkerchief, which gave the Mexicans the excuse to put down their weapons. At the end of a day of intense fighting, both sides counted heavy casualties: the Mexican forces had ten thousand fewer soldiers, a third of their strength. Scott's much smaller force of eighty-five hundred had been decimated. But the way to the capital now lay open.[48]

Undecided as to what avenue of attack to take on the city, Scott once more sent Beauregard and Lee out on reconnaissance. The latter recommended an assault from the south. Beauregard favored an attack from the west, against the Molino del Rey buildings in the walled park of Chapultepec, where the Mexicans had constructed earthworks anchored by massive stone structures. His counterintuitive argument of feinting from the south, then attacking the Mexicans' stronghold at daybreak, won Scott's approval. The battle for Chapultepec lasted for ten days. During the final assault on September 13, the Irish-born Colonel Timothy Patrick Andrews led the Ninth and Fifteenth infantries through the swamp onto the western edge of the grove. James Shields and Lt. Col. J. W. Geary led New York and Pennsylvania regiments in flanking the Mexican defenses to provide an opening for the rest of the division. They navigated the mined field safely and reached the walls of the fortress, which they scaled with ladders, thus breaching the well-laid defenses of Mexico City. Both Shields and Geary were wounded in the action.[49] John Howard of the Maryland Volunteers was among those successfully scaling the walls at Chapultepec.[50] James Longstreet, carrying the regimental flag of the US Eighth Infantry, was hit in the thigh as he charged up the hill toward the wall. He passed it on to George Pickett, who took it over the wall with him.[51] Beauregard rallied Joe Johnston's troops by seizing a rifle, then mounting the parapet of Chapultepec, just behind the first unit to scale it. He had vowed to tear down the Mexican flag waving over the citadel but was greatly disappointed to find another captain had preempted his feat. By evening, a mud-covered Beauregard was in the Grand Plaza of the city, celebrating the war's end as the bells of the cathedral struck seven.[52]

Chapultepec was a Pyrrhic victory for the Americans, who suffered more than 700 casualties, including 116 killed, in a reckless attack against entrenchments, without any prior artillery bombardment or support during the charge. The Catholic press noted that Irish volunteers had played an important role in the capture of Mexico City, pointing in particular to those in the Second New York, the First and Second Pennsylvania, and the Palmetto Regiment of South Carolina.[53] In the fighting around the capital the Second New York had suffered the highest casualties of any American unit during the war. The Valley of Mexico campaign had ended in an American triumph, but one that had cost Scott more than a quarter of his army.[54]

CONSEQUENCES

Among the nearly thirteen hundred Mexican prisoners taken at Churubusco were the surviving San Patricios. Colonel Bennet Riley presided over one of the two courts-martial that tried the seventy-two San Patricios for desertion in the weeks following the climactic battle. Forty-nine of them were sentenced to hang.[55] There were two mass hangings, the larger of which Colonel William Selby Harney orchestrated in s particularly sadistic manner. Harney ordered that it coincide with the assault on Chapultepec Castle some two miles distant from the place of hanging. Those to be executed were to remain in position with nooses around their necks until the American flag was raised above the castle. They waited several agonizing hours before the sight of the raised flag finally brought the order to spring the trap door.[56]

Winfield Scott's successful campaign had fed James Polk's appetite for Mexican territory. Some in his cabinet, including James Buchanan, were pressing for all of it. At the same time, nativist sources persisted in accusing the president of conspiring with Catholic authorities to augment the Roman Catholic population by the annexation of much of Mexico. When John Hughes was invited to preach to Congress in December 1847, speculation grew that the New York prelate was shortly to replace Nicholas Trist, the US commissioner dispatched to negotiate the peace. Such an appointment seemed more likely in the wake of Polk's appointment of a US minister to the Papal States in 1848.[57] The president justified the ministry as a promoter of America's economic interests in Europe as well as an encouragement to the new pontiff, Pius IX, to expand the liberal policies he had begun implementing in his temporal realm.[58] Opponents of any such US representation to the Holy See saw it as abetting the papist plot to subvert American republicanism.[59]

In Mexico, Winfield Scott and Nicholas Trist had a very different perspective than Polk and his cabinet had about peace prospects. To Scott and Trist, the formidable guerrilla activity as well as the racial character of the Mexicans very much weighed against any annexation of Mexico in its entirety. The only way the United States could do so was to commit to a permanent army of occupation. To both men, this was far too high a price to pay. Trist determined to make a treaty that would dismember Mexico to the least degree possible.[60] The Mexican negotiators, conscious of the virulent anti-Catholicism in America, insisted that the treaty contain specific protections for Catholics in the newly acquired territory. Thus Article IX guaranteed that Catholic priests would be free to practice their ministry, that Catholic property would be respected, and that Mexican bishops would not be restricted in their dealings with the priests in the region.[61] To Polk's dismay, with antiwar Whigs now in control of Congress, he had little choice but to scale back his territorial aspirations and submit Trist's treaty to the Senate for ratification.[62] As Amy Greenberg concludes: "It was not the most generous treaty Trist could have negotiated, but it was perhaps the most generous the president would accept."[63]

The Mexican-American War made the United States the master of the North American continent. The American flag now flew from the Great Lakes to the Rio Grande and Baja California, from the Atlantic to the Pacific. Within two years the United States had increased its territory by a third. The official boundaries of the American Catholic community expanded accordingly. In the Oregon Territory, the Holy See had created an archdiocese even before it was determined under whose sovereignty the territory would fall. François Blanchet became the first ordinary in an area with precious few Catholics, but with a strong tradition of anti-Catholicism. The institutional church in the New Mexico territory had long suffered from neglect, first of the Spanish, then the Mexicans. Shortly after a Frenchman, John B. Lamy, was appointed bishop in 1851, the delegate from that territory, a Roman Catholic priest, José Manuel Gallegos, challenged Lamy's authority in Congress. Lamy, according to Gallegos, was destroying the Catholic Church in New Mexico by imposing his alien Gallican standards on the local religious culture. A New Mexico businessman, Miguel A. Otero, testified that the new bishop was merely carrying out long overdue reforms against an immoral clergy. Moreover, Otero charged Gallegos with having secured his office through election fraud. The House subsequently not only heeded the treaty provision in supporting episcopal authority but ousted Gallegos in favor of Otero. Lamy gradually replaced the clergy he inherited with priests from Europe and the eastern United States. He also brought in male and female religious to provide for the educational and social needs of his people. The official church may have failed to enculturate in New Mexico but, through Lamy's zeal and adept organizing, it revitalized institutionally and spiritually.[64]

In California, the new bishop was a Catalan Dominican, Joseph Sadoc Alemany. He estimated his new see contained some 40,000 Catholics amid a highly transient and rapidly growing population of some 200,000. He had three colleges, and two academies for girls, one run by the Dominicans in Monterrey; and Notre Dame at San Jose, operated by the Sisters of Notre Dame de Namur. The diocese was plagued with the racist crusades of Irish miners to drive Hispanics out of the gold fields. Vigilante groups served as enforcers of a social order in which the proper place for people of color was at the bottom.[65]

Winfield Scott, who had exhibited nativist tendencies before the war, confessed in later years how the war had changed his thinking: "I can say the Irish, the Swiss, the French, the Britons and other adopted citizens, fought in the same ranks, under the same colors, side-by-side with native born citizens, exhibiting like courage and efficiency. . . . all proved themselves the faithful sons of our beloved country."[66] In James Shields the war created the first Catholic military hero since the Revolutionary War.[67] He returned from Mexico to embark on a nationwide tour celebrating his gallantry. Shields quickly reaped the political spoils that military fame brought in the nineteenth century. The Illinois legislature elected him to the US Senate in 1848. Some among his Irish colleagues regretted that his immigrant status deprived him of the opportunity of becoming a presidential candidate, as Zachary Taylor had become.

Despite Scott's change of heart and Shields's success, Tyler V. Johnson contends that the Mexican-American war, unlike most American wars, did not bring about any ethno-religious détente, but rather intensified, at least in the eyes of many Catholics, the nativist animus.[68] The total victory that the American expeditionary force achieved in Mexico was convincing proof, for American evangelicals, of the providential expansion of the "Protestant Empire" at the cost of a despotic Catholic power. This republican triumph, they were sure, was of a piece with the European Revolutions of 1848 that were dethroning monarchial Catholic governments. As Pinheiro notes, "Expansionist ambitions during the war combined almost effortlessly with American suspicions that the Catholic Church, having already impeded Mexico's economic, social, political, and religious progress, aspired to do the same to the United States."[69] As William Kurtz concludes, "the war had little positive impact on tolerance for Catholicism in American society."[70] To say nothing of equality.

†

CHAPTER 2

The Remaking of
the Catholic Community and
Nativist Backlash

This election has demonstrated that by a majority,
Roman Catholicism is feared more than American slavery.
—J. W. TAYLOR, NOVEMBER 11, 1854

THE SHIFTING CENTER OF
CATHOLIC AMERICA

Over the course of two decades, from 1840 to 1860, there was a seismic change in the demographics of Catholic America. By the 1850s Catholics were no longer a tiny, seemingly genteel community easily absorbed into the larger society. From the thirty thousand or so Catholics in the new republic of the 1780s, within six decades the Roman Catholic Church had become the largest denomination in the United States, with more than three million adherents. By the eve of the Civil War, Catholics made up nearly a ninth of the population.

Obviously, natural growth alone could not explain this stunning development. New territories acquired from the Mexican-American War added scores of thousands to the US Catholic population. In the fifteen years before the Civil War, an estimated sixty thousand Americans converted to Roman Catholicism. The two groups most susceptible to conversion were those at the extremes of the American Protestant spectrum: Episcopalians and Unitarians. The former denomination was experiencing the full impact of the transatlantic Oxford Movement that was shaking the Anglican tradition to its core in its quest to recover its more Catholic elements. That movement precipitated a substantial exodus from the Episcopal Church to Roman Catholicism that swept up seminarians at New York City's General Theological

Seminary like James McMaster; ordained members, including a bishop; and West Point cadets, such as William Rosecrans and Amiel Whipple.

Those converts associated with the Protestant liberal tradition, such as Orestes Brownson and Isaac Hecker, were drawn to Rome because of its assertion of unifying authority against a Protestant-cultivated self-sovereignty, which inevitably produced the centrifugal forces creating an ever more divided religious landscape in America. Hecker, who was ordained as a Redemptorist in 1849, founded in 1858 the Missionary Society of St. Paul the Apostle (Paulists), a religious congregation of converts dedicated, in part, to the conversion of America to the Catholic Faith, convinced that religious unity alone held the key to the United States realizing its promise.

Upon no group did the Catholic Church in America expend more personnel and energy on converting than indigenous Americans. When the US government brought a band of Jesuits, including Pierre-Jean De Smet, to Missouri in 1823 to operate a boarding school for Indians, it marked the renewal in the Plains and Mountain West of the United States the commitment of the Catholic Church to evangelize the indigenous peoples.[1] From his early days working among the Rocky Mountain tribes, De Smet accomplished conversions on a Xaverian scale. But De Smet also came to epitomize in the American West the Jesuit tradition of acculturating Christianity to the host societies they hoped to convert. No one came to have more influence, not only with Native Americans, but with government officials, both the politicians in Washington and the Indian agents and military in the West.

But immigration was, by far, the key element in the quantum leap in the Catholic presence during the late antebellum era. Nearly three million immigrants arrived in the decade from 1845 to 1855, more than the country had recorded over the previous seventy years. In sharp contrast to earlier waves of immigration, the majority of the newcomers, perhaps as many as two-thirds, were Roman Catholics. By the late 1850s, immigrants comprised nearly 15 percent of the population, a proportion far above anything the nation had seen before. Over 86 percent of the immigrants settled in the North, most in urban areas. By the mid-1850s, immigrants, in cities from New York to Milwaukee, were threatening to become a majority, or had already become one.[2] Urban immigration in the South was largely a feature of cities in the border area that had been the Catholic heartland, as well as of the port cities from Richmond to New Orleans. In all these places, Catholics made up a majority of immigrants, who ranged from 15 to 30 percent of the municipal populations.[3]

Ireland was the primary source of immigration. Of some 5 million people who came to the United States in the three decades before the Civil War, nearly 40 percent were Irish.[4] By 1860, there were more than 1.6 million Irish immigrants in America. Over 90 percent of these Irish newcomers were Catholics. The Irish-born made up more than a quarter of the populations of New York City and Boston.[5] As Hasia Diner notes, New York became America's Most Irish City.[6] Becoming "the Dublin of America" was a dubious distinction that Theodore Parker, Boston's most prominent Unitarian minister, feared that his city would all too soon be able to claim.

Urban America's first large-scale experience of Irish papists flooding their ports came amid the worst possible circumstances: the potato blight and subsequent famine that swept across Ireland in the mid-1840s, which killed between one and a million and a half persons, perhaps as much as a sixth of the population. Even more, perhaps two million, left Ireland. About 75 percent ended in the United States. As a group, they were the poorest newcomers America had seen. More than four-fifths were unskilled laborers. Many, if not most, were illiterate.[7] Adding to their alien character, about a quarter of them were Gaelic speakers. They tended to settle where the opportunities for work were—in the cities, although many, at least initially, lived transient lives, building the canals and railroads that were transforming America in the antebellum period, or working as longshoremen and the like in ports from Boston to New Orleans.[8] Irish women quickly dominated urban domestic service.

Aggravating the peril that many of the native-born saw in the Irish was their susceptibility to disease, in particular their vulnerability to the seasonal epidemics that terrorized cities in the antebellum decades: cholera, yellow fever, malaria. Upon their arrival in America, the Irish, so many of them malnourished, typically moved into quarters hardly made for living, where unsanitary conditions cultivated all the diseases of the local environment to the most lethal effect. Typhus, typhoid, dysentery, consumption—all contributed to the incomparable mortality rate that the Irish suffered, from Boston to New Orleans. New York City, by 1860, had a death rate of one in thirty-five, one of the highest in the world. Fewer than half the children lived to be six. For Irish children, the death rate was even worse. Poor sanitation accounted for much of the mortality.[9] When epidemics of cholera or yellow fever struck cities with large concentrations of Irish, their mortality rate was staggering. In 1853 yellow fever killed 20 percent of the Irish in New Orleans.[10] In Charleston the Irish accounted disproportionately for more than a third (36 percent) of the deaths from yellow fever in the decade between 1849 and 1858.[11] In Savannah, when yellow fever struck in August of 1854, at least 40 percent of the thousand victims in the city were Irish born.[12] The Irish quickly found disproportionate representation in the asylums, the hospitals, the prisons. In Baltimore, the Irish were the major cause for the doubling of the prison population from fifteen hundred in 1844 to thirty-one hundred in 1854. Immigrants, most of them Irish, comprised nearly 40 percent of the inmates, far above their proportion of the general population.[13] By 1852 the Hibernian Society of Baltimore was supporting no fewer than seven hundred destitute Irish.[14]

Nearly one and a half million Germans emigrated to the United States between 1843 and 1861. Like the Irish, the precipitant for emigration was potato rot, beginning in 1842. Although there was considerable "poor dumping" upon American shores by German states, their emigrants tended to bring more skills and capital with them.[15] Unlike the Irish, two-thirds of the Germans preferred to continue in America the rural life they had cherished in the German states. In cities from New York to Baltimore to Cincinnati to Milwaukee, the minority of German immigrants established their own colonies in urban neighborhoods.[16] Two-thirds of the antebellum emigration was from the southern German states, such as Bavaria and Baden. Hence the relatively high proportion of Catholics among German immigrants. In New York City's *Kleindeutschland* on the lower East Side, at least a third were estimated to be Catholic.[17] In Cincinnati and Milwaukee, the Catholic proportion was much higher.[18]

It was not merely the Catholic profile of this mass immigration that was disturbing resident Americans. Immigrant Catholics seemed to be reconfiguring every dimension of the American Catholic community, making it less and less American. Consider the communities of religious women. In the early republic, the native-born had made up the overwhelming majority. The first such community, the Carmelites at Portobacco, Maryland, although an offshoot of a monastery in Flanders, was started by a band of four nuns, three of whom were native Marylanders who had joined the Carmel at Hoogstraten as part of the wave of Maryland Catholic children sent abroad for a Catholic education unavailable to them in their own land. The other Catholic women's religious communities with origins in the first three decades of the nation's existence were largely American creations, with native founders and a vast majority of native members.[19] From the 1830s on, it was quite a different story, with religious communities in Europe accounting for the vast majority of new foundations of Catholic religious women across America.

The Catholic Church in America had always been heavily dependent on an immigrant clergy. In 1838, foreigners made up four-fifths of the Catholic clergy in the United States.[20] That dominance continued in subsequent decades. By 1860 immigrant clergy dominated the faculties of most Catholic colleges, including the Jesuit institutions, as well as Notre Dame and Villanova.[21] At the higher episcopal tier, immigrants also prevailed. Of the eighty bishops named between 1830 and 1866, three-quarters were foreign-born.[22] At the same time, Catholic monarchs in Europe were forming foreign aid societies precisely to aid and support immigrant groups in the United States.

This foreignization of the Catholic Church seemed, to many careful observers, a growing threat. A body which had never completely established its bona fides as a community whose loyalty could be trusted, if not taken for granted, now seemed to be flaunting its foreign character, becoming more aggressive in its plan to make America Catholic.

THE ROMAN MENACE

Between 1840 and 1860, Catholic religious orders established more than forty institutions of higher learning in America. The sudden influx of Jesuit refugees from the European revolutions of 1848 enabled the Society of Jesus to accelerate the expansion of their US colleges that had begun at the start of the decade. By 1860, Jesuits were conducting fourteen institutions of higher learning from Worcester, Massachusetts, to San Francisco. The Augustinians, the Congregation of Holy Cross, the Benedictines, Vincentians, Franciscans, and Christian Brothers made their own contributions to the establishment of an educational empire that challenged the ones that Episcopalians, Baptists, and especially the Presbyterians were building in America in the antebellum era.

Paralleling this spurt of Catholic colleges for males was the even greater spread of Catholic female academies, run by orders of religious women. Catholic female academies in North America trace back to the eighteenth century, but, as with the male religious orders, it was the unprecedented influx of women religious in the three decades before the Civil War that occasioned a profusion of academies, many in the southern states, as the vast majority of the Catholic female academies had been before 1840.[23] In 1850, there were 158 convents, 1,664 nuns, and 91 academies. A decade later those numbers had more than doubled, thanks to the foundings by Ursulines, Visitandines, the Religious of the Sacred Heart, the Sisters of St. Joseph, the Daughters of Charity and its offshoots, the Sisters of Mercy, the Sisters of Notre Dame de Namur, and the School Sisters of Notre Dame.

The "escalating grandeur" of the architecture of new Catholic churches reflected the sudden prominence of the Church in America, which many found alien to American values. Churches increasingly were built in the Gothic style, such as Patrick Charles Keely designed for Charleston's Cathedral of St. John and St. Finbar in the early 1850s. Such magnificent edifices, with their multiple altars interspersed among sacred paintings and statues, and with spires soaring skyward, visually trumpeted their Roman connection, a sharp contrast to the much plainer styles of earlier Catholic churches, often with the modest exteriors and stark interiors befitting a republican society. Of course, Roman Catholics were not the only Christian denomination in America to turn to the Gothic tradition. The Catholic movement within the Episcopal Church had its own Gothic churches that Richard Upjohn and others designed, such as Trinity Church in New York City. But to many Americans, such papist architecture was a constant reminder of the alien nature of Roman Catholicism, now commanding, through a flood tide of immigrants, an unprecedented presence and threatening a future in which the church would make ever more inroads upon American society. Nothing seemed to flaunt the growing power of the church in America as did the First Plenary Council of the hierarchy in Baltimore in May of 1852. The assembled prelates, clergy, seminarians, and altar boys processed in full ecclesiastical dress, accompanied by a German band, through crowds that packed the streets surrounding the Baltimore cathedral, whose bells continued to peal throughout the procession. It was a sight, a New York journalist noted, that people in a republic were not accustomed to seeing.[24] For many it was quite ominous and disturbing.

For nativists the conquest of Mexico was a confidence booster in the struggle against the domestic subversive forces of Catholicism. What the victory against Mexico did not do was to popularize nativism as a political movement. Nativist politics remained local and decentralized into the 1850s. That all changed in the mid-1850s with the rise of the American Party, or the Know-Nothings, as they came to be known. Several factors were at play in the national politicization of nativism, including immigration and slavery. But the immediate catalyst for its political institutionalization may very well have been a well-publicized tour of America in 1853–54 by a delegate of Pope Pius IX. In the spring of 1853, the pontiff sent the newly appointed nuncio to Brazil, Archbishop Gaetano Bedini, to the United States, supposedly to investigate certain issues concerning the Church in that country. Evidence suggests, however, that Bedini's primary mission was to ascertain the American government's position on the establishment of full diplomatic relations with the Holy See.[25]

Reconciling long-running disputes between church officials and the trustees of two German parishes in Philadelphia and Buffalo had been a major charge that Bedini had been given in his instructions. Despite all his diplomacy, Bedini's intervention served mainly to reanimate the opposition to the bishops' continuing attempts to secure court recognition of the local prelate's right to own church property as a "corporate sole." To nativists this seemed a subversion of republican principles in which church members or their representatives were the legal owners, not a single ecclesiastic. The Catholic Church's consolidation of power within the episcopacy was a grave threat to the republican principle that property is the *sine qua non* of independence. For bishops to control church property was ultimately to usurp authority which rightly belonged to the laity.[26] In New York it led eventually to the state legislature's passage of the Putnam Bill in 1854 which banned any episcopal ownership of church property.[27]

Beginning in Pittsburgh in December 1853, Gaetano Bedini's tour of America encountered increasingly hostile crowds, their paranoia fed by stories that Catholics were infiltrating government at an alarming rate. It didn't help that the first elected governor of the newly admitted state of California was a Catholic. Most prominent of the national Catholic officials was James Campbell, President Franklin Pierce's postmaster general, the first Catholic to hold a cabinet position. That the postmaster general controlled more patronage than any other government official, besides the president, only inflamed nativists the more about the rise in Catholic power. The worst for Bedini came on Christmas night in Cincinnati. Close to a thousand German protesters marched on Archbishop John Purcell's residence, where the nuncio was staying. They bore with them the time-honored grammar of anti-Catholicism: signs and banners proclaiming: "Down with Bedini," "No Priests," "No Popes." Some carried a haunting revival of the centerpiece of Pope's Night parades in eighteenth-century cities: a light-frame wood scaffold, from which the effigy of a mitered Bedini hung by his neck. Purcell was certain they intended more than a ritual killing. Whatever their goal, police broke up the march a block short of the episcopal residence, not without casualties: one dead, fifteen wounded. Bedini left the city safely three days into the new year, but the protests grew larger, with their ritual hangings in cities in the region with large German populations: Louisville, Covington, Cleveland, Baltimore.[28] In Wheeling, Virginia, only the intervention of hundreds of Irishmen saved Bedini from bodily harm. The nuncio escaped his last threatening mob in New York harbor by being secretly spirited by rowboat and tugboat to the safety of a Liverpool-bound British three-master.[29]

THE POLITICIZATION OF
ANTI-CATHOLICISM

The Order of United Americans, or American Party, had become a formal political party in 1852, a year before Gaetano Bedini's arrival. In the aftermath of the nuncio's disastrous tour, the party seemingly overnight became a major political force, as the providential response to the growing threat that Rome posed for the American republic.[30] In a six-month stretch from May to October of 1854 membership in the American Party soared, in rural and urban areas alike, from New England to Louisiana, from 50,000 to more than a million.[31] The party had at least 121 representatives in Congress and controlled nine governorships, twelve legislatures, municipal governments in Boston, New York, Philadelphia, Baltimore, and New Orleans.[32] With shocking suddenness the American Party had established itself as the dominant party in half the states of the North, with particular success in New England. It seemed to have all the political tailwinds. As one Whig member remarked to another in the wake of their party's devastating electoral losses in 1854: "This election has demonstrated that by a majority, Roman Catholicism is feared more than American slavery."[33]

The American Party uniquely confined membership to native-born and -reared Protestants without a Catholic spouse who were willing to pledge to combat "the insidious policy of the Church of Rome, and all other foreign influences against the institutions of our country," mainly by voting for only native-born Protestants.[34] To the Know-Nothings, Anglo-Saxon Protestantism defined American nationality. It represented a return to the colonial understanding that religion and race determined citizenship, that Anglo-Saxon Protestantism embodied the liberal values at the core of republicanism, while Catholicism epitomized the tyranny ever in mortal combat with liberty. As Anna Carroll, the party's chief propagandist, boasted in her 1855 polemic, *The Great American Battle,* America was not only a Protestant nation, but an Anglo-Saxon one, its core being the descendants of the largely Anglo-Saxon settlers of the colonial period. An immigration dominated by Germans and Irish with ties to Rome was a mortal threat to the republic's survival. The key to resisting the Catholic immigrant tide was to control the gateway to citizenship. So, the party pushed to extend the naturalization waiting period to twenty-one years, the exact time it took for the native-born to achieve the vote by reaching maturity. And to ensure that only the best governed, the Know-Nothings excluded the foreign-born from ever holding any office.

THE COMMON SCHOOL AND
PAROCHIAL FUNDING

Besides immigration, the issue of public funding for parochial schools was a major concern for nativists. Education resurfaced in 1852 as a wedge issue when the First Plenary Council of Baltimore urged that bishops seek government aid. That subsequently ignited opposition in cities from Baltimore to Cincinnati. Protestants read such attempts to siphon off monies from the common school as an assault on the nursery of an educated citizenry. When Archbishop Purcell, whose parish schools were already accommodating over 40 percent of Cincinnati's school-age population, launched a campaign to secure funds from the legislature, the Whig-controlled government introduced legislation that would require all children in the state to attend public schools.[35] The Democrats ensured that that bill failed, but Purcell came no closer to securing funding.[36] In neighboring Kentucky, Bishop Martin Spalding, frustrated by the mandatory use of the King James Version of the Bible in the public schools, in 1854 called for public funding of all schools, including parochial ones. The subsequent state election proved a disaster for any Catholic hopes of securing public aid as the nativists enjoyed extraordinary success at the polls in the state's three largest cities: Louisville, Lexington, and Covington, where the vast majority of immigrants were concentrated.[37] A Catholic attempt to secure aid for its schools became a catalyst for nativism's spectacular rise in Maryland.[38]

NATIVISM AND VIOLENCE

In Maryland, startling Catholic political success propelled voters into the American Party.[39] In 1850, Maryland had elected its first Catholic governor. Two years later, a Catholic, Jerome Hollis, became mayor of Baltimore. To many Marylanders, the twin elections were dramatic signs of rising Catholic power.[40] The American Party promised to restore the republican values and order that had marked the state's origin, when Catholics were regarded as a genteel, nonthreatening minority.[41]

By the summer of 1854, Baltimore was becoming an epicenter of nativism. In the fall, Samuel Hinks, a virtual unknown who had publicly announced his candidacy just two weeks earlier but did no campaigning, defeated the incumbent Catholic mayor, Jerome Hollis. The next year the new party swept races across the state to gain majorities in the congressional delegation, as well as in the general assembly and state senate. Except for the historic Catholic areas of southern Maryland and the Eastern Shore, the Know-Nothing Party dominated the state.[42]

Archbishop Francis Kenrick reported to a Roman friend the terror the Catholic community in Maryland and elsewhere was enduring under nativist rule. "Churches have been burned, the cross has been torn down from their roofs and trampled under foot and Irishmen have been shot down or poniarded, on the slightest pretext. . . . Armed men have paraded the streets to provoke and punish the least manifestation of displeasure. . . . The clergy are frequently insulted in the streets throughout the whole country . . . and a few weeks ago a committee of twenty-five took [it] on themselves to visit the convent of the Visitation at Frederick."[43] In the neighboring District of Columbia, a mass meeting calling for federal legislation to regulate immigration ended with the group depositing into the Potomac the marble stone that the pope had contributed to the Washington Monument then under construction.

Indeed anti-Catholic sentiment in much of the country, including the South, was strong enough that it became common practice for nuns and sisters traveling by train or boat through the South or Midwest to dress in secular clothes.[44] In Kentucky, anti-Catholic feeling forced Bishop Martin Spalding to advise the seven Xaverian Brothers whom he had recruited from Belgium to live with private families rather than in community.[45] Archbishop John Purcell of Cincinnati confessed in 1854 that he had not felt safe in Cincinnati for some years.[46] A Belgian-immigrant Jesuit, Pierre-Jean De Smet, was so exasperated by the anti-Catholic animus infecting the country that he confessed to a friend, late in 1854, "I cannot say much about the United States. American liberty and tolerance, so highly boasted, exists less in this Great Republic than in the most oppressed country of Europe."[47]

In Ellsworth, Maine, a Swiss Jesuit, John Bapst, discovered just how traumatic a backlash any challenge to Protestant-controlled public education could generate. Bapst had been among those forced into exile in 1848. In Maine he was responsible for covering thirty-three missions, serving Penobscot Indians as well as Euro-Americans, mostly immigrants. Initially welcomed, particularly for his organizing of temperance societies which sharply reduced alcohol abuse, John Bapst began to lose local favor in the course of a wave of conversions of young people, particularly females, attributed to his influence. Bapst had public opinion turn decisively against him when he insisted that Catholics students, out of respect for their religious freedom, be given the option of using the official Catholic Bible or be excused entirely from the daily Bible reading. When school officials refused to make any alterations in their traditional practice, Bapst orchestrated the withdrawal of

Catholic children from the school and sued the school board. The Maine Supreme Court ruled that reading the King James Bible was an essential propaedeutic for an informed, virtuous citizenry.[48] Tensions rose, especially as Know-Nothing militias in Maine exacted vigilante-style justice where they saw fit. During the summer of 1854 two Catholic churches in the area went up in flames. Jesuit officials, concerned for Bapst's safety, removed him to Bangor. Then the following October, Bapst foolishly returned to Ellsworth. The news quickly spread. A mob surrounded the house where the Jesuit was staying, dragged him out, applied tar and feathers to his body, and paraded him on a plank around the streets of Ellsworth for some hours. No arrests followed. The ordeal left the priest with lifetime psychiatric scars that eventually brought him to a mental asylum outside of Baltimore, where he spent his final tortured days.[49]

Between 1834 and 1852 there was but one major political riot in the United States, with a dozen deaths. In the middle 1850s the American Party was involved in twenty-two, accounting for seventy-seven deaths and several hundred injured. Significantly, the violence was almost exclusively a southern phenomenon. Nineteen of the riots occurred in New Orleans, Washington, St. Louis, Louisville, and Baltimore: all important centers of pre-1840s Catholic America. The identification of the Catholic Church with slavery was a powerful fomenter of violence. In St. Louis, the rioting grew out of a standard election day strong-arming disfranchisement tactic: denying access to the ballot box to persons trying to cast votes for the opposition. When nativists turned away a group of Irishmen, the ensuing argument turned lethal when one of the Irish stabbed a very young nativist. That unleashed three days of fierce fighting and destruction, mostly in Irish neighborhoods. In all, several blocks were leveled, ten persons killed, at least twenty seriously injured.[50] In Cincinnati, at the beginning of April 1855, American Party leaders brought in gang members from across the Ohio River in Kentucky to "monitor" the polling places in certain heavily Catholic German wards. When rumors circulated of voting fraud in one such ward, the Kentucky mercenaries, with an arsenal of cannon, pistols, and knives, stormed the polling place and destroyed the ballots, before setting out on a rampage through the German district. German militias erected barricades to prevent any further incursions. The American-initiated violence left two dead and an unknown number of wounded but failed to keep the party in power.

Approaching the August municipal elections, the editor of the *Louisville Journal* warned that the vote would decide whether religious freedom or papal tyranny would prevail in the city. "The Romish corporation," he asserted, "has always been the prostitute of Satan," ever using its local agents to undermine democracy.[51] The *Journal*, in its final editorial before the election, had this advice: "So go ahead Know-Nothings, and raise just as big a storm as you please."[52] Raise it they did, to an unprecedented level. Election day dawned with the nativist gangs controlling all the polling places across the city. Fighting commenced when nativists attempted to bar immigrants from voting. In one German ward, rejected voters fired pistols at their rejecters. Another group of Irish fatally beat up a nativist blocking access to a polling station. In retaliation, a nativist mob, dragging a cannon, headed toward an Irish ward. On their way they set fire to an Irish tenement, then shot fatally about a dozen persons fleeing the burning building. When another crowd passed a German brewery, shots from inside the building caused the marchers to storm the building and put it to the flames. In the melee ten persons died, most of them Germans. The wealthy Irish owner of one set of tenements tried to save his buildings by bribing the would-be arsonists; they killed him and took the money as well. Darkness brought the mayhem to an end. The actual death toll was never established. At least twenty-two fatalities were counted, two-thirds of them Catholics. Some estimates went as high as a hundred. The racism underlying the violence came out in one witness's account. When asked whether he had observed any persons in the burning buildings, the witness replied: "Not many whites, just Irish."[53] "We have just passed through a reign of terror," Spalding wrote Purcell of Cincinnati. There were at least a hundred victims, dead and maimed, of the violence. One was a priest who had been killed while administering the last rites to a dying parishioner. "I am told that 1000 houses are now vacant," Spalding reported.[54] Eighteen-fifty-five turned out to be the high-water mark of the American Party in Kentucky, but that year's violence left Martin Spalding with the post-traumatic stress syndrome that the nativist-induced violence affected in so many American Catholic leaders.

Nowhere did the American Party, as well as the violence its members occasioned, persist as long as it did in Baltimore, where immigration was growing the Catholic population well beyond the small presence it had historically had in the largest city of a state associated, from its planting, with the Catholic Church. Baltimore had nearly the perfect environment for political mayhem. The city was awash with gangs, marked by colorful names: The Rip Raps, Gladiators, Red Necks, Butt Enders, Hard Times, Plug Uglies, Blood Tubs, Bloody Eights, and so forth. Most gangs were volunteer firefighting companies which had connections with the political parties. Know-Nothing gang members also pervaded the police department.[55] It made for institutional violence that rendered fair and free elections unattainable. In the October election of 1856, in pitched battles with knives, chains, bricks, clubs, and cannon, gangs waged battle for control of voting precincts.[56] In the end the American gangs prevailed over their outnumbered, out-armed Democratic counterparts. Seven combatants had died in the course of the day. A month later the presidential contest brought violence on a greater scale. Once again American gangs seized more voting places than their Democratic opponents to consolidate the Know-Nothings' control of municipal government and to help make Maryland the one state to support the American candidate, former president Millard Fillmore. Citywide fighting left 10 dead and over 250 wounded. Police subsequently arrested Democratic gang leaders and confiscated arms from immigrant militia companies.[57]

Over the next three years, Know-Nothing gangs all too efficiently ensured enough "franchise cleansing" to keep the party in power.[58] Then, in October 1859, their intimidation and lethal violence overreached when their fatal victims included two policemen. That proved the last straw for a majority of Baltimoreans. The following October, 1860, with the police department no longer under Know-Nothing control, a coalition of Democrats and former Whigs swept to power. The election of the banker George William Brown as mayor and George Kane, a second-generation Irish merchant, as police commissioner showed that "Baltimore was herself again," the *Catholic Mirror* commented.[59]

NEW ORLEANS'S DISTINCT
BRAND OF NATIVISM

In New Orleans, where Catholics constituted a large minority of the population, the American Party attracted thousands of them, predominantly by promoting itself as a reform movement and vehicle for preserving national unity.[60] That did not spare the city from the violence that marked the party's rise in Baltimore and elsewhere. Five nativist-related riots wracked New Orleans between 1853 and 1856.[61] In September of 1853, rumors spread that the Know-Nothings were plotting to massacre the Catholics in the city, which touched off rioting for a week. That led to a clash of arms between nativists and Irish Catholics that left two dead and many injured.

Charles Gayarré was among the six-member Louisiana delegation to the American Party convention in Philadelphia in 1855. The lone Catholic in the group, Gayarré was denied a seat because of his religion. Gayarré, from the convention floor, condemned the party for its bigotry, at which point the

Louisiana contingent withdrew from the convention and the Louisiana council of the Know-Nothings eventually withdrew from the party.[62] Nonetheless, the city remained a Know-Nothing stronghold through the 1850s.[63] Harassment of Irish Catholics became so extreme in New Orleans that a group of Irish, in a move echoing Maryland Catholics a century earlier, petitioned the government of Mexico for permission to colonize. The *Orleanian* commended the move to emigrate as a wise one in seeking a land where "they will be treated less as an inferior caste than they are here."[64] When the nativists prevailed again in the mayoral race of 1856, it proved the swan song for the American Party in the region, as the violence that once more ensured a Know-Nothing victory led to mass defections by former Whigs, including Gayarré and Judah P. Benjamin, a US senator and Whig planter from New Orleans, who blamed the Know-Nothings for their abolitionism and anti-Catholicism.[65]

THE COLLAPSE OF THE
AMERICAN PARTY

The concern that the party serve, if not primarily, at least substantively, as a party dedicated to preserving the Union, led to the establishment, in November 1854, of a Third Degree in the party membership, the "Union Degree," which required the degree recipient to pledge to work against any effort to destroy or weaken the Union.[66] This aim came to its ultimate test at their Philadelphia convention in early June of 1856, when the delegates adopted the controversial "Section Twelve" of their platform, which repudiated any congressional power to prohibit slavery in the territories. That attempt to bury the slavery issue met a subsequent general repudiation by northern Americanists. It began a fatal sectional split for the party.[67]

As meteoric as was the American Party's rise, so was its fall. In the three-way presidential election of 1856, the party's candidate, Millard Fillmore, received just a quarter of the popular vote. No longer were Catholic immigrants a prevailing political issue. The slavocracy now cast far larger shadows over the future of the republic than did popery. As Charles Dana observed to Henry C. Carey in the wake of the Know-Nothing implosion, "neither the Pope nor the foreigners ever can govern the country or endanger its liberties, but the slavebreeders and slavetraders do govern it, and threaten to put an end to all government but theirs."[68]

Eighteen-fifty-six proved to be the last presidential election in which the party ran a candidate. As with the Whig Party, it simply could not keep its members North and South together over the slavery issue. The party fragmented, its northern members finding compatibility in the Republican Party, its southern ones becoming Democrats and ultimately reluctant secessionists.[69] The collapse of the southern wing of the Know-Nothings effectively made the South a one-party region. It may also have facilitated the acceptance of Catholics by the Protestant majority in the region. With Democrats as the hegemonic political force in the region, a party traditionally friendly to immigrants, southern Catholics did not face the organized hostility that persisted in the North, as American Party members largely were absorbed in the Republican Party that came to dominate the northern section of the political landscape.

†

CHAPTER 3

The Slavery Crisis
and the Taney Court

Freedom has been a serious misfortune to the manumitted slave;
and he has most commonly brought upon himself privations, and sufferings
which he would not have been called on to endure in a state of slavery.

—ROGER B. TANEY, 1857

CATHOLICS AND THE
POLITICAL REALIGNMENT

The political divisions that immigration and slavery caused in the 1850s produced "a kaleidoscope of parties and fusion groups" so byzantine that the *Congressional Globe* gave up trying to identify representatives with existing parties.[1] Eventually there emerged a political realignment, the third-party system that the country had known since its beginning as a republic. Of the two parties that emerged in the new configuration, the Democrats were a survival from the old system, the Republicans a new creation, a sectional party born of the paramount issues of the decade. For Catholics, the realignment found them representing a greater portion of the Democratic Party, as the party saw serious Protestant defections over immigration, abolition, and temperance. In the North, Catholics rose from an exotic minority in the party to its backbone by 1860.

COMPROMISING THE NATION

The realignment stemmed from the issues raised by the vast territories acquired from Mexico. Until the Mexican-American War the country had maintained a balance of political power through an equal number of slave and free states. The southern congressional bloc wanted the assurance that slavery would be able to expand into the western territories, including those just acquired from Mexico, to maintain the traditional balance in the US Senate.[2] The mounting sectional discord over the issue fueled speculation that the Union was in danger of coming apart. When Lieutenant William Tecumseh Sherman brought dispatches from Washington to General Winfield Scott in New York City in January 1850, the general startled the young officer by telling him that "our country was on the eve of a terrible civil war."[3] At the time, Henry Clay had initiated a series of bills in the Congress that included the admission of California as a free state; the division of the rest of the Mexican cession into two territories, whose citizens would themselves decide the status of slavery within their borders; abolishment of the slave trade in the District of Columbia, and a fugitive slave law that favored the slave owner trying to retrieve his "property." The bills collectively failed to gain any traction within the Congress. Later that summer, Stephen Douglas managed by a bit of legislative legerdemain to find shifting majorities to support individual parts of Clay's original comprehensive plan. The consequence was a compromise that left majorities in both North and South unhappy: the South over the failure to get a firm commitment to slavery's right to expand into territories outside of the Mexican cession; the North over the fugitive slave law that seemed to confirm the incomparable power of the slavocracy to secure its property—whether human or otherwise—in the North, South, or West.

An early challenge to the Fugitive Slave Act occurred in Lancaster County, Pennsylvania, in September of 1851 when members of the sizable African American community in Christiana rose up in arms to prevent a posse from retrieving four escaped slaves of Thomas Gorsuch, a farmer in northern Maryland. When Gorsuch's party attempted to apprehend the quartet, Gorsuch and his son were both clubbed and shot. The four fugitives escaped to Canada. Gorsuch subsequently died; his son miraculously survived. Maryland was in an uproar. At a meeting in Monument Square in downtown Baltimore, more than five thousand called for the breaking off of all relations with the North, including the withdrawal of all students in northern institutions. As the Catholic governor of Maryland, Enoch Lowe, wrote to President Millard Fillmore, "I do not know of a single incident that has occurred since the passage of the Compromise measures, which tends to weaken more the bonds of union." Unless the government secured the severest retribution for the "murderous treason" committed in Pennsylvania, Lowe saw only a "crumbling Union" in the near future.[4] Thirty-eight persons were subsequently indicted on multiple charges of treason. None was convicted. Lowe found the jury's failure to convict ample evidence that "the whole state [of Pennsylvania] is tainted and rotted."[5] For Marylanders, the lesson of Christiana was that the law had failed to do justice. They would have to look to themselves.[6]

Successful rescues proved to be the rarity. Despite personal liberty laws in many northern states which forbade state officials to cooperate in such apprehensions and transfers, of the two hundred or so Blacks claimed under the law, the vast majority, whether fugitives or not, found themselves back in slavery.[7]

CATHOLICS AND THE
SLAVERY CRISIS OF THE 1850S

Until the 1840s the Roman Catholic community in British America and then the United States had been concentrated in the South. Slavery was an institution with which Catholics were involved, both as enslavers and the enslaved. From John Carroll on, many southern bishops owned slaves. As bishop of Charleston, Patrick Lynch inherited nearly one hundred South Carolina Blacks on his two upland plantations.[8] Slaveholding was also widespread among religious communities, both male and female. The Jesuits had been among the country's largest slaveholders before their notorious mass sale of more than 270 laborers from their Maryland plantations to ones in Louisiana. Jesuits in Missouri, Alabama, and Louisiana continued to own enslaved persons throughout the antebellum era, as did the Vincentians in Missouri, the Sulpicians in Maryland and Kentucky, and the Capuchins in Louisiana. Slaveholding by religious women had originated in the United States with the Carmelites in Maryland. That tradition spread to the other early Catholic women's communities, composed typically of the native-born. When religious communities of immigrant women began to arrive in America, unlike their male counterparts, they did not take easily to this peculiarity of American culture, but in most cases they eventually made their separate peace with it.[9]

Before the 1820s, southern Catholics such as Charles Carroll, William Gaston, and Roger Taney had been prominent figures in the colonization movement, which promoted emancipation and removal as the solution to the slavery dilemma. Gaston regarded slavery as "the worst evil" afflicting the South; Taney indicted it as "a blot on our national character." The forces polarizing the nation over slavery had increasingly undermined colonization as a remedy. Many of its advocates, like Taney, by the 1830s were ardent defenders of southern "rights."

At least two American bishops, Michael O'Connor of Pittsburgh, and John Miege, SJ, of the Kansas Territory, complained to Rome in the early 1850s about the hierarchy's collective failure to address the slavery issue. With the Bedini visit impending, Roman authorities apparently decided to await the nuncio's finding about the matter.[10] In his 1854 report Bedini concluded, "The problem of the negro slaves in the United States is so delicate that it might be considered dangerous. . . . As matters stand, we must admit that the Bishop, who uses too much zeal in defending one cause or the other is imprudent. . . . Therefore, it might be better for the Bishops to show and profess a marked neutrality." To take one side or the other, Bedini warned, would open the bishop to being used or attacked by one side or the other. Better to avoid it altogether in a society whose hostility to Catholics the archbishop had just experienced in spades.[11]

The American bishops took Bedini's advice and directed their clergy to do the same. As Archbishop Francis Kenrick reported in his pastoral letter about the Ninth Provincial Council of Baltimore in 1858, "our clergy have wisely abstained from all interference with the judgement of the faithful, which should be free on all questions of polity and social order, within the limits of the doctrine and law of Christ. . . . Leave to worldlings the cares and anxieties of political partisanship." No political party, Kenrick implied, could be the channel for implementing the doctrine and teaching of the Church.[12] That letter echoed Kenrick's introduction to his translation of the Epistle of St. Paul to Philemon (1851), in which he had argued that "the Gospel is not directed to disturb the actual order of society, by teaching men to disregard their obligations, however severe their enforcement." The social order took precedence over "theories of philanthropy."[13] The church was above politics. Its sacred charge was to save souls, not redeem the social order. Kenrick's position was a recipe for apathy.[14]

Archbishop Anthony Blanc of New Orleans, in his pastoral letter of 1852, defended slavery as part of the order which is essential in civilized society. To the prelate slavery provided the ideal institution by which the reciprocal deference and benevolence between inferior and superior are guaranteed.[15] Any activity regarding the reform of slavery needed to be restricted to improving the conditions under which the enslaved lived, particularly their right to religious ministry. Seven years later, the priest editor of the *U.S. Catholic Miscellany* pronounced abolition and Catholicism to be utterly incompatible. "No man can be an Abolitionist and a Catholic together. He might as well expect," James Corcoran explained, "both to remain in her communion and at the same time be allowed to profess Protestantism."[16]

What united white Catholics, whether slave owner/hirer or not, whether of North or South, was the commitment to white supremacy. The sections merely attempted to secure its permanency in different ways. In the South, slavery was the major mechanism; in the North, the exclusion or segregation of Blacks maintained the traditional racial order.

BLACK CATHOLICS

African Americans had been an integral, if largely a subordinate, part of the American Catholic community from its colonial beginnings. At the time of the American Revolution, African Americans, mostly enslaved, constituted about a tenth of the Catholic population. That proportion steadily declined as European immigration drove Catholic population growth in the United States. By 1860, the estimated 100,000 Black Catholics made up less than 5 percent of the Catholic population. As the center of the general Catholic population continued to shift northward during the antebellum period, the vast majority of Black Catholics remained in the South. Most were in bondage, but there was a significant free minority, particularly in Maryland, Missouri, and Louisiana. In the latter state there were communities of free people of color, mostly the descendants of unions between African slaves and French planters or traders.[17]

Free Catholics of color, predominantly of mixed race, tended to be found in the cities. St. Louis had a large community of free mixed-race Catholics, whose ancestry traced back to Missouri's French colonial past. Most of the free Black Catholic urban presence traced back to the 1790s when those of African descent, both free and bonded, were among the refugees from the revolution in Saint-Domingue who found sanctuary in cities from New York to New Orleans.

Segregation by custom in public transportation, hotels, restaurants, churches, schools, and theaters kept northern Blacks apart. They were legally free but socially far from it in their access to so much of urban public life. This apartheid was a constant reminder to Blacks of their inferior status. In 1853, a Black Catholic in New York, Harriet Thompson, along with twenty-six other Black Catholics, appealed to Pope Pius IX to order Catholic authorities in the United States to provide the same spiritual care for Blacks as they did for whites. A particular problem, she pointed out, was the tribal mentality of the heavily Irish US clergy. They could not see beyond their own kind. Archbishop Hughes himself she accused of dismissing Blacks as nonmembers of his flock. "Rev. Abp. Hughes . . . [hates] the black race so much that he cannot bear them to come near him." Thus Black Catholics were kept out of parochial schools. They were segregated in church. The consequence,

Thompson claimed, was mass defections among African Americans from the Catholic Church.[18]

The largest Black Catholic community was in Maryland. Black Catholics here fared better than their brethren in New York. Baltimore housed the Black congregation of the Oblates of Providence. In the 1840s the Queens, Butlers, Berrys, and other Black families established the Holy Name Society of Colored People, in Calvert Hall, the archdiocese's social center. For its 270 members Holy Name sponsored a chorale society, library, sodality, and other activities.[19] Even in Baltimore, institutional racism ran deep. In 1845, Holy Name lost its social, spiritual, and intellectual home when Calvert Hall was given to the Christian Brothers as the site for their college for white boys. The situation for Black Catholics in Maryland improved with Francis Kenrick's ascent to the see in 1853. Kenrick became a staunch supporter of the Oblates, partly to encourage their work in securing converts among African Americans. Moreover, he exhorted white Catholics to accept Black converts as fellow Catholics. One seventeen-year-old Black convert, William Augustine Williams, who wished to be a foreign missionary, Kenrick recommended in 1855 for the Urban College of Propaganda, but, given the increasingly charged racial climate, Kenrick thought it expedient that Williams be ordained for Liberia.[20]

A unique free Black community, the Afro-Creoles, a majority of whom were Catholic, developed in southern Alabama and the Natchitoches and New Orleans regions of Louisiana. These French Africans constituted, by law and custom, a *tertium quid* in Louisiana society between whites and enslaved Africans. Indeed Afro-Creoles were often enslavers. Literate and relatively prosperous, the Afro-Creoles enjoyed certain civil rights, such as owning property, making contracts, and testifying in court. They also developed a web of community institutions—schools, literary societies, benevolent organizations—which repressive legislation late in the antebellum era began to shut down.[21]

The Church afforded particular opportunities for Black Catholics of mixed-race origins to find their own niche in religious communities and apostolates. Marie Lange and two other Saint-Domingue exiles had done so in establishing the Oblate Sisters in 1829. In New Orleans, Henriette DeLille and Juliette Gaudin in the 1850s formed the Congregation of the Holy Family. Mixed-race Catholics of sufficiently light complexion could enter white religious communities by passing. Shannon Dee Williams has identified at least twenty-nine women with African American ancestry who were accepted into white religious communities in the antebellum period. Superiors in most of these cases chose to ignore the ethnic background of those entering. As Williams notes, not only were sisters who passed for white forced to endure a type of social death, but also the election of a new superior, the regular admission of new candidates into orders, and the appointment of new ecclesiastical authorities regularly put sisters whose African heritage was known by anyone at risk of hostility, expulsion, or worse. Mother Theresa Maxis, the founder of the Immaculate Heart of Mary Sisters, made that discovery in the late 1850s, when her ecclesiastical superiors in Detroit threatened to reveal her African heritage in retaliation for her challenging their authority.[22]

No mixed-race family took better advantage of opportunities for social mobility within the Church than did the Healys. Of the ten children of the Irish Georgia planter, Michael Healy, and his slave wife, Eliza, five became priests or nuns. The priests all rose to high positions within the Church. James became Bishop of Portland, Maine; Patrick became president of Georgetown University; Sherwood became the chancellor of the Archdiocese of Boston. Of the two sisters who became nuns, one, Eliza (religious name: Mary Magdalen) became the mother superior of several Canadian communities of the Congregation of Notre Dame. The key to the remarkable advancement of the Healys within the institutional Church lay in their self-identification as white and their limited success at presenting themselves as such. That ability also allowed Michael Healy Jr. to become a Coast Guard commander and Martha Healy to marry a white businessman, James Cashman. Even with the Healys there was inequity in their passing. The two sisters who entered the white world of female religious orders had to do so in Canada, where race did not loom nearly as large as it did in their homeland.[23]

DEMOCRATS
BACK IN POWER

The Election of 1852 proved to be a referendum on the Compromise of 1850, with the Democratic candidate, Franklin Pierce, pledging not only to support it in its entirety, but also to apply the principle of popular sovereignty to the organization of all the country's territories, not just those in the Mexican cession. The Whigs, courting the growing Catholic vote in the North, nominated Winfield Scott, the late hero of the Mexican War whose efforts to protect the persons and property of the Catholic Church in Mexico were well known. While an Episcopalian himself, the general had educated two of his daughters in convents. One daughter, at Georgetown Visitation, had converted and joined the Visitandines. This play for the Catholic vote likely alienated more anti-Catholic Whigs than it attracted Catholic Democrats. The election proved a Democratic landslide, with Franklin Pierce carrying the Electoral

College, 254–42. The Democratic Party was reaping the fruit of its proslavery agenda, not only in the South, but the North as well, particularly among Catholics who were becoming an increasingly important constituency.[24]

Early in 1854 Stephen Douglas introduced his Kansas-Nebraska Act, a clever ploy meant to relieve Congress of the responsibility of deciding whether a state was to be free or open to slavery by putting the responsibility on the people of the territory itself. The bill was passed by both houses of Congress, thanks to overwhelming support from southern Democrats and Whigs, along with half the northern Democrats. But Douglas had badly overestimated popular sovereignty's intersectional appeal. The Kansas-Nebraska Act stirred a backlash against slavery even fiercer than that produced by the Fugitive Slave Act. The congressional elections of 1854–55 proved to be the Whigs' political Waterloo.[25] For the Democrats it marked the beginning of mass defections of northern voters from the party that by the end of the decade reduced it to minority status in the region, with Catholics now its core.

Two years later, James Buchanan kept the presidency in Democratic hands by making the protection and expansion of slavery a central issue. In a three-way race among the American, Democratic, and Republican parties, Buchanan won 45 percent of the popular vote but 174 of the electoral votes to John C. Frémont's 115, thanks to carrying all the slave states, except for Maryland, which was the lone state that Millard Fillmore, the American Party nominee, won. The five free states Buchanan won—Pennsylvania, New Jersey, Illinois, Indiana, and California—all had populations significantly Catholic as well as southern in their origin.[26]

Both Pierce and Buchanan acknowledged their debt to southern support not only by their policies, but their appointments as well. Southerners particularly dominated Buchanan's cabinet. Patronage favored southerners and Catholics. In Washington's official society, the southern grand dames continued their reign. One whose status rose among her peers with Buchanan's ascent to the White House was Rose O'Neal Greenhow, a forty-four-year-old Irish Catholic widow who had deep roots and growing influence within Washington's sociopolitical sphere. Greenhow was the daughter of a middling planter, John O'Neale, in Montgomery County, Maryland, about fifteen miles south of Frederick. When Rose was five, her father, a habitual drunk, fell from his horse as he was returning home from a drinking spree and split his head on a rock. The enslaved boy accompanying him raced home to report the accident to his mother, who, so it was claimed, instructed him to return and finish off his master. Which he reportedly did, and for which he was subsequently hanged. When Rose was sixteen, her mother sent her and her older sister, Ellen, to live with a relative who conducted a boardinghouse which catered to congressmen, the most prominent of whom was John C. Calhoun of South Carolina. Rose particularly took to Calhoun as her political guru as well as the father she never really knew. Years later, Rose and her husband, Robert Greenhow, became prominent hosts of Washington's social, political, and diplomatic elite, including Calhoun, Taney, and Buchanan. During the presidential campaign of 1856 she served as an unofficial consultant to the latter. With Buchanan in the White House, Rose O'Neal Greenhow became one of his most trusted advisors.[27]

TANEY AND DRED SCOTT

In his inaugural address at the beginning of March 1857, the newly sworn president advised the nation that the question of the constitutionality of slavery in the territories was one that the courts were best able to settle. Presiding over the US Supreme Court was Roger Taney, the first Catholic to serve as chief justice. The eighty-year-old Taney had grown up on a tobacco plantation in Calvert County, Maryland, had graduated from Dickinson College, and after reading law in Annapolis for three years, began to practice in Frederick in 1799. Taney served single terms in both the Maryland House of Delegates and the Senate as a Federalist. Along with his brother-in-law, Francis Scott Key, Taney became involved in efforts to reform slavery, from the personal, including protecting free Blacks from kidnapping, and emancipating his own seven slaves, to the institutional, with Taney and Key helping to establish the Maryland branch of the American Colonization Society in 1819. Taney's linking his political aspirations to Andrew Jackson's proslavery Democratic Party in the 1820s seems the biggest factor in his evolution from gradual emancipationist to full-blown protector of "southern rights." By 1857 Taney was in his twenty-second year of heading the court. Five months before the court's ruling on *Dred Scott v. Sanford,* Taney had written a friend: "it is my deliberate opinion that the South is doomed, and that nothing but a firm united action, nearly unanimous in every [Southern] state, can check Northern insult and Northern aggression."[28] *Dred Scott v. Sanford* proved to be Roger Taney's contribution to that effort, from his unique place of power as chief justice.

By a seven-to-two majority the Supreme Court ruled against Dred Scott, who based his claim of freedom upon his master having taken him into a free territory. Taney declared, in effect, that the Missouri Compromise had been unconstitutional, along with the mechanism of popular sovereignty as a means of determining whether slavery would be legal in a state or not. Confirming a slaveholder's constitutional right to transport his property, including humans, into the country's territories was a primary objective of Taney's in crafting his opinion.[29] In addition, in an obiter dictum that consumed nearly half of the opinion, the chief justice ruled that Blacks were never intended to be citizens of the United States. Two years before *Scott,* the court had ruled unanimously that the Treaty of Guadalupe Hidalgo incorporated nonwhite Mexicans as citizens of the United States. Now Taney affirmed that Blacks, whether bonded or not, belonged in a special racial category that ruled out the possibility of citizenship.[30] In effect, the Taney Court had not only authorized the free spread of slavery but had "fixed the *status* of the subordinate race *forever.* The decision recognized the status of the black as nature had ordained."[31] The *Baltimore Sun* concurred that it was "impossible" to recognize "negroes as citizens."[32]

JOHN BROWN AND
THE FAULT LINES OF UNION

In Harpers Ferry, Virginia, the church for the six hundred or so Catholics who had found employment at the town's armory sat on a rocky promontory which overlooked the confluence of the Shenandoah and Potomac rivers. It was, as its Irish-born pastor, Michael Costello, once wrote, "one of the most beautifully wild scenes in the United States," echoing Thomas Jefferson, who eighty years earlier had judged the sublime view worth a trip across the Atlantic. On Monday morning, October 16, 1859, Costello had awoken to see armed men patrolling the streets in the town below. Then a gun battle developed around the armory between these strangers and locals, some of whom the priest recognized as parishioners. When one of them was struck down in the crossfire, Costello raced down the hill from the church to minister to him. As the priest approached the fallen Catholic, he expected to be captured by the outsiders, as he had seen happen to others. To his surprise they allowed him to minister the last rites to the dying man.

As Costello soon discovered, the strangers were a multiracial band of would-be revolutionaries, led by "Captain" John Brown, the abolitionist made infamous three years earlier for his execution of five Kansas settlers along Pottawatomie Creek in retaliation for proslavers burning the town of Lawrence, Kansas. Now Brown had led twenty-two others into isolated Harpers Ferry, home to a major arsenal of the US government, as well as to the largest armory in the country. John Brown and his men seized the two principal installations of the town, commandeered its weapons, and sent out parties to round up slave owners as hostages and their slaves as the first recruits in the revolution they hoped to initiate. Then Brown waited for the word to spread, to the slaves in the countryside, to abolitionists northward, that the year of jubilee had begun. Harpers Ferry was to be the capstone to the decades-long crusade against slavery that Brown had waged, the launching of the revolution that would bring down slavery throughout the land.[33]

The only persons to respond were the militia throughout the region, who poured out of the towns and villages of Virginia and Maryland to lay siege to Brown's small band. Sixty-five miles away in Baltimore, news of "a Negro insurrection" at Harpers Ferry had thrown Baltimore into a panic. Five companies of militia, including the McComas Riflemen, rushed by train to the beleaguered town. Henry Chatard Scott, of a prominent Catholic family which had been forced to flee Saint-Domingue during its slave uprising, was a surgeon for another company, the Baltimore City Guard, and reportedly treated the wounded, including Brown. In Richmond, the Montgomery Guards, the militia company that had been formed in 1850 in the basement of St. Peter's Church, were among those who responded to the governor's call for volunteers but reached Harpers Ferry too late.[34] After a day and a half of sporadic fighting, a company of marines successfully stormed the engine house on the armory grounds where Brown and the remnants of his raiders had barricaded themselves. Fourteen people lay dead, including ten of Brown's men. Costello was called to minister to two marines, both Catholics, who had been wounded, one of them, Private Luke Quinn, mortally. He was laid to rest in the Catholic cemetery up the hill from the engine house.

Michael Costello visited John Brown in his Charlestown cell while he was awaiting execution, to offer his priestly services. Brown declined to have the ministry of any clergy, all of whom he considered to be apologists of slavery. As such, they were, to Brown, "as bad as murderers, fornicators, adulterers, etc." Let them first "sanctify themselves by becoming abolitionists," Brown informed Costello, and then they might "be worthy to minister unto him." They then fell to trading biblical passages concerning slavery. Brown's invocation of St. Paul instructing ministers of religion to first break the chains of slaves before presuming to preach to others was, the priest responded to Brown, nowhere in any Bible he had ever read. Costello did remember that Paul, in one of his epistles, had sent back a fugitive slave to his master. Brown ended the conversation by replying that "he did not care what St. Paul did . . . and not even what he said if it was in favour of slavery!"[35]

If various events of the 1850s—the Fugitive Slave Act, *Uncle Tom's Cabin*, the Kansas-Nebraska Act and the subsequent civil war in Kansas, *Dred Scott v. Sanford*—had intensified the polarization of the country, John Brown's raid proved to be the earthquake that shattered the fault lines of union. In early December, the *Baltimore Sun* editorialized that the South could not afford to "live under a government, the majority of whose subjects or citizens regard John Brown as a martyr and a Christian hero, rather than a murderer and robber."[36] Northern Democrats used the occasion to tar Republicans in general as "lawless, murderous abolitionists bent on race war and disunion."[37] As William Evitts has observed, Brown's raid was the worst realization of chronic southern fears of another Haiti uprising or Nat Turner killing spree. Now, not only had it occurred, but northerners had funded and aided it.[38] The Catholic newspapers, both those with official diocesan connections and those merely edited by Catholics, faulted the Republicans for the attempted uprising. The Baltimore *Catholic Mirror* deemed it "an insane attempt made by a monomaniac and a few deluded followers to liberate the slaves and overthrow the United States Government."[39] The *Pittsburgh Catholic* found it hypocritical that "the entire secular press condemned in Virginia what it applauded in Italy" when the evils in both places were seen as identical. "When evils are at a distance," the paper concluded, "liberty is a sacred name" which exonerates the violent means employed to secure it. "But we see more clearly the evils of rebellion nearer home, and . . . the good sense of all condemns Captain Brown." Only anti-Catholic and anti- monarchical bias prevented a condemnation of the revolutionaries in Europe, the paper concluded.[40] The *Boston Pilot* took ethnic pride in finding no "shadow of an Irish name" among the insurrectionists." In contrast "the gallant Sgt. Quinn" had been the first US marine to "patriotically charge the engine house," and paid with his life for his gallantry.[41] In its immediate reaction to the raid, the *Freeman's Journal* deemed it "A Result of the 'Irrepressible Conflict' Theory," a cautionary tale for both North and South to tamp down their passion. Otherwise the "bloody fanaticism" would be even worse next time.[42] A month after the raid, James Gordon Bennett of the *New York Herald* confessed his dismay that Republicans were more and more being "abolitionized" at a "fearful speed."[43] The *Metropolitan Record* of New York editorialized: "We would not be alarmists; but we have no hesitation in saying that the worst symptom that has yet turned up indicating the condition of the body politics [*sic*] . . . is the bad and bloody business at Harper's [*sic*] Ferry. For the remedy, we should recommend forbearance and patience to the North—patience and forbearance to the South."[44] Patience and forbearance were, at least for the South, the last advice it wanted to be given, when Brown's raid seemed but the precursor of the general insurrection to come, if the abolitionists had their way.

†

CHAPTER 4

The Election That Rent a Nation

Our once great and glorious Union is severed,
perhaps forever. . . . [The Church] remains immovable.
—*CATHOLIC MIRROR*, MARCH 23, 1861

THE COLLAPSE OF
THE LAST NATIONAL PARTY

In April of 1860, 303 delegates to the Democratic National Convention convened in Charleston to nominate a candidate for the presidency who could
unify the sectional wings of the party to ensure victory against the regional
candidate the Republicans would select. As it happened, unity never had a
chance. Robert Barnwell Rhett, the owner of the *Charleston Mercury* and
a leading fire-eater, along with a fellow radical, William Lowndes Yancey
of Alabama, were determined to split the Democrats in order to assure the
secession of the slave states. Their chosen instrument of division was an insistence on a plank in the Democratic platform that called for the protection
of slavery in the territories.[1]

The candidate of the northern Democrats was Stephen Douglas, the US
senator of Illinois, the savior of the Compromise of 1850 and the instigator of
the Kansas-Nebraska bill. The forty-seven-year-old Douglas was married to
his second wife, Adele Cutts, a Catholic, whose brother, Madison, was the
brother-in-law of Rose O'Neal Greenhow.[2] Douglas and his northern supporters prevailed in keeping any such language as the fire-eaters wanted out
of the platform. That was enough to send 118 delegates, a third of them from
New York, on a planned exit from Institute Hall. As the seceders left the building, Maryland delegate Robert Brent, the former attorney general of Maryland and a collateral descendant of John Carroll, warned them that, by their
walkout, they were guaranteeing that the nation would have an abolitionist
president and Congress.[3] A month later, when the Douglas and walkout fac-

tions regathered in Baltimore at separate locations to choose Douglas and John Breckinridge respectively as competing Democratic candidates, they confirmed Brent's prediction.

CATHOLICS
AND THE ELECTION

During the presidential campaign of 1860, Abraham Lincoln came to New York City. His tour of the city took him to Five Points, the nadir of Irish settlement in New York. The wooden hovels, the garbage- and excrement-filled streets, all the detritus of raw poverty shocked the presidential candidate. When he was invited to speak to a Sunday school class at an industrial school for boys in the neighborhood, he found himself momentarily at a rare loss for words. He later said that encountering those children was something he would never forget. Somehow their desire for education had moved him, "given me courage," in continuing his campaign for the presidency. They had "inspired" him that, if elected, he could make a difference in improving their lives and the life of the nation.[4] He little realized, then, how the course of the war would lead him to redefine the nation by legitimizing the rights of the Irish and of everyone else on the underside of American society to share fully in its fruits.

Catholic officials, predictably, stayed quiet about the choice the nation faced. The superior general of the Society of Jesus, Peter Beckx, instructed Jesuits in the United States not to "manifest or entertain any leaning or partiality towards either party," and forbade his subjects from voting in the election. The bishops and clergy in the border states especially strove to be apolitical, convinced that the involvement of clergymen with politics had produced nativism, abolitionism, and secession. A truly neutral hierarchy could best promote union and peace, as well as preserve collegiality within the American Catholic community. John Purcell broke with the prevailing noninvolvement policy of the American hierarchy by publicly supporting Lincoln. Among the clergy the priest-president of Mt. St. Mary's, John McCaffrey, stood out for his public warning that Lincoln's election would mean civil war.

The Catholic laity were overwhelmingly Democratic partisans, especially the Irish.[5] The Catholic newspapers made clear their Democratic bent. The *Boston Pilot* regarded Abraham Lincoln as the candidate of the "John Brown clique" and a tool of the British. At the *New York Herald,* James Gordon Bennett defended the South's interest in protecting its peculiar institution as a reasonable one. "When it ceases to be their interest to remain," the paper warned a week before the election, "the Union is but a rope of sand."[6] To Bennett, Lincoln and the Republicans championed "perfect equality" for Blacks "in all things with the whites."[7] Thomas Francis Meagher and the *Irish News* strongly supported Stephen Douglas.[8]

Lincoln got less than 40 percent of the popular vote, but he carried every state above the Mason-Dixon Line (except for California, Oregon, and New Jersey). John Breckinridge, the southern Democratic candidate, carried all the states of the Deep South, as well as Maryland. John Bell, the candidate of the Constitutional Union Party, a mix of old Whigs and Know-Nothings, carried Kentucky, Virginia, and Tennessee. Douglas got only Missouri in addition to half of New Jersey. Despite winning New York State, Lincoln lost New York City by over 30,000 votes. New Yorkers also defeated a municipal proposal to enfranchise Blacks.[9] In the Irish-heavy Sixth Ward, in which Five Points was located, only 12 percent of the voters chose Lincoln, which was more than he received from the Points district itself.[10] The German wards, by a small majority, also went for Douglas, whom the Catholic *Staats-Zeitung* had endorsed.[11] In Boston, Douglas carried the two Irish wards; he lost the other ten to Lincoln. In Missouri, German Catholics went heavily for Douglas, who carried the state. Lincoln pockets in Catholic America were rare. In Cincinnati, Judge Johann B. Stallo, who had been a delegate to the Republican convention, had great influence in the German Catholic community, which made up a majority of the Germans there. Buffalo also proved a Lincoln stronghold among German Catholics, perhaps in part because of the long battle that trustees at the German Catholic Church, St. Louis, had waged with the hierarchy in the 1840s and 1850s.[12]

Breckinridge especially wanted to win the border states of Maryland, Kentucky, and Missouri. A plurality of Maryland voters delivered the state to him, by 720 votes. Baltimore made the difference. Two of Breckinridge's three strongest wards were the immigrant-heavy Second and Seventeenth, where he won 76 percent and 64.4 percent of the vote respectively. Also crucial for him were the more than 60 percent of voters who went for him in the two Catholic-heavy counties, Charles and St. Mary's.[13] Significantly, at least four of Breckinridge's electors from Maryland were Catholics: E. Louis Lowe, James L. Martin, John Brooke Boyle, and T. Parkin Scott.[14] Breckinridge probably carried a large portion of the Catholic vote in his native state, Kentucky, but barely failed to repeat his success in Maryland. Missouri was a bigger disappointment. Unionist candidates Douglas and Bell garnered over 70 percent of the votes, the Irish vote going heavily for Douglas.

SECESSION

The bishop of Charleston, Patrick Lynch, like his diocesan newspaper, the *United States Catholic Miscellany,* had remained on the political sidelines throughout the 1860 campaign. With Lincoln's victory, the paper's editor, James Corcoran, broke the silence by spelling out in an editorial the only honorable course that South Carolina, and the South, could take: "Long years of menace, insult, outrage and unconstitutional aggression have become at last, certain political as well as social evils which it is wiser to obviate before-hand, than to wait hopelessly in search of their remedy. . . . [T]hat evil day has come upon us, sooner than we would have wished, in order that with free counsel and untrammeled hands, we may deliberate upon and work out our future destiny." That destiny, Corcoran concluded, called them, with their sister "Sovereign States," to take up "a way that will leave untouched the honor and happiness of the South."[15] The "way" needed no explanation. Secession hung over South Carolina like a bright sun's promise of a fair future. Now a Catholic priest was urging the state to take that unprecedented step as the only course that honor would allow. On December 20, the delegates to the Secession Convention assembled in the hall of the St. Andrew's Society on Broad Street, next door to Bishop Lynch's residence. There they unanimously adopted the Ordinance of Secession.[16] Two days later, in the *United States Catholic Miscellany,* Corcoran celebrated the epic event: "South Carolina has, at last, in solemn convention of her people, resumed the portion of her sovereignty which she surrendered in 1789; and now stands before the world, a free independent sovereign State."[17] When the paper next appeared, it had a new name on its masthead: *Charleston Catholic Miscellany.*

In New York, Archbishop John Hughes expressed to Patrick Lynch his shock that his fellow friend and Ulster émigré would have permitted such a radical piece in his diocesan paper. Lynch, in his response to Hughes, articulated for the first time his opinion about the crisis the nation was facing. Fear of the damage a Republican administration could inflict upon the South's slave economy, as well as the appeal of a free-trade Confederacy which would eliminate the heavy burden of inflated tariffs to prop up northern industries—these, Lynch warned, were powerful incentives for the South to secede. Abetting those motives was the unspoken assumption that the joining together of a critical mass of seceding states would deter any attempt by those remaining in the Union to resort to force to preserve the present republic. Lynch himself hoped the Union would somehow hold together under the present crisis, but Union was not an end in itself. The South had to consider its own best interests.

In November 1860, William Henry Elder, bishop of Natchez, advised his priests that only the Mississippi legislature had the competency to know whether secession was the proper course of action to take. What they and their congregations could do was to pray, fast, and give alms, that such Christian works might inspire the lawmakers to do God's will in deciding Mississippi's future. To the private judgment of his people, Elder left the question of secession, but did tell them that, if they were "dispassionately" convinced "that secession was the only practical remedy," for protecting their basic interests, then they had the duty, as citizens, to support the movement.[18] In the mid-1850s, when Elder was president of Mount St. Mary's College, he had considered secession a rash action for the South. Then, as northern states passed Liberty Laws to thwart the Fugitive Slave Act and pilloried Roger Taney for the Dred Scott decision, Elder grew much more sympathetic toward those clamoring to secede.[19] After Mississippi voted overwhelmingly to secede, Elder was "satisfied that the great body of the people have acted conscientiously."[20]

In Mobile, Alabama, Bishop John Quinlan issued a pastoral letter in early January to present his position on the impending breakup of the Union, in which Alabama was a central player. In veiled language Quinlan lamented that the relentless attacks of northern fanatics upon the Constitution of the United States had brought the country to the breaking point. Catholics, the bishop counseled, had the consolation of knowing that they had contributed in no way to the present crisis now confronting the country. If the preservation of the Union could only happen by the forfeit of the South's rights, then better the Union should collapse than that such injustice prevail. God could raise up a new republic.[21]

Senator Stephen Mallory of Florida felt that secession was only justifiable as a last resort. Not until it became obvious in January that his state would become part of the parade of states withdrawing from the Union did Mallory join the movement. In February, he made his resignation speech on the Senate floor. He reminded his audience that it had been but fifteen years since Florida had entered the Union. But although it was one of the youngest states, it enjoyed all the rights of which the original thirteen rightly boasted. Now, Mallory contended, it was all too clear to Florida and the other southern states withdrawing from the Union that their rights were being threatened. "The people of the South," Mallory declared, "will not as freemen submit to the degradation of a constrained existence under a violated Constitution."[22]

In the border states, Union and Confederacy competed for the allegiance and commitment of citizens. Choices were made, more by the subconscious workings of mores, emotions, recent experience, and memory than by any conscious self-debate. If the federal government was the stronger magnet of identification for the majority of border-state inhabitants, among Catholics (a fifth of the population in Maryland and Missouri; 7 percent in Kentucky) the Confederacy had the decidedly greater attraction for various reasons: tradition, race, the conflation of the Republicans with the Know-Nothings, the similarity of the South's position vis-à-vis the United States and Ireland's with Great Britain.

In the wake of Lincoln's election, the publishers of the *Catholic Mirror* brought out a pamphlet defending secession as a legitimate means of preserving the fundamental rights of citizenship that the Constitution was framed to ensure. Thomas Parkin Scott, a prominent Catholic lawyer who had been a Breckinridge elector, contended that, when the states formed the Articles of Confederation in 1778, they did so as "FREE AND INDEPENDENT STATES." Moreover, in framing that compact, they stipulated that "each state should retain its Freedom, Sovereignty, and independence." The Ninth and Tenth amendments to the Constitution declared explicitly "that all powers not granted were reserved to the States or to the people." Equality, sovereignty, and independence are all among the powers reserved by the individual states. Nonetheless, Scott argued, "we of the South have experienced from 1790 to the present day" an assault upon its keystone institution, slavery. With the election of Lincoln, the "Executive Power of the General Government" was "in the hands of those who have . . . avowed 'an irrepressible conflict' with the institutions and rights of the South." That, to Scott, was a clear breach of the compact twice made among the states to ensure "a peaceable Constitution." If the North did not repeal its "unconstitutional legislative acts" regarding fugitive slaves and recognize the "equal rights" of all states "in the common territory," then the South would have no choice but to secede. "Separation is better than subordination or peace." Whenever a government fails to protect the rights of its citizens, Scott concluded, "allegiance is forfeited" and citizens must "change the government" which is not accomplishing "the object for which it was instituted."[23]

Scott's argument was one to which the vast majority of Catholics, to the extent that they reflected upon it, assented. Secession was no arbitrary action being taken freely by the South. The decades-long determination of a minority of abolitionists in the North to undermine slavery, an institution protected by the Constitution itself, had finally forced the South to invoke its Constitutional right to separate. Unions were as permanent as the willingness of all their members to abide by the laws and spirit of the constitutions which had created them.

Pressure continued to mount on Maryland's governor Thomas Hicks to call the legislature into session, presumably to follow Maryland's fellow southern states into secession. On February 1, there was a new attempt at secession made at the Maryland Institute. By this time seven Deep South states had seceded, and the participants evidently felt that Maryland was being left behind in the rush to form a new republic. William Henry Norris told the assembly that the country was on the brink of "dismemberment." He reminded them that the Bill of Rights guaranteed the people's right to assemble to take governance into their own hands when their representatives failed to do their duty. Then Enoch Louis Lowe, the former governor, electrified the crowd by asserting that, should Hicks continue to prevent the people from the opportunity to express their opinion through their representatives, he would personally lift "the banner of revolt against him."[24]

No one strove harder to stay above the political turmoil than did Martin John Spalding, the Catholic bishop of Louisville. Spalding, who, as bishop, had inherited at least twenty slaves, found it incomprehensible that abolitionists could succeed in tearing the country apart. The graver the secession crisis became, the more Martin Spalding conflated abolitionism and Protestantism in assigning blame. They would "destroy the Union and bring about a bloody civil war, in order to confer a boon of most problematic benefit on the slave population." To Spalding, that was seeking to remedy one evil by a greater one.[25] When the special convention that Kentucky had called voted not to secede in late February, that action convinced Martin Spalding that there would be no civil war in which Kentucky would find itself in the middle. Still, he regarded Lincoln and his supporters as "aggressive fanatics determined to commence war with the South."[26]

As in Baltimore, St. Louis Catholic secessionists were mainly a working alliance of monied, old family gentry and recent Irish immigrants. Irish-born Archbishop Peter Kenrick, Francis's brother, in January 1861, issued a pastoral letter in which he urged Catholics essentially to stay out of politics by avoiding "occasions of public excitement . . . and . . . public gatherings where words of passions might endanger tranquility."[27] He might as well have counseled them to stop breathing. The Jesuit community at St. Louis University, despite the superior general's admonition, quickly gained the reputation as a Confederate stronghold. In February, William Stack Murphy was named head of the Missouri Province of the Society of Jesus. The new provincial's sympathies were clearly with the South. A decade earlier, he had written the superior general that, regarding the North and the South, "one would call them in many respects two distinct peoples; very probably their political and national union will one day cease."[28] When the split came, Murphy regarded the Confederacy as the successor to the colonies which had declared their independence of Great Britain. "According to principles of international law," Murphy wrote the superior general in March of 1861, "and the example set by the fathers in formerly driving out the English, the Southern states have seceded with the best of right." At present, only the fear of losing their slaves to the free states which bordered them kept Missouri and Maryland from joining their sister states to the south. Murphy expected the pair to secede eventually, as part of the balkanization of the United States, which seemed inevitable.[29] Jesuit superiors thought it prudent to transfer another St. Louis Jesuit, Ferdinand Garesché, to Louisiana, where his pro-Confederate views would be more widely acceptable.[30] Pierre-Jean De Smet and Francis Weninger, by contrast, were two powerful dissenting voices among Missouri Jesuits, particularly the latter in his antislavery opinion. They were exceptions to the opinion prevailing among their brethren.

Although southern sentiment was widespread in the lower portions of the Old Northwest—Ohio, Indiana, and Illinois—John Purcell, the archbishop of Cincinnati, had no sympathy for those pushing disunion. That he had chosen to vote in the presidential election of 1860, his first such vote in two decades, was stark evidence of how important the archbishop considered the election to be for the country's preservation. As the *Freeman's Journal* quoted Purcell early in 1861: "The Catholic Church is conservative and all its principles revolve and gravitate around the idea of union. What is the principle of secession but the carrying out of the principle of private judgment?"[31] It had no more place in a republic than it had in the Church. The archbishop had been considerably blunter in remarks he made to a gathering at the Catholic Institute three weeks earlier when he had hoped "that the hideous rattlesnake of secession may be crushed to death." That remark produced much consternation among his fellow prelates, which may explain Purcell's offer of his resignation to Pope Pius IX, who refused to accept it.[32]

As South Carolina moved swiftly to launch the secession of southern states, the *Irish-American* told its readers to beware of allowing their instinctive sympathy toward the South blind them to the stark consequence of secession. "Secession means revolution; there can be no doubt of this; and we cannot be induced to forswear the allegiance we have pledged to our adopted country to gratify the secessionists, by abetting them in their unwise and anti-national proceedings." The paper pleaded with the southern states to reconsider what they were doing, before it was too late; to recognize the economic havoc that division and war would have on the working people of the North, not least the Irish, "among the best friends the South could claim in the North."[33]

As indicated by the prominence of New York delegates in the walkout at the Charleston convention, there was much sentiment among Democrats in that state to align with their southern counterparts. In January of 1861, a Catholic member of the New York Board of Aldermen, Francis Boyle, in expressing his sympathy for South Carolina's action, called for a state convention to deal with the crisis. Immediately, a fellow board member, James Brady, demanded to know why he wanted to call a convention. To secede from the Union? "Never allow South Carolina or no slave, nor no nigger of any description to interfere with our stars. . . . I go for my country. . . . they are only fighting for niggers." To Brady, if secession was really about protecting one's investment in human property that was Black, he wanted to have nothing to do with it. It had nothing to do with him or his adopted country.[34] Brady later was the main speaker at a mass "Union Meeting" at Cooper Institute at the end of January, in which Brady made clear that preserving the Union did not mean coercing the states of the emerging Confederacy to return.[35] The editors of the *Irish-American* agreed with Brady that "this Confederation can [not] be held together by armed force." Their very use of the word "Confederation" implied their subscribing to the compact theory as an explanation of the origin of the union of states and of those states' right to withdraw when necessary.[36]

Other important local officials, who did not favor secession, looked to compromise to defuse the crisis. Charles Daly, a Catholic justice of the Court of Common Pleas, thought that the Crittenden Compromise in the US Congress was the only way of preventing civil war.[37] He pressed his case in several meetings with the incoming secretary of state, William Seward, who was looked on as holding the real power in the Lincoln administration. Daly found Seward unshakable in his conviction that there was no danger of war. The crisis, Daly's wife reported Seward to have said, "will all be over in six weeks." When the judge asked Seward what the administration intended to do, should Sumter be attacked, Seward rebuked Daly for even considering the possibility. "They won't do it," the former governor told the judge, "and if they do, it will be time enough to think about it." Such was Seward's confidence in his ability to navigate the roiling waters that secession had stirred. By coincidence, that same day, upon leaving his meeting with Seward, Daly had, by chance, encountered Judah Benjamin, then a US senator from Louisiana. While walking up Pennsylvania Avenue together, Benjamin remarked: "We shall all be back here in two months, and you will join us. New York and several other states will come in." Benjamin had reason to believe that Washington, by March, would become the capital of the Confederacy, which would include among its member states New York, which, with its economic ties, would see that its best interests lay in the new confederation.[38]

In Philadelphia, Bishop William Wood wrote to Patrick Lynch in late January 1861: "There is a strong feeling here that we should hold fast to the South, and some propose that when it is formed, we should join the Southern Confederacy. . . . I am a peace man, under all and every circumstance, and I hope no gun will be fired unless it be for union restored, or secession permitted and consolidated."[39] Wood's enigmatic statement would have greatly disturbed a fellow Pennsylvania bishop, Joshua Young of Erie, who had no intention of holding "fast to the South." Young informed Francis Kenrick that he considered secession "a most criminal and treasonable outrage."[40] Other Catholic voices in the northern states, if not sharing Young's contempt for secession, still rejected it as a constitutional course of action. Orestes Brownson regarded sovereignty as a continuum that had passed from the British crown to the states collectively. "The people of the United States have . . . always been and are one political people, and have never existed as separate, independent and sovereign states."[41] De Smet understood that the US Constitution created a "perpetual" Union, from which no member state could secede.[42]

The Catholic press was badly divided over the issue of secession. In the border states diocesan papers were aghast at the rush toward war. The *Western Banner* of St. Louis took great umbrage at the mere discussion of political issues by Catholic papers, no matter their viewpoint. The *Guardian* of Louisville, reflecting the irenic bent of its bishop, Martin John Spalding, editorialized that the Church should "steer clear of all this irritating discussion" about whether there was a Constitutional duty to coerce the states who had seceded back into the Union.[43]

To John Duffey, the editor of the *Catholic Herald* of Philadelphia, sovereignty lay primarily with the individual states. Hence the regulation of slavery was a responsibility of the state, not the central government. For the central government to claim the authority to regulate it was, in effect, to sound the death knell for the republic, to "overthrow the entire system of government," and to "consolidate a despotism on the ruins of the present Union of confederated republics. *United we stand, divided we fall.*" What Duffey could not admit was that the United States was not a "Union of confederated republics" but a republic in which sovereignty was distributed between the federal government and the individual states. The crucial question was whether the federal government had the authority to require individual states to comply

with laws or regulations established at the national level. This was a controversy that went back at least to the late 1790s when two states, Kentucky
and Virginia, had passed resolutions asserting the right of individual states
to nullify laws passed by the federal government. That challenge had never
been effectively resolved; indeed, it had been reasserted periodically, with
threats to secede if the protests of the individual states failed to receive a fair
hearing. The *Herald* editor, along with those advocating nullification, were,
unwittingly or not, assuming that these republics or states possessed a certain
autonomous authority which ultimately the national government could not
challenge. With that perspective Duffey thought the proper course of the
federal government was to let the come-outer states depart in peace.[44]

By and large, the Catholic press, whether it supported secession or not,
condemned the resort to any coercion to bring back the departing states.
James Gordon Bennett thought it unthinkable that the South could be co-
erced back into the Union, convinced as he was that nine out of ten northerners opposed it.[45] James McMaster, states-right Democrat and anti-abolitionist
that he was, nonetheless had no truck with secessionists. To McMaster, as
with Brownson, the Union was indissoluble. But, if he opposed secession
he also was against any use of force to bring the seceding states back into the
Union, which he considered permanent.[46] Even the *Catholic Telegraph,* which
condemned secession, judged that "coercion, by renouncing the principle
of self-government, would shatter [our free government] to fragments, and
scatter its poor ruins to the winds."[47] In attempting to preserve the Union by
force, Lincoln would destroy it. The *Catholic Mirror* declared in early February, "We are the advocates of no party, but we are faithful adherents of the
republic, devoted to . . . peace and union. . . . We think that *every voice* should
be raised against civil war." It urged the incoming Lincoln administration to
conciliate the South to prevent it.[48] A month later, as the prospects for the
Peace Conference dimmed, the paper warned, "If war comes among us . . .
ruin will be on both sides; horrors there will be in abundance."[49] By the latter
part of March, the editor was forced to admit that "our once great and glorious Union is severed, perhaps forever." What would rise out of the wreckage,
no one knew. The only consolation he could take was in the faith that, while
"all things perish, peoples, states, dynasties, and sects," the Church "remains
immovable."[50]

In New Orleans the Catholic paper *La Propagateur,* in late January 1861,
published a list of principles to guide southern Catholics in the current crisis. "1. Each state is sovereign. 2. [As such the states] maintained the right to
secede from the Union whenever they judged that reasons of honor, liberty,

or security were sufficient to warrant such a separation. 3. For the Southern States, these sufficient motives exist today. . . . 4. residents of a state could recognize no other sovereign authority [but the state. For Catholics] patriotism is . . . a religious duty."[51]

PLOTTING A COUP

By 1860 the growing sectional crisis caused the Knights of the Golden Circle, a secret society which had promoted the expansion of slavery into Central America and the Caribbean, to make military preparedness to defend and promote the interests of the slave states its top priority. Organization members, many of them Catholics, formed militias. They also served as officers in militias springing up throughout the South, such as the "Southern Guide," the brigade that Paul Semmes was organizing in Georgia.[52] In Baltimore, at a preelection rally for Breckinridge in late October, it was announced that a new paramilitary organization was being formed, the National Democratic Volunteers, under the command of William Byrne, a Baltimore businessman and a Breckinridge delegate. Just weeks later, as a southern version of Lincoln's Wide Awakes, more than five thousand National Volunteers marched in a torchlight parade for Breckinridge, led by Byrne on horseback. The District of Columbia had its own branch of the National Volunteers, headed by Cornelius Boyle, a doctor.[53]

By the end of 1860, the Knights of the Golden Circle were plotting to use its military power to seize federal forts and other facilities in the South, as well as to make plans to prevent Lincoln from taking office, including the takeover of Washington, DC, where, by Cornelius Boyle's optimistic calculation, about four-fifths of the population, including many government officials and workers, supported secession. Indeed, Secretary of War Floyd had for over a year been diverting arms to federal arsenals in the South, where they might easily be taken possession of by southern state militias. Meanwhile in Georgia, Paul Semmes had been ordered north by Governor Joseph E. Brown to acquire weapons. Once there, Colonel William J. Hardee, recently commandant of cadets at West Point, assisted Semmes in his arms quest. Through Hardee's contacts, the pair entered into contracts with gun manufacturers. Hardee also enabled Semmes to acquire six Columbiad cannons, from the government's own Fort Pitt foundry.

From late December through January, the seizures of federal installations—no less than twenty forts and arsenals—came in more rapid succession than the secession of the slave states. Several takeovers occurred in states that had yet to pass ordinances of secession. The Knights of the Golden Circle were likely involved in most, if not all of them.[54] In Alabama, the editor of the *Mobile Daily Register* was a Kentuckian, Theodore O'Hara, who had been involved in several filibustering expeditions to export slavery to Central America. O'Hara regarded Lincoln's election as a direct threat to American republican government. In the wake of the election, O'Hara recruited a company of cavalry, some of them students at the Jesuits' Spring Hill College. Subsequently, O'Hara's Mobile Light Dragoons participated in the seizure of several forts in Alabama and Florida and was engaged in the siege of Fort Pickens.[55] At Pensacola, O'Hara was given command of Fort McRae, until Braxton Bragg's arrival as area commander.[56]

As the prospect of a new republic consisting of seceding states became a near certainty in January, a congressional select committee held hearings to determine the existence and extent of secessionist conspiracies to attack Washington itself. In the course of the committee's investigation, several Marylanders, known to have secessionist sympathies, including former governor Enoch Louis Lowe, Cypriano Ferrandini, and Otis K. Hillard, were called to give testimony. At about the same time, John H. Hutcheson had opened a stockbroker's office just south of the center city. Hutcheson was the alias of Allan Pinkerton, who had been hired by Samuel M. Felton, the president of the Philadelphia, Wilmington, & Baltimore Railroad, to ferret out any plans to disrupt Felton's line between Philadelphia and Baltimore in order to isolate the North from the nation's capital. Pinkerton and his agents soon discovered a much deadlier plot than the disruption of transportation. Local secessionists connected with the National Volunteers were planning to assassinate Abraham Lincoln during his stop at Baltimore, the last of his epic succession of appearances across the country on his way to Washington. Specifically, one agent, Harry W. Davies, reportedly an ex-Jesuit seminarian, had worked his way into the circle of conspirators. He had identified Hillard and Ferrandini as key figures in the plot, with Ferrandini, who operated the barber shop at Barnum's Hotel, as the head of the operation. Ferrandini expressly vowed, in the presence of both Davies and Hutcheson, to kill Lincoln. "If I alone must do it," Pinkerton reported the barber as saying, "I shall—Lincoln shall die in this city."[57]

Differing accounts of the intended plan of assassination emerged from not only Pinkerton's investigation, but that of other intelligence agencies, including the New York City Police Department, who also had agents in Baltimore. The National Volunteers, the Baltimore police commissioner (George Kane), Custom House officials—all were reported to be somehow involved.[58] The upshot was that alarms began to be sent to Lincoln, concluding a twelve-day, nineteen-hundred-mile victory train tour on his way to Washington for his March 4 inauguration. By the time the Lincoln party reached Philadelphia on February 22, sufficient intelligence of a plot to waylay and kill the president during a Baltimore stopover convinced Lincoln's advisors that they needed to change his itinerary to take him through the city, unannounced, by a different route during the middle of the night. Thousands of Baltimoreans turned out at the Calvert Street station on February 23 to await the president-elect's arrival, from which there was to be a parade that would terminate at the Eutaw House, where a dinner with local dignitaries was to take place. The crowd waited for hours, only to be told eventually that Lincoln was already in Washington. There would be no Baltimore stop.

BEAUREGARD TO CHARLESTON

The previous December, thanks apparently to the influence of his brother-in-law, Senator John Slidell of Louisiana, P. G. T. Beauregard had been appointed superintendent of the US Military Academy. Beauregard had barely arrived in West Point when he learned that his appointment was being revoked. During a stopover in Washington on his way to his new post, Beauregard had confessed to a military superior that, should Louisiana secede from the Union, he would have to follow his home state. Now Beauregard felt dishonored that that superior had terminated him, even though Louisiana was still in the Union. Nonetheless, he headed for home three days after Christmas. Back in Louisiana, he sought to have the governor appoint him head of the new Louisiana army but lost out to Braxton Bragg. He soon had the consolation of winning an even more important post, besides making a quantum leap from captain to brigadier-general, when Jefferson Davis named him commander of the Confederate forces in Charleston, who were besieging the federal garrison at Fort Sumter.[59]

$$\dagger$$

CHAPTER 5

War Fever

The persistent heresy of state supremacy over the
general law . . . shall perish in the flames.
—*BROOKLYN TABLET*, 1861

FORT SUMTER

In early February, Charleston Bishop Patrick Lynch informed Archbishop
Francis Kenrick of Baltimore: "we are all agog here, and things look warlike
as they have for five weeks past. Six Batteries of Columbiads and heavy cannon are planted around Fort Sumter, and are ready to open fire, whenever
the word is given." From what the bishop had picked up from the authorities,
"four days will end the business—too quickly for troops to be sent on to take
part in it."[1] The Confederate officials had reason to believe, from William
Seward and others, that the new administration would eventually cede the
two forts in South Carolina and Florida that federal military forces were still
holding. That is, until Lincoln's inauguration when, despite his calling upon
"mystic chords of memory" to reunite North and South, the new president
made it as clear as he could that there would be no voluntary cession of the
forts, nor any recognition of secession. Even then, Seward kept sending signals that, in the end, the federal forces would withdraw, no matter what Lincoln had asserted.

Since the beginning of March, Brigadier General P. G. T. Beauregard had
commanded the Confederate forces in Charleston. When the Confederates
learned that a supply ship was headed toward Fort Sumter in early April, they
seized upon that action as an excuse to move against the fort.[2] At 4:30 a.m. on
April 12, guns from the quay and surrounding islands opened fire on the brick
fort in Charleston harbor. The fort's shore-facing batteries responded. All
through the day, the cannonading of the fort continued. Anderson at first kept
his guns silent, then unleashed all of the firepower from the fort's shore-facing

batteries. Fortunately, virtually all the cannon in play were smoothbores, little capable of inflicting decisive damage on either the fort or the shore. Amid all the shelling, the federal relief fleet arrived but dared not attempt to reach the fort itself. At one point, early on April 14, the shelling caused the barracks in the fort to catch fire. General Beauregard sent a delegation to assist in combating the fire. Anderson politely declined. Shortly afterwards, a white flag went up over Sumter. Anderson had finally decided that he had done all that duty required and could, in honor, give up the fort. Beauregard allowed its commander to have an artillery salute for the American flag. On the fiftieth round of the salute, a gun exploded, killing one Union soldier and wounding five.[3] The "battle" ended with Confederate soldiers and Charleston citizens doffing their caps in honor of the Sumter defenders as they sailed out of the harbor to make their way north on the fleet that had intended to enable them to maintain a federal presence in the heart of the Confederacy.[4]

A PANDEMIC OF PATRIOTISM
IN THE NORTH

The day after Major Anderson surrendered Fort Sumter, Lincoln issued a proclamation that an insurrection existed in seven states and called on *all* the states to provide a total of seventy-five thousand volunteers for three months in order to suppress it. When Cump Sherman had the opportunity to meet the president shortly afterwards, he did not hesitate to point out to Lincoln how inadequate was his response to the attack on Fort Sumter. "You might as well try to put out a fire with a squirt gun as put down this rebellion in three months' time." "I guess," Lincoln responded to an unimpressed Sherman, "we'll manage to keep house."[5]

Lincoln's expectation about what it would take to put down the rebellion may have been obviously unrealistic to a military veteran, but such a calculation had no chance of influencing a northern public driven to a frenetic pitch of patriotism by the Confederate attack. Two days after the attack on Fort Sumter the Jesuit Pierre-Jean De Smet returned to New York from another recruiting trip to Belgium and the Netherlands. On his subsequent thousand-mile trip home to St. Louis, De Smet found "nothing but the clang of arms . . . & the war-cry repeated in every city, town & hamlet." In a divided country in which both sides had expected a peaceful resolution, Sumter-inspired war fever had become a pandemic that respected no portion of it.[6] Nowhere was that truer than in New York City, where the shock of the attack on Fort

Sumter produced "an unprecedented outburst of patriotism" that overnight had American flags and bunting adorning everything from public buildings to omnibuses to churches and synagogues.[7] In Buffalo, where approximately half of the population was Catholic, news of the attack on Fort Sumter brought a crowd to Buffalo bishop John Timon's residence. Timon, the son of Irish immigrants, immediately displayed the American flag over the episcopal residence. In a prepared speech before a crowd who had gathered in front of the residence, Timon denounced the radical minority in the South who had set off this conflict and pledged his support for the government.[8]

Bishops and priests from Boston to Pittsburgh to Milwaukee, some under more pressure than others, flew flags from their cathedrals and churches as a totemic expression of allegiance. In the Republican stronghold of Pittsburgh, Bishop Michael Domenec reported: "Our churches were in danger of being burnt; we were obliged to raise the Union flag on the Cathedral and on all the churches."[9] The bishop himself took a public oath of fealty to the United States and urged his fellow Catholics to do the same.[10] No bishop was more supportive of the war than was Archbishop John Purcell, who told the Catholics of the Cincinnati Archdiocese that "it is our solemn duty as good and loyal citizens to walk shoulder to shoulder with all our fellow citizens in support of the national honor."[11] To leave no doubt about the loyalty of Cincinnati's Catholics, Purcell had a gigantic American flag, some ninety feet in length, displayed from the spire of the cathedral. In Wisconsin, where rumors circulated that Bishop John Henni had instructed his priests to discourage enlistments, Henni directed that every church in the diocese publicly display the American flag.[12]

The *Pittsburgh Catholic* editorialized that the federal government had no recourse but "to take strong measures" against those who would seize US property and fire on its flag. "We have to select," it concluded, "between a legitimate government, and an unjustifiable rebellion." That choice was an easy one, it added, when the Confederacy "has African Slavery for its cornerstone."[13] Of all the Catholic papers, perhaps none proved more prophetic than did the *New York Tablet* in its editorial on May 4, 1861, in which the editor predicted that the war would be a "fiery ordeal" out of which the country would at last become a true nation, one in which "the persistent heresy of state supremacy over the general law, of the nonexistence of any obligation on the part of one state . . . toward all the others, shall perish in the flames. Liberty will thenceforth be the rule, slavery the exception." Slavers would no longer be favored over white laborers in having access to the public lands. "The great republican principle, that the majority shall rule and the minority submit, will be thoroughly and firmly established as the keystone of our republican arch." It was a clarion call for a *herrenvolk* democracy. It promised nothing to those who did not fall within the racial circle, to whom the *Tablet* limited its concerns.[14]

In the North, Sumter brought an outpouring of Irish volunteers. Ryan W. Keating, who has intensely studied Irish regiments in the Union armies, found that over 150,000 Irish-born males served in the Union forces.[15] As the *Irish News* reported, immediately after Sumter: "The Celtic element is on fire throughout the city."[16] With the largest Irish population in the country, New York raised more Irish regiments than any other locality. The Irish Revolutionary Brotherhood (Fenians), the New York–based nationalist organization committed to Ireland's liberation, was a major contributor to the New York Irish response. One of their leaders, Michael Corcoran, commanded the New York Sixty-Ninth Regiment.

The four Irish regiments were not the only Catholic ethnic ones organized in New York. The French community in New York City, led by immigrant Philippe Régis de Trobriand, organized a multiethnic regiment, the New York Fifty-Fifth, in which men of French origin were the majority. Edward Ferrero, whose Italian parents had brought him to New York City as a young child in the early 1830s, recruited a regiment in the first summer of the war, the New York Fifty-First.

In New Haven, Connecticut, where five years earlier the governor had disbanded the Irish militias as being "detrimental to the military interests of our State," another Irish nationalist and community leader, Thomas Cahill, took the lead in July 1861 in forming a regiment composed of his fellow countrymen.[17] In Massachusetts, Irish community leaders raised two regiments, the Ninth and the Twenty-Eighth.[18] As a sign of the city's appreciation, in its celebration of the Fourth of July a week later, the Irish flag was raised on Boston Common, along with the flags of the nations. Further recognition of the Catholic community's patriotism came later that month when Harvard College awarded Bishop Joseph Fitzpatrick an honorary degree, the first ever accorded to a Catholic ecclesiastic.[19]

In Chicago, the Irish politician James A. Mulligan raised a regiment which became the Illinois Twenty-Third. In 1862, the vicar general of the Chicago Diocese, Dennis Dunne, led a campaign to form a second Irish regiment, which he dubbed "the Irish Legion." There was distinctly less enthusiasm for the war among the Irish in Indiana, where John C. Walker and Bernard F. Mullen, who had been trying to raise regiments for months, finally had to combine their recruits to form the Indiana Thirty-Fifth.[20] In Wisconsin, persistent nativism hampered Irish enlistments.[21] In Fond du Lac, Wisconsin, a local Irish Catholic militia, the Hibernian Guard, attempted to volunteer their services at a Union rally, only to be told by the quartermaster general of the Wisconsin State Militia that "there are enough young Americans to put down this trouble inside of 90 days and we do not want any red faced foreigners." It took John Doran, an Irish immigrant and Milwaukee lawyer, nine months to enlist enough of his countrymen to form the Wisconsin Seventeenth.[22] Doran's experience foreshadowed the overall war record of the Irish. Of the estimated 200,000 Catholic Americans who served in the Union military, the Irish were the most underrepresented ethnic group, despite persistent efforts of clergy and bishops to encourage enlistments.[23]

No immigrant group had as many of its men in Union armies as did the Germans, with as many as 216,000 estimated to have been in their ranks.[24] In general, Catholics ranked among the lowest of German subgroups in their enlistment rate.[25] As in an earlier civil war, the American Revolution, there was a strong current among German Catholics that this was not their war, particularly if it involved emancipation. A Jesuit, Francis Weninger, admitted that the German Catholics shared with their Irish counterparts a distinct aversion to making abolition a war aim. Recruitment efforts met with little success. If northern Catholics saw the war as an opportunity to prove their loyalty, the enlistment rates of both German and Irish Catholics failed to demonstrate it.

SOUTHERN CATHOLICS
EMBRACE THEIR NEW NATION

Within the eleven Confederate states there were eleven dioceses. Eight of the eleven prelates were foreign-born (four French, four Irish); three were natives. Whether immigrants or native-born, with one exception, they became staunch supporters of the Confederacy. The exception was James Whelan, OP, of Nashville. Whelan made no attempt to hide his Unionist leanings. When Union forces in 1863 occupied most of his diocese, Whelan freely fraternized with the occupiers. That disloyalty so outraged both Catholics and non-Catholics that the bishop was forced to resign in May of 1863.[26]

Typical in his overt support of the Confederacy was the French-born Bishop Auguste Martin of Natchitoches, who declared in a pastoral letter in the summer of 1861 that the southern states had seceded to escape the tyranny which the North threatened to impose upon them. According to Martin, Catholics in those states had the obligation in conscience to take up arms for their new country. "Justice and truth," he assured them, "are invincible."

Those principles gave them a strength greater than arms could ever provide.[27] Richmond bishop John McGill, Philadelphia-born but raised in Bardstown, was sure, like Martin, that the Constitution and justice were on the side of the Confederacy. McGill even became a significant purchaser, for the diocese, of Confederate bonds.[28]

The French Redemptorist archbishop of New Orleans, John Mary Odin, abhorred slavery as a state into which human beings should never be put, but he came to recoil even more so from abolitionists, whom he blamed for the war.[29] Charleston, with its estimated twenty thousand Catholics within its boundaries of the Carolinas, was hardly the most important Southern see, but its ordinary, Patrick Lynch, became the most noted episcopal apologist for the Confederacy. In celebration of the fall of Fort Sumter, Lynch ordered a *Te Deum* solemnly sung at his cathedral. Days later, he was among the dignitaries touring the site of the first battle for southern independence. Like McGill, Patrick Lynch heavily invested his diocesan funds in Confederate bonds as a telling sign of the collective loyalty of Charleston Catholics.[30]

The religious orders, both male and female, became some of the strongest adherents of the Confederacy. As the Ursuline nun Baptista Lynch, Patrick's sister, wrote her bishop brother in early June of 1862 when Confederate prospects seemed increasingly bleak, "I am a very strong secessionist."[31] Her community demonstrated its patriotism by sewing regimental and national flags for Catholic units. In Alabama, the Jesuits at Spring Hill made no pretense of observing the neutrality that their superior general was prescribing, but were, as an early historian of the school judged, "ardently Confederate as the most enthusiastic of their pupils."[32]

IRISH IN
CONFEDERATE SERVICE

Fewer than 7 percent of the Irish-born lived below the Potomac, but, like their northern counterparts, they were concentrated in urban areas.[33] Estimates of the number of Irish and Irish Americans who served in the Confederate armed forces range as high as forty thousand, but such estimates include Protestants as well as Catholics. Catholics likely comprised but a half or so of Irish Confederate enrollment. At the same time, the percentage of eligible Irish in the South, as in the North, who fought in the war was significantly below that of the general eligible population of the region. That lower service rate may, in part, have reflected the tendency of some Irish to claim exemption from service as noncitizens.[34] At the same time, Irish Catholics in the South seemed to have a higher proportion of their eligible population in military service than did those in the North. This regional disparity would seem to apply to the eligible Catholic population. As Gracjan Kraszewski suggests, this might have reflected the Catholic sentiment that found southern society more congruent than it found its northern counterpart. Catholics, given their own institutional structure and teachings, were more drawn to the values of tradition, conservatism, and hierarchical order that the South promoted than they were to the materialism, liberalism, and centralization that the North increasingly embodied.[35] An important attraction for the Irish to the Confederate cause was the parallel that the southern Irish saw between the Confederacy's struggle for independence and their native Ireland's fight against their British occupiers. As Thomas McMahon pointed out to Thomas Francis Meagher, upon hearing that the veteran of the Revolution of 1848 was enlisting in the Union Army, it was pure irony that he who had fought so valiantly for Irish independence against English oppression was now himself abetting the effort to strike down the South's struggle for self-government.[36]

In New Orleans, Irishmen could be found in all of the regiments raised in the city and dominated some, such as the Louisiana Sixth. Indeed, Louisiana provided more Irish for Confederate service than did any other Confederate state. The Seventh Louisiana was more than a third Irish-born. Irish formed a substantial part of what became known as the "Tiger Battalion." Patriotism and ethnic pride were hardly the sole reasons the New Orleans Irish enlisted. Economic necessity drove many into Confederate ranks. Others were dragooned into the army from the saloons, jails, and alleys of the city. The forced enlistments certainly contributed to the high rate of criminal behavior and desertion among noncitizens in the Louisiana regiments.[37] Irish Catholics, located so heavily in port cities of the Confederacy, unsurprisingly were overrepresented in the country's naval and marine forces, with more than 600 (out of 4,000) in the navy and some 150 (of 560) in the Marines.[38]

At the war's outbreak, Louisiana's governor, Thomas D. Moore, asked the heavily Catholic Afro-Creole community to raise a regiment. More than 1,000 responded by forming the Native Guards, with a white commander, Félix Labatut.[39] The *New Orleans Daily Crescent* predicted, "Our free colored men . . . will fight the Black Republicans with as much determination and gallantry [as whites]."[40] They never had the chance, as it quickly became clear that the Native Guards, used almost exclusively as a ceremonial home guard, were window-dressing for the Confederacy, a public relations prop to show the world that this was not just a white man's war. The Confederacy had no intention of testing the willingness of any Blacks, whether free or bonded, to fight for a republic whose cornerstone was slavery.

GRASPING AT NEUTRALITY

The slaveholding border states supplied more than twice as many whites for the Union forces (approximately 200,000) than they did for those of the Confederacy (90,000 or so).[41] Had Maryland, Kentucky, and Missouri all eventually cast their lots with the new nation, those figures would have been a great deal more favorable to the Confederacy. In late February a rumor circulated broadly that Maryland planned to secede, should peace negotiations come to nothing. Maryland, Kentucky, and Missouri all remained within the Union, although all three made early attempts to be neutral in the war between the federal government and breakaway states, a tacit recognition of their divided citizenry. The citizens of all three border states were indeed badly divided, with a significant majority loyal to the established republic and a considerable minority identifying with the new confederacy below the Mason-Dixon Line. The Catholic communities, however, did not mirror the split of the general populations of these border states. Tradition, kinship links, ideology, and race combined to orient most of the white Catholics toward the South. The Confederacy had their sympathy, if not their formal allegiance, as their enlistment patterns and their opposition to the war policies of the Lincoln administration demonstrated.

Martin Spalding, the bishop of Louisville, kept hoping, even after Sumter, that sanity would prevail. "I think it would be *madness* for us to secede now," he wrote his brother in late April. We would become the theatre of a terrible war, & our slaves would be emancipated, or at least our safety would be imperiled. . . . We should keep cool & remain neutral as long as possible; though I think that *ultimately* we will have to take sides."[42]

In its first edition after the firing on Fort Sumter, the Baltimore-based *Catholic Mirror* had a long editorial on "The War," in which it admitted that slavery was at the root of the conflict, but blamed northern preachers and newspapers for inciting it. To the editor, southern slavery was an idyllic state of life for the Black laboring class, far better than the one the white laborer knew, either in the North or in Ireland. If within their rights as sovereign states, the South, the editor owned, "were ever hasty in withdrawing from the great American republic, but they have gone." It was simple madness to suppose "to bring them back by force." That editorial appeared on Saturday, April 20, a day after the first blood of the war had been drawn on the streets of Baltimore itself because a large portion of the community shared the editor's opinion.

Tensions had been rising in Baltimore since the news from Charleston had rocked the city. The extreme difference in sentiments between Unionists and secessionists led to large-scale fighting in the days leading to the nineteenth of April. Well before the firing commenced at Sumter, the rival Confederate and Union governments had been openly recruiting soldiers in the city. Groups of volunteers were regularly departing Baltimore on ships heading toward Charleston and points south. Demonstrations of support for the Confederacy continued in the city, including mass meetings in Monument Square. On the afternoon of Thursday, April 18, several hundred Pennsylvania troops came into the Bolton Street depot of the Northern Central Railroad, where they were greeted by locals singing "Dixie's Land" and sending up cheers for the Confederacy. With a police escort, the soldiers made their way through the jeers, groans, and Confederate cheers of the onlookers to Mt. Claire Station, where they boarded cars to the District of Columbia.

The following morning, the National Volunteers staged a mass rally at Monument Square to organize resistance to any further passage of troops.[43] Monument Square was but a few blocks east of the President Street Station, to which most of the crowd headed, in anticipation of the arrival of more troops. At around 11 a.m. a train arrived at the station with about twenty-two hundred soldiers from Pennsylvania and Massachusetts.[44] At the station the cars were hitched to horses who conveyed them along Pratt Street to Camden Station where a train would take them the last thirty-six miles to Washington. The nine first cars carrying some seven companies of the Sixth Massachusetts managed to get to the connecting station. Then the rapidly swelling crowd, with a fusillade of stones that broke all the windows of the lead car, forced authorities to order the soldiers from all the remaining cars to take to the streets for the final mile to Camden Station.[45]

With Mayor George Brown and some police leading, the troops made their exposed way west along Pratt Street, through "an immense concourse of people" that pressed upon them from all sides. They found themselves increasingly vulnerable, not just to shots and missiles from the crowds along the sidewalks, but from the upper stories of buildings. At one point, after a soldier bringing up the rear was struck by a bullet, his fellow soldiers wheeled and fired point-blank into their pursuers. At another, civilians seized guns from fallen soldiers and fired them lethally at the Sixth. Francis X. Ward of the Maryland Guard led a charge on the Massachusetts regiment. When he grabbed their flag, a bullet passed through his hip before fatally striking another citizen.[46] At still another point in the desperate march, a Massachusetts soldier dropped his weapon, which Edward W. Beatty immediately picked up and fired at the soldiers.

Historians have concluded that the crowds, estimated to be between eight thousand to ten thousand, were largely composed of middle-class Democrats, many of them Catholics from the Custom House or street gangs.[47] A great number of those who had participated in the late February gathering, such as the National Volunteers and Maryland Guard, were on the streets on April 19.[48] George Konig, an Alsatian Catholic who operated a saloon and brothel on Canton Avenue in the Fell's Point section, led a large group of toughs behind a "secession flag" to the President Street Station and onto Pratt Street, where they began to taunt and throw missiles at the soldiers, including paving stones, a traditional weapon in the street wars of the 1850s.[49] An Italian, Cypriano Ferrandini, the Barnum Hotel barber who was reputedly the ringleader of the February plot against Lincoln, was also a prominent participant in the April 19 rioting.[50] As the mob continued to attack the Massachusetts regiment, the police did little to contain them. Some refused to arrest rioters or released them shortly after making perfunctory arrests.[51] By the time the train pulled out of Camden Station at 12:45 p.m., thirteen civilians were dead, as were four of the Massachusetts Sixth. Most of the civilian dead were Irish.

With Confederate fever running rampant in the city over the "massacre" perpetrated by northern troops, a temporarily united Baltimore community prepared to do everything to prevent a replication of Friday. The city council appropriated a half-million dollars for the defense of the city. Bank presidents Columbus O'Donnell, Johns Hopkins, and John Clark offered a loan of an equal amount for the same civic purpose. Confederate flags flew everywhere. By Saturday, Baltimore officials were claiming that they had twelve thousand citizens under arms.[52] So thoroughly did pro-southern sentiment dominate the city in the immediate aftermath of the riot that, in the election to choose delegates to the state assembly, the slate of Democratic candidates running under the title of the Southern Rights Party, including the Catholics, John C. Brune (the president of the Board of Trade), and T. Parkin Scott, was uncontested. The press, north and south, was convinced that Maryland's secession was a fait accompli.

If secessionists remained in control of the city, they would isolate the nation's capital from the loyal states. Subduing Baltimore became a prerequisite, even if that involved massive bombardment, as President Lincoln himself instructed his commanding general. That proved unnecessary. Even before federal troops occupied the recalcitrant city, secessionist fever was fading.

Francis Kenrick reported to Martin Spalding on May 4, 1861: "Our citizens became sensible that they must yield to the overwhelming force of the General Government, and our Legislature has adopted conciliatory measures. Yet we are not without fear that troops from the North may inflict some retaliation."[53] On Monday, May 13, General Benjamin Butler's troops, under the cover of rain and darkness, occupied Federal Hill overlooking the central city and trained fifty cannon on downtown Baltimore. In late June, military authorities, acting on information that Marshal George Kane and the police commissioners were working hand in glove with secessionists, had them arrested and the city placed under martial law.[54] Baltimore became the first area in the South to experience the "hard-war tactics" that the Lincoln administration was willing to deploy to end the rebellion.

RECRUITMENT IN
THE CHESAPEAKE REGION

Even before Sumter, the Confederate government had been successfully recruiting in Baltimore. Compared to the Confederate efforts, Union forces were very slow to organize in the state. Most federal regiments were not formed until the winter of 1861–62.[55] In all, about 41,000 or 63 percent of those who fought in the war did so for the Union (of those 41,000, over 9,000 were Blacks). Approximately 22,000 served in the Confederacy's armed forces. Thus 43 percent of the white enlistments were for Confederate service.[56] The bulk of Maryland Confederates signed on to the war in its first two years; the bulk of Union inductions took place in the latter half, after the Lincoln administration had been forced to institute conscription in order to meet its manpower needs for its armies. German immigrants in Baltimore outnumbered the Irish by two to one. A large minority of the Germans were Catholic. Like their brethren elsewhere in the border states and those of the old Northwest (Ohio, Illinois, Indiana), they lagged behind their secular ethnic brethren in their enlistments and support for the war. Of the nearly 1,400 Maryland Germans and Irish who responded to Lincoln's call in 1861, Germans accounted for nearly 80 percent of the recruits. Only after conscription began in 1863, with its opportunities for bounties and substitution fees, did the enlistment of the Irish begin to approach that of the Germans. The statistics bear out the complaints of officials like Governor Bradford that the Baltimore Irish were not bearing their share of the burden of defending their adopted country.[57] At the same time, the Irish constituted a higher proportion of deserters than their enlistment rate would have predicted.[58]

73

Conversely the Irish were overrepresented in the Confederate ranks, with those in Maryland-based units nearly doubling their German counterparts (432 to 241).[59] In Baltimore, and even more so on the Eastern Shore and in southern Maryland, those actively identifying with the South and willing to commit themselves to the region's efforts to achieve independence outnumbered those who identified with the North and were willing to commit their lives and honor to the Lincoln administration's war to preserve the Union, with the disparity least in Baltimore among these three sections. In northern and western Maryland, there was more ambivalence, but overall a leaning toward the maintenance of the Union prevailed. In the statewide Catholic community, secessionists greatly outnumbered Unionists.

Catholics, particularly those from old families like the Edelins, Digges, Howards, and Dorseys, were prominent in the initial companies that became the First Maryland Infantry Regiment (CSA). Francis Xavier Ward, a prominent riot participant, within the month was at Harpers Ferry, a first lieutenant in the First Maryland Regiment which was being organized for Confederate service. In mid-May, John White Scott, the son of Thomas Parkton Scott, quit a law apprenticeship to head south to join the rebel army. On May 4, Edward R. Dorsey, a first lieutenant in the Baltimore City Guard, offered his company's service to the Confederacy. Four days later Francis J. Thomas, a West Point graduate and veteran of the Mexican-American War, who listed himself as "Adjutant General of Maryland," offered his service to the state of Virginia, with the dubious promise that at least 1,500 more recruits were in transit from Maryland.[60]

Many Anglo-American Catholics in southern Maryland prepared to go south within days following the bombardment of Fort Sumter.[61] By 1862 the Jesuit seminarian John Abell Morgan reported that most of his friends in his native St. Mary's County were fighting with the Army of Northern Virginia. They were part of the rural and urban gentry who formed the nucleus of the Maryland officer corps in the Confederacy.[62] Indeed available evidence points to Catholics constituting a large portion of the two major units that Maryland contributed to the Army of Northern Virginia: the First Maryland Regiment and the Maryland Battalion. Kevin Conley Ruffner found in his study of Marylanders who served as Confederate junior officers that at least a dozen were Georgetown College alumni.[63] In all Ruffner discovered at least seventeen Catholics among the Confederate officers he studied, or 12 percent of the cohort. He thought it likely that this was an undercount.

Maryland chronically failed to meet its recruiting quotas set by the Lincoln administration. As a result of this shortfall of three-year enlistments, it was forced to form units with short-term commitments, as brief as ninety days. By 1863 authorities became so desperate that they even reached into the prison camp at Point Lookout in southern Maryland in their manpower search.[64] Charles Aloysius Deitz, an immigrant from Saxony; Charles Edwin Dudrow, a cigar maker from Frederick; and Robert McIntire Gorsuch, a tobacconist, were notable Catholic officers of Maryland Union units.[65]

KENTUCKY

"We should keep cool & remain neutral as long as possible," Bishop Martin Spalding wrote his brother, Benedict, in late April. To join either side, the bishop feared, would make Kentucky "the theatre of a terrible war & our slaves would be emancipated, or at least our safety would be imperilled."[66] Kentucky's governor and legislature, sharing Spalding's fears, adopted a policy of neutrality, as though the state was not an integral part of the United States but an external body that would be willing to act as a third party.[67]

Bishop Spalding, on his visitation of congregations in Western Kentucky immediately after the firing on Fort Sumter, found a pervasive display of Confederate flags in this hotbed of southern affinity.[68] That portion of Kentucky, like the area around Bardstown, hardly mirrored the sentiment of the state as a whole, where a conservative Unionism prevailed. A large majority of Kentuckians chose to remain loyal, not only because of the economic and social ties they had to northern states, but in the calculation that the federal government would not only prevail in putting down the rebellion, but also preserve slavery in doing so. As James W. Finck has argued, "the question was not whether Kentucky believed in slavery, but which side offered the most protection to slavery" as a guarantor of white supremacy and control of Blacks.[69] Kentucky had far more slaves than Maryland, 225,000 to 87,000, and far fewer free Blacks than Maryland's nearly 84,000. A state with such a large slave population, which annually counted the largest number of runaways (1,200), understandably feared slave insurrections. To join the Confederacy would very likely just make matters worse.[70] They sensed that, even though they by and large identified with the South, the Union was their best bet for protecting their investments in a slave economy that was steadily shrinking and facing a precarious future. The majority of Kentucky slave owners were betting not only that the Union would prevail in the war, but that the federal government would not punish the loyal by taking their most valuable property.

The 66,000 white Kentuckians who fought for the Union, as opposed to the top estimate of 40,000 who went South to defend the Confederacy, speaks to that decided preference, however qualified, for the Union.[71] They were for the preservation of the Union as it was, with slavery intact. Enslaved labor in Kentucky was a major part of the workforce (one of every five Kentuckians was enslaved) but was largely the province of small farmers.[72] Like Maryland, it was shrinking as a proportion of the labor force, particularly as the demand for and price of slaves was fueling their sale to the Deep South.[73] The state was becoming less and less dependent on enslaved labor, particularly as Kentucky agriculture diversified to include less labor-intensive staples.[74] That diversification led to greater hiring out of enslaved labor, which ironically brought a larger proportion of white society into slavery's orbit.[75]

The Kentucky Catholic community, on the other hand, had a greater investment in slavery than did its non-Catholic counterpart, one reason for its greater commitment to the Confederate cause. C. Walker Gollar found that, in the historic heart of Catholic Kentucky, Washington and Nelson counties, Catholics tended to be slavers in a greater proportion than did the general white population.[76] That demographic evidently weighed heavily in shaping allegiance within Kentucky's Catholic community.[77]

MISSOURI

The stained-glass window bearing the stars and bars of the Confederate flag in St. John the Apostle and Evangelist Church in St. Louis is an enduring witness to the prevailing sentiment of the Catholic community during the Civil War. Its pastor at the outbreak of the war, John B. Bannon, was the only diocesan priest to become a full-time chaplain for the Confederacy. The state, because of its heavy concentration of Germans as well as migrants from the free states, experienced the greatest division of the border states. In St. Louis, riots occurred between rival factions, beginning in late April. Governor Claiborne Jackson, at month's end, declared that "Missouri . . . in concert with Tennessee and Kentucky . . . are all bound to go out and should go together if possible." The governor called for the southern-committed state militia brigade, including the St. Louis Grays, the Laclede Guards, and the Washington Blues, under the command of the career military and converted Catholic general, Daniel Morgan Frost, to muster at Camp Jackson just outside the city, as the prelude for an attack on the US arsenal, whose sixty thousand muskets equaled more than half the existing supply in the entire Confederacy.[78] On May 10, before the state militia could move out for their assault, some eight thousand Union troops surrounded the seven hundred insurgents and forced their surrender. As the local rebels were being marched through the city, supporters of the prisoners began heckling on the streets and firing from flanking buildings upon the largely German troops. Instantaneously there was indiscriminate shooting between troops and protestors. When the firing stopped, fourteen persons were dead and forty wounded, many mortally. St. Louis's violence had produced casualties that surpassed Baltimore's of the previous month. Among the spectators were William Tecumseh Sherman and a son.[79]

The Unionist cause fared badly in the immediate fallout of the Camp Jackson attack. The Jesuit provincial superior, William Murphy, a Confederate supporter, wrote the superior general: "By force of arms and at the cost of the slaying of some thirty citizens of both sexes, the troops of the general government, made up almost entirely of a rabble of non-Catholic Germans, have effected a military occupation of the city."[80] The following day, Governor Jackson declared war on the United States and issued a call for fifty thousand Missourians to defend the state against federal troops. Secessionist sentiment surged, as did enlistment in the Confederate forces or pro-Confederate militia. Frost went South, as did most of the militia. Among them were Catholics William Wade, Richard C. Walsh, John Kearny, Patrick Canniff, and Henry Guibor. Catholics comprised a substantial proportion of the First Missouri Brigade of Price's Army of the West. John Bannon, who became the unofficial chaplain of the brigade, estimated that there were approximately fifteen hundred Catholics in Price's force.[81] Most were undoubtedly Irish. Of the eighteen hundred Irishmen in the border states that David Gleeson estimates were in the armed services of the Confederacy, the majority would have been Missourians.[82]

More violence occurred the following month. In mid-June, Governor Jackson abandoned the state capital, Jefferson City, and relocated his government in southwestern Missouri near the Arkansas border. Unionists reassembled a major portion of the anti-secession convention in the capital as a provisional government of Missouri. Pro-southern forces proved victorious twice that summer at Wilson's Creek in August and at Lexington in September, where the commander of the Union forces, Colonel James A. Mulligan, surrendered his garrison of thirty-five hundred to a besieging force under General Price. In November, Jackson's competing government passed an ordinance of secession. The Confederate Congress subsequently admitted Missouri as its twelfth state, but it was essentially an aspirational gesture. The federal occupiers' suspension of habeas corpus, imposition of loyalty oaths, and arresting of any citizens whose loyalty was suspect all served to suppress dissent and keep the state within the Union.

The Missouri German Catholics were the least likely of their ethnic bloc to enlist in the Union forces, or to vote Republican.[83] In general, where Germans, often Catholics, tended to be Democrats, they were least likely to support the war. That was particularly true of German Catholics, who had the highest rate of Democratic affiliation in their ethnic cohort. As Walter D. Kamphoefner concludes: "There can be no doubt that political affiliation played heavily" in determining the level of one's commitment to the war, or the lack of it.[84] In St. Louis, German Catholics got caught up in the war within the war that developed within the German community. The Catholic *Tages-Chronik* made no attempt to hide its Confederate sympathies, although never coming out for secession.[85]

PRESERVING CATHOLIC UNITY
IN A DIVIDED NATION

As Catholics rallied to the competing governments or attempted to avoid any such choice, Patrick Lynch, writing to his old friend John Hughes, took comfort in the conviction that there was still one community in the nation that civil war could not divide. The "bridge of Catholic union," founded on the faith they continued to share even though they might now be formal enemies, could uniquely "span the chasm" that separated North and South.[86] Dual allegiance, it turned out, had its saving grace. Catholics might now acknowledge different presidents, but they still professed spiritual fidelity to the same pope, preserving a bond that eluded most other Americans. As John Hughes told a Catholic group in New York City on St. Patrick's Day, less than a month before the attack on Fort Sumter, "There is no geography for the Catholic as a Catholic. . . . he embraces his brother Catholic . . . in the capital of China . . . the same as if he were in New York. He believes all that we believe." Theology was the ultimate bond.[87] Strengthening this bond was the network of institutions—the academies, colleges, seminaries, and houses of religious men and women—in which the Catholic elite had formed their worldview. Moreover, so many of the priests and the active religious women were accustomed to serving in dioceses other than their own. This was particularly true of the women religious. That kind of movement widened the circle of acquaintances and broke down a local sense of belonging that tended to look inward rather than outward.

As Confederacy and Union prepared for war, Catholics on both sides could take consolation in the unique cord of union which their Church provided them. What remained to be seen was how that bond would affect the hard choices that war would inevitably raise.

†

CHAPTER 6

First Season of War

Come on! Why do you not come?

—ROSE O'NEAL GREENHOW
TO P. G. T. BEAUREGARD, AUGUST 1861

BUILDING AND LAUNCHING
A CONFEDERATE NAVY

Stephen Mallory began to assembly a navy, first in Montgomery, then in May 1861 in his quarters on Ninth Street, between Main and Franklin streets, in Richmond. The highest priority was ironclads that would enable the Confederate Navy to offset the great advantage the US Navy had in the quantity of ships it already possessed. Two ironclads were ordered built: the *Virginia* in the Norfolk shipyard and the *Mississippi* in New Orleans. Mallory also dispatched two agents to England to purchase ironclads. In addition, he awarded contracts for the construction of scores of gunboats, floating batteries, and other war vessels. Finally, he built eighteen shipyards, as well as boiler, ordnance, and machine shops for the supplies needed to keep a navy afloat. Over the next three years Mallory oversaw a naval service of nearly five thousand personnel and some forty ships, most of which were gunboats used to defend inland waterways like the Mississippi and the James. But the greatest naval weapon, in Mallory's vision, was the commercial raider, with which the secretary hoped to severely damage the United States' shipping around the world.[1]

On June 30, the newly commissioned Confederate States Steamer *Sumter,* a converted packet ship, slipped past the Union blockade of New Orleans to begin a unique mission: to disrupt enough northern maritime commerce to force the US Navy to divert ships from its coastal blockade of southern ports in order to protect merchant ships. The *Sumter*'s commander, the fifty-two-year-old Raphael Semmes, was being asked to be a nineteenth-century Francis Drake, effectively a privateer who would internationalize the war by attacking US commercial ships wherever the trade routes took them. Mallory also charged Semmes "to show the Confederate flag" in ports around the world, to give the Confederacy a global military presence.[2]

Raphael Semmes set the *Sumter* toward the West Indies and the Brazilian coast.[3] It proved to be an area abounding with quarry. In two days, Semmes captured seven ships. The first ship he seized, on July 3, 1861, he ordered burned. When Semmes learned that the ship was uninsured, he had the *Sumter*'s officers take up a collection for the captain and crew. When Semmes tried to take his prizes into the Dutch island of Curaçao in mid-July, the governor refused to allow the *Sumter* to dock. Semmes reminded the official that several major European countries, including the Netherlands, were allowing Confederate ships the use of her ports. While town officials were deliberating what to do, Semmes had the *Sumter* bombard the hillside just above their meeting place. Permission promptly came for Semmes to bring his ship into the town.

By midsummer, Semmes's seizures were causing a major panic among US shippers. A warship, the USS *Powhatan,* began a search for the Confederate raider. With the *Powhatan* on his track and ships avoiding the West Indies, Semmes took the *Sumter* across the equator into the South Atlantic. In mid-November, Semmes recrossed the equator and made a call at Saint-Pierre in Martinique. There the USS *Iroquois* found the *Sumter* and had it trapped in the harbor. Once more Semmes managed to slip a blockade, on a moonless night in late November. With several federal ships tracking it in the West Indies, Semmes decided to cross the Atlantic to Europe, where the US Navy would not have the presence it had off the coast of the Americas. Here he resumed the practice of burning enemy ships with their cargo after taking their crews captive. By December the *Sumter* was housing forty-three prisoners. A cyclone they encountered off the coast of Spain in mid-December badly damaged the ship. On January 3, Semmes took the *Sumter* into Cádiz harbor where Spanish officials reluctantly allowed the captain to remain long enough to have his vessel repaired. When he docked at Gibraltar, he learned that Mallory had a new ship being built for him in England.[4]

MANASSAS

On July 4, twenty-five miles south of Washington, DC, the major Confederate force in northern Virginia celebrated the day as they had traditionally celebrated it before the war. Indeed, they felt they had a better claim on Independence Day than did the federals, inasmuch as they saw themselves replicating their forefathers' revolt against Great Britain in their quest for independence. At a battalion barbecue, Lt. Col. Charles Dreux of the Seventh Louisiana Infantry made a toast honoring George Washington and the occasion, which concluded: "This is our day, and we will have it." The very next day Dreux was killed in an abortive attempt to ambush a federal cavalry patrol. The first Confederate soldier to die in the war, Dreux instantly became a national hero. A black-draped train bore his remains back to New Orleans. There he lay in state at city hall for days. Then, following a funeral Mass at St. Louis Cathedral, a procession which included forty priests, a squadron of cavalry, and two hundred carriages accompanied his body to the cemetery, with a reported ten thousand following behind. Some sixty thousand persons lined the route of black-crepe-covered buildings and flags at half-mast. Church bells throughout the city tolled.[5]

Two months after his call for three-month volunteers, Abraham Lincoln was coming under growing public pressure to use them to put down the rebellion. Despite a lack of staff officers to plan the campaign, a dependence on raw troops to execute it, and commanders who could scarcely operate effectively above the brigade level, General Irwin McDowell prepared to start his thirty-six thousand troops, whether battle-ready or not, from Washington into northern Virginia to engage the Confederates.[6]

In mid-July, P. G. T. Beauregard, now commanding the Confederate troops around Manassas Junction, began receiving covert messages from Washington about the plans and timetable of the Union Army. It was not an unexpected development, but one which gave him a decided advantage as the two armies maneuvered toward the long-anticipated battle which many, if not most, expected to settle the fate of the rebellion and the Republic. At the outbreak of the war, there were significant numbers of government personnel and local militias whose primary allegiance was to the Confederacy. A disproportionate number were Catholics, reflecting the historic concentration of Catholics in the Chesapeake region, as well as the Buchanan administration's packing of the government bureaucracy with southern sympathizers. When Charles P. Stone was appointed by General Winfield Scott to be inspector general of the District of Columbia's militia, he quickly discovered that the National Volunteers were "a hotbed of disloyalty."[7] Stone, a career soldier and a Catholic convert, managed to remove some key officers, including F. B. Schaeffer and Cornelius Boyle, and eventually reorganized the Volunteers as a loyal militia.[8] But the spy network that infested Washington's bureaucracy quickly gave cause for the Congress to establish a Select Committee on Loyalty of Clerks.

The person who became the most notorious spy during the first year of the war held no government position but had the extensive government connections and commitment to the Confederacy that made her a natural target for Confederate authorities to recruit to their service: Rose O'Neal Greenhow. No one was more furious about the sociopolitical impact of the Republican ascendancy than this deposed grand dame of the Buchanan administration, who also happened to be the aunt of Adele Douglas. To Greenhow the Republicans were a sorry bunch of abolitionists, prohibitionists, and Catholic haters, the "new barbarians" whose invasion was threatening the civilized social, moral, and racial order that had marked the capital when Greenhow and her peers were setting the standards for high society.[9]

Sometime shortly after war broke out, Captain Thomas Jordan, the quartermaster of the US Army, apparently on instructions from Confederate officials, approached Greenhow about organizing an espionage ring in the capital.[10] Rose Greenhow subsequently put together a team of operatives, both men and women, to observe military movements around the district and exploit their connections with public officials to secure vital information. On July 9 Greenhow dispatched a sixteen-year-old girl on horseback with a coded message warning General Beauregard that federal forces would begin their march on Manassas a week later. With that information the commanding general telegraphed Jefferson Davis to rush reinforcements from General Joseph Johnston's army some sixty miles to the northwest.[11]

The fifty regiments of the Union Army of Northeastern Virginia began the march south with the regimental bands serenading the motley uniformed troops, ranging from the grays of the New York Sixty-Ninth to the red-panted New York Zouaves, to the New York Seventy-Ninth, some of whose Scottish members sported kilts. The pace to Manassas proved agonizingly slow. They made twelve miles the first two days out. They had no experience whatever with carrying heavy knapsacks on long marches, particularly one made in the midsummer Virginia heat, with Confederate snipers about, together with fence rails and felled trees blocking their route. The well-advertised battle-in-the-making had attracted a throng that added to the congestion. It became almost impossible for the quartermaster's wagons to get food to the marchers when they exhausted their rations. Quickly, the undisciplined troops turned foraging into indiscriminate vandalism. William Tecumseh Sherman was outraged that federal troops would stoop to such barbaric behavior. "No Goths, no Vandals ever had less respect for the lives & property of friend and foe," he wrote his wife.[12]

At Manassas, General Beauregard had positioned his Confederate force in a serpentine line that paralleled eight miles of a creek called Bull Run, but he had no intention of simply taking the brunt of any Union assault. Putting the bulk of his twenty-thousand force on the right of his line, he planned to strike the federals across two fords, Blackburn's and McLean's, before McDowell could begin any offensive.[13] Along Bull Run, James Longstreet's brigade had hidden themselves above the banks of Blackburn's Ford. When the first federals approached the ford on Thursday, July 18, Longstreet had the First Virginia, commanded by Patrick Moore, up front to repel the Union assault. Springing up from their cover, the Virginians surprised their attackers. In the heat of the battle, Company C (the Montgomery Guards), under the command of Captain John Dooley, deployed the ancient Irish war cry: "Faugh a Ballagh!" (Clear the Way). In the skirmish, which lasted over two hours, the Virginia First played a major role in repulsing the Union probe. For their being in the thick of the action, the Virginia regiment bore the brunt of the Confederate casualties, with thirteen dead. Its Irish colonel, Patrick Moore, was among the badly wounded. John Dooley was promoted to major.[14]

As the armies drew closer together, spectators, ranging from congressmen to kinsfolk to would-be witnesses of history, gathered behind both lines of battle. It was Charleston harbor anew, now with crowds of spectators on each side, as though settling in for a sporting event, making a reaffirmation of the romantic nature of war. The Union struck first, in the predawn on the Confederate left, which Beauregard had left underdefended, since he intended to deliver the first blow to the Union left and rear. The Union attackers encountered Wheat's Louisiana battalion of Early's brigade. In rallying his greatly outnumbered troops to resist, Wheat was disabled by a bullet to his chest. As the battalion began to fall apart, someone yelled: "Tigers, go in once more, . . . I'll be gloriously God damn if the sons of bitches can ever whip the Tigers." Fortuitously, reinforcements joined them just as they started their frantic countercharge. Thus was born the title of "Fighting Tigers" that the Louisiana units proudly bore for the rest of the war.[15]

About noon, William Tecumseh Sherman's brigade was ordered to cross Bull Run and support the assault on Matthews Hill. Sherman, in reconnoitering the terrain that morning, had discovered Farm Ford about a half-mile from the Stone Bridge. The brigade, with the New York Sixty-Ninth leading the way, crossed the Run at the ford and joined in the pursuit of retreating Confederates. The brigade continued along the Sudley Road toward Henry Hill, where McDowell's forces appeared on the verge of breaking through the enemy defenses.[16] At least, that was the sense that Sherman got from seeing General McDowell and his staff racing back and forth, waving hats and swords with cries of "Victory! Victory! The day is ours!" The Confederates were under great pressure on Henry Hill as Beauregard arrived. Typically, the commander immediately rode along the line imploring them to stand firm and ordering the regimental colors to be displayed boldly, as though daring the enemy to continue the attack.[17]

In the end, it came down to Henry Hill. Hours of assault and counterassault had left the Confederates still in possession, if ever so precariously. McDowell had virtually used up all his available units in prosecuting his offensive but could not yet bring himself to let victory, which had seemed within their grasp more than once during this long day, slip from them for want of one last effort. So he turned to Sherman, whose brigade was virtually the only one not to have been bloodied in the earlier action. With him and his three thousand or so men would hang victory or defeat. McDowell was still confident that victory could be theirs. If anything, Sherman was even more so.

Michael Corcoran, commanding the Sixty-Ninth, sensed disaster. The brigade waited on a road already packed with dead and wounded, hardly an ideal environment from which to launch yet another attack on an enemy position that had already repelled a series of federal assaults with devastating casualties for the attackers. Sherman ordered one of his four regiments, the New York Thirteenth, to make its ascent up the northwestern slope toward Henry House on its own, with the others to follow when ordered. That had been standard procedure in the Mexican War. But those were far smaller armies, where most of the fighting was at the regimental level. Indeed, military theory taught that the regiment was the ideal size for efficacious command management. Here, with much larger forces involved, that orthodoxy was the recipe for failure, as the assaults had shown earlier in the day, but Sherman had been in no position to learn from it, and so now paid a dear price for his education.

Without support, the Thirteenth remarkably closed to within seventy yards of the Henry House when rebel infantry volleys and artillery forced the attackers to hug the ground to avoid the withering shot and shell. All they could do was wait for reinforcements who might draw off enough fire to allow their escape. The Second Wisconsin regiment tried to do just that but failed, because their line became misaligned, and their gray uniforms drew fire from federal units in their rear. Sherman called up the Seventy-Ninth New York, but it fared no better than its brother regiments. Only the Sixty-Ninth remained for Sherman's last grasp at victory. In both Gaelic and English, they shouted their war cries and made for the crest, in shirt sleeves, having jettisoned their heavy coats in a concession to the heat. Thomas Meagher shouted:

"Come on, boys, you've got your chance at last!"[18] They made the most of it, thanks to artillery support denied the earlier assault efforts, as well as their gray uniforms, which the Confederates mistook as their own. The Thirty-Eighth New York had simultaneously with the Sixth-Ninth reached the top of Henry Hill and made an oblique move toward Confederate defenders opposing the Sixth-Ninth. The combined pressure broke the Confederate line.

The two New York regiments had cleared the crest of Henry Hill of its Confederate defenders, or so they thought. The reality was that a formidable force, including the majority of Thomas Jackson's brigade, remained on the right. More ominously, Beauregard and Johnston were preparing to send in fresh troops all along the line. McDowell, of course, knew nothing of these Confederate plans. He was happy enough that some of his units were at the top of Henry Hill, and congratulated Corcoran for the Sixth-Ninth's success. His reverie was short-lived as the Confederate commanders sent in the remnants of regiments and other units as part of what they hoped to be a final counterattack. The First Maryland Infantry was among them, having just arrived by train. They led the flanking charge that finally took Henry Hill for good.[19] It was not a closely coordinated textbook counterattack, but serendipity produced enough units, including the Louisiana Seventh, attacking more or less simultaneously to sweep all before them, including the New York Sixty-Ninth, which not only resisted but managed not one but two counterattacks that slowed the inevitable. Then two things occurred that broke the Sixty-Ninth. The regiment had its banner taken.[20] Almost simultaneously, Thomas Meagher's horse was shot from under him, and the major fell unconscious to the ground. That was the last straw. The Sixty-Ninth became the rear guard for the ignominious retreat of the Army of Northeastern Virginia to its Washington base.[21] When the Sixty-Ninth arrived back at Fort Corcoran early Monday morning, it had two hundred fewer members than it had started with the previous day. The Confederates had captured sixty of them, including their commander, Colonel Corcoran.[22]

Longstreet attempted to cut off the Union forces at Blackburn's Ford, but, on this day, it was Longstreet who was repulsed. The retreat, in part orderly, in part panicked, continued unchallenged. Animals, wagons, soldiers, and a few civilians all ran pell-mell to put whatever distance they could between the pursuing rebels and themselves. Cump Sherman told his wife: "I have read of retreats before . . . but nothing like this. It was as disgraceful as words can portray, but I doubt if volunteers from any quarter can do better."[23] This had been Sherman's first experience of battle. He had performed courageously, despite being twice grazed by bullets and having a horse shot under him. But he felt only the defeat and disgust at what came of relying on a volunteer army.[24] The day had also left him convinced that he would not live to see the war's end.[25]

For the army, the rout was terror enough, causing thousands to abandon to the roadside all manner of clothing, equipment, and artifacts (including official documents), a ready-made supply center for the pursuing Confederates. There were four thousand rifles and muskets, enough to equip a division, 500,000 rounds of ammunition, twenty-seven guns. The official casualty list for the federals was 481 killed, 1,011 wounded, and 1,216 missing. The actual casualty count was almost certainly higher, especially for captives. The Confederates had 381 killed, 1,582 wounded, 13 missing. For a divided nation that had mostly romantic notions of war, the numbers were shocking. Only the commanders' inability to utilize their manpower to the maximum prevented them from being even higher. (Both sides deployed fewer than half their troops.)[26]

Throughout that Sunday, in the Indian Office in downtown Washington, the Jesuit Pierre-Jean De Smet could "hear distinctly the cannon from Bull Run."[27] When late in the day the sounds began getting louder, Father John Early, Georgetown's president, watched from the hilltop overlooking the Potomac as federal cavalry appeared in ever thicker numbers racing across the Aqueduct Bridge toward Washington. He remarked: "the Union forces evidently have met with a serious reverse. They may be in here before night."[28] And so they were, as the demoralized, bedraggled survivors straggled into the capital throughout the night. The routed army had, for the most part, left their wounded and dead behind them. The next day Lieutenant Julius Garesché, a Georgetown alumnus, wrote Father Early, "All our sick and wounded, I suppose, are in the hands of the confederate army—At least one third of them must be Catholics—with no Priests to care for them! There is work for half a dozen."[29] That same day three Jesuits set out from Georgetown to the battlefield.

CONSEQUENCES

What the Federals came to call Bull Run and the Confederates, Manassas, was a battle one could have predicted of two hastily prepared forces, most of whom expected their service to be no longer than it took to fight one battle. That was especially true of the Union force, composed, as it was, overwhelmingly of ninety-day men whose time was near expiring. Add to that the miscommunication, ignorance of the terrain, lack of discipline, and confusion in properly identifying uniforms and banners that marred the performance in battle of both sides. The Confederates had three advantages which proved vital to their success: the six-months start in organizing its army and equipping it with the property from all the arsenals James Buchanan had chosen not to defend; the better intelligence, thanks to Rose Greenhow and the Confederate network within the District of Columbia; and the better concentration of their manpower.

Manassas made Beauregard's star soar even higher than it had risen after Sumter. Lost in the decisive Confederate victory was the evidence that its commander had performed poorly in managing an army far larger than he or any general had had in the past. The government, nonetheless, rewarded Beauregard by a promotion to full general. Songs were written in his honor ("General Beauregard's Grand Polka Militaire," "The Beauregard Manassas Quick-step"). Steamboats, racehorses, male children were all named for him. He suddenly became a people's choice for the presidential election in November.[30] All this public adulation emboldened Beauregard to go over President Davis's head by complaining to Congress that the failure to provide adequate food and transportation for the army had prevented it from reaping the full harvest of victory, presumably the taking of Washington. If the great victory they had secured at Manassas had not translated into the ending of the war, as so many had expected, Beauregard was telling them whom to blame: Lucius B. Northrop. Beauregard's claim that only the failure of the Confederacy's commissary general to supply the food and transportation vehicles to enable the army to cross the Potomac, seize the federal capital, and allow Maryland to become the twelfth state of the Confederacy provided the southern public with an explanation for why Manassas had not brought the peace that a decisive victory was supposed to bring. The secretary of the navy, Stephen Mallory, surely had Beauregard in mind when he remarked, in the wake of Manassas, that the nation's fate was now in the hands of vain military idiots.[31] For the Confederate public, it just made Beauregard an even greater hero.

Rose Greenhow was in New York City when news broke about the federal rout. "The whole city seemed paralyzed by fear," Greenhow wrote. "A thousand men could have marched from Central Park to the Battery without resistance."[32] Marie Daly learned that one casualty of the battle was the regimental flag that she had presented to the New York Sixty-Ninth before they headed south. That, to Daly, was a small loss, considering the major consequences of the defeat. "Never in my life did I feel as badly as when I saw this fearful, disgraceful news in the paper yesterday," she wrote. "It will prolong the war another year, if not three, and give European powers cause to consider the matter of recognizing the Confederacy as very probably their best policy."[33]

Most of the seriously wounded, including many federal soldiers, ended up in Confederate hospitals. A Charity Sister, Rose Noyland, remembered that at the Richmond Alms House, which had become the Richmond General Hospital, "We found three hundred sick and wounded Confederate and Federal soldiers." Many of those poor soldiers lay on the battlefield several days under sun and rain. Their wounds were filled with maggots and gangrene. We spent days scraping maggots and cutting away rotten flesh. . . . Sunday night, eleven prisoners were brought to the Hospital. . . . They didn't know where they were being taken to, but when they saw the cornettes . . . they gave three cheers for the Sisters of Charity at twelve o'clock at night!" They later told the sisters that they had survived the battle thanks to the scapulars and medals they had been given.[34]

SUNSET FOR A SPY RING

Buoyed by the wild tales of impending disaster for the Union in the wake of the debacle at Bull Run, Rose Greenhow took the train from New York to Washington, fully expecting to find the Confederates in control of the federal capital. General Beauregard was not there to greet her but upon reaching home she found an encrypted message from her Confederate contacts at Manassas: "The Confederacy owes you a debt."[35] For weeks following the federal disaster at Manassas, Greenhow, along with many in Washington, both in and outside of government, expected the Confederates to storm the city. She sent messages to Beauregard urging him to strike. "Come on! Why do you not come?"[36] Greenhow kept sending information to Beauregard, including the message on August 5 that her group was planning a campaign of sabotage (cutting telegraph wires, spiking guns, and so forth) as a prelude to the Confederate attack. By this time, Allan Pinkerton and his agents were surveilling Greenhow's house on Sixteenth Street, just above Lafayette Square. Before the month's end, the stakeout had recorded enough suspicious visitors to put Greenhow under house arrest for five months, before she was moved to the Old Capitol Prison in mid-January of 1862.

Finally, Greenhow was given a hearing in mid-March. With all the hauteur she could muster, Rose denied she had ever engaged in espionage, and demanded that they show proof of her alleged treason.[37] It was a performance bold enough to reduce the commission to recommending that she be sent beyond the lines, to remove this regal rebel from the heart of the Union. Weeks later, she finally agreed to exile in the South. When she arrived in Richmond in early June, Jefferson Davis was one of her first visitors at her hotel, to convey the Confederacy's gratitude for all she had done to ensure that it would prevail.[38] He found, not the defiant grand dame that had performed for her federal inquisitors, but a shrunken woman who gave every appearance of someone who had been "shaken by mental torture." She was also penniless. Davis had Judah Benjamin dispatch $2,500 to her as a token of the Confederacy's gratitude for what she had done.[39] As a historian who has studied her espionage remarks, "one major service performed by the Greenhow ring was their engaging of the full-time attention of so many Federal secret-service people that they seriously held back the Federals' own intelligence collecting." Once the ring was broken through Greenhow's arrest and exile, Confederate intelligence about Washington's plans and intentions was never the same as it was during the short time in which the grand dame of Washington society was supplying it, although it was never on the scale that she herself and the myth she helped fashion made it out to be.[40]

THE WAR IN WESTERN VIRGINIA
AND ON THE POTOMAC

For many northern Catholics, the convert general William Rosecrans became the avatar of Catholic patriotism. Commanding a brigade of Ohio regiments, including the Thirtieth Ohio under Col. Hugh Ewing, Rosecrans had early on displayed the ability to concentrate his forces so as to gain an advantage over a foe, even when the opponent had superior numbers. In August at Rich Hill Mountain, Rosecrans, through adroit maneuvering, defeated John Floyd's larger force. Then, in late September, on Big Sewell Mountain, Rosecrans inflicted a heavy blow on a Confederate reconnaissance, then withdrew before Robert E. Lee could bring his entire army against him.[41] The Confederate resistance soon turned into guerrilla warfare, which forced Rosecrans to inflict punishment on those suspected of aiding the guerrillas, including the burning of homes.[42] By the end of 1861, he was arguably the most successful general that the Union forces could claim. Yet his success seemed to earn him little recognition or advancement. When Lincoln removed Irwin McDowell following the shocking defeat at Bull Run, it was not William Rosecrans but George McClellan whom Lincoln named to replace him, even though some attributed McClellan's success in western Virginia more to Rosecrans than to the wunderkind of the Union armies.

At Manassas, P. G. T. Beauregard, despite Rose Greenhow's pleas, was not preparing to liberate Washington, but he did have a plan to end the war before the federals could bring to bear all their manpower and industrial potential.

He intended to put his army across the Potomac, upriver from Washington, and maneuver his way into Maryland, to a position north of the capital which would force McClellan into marching his still-not-ready troops into unfavorable terrain where the Confederates could achieve the decisive victory that would win independence for the Confederacy. Joe Johnston, Beauregard's co-commander at Manassas, liked the idea. Jefferson Davis came to Fairfax Courthouse to hear the proposal. In the end, the president turned it down. The Confederacy simply did not yet have the capability of fielding an army of sixty thousand to carry out Beauregard's plan.[43]

One accomplishment that Beauregard was responsible for in the interlude was to devise a flag that would clearly identify the forces beneath it, far better than the standard used during the Battle of Manassas which too closely resembled the US flag. The result had been confusion that occasionally proved deadly. Beauregard first approached the Confederate Congress about securing a new flag for combat, but found no support in that body, whose members informed him that the people wanted a flag that approximated that of the United States. So, left to his own devices, Beauregard himself worked up a design for a battle flag. On a bright red background, Beauregard placed a cross of blue bars with white stars embossed. It was the stars-and-bars flag, which, for most citizens of the Confederacy, became the Confederate flag. At the end of November, the new flag had its formal unveiling at a solemn ceremony in Centreville, with Beauregard exhorting his troops to regard that flag as the emblem of all they held dear and, under that banner, to beat back "the invader, and find nationality, everlasting immunity from an atrocious despotism, and honor and renown for themselves—or death."[44]

In late October, Gen. George McClellan ordered Brig. Gen. Charles Stone to make a reconnaissance of the Virginia side of the Potomac near Leesburg. Stone sent a probing force under Col. Edward Baker, a sitting US senator from Massachusetts. Through a series of miscommunications, Baker's soldiers were surprised by Confederates at Ball's Bluff. The resulting rout of the Union forces produced over one thousand casualties. Baker was among the fatalities. Stone became the scapegoat for the Union disaster. That the Democratic Stone had earlier infuriated congressional abolitionists by returning escaped slaves to their owners made him particularly vulnerable to charges of misconduct. It also did not help his standing with his critics when, in his official report, he pointed out Baker's shortcomings as a commander. In early February, on orders from Secretary of War Edwin Stanton, Stone was arrested. He spent the next six months in prison, without any charges being lodged against him. His release was finally forced upon the Lincoln administration by legislation that required charges to be filed and a trial held within thirty days for any military officer. Stone held several positions of command later in the war, but his career had basically been ruined by political revenge.[45]

HUGHES AND LYNCH
DEBATE THE WAR

On September 5, the *New York Daily Tribune* published an exchange of letters between Bishop Patrick Lynch of Charleston and Archbishop John Hughes of New York. In a separate editorial, the paper saluted the prelates for taking seriously their responsibility of speaking out on the crucial moral issues of the origin and prosecution of the war.[46] Patrick Lynch's letter made an informed, well-reasoned case for the South's quest for independence. The bishop argued that, having exhausted every constitutional avenue for defending their rights, the South had no other choice than to uproot itself from the Union it had played such a vital part in forming. Having attempted to withdraw peacefully, the Lincoln administration forced war upon it. He confidently predicted that the major remaining slave states—Maryland, Missouri, and Kentucky—would all join the Confederacy before year's end. As for the war, he argued that the North lacked the military leadership or the economic weapons to impose its will upon the South. This war, he presciently diagnosed, would be fought on an unprecedented scale in American history, with armies of fifty thousand or more opposing each other. The debacle at Manassas showed all too clearly that neither side had generals capable of managing armies of that size. The result could only be a bloody stalemate. Economically, the South held a winning hand with its cotton production. Cotton exported to Europe would provide the Confederacy with the means for prosecuting the war that the Union could not match. Conversely, should a Confederate embargo or Union blockade prevent King Cotton from reaching European markets, economic pressure would force England and France, no matter their thoughts about slavery, to intervene on the South's side. "The separation of the Southern States is *un fait accompli,*" Bishop Lynch concluded. "The Federal Government has no power to reverse it."

John Hughes, in his equally lengthy reply, argued that the original compact between the states that produced the Constitution preempted secession as a possible course of action by any of the states who were party to it. Even if one conceded that the Constitution allowed it, the South had no justification for invoking it. Hughes reminded his friend that the southern states had dominated the governance of the United States over its first eight decades and more. The 1860 election had been an anomaly caused by having three candidates on the ballot who split the Democratic vote. If the South had remained within the Union, the odds were that in the next presidential election the normal political calculus would again prevail. But, realizing that these were anything but normal times, Hughes quixotically suggested that both sections, despite being at war, call separate conventions to examine the Constitution of the United States, to determine what amendments were needed to make reunion possible.

SHERMAN ON THE BRINK

In mid-August, William Tecumseh Sherman was promoted to brigadier general of volunteers. The higher rank Sherman much valued. The same could not be said for the soldiers he would be commanding. Then came an invitation from Robert Anderson, the hero of Fort Sumter, to meet him at the Willard Hotel, across from the White House on Pennsylvania Avenue. Anderson wanted Sherman to be his top aide in his new post, heading the Department of the Cumberland. Sherman, who had vowed after the fiasco at Bull Run not to take any field command involving volunteers, all too happily agreed.

It took Sherman little time in Louisville to conclude that there was much more intensive sentiment for the Confederacy in the state than for the Union. Unionists were lukewarm in their allegiance; Confederates, by contrast, were fervent in their support. "If they are united, and we disunited or indifferent, they will succeed," he wrote his brother.[47] That appraisal of public opinion caused Sherman to exaggerate greatly the numbers and infinite threat that Confederate forces posed to Kentucky. Alerted that a Confederate Army was advancing on Louisville in September, Sherman set out with a ragtag force of some five thousand militia and volunteers to meet the invaders, only to discover that his intelligence had concocted a phantom enemy army. But, far from easing Sherman's concern about Confederate threats, the incident only provided an occasion for imagining the worst when the Confederates really came. Sherman kept pleading, ever more urgently, for Washington to send troops, and lots of them, to ensure that the Confederacy would not soon claim Kentucky as its twelfth state. When his pleas brought no relief, he began to question his ability to do what he had been charged to do. Barely a month after succeeding Anderson, Sherman's growing mental anguish and erratic behavior led to his reassignment to St. Louis, as an aide to General Henry Halleck. Then newspapers published a statement, supposedly from Halleck, in which the general alluded to Sherman as "completely broken" physically and mentally. He was, the general concluded, unfit for duty. Reports began to swirl about Kentucky and beyond that Sherman had had a mental breakdown. He himself was shocked to see a headline in the *Cincinnati Commercial* at the beginning of December which referred to him as "insane."[48]

Sherman may well have been suffering from what one of his biographers has judged to be clinical depression. A change of skies did not improve his mental state. When Ellen and John Sherman traveled to St. Louis to boost his spirits, they could not dent his insistence that the Confederates were on the brink of multiple invasions of the western cities of St. Louis, Louisville, and Cincinnati. Halleck sent him home with his wife on a three-week furlough. Whatever his mental condition, his family would not allow his wartime service to end in such a dishonorable manner. They were convinced that a conspiracy of generals (Halleck, McClellan, John Pope), with certain newspapers as their promulgators, were at the root of Cump's anxiety and depression. Ellen and her father, Thomas Ewing, took themselves to Washington to plead Cump's case with everyone in the administration's orbit who was willing to listen, including the new secretary of war, Edwin Stanton, who was a close friend of Ewing. Hugh Ewing secured a leave from the Army in western Virginia to head east to defend his foster brother. Thomas Ewing was in particularly good standing with Lincoln, having been a valuable advisor to the president in dealing with the *Trent* crisis. The elder Ewing assured Lincoln that his son-in-law had promised to be more circumspect in his speech and behavior in the future.

SECURING MARYLAND

In September, President Lincoln proclaimed a day of prayer and fasting. Archbishop Kenrick ordered all the churches in the Province of Baltimore to offer several prayers, including John Carroll's prayer for the president and the preservation of the Union. How widely this was observed throughout the province, which included Richmond, Charleston, and Savannah, can be gleaned from the effective refusal of all the priests of the Baltimore Cathedral to do so. It was left to Kenrick himself to carry out his own observance of the president's day. When the archbishop read the contested portions of Carroll's letter, most of the congregation expressed their displeasure either by walking out or by an exaggerated rustling of papers and silks.[49] Earlier Kenrick had urged his own clergy and religious not to get involved in the politics which had riven the country, but to pray for peace and "the constituted authorities." For many in Maryland, especially Catholics, Lincoln was not their constituted authority.

But the pro-Confederates in Maryland no longer held the same power they had had the previous spring. Later that September, federal authorities conducted a mass roundup of state legislators before the General Assembly could consider an ordinance of secession. Then, in November of 1861, the Unionist Party gained political dominance in the state. A Catholic, Benjamin C. Howard, the son of a Revolutionary War hero, became the reluctant States' Rights Party's candidate for governor. Howard had two sons in Virginia, fighting for the Confederacy. With so many former Democrats, both leaders and rank-and-file, now gone south, the outcome seemed preordained, especially with numerous Democrats boycotting the election. That the Lincoln administration militarized the election, by giving all Maryland Union units three-day furloughs to vote, as well as posting soldiers at precincts throughout the state to ensure that no returning Confederates could vote and to discourage southern sympathizers, also suppressed the States' Rights' vote. The Union Party's candidate, William Bradford, won with nearly 70 percent of the vote, producing the very "killing majority" against secession in the legislature that Hicks had been looking to secure.[50] Howard carried four counties, three in southern Maryland and one on the Eastern Shore. All four had significant Catholic populations. Federal intimidation, with troops at the polls and the arrests of Confederate soldiers returning to cast votes, no doubt padded Bradford's margin of victory, but did not change the outcome.[51] Too much of the Democratic Party was below the Potomac, ensuring that Unionist opposition was enfeebled for the war's duration.

THE *TRENT* AFFAIR

On November 8, a US steamer, the *San Jacinto,* had intercepted a British ship, the *Trent,* off the Bahamas and forcibly removed two commissioners of the Confederate government, James Mason and John Slidell. The British government demanded their release and dispatched troops to Canada as a prelude to a declaration of war against the United States. The Lincoln administration, although it had not ordered the seizure, refused to apologize for the incident and continued to hold the Confederate pair. The drums of war began to beat in both the United Kingdom and the United States, nowhere more so than in the pages of the *New York Herald,* where the *Trent* affair became the perfect occasion for bringing James Gordon Bennett's Anglophobia into full play by goading the United States into opening a new front for the war against Great Britain.[52] Secretary of State William Seward had considered sending three emissaries to London, including Archbishop John Hughes, but had been dissuaded by his minister in the United Kingdom, Charles Francis Adams. Finally, multiple figures, including Judge Charles Daily and Thomas Ewing, were instrumental in persuading Lincoln and his cabinet that retaining Mason and Slidell would bring armed intervention by not only Great Britain but France. Shortly after Christmas, the commissioners were freed.[53]

FIRE IN CHARLESTON

In mid-December, Francis Lynch wrote from upcountry Carolina to his bishop brother in Charleston: "It was with profound grief that we heard of the awful fire in your city, spreading so much destruction in its way, heightened by the calamitous destruction of your premises and our grand Cathedral."[54] Disaster had struck Charleston in the form of a wind-fueled fire that swept the old district of the city, leaving behind a skeletal landscape and swelling the refugee tide heading upstate. Among the most conspicuous casualties were the core structures of the Diocese of Charleston: cathedral, bishop's residence, seminary, free school, newspaper offices, and orphanage. "I did not think that *you* required so stern a lesson in 'holy indifference,'" his sister, Baptista, wrote. "Well! You are the very one to say 'Fiat voluntas Dei' in all things."[55]

On Christmas Eve, Patrick Lynch was one of seventeen persons appointed by Mayor Charles McBeth to a Committee of Citizens' Relief for victims of the conflagration which had ravaged 540 acres of the heart of the city.[56] A week later, the committee issued a report, which bore all the marks of Lynch's authorship, announcing the relief they had already begun to provide and the plans they had for Reconstruction projects, which would, among other things, "lessen the probability of a pestilential outbreak," of yellow fever in the coming summer, such as Charleston had too often experienced in the past.[57]

✝

CHAPTER 7

Grand Campaigns

What horror is war!

—EDMOND ENOUL LIVAUDAIS,
SHILOH, APRIL 7, 1862

TO END A REBELLION

"The Judge came home last night . . . [from Washington], entirely disheart-ened. The corruption of every part of the government and the country is so great that he despairs of it altogether . . . For my part, if they would consent to yield the border states, the rest of the slave states might go. They would soon revert to us again, in all probability. For what can we do with them if we conquer, or with their black chattels if we free them?" So Marie Daly summed up the situation as the first month of 1862 neared its end. Letting the Confederacy be, in the expectation that its states would soon return, was, to her, a far better alternative than occupying the South and freeing its slaves.[1]

Occupying the South, or at least critical portions of it, was indeed the Lincoln administration's goal for 1862. Emancipating its slaves was not. In his message to the Congress on December 3, 1861, President Lincoln had made clear that he "thought it proper to keep the integrity of the Union prominent as the primary object of the contest."[2] To achieve that end, over the first five months of the new year, Union forces in the East established beachheads from Roanoke Island in North Carolina to St. Augustine in Florida, the big-gest of them on the Virginia Peninsula between the York and James rivers, where George McClellan assembled a massive army to march on Richmond. In the West the seizure of key forts guarding the Tennessee and Cumberland rivers opened those waterways for Union forces to penetrate deeply into the South. Nashville fell to Union forces in the late winter, putting a particularly productive breadbasket and iron-producing region of the Confederacy in federal hands. Confederate morale plummeted.[3] No less an authority than retired general Winfield Scott told Charles Daly at the beginning of March that, "by May it will all be over; they must submit."[4]

SHILOH

In the late winter of 1862, P. G. T. Beauregard, now assigned to the Western Theater, joined his army with that of General Albert Sidney Johnston to establish a defense line at Corinth, a vital rail center just inside the Tennessee-Mississippi border, toward which federal armies were reportedly moving. By the end of March, Ulysses Grant was at Pittsburg Landing on the Tennessee River, some twenty miles above Corinth. Confederate intelligence had twenty-five thousand reinforcements on route to supplement the fifty thousand Grant already commanded.[5] Beauregard and Johnston agreed that they could not wait for the federal armies to reach them. They alerted their troops to be ready to march out on April 3. As they marched north, the Jesuit chaplain, Ignace François Turgis, who estimated that nearly half of the forty thousand Confederates were Catholics, raced from regiment to regiment, hearing the confessions of all who desired to make them. "I was the only priest," he later said. "I gave absolutions for forty-eight hours without stopping."[6]

It took the forty thousand Confederates nearly three days to cover the twenty-two miles. They moved into position late on Saturday, April 5. The federals had no idea that four corps of Rebels were within a couple of miles of their camp. At a little after 5 a.m. on Sunday, the first line of the massive Confederate attack struck the Union right. Reports of full-scale fighting began to reach Sherman shortly afterwards. For three hours he refused to believe that battle was underway, even after his orderly was killed by enemy fire at Sherman's side when the division commander rode out at 7 a.m. with his staff to investigate the persistent reports of fighting. At 8 a.m. the gleam of thousands of approaching bayonets finally left no room to doubt that they were under a major attack. In his desperate attempts to rally the panicking, inexperienced Union troops, Sherman had no fewer than three horses shot out from under him. Unfazed, he rose from the side of one fallen animal to mount a fresh one and repeated the switch all too soon afterwards. As the storm of battle howled about him, Sherman, his arm in a sling to support his bleeding hand, was an island of calm focus and command, directing troop alignments, reviving spirits, being everything a commander under attack should be.[7]

Around midday, after both Union flanks had collapsed, the Confederate command ordered a frontal assault on the Union center, a scrubwood forest intersected by a wagon trail, that became known as "The Hornet's Nest" for the waves of attacks (at least eleven) that the Orleans Guard and other Confederate units furiously mounted. At one point, the blue uniforms of the Guard made them perfect targets for friendly fire, until they managed to turn their coats inside out, with only two fatalities due to the mistaken volleys they had attracted. It was but one small part of a day in which both sides were seeing the elephant for the first time. One that for all too many evoked a primal fear that sent green recruits, some of whom had received their weapons on the previous day, running for their lives. One that would leave Private Edmond Enoul Livaudais of the Guard recording: "What horror is war!"[8]

Early in the afternoon, Albert Sidney Johnston learned that a Tennessee regiment was refusing to attack the Union line in a peach orchard just to the right of the Hornet's Nest. Johnston rode furiously to the recalcitrant unit and proceeded to lead them personally into battle. About two o'clock, as he returned to his observation point, the commanding general suddenly slumped in his saddle. When aides lowered him to the ground, they discovered him bleeding profusely behind his knee. Theodore O'Hara, now a member of Johnston's staff, galloped off in search of a surgeon to deal with his commander's wound. By the time he returned, Johnston had bled to death from a severed artery.

With Johnston's death in midafternoon, Beauregard took command. He ordered an artillery barrage against the Hornet's Nest. William Lynch's Fifty-Eighth Illinois was on the right edge of this vortex of the Confederate attack. As Confederate forces encircled the "Nest," the Fifty-Eighth tried to break out of the entrapment but failed. Along with the other defenders along the Sunken Road, the Fifty-Eighth held out for several more hours, before surrendering at 5:30 p.m. The Confederates drove the remaining Union forces nearly three miles before Grant established a new line, a semicircle that had his left flank anchored on the Tennessee River.

Beauregard ordered the attacks suspended until the next morning and the army to retire to the federals' former camp. He considered the enemy defeated. Tomorrow would be a mop-up operation. The commanding general wired Richmond that they had won "a complete victory." Scarcely had that celebratory message been sent when Bedford Forrest reported to General William Hardee, corps commander on the Confederate right, that Buell's army had arrived, which would give the federals a decisive advantage in any renewed conflict. Forrest urged a night attack before that occurred. Hardee pondered the suggestion, but ultimately did not even convey the information to Beauregard.[9] With nightfall came rain, gently at first, then gradually harder until it came down in torrents. Left untended were the thousands of wounded, dying, and dead between the lines—a perfect nightcap for a day straight out of hell.[10]

Early the next morning, Theodore O'Hara led an escort taking Johnston's body to Corinth, to be shipped to New Orleans.[11] As O'Hara's party headed southward, the Union forces, now with twice the men the Confederates had, launched an attack. Despite a valiant Confederate effort to repel the offensive (Beauregard himself twice seized the colors of regiments he considered going into action too slowly to lead them forward), physical fatigue and psychological shock at having victory snatched from them when it seemed well in their grasp forced Beauregard, by midafternoon, to order a retreat to Corinth.[12] A barefoot Private Livaudais marched toward Corinth with the New Orleans Guard, now with a third fewer men than had made the march to Pittsburg Landing. It took them four days to get there. When they arrived, Livaudais dropped to his knees in prayer, thankful that his life had been spared. "Everywhere prevailed a mournful silence," he wrote.[13]

Shiloh was the first battle of the war in which armies of Napoleonic size had fiercely battled each other for two days with staggering costs. Casualties for the two armies approached twenty-four thousand, five times what they had been at Manassas. A team of four Sisters of Charity, led by Sr. Anthony O'Connell, went South from Cincinnati to serve on the floating hospitals in the Tennessee River above Pitts Landing. "The battlefield of Shiloh," O'Connell remembered, "presented the most frightful and disgusting sights that it was ever my lot to witness," as they gathered up the wounded among the hundreds of dead. The stench from the human and animal corpses was so terrible that they had to move their ship upriver to get beyond it.[14] Sr. Theodosia Farn remembered, "At one time our boat's deck looked like a slaughter-house. Wounded, wounded everywhere!"[15]

Sherman's extraordinary actions during the first day of Shiloh did not go unnoticed, by his men or by superiors. Thanks to Halleck's and Grant's fulsome praise of Sherman's battlefield valor, as well as pressure exerted by John Sherman and Thomas Ewing on Abraham Lincoln, he was promoted from brigadier to major general.[16] Shiloh became the great watershed for Cump Sherman's military fortunes. It also left him with haunting images of the horrific character that the war had assumed which reinforced his sense that he would not survive it.[17]

Sherman commanded the right wing of the 125,000-man Union force under Halleck which took a month to cover the twenty-five miles to Corinth. As the federals moved ever so cautiously toward Corinth, a typhoid epidemic swept the town. The epidemic, along with rampant dysentery, killed more Confederates than the two-day battle at Shiloh had claimed. Still, Beauregard kept his army there until April 25, when he ordered a retreat.[18] When Halleck's gargantuan force finally reached the town, the enemy was long gone. Beauregard considered his strategic retreat a grand coup. That sentiment was not shared in Richmond, particularly when Memphis surrendered to federal forces weeks later, opening the Mississippi to federal vessels as far south as Vicksburg.

NEW ORLEANS

That same April, on Ship Island, a barrier isle in the Gulf of Mexico some fifty miles east of New Orleans, over fifteen thousand Union troops, including the Ninth Connecticut Volunteers, boarded ships to head to the mouth of the Mississippi, where they witnessed the federal fleet quickly subdue or bypass the Confederate forts guarding the approach to the Emerald City. Thomas Cahill and the Connecticut Ninth were finally sent ashore to subdue the bypassed forts. Rumor had it that the forts mounted three hundred guns and were surrounded by an alligator-filled moat.[19] To Cahill's great relief, the Connecticut Ninth found them abandoned. General Benjamin Butler, sensing that the Irish community in New Orleans was the weak Confederate link among the local citizens, had Cahill's Irish regiment lead the federals into the city.[20] The Ninth's band played all the Irish airs they could remember, as well as a medley of national tunes, including "Dixie." "Our men find lots of old acquaintances here," Cahill happily wrote his wife. "I think we were here another week we would have the biggest half of the Irish here with us."[21] By the beginning of June, Cahill had enlisted nearly two hundred.[22]

The Irish behavior was hardly typical of the reception that the Catholic community of New Orleans gave their federal occupiers. Abbé Perché's *Le Propagateur Catholique* was so hostile to the occupying Union forces that Butler suspended the paper and placed the editor under house arrest for over a month.[23] Many Catholics joined the thousands of residents who sought refuge inland. Herminie Blanchard, the wife of Confederate General Albert Blanchard, had been out of the city when it fell. She daringly returned, using her maiden name (Benoist de la Salle), in order to secure valuable papers as well as to check on her daughter in the Ursuline Academy there, before somehow making her way back out of the city to Confederate territory.[24] Among those who escaped from the federal occupation of New Orleans was the writer Florence Jane O'Connor, who became an expatriate in London, where she published *The Heroine of the Confederacy.*

Another Catholic group that largely welcomed the federals to the Crescent City was the *gens de couleur*. At the outbreak of the war, the Confederate government had mandated that the free Blacks of the city raise a regiment, the Native Guards, who subsequently were utilized only to participate in ceremonies. Unsurprisingly, when the federals were on the doorstep of the city in April of 1862, Confederate officials ordered that they disband. The Native Guards disposed of their Confederate uniforms but hid their muskets in various venues, including the Institute Catholique, with the obvious intention of using them again in the service of their soon-to-be occupiers, if they would accept them. Three months later a delegation of former officers of the Native Guards offered their services to General Benjamin Butler. Butler in turn sought permission from the secretary of war, Edwin Stanton, to enlist the former regiment under US colors. When no response came from Washington, Butler took matters into his own hands by advertising for all free men of color who were veterans of the Louisiana militia to enlist in the Union Army, "subject to the approval of the president." Those who enlisted were promised 160 acres of land, a bounty of a hundred dollars, and food rations for their families. Two thousand initially applied, including about a quarter of the Native Guards. Among the applicants were the members of a hundred-man company that a thirty-eight-year-old Black Creole cigarmaker, and former lieutenant in the Native Guards, André Cailloux, had raised. Cailloux's company became part of the First Louisiana Native Guard Infantry. Most of the members of the First were Catholics.[25] By August more than three thousand Afro-Creoles had enlisted for the three Afro-Creole regiments.

White New Orleans was not ready for racial equality, particularly in the military. Whites insulted Black troops on the street. Landlords used economic pressure by various forms of harassment of their families, with eviction the ultimate punishment. Catholic clergy made plain to family members their antipathy toward the very notion of Black troops. An exception was Claude Paschal Maistre, who became a kind of chaplain to both the Black regiments and their families while championing their equal rights.[26]

The Louisiana First (USA), after a month of training, in late October of 1862 were detailed to repair infrastructure (bridges and railroad tracks) west of New Orleans. Their presence quickly became a lure for runaways from plantations in the region. Planters pleaded in vain that military authorities remove the Black troops. The First's white commander was himself complaining to the same authorities on behalf of his regiment: that they had not yet received their promised bounties nor any regular pay to assist their families back in New Orleans, who were suffering. He begged that they be integrated into the front-line troops. Instead, the regiment was ordered to construct three forts, the very kind of behind-the-lines labor in which the Confederates had so many of their slaves engaged. The New Orleans Afro-Creoles had been given uniforms and weapons, but they might as well have been enslaved, working for the Confederacy. It was clear that General Nathaniel Banks, who had succeeded Butler, regarded Black officers as a threat to social order. He began a campaign to purge them.[27] Through threatening hostile reviews of their aptness for command, Banks pressured most of the officers in the Second and Third Louisiana regiments to resign. Cailloux, like most of his fellow officers in the First, held firm.[28]

CLEARING HAMPTON ROADS

With Roanoke Island in Union hands by mid-February, the Confederate shipyard at Norfolk was suddenly exposed to a rear attack by canal and river. The secretary of the navy, Stephen Mallory, had one resource at the Norfolk yards that might conceivably change the war's dynamic: the *Merrimac,* a wooden ship converted into an ironclad, the *Virginia.* If the *Virginia* could somehow fight its way out of the naval blockade at Hampton Roads, Mallory informed Captain Franklin Buchanan, commander of the vessel, it could proceed to New York City and, with its guns, "strike a blow from which the enemy could never recover. Peace would inevitably follow. . . . Such an event . . . would do more to achieve our immediate independence than would the results of many campaigns."[29] On March 8, the day after Mallory had written, the *Virginia* steamed out of Norfolk to challenge the federal armada at Hampton Roads.

Over the next few hours, the unwieldly vessel terrorized the five wooden ships guarding the passage to the ocean. The *Virginia,* by several broadsides and a ramming with the iron plate of its prow, sank one of the sailing vessels. Further broadsides eventually exploded the boiler room of another and sent it to the bottom as well. Then it closed on a steam ship, the *Minnesota,* which had run aground. But the *Virginia*'s twenty-two-foot draft prevented it from navigating the shallow waters in which the *Minnesota* was trapped. As night closed on Hampton Roads, the Confederate ironclad reluctantly retreated into its port, content to finish its work on the morrow.

When the sun rose, there was another ship guarding the *Minnesota,* such a strange craft that the crew of the *Virginia* at first mistook it for a boiler from the *Minnesota* sitting atop a raft. They were soon disillusioned by a gun emerging from the "boiler" to fire at them. That began a naval battle the likes of which had never been seen, with both ironclads firing shells and attempting to ram with no lethal effect. At last, the *Virginia,* its engines barely operating, returned to port. Mallory's *Virginia* had dramatically demonstrated the potency of ironclad vessels, but there would be no war-ending bombardment of New York City.[30]

THE PENINSULA CAMPAIGN

In the first week of April, the Ninth Massachusetts became the lead unit of the Army of the Potomac to reach the Confederate fortifications that stretched from Yorktown to Williamsburg, on the Virginia peninsula framed by the James and York rivers. It marked the beginning of George McClellan's grand campaign to end the rebellion by marching an enormous army of 100,000 troops up the peninsula to the Confederate capital of Richmond. Gen. John Magruder, the commander of the Confederate forces on the peninsula, had fewer than 15,000 men to deploy along the six miles of fortification. Magruder, through the theatrics of parading troops to create the illusion of arriving reinforcements, convinced George McClellan that a siege was the best lifesaving tactic, to maximize the damage done to the enemy while keeping his own casualties to a minimum. For a month, the siege dragged on, as McClellan meticulously got all his pieces in order. Patrick Guiney's Massachusetts Ninth was on the front line opposite the Confederate redoubts at Yorktown. He wrote his wife, Jenny: "When our army opens upon the enemy *in earnest* Yorktown will be too hot for a human being to live in it."[31] Perhaps Yorktown would be the place where this rebellion was put down, just as Yorktown had sealed the success of one eighty years earlier at the dawn of the republic.

Unlike the British, the Confederates were not encircled at Yorktown. Before the Army of the Potomac could bring its immense firepower to bear on the Yorktown defenses, the Confederates abandoned their lines to retreat to Richmond. As the Confederate forces withdrew up the peninsula, James Longstreet's division was part of the Confederate force manning the fortifications around the colonial capital of Williamsburg, to slow the Union pursuit. Joe Hooker's division led the Union attack. When Longstreet's division threatened to turn Hooker's left flank, the Excelsior Brigade, which included the New York Seventy-Third, was ordered forward. The Seventy-Third's chaplain, Joseph O'Hagan, SJ, had the Catholic majority in the regiment kneel and make an act of contrition. Hundreds instantly fell to their knees in the mud to receive absolution from the priest, while their non-Catholic comrades removed their caps in respect. Within minutes the brigade was being pressed to contain the Confederate assault. More reserves were brought up to protect the flank, including the New York Thirty-Seventh. Ten years later the regiment's Jesuit chaplain, Peter Tissot, vividly remembered "the awful impression made on me when we were told that we must 'go it.' I felt as if my heart were sinking into my boots. Many of my poor men seemed to feel pretty much the same." The rattle of musketry and booming of artillery were deafening. They could see nothing.[32] The fighting went on until darkness fell, about 6 p.m.[33] When daylight returned on May 6, the Confederate rearguard had pulled out of Williamsburg to join the main army on its way to Richmond.

The First Virginia had been in the forefront of the Confederate oblique attack on the Union center. The captain of Company C was James Dooley, a former student of Joseph O'Hagan at Georgetown. The First found itself under heavy fire from encircling federals. The regiment managed to escape, but Dooley, whose right wrist had been shattered during the fighting, was left on the field of battle, along with many dead or wounded fellow soldiers. Dooley was taken to Williamsburg, to Bruton Parish Church, which was serving as a federal field hospital.[34] There he managed to avoid having his arm amputated, but his service in the Army of Northern Virginia had ended, after barely a month.

FROM DREWRY'S BLUFF
TO SEVEN PINES

Ten days after Williamsburg, the federal navy attempted to run the Confederate batteries on Drewry's Bluff, some ninety feet above the James. They even brought up the *Monitor* to employ its rotating guns to take out the Confederate artillery. Two days before the federal fleet arrived, Stephen Mallory, instead of attending Sunday Mass, had "hurried off guns, men and materials to meet the enemy at Drewry's Bluff."[35] Mallory's attention to Richmond's chief defense against a naval incursion quickly paid dividends. The guns on the bluff took a deadly toll on the federal invaders, while the bluff itself proved to be too high a target for the guns of the ironclad to get into position to reach. Union sailors were all too vulnerable to Confederate sharpshooters on shore. Daniel Carroll, of the Maryland Carrolls, was manning a gun on the bluff when a shell fragment from a Union gunboat killed him. But the Confederate batteries forced the Union fleet to abandon its plan of putting Richmond itself under its bombardment.

Despite the successful turning back of the federal fleet at Drewry's Bluff, it seemed but a matter of time before Richmond and then Petersburg would fall to McClellan's mega-army. Not only were ordinary civilians fleeing Richmond, but the Confederate Congress itself. The records and other valuables of the government were all packed, ready to be relocated should McClellan take Richmond.[36]

As George McClellan positioned his grand army for a siege of the Confederate capital, Joseph Johnston determined that, as at Yorktown, he could not afford to allow that to happen. This time, however, retreat was not an option. Instead, on the last day of May, Johnston launched a mass assault of two-thirds of his force, some fifty-five thousand men, against two corps on the Union left at Fair Oaks or Seven Pines, some five miles east of Richmond. Johnston's complex plan was to have three divisions, including Longstreet's, proceed on separate roads to converge on the right flank of the Union's Third Corps. Longstreet was to initiate the movement at 4:30 a.m. For a variety of reasons, the attacking columns started hours after they were scheduled to begin, and, because of miscommunications, all three ended up creating gridlock on a single road. Not until 1:00 p.m. did the attack start, with relatively few of the intended strike force involved, only nine of the twenty-two brigades. More than thirty thousand Confederates never saw action. Longstreet's total inexperience at handling so many troops showed in his allocation of troops and his passivity in directing the many soldiers under his command. Despite the blunders, the Confederate assault caught the Army of the Potomac utterly unprepared. The New York Sixty-Ninth, for one, was hosting a steeplechase when the Confederates struck. The Confederate attackers drove the Union corps back a considerable distance, some two and a half miles. Peter Tissot remembered the beginning of the fighting around 1:00 p.m. As the men constructed rifle pits, the chaplain rode along the improvised line, imparting absolution. Then late in the afternoon they were ordered forward. As Tissot, with some surgeons, watched the advance, five or six shells landed near them. Fortunately, they were already spent. When several more balls whistled by him, he thought it prudent to seek shelter in a ravine. But a shell found his horse there and killed him.[37] Eventually, however, reinforcements reached the endangered corps from across the river to stem the Confederate offensive. The next morning, June 1, the Confederates renewed their attack to break the siege, but gave it up before noon. By the end of the day, they were back in their Richmond trenches.

WAR COMES TO
THE SHENANDOAH

"Your long & exceedingly interesting letter was such a relief to us!" Baptista Lynch wrote her brother, Patrick, in late May. "We had heard of your narrow escape with the sisters, but . . . we had almost concluded that you must have been overtaken by the Yankees."[38] Patrick Lynch had, earlier that spring, traveled to Greenbrier, Virginia, where a group of his diocesan Sisters of Our Lady of Mercy had, since the previous fall, been administering a military hospital. By early May the hospital found itself in the middle of armies maneuvering to gain control of the vital Shenandoah Valley. Bishop and sisters had to relocate their hospital in Montgomery White Sulphur Springs in the westernmost part of the state.

A major change in Confederate strategy had been responsible for disrupting the Mercies' hospital ministry. As McClellan inched his grand army up the Peninsula toward Richmond, Irvin McDowell was preparing to march his corps south for an eventual linkup with the Army of the Potomac. Well before McDowell had his troops at Fredericksburg, some fifty miles north of Richmond, the Confederates had intelligence of the pincer strategy that the federals were planning to spring on them. Robert E. Lee, Jefferson Davis's chief military advisor, persuaded the president to reinforce Thomas Jackson's small army in the Shenandoah Valley so that it could open a second front in the Eastern Theater that would force the federal government to shift military units to the valley, and thus relieve Johnston's army defending Richmond. Jubal Early's division subsequently joined Jackson's force, bringing Jackson's total to some seventeen thousand. Jackson thereupon headed east with his enlarged army, which fed speculation that they were headed toward Richmond. At Charlottesville, however, the army boarded trains that took them west, over the Blue Ridge to Staunton. From Staunton, Jackson led about half of his force through a mountain pass to McDowell, where they quickly subdued a surprised, outmanned portion of John C. Frémont's army.

Aided by the maps that his topographical engineer, Jedediah Hotchkiss, had provided him of the region, Jackson carried out a series of cat-and-mouse maneuvers that enabled him not only to prevent three separate federal armies operating in the valley from combining their forces to confront him, but to engage them separately when he had the advantage, either in position or numbers or both. Compounding the federal disadvantage was the capture of several of their scouts, including John James Murphy and James J. Callahan, whose intelligence may have altered the course that Jackson's lightning campaign took.[39]

On May 23, 1862, Jackson's foot cavalry surprised the Maryland First Union Regiment, which was serving as the garrison at Front Royal, in the lower valley. The First Maryland Infantry (CSA) led the attack, followed by the Louisiana Tiger Battalion. That the Maryland First was even taking part, having a key role in the Confederate assault, was remarkable. Regiment morale had been notoriously bad for some time, stemming from the very nature of the Maryland unit. It was not an official regiment of the state, but self-supported. Being an orphan regiment had its romantic appeal, but romance could not provide the clothing, provisions, arms, furloughs, and financial support that a state government was expected to do. That took its toll over time. By the spring of 1862, desertions were rampant among the First Maryland. Requests for discharges were also soaring. As the battle at Port Royal was taking shape, the First's commander, General Bradley Johnson, told his disgruntled troops that General Jackson desperately needed them, but he himself had no intention of leading unhappy troops into battle. He then reminded them of what their fellow Marylanders were suffering in Baltimore under Union occupation, including imprisonment and exile. At the end of his fiery speech, the regiment let out the roar of a band of men ready to drive the enemy clear across the Potomac to their home state.[40] Together with Wheat's Battalion of the Louisiana Brigade, the First Maryland drove federal troops, including their Maryland counterpart, through the streets of Front Royal.[41] More than seven hundred of the garrison became captives.[42]

Two days later Jackson had his troops outside of Winchester, twenty miles to the north of Port Royal. On the morning of May 25, the Louisiana Brigade broke Banks's right flank, which sent his whole force racing through the town in retreat.[43] Jackson pursued the defeated federals over twenty-five miles to the Potomac River, at Harpers Ferry. Standing on the Bolivar Heights above the town, William H. Murray of the First Maryland shed tears as he looked upon his native state for the first time in more than a year. As he later wrote his mother, "I thought Oh could I but stand once more upon her soil and say Thy Will be done I could be happy."[44]

"We are all charmed at Stonewall Jackson's bravery," Baptista Lynch wrote her bishop brother on June 4, "& hope that Maryland will as the song says 'arise in majesty.' I do hope the Washingtonians & Philadelphians may feel a little of what we have suffered from their aggression."[45] Jackson had too few men to consider any invasion of the North. Rather, on the last day of May he began retreating up the valley. He had intelligence that two Union armies were converging on him, Frémont's from the west and Shields's from the east, the latter closing on Front Royal. Jackson's army, including its eight-mile-long wagon train, somehow managed to reach Port Republic, in the upper valley, which held the only remaining bridge spanning the Shenandoah River. On each side of the river was a Union force, Frémont's on the west bank, Shields's on the east. On June 8th, Frémont inexplicably committed but a fraction of his

11,000 men to attack Ewell's division at the crossroad aptly known as Cross Keys. The Louisiana Seventh took the brunt of the Union assault, with its lieutenant colonel, Charles de Choiseul, mortally wounded. After being repulsed by the Confederates, Frémont made no further assaults. Jackson left a token force to oppose Frémont, then moved against James Shields at Port Republic. Shields's force, outnumbered by more than two to one, nonetheless held off the Confederate attack for more than three hours.[46] Jed Hotchkiss guided the Louisiana Brigade over a mountain road, which put them opposite the plateau on which Shields had his artillery. A ravine stood in their path to the guns. The brigade came charging out of the woods with a sustained rebel yell. The attack reached the federal batteries but was repulsed. A second charge replicated the outcome of the first. Finally, Confederate reinforcements enabled a third charge to send the Federals scurrying northward.[47] It marked the end of the Shenandoah Valley campaign.

SEVEN DAYS

Robert E. Lee had replaced Joseph Johnston as commander of the Army of Northern Virginia, after Johnston's severe wounding at Seven Pines. Lee spent the first three weeks of June strengthening his fortifications around the capital. But he had no interest in just being as prepared as possible for McClellan's ultimate bombardment of the city. Nor did he intend, like Johnston, to mount an offensive to break the siege. He was playing for much higher stakes: a massive assault that would destroy the Army of the Potomac and effectively end the war, at least in the East. And so, he recalled Jackson's army from the Shenandoah Valley. Additional reinforcements from the Carolinas brought the Army of Northern Virginia to more than 92,000. Opposing him, McClellan had nearly 106,000 men, but at least 11,000 were ill, victims of the fever-ridden Peninsula. Moreover, the Union Army was divided by the swollen Chickahominy River, with but one corps north of it. That was the weak link Lee intended to strike.[48]

Thursday, June 26, was the day chosen by Lee for the grand assault, bringing more than 55,000 troops, including those of Jackson's Valley army, against Fitz John Porter's Fifth Corps isolated above the Chickahominy. As at Seven Pines, the Confederate battle plan was complex. Jackson was to strike first, turn the Union right flank, and force a retreat. As he swept southeastward, he would be joined echelon-fashion by the two Hill's and Longstreet's divisions to form a massive force overwhelming the federals. But the execution of the plan proved another matter. Jackson, exceedingly behind schedule in reaching the main army, for whatever reason, halted his troops in late afternoon, before reaching the battlefield. When morning became afternoon with no action, John Magruder, commanding a division below the Chickahominy, sent Major Joseph Brent out the Mechanicsville Turnpike to find the cause of the delay. Brent found Confederate troops massing in the woods on both sides of the pike and President Davis, his secretary of war Randolph, and secretary of the navy Mallory in a grove near the Chickahominy looking as gloomy as Brent could ever remember seeing anyone. Around four o'clock Brent heard the crack of sustained rifle fire. It was A. P. Hill's division. Tired of waiting for Jackson, Hill had put his men in motion.

The battle was on, soon joined by Longstreet, at Lee's directive. Hill, still expecting that Jackson would arrive on his left sometime soon, was intending only a demonstration in force until Jackson could show up and send the federals to the rear. But the Confederate division soon found itself under the devastating shelling of Union artillery. To prevent a counterattack, Lee directed A. P. Hill to press his offensive. When Hill's division came under a heavy fire from the federal artillery, he sent William Peagram's Purcell battery forward to provide a counterfire. As the newest member of the battery, Francis Dawson became an ammunition supplier. "There was no thought of danger," Dawson remembered, "though the men were falling rapidly on every side." The battery, in attempting to close on its infantry, had exposed itself to an enfilading fire. Dawson himself went down, struck in the left leg below the knee by a shell, leaving a gaping gash from which blood was gushing. Dawson used his handkerchief as a tourniquet around his leg and went back to manning the gun.

After several efforts to break through, with heavy losses, Hill called off the attack, having lost 553 men in the effort. Because of the botched execution, the assault had ended up involving but a fifth of the intended 55,000, of whom nearly 1,500 were casualties.[49] Purcell's Battery had more than its share. As night fell around 9 p.m. the battery had lost nearly two-thirds of its 75 men. Francis Dawson began dragging himself back to Richmond. On his way he passed some field hospitals where he had his first view of "scientific butchering": blood-saturated surgeons, working on plank tables, sawing away. "Under the table lay arms, hands, feet, and legs, thrown promiscuously in a heap, like the refuse of a slaughter house." Finally, an ambulance picked Dawson up to carry him the remainder of the way to town.[50]

The next morning, Lee ordered a continuation of the previous day's attack plan, this time with all units deploying at the appropriate times in the grand turning movement. Once again, Jackson failed to initiate the assault.

Once again it fell to A. P. Hill to give the signal to attack, at 2:30 p.m. The First South Carolina, for whose Irish company the Columbia Ursuline nuns had sewn a flag, had the dubious distinction of leading the attack. At Gaines' Mill, they encountered the Massachusetts Ninth, who had been posted there to protect the bridge over the creek. The Ninth had expected other regiments to join them, but they failed to show. The Massachusetts Irish prudently retreated nearly a mile to the center of the Union line. For two hours, the Confederates pressed the Union center to the breaking point. With little artillery support, the First South Carolina lost 57 percent of its manpower in the subsequent fighting, which stretched over two hours with precious little ground gained. At 3:30 p.m., Lee had Ewell commit his three brigades on the Confederate left flank, with the Louisiana Brigade in the lead. Attacking across Boatswain's Swamp, the brigade ran into a federal firestorm. "Many of us of us were wounded," Lt. Blayney Walsh wrote, "all within a space of thirty yards." The Sixth Louisiana's commander, Col. Isaac Seymour, on horseback, took shots in his head and chest. Walsh himself was severely wounded in the foot.[51] Further efforts to break Porter's line only accelerated Confederate casualties. That took all the fight out of the Fighting Tigers, who retired from the field.[52]

About 7 p.m., with about an hour and a half of daylight remaining, Lee sent in his remaining sixteen brigades, 32,000 men. Many of the federals, if not most of them, had been under the strain of attack for hours. What followed was hardly a coordinated general assault but a series of partial attacks. Longstreet had the worst position, close enough to the river to be vulnerable to federal artillery south of it.[53] Chase Whiting ordered Law's and Hood's brigades to cover the open ground down to Boatswain's Swamp without pausing to fire. It worked, at a terrible cost of a quarter of the members of their brigades. The Confederates overran the Union defenses, and a general stampede set in all along the corps' line, with more than twenty guns abandoned in their flight.[54] The Ninth Massachusetts found itself being engulfed by Confederates. Patrick Guiney, having taken over for Thomas Cass, whom illness had claimed, ordered the regiment to fire a volley at the closing Confederates, then to charge. That drove back the rebels enough for the Ninth to withdraw from their line of battle some distance. Guiney repeated the same tactic several times, before relief arrived from two other regiments. Guiney instantly recognized the Irish flag. He shouted out: "Hello, General Meagher, is this the Irish Brigade? Thank God we are saved."[55] Not all of them. When the Ninth finally crossed the Chickahominy in the first hours of June 28, they had 252 fewer men than they had had the previous day. Guiney himself became extremely sick and relinquished command of the Ninth. The extraordinary exertion that the battle had demanded of him had greatly exacerbated the malaria that he had contracted on the Peninsula.[56]

In nine hours of furious warfare, the combined casualties surpassed 15,200. Lee's grand assault had carried the day, but his dead and wounded far surpassed that of McClellan's. The surviving members of Porter's corps headed south to cross the Chickahominy and rejoin the rest of the Army of the Potomac in seeking the safety of the Union gunboats on the James River at Harrison's Landing.

Over the next three days the Army of the Potomac struggled to transport a Napoleonic-size army with its heavy artillery, ambulances, and miles-long baggage trains across bodies of water swollen from the heavy rains that pelted the region on the nights of June 28 and 29.[57] In negotiating the fifteen miles to Harrison Landing, most of the army found itself serving as a massive rear guard. On June 29, below the Chickahominy, in the area known as White Oak Swamp, Lee's forces had their best opportunity to bag their foes. But, as had happened more than once before on the Peninsula, the inability to coordinate dispersed units for a mass attack enabled the federals to continue south over White Oak Bridge and other crossings toward the landing.

At Glendale, a crossroads about ten miles north of the James, Lee determined to drive a wedge between the still-scattered elements of the Army of the Potomac by attacking certain portions of it from the north and west, thus seizing the numerical advantage. Yet again, Confederate commanders failed to carry out their assignments. This time the culprits were Jackson and Huger. When those two failed to set their troops in motion, Lee turned to Longstreet. At 5 p.m. the battle finally got underway. A. P. Hill soon committed his division to the desperate fighting. The Confederates nearly achieved splitting the Union Army, but the failure of the other divisions to engage, even though they were within a couple of miles of the fighting, allowed the federal Second Corps to hold together until darkness fell around 9 p.m. Of the nearly 3,700 casualties of the Confederates, Longstreet bore the brunt, losing a quarter of his division over the course of the day.[58]

July 1 dawned with about 18,000 federals and thirty-seven artillery in battle line atop Malvern Hill, overlooking a mile and a quarter of open ground, eight miles north of Harrison's Landing. For the first time in the week of battles, all the units of the Army of Northern Virginia were on hand and in easy communication. Whether to make another mass assault on such a strong position was the question the Confederate commanders debated. D. H. Hill cautioned that the better part of valor would be to forego an attack in which infantry would need to charge up several hundred yards of open ground under rifle and cannon fire. Longstreet was of a different mind. To him, McClellan was whipped. (He would have been even more convinced of this had he known of McClellan's absenteeism during the week, an absence that would continue that day as well.) "Don't get scared," Longstreet insisted, "now that we have him." That logic prevailed.[59]

The freshest divisions, those of Jackson, Magruder, and Huger, were given the responsibility of making the assault. Almost immediately things went awry. Longstreet himself had to chase after Magruder's division, which set off on a road leading away from Malvern Hill. The Confederate guns never mounted an effective artillery barrage on the Union line to render it vulnerable for any grand assault. In the event, there was no such assault, but, as had happened too many times that week, miscommunication and false reports produced piecemeal charges, each cruelly cut down by the ball and canister fire of the artillery. At 4:45 Huger's division, including the Louisiana Brigade, ran out of the woods to take their turn at gaining the hill. Before the brigade and their comrades got to within three hundred yards of their destination, federal artillery and the long-range rifles tore gaps in their line.[60] The Ninth Massachusetts, in the second line of the four-deep Union defense, countercharged with bayonets several times to turn back the remnants of Confederate waves.[61] During one such maneuver, Colonel Cass was mortally wounded.[62]

The Tenth Louisiana was part of the last desperate twilight assault against the entrenched federals. Their commander, Eugene Waggaman, had them double-quick across half the open ground to a gully, which could afford some protection. Most made it to the ravine. Then Waggaman gave the final instructions: "Not a shot must be fired until we get to the guns. . . . Remember Butler and the women of New Orleans. Forward, charge!" They went up into the ball and shot blasting from the massed cannon. Somehow, about a score or so of the Tenth, including Waggaman, made it to the part of the hill held by the Irish Brigade. Furious hand-to-hand combat ensued, with Waggaman slashing away at the Union Irish with a family sword before finally being subdued. It fell to the Irish of the Union and the Confederacy to terminate the week-long carnage.[63] The Confederates, as the attackers, had suffered the greatest number of casualties, more than 20,000. In one week, the Army of Northern Virginia had lost a fifth of its manpower. Longstreet's division, which had borne so much of the fighting, lost at least 40 percent of its force.[64]

Stephen Mallory saw God's hand in the disaster that the three-month campaign had proven to be for McClellan's grand army: "a just and all wise God has brought home to them their guilt in a manner the most impressive. The unburied forms of thousands of Yankees, strewed throughout a line of nearly twenty miles, are eloquent though silent monitors of the justice of Heaven."[65] Robert E. Lee no doubt shared Mallory's appreciation of God's providence but was more focused on the human failings that had prevented Lee from destroying McClellan's grand army. The reorganization of the Army of Northern Virginia that Robert E. Lee carried out in the wake of the frustrating outcome of the campaign said volumes about Lee's assessment of performance. The major change came in the reallocation of divisions. Thomas Jackson, who had had fourteen brigades under him, was reduced to seven; James Longstreet, who had had six, now commanded twenty-eight. Longstreet had become Lee's right-hand man.[66]

†

CHAPTER 8

Slavery and the
Shifting Goals of the War

[It] is impossible to save both the
integrity of the Nation and southern slavery.

—ORESTES BROWNSON, OCTOBER 23, 1861

THE PENINSULA CAMPAIGN
AS A CATALYST FOR EMANCIPATION

At the war's outset, George McClellan had written his wife: "Help me to dodge the nigger, we want nothing to do with him." But events during the four-month campaign overtook McClellan's prejudice. Ironically, the campaign itself became a catalyst for emancipation. The use of slave labor by the Confederates and the valuable intelligence runaways provided to the federals during the campaign convinced many in Congress, including moderate and conservative Republicans, to advocate abolition as a war measure. These contributions of free Blacks and fugitive slaves, whether of intelligence or physical labor, began to shift opinion within the Army of the Potomac about the advantages of emancipation. The fierce Confederate resistance to McClellan's grand army also went a long way toward burying the prevailing notion within the Lincoln administration and beyond that secession had been the work of an extremist minority; that a limited war which respected southern property, including the enslaved, could persuade the seceded states to return to the Union.[1]

By seizing the initiative to preempt the siege that George McClellan was sure would spell the end of the Confederacy, Robert E. Lee had not only saved Richmond but reversed the tide of war in the East, a shift that had begun in the Shenandoah Valley with Jackson's stunning success against three Union armies. When Lee calculated that the Army of the Potomac no longer represented a threat to Richmond, he began to shift his forces westward to prevent John Pope's new army from seizing Gordonsville, a key rail center, northwest of Richmond. By the end of July, most of the Army of Northern Virginia was in transit toward the piedmont, or already there.

HARD WAR IN
PIEDMONT VIRGINIA

The Army of Virginia under John Pope began operations at the end of June. Pope, who made no attempt to hide his Republican affiliation, had been brought east by Lincoln, in part to prosecute the war on the assumption that not just the southern military was the enemy, but the entire community. So Pope's army would not respect property as untouchable but would reserve the right to utilize whatever it needed to live off the land. For any harm done to Union soldiers by guerrillas or partisan units, the community would be held accountable. In mid-July, Pope promulgated the new rules by which his army would operate. The Army of Virginia would provide vouchers for any property they confiscated, with the vouchers redeemable at the end of the war, provided those holding them had been loyal to the Union; those who harbored or assisted guerrillas would be prosecuted; their homes burned, in some circumstances. Those who demonstrated disloyalty would be arrested and compelled to take a loyalty oath. If they refused, they would be sent South. If they complied with the oath, they would be able to remain in the community. Those who took the oath, only to relapse into rebellion, would be shot.[2] By the time Longstreet's wing of the army arrived in the piedmont in mid-August, the signs of Pope's hard war upon the population were all too visible. The Redemptorist chaplain of the Fourteenth Louisiana, James Sheeran, remembered "the devastating marks of the enemy . . . along our route. The fences were torn down, corn trampled under foot and houses gutted of their furniture. They even destroyed a mill and then threw the wheat it contained into the Rapidan." A plantation owner reported that Pope's men had "plundered him of all he had: his corn, wheat and pork; killed his hogs; drove off his beef cattle and even his milch cows." When the owner directed his slaves to put back the fences the Union troops had thrown down, the troops refused to allow the Blacks to do it, unless "he would pay them regular wages."[3]

The day after the conversation with the plantation owner, the Louisiana Brigade made a nearly twenty-mile forced march to Cedar Mountain, where two federal divisions under General Banks had surprised Jackson's superior force and, in two hours of fighting, steadily drove them back. The Louisiana Brigade had enough energy left to be part of a Confederate ambush on Banks's left flank, which caught the pursuing federals in a cross fire and helped turn the federal advance into a headlong flight of several miles.[4] The Tenth Alabama was part of the chase. The Jesuit chaplain Hippolyte Gache, following his regiment, was taking particular pleasure in the rout of "an insolent enemy who had come to slaughter us. . . . I think this was the greatest thrill of my life, seeing our shells exploding in the midst of those confused and terrified troops!" Later in the day, Gache searched out the wounded and dying on the ground over which the battle had taken place. "The scene which now confronted me was no less horrible than what I had witnessed on the banks of the Chickahominy. . . . Faced with this carnage, I quite forgot the joy I had experienced when first I heard the sound of cannon and fusillade. All at once I was overwhelmed by a profound sadness." Sadness turned to disgust when Gache spotted Confederate soldiers stripping corpses of their clothes and other valuables.[5]

THE ROAD
TO EMANCIPATION

In his inaugural address, President Lincoln had announced that he had no intention of interfering with slavery in the states where it existed. But Lincoln knew the quarrel of the newly formed Confederate States of America with his administration was not the status of slavery in the states but rather in the territories. Was slavery to be free to expand into those territories and be protected there, as the seceded states insisted, and the Supreme Court had ruled in its *Dred Scott v. Sanford* decision in 1857? Or was Congress to take the appropriate steps to preclude such expansion and protection, as the Republicans had pledged in their platform? Lincoln went on to point out that *Dred Scott v. Sanford,* the 1857 Supreme Court decision which had sanctioned slavery in the territories, should not be the last word. "If the policy of the Government is to be irrevocably fixed by decisions of the Supreme Court," he noted, "the people will have ceased to be their own rulers, having to that extent practically resigned their Government into the hands of that eminent tribunal." The president was suggesting that the Congress, the branch most beholden to the people, had the power to change that decision by their own action.[6]

When Congress met in July 1861 in special session, both houses passed resolutions that reaffirmed Lincoln's assurance that the government had no intention "of overthrowing or interfering with the rights or established institutions of [the seceded] States."[7] The day before the first of those resolutions, the stunning Confederate victory at Bull Run had been a distressing revelation that this would be no one-battle war won by seventy-five thousand volunteers engaged for ninety days. That realization occasioned a rethinking by congressional Republicans of how sacrosanct the institution of slavery should be in crafting a strategy for ultimate victory. Little by little, Congress began to take up Lincoln's threat to whittle away at slavery, both in the territories as well as in the seceded states themselves.

On August 6, less than three weeks after Bull Run, the Congress had passed a Confiscation Act, which effectively treated as contraband any runaway slaves who had been employed by the Confederate armed forces. Eight months later it emancipated all the three thousand enslaved persons in the District of Columbia with limited compensation (a maximum of $300 per slave) to those who had held them as property and took the oath of allegiance.[8] For the first time in the country's history, the federal government had abolished slavery in a jurisdiction.[9] Then, two months later, Congress took the bolder step of nullifying the *Dred Scott v. Sanford* decision by emancipating all enslaved individuals in the country's ten territories. In mid-July, Congress passed a second Confiscation Act, which authorized the seizure of all those enslaved by those engaged in rebellion. Lincoln signed that measure into law as well as a Militia Act, which approved the enlistment of African Americans.

For his part, Lincoln had been reluctant to embrace emancipation efforts that could prove to be counterproductive. He had been quick to countermand emancipation orders by Union generals in South Carolina and Missouri in 1861–62. In his report to Congress in December 1861, Lincoln had rejected emancipation as a military necessity. On Ship Island the commanding general had issued his own emancipation directive, which had produced an instant firestorm, not least among his own men. The regiment's Catholic chaplain, Daniel Mullen, instantly took issue with it as being contrary to Catholic teaching. Individual soldiers were threatening to resign. Thomas Cahill, commanding officer of the Ninth Connecticut, found himself at sea over the controversy. Above all he was determined not to endorse "Abolition or infidelity or sectarianism."[10] To Cahill all three were equally heretical. As for General Phelps, Cahill considered him a "monomaniac."[11]

Since early 1862, Lincoln's own emancipation efforts had been concentrated on the border states, where he had determined the key to defeating the South lay. If Lincoln could persuade Delaware, Kentucky, Maryland, and Missouri to accept compensated emancipation for their slaveholders, it would be a decisive signal to the Confederacy that these four states, whom it badly needed to prevail in the Civil War, would not be joining it. For months he tried to coax legislators from the border states to accept the compensated emancipation for their slaveholders which the Congress had approved in April 1862. In the end not one of the four was willing to participate.[12]

Had McClellan succeeded in taking Richmond and thereby virtually ending the war, it would have restored the Union "as it was antebellum." Instead, his failure on the Peninsula put pressure on Lincoln to pursue limited emancipation as a military necessity.[13] In early July he told Senator Charles Sumner of Massachusetts, a leading abolitionist, that he hesitated to invoke such a policy for fear that half of his officers would "fling down their arms and three more States would rise" against the Union.[14] Further reflection apparently convinced Lincoln that the benefits that emancipation would bring to the Union's war effort outweighed any risk of defections among officers or border states. And so, in the latter part of July he confided to his cabinet his plan to exercise his authority as commander-in-chief to free the 3.5 million enslaved persons in areas that were in rebellion against the United States. Such a proclamation, so Lincoln hoped, would undermine the Confederacy's use of slave labor to support Confederate armies. Secretary of State William Seward cautioned that to issue it at this time of "our repeated reverses" would simply fuel the charge that it was "the last measure of an exhausted government, a cry for help." Lincoln deferred to Seward's suggestion that he bide his time "until the eagle of victory takes his flight."

CATHOLICS AND EMANCIPATION

The Catholic position on slavery in the nineteenth century developed out of its traumatic experience with the forces of enlightened liberalism, epitomized by the French Revolution. "Catholics lumped immediate slave emancipation," John McGreevy has noted, "with a religious and political radicalism that threatened the foundations of society," including the hierarchical order of which slavery was an evil necessity in a bi-racial society in which one race was superior to the other.[15] Publicly the American hierarchy in the antebellum period had regarded slavery as basically a political issue over which the state alone had jurisdiction. As for the immediate abolishment of slavery, most Catholics would have agreed with Patrick Lynch's dismissal of the notion as a mere "speculative idea," with no bearing on the sociopolitical order. That all changed with Lincoln's election and his party's commitment to prevent the spread of slavery. The South, according to Lynch, had no choice but to strike out on its own.[16]

Orestes Brownson, long before his conversion to Catholicism in 1845, had judged slavery to be morally indefensible but condemned abolitionism as a means of eradicating it, not only because of the anti-Catholic sentiments of most of its promoters, but also because Brownson regarded slavery as an institution protected by the Constitution. As such, it could not be undone by the moral judgment of a minority. In addition, Brownson considered Blacks, as moral and intellectual inferiors, to be problematic candidates for freedom.[17] The war changed his thinking mightily. In his August 1861 essay "Slavery and the War," Brownson made a strong case for abolition as the only way to save the Union. The fear of pushing the border states into the Confederacy by making emancipation a war goal had limited the Union's ability to prosecute the war. The Union people, Brownson argued, had to avail themselves of every advantage allowed by the laws of civilized warfare. Those who sought to destroy the Republic could not hide behind the Constitution to protect their property. Brownson called on Lincoln "to liberate all the slaves of the Union."[18] As Brownson wrote Senator Charles Sumner in October of 1861, "the great question before us now is, whether we shall sacrifice the nation to slavery, or slavery to the nation."[19] Like Lincoln, emancipation for Brownson became a military imperative.[20] That essay evoked a bitter response from Archbishop Hughes in the *Metropolitan Record*. Hughes found Brownson's piece "untimely and mischievous." The archbishop reminded the editor that abolitionism, not slavery, had caused the war. Immediate emancipation would gravely damage the war effort, inasmuch as a great many troops, especially Catholics, would not fight to end slavery. Anyone advocating it "stands in need of a straight-jacket, and the humane protection of a lunatic asylum." One did not overturn past wrongs by revolutionary means, the archbishop instructed.[21] Brownson was having none of it. Secessionists were the actual instigators of the war. By repudiating the Constitution through that action, the South had forfeited the Constitution's protection of slavery. To sustain the Union, Catholics had no choice but to join the abolitionist cause.[22]

The backlash within the Catholic community to Brownson's call for abolition was loud and immediate, going beyond episcopal rejoinders to canceled speaking engagements and dropped subscriptions to his quarterly magazine. By one estimate, during the first two years of the war, his quarterly lost two-thirds of its subscribers.[23] Most of the Catholic press strongly opposed any steps, taken either by the Congress or the military, that involved emancipation. John Mullaly of the *Metropolitan Record* denounced the Confiscation Acts as unconstitutional, parts of the Abolitionists' "grand project of social amalgamation and equality between blacks and whites."[24] The *Catholic Mirror* warned that the bill emancipating the slaves of the District of Columbia was but the first step toward a general emancipation, which gave the lie to prewar Republican claims that they would honor the Constitution by not interfering with slavery in the states.[25] The *Boston Pilot,* in its opposition to the first Confiscation Act, insisted, "The truth is no government suits the Negroes of the South, but the domestic government they have," that is, slavery.[26] Three months earlier the paper had declared that "the complete safety and integrity of the Union require two things, each of them absolutely; the overthrow of rebellion in the south, and the overthrow of abolitionism in the north."[27] For Boston's Catholic paper, there was no using one to achieve the other. In response to Gen. David Hunter's proclamation freeing the enslaved in Beaufort, South Carolina, James McMaster of the *Freeman's Journal* found "there is deep disgust felt by white men from the North at being transmuted into the servants of the Cuffies and Sambos of South Carolina, instead of being . . . the soldiers of a *white man's country.*"[28] James Gordon Bennett had bluntly declared, in July 1862, that the federal government's fundamental war policy should be the preservation of white supremacy in a restored Union. Any calls for abolition, enlisting Blacks, or Black citizenship would only "drag down the white man to the level of the negro, or rather to produce . . . by amalgamation, a mongrel breed inferior to either."[29]

A few Catholic weeklies supported, to some extent, the abolition strategy of the Lincoln administration. In late July of 1862, the *Pittsburgh Catholic,* edited by a diocesan priest, James Keogh, pointed out that "he who stops to make distinctions, to say that he will fight for this, but not for that, is helping, though perhaps unconsciously, to destroy the Union, for, before the questions thus raised can be settled, the battles on which the great issue depends, will have been fought. Now, there should be but one party, with the simple creed that every sacrifice must be made, every measure taken which may be necessary to ensure the success of the legitimate Government." Drawing a line to exclude emancipation as a war aim was to abet the destruction of the Union.[30]

While making a visit to Rome in the summer of 1862, Archbishop Purcell encountered Félix Dupanloup, the bishop of Orléans, France, who had just issued an antislavery pastoral.[31] In it the French bishop had contended that history showed that slavery has never been the pathway to liberty. "The longer it endures the more it oppresses."[32] The meeting appears to have been a major contributor to the sea change in Purcell's thinking about slavery. In a pastoral letter published in early September 1862 the archbishop flatly blamed the southern states for starting the war. The South, he charged, had, decades earlier, decided upon secession as the best protector of slavery and systematically prepared for war from the late 1850s on. The North had no choice, according to Purcell, but to fight. And the only way to victory for the North lay through abolition.[33] Unlike his fellow prelates, Purcell now felt that slavery was a critical issue that the Church needed to address. Indeed, throwing caution to the wind, the archbishop added, "He who tries to perpetuate slavery disrespects the doctrine and example of Christ."[34]

Archbishop Purcell spoke for a distinct minority among white American Catholics. A Fourth of July celebration by New York Democrats at a packed Tammany headquarters in 1862 highlighted mainline Catholic opinion. The program opened with a sung poem entitled: "The Union as it was, and the Constitution as it is." The anti-abolition message could not have been clearer. Judge Charles P. Daly told the crowd that the Democrats had a solemn duty to demand that the war be carried on "not as a political speculation, but as a great national work." Congress was wasting its time in devising measures for the confiscation of property and the emancipation of slaves in territory controlled by the Confederates. As it was, nothing less than the principles of republican government were on trial in "this great contest."[35]

That same week the *Catholic Mirror* reported that the state of Illinois had just voted to bar Blacks from the state, and to deny to any resident African American "the right of suffrage, or hold any office therein." To the editor of the *Mirror,* Illinois's referendum pointed up the hypocrisy of the North in waging a war to free a race while passing legislation to ensure that the freedmen would never darken the northern states' own soil, much less enjoy the rights of citizens. It was also a harbinger of what one could expect should the abolitionists succeed in gaining their objective: "an irreparable evil" that would breed "a policy of antagonism to the negro" in all the free states. The abolitionists had already been responsible for plunging "the country into a civil strife, which is engendering the passions of a hatred and revenge that years of peace will not eradicate or extinguish." By forcing the enslaved to care for themselves would be to put them on a path to "sink lower and lower in the scale of civilization," accelerated by hostile legislation that would render their situation more and more dire. Such would be the tragic consequences of emancipation.[36]

To William Tecumseh Sherman, who had spent a good portion of his adult life in the South and had been the owner of slaves during two of his postings, in Mobile and Charleston, slavery was simply an economic necessity. As he had written his brother, John Sherman, in December 1859, "I would not if I could abolish or modify slavery. . . . Negroes . . . must of necessity be slaves."[37] "A nigger is not a white man," he told his wife, "and all the Psalm singing on earth won't make him so."[38] His wife, Ellen, may have agreed with her husband about the inferiority of Blacks, but, by the spring of 1862, she had already become an emancipationist, if only as a war aim. "The rebels," she wrote Cump, "ought not to be protected in their property, especially that property which enables them to keep up the means of carrying on this warfare. . . . I, for one shall be sorry to see the South received into the Union again until her slaves are free & she is humbled. . . . Miserable people I feel no compassion for them."[39]

As Confederate armies moved north in Virginia and Tennessee, the secretary of the navy, Stephen Mallory, reported to his wife that the slavery issue was so dividing the North that "we are stronger today than we have ever been, while our enemy is weaker. . . . Lincoln has at last quailed before the fear of driving off the border states has declared that the negro is not an essential element of the war, but is secondary to the Union." Lincoln's rejection of abolition, Mallory assured his wife, would be the final straw in the disuniting of the North.[40]

SECOND BULL RUN/MANASSAS

On August 24, as the Army of Virginia and the Army of Northern Virginia were facing each other in the vicinity of the Rappahannock River, Lee sent Jackson's wing of the army westward to circle around the federal army and get between it and Washington to force Pope to deal with this new threat. Jackson subsequently seized Manassas Junction, with its massive store of supplies, for the Union Army. Two days later, Lee sent his other wing, under Longstreet, on the same circling route that Jackson had taken, while leaving a single division along the Rappahannock to contest Pope. When Pope got word of Jackson's presence at Manassas Junction, he perceived the opportunity to overwhelm the isolated Confederate wing. On the morning of August 28, the Army of Virginia began heading north toward the Junction, twenty miles distant. Meanwhile, elements of the Army of the Potomac were ordered to march westward to trap Jackson from the east. Eighty thousand federals were soon bearing down on him.

Jackson was waiting, his 24,000 men concealed in the woods and behind the embankment of an unfinished rail line that paralleled the Warrenton Turnpike, a few hundred yards south. As Pope's lead division headed east along the pike, Jackson struck, signaled with an artillery volley. When the Second Wisconsin, led by Col. Edgar O'Conner, was sent to silence the artillery, suddenly the Stonewall Brigade, now reduced to 800, emerged from the woods in battle formation. Confederate and Union forces faced each other, closing to fifty yards, as they fired volleys. More units joined each side as twilight deepened. O'Conner fell, mortally wounded in the groin. After nearly two hours of close-up volleys, night finally ended the deadly exchange. Of the two units that had begun the fight, the loss was staggering. The Second Wisconsin had lost more than 60 percent of its men; the Stonewall Brigade had lost 40 percent.[41]

The next morning, Pope, thinking that Jackson was withdrawing from the Manassas area, ordered Franz Siegel's division to pursue him. By 10 a.m. Longstreet's wing arrived, unbeknownst to Pope. Longstreet put his troops into a line looking east. On the Confederate left, Pope, still oblivious to Longstreet's presence on his front left, made matters worse by issuing ambiguous, if not contradictory, orders to his corps commanders. He persisted in ordering diversionary attacks against Jackson, which became earnest ones, as Pope awaited Porter's corps to strike the decisive blow from the west on Jackson's rear. Col. Wladimir Krzyzanowski's brigade had marched unawares into Jackson's line, yet again concealed in the woods. Nonetheless, the initial fighting seemed to favor the Union forces as they pushed the Confederates back. As the Louisiana Brigade, at the center of Jackson's line, took part in a counterattack late in the afternoon, their commander was wounded; Charles Strong, the Louisiana Sixth's leader, took over. The net result of the morning and afternoon's action was a series of attacks, such as the one undertaken by James Nagle's brigade of Reno's division of the Ninth Corps: some initial success, undone by the lack of timely support, leading to retreat, all at the cost of a third of its manpower.[42]

Longstreet, meanwhile, had his wing also concealed in woods, in perfect position to pounce on the Union left whenever he chose. Lee wanted to have him do so immediately to relieve Jackson, but Longstreet convinced him to delay any such attack until they knew better how Pope intended to deploy his various corps. When Longstreet observed a division of McDowell's corps moving north to attack Jackson, Lee ordered Longstreet to make a "reconnaissance with force" against the division as a prelude to an all-out attack the following morning. Longstreet sent seven of his twelve brigades forward to initiate the probe. As darkness put an end to the fighting, 10,000 of Longstreet's wing had gotten themselves virtually cheek by jowl with the left wing of the Union army, by now totally disorganized, and still with little sense of the peril they faced on the morrow.[43]

That night, Pope, informed that Longstreet had arrived, assumed that he was there only to provide support for Jackson, not extend the Confederate line a mile southward. If anything, Pope still thought a Confederate retreat the most likely development. When, before dawn, one of Jackson's divisions was spotted repositioning itself, the movement was taken to be the beginning of Jackson's withdrawal, a replication of Cedar Mountain. Pope ordered three corps to attack Jackson. Before that order could be executed, Porter arrived at Pope's headquarters to announce that Confederates were threatening his flank. Pope had a skirmish line sent out on the right to test Porter's claim. Even when it was immediately challenged, the commanding general remained unconvinced that Longstreet's wing could really be there. The morning passed, with no major action.

Finally, around noon, Pope directed the entire army to take up the pursuit of the "retreating" Confederates. The movement had barely gotten underway when the lead Union column ran into heavy Confederate fire. Pope received intelligence that the Confederates were turning the federal left. Pope refused to believe that his flank was in grave danger of being overwhelmed by a Confederate force more than three times larger than the 8,000 of his own troops which he had on his left. On the Union right, two New York regiments, the Twenty-Fourth and the Thirtieth of the Second Brigade of the First Division of the Fifth Corps, led by Col. Timothy Sullivan, were driving the Confederates back on their left. The Louisiana Brigade, which had been involved in repelling Union attacks that day as well as the previous one, at last ran out of ammunition. They turned to rock throwing. Since rocks could be thrown at a more rapid rate than rifles could be fired, the rocks proved effective for a time, until Confederate artillery blunted the Union attack.[44] Porter and then McDowell sent in additional reserves, further reducing the Union left to barely a couple of thousand men to confront Longstreet's entire wing. At 4 p.m. Longstreet finally committed his wing to an all-out assault. Their objective: to seize Henry Hill, the ground around which so much of the first battle of Bull Run had been fought. With the hill in Confederate possession, they could prevent Pope's army from escaping, as McDowell's had been able to do a year and a month earlier.

The Confederate avalanche came across undulating ground that ranged from a mile and a half to two miles, which made Longstreet's coordination of the movement of 25,000 troops a remarkable feat which was key to the Confederate success. Perhaps it was poetic justice that the defense of Henry Hill fell to Irvin McDowell. McDowell quickly decided to make Chinn Ridge, some five hundred yards west of Henry Hill, his major line of defense, eventually positioning about 7,000 infantry backed by artillery. At 4 p.m. the First

Virginia was ordered into the assault. John Dooley, seeing the elephant for the first time, remembered rushing toward Chinn Ridge, "completely bewildered and scarcely heeding what takes place around. . . . I catch a glimpse of the battery . . . on a hill . . . as we approach, at a double quick." A brigade, which had gone into action just before the First, came down the hill in disarray, some shouting for the Virginians to advance, others to go back, still others to hit the ground. The First kept charging up the hill, their ranks thinning from the artillery shells and rifle fire, then halted momentarily for a volley against their target. The next thing he knew, Dooley was standing among a wrecked battery, with "broken caissons, bleeding horses, the dead & the dying."[45]

For an hour and a half, fighting raged around the ridge before the Confederates forced the last Union force, Krzyzanowski's brigade, to withdraw. By that time, McDowell had gained enough time for Pope to position four brigades and two batteries on Henry Hill. The Union commanding general was able to do so because Jackson did not complement Longstreet's assault on the Union left with one on its right that should have crushed the Army of Virginia. The defenders of Henry Hill managed to ward off the less-than-all-out attacks by Confederate brigades, until darkness eliminated any possibility that the Confederate tide would roll up Pope's army.

The bloody day ended with the Union forces forming a battle line a mile long between Poplar Ford and Henry Hill. Barely were they in position before the order came to retreat to Centreville. The Ninth Massachusetts had been on guard duty along the Rappahannock River when the battle commenced. They marched north to join the fighting but through faulty directions did not arrive at Centreville until late in the afternoon of the thirtieth. Finally ordered to the front, they had barely begun moving when the road suddenly became impassible; thousands of soldiers, hundreds of artillery batteries, ambulances, and other wagons were in a wild, full-scale flight from the plains of Manassas. In this mad gridlock the best that the division commander could do was to improvise a rear guard by drawing his men up in battle formation prepared to contest any pursuing rebel units. They never showed.[46]

The next day, Lee's final attempt to cut off the Union Army before it could get back within its District of Columbia fortifications failed during a thunderstorm at Chantilly. Nonetheless, the Confederacy had won its most decisive victory and had radically changed the tides of war. In late June, a federal army had been at the gates of Richmond; two months later, the federal government was shipping its Washington arsenal to New York City, to keep it out of the hands of Confederates who were now threatening its capital. As the Confederate Congress had abandoned Richmond in May in the fear that it would fall to McClellan, now a steamer was standing by, in the Potomac, to carry the president and his cabinet to safety, if need arose.

The three-day battle had cost the two armies more than 22,000 casualties. Once again, the Confederate Army was left in possession of the field of battle as had been true since the first major action in the East. Two days after the conclusion of the fighting at Manassas, James Sheeran had gone over the terrain where Jackson's wing had been assaulted to see whether there were still any wounded there. He encountered "a shocking spectacle." Despite the work of burial details, there were still bodies everywhere "scattered through the woods and over the field . . . some with their brains oozing out; some with their face shot off; others with their bowels protruding; others with shattered limbs." Many of the wounded "had been without food for three or four days and had no one to hand them as much as a drink."[47] Five Sisters of Charity arrived from Richmond at the battlefield shortly after its conclusion to establish a field hospital to tend to the wounded and dying.[48]

AWAITING
THE CONFEDERATES

Most of the Union wounded as well as some captured Confederates were taken back to Washington, where the government had appropriated nearly every large structure in the area, including most of the buildings on George-town College's campus and villa, Holy Trinity Church in Georgetown, and St. Aloysius Church near the Capitol. Five hundred of the wounded were brought to the college. Hundreds of them converted to Catholicism, including virtually all of the hundred-plus who died. The only thing apparently that prevented the complete takeover of the facilities of the college (as happened at Columbian College in the District) was the intercession of a Union general, A. W. Whipple, who had two sons in the college. The college continued to function as a military hospital for the remainder of the year.

In Washington, on August 29, Bernardine Wiget had accompanied John Abell Morgan to the station to catch a train to Baltimore. As a member of the faculty, Morgan was returning to Loyola College for the opening of its school year. "There was considerable excitement in Washington today," he wrote, "as Jackson was expected to be near at hand." At the Old Capitol Prison, Dennis Mahoney, the editor of the *Dubuque Herald*, who had been arrested in mid-August for editorials deemed manifestly disloyal, recorded in his diary on August 31: "Hundreds of the inhabitants of Washington left the city yesterday, and more are leaving to-day, in apprehension that the city will be taken by the Confederates who are understood to be but a few miles distant . . . and they are preparing to shell the city. The Capitol is to be converted into a hospital, for the purpose . . . of preventing its destruction in case the Confederates should get near enough to fire upon it." The next day, September 1, Mahoney recorded: "The road towards Bladensburg was thronged all day with vehicles carrying household goods and their owners away from Washington. It is understood that the city is invested by the Confederates."[49]

"We have the most harassing rumors this morning," Ellen Sherman wrote her husband on August 30.

> It is said that Cox's Division has been cut up by the Rebels and forced to retire. Boyle [Hugh Ewing] & Col Scammon were of that Division. I trust in God they are safe but think of the poor fellows who went on but ten days ago full of hope & ardor to offer their lives for their country being slaughtered by base & diabolical rebels. I hope this may be not only a war of emancipation but of extermination & that all under the influence of the foul fiend may be driven like the Swine into the Sea. May we carry fire & sword into their states till not one habitation is left standing. My boys shall go when strong enough to carry a musket.—Would they were all boys to offer their lives in exterminating & punishing foul treason.[50]

A year's fighting with mounting casualties scarcely imaginable when the war started had turned Ellen Sherman into an advocate of punitive warfare in all its raw, unforgiving vengeance. In the Confederacy itself, battlefield success bred not vindictive sentiments toward the opposition, but thanks to a gracious God who had deigned to favor them. So, in the late summer of 1862, Bishop Augustin Verot ordered a *Te Deum* to be performed in all the churches of the diocese and vicariate for the Confederate victories that the season had brought.[51]

†

CHAPTER 9

The War Comes
to the Catholic Heartland

I wish the army would take Washington and defend it
for the nation and drive Lincoln and his host of locusts, like
those which infested Egypt of old, into the sea.

—MARIE DALY, SEPTEMBER 11, 1862

THE MARYLAND CAMPAIGN

On September 7, 1862, Madge Preston and her daughter, May, were planning to take the Western Maryland Railway from its Baltimore station to the line's terminus. From there they would go by buggy the last sixteen miles to Emmitsburg, to enter May at St. Joseph's Academy, run by the Daughters of Charity. Late in the day, they discovered that the railway had suspended all traffic to western Maryland. The Army of Northern Virginia had occupied the area. What Martin Spalding had long feared for the Catholic heartland—that it would become the battleground over which the war would be fought— was now becoming grim reality. By the first week of September, Confederate armies were on the offensive in both Maryland and Kentucky.[1]

Despite debilitating losses in the Manassas campaign, Lee determined the potential gains to be had from invading Maryland, from the acquisition of recruits to the weakening of northern morale, far outweighed the limitations constraining his army.[2] And so Lee had taken his soldiers, now reinforced to more than 75,000, across the Potomac forty miles above Washington on September 4, heading for Hagerstown, just a few miles south of the Pennsylvania border.

The latest Union military debacle did force Lincoln, more than a week after the second failure at Bull Run, to put George McClellan back in command of the major army of the Eastern Theater, despite his failure on the Peninsula and his recalcitrance in making his army available for the Manassas Campaign. On September 11, James Gordon Bennett editorialized that McClellan should insist on Lincoln's making a long-term commitment to him as commander of the Army of the Potomac. As a show of his faith in McClellan, the president should purge the radicals from his cabinet. That led the *New York Tribune* the next day to charge the *Herald* with promoting a military *putsch* by the generals to "subvert the Republic and establish a Proslavery despotism on its ruins."[3] Marie Daly, for one, found that an inviting prospect. "The wretched heads of departments know nothing of their duties and the *honest* fool at their head is content playing President. . . . I wish the army would take Washington and defend it for the nation and drive Lincoln and his host of locusts, like those which infested Egypt of old, into the sea."[4]

McClellan's restoration to command quickly revived morale. On September 7, the Army of the Potomac, one-fifth of whose regiments had little or no training, set out for Frederick, forty-five miles to the northwest, where the army would be positioned to protect both Washington and Baltimore. As it happened, Frederick, Maryland's second-largest city, was the place where the invading Confederates had first made camp. When Longstreet's wing marched through the town on September 10, John Dooley observed that "the large majority of the people were silent." He suspected that some feared to show any support, lest they be reported to federal authorities when Frederick fell back into Union control.[5] The truth was that this portion of Maryland, with its large German settlement, was little disposed to greet the Confederates as liberators. Most of the males willing and able to serve the Confederacy had already gone South, like former governor Lowe. The invading army harvested but a few hundred recruits, far less than the thousands they had anticipated.

The sustained cheers that greeted the Army of the Potomac's entry into Frederick was in stark contrast to the scattered demonstrations of support Lee's forces had received a week earlier. When the army made camp on the outskirts of the town, a soldier chanced upon a communiqué from General Lee which indicated that he had dispatched his army to several different locations, including South Mountain and Harpers Ferry. When the information was brought to McClellan, the Union commander instantly realized how vulnerable the enemy was to any of its separate elements being overwhelmed by the superior federal force. McClellan decided to attack in two directions, sending the main portion of his troops along the National Road toward South Mountain, while the Sixth Corps moved down Pleasant Valley to attack the Confederate force occupying Maryland Heights overlooking Harpers Ferry, where Lee had dispatched Jackson's wing of the army to capture its 12,000-man garrison.

In Emmitsburg, as Mount St. Mary's students were making their way early Sunday morning, September 14, to the college chapel for Mass, they heard the continuing boom of cannon to the south. Despite the sounds of war, college life on the mountaintop went on normally throughout that Sunday. Finally, at 3 p.m. a few students, accompanied by a prefect, made their way down the Frederick Pike to perhaps get a glimpse of the battle. Their rector, John McCaffrey, had told them that the Confederates had taken Baltimore. Now this army, which some of their classmates the past week had been running off to join, was coming to liberate them! Even on the closer mountain side they could see nothing. But the sounds were much more distinct, "sharp, ringing volleys of musketry and then the quick, sullen booming of the cannon, as they came along the reverberating sides of the mountain."[6] The Mount St. Mary's contingent were aural witnesses of the battle for South Mountain some twenty miles distant, where D. H. Hill's division of 4,000 Confederates defended the range of large hills, interwoven with a labyrinth of roads transecting its hardwood forest.

The first action in the morning had taken place at Fox's Gap, a half-mile south of the National Road. Hugh Ewing led the Thirtieth Ohio of Cox's division toward a gaping hole of several hundred yards in the Confederate defense. Immediately he found his regiment in an enfilading fire from the left and rear. Fortunately, the Twenty-Third Ohio came to their rescue and drove back the Confederates to the left of the gap. But, through miscalculations about Confederate strength in the immediate area, the federals failed to exploit the opening they had been given. Artillery from the heights rained down on the outnumbered Union infantry. Fixing bayonets, the First Brigade charged into Confederate artillery and infantry, with the Twenty-Third Ohio on the left flank, the Twelfth Ohio in the center, and the Thirtieth Ohio on the right. Over an open field, the Thirtieth Ohio headed toward concealed Confederate cannon in the woods. They gained their objective, then held off several counterattacks over eight hours. In their first major combat, their casualties were heavy—21 killed and 65 wounded. The division lost 106 killed in action, 336 wounded, and 86 missing and presumed dead. At 34 percent, it was the highest Union casualty rate.[7]

John Dooley and the First Virginia were with Longstreet's eight brigades in Hagerstown, when, in the late morning, orders suddenly came for them to double-march. Once started, Dooley knew they were retracing their steps on the National Road but unsure whether they were going toward Harpers Ferry or elsewhere. Not until they approached Boonsboro did the boom of cannons identify their destination: South Mountain. Dispatched south to reinforce those holding Fox's Gap, the Virginia First was suddenly ordered to return to the National Road and Turner's Gap. Longstreet had concluded that Fox's Gap could no longer be held.[8] When darkness provided cover, the Confederates along Turner's Gap retreated silently through Boonsboro and turned due west to the village of Keedysville, five miles from the Potomac and safety.

North of the National Road, George Meade's division was poised to attack the Confederate defenses at Turner's Gap. Col. Hugh McNeil's Thirteenth Pennsylvania was ordered to "feel out" the area. The Thirteenth quickly became the target of Confederate artillery as well as of skirmishers. Feeling out soon became a full-scale engagement with Col. Thomas Gallagher's Tenth Pennsylvania among the regiments sent to aid McNeil's Thirteenth. Gallagher was soon out of the fight with a bullet wound to his arm, but the assault finally drove the Confederate left at the gap down the hillside to join the retreat to Keedysville. George McClellan ordered the pursuit of a foe that all the signs indicated was desperate to get back to Virginia. Chaplain William Corby's regiment was the lead unit in the pursuit of the Confederates. Corby remembered how "wild" his men were to bag the retreating rebels. They found themselves cutting a path through "men and horses, dead and dying." Corby dismounted whenever he came upon a dying man, heard his confession, if Catholic; baptized him, if Protestant, "as individual cases required."[9] On the morning of the fifteenth, as McClellan and his staff rode along the turnpike from Boonsboro to Keedysville, wild cheering from the troops accompanied them, as though sensing that the end of the war might at last be near, perhaps as near as the next battle.

TO STAND AT SHARPSBURG

At 10 p.m. on the fourteenth, Robert E. Lee learned that the federals had forced Crampton's Gap and trapped McLaws's division on Maryland Heights. Paul J. Semmes's brigade had been unable to prevent the Union assaults from finally breaking through the gap. The brigade moved south to form a buffer between the attacking Union troops and McLaws's artillery. To give McLaws time to extricate his men and rejoin the main army, Lee, at dawn on the fifteenth, decided to form a new line at Keedysville, He had barely sent that information off to McLaws when he learned that the only road open from Maryland Heights was the Harpers Ferry–Sharpsburg Road. Accordingly, Lee ordered the army to withdraw an additional three miles to the village of

Sharpsburg, which afforded far better ground for mounting a defense, but was only two miles from the Potomac.[10] Later that morning, a message came from Jackson that the Confederate forces at Harpers Ferry were at last in position to subdue the federal garrison there. That news bolstered Lee's decision to remain at Sharpsburg.[11]

With at least half his army still besieging Harpers Ferry, Lee boldly threw up lines stretching for five miles in a north-south direction on high ground beyond Antietam Creek in front of and north of Sharpsburg. There Lee, with his 15,000 or so troops strung out along the sprawling line, waited for Jackson. McClellan methodically brought up his 80,000 troops. By midday of the sixteenth, most of Jackson's troops had arrived, but that still brought Lee's force to a maximum of 25,000. McClellan had at least 60,000. Finally, in midafternoon, McClellan sent Joe Hooker's First Corps across Antietam Creek. Col. Hugh McNeil's Thirteenth Pennsylvania of Seymour's First Brigade was one of the first units to cross the Upper Bridge and head north along the Williamsport Turnpike toward what became known as the East Woods. The courage and leadership that thirty-two-year-old McNeil had displayed over the first year and a half of the war had elevated him from private to colonel. As his regiment prepared to advance into a plowed field, McNeil, at the head of his regiment, ordered a charge. They went into the best double-quick they could execute in an uneven field. From more than a hundred yards away came the fire of Confederate rifles and muskets. Seventy-five yards from the Confederate line, the Thirteenth Pennsylvania reached a rise that afforded them protection once they fell to the ground and began responding to the Confederate volleys. Into the night they fired away at each other, with South Carolina gunners feeding canister into the Pennsylvanians' ranks. Sensing the tide of battle shifting their way, thanks to the superior firepower of their Sharps rifles, McNeil ordered the Thirteenth to resume their charge toward the woods. Nearing the edge, McNeil shouted "Forward, Bucktails, forward," only to be struck down by a bullet through his heart. His death bred an instant fury which drove his troops into the woods intent on avenging their colonel's death. Slowly they pushed the Confederates out of the woods. At the end of the fighting, the First Corps had established itself in the East Woods.[12]

Night brought little or no sleep to the edgy soldiers on both sides of Antietam Creek, sure that the dawn would bring a major battle. The Louisiana Sixth, down to company size, had arrived on the north end of the five-mile battlefront on the evening of the sixteenth.[13] As the first light appeared on the horizon, scarcely minutes past five, fighting broke out in the East Woods. Not until 6:45 was the regiment ordered forward into a cornfield abutting the woods. They succeeded in turning back a Union brigade into the West Woods. There artillery fire drove them back to the Dunker Church. In about twenty minutes, the Sixth Louisiana lost half its shrunken numbers. The lethal fire spared no one. Col. Henry B. Strong, whose white horse presented a particularly conspicuous target, was among the first to fall. Gen. Harry Hays finally ordered the brigade to withdraw. A captain took command of the remnant of what had been a regiment, only to be killed in the next charge the Sixth attempted. The few survivors hunkered down at the front until evening. The Sixth Louisiana suffered 11 killed and 41 wounded, about half the men who went into action. And all in barely an hour.[14] As both sides savagely attacked and counterattacked, casualties mounted as they never had. Within the first two hours, they approached 4,400, or 32 percent of those engaged.

About the same time as the Louisiana brigade had engaged the enemy, Starke's brigade was sent into the intensifying battle. Even before they were called forward, artillery fire had wreaked havoc. Charles Behan, on his eighteenth birthday, became one of its fatalities. In the ensuing movement into the woods, Starke on his horse was mortally wounded. Approximately 550 Louisianans of Hays's brigade had double-quicked into Miller's cornfield. A half-hour later, there were barely forty left to reform around the Dunker Church.[15] By noon the federals controlled the East Woods but lacked the reinforcements to take any further ground. The units that had been engaged in the fierce combat that seesawed for nearly seven hours through the woods and cornfield were effectively rendered *hors de combat.*[16]

As the fighting petered out at the northern end of the battlefield, it intensified more than a mile south, along a depressed portion of the Hagerstown Pike that formed a natural fortification for the Confederates, who had failed to entrench their position all along the line. Beginning at 9:30 a.m., different federal units carried out a series of near-suicidal attacks. About 2,500 Confederates along the sunken road cut down wave after wave of federal brigades trying to break the Confederate center. Francis Meagher had arrived at Antietam Creek with his Irish brigade just in time for the battle. Late in the morning, when the center of the action had shifted southward to the sunken road, the brigade was ordered forward. As they came over the rise, they marched into a storm of canister and shell from the batteries on the hill beyond the Confederate line. At General Meagher's command, the brigade's double line fired a volley, then charged, then stopped to deliver another volley, much closer to the road. As they charged, one regimental flag bearer after another was struck down. Meagher, as always on horseback, had his mount once more shot from under him. The fall stunned the commander, whom two of his privates dragged to the rear to seek treatment amid the haystacks serving as a field hospital.[17] Shortly afterwards, the Irish Brigade ran out of ammunition and withdrew. The brigade's return to the rear was in grand Celtic style, with ordered arms, flags proudly flying, in columns of four.[18] As the remnants of the Irish Brigade gathered to ascertain their losses, the cost shocked even the battle-hardened veterans. Both the Sixty-Third and Sixty-Ninth New York lost 60 percent of their numbers, suffering 202 and 196 casualties, respectively, most cut down within the first five minutes. In all the brigade recorded 540 casualties.[19]

Behind the Sunken Road, James Longstreet with surreal composure ordered infantry reserves forward to relieve the exhausted survivors. He repositioned artillery to counter the punishing shelling coming from the farther side of the creek. Then suddenly an all-too-familiar misunderstood order put the entire thin rebel line in imminent peril. A Confederate colonel, thinking he had been ordered to pull back his regiment, withdrew them from their central position along the Sunken Road, opening a huge gap into which federal troops quickly poured. The Confederates fell back nearly a half-mile. It was clear to all, including those at McClellan's headquarters, that this was the breakthrough they had hoped for. General William Franklin pleaded to send his corps in to seal the victory. Incredibly, McClellan responded, "It would not be prudent to make the attack." Still assuming that Lee's forces outnumbered his own, McClellan feared a trap by Lee that would doom his army, and with it the Republic.[20]

The only force preventing the Union attackers from rolling up the collapsing Confederate line was a single artillery battery and a few hundred infantry. Longstreet directed the battery fire into the oncoming federal horde. When several gunners were cut down by Union gunfire, Longstreet's own staff took over the guns. The lone battery held long enough for additional Confederate batteries to join in and finally stanch the nearly fatal opening. Col. Thomas Welsh, commanding a brigade of the Ninth Corps, was convinced that "the whole Rebel Army could have been captured or destroyed easily before it could have crossed the Potomac—but indeed it seems to me that McClellan let them escape purposely."[21]

George McClellan's original battle plan had been for simultaneous assaults to be made at both ends of the battlefield, but Ambrose Burnside had failed to execute his assault at the southern end. Burnside's engineers had found no ford below the lower (Rohrbach) bridge to enable his troops to navigate the creek. At around 10 a.m. Burnside finally began sending troops across the bridge. For nearly three hours various regiments of the Ninth Corps attempted to negotiate the narrow passage of the Rohrbach Bridge. Four hundred Georgia riflemen in thick woods on the bluffs on the west side of the creek continued to stymie their crossing. The Kanawha Division, waiting its turn to cross the bridge, was increasingly frustrated by the serious casualties it was sustaining from the Confederate artillery from the bluffs beyond the creek. Finally, around 1 p.m. they had suffered enough, and began their own search for a place to cross. They soon discovered several shallow spots in the creek. Hugh Ewing led the First Brigade across Antietam Creek amid "a shower of grape." Two staff officers from the Thirtieth Ohio died during the crossing, as did two of the regimental color bearers.[22] With the Kanawha Division now outflanking the Confederate right, shortly afterwards there was a breakthrough at the bridge and Burnside's corps began pouring across to initiate their long-delayed assault. The Army of the Potomac seemed on the cusp of the total victory Lincoln had been seeking in vain throughout the summer.

Kemper's brigade, stationed a half-mile behind the sharpshooters, with barely 200 men and three cannon, were all that stood between the Ninth Corps and the Potomac River. John Dooley's First Virginia, part of the brigade, counted 17 men. For a short time, the tiny Confederate force with its cannon and muskets stopped in their tracks Burnside's men, many of them raw recruits. But once the superior Union artillery silenced one of the Confederate guns, the others beat a hasty retreat, soon to be followed by the entire brigade, "in great disorder," as Dooley remembered. "Oh, how I ran! Or tried to run through the high corn, for my heavy belt and cartridge box and musket kept me back *to half* my speed. I was afraid of being struck in the *back,* and I frequently turned half around in running, so as to avoid if possible so disgraceful a wound."[23]

As the Confederates fell back through the village, the Army of the Potomac was poised for a general assault along the entire line, which no shifting of troops would blunt. Then McClellan, fearing that Lee had reserves he had yet to commit to the battle, called off the attack on the north end of the field. The Massachusetts Ninth was among the troops of Porter's Fifth Corps that were held in reserve throughout the seemingly endless day. Late in the afternoon, orders came for the corps to relieve the Second Corps around the West Woods, but the Ninth had moved but a short distance when they were sent back to their former position behind McClellan's headquarters.[24]

Cox's division, once up the south side of Antietam Creek below Rohrbach Bridge, was in position to cut off the Army of Northern Virginia from its escape point across the Potomac at Boteler's Ford. The division, however, had exhausted their ammunition, which had not been resupplied after South

Mountain. In addition, the Twenty-Third Ohio was in a state of collective shell shock. Finally, in late afternoon, additional ammunition arrived and at least some of the Twenty-Third recovered psychologically. Before they could execute their trapdoor movement, AP Hill's division completed their thirteen-mile forced march from Harpers Ferry to put an end to any such closure. The division found itself guarding the frantic retreat of federal units that had penetrated farthermost through Sharpsburg.

THE END OF A CAMPAIGN

When James Longstreet joined the rest of the Confederate high command late that evening at Lee's headquarters to discuss their options for the morrow, Lee cried out: "Ah! Here is Longstreet," as he threw a shoulder around his favorite lieutenant; "here's my old war-horse—Let us hear what he has to say." As though sure that the warhorse who, barely two months earlier at Malvern Hill, had urged the final assault that would surely bring victory, was still of that mind. But Longstreet knew too well the devastation his wing had taken over the endless day that had, mercifully, just closed, his effectives reduced, as he put it, to "a good skirmish line." He could only second those pressing to recross the Potomac into Virginia.[25] The carnage of 24,000 casualties surpassed that of any previous day in the nation's war experience. Lee had lost 28 percent of his army, McClellan 24 percent. The losses were particularly high for Longstreet's and Jackson's commands. They both suffered a casualty rate of slightly over 40 percent.[26]

The casualties of the battle overwhelmed the healthcare facilities of the area. In Frederick portions of the Jesuit novitiate and of the Visitation Academy were both converted into hospitals. A Vincentian, Edward M. Smith, pastor of St. Joseph's Church in Emmitsburg, along with two Charity Sisters, brought clothing, medicines, and money to Sharpsburg. Smith tended to the wounded in the seven hospitals set up in Boonsboro. The two Sisters set up temporary shelters, of blankets mounted on rails, for those still lying under the boiling sun on the battlefield. Two days later, ambulances removed their patients to more permanent facilities in Frederick and Hagerstown. The sisters turned their attention to the wounded in the barns of the vicinity. For six weeks Charity Sisters divided their time between the field hospitals in barns and tents and the facilities in Frederick.[27]

The *New York Herald* declared that "the battle of Antietam has broken the back of the rebellion" and "changed the tide of affairs."[28] That proved to be a serious misdiagnosis of the condition of the Army of Northern Virginia as well as the state of the war. The army had been badly bent by the fierce daylong fury, but hardly broken. That would have taken the vigorous renewal of the battle on the following day, which McClellan refused to order, despite having the luxury of thousands of troops who had seen no action on the seventeenth. McClellan's remote and supercautious leadership both during and after the fighting left Hugh Ewing disgusted with eastern commanders. If Lincoln wanted to prevent the country from becoming hopelessly divided between those committed to the pursuit of victory and those seeking peace at whatever price, he had to remove McClellan.[29]

RECLAIMING THE CONFEDERACY'S TWELFTH STATE

Many Kentuckians who had gone South, like their Maryland counterparts, kept lobbying for an invasion of their state. At a meeting with Braxton Bragg in Tupelo, Mississippi, at the end of July, a group of Kentucky expatriates implored the Confederate commander to rescue their state from the iron-heel rule of the Union military governor, Brig. Gen. Jeremiah Boyle. A majority of Kentuckians, these émigrés insisted, would greet them as liberators. The cumulative lobbying persuaded Bragg to have Kirby Smith lead his 8,000 men toward Lexington. In the end, the Confederacy sent not one, but two armies into Kentucky in August 1862. Kirby Smith's army took advantage of a mountain gap that set them on a path toward the Bluegrass region, a hotbed of secession in the state. At Richmond, a county seat twenty miles south of Lexington, Smith routed a small Union force of recent recruits. The next day the Confederates received an exuberant welcome in Lexington, with women wildly cheering their liberators from windows and doorways. On September 1, they claimed Frankfurt, the federal capital of the state, as well.[30] The way seemed clear to the Ohio River ports of Newport and Covington, as well as Cincinnati on the river's northern shore. In Columbia, South Carolina, Mother Baptista Lynch couldn't resist telling her brother Patrick, "How I would enjoy seeing Mr. E[ward] Purcell when Cincinnati was demanded!"[31]

If a great many Kentuckians, particularly women and children, were ready to cheer their Confederate "liberators," all too few Kentucky males were interested in availing themselves of the arms that the invaders had hauled into the state in the expectation that they would enrolling thousands who would need weapons. If Maryland yielded few recruits for the Confederacy because the hearts of the residents of western Maryland were not with the South's cause in the first place, in Kentucky it was a more complicated picture. "Their hearts were evidently with us," Smith reported to Bragg, "but their blue-grass and fat-grass cattle are against us." There was a limit to Kentucky's southern leanings. Volunteering was an action far beyond the will or capacity of most Kentuckians, at least short of a victory by the Confederates in the Bluegrass region. In all, some 2,500 Kentuckians enlisted in the Confederate armies during their two months in the state, ten times what they had garnered in Maryland, but only a tenth of the number that Confederate authorities had anticipated.[32]

As the Confederate armies pushed aside the impotent Union opposition to make their way toward Lexington and Louisville, Bishop Martin Spalding wrote in his journal: "I will not leave my post, nor the sanctuary which I love! There my bones may be laid, in the tomb prepared for me. . . . God help me & my people!"[33] A week later he could only add to his journal: "K[entuck]y to be drenched in fratricidal blood!"[34]

Braxton Bragg had reorganized the Army of the Mississippi into two wings, the Right Wing under the command of Leonidas Polk, the Left Wing under William J. Hardee. The forty-six-year-old Hardee, a convert to Catholicism, had formerly been the commandant of the US Military Academy, where he had authored *Hardee's Tactics,* a valuable instrument for the training of soldiers that both Union and Confederacy had utilized. Hardee himself had distinguished himself by his courageous performance at Shiloh. The 30,000 troops of Hardee's wing had left Chattanooga, Tennessee, on August 28 to invade central Kentucky. That same day Don Carlos Buell's federal army had headed toward Kentucky from Nashville. For two weeks in September, Buell's Army of the Ohio pursued Bragg's army, intent on preventing it from taking possession of Louisville, which seemed receptive to Confederate rule, given the persistent sympathy of its residents toward the Confederacy (with thousands turning out for funerals of Confederate soldiers), and the rising opposition to Union occupation, particularly after the military governor, Jeremiah Boyle, had imposed the conscription of all males between eighteen and twenty-one.[35]

By the latter part of September, the Army of the Ohio was closing on Bragg's army at Munfordville. The night before the federals expected to confront the Confederate Army at the town, the Holy Cross priest, Peter Paul Cooney, the chaplain of the Twenty-Third Brigade of the Second Corps, spent eight hours in a makeshift confessional consisting of blankets draped over three stacks of guns, forming a horizontal *V.* "About twelve o'clock," he wrote his brother, "my legs were perfectly benumbed, until one of the poor soldiers brought me a blanket to roll around my thighs. . . . Here the poor fellows came, impressed with the idea that perhaps this would be the last confession of their lives. Some of the officers gave me their wills and then went to confession."[36] The next morning, by the time they reached Munfordville, the Confederates were gone.

Bragg had led his army northeast to Bardstown, where he expected to find Smith's force. The market town was the hub of Catholic settlement in Kentucky. From the 1780s on, Maryland Catholics had migrated there in search of new fields to cultivate tobacco. Over the first five decades of the century, these ex-Marylanders and their French priests had worked an institutional miracle in the churches and women's religious orders and colleges and academies they had established, meriting the "Holy Land" title by which the area came to be known. On September 22, the first units of the Army of the Mississippi marched into Bardstown to a raucous reception that rivaled the joyous celebrations in the Deep South during the opening days of the war. As one Louisiana soldier noted, "the people of this section are nearly all secessionists. They received us with the wildest demonstration of delight." Brig. Gen. Sterling Wood, an alumnus of the town's St. Joseph's College, noted the correlation between allegiance and religion: "All the Catholics in this country are Secesh, the Protestants Union." Unfortunately, for those hoping to bring Kentucky into the Confederacy, there were more Protestants than Catholics, even in the "Holy Land."[37]

IUKA AND CORINTH

Part of the Confederate plan for the Kentucky Campaign had been for Generals Sterling Price and Earl Van Dorn to bring their forces from Mississippi to western Kentucky to provide a third force invading the state. In mid-September, Price's troops had cleared a small Union garrison from Iuka, a railroad town in northern Mississippi. General Ulysses S. Grant ordered Generals William Rosecrans and Edward Ord to bring two divisions each in a pincer move against Price's 15,000-man army. Rosecrans marched his divisions from Corinth twenty miles to the south of Iuka while expecting Ord to position his two divisions to the north of the town. On September 19, as Rosecrans's lead units were approaching Iuka, Price ambushed them. The subsequent fighting cost Rosecrans's divisions some 800 casualties, but Price lost nearly double that amount before he managed to slip away southward after night fell. Ord never showed, whether, like Buell, the victim of an acoustic shadow which left him unaware that a battle was taking place about three miles from him, or of a false report that McClellan had destroyed Lee's army at Sharpsburg just two days earlier.[38] Rosecrans claimed victory at Iuka, even citing divine intervention. Still, he was livid at Grant, who, he was convinced, had called Ord off the operation. Relations between Grant and Rosecrans were never the same following Iuka.[39]

Two weeks later, on October 3, Price and Van Dorn, outnumbering Rosecrans with 22,000 to his 18,000, struck from the north and drove the federals back into the earthworks that Rosecrans had compacted to better concentrate his troops. At 4:30 the next morning, a two-hour artillery exchange renewed the battle. Then came the Confederate assault. Chaplain John Bannon, with crucifix and Bible in hand, went through the ranks of the Missouri Brigade, blessing and encouraging them as they waited to go into action. Just before the command to advance was given, Bannon had them all kneel for absolution. Then they went forward and seemingly in no time had broken through the Union lines and captured scores of artillery pieces.[40] As the federal salient began to collapse, Rosecrans raced his horse to the front and heroically urged his men to "Stand by your country." A volley of bullets tore away his hat, but miraculously missed him. His brave leadership rallied his troops; the line held. Van Dorn later expressed his wonder at Rosecrans's bravery in holding the federal line together. "I don't see how the devil [Rosecrans] held the place," Van Dorn admitted, and went on to opine that "I don't believe any other man in the service but Rosecrans could have done it."[41]

Concentration of resources in shorter lines, including reserves, proved decisive for the Union victory in the two-day battle, during which the Confederates sustained four times the casualties that the federals suffered. Rosecrans started in pursuit of them, only to have Grant order him back to Corinth. Rosecrans could not believe Grant could be blind to their golden opportunity: "The whole rebel army of the West, and certainly the whole flower of it, is in our front, whipped and demoralized. We could drive them like a flock of sheep. It seems to me that the time has come to win the war in the west."[42] Grant was unmoved. Back they went to Corinth. For Rosecrans it proved a short stay. Halleck ordered Rosecrans to return to Cincinnati, where he was given command of the new Army of the Cumberland, with responsibility for securing not only Kentucky, but middle and eastern Tennessee as well.[43]

PERRYVILLE

On October 6, General William J. Hardee led the Left Wing of the Army of the Mississippi into Perryville, a village in the center of Bluegrass country, just west of Danville, along the Chaplin River. They stopped there to refresh their water supply from the many potable streams in the vicinity. When Union cavalry began shadowing Hardee's left flank, Leonidas Polk, commanding the Right Wing, sent a division to reinforce Hardee. As it happened, Hardee had three corps of the Army of the Ohio behind him. They also were urgently seeking water.[44] As Kenneth Noe wrote of the prelude to the Battle of Perryville: "no one in the Confederate high command had an adequate grasp of the situation."[45] One could have said the same of the Union command as well.

At 11 a.m. on October 8, Hardee sent his Left Wing across dried-up Chaplin River to form a line between the river and Doctor's Creek west of the village. On the north end of the field, Polk, at 2 p.m., prepared to attack what he perceived to be the highly vulnerable left flank of the Union Army. The Confederates were marching into the well-positioned First Corps of the Union Army. Nonetheless, after persistent assaults for over an hour and a half the Confederates drove back the Union left but failed to turn it. Neither army commander realized the extent of the battle that was developing. In midafternoon, Bragg still had no idea that he was facing Buell's whole army. Still, he knew more than Buell, who remained ignorant of the very battle that was raging near him.[46] Acoustic shadow refracting the sound as well as the constant wind that dissipated the smoke over the field hid from Buell the vital signs of battle.

On the southern end of the field, Hardee opened his attack at 2:30 p.m. Confusion galore marked its execution. Intended to be an echelon-style assault with Buckner's veteran six-regiment brigade leading the attack, miscommunication apparently resulted in Thomas Jones's inexperienced, undermanned three regiments leading the way, only to quickly suffer 50 percent casualties and fall back. When a larger, veteran brigade attacked in the wake of Jones's brigade, it was caught in the friendly fire of a Confederate battery which disorganized their ranks. Eventually, however, in large part because of the superior performance of Confederate artillery, the Union right began to fall back as well. The newly appointed division commander, Phil Sheridan, content to let his artillery do the work and expecting an imminent attack on his own position, failed to commit his infantry as reinforcement at a critical time.[47] The Union left collapsed around 3:30 p.m. About the same time, the Confederate Right Wing renewed its assault, having gained some three hundred yards in the earlier fighting. An hour of unsuccessful assaults out of a ravine up a steep slope ended the fighting on the northern end of the battlefield. The federal line had been bent in a ninety-degree angle but still held.

The Union situation was much more critical on its right, with a huge gap in its line. As federal units began to withdraw, the Ohio Tenth remained to contest any new Confederate attack. Despite the gathering darkness, the Confederates made one last assault. As two Confederate regiments led the charge up a hill, Lt. Col. Joseph W. Burke of the Tenth ordered his men to rise and charge down the hill. The desperate measure blunted the attack. Burke then grabbed the bugle from an aide, sounded the halt for the counterattack, redressed his line, assigned skirmishers, then led the retreat up the Mackville Road, as a grassfire broke out around them.[48]

The casualties for the day were 4,200 for the Union; 3,400 for the Confederates, despite the Confederates having been the attackers for most of the four hours of fierce fighting. Nonetheless, it proved an exorbitant cost, with the Army of the Mississippi having lost a fifth of its force in the fighting.[49] Sisters from St. Catherine's convent, fifteen miles from the battlefield, came in wagons to transport the wounded back to their convent. "Long after midnight," the annals for the Dominican community recorded, "wagon loads of bruised and shattered heroes were still being brought to St. Catherine."[50]

Bragg, under cover of night, retreated a dozen miles to the northeast, where he linked up, at last, with Kirby Smith. Smith wanted to renew the fight, confident that the Confederates had the numbers and experienced troops to defeat Buell. Bragg had already seen enough of Kentucky to convince him that no additional battles would win the state for the Confederacy. As he reported to Confederate officials, the people of the state "are neither disposed nor willing to risk their lives or their property" to join the rebellion.[51]

†

CHAPTER 10

Emancipation

The Negro family is certainly inferior to the White, and a
persistent attempt at their immediate emancipation, without authority,
and in violation of laws and solemn compacts, would be attended
with fearful mischief, and end in their destruction.

—THOMAS PARKIN SCOTT, JANUARY 11, 1863

LINCOLN'S PRELIMINARY
PROCLAMATION

Union success at Antietam, limited as it was, enabled Lincoln to proclaim
that, if the Confederate States failed, by January 1, to call off their effort to
gain independence, Lincoln would sign the order officially freeing, as a military necessity, all those held in bondage beyond Confederate lines. In addition, all those freed under the order would be eligible to serve in the Union's
armed services. That changed the nature of the war. It may have freed not
one slave throughout the Confederacy, but it told the South and the world
that abolition was now an explicit war goal of the US government, and that
that government wanted able-bodied formerly enslaved males to be part of
its effort to end the rebellion.

In the wake of the president's proclamation, Archbishop Hughes reiterated his warning of the previous year that "we Catholics, and a vast majority
of our brave troops in the field, have not the slightest idea of carrying on a war
that costs so much blood and treasure just to gratify a clique of Abolitionists."[1]
When a Kentucky abolitionist, Cassius Clay, spoke at an Irish freedom rally in
New York, a month after Lincoln had made his announcement, he attempted
to appeal to their own subjugation in Ireland by the British. "I would not
enslave neither the Irishman nor the negro," Clay told them. "If you want to
make labor respectable, make it free and God will prosper it." For his efforts,
Clay got hisses, groans, and shouts for his removal.[2]

The Catholic press, with two exceptions (*Catholic Telegraph* and *Der Wahrheits Freund*), condemned Lincoln's executive order. The most critical of the Catholic weeklies was James McMaster's *Freeman's Journal*. About the proclamation the *Freeman's Journal* predicted: "Its effect at the North will be one of wide-spread demoralization of forces, and division of parties. As a document of state it is beneath either discussion or even simple contempt."[3] Lincoln's efforts to put Blacks on an equal level with whites through emancipation and enrolling them as soldiers were two straws too many for the *Pilot*'s support of the war. The enslaved, Patrick Donahoe insisted, did not want freedom. Nature intended the planation to be their habitat.[4] For the leading Irish journal, the *Irish-American,* the Emancipation Proclamation was nothing more than a demonstration of the radical "Negrophilism" of the administration and "the irredeemable malignity of the Abolition hatred of our race." What putting Blacks on an equal level meant for the Irish was increased competition for jobs and military service.[5] Dennis Mahoney of the *Dubuque Herald* judged the proclamation the "crowning act of Lincoln's folly." Mahoney had no doubt that the president's executive order was unconstitutional, freeing citizens from any further obligation to support the war.[6]

The editorials of the *Wisconsin Daily Patriot* were a barometer of Catholic opinion in the wake of Lincoln's proclamation. In late August 1862, the paper declared that "Catholics have shown their loyalty to our Government, without flinching. They are ready to fight for the Government and its institutions and laws, as established by our forefathers."[7] Three and a half months later, the paper was defining loyalty much more narrowly: "Loyalty . . . means devotion to the Union, and the legitimate government of the United States. It does not mean the adoption of any peculiar theory."[8]

ANOTHER MARCH

ON RICHMOND

On November 5, Abraham Lincoln removed George McClellan as commander of the Army of the Potomac. McClellan's failure to vigorously prosecute the war in the East had finally exhausted the president's patience. Lincoln's removal of McClellan probably disturbed the Catholic community more than any other cohort within the North. Most Irish in the Army of the Potomac deeply resented it. The Irish Brigade made its protest by lowering their regimental flags when McClellan took his official leave of the army he had created.[9] "Those whom the Gods wish to destroy," Marie Daly commented about the change, "they first make mad." All Daly could do was hope that Ambrose

Burnside, McClellan's successor, would "not allow himself to be goaded on by the public clamor to do anything rash."[10]

Burnside quickly devised a plan to have his unprecedentedly large army (120,000) execute a flanking move on the Confederates by striking east toward Fredericksburg, fifty miles north of Richmond. Two weeks after taking over, Burnside had two corps of his army occupying Falmouth Heights, on the Rappahannock River opposite Fredericksburg. That river proved the rub. The Army of the Potomac needed pontoon bridges to cross. By the time they arrived in late November, James Longstreet had most of his corps occupying the hills behind the town. As the calendar turned to December, both sides expected that they were settling into winter quarters. But pressure from many quarters was building on the commander of the Army of the Potomac to strike.[11] His generals' consensus, that it would be foolhardy to attempt a frontal assault, given the formidable Confederate defenses on the heights behind Fredericksburg, merely strengthened the insecure Burnside's commitment to attack.[12] Chaplain Joseph O'Hagan, from Falmouth Heights, watched warily as the Army of the Potomac made its initial preparations to cross the Rappahannock and storm the seemingly impregnable Confederate defenses. "If [Burnside] attempts it here," O'Hagan wrote Bernardine Wiget at the end of November, "it will be at a terrible sacrifice of life."[13]

On picket duty on December 12, John Dooley could hear, for hours, the muffled sound of troops crossing the pontoon bridges. Behind him, Confederate comrades took their positions along the four-foot-high stone wall and other fortifications which ran along Marye's Heights. But the day passed with the federal troops still settling into the lower town and at the bottom of the hilly plain that separated them from the Confederates on the higher elevation. Snow fell, making an impending battle even more incongruous. The next morning, thick fog covered the town and hillside. Not until nearly an hour past midday did the attack on the Confederate right, east of the town, begin. George Meade's division broke through a gap in the rebel line but, lacking the support to sustain the breakthrough, the attack faltered, and Meade withdrew his surviving troops. In the afternoon the Union assault shifted westward a half-mile, where the attack route ran up five hundred yards of exposed ground that provided little or no cover.

As the Irish Brigade made its way along Hanover Street in four columns, a soldier approached Chaplain Corby. "Father," he reported, "they are going to lead us over in front of those guns which we have seen them placing, unhindered, for the past three weeks." Corby tried to assure the soldier: "Do not trouble yourself; your generals know better than that."[14] The embalmers thrusting cards advertising their morbid trade into the palms of soldiers as they headed toward the guns must have stirred doubts about the wisdom of their commanders, but on they marched. A band playing "Gary Owen" in the brigade's honor boosted its morale, for the moment, as the sun finally took command of the frigid day.[15]

The 116th Pennsylvania, which had become part of the Irish Brigade, brought up the rear of the five-regiment, 1,200-man unit as they waited on the town's main street. The entire brigade was in the range of Confederate artillery which flew past and exploded below them. Finally came the order to advance, with fixed bayonets, up the hill. Federal guns suddenly revived to provide cover. That seemed only to increase the shot and shell coming from Marye's Heights at this new threat emerging from the town.[16] The brigade, with sprigs of green boxwood in their caps, went into a double-quick pace as they crossed the tracks of the Fredericksburg & Richmond Railroad. Then they had to navigate a small canal before making a final charge, in tandem with two other brigades. Too soon they encountered a storm of musket fire, under which the brigades staggered before resuming their climb in a double line of battle. Gen. Thomas Meagher's ulcerated knee made it impossible for him to negotiate the hill. Then Meagher's final order: "Load and fire at will," before he reluctantly returned down the hill to retrieve his horse.[17] The brigade got within twenty-five yards of the wall, closer than had most of the dozen other assaults that were made on that late wintry afternoon. Confederate muskets made them pay an immense price for the ground that they covered.[18] Nearly half the members of the five regiments who stormed the Confederate line fell dead or wounded. In barely a half-hour the brigade had been virtually destroyed, perhaps barely a sixth still countable as effectives.

The Massachusetts Ninth had set out for Fredericksburg before dawn on the thirteenth. They crossed the river between 2 and 3 p.m. passing many of the wounded from the Irish Brigade heading back to Falmouth. As they moved up the hill to Marye's Heights, they came under heavy shelling and rifle fire. A shell fragment broke Patrick Guiney's sword scabbard in half but left him untouched. With the sun setting, a staff officer notified Guiney that the regiment was ordered to charge the hill. Guiney had no intention of adding to the horrific carnage. "You go and tell your general that I take orders from my immediate superiors," Guiney told him. The officer left; the Ninth remained in its prone position throughout a seemingly endless, frigid night. Over the next two days they stayed rooted on the hill before finally withdrawing to Falmouth Heights.[19]

One gets some sense of the magnitude of the Union's losses at Fredericksburg from the grim fact that five other Union brigades suffered more casualties in the battle than did the Irish Brigade.[20] In a pathetic demonstration of military insanity, fourteen brigades had, seriatim, stormed up Marye's Heights to be mowed down by the murderous cannon and rifle fire of the stonewall-protected Confederates. Five days after the disaster, O'Hagan wrote again to Wiget: "I never imagined that so many dead could be left on our field. They were actually in heaps. . . . I am only surprised that the entire nation does not rise up against it unanimously."[21] The nation did not rise, but Fredericksburg proved, for a great many in the Catholic community, especially in the Irish neighborhoods of New York and other cities, to be a particularly disheartening test of their patriotism. Indeed, the near annihilation of the Irish Brigade provided opponents of the Emancipation Proclamation with the opportunity to charge the Lincoln administration with sacrificing Irish lives in its desperate attempt to secure a military success that would legitimize the clearly unconstitutional executive order Lincoln was poised to put into effect in less than three weeks.

STONES RIVER

In the wake of Union failures at Fredericksburg and Chickasaw Bluffs, where William Tecumseh Sherman's attempt to seize Vicksburg at the end of December had replicated Burnside's disaster on a smaller scale, Lincoln's hopes for a victory to offset the political and military setbacks he had suffered in the past three months fell upon William Starke Rosecrans, now commanding the Army of the Cumberland. His charge from Washington was to liberate middle and eastern Tennessee, thereby creating a wedge in the Confederacy, isolating Virginia, the Carolinas, and Georgia from the rest of the Confederacy.[22] Henry Halleck told him: "If the enemy be left in possession of middle Tennessee, which we held last July, it will be said that they have gained on us. . . . Your movements have an importance beyond mere military success." Public morale in the North and possible international intervention were also at stake here.[23] And, of course, there was the looming proclamation. With Nashville his base and Julius Garesché his chief of staff, Rosecrans began an eighteen-hour-day work schedule in preparing his comprehensive plan for the campaign. Two days after Christmas, Rosecrans led his army out from Nashville in three columns toward Murfreesboro, twenty-five miles to the southeast, where Braxton Bragg's 35,000 troops of the Army of Tennessee awaited.

Rosecrans's force took up a position a couple of miles north of Murfrees-boro, astride the Stones River, which snaked its way northward a mile west of the town. On the morning of December 31, Rosecrans and Gareské heard Mass in a small tent as other military stood reverently just outside. Gareské issued a message in which he told the troops that Rosecrans "feels perfectly confident, with God's grace . . . of striking this day a blow for the country the most crushing, perhaps, which the rebellion has yet sustained. . . . the very fate of the nation may be said to hang on the issues of this day's battle."[24]

Both Bragg and Rosecrans had the same battle plan: hit the opponent on its left flank and *en echelon* roll up his forces in a wheel movement. Bragg struck first. In a reprise of Shiloh, his 13,000 troops surprised the federals east of the river as they breakfasted. Bragg quickly broke through the Union left. Rosecrans ordered a counterattack. With his signature unlit cigar in mouth, he calmly rode to the front to personally direct the deployment of troops and batteries. Despite a heavy fire from the nearby enemy, Rosecrans, with an al-most eerie calm, continued to direct and encourage his embattled troops. Not so his cavalry commander, Phil Sheridan, who began cursing and screaming amid the roar of battle. "Watch your language," chided Rosecrans. "Remem-ber, the first bullet may send you to eternity." "I can't help it," responded the bantam Sheridan to the nearly six-foot Rosecrans. "Unless I swear like hell the men won't take me seriously."[25] In the event, the officers checked the retreat. Later, seeing that a Union brigade was struggling to hold its ground, Rosecrans, with Gareské right behind, raced toward the brigade. An unex-ploded shell roared past Rosecrans's head but tore off Gareské's. In all, four of Rosecrans's escort were killed during this phase of the battle, not sharing their commander's "charmed life," as his surgeon described it.[26]

Theodore O'Hara, now on Breckinridge's staff, spent the first day of battle as a courier between Generals Breckinridge and Bragg. That did not keep him from the action. When one of the brigades of Breckinridge's division was on the verge of collapsing, O'Hara courageously went to its front to reform its ranks.[27] Several hours of fierce fighting pushed Union units three miles to the rear. All except for Phil Sheridan's division, which, at great cost, held its ground for two hours before superior Confederate numbers forced Sheridan to withdraw northward as well. But success proved too much for the attack-ers as the Confederate pursuers finally exhausted themselves in their pursuit and, with no reinforcements to supplant them, had to pull back as nightfall overtook the brief hours of daylight marking December's end.

During the long night, Rosecrans contracted and entrenched his line of defense to take maximum advantage of his greater numbers. The first day of the New Year passed with both armies trying to outwait the other. Bragg was confident that Rosecrans would inevitably have to retreat. By January 2, the Confederate commander, realizing that Rosecrans was going nowhere, decided to force him to it by renewing his attack. Bragg waited until 4 p.m. to initiate it, less than an hour before sunset, which would virtually rule out any federal counterattack. What Braxton Bragg did not take into account were the extent and deadliness of the Union artillery, which quickly turned the Confederate assault into a panicked race to the rear. A day later, Bragg withdrew his forces south of Murfreesboro.[28] By January 4, the Confederates were forty miles farther south than they had been at the end of the year.

Perryville had been a tactical victory for the Confederates which turned into a strategic defeat by Bragg's withdrawal from the field. Stones River was a tactical draw that became another Confederate defeat when Bragg once again retreated such a great distance from the field of battle. As for casualties, Rosecrans's forces were the worse for it, 12,706 men or 29 percent of those involved in the battle, as opposed to Bragg's 9,870 or 26 percent. The federals' casualties were surprisingly large, considering they were on the defensive. For both sides, the casualty rate was an unsustainable one, more so for the Confederates than the Union troops, at least in terms of the finite manpower pools available to the two governments. And for the federals, the losses suffered at Stones River, on top of those at Fredericksburg two weeks earlier, served to accentuate the terrible price the country was paying to become whole again. But in the Western Theater and on its northern home front, Stones River became a "victory." "I can never forget," President Lincoln wrote to Rosecrans many months later, "that you gave us a hard-earned victory, which had there been a defeat instead, the nation could scarcely have lived over."[29] Coming barely two weeks after the Union disaster at Fredericksburg, Stones River proved to be a military, economic, and diplomatic stabilizer. A certain equilibrium returned to the stock and gold markets. The northern press, desperate for a general who could delivery victories, hailed Rosecrans. As *Harper's Weekly* declared, as "a strategist Rosecrans has proved himself second to none." The *New York Times* wrote: "General Rosecrans, if success be the standard, stands at the very head of the Union Generals."[30] Among his advocates, Rosecrans could still count those high in the Lincoln administration. Both Secretary of War Edwin Stanton and Henry Halleck wanted Rosecrans to replace Ambrose Burnside as commander of the Army of the Potomac, but the majority of the president's advisors, no doubt with John Pope's recent disastrous tenure in mind, thought it ill-advised to appoint a westerner to lead an eastern army.[31]

EMANCIPATION
BECOMES OFFICIAL

Biracial crowds in Washington and other cities across the North gathered at midnight of the new year to celebrate the official freeing of millions of slaves. Few white Catholics were among them, in person or in spirit. William Rosecrans was a notable exception. Indeed, the general viewed his victory at Stones River as a confirmation of the providential character of Lincoln's proclamation. It was a proleptic event, according to Rosecrans, one that told the world, "Slavery is dead. Nothing can resuscitate it." God Himself had "ordained its destruction."[32]

General Rosecrans, together with his brother Sylvester, the auxiliary bishop of Cincinnati, both became public supporters of Lincoln's proclamation, as did the Purcell brothers, Archbishop John Baptist Purcell and his brother Edward, editor of the *Catholic Telegraph*. In Philadelphia, Augustinian Patrick Moriarty, the president of Villanova College, told a largely Catholic audience that fighting a war to abolish slavery was a just and necessary goal.[33] In New Orleans, Claude Paschal Maistre advertised a High Mass of Thanksgiving to be offered on April 9, 1863, to commemorate Lincoln's proclamation. An overflow crowd packed the church for the Mass. Maistre, in his sermon, pronounced the proclamation as the initial step on the road to equality. "God watches and His justice finally prevails. Men might perish in the work, but a principle—a faith set loose—spreads and bears fruit."[34] By April most of Maistre's white parishioners had already deserted him over abolition and Black enlistment. Some of them even talked about lynching as a just punishment, a retribution in which some of Maistre's fellow priests concurred.[35]

By and large, the Catholic response became increasingly alarmist about the horrific consequences emancipation would set loose. Ten days after Lincoln signed the proclamation, Thomas Parkin Scott, a Baltimore lawyer, with ties to Saint-Domingue refugees, gave a lecture to the Catholic Institute. His stated topic was "Authority and Free Will," but his actual remarks pertained much more to the president's recent executive action regarding slavery. The Founders of the United States had deliberately restricted citizenship to white men, Scott began. Within that circle all were indeed equal. More broadly speaking, society demanded a hierarchical order. In any society a certain subordination of some individuals to others was natural. "High and low, bond and free, are alike acceptable before the Deity; but a degree of subordination is necessary for the preservation of that order which is essential to the existence of society. Slavery," Scott reflected, "has been with us as far back as we can reconstruct history, as both the Old and New Testaments attest." Given that lineage, "it is dangerous for one community to attempt to interfere with another, and in our case morally and legally wrong. . . . The Negro family is certainly inferior to the White, and a persistent attempt at their immediate emancipation, without authority, and in violation of laws and solemn compacts, would be attended with fearful mischief, and end in their destruction." It would also justify a resistance to that government bent upon taking actions "without any warrant in the Constitution and the laws of the country to justify it."[36] For Scott, history, scripture, republicanism, nature, and the Constitution all served to repudiate Lincoln's proclamation. In Chicago, Richard Merrick found the proclamation to be such a threat to the Constitution and republican governance that he concluded the best option for opponents of the administration had become what many considered treason.[37]

The *Irish-American* reported in early January: "The Emancipation Proclamation is universally condemned as one of the worst acts of the president's administration. . . . Clearly illegal, it gives the South every incentive to fight with greater desperation than ever."[38] To the *Metropolitan Record,* Lincoln's proclamation was perverting a war to restore the Union into an "emancipation crusade."[39] In February of 1863, Chaplain Joseph O'Hagan returned on a short furlough from the Fredericksburg front to Washington. Riding the train, then boat, from camp to the capital, the chaplain heard nothing but soldiers venting "all their spleen among the Negroes. Nothing is heard . . . but imprecations on the 'woolly heads!'"[40] The formal proclamation of emancipation no doubt accelerated resignations and desertions within Union armies. The heavily Irish Illinois Ninetieth had several of its officers resign in protest of the proclamation. The regiment, for the war, had an unusually high desertion rate of nearly 40 percent, about five times the average. Emancipation seems to have been a major precipitant.[41] Sergeant Charles Woollett noted the negative effect the proclamation had on the regiment: "The emancipation policy and proposed arming of negroes is causing deep dissatisfaction, which, I fear will bear bitter fruits."[42] Peter Welsh wrote his wife in early February 1863 that there was "dissatisfaction and loud denunciation" of the president's proclamation. Welsh, a McClellan man, thought that if slaves and slavery were disrupting the Union then the nation needed to "sweep both from the land forever rather than the freedom and prosperity of a great nation . . . should be destroyed." Welch was a conditional abolitionist, the condition being the deportation of all the emancipated, an event he fully expected to see accomplished, once the "incompetent . . . and fanatical nigar worshippers" of the Lincoln administration were turned out by the majority of citizens in the North.[43]

Most Catholic military who supported emancipation found their opinion an unpopular one among their fellow soldiers. Colonel Patrick Guiney told his wife that, within his regiment, "I find but very few whose views are congenial to me," he wrote his wife; "how painful [to be] in the midst of men who are constantly talking down the Government!"[44] His worst fear was that the generals on both sides would agree to an armistice, "on God knows what terms," in order to subvert Lincoln's proclamation.

A particularly alarming provision of the Emancipation Proclamation was its call to enlist Blacks for military service. Given that military service was commonly considered a prerequisite for citizenship in a republic, the vision of Black soldiers raised fears among whites, North and South, that nonwhites were permeating the circle of citizen-soldiers. When the first Black regiment marched down Broadway, John Mullaly's headline in the *Metropolitan Record* read: "New York Disgraced." The story below found "this infamous parody of patriotism" sad proof "of the degeneracy of our Government."[45] The *Boston Pilot* had no doubt that "one Southern regiment of white men would put twenty regiments of them to flight in half an hour. Twenty thousand negroes on the march would be smelled [*sic*] ten miles distant. . . . There is not an American living that should not blush at the plan of making such a race the defenders of national fame and power." There was the racist trifecta: Blacks were inferior, they were un-American, and their offensive odor disqualified them as soldiers.[46]

For many whites in the border states, Black enlistment became the bridge toward citizenship and full equality—social, cultural, political—that could not stand.[47] In February 1864, an amendment to the Enrolling Act of March 1863 authorized the enrolling of African American slaves, with compensation to owners. The amendment did not require the permission of owners for their slaves to be taken for military service. In southern Maryland the inclusion of slaves as potential draftees only intensified the opposition to the war, particularly where the recruiting officer himself was Black. In St. Mary's County, two whites killed a Black lieutenant they accused of persuading their slaves to enlist. Other slave owners sought to have their adult males drafted for the $300 they received for each slave, given the increasing instability of the institution by the late stages of the war.[48] Eventually Maryland fielded six Black regiments, totaling nearly 9,000 members, many of them from southern Maryland.

In Kentucky and Missouri, where the rate of Black enlistments was the highest among the slave states, Black soldiers became the chief targets of guerrilla violence.[49] By the summer and fall of 1864, guerrillas conducted a brutal terror campaign against the African American communities in Missouri and Kentucky, a sign of things to come in the states that had composed the Confederacy. As Paul Cimbala notes: "The racial violence at the heart of the border states and the heart of the country as a whole symbolized the fervent opposition to radical egalitarianism in the American heartland and directly inspired the resurgence of a new racial conservatism at the national level."[50]

The looming horror of a Saint-Domingue writ large was a trauma to which most southerners would not admit to harboring. The standard profession was that their slaves were utterly happy with their lot and hence unshakably loyal. Rarely would the ideological guard come down to reveal their inner fears, as it did for Margaret Brown Loughborough, a Catholic woman working for the War Department in Richmond when she wrote: "The negro men had to go to work on the fortifications . . . to rid the women of the menace of their presence and left us a city of women."[51] To those casting Saint-Domingue as a cautionary tale about emancipation, Orestes Brownson pointed out that the horrors of Saint-Domingue were not the consequence of giving freedom to the enslaved but rather the obstinacy of the slavers in resisting the partial abolition that France had decreed.[52]

At the May Convention of the New England Anti-Slavery Convention in May 1863, William Lloyd Garrison arose to rebut an Irish abolitionist who was defending his fellow Irish against charges of their proslavery obstinacy. "Priests and people," Garrison asserted, "political leaders and followers [are] the very bitterest enemies of the anti-slavery cause. Almost universally, they have exhibited an infernal spirit in regard to the colored population. We know the causes which have made them such; we know that they are the tools of priests and politicians."[53] Garrison could not have asked for a stronger affirmation of his charge than the one the archbishop of New York provided him. It was not true, the archbishop responded to Garrison, that "slavery having been wrong in its inception can never become lawful by prescription. . . . Slavery having existed almost from the beginning, the Church may employ only religious and moral suasion to remove the dangers surrounding masters and slaves in their relations with each other." To institutionalize a state of life was to legitimize it. For Hughes the permanency of slavery was akin to that of original sin for humanity. With the exception that the slaves, unlike the baptized, had no hope of being liberated from their condition. Regarding the war, Hughes declared, once again, "We Catholics, and a vast majority of our brave troops in the field, have not the slightest idea of carrying on a war that costs so much blood and treasure just to gratify a clique of abolitionists in the North." Abolition as a war goal simply alienated troops and potential volunteers. It also worsened conditions for the freedmen. The only legitimate war aims for Hughes remained the preservation of the Union and the Constitution.[54]

MARTIN SPALDING AND
THE PERILS OF THE PROCLAMATION

To no prelate was the Proclamation more repulsive than to the bishop of Louisville, Martin John Spalding. Although a southern sympathizer, with several family members fighting for the Confederacy, he was of the firm belief that the hierarchy had no business involving itself in political matters. As he told the cathedral congregation in Louisville during a Pontifical Requiem Mass for the war dead, the mission of the Church was to preach peace and good will, to soothe the cruelty of war by her ministrations to the wounded and the dying. With that mission ever in mind, the bishop had told his audience that he considered it his sacred duty to confine his words and actions to the spiritual sphere.[55] Spalding had accordingly adopted a public posture of strict neutrality during the early course of the war. The Emancipation Proclamation radically challenged Spalding's position. On the day the proclamation became official, Spalding wrote in his journal: "While our brethren are thus slaughtered in hecatombs, Abraham Lincoln coolly issues his Emancipation Proclamation, letting loose from three to four millions of half-civilized Africans to murder their masters & mistresses!! . . . Verily this is a bloody New Year!"[56] Still Spalding remained silent. Then in early April an editorial appeared in the *Catholic Telegraph* of Cincinnati advocating the abolition policy promulgated by the president three months earlier. In subsequent weeks Edward Purcell defended the administration's policy as a legitimate use of federal power to achieve victory in a civil war.[57]

The *Telegraph*'s editorials, to Spalding, were elaborating upon an earlier statement of Archbishop John Purcell. In his pastoral letter issued in late January, the archbishop had declared that "we go, with our whole heart & soul, for the maintenance of the Union & the Abolition of Slavery—against neither of which does the Supreme Pontiff of Christendom utter a single word."[58] That stirred Spalding to write, not to his own metropolitan, Archbishop John Purcell, but to the metropolitan of the Baltimore Province, Archbishop Francis Kenrick. Spalding was seeking Kenrick's advice about writing to Propaganda Fide in order to persuade the Roman congregation to instruct prelates like Purcell not to engage in the discussion of political matters in the public square, where, in Spalding's view, the archbishop was "run[ning] mad with this insane abolitionism."[59]

Francis Kenrick, who had more than anyone in the antebellum era set the apolitical policy for the hierarchy, predictably encouraged Spalding to provide Rome with "a full and candid exposition of the facts."[60] Kenrick himself had written to Rome suggesting that officials issue some directive "that the Catholic prelates abstain from those discussions which excite the slaveholders and sometimes aggravate the conditions of the poor slaves."[61] Within the month Spalding had dispatched a twenty-three-page report to Cardinal Alessandro Barnabò, prefect of Propaganda Fide. In it, Spalding admitted that a principal cause of the war was slavery, a system that "all good and moderate men" recognize as a "great social evil." The problem was how to rid the country of it without destroying the country in the process. If the United States were Catholic, Spalding went on, and guided by the Church's spirit and practice, real reform and gradual improvement in the lives and character of the slaves would lead benevolent masters to emancipate them gradually. But America being fundamentally a Protestant society, even were Catholic masters to emancipate their slaves, these freed persons would experience "moral and physical regression" in the North, where segregation and hostility to Blacks prevail. Immediate emancipation would immensely magnify the evil.

President Lincoln's Emancipation Proclamation, Spalding asserted, was nothing less than an instrument of terror to be employed against "obstinate rebels." It was an invitation to the more than three million slaves to rise and massacre the whites in their midst, to replicate the horrors of Saint-Domingue. Fortunately, the slaves had repudiated the call to insurrection, in a striking affirmation of their loyalty to the peculiar institution of the South. Spalding then took up the question of the Church's relation to the war. In a country that enjoyed the separation of Church and State, religion and government had nothing to do with each other. During the war, he reported, Catholic prelates and priests, with few exceptions, had been faithful to their tradition of restricting themselves entirely to the spiritual sphere, by praying "for the return of peace and prosperity." By inserting themselves into the "political agitation," Purcell and his allies were providing the enemies of the Church an excuse to renew the attacks in the postwar period that had plagued antebellum society by blaming Catholic leaders for all the human and material loss that the war has brought.[62]

Spalding had hoped that his arguments would lead Propaganda to censure Purcell and thus weaken the forces championing abolition as a war goal. The cardinal prefect did not do so, but he did share Spalding's piece with Pope Pius IX and had it published seriatim in the *Osservatore Romano*.

In April, President Lincoln proclaimed a day of fasting and humiliation to atone for the national failings that had moved God to inflict such a devastating war upon the country. The *Pittsburgh Catholic* applauded the president's acknowledgment of the need to do penance for the nation's sins. "Our sins," it confessed, "as a people, have been many and great. . . . We know," the editor continued, "that many persons place slavery as the first among the sins for which God is punishing us. . . . This, we believe, on reflection, must be rejected as false." The Constitution's recognition of slavery absolved individuals as well as sections from any responsibility for its existence. Hence, the editorial concluded, its readers needed to avoid the pharisaical trap of condemning slavers while ignoring one's own sins, for which one has full responsibility: the infidelity in the practice of one's religion, materialism, national pride, and so forth. It was as though the Constitution had been received by the Founding Fathers on some mountaintop, that it had a divine sanction that rendered it beyond the realm of blame or reform. The historical reality was that men had made the Constitution, and slavery had shaped the form that the Constitution took. To the editor, that paled against the personal moral failings in both North and South.[63] Lincoln's limited emancipation might be acceptable as a war measure. But any goal to eliminate slavery as an institution from the land could not be justified under this rationale. Four months later, the editor could write: "the vast majority of the people of the North wish [the South] no greater harm than a speedy return to the Union under which it has grown prosperous and great."[64] The editorial still assumed that abolition had not become a war goal; that the invitation that Lincoln held out to the South, before January 1, 1863, still held: that all they needed to do was to lay down their arms and return to their proper place within the union of states. But the expiration date of that offer had long since passed. Peace based on the *status quo ante* was no longer possible, no matter how much white Catholics persisted in wishing it.

CHAPTER 11

1863

The War in the East

Gettysburg, the evening of July 3rd, were the time and place
to ruin [Lee's] army. We saw his Army flying from the field, broken,
beaten, terrified! . . . But Meade allowed it to pass . . .
and gave us—another year's work."

—PATRICK GUINEY, JULY 16, 1863

CHANCELLORSVILLE

Joe Hooker, utilizing the information he was getting from the Bureau of Military Information (BMI) which he had established upon taking command of the Army of the Potomac, knew that Robert E. Lee had once again dispersed his army, this time dispatching a third of his force on a foraging mission hundreds of miles distant. On April 12, Hooker sent his cavalry across Kelly's Ford to destroy the rail, telegraph, and other lines of communication between Fredericksburg and Richmond. That, Hooker reasoned, would force Lee to evacuate his lines along the Rappahannock. Once he retreated south, Union cavalry would stand in his way. Two weeks later the infantry of the Army of the Potomac followed the cavalry across the river, to be in position to strike Lee's flank or rear.[1]

On May 2, Lee, having discovered Hooker's bold flanking movement, sent Jackson with his corps of fifteen brigades along an obscure, twelve-mile path which brought him west of the Union's Eleventh Corps. Hooker at first took the Confederate movement to be the beginning of Lee's anticipated retreat, but eventually warned O. O. Howard, commanding the Eleventh, that his right was in danger of being flanked. Howard assured Hooker that he was taking appropriate precautions.[2] He took none. At 5:30 p.m., Jackson unleashed a massive assault that proved even more overwhelming than Longstreet's at Manassas the previous August.[3] James Emmons of the New

York 154th remembered the rebels swarming "like flies on a dead horse."[4] Maj. Peter Keenan of the First Cavalry Battalion of the Eighth Pennsylvania and three other officers were playing high stakes draw poker on a cracker box when the Confederate dam burst. Keenan shouted: "Draw sabers and charge." The battalion, with sabers aloft, headed toward the Plank Road and the butternut tidal wave. They cut their way through the sea of assaulters for about a hundred yards before a Confederate volley brought down Keenan and perhaps a third of the battalion. John Collins, in the trailing battalion, had his horse shot out from under him as he tried to reverse course. Collins took to the woods and made his way to a picket line improvised by General Howard. That defense, too, quickly collapsed in the face of the Confederate wave that seemed to gain force as it went.[5]

After some initial resistance to the two-mile-wide, rebel-yelling Confederate onslaught, general panic set in, with troops discarding their rifles and tearing off their corps badges, as though to spare the Eleventh Corps the ignominy of such a complete rout. Over the next hour and a half, Jackson's 20,000 or so attackers drove the federals over a mile and a quarter east. The Chancellor House, where Joe Hooker had established his headquarters, was less than two miles distant, but the prevailing wind patterns created, as at Perryville, an acoustic silence that kept the Union commander ignorant of what was happening in his immediate rear.[6] Fewer than four miles separated Jackson from Lee. About three-quarters of an hour of daylight remained to perhaps crush the Army of the Potomac between the Confederate pincers.[7] General Billy Mahone's brigade on the Confederate front east of Chancellorsville began making demonstrations of a second attack. For Lee, who was always looking for the right circumstances to destroy his opponent, never had the stars seemed so well aligned. Unfortunately, the entangled terrain proved a greater foe to the attackers than did the uprooted Union units. As the Confederate pursuers got increasingly disorganized among the undergrowth in the falling darkness, the command came to halt and restore order.[8]

By the morning of May 3, both armies were fragmented, with the opposition between their several components. Jeb Stuart, who had taken command of Jackson's forces in the wake of Jackson's wounding by friendly fire, faced an entrenched enemy holding the interior lines. Nonetheless, he prepared to carry out Lee's earlier order to attack at dawn. Fighting erupted all along the mile-wide battlefield, as Stuart threw his entire corps against the Union line in three waves. The first two assaults of three-deep columns had temporary success, then stalled. As part of Stuart's third line, Edward A. O'Neal led his Alabama brigade. After crossing the open field at a double-quick they assaulted the next federal breastwork. A frenzied contest for the work followed. At last, the rebels summoned the energy for a final charge which broke through Hooker's ring defense.[9] The breach had exposed the flank of John Geary's Twelfth Corps division, which soon found itself under a series of Confederate charges and terrible shelling from the high ground of Hazel Grove, which Hooker had abandoned. Geary's three brigades fell back toward Chancellorsville. By 10 a.m. the federals were in general retreat, allowing the Confederates to join their wings to pin the main body of the Army of the Potomac against the Rappahannock.[10]

By evening, fires started by Confederate shelling spread throughout the woods, burning alive the wounded of both sides caught in its relentless, impartial path. The final horror of a horror-filled day.[11]

WAITING TO BAG THE TWO WINGS OF
THE ARMY OF THE POTOMAC

On Monday morning, Union General Amiel Whipple, commanding the Third Division of the Third Corps, was overseeing the strengthening of breastworks in the Union line above Chancellorsville. A rebel sniper in a tree began firing at Whipple and his staff. Whipple began writing an order for his sharpshooters to respond to the sniper when one of the sniper's bullets struck Whipple in the abdomen. Whipple died in a Washington hospital three days later. Patrick Guiney had been close to Whipple when he was hit. Guiney judged his death "a great loss. He was a very pious Catholic," he added.[12]

Meanwhile, Lee was waiting for Jubal Early to dispose of Sedgwick's corps at Fredericksburg before rejoining the main army for the final assault on Hooker's entrapped army. Late on the afternoon of May 4 the Confederates were in place to assault the trapped Union Sixth Corps. At 5:30 p.m. three guns, fired in rapid succession, signaled the attack to begin. The Louisiana Sixth, in the middle of Early's line, at the order of "Forward, double-quick!" started the ascent of the steep slope at the top of which the Sixth Corps lay in wait. Screaming the rebel yell, the Louisiana Brigade went up the hill, amid a punishing barrage of shot and shell that left a blanket of dense smoke. Reduced in numbers as they were, the brigade lived up to its reputation of "Fighting Tigers" by routing the Union defenders from their first line and then from their second as well. Only at the third and last line did the accumulation of the human damage done by the Union firepower force the Louisianans to stall in their drive.[13] Chancellorsville cost the Sixth Louisiana nearly two-thirds of its 275 men. The Louisiana Brigade lost about 45 percent of its 1,500 effectives.[14] Before the surrounding Confederates could attempt another assault, the Sixth Corps managed to slip across the Rappahannock, leaving a thousand or so captives behind. The next day, Hooker withdrew the rest of the Army of the Potomac to the north side of the river, an inglorious end to the campaign that had seemed destined to be the decisive one for the Union in the Eastern Theater. Only the Peninsula Campaign had been costlier for the two armies.[15] As on the Peninsula, Lee had won a pyrrhic victory, losing over a fifth of his army in the inhospitable terrain around Chancellorsville.

A NEW INVASION

In August of 1862, Robert E. Lee had maneuvered the mass of his army from its position along the Rapidan River without John Pope's detection until Thomas Jackson was well in Pope's rear, the prelude to the epic second victory at Manassas. Now in early June, history seemed to be repeating itself along the Rappahannock River as Joe Hooker began receiving reports of Confederate movements in various directions. But, thanks to the Bureau of Military Information, Hooker was in a far better position than Pope to learn of Lee's general destination. One person key to this discovery was Martin Hogan, a private in the First Indiana Cavalry who had been operating as a scout and spy for the BMI. In mid-June, Hogan and Yaller Carney penetrated into Confederate territory to observe dust clouds in a northerly direction over the Blue Ridge chain. At the same time, Hogan got information from a runaway male slave that Lee's army was heading toward the Potomac. Two other Black escapees from the Army of Northern Virginia provided confirmation of the intelligence. Hooker had no doubt that a second invasion of the North was imminent.[16]

As James Longstreet wrote to a government official: "If we could cross the Potomac with one hundred & fifty thousand men," such a huge invasion force might in itself force Lincoln to negotiations; if not, there was the good prospect of being able to "destroy the Yankees," ideally from maneuvering the enemy into attacking the Confederates on ground of Lee's choosing.[17] Then too, the North had the plentiful means to feed and maintain the Army of Northern Virginia, something the Confederacy was increasingly failing to do. And there was yet another reason Lee wanted to head north again. He had recently learned about McClellan's coming into possession of his secret orders to his lieutenants during the Maryland campaign. Had that not happened, so Lee reasoned, his Maryland plan would very likely have succeeded. The knowledge shored up Lee's determination to embark on an invasion of the second largest state in the Union, Pennsylvania. Victory there might compensate for any loss of Vicksburg, and it just might be the tipping point to the collapse of northern support for the war and eventual independence for the South. Risks were well worth taking for stakes that could not be higher.[18]

When James Longstreet's corps arrived in the Pennsylvania town of Chambersburg in late June, the commander, with Robert E. Lee at his side, demanded that the town provide him with 60,000 rations. This, in the wake of Richard Ewell's commandeering from the people of Chambersburg staggering amounts of clothing and food just days earlier.[19] As the three corps of the Army of Northern Virginia fanned out north and east across the state, they requisitioned tens of thousands of cattle, sheep, and hogs in Pennsylvania, although Confederate officials put a patina of legitimacy on the confiscated goods by paying for them with Confederate money.

Worse than the property seizures was the kidnapping of Blacks in the region. Word of the Confederate invasion set in motion a stream of refugees, Black and white, as far north as Harrisburg, fleeing the threatened territory with all the valuables that they could salvage on wagons.[20] Confederate units, with the authorization of top commanders, including Longstreet, deliberately searched for Blacks to capture and transport to Virginia. In Mercersburg and McConnellsburg, the Second Maryland Battalion threatened to burn down every house suspected of harboring a fugitive slave. For too many Confederates, differentiating between enslaved and free Blacks was a distinction they cared not to make. It was as though the Emancipation Proclamation had driven white southerners to take ever more radical steps to save their way of life in this matter, by an act which left no doubt about their conviction that slavery was the natural condition of the African. Multiple sources indicate that hundreds of free Blacks, as well as long-transplanted runaways, were shipped south.[21]

A NEW UNION COMMANDER
AT A CRITICAL HOUR

Late in the evening of June 28, amid a rainstorm, a seedy-looking civilian arrived in the encampment of James Longstreet's corps outside of Chambersburg. Henry Thomas Harrison was a Tennessee actor serving as an intelligence agent for Longstreet. Now he reported that Hooker's army was in Maryland, heading toward Pennsylvania, with the various corps of the Army of the Potomac making their separate ways north. It represented the Confederate version of the discovery of Lee's order outside of Frederick the previous September. Lee, the next day, summoned his dispersed corps to congregate at the crossroads of Gettysburg.[22]

As the Irish Brigade marched on the morning of June 29 out of Frederick toward Emmitsburg, rumors began to circulate that George McClellan was once again in command of the army.[23] The Army of the Potomac did have a new head, but it was not their former commander for whom so many in the ranks still longed to lead them once more. The night before Harrison made his appearance at Longstreet's tent in Chambersburg, Maj. Gen. George Gordon Meade of the Fifth Corps had been awakened with the news that President Lincoln had appointed him commander of the Army of the Potomac. Meade, of an old Philadelphia Catholic family who had followed a schismatic priest, William Hogan, out of the church in the 1820s, had become Joe Hooker's most reliable corps commander during the past year. Hooker himself had steadily lost the president's confidence in the wake of the Chancellorsville defeat, especially after Hooker had attempted to scapegoat others of his top command. When Hooker submitted his resignation as a ploy to get a free hand in planning strategy, Lincoln took the opportunity to change commanders.[24]

AN UNINTENDED
BATTLE BEGINS

Gettysburg, like Sharpsburg, was a market village at which multiple roads met. It was the natural place for Lee's scattered troops to reconvene, just as Sharpsburg had served as the intended point of convergence. At 4 a.m. on July 1, Maj. Gen. John F. Reynolds, commanding the First Corps of the Army of the Potomac, received an order from General Meade to advance his own corps as well as the Eleventh toward Gettysburg. An hour later Gen. Henry Heth, a Georgetown alumnus, led his Confederate division from Cashtown toward Gettysburg. When Heth encountered some initial resistance, he assumed it was local militia which could be easily brushed aside. When the subsequent fighting made it clear that he was facing a significant portion of the Army of the Potomac, Heth ordered his division to "move forward and occupy the town."[25] The battle thus began without Lee's knowledge, much less his direction. Once started, it took on a life of its own. Lee chose then to pursue the attack on the federal defensive position, because the Army of the Potomac was there, presenting an opportunity for a decisive victory, one Lee had confidence his soldiers could achieve, no matter how daunting the circumstances.

Reynolds arrived at McPherson's Ridge, west of Gettysburg, around 10 a.m. He was urging the Second Wisconsin Regiment forward when he was killed instantly by a bullet to his head. Despite Reynolds's death, the First and Eleventh corps held off the Confederates for the next several hours.[26] Around 2 p.m. Rhodes's division of Ewell's corps began to arrive from the north. One of Rhodes's brigades was led by Col. Edward A. O'Neal. The Union defenders found themselves being pressed from both the west and the north. Rhodes's initial assault failed, with O'Neal's Alabama brigade routed. Further Confederate reinforcements brought a new wave stretching from west to north that threatened to engulf the outnumbered Union troops. Wladimir Krzyzanowski, commanding the reserve brigade of Carl Schurz's division, blunted the Confederate drive on the Union right, but was eventually forced to join the rest of the First and Eleventh corps as they retreated through the streets of Gettysburg. Hays's brigade was part of the flanking movement against the Eleventh Corps and managed to get into Gettysburg before the retreating troops of the Eleventh reached it. Hand-to-hand combat ensued, with 3,000 Union prisoners bagged. The remainder of the corps continued down the Baltimore Pike to Cemetery or Culp's Hill.[27]

Twenty-three thousand Confederates had forced 18,000 Union troops to retreat nearly two miles to a hill immediately to the south of the town. The casualty rates of the two Union corps were astronomical: 69 percent for the First, 53 percent for the Eleventh.[28] By 4:30 p.m. the general Confederate sentiment in the field was that it was Chancellorsville redivivus. Four hours of daylight remained to carry Cemetery Hill. But five divisions of Lee's own force had still to arrive. Of the ten brigades of his army that had been engaged in the fighting, the casualty rate was 40 percent. Moreover, Lee did not know how many reinforcements the Army of the Potomac had in the immediate area. These factors prevented the commander from ordering an all-out attack to complete the day's success.

IN SEARCH OF
AN AMERICAN WATERLOO

As Lee and Longstreet watched through field glasses from Seminary Ridge the two Union corps settling into improvised works on Cemetery Hill, they discussed what seemed their best option for the morrow. Longstreet could not have been more negative about the prospects of any Confederate attacks upon the formidable federal defenses on the opposite hills. In his mind their only hope for securing a major victory was another turning movement. But this time, to the right, not to the left, as Lee had consistently favored in previous flankings. That would put the Army of Northern Virginia between the Army of the Potomac and Washington, on ground of their choosing, which Meade would attack at the peril of duplicating the horrendous carnage the federal army had suffered at Fredericksburg.[29] Lee rejected Longstreet's proposal. Ever since Lee had taken command, his constant goal had been to seek the right set of conditions in which to destroy the army opposing him. Riding the crest of his army's latest demonstration of their superiority, Lee decided that, no matter who held the high ground, he would go for that final peace-sealing victory which had eluded him over the past year.[30]

By 5 a.m. on July 2, corps commanders Longstreet and Hill, and division leaders Hood and Heth gathered with Lee under a tree to discuss operations for the coming day. Longstreet renewed his reasons for a flanking movement, which Lee once again dismissed. At 5:30 Longstreet sent Capt. S. R. Johnston, an engineer of his staff to reconnoiter the Union left flank. Over three hours later, Johnston returned to report that the outcropping at the southern end of the Union line was unoccupied. Lee determined to launch the attack as soon as possible.[31] It was to be *en echelon,* with Longstreet's brigades striking in waves from the Confederate right, followed by Ewell's corps attacking in similar fashion on Culp's Hill, resulting, if all went as planned, in rolling up both flanks of the Union Army.[32]

Nothing went as planned. Not until nearly 4 p.m. were all the units in place. Porter Alexander began the Confederate bombardment of the Union defenses on the southern portion of the Union defenses running from Cemetery Ridge to Little Round Top. Then Longstreet began to commit his 14,500 troops to their seriatim assaults. The fighting at Little Round Top swayed back and forth. With the Union line threatening to collapse, Brig. Gen. Gouverneur Warren went off in search of help. Spotting a column of troops heading for the Peach Orchard, Warren rode to intercept them. It was his old brigade in the Second Division of the Fifth Corps. Warren spotted Col. Patrick H. O'Rourke of the 140th New York regiment. Warren told O'Rourke of his critical need for reinforcements at Little Round Top. When O'Rourke pleaded that his regiment had been ordered to provide relief in the Peach Orchard, Warren replied: "Never mind that, bring your regiment up here and I will take the responsibility."[33] When they reached the top of Little Round Top, O'Rourke, seeing how severely the Confederate assault was pressing the Union left, ordered the 140th New York to charge. He was leading his men down the boulder-strewn hill when he suddenly keeled over, a bullet having pierced his neck. Remarkably his men rushed past their fallen commander to club the oncoming Confederates with their rifles, as the exhausted rebels tried to complete their climb. The valiant work of the 140th in shoring up of the imperiled southern end of the Union line proved crucial in turning back Longstreet's assault, but the regiment lost more than a fifth of its force in the counterattack. Patrick O'Rourke was among the fatalities.[34]

At the Peach Orchard, Gen. Dan Sickles's corps had established a salient with two brigades, including the 1,800-man unit led by Gen. Philippe Régis de Trobriand. In the course of the fighting, three of Trobriand's five regiments were deployed to shore up gaps in the line. That left but two regiments to defend the center, along with the First Division of the Fifth Corps. When the commander of the division inexplicably ordered a retreat, Trobriand's unit was forced to abandon the Wheat Field, as well as Devil's Den. As the crisis around the salient worsened in the late afternoon, Meade and Hancock made quick adjustments to stabilize their defense of the wheat field, including bringing in the Irish brigade, reduced by their losses in previous battles to barely regimental size. William Corby happened to be the sole chaplain with the brigade that day. Corby climbed onto a boulder as the brigade prepared to move forward. Holding his arm aloft, the Holy Cross priest managed, for a moment, to halt the march into the killing grounds that awaited them. The priest had the Catholics in the brigade kneel as he imparted a general absolution.[35]

The Twenty-Eighth Massachusetts found itself in the thick of the fighting "in a skirt of woods where the enemy was pressing our lines hard." "Our little brigade," Peter Welsh later wrote, "fought like heroes and we drove the . . . enemy nearly a quarter of a mile when he threw a heavy force against the brigade on the right of ours . . . which let him in on our flank by which we were compelled to fall back." The fighting lost any semblance of order, the whole bloody scene one of indiscriminate firing and general chaos. Somehow the brigade advanced to threaten a Confederate gap in the line of attack, around Rose's Woods, a forbidding space full of trees and uneven, rocky interstices. In this hellish terrain, the Irish, with their smoothbores, fired as best they could through the smoke-filled air.[36] Their opposing division leader, Joseph Kershaw, was meanwhile frantically attempting to locate Paul Semmes in order to have his brigade repair the gap that the Sixty-Sixth was trying to exploit. Remarkably, through the smoke and din of the fighting raging about him, Kershaw found Semmes, who immediately ordered his brigade to seal the breach. Scarcely had Semmes sent them forward when a bullet struck his left leg. Semmes improvised a tourniquet to stanch the bleeding but had to be carried from the field.[37] The Confederates failed to close the gap. The Fifth Corps pressed forward. Kershaw gradually withdrew his men toward the Rose farm, and the federals had their first major gain of territory in the day's fight. They had claimed the Wheatfield and most of Rose's Woods.[38] Longstreet sent in Barksdale's brigades, and they gave testament to the effectiveness of the *en echelon* tactic, as this follow-up assault found the federals with no reserve force available. The Irish Brigade fell back north of Little Round Top, where they remained. The holding action of the Twenty-Eighth Massachusetts had cost the regiment nearly 40 percent of its 530 men.[39] As sundown approached, the rebels, having gained Devil's Den, Houck's Ridge, Rose's Woods, and the Wheatfield, prepared to take Cemetery Ridge. The last Confederate assault against Cemetery Ridge got as far as the copse of trees on Cemetery Hill before Meade and Hancock secured additional forces to mount a successful counterattack to save the day.

At the northern end of the Confederate line, Richard Ewell's corps had been given the charge of completing the *en echelon* attack which James Longstreet's corps had begun on the southern end. Once again, a Confederate plan of attack that depended on close execution faltered on the failure of a link in the command chain. Not until 6:30 p.m. did Ewell send Johnson's division up Culp's Hill. The Second Maryland was among the units. "Scarcely had we reached the creek that runs by the foot of the mountain when we were fired upon by the Enemy," William Stone recalled. Instantly, four members of his company fell, but the battalion was soon chasing federals up the hill. Among the battalion's dead was Capt. William A. Murray, who, thirteen months earlier at Harpers Ferry, had expressed to his mother his frustration in being able to see his native Maryland across the Potomac but unable to walk once more on its soil. Now he had died just a few miles north of the Maryland state line.[40] Meanwhile, the Sixth Louisiana, reduced to 220 effectives, had stormed up Culp's Hill and broken the federal line, capturing scores of defenders and several cannon. From this height the Confederates were in a nearly perfect position to train the captured artillery to enfilade the Union line stretching along Cemetery Hill to Little Round Top.[41] That possibility proved an evanescent one. Samuel Carroll led his Union brigade from four hundred yards to the west across the Taneytown Road to the Baltimore Pike, where they formed a line to force the Louisianans back down the hill they seemed on the cusp of claiming.[42] The Louisiana Sixth lost about a quarter of its members in the night's fighting, including its lieutenant colonel, Michael Nolan.[43]

George Meade was in the saddle most of this long afternoon and evening, directing specific units to endangered positions in the rapidly changing fortunes of battle. At one point Meade rode so close to the fighting that his horse was wounded.[44] By contrast, Lee remained on Seminary Ridge. An English observer remembered that the general spent much of the afternoon sitting alone under a tree, as though he were a mere spectator. Overall, the commanders of the federal units outperformed their Confederate counterparts, particularly in their ability to make rapid adjustments to changing conditions on the battlefield. That was a trait that had distinguished Confederate generals in the Army of Northern Virginia over the course of the war's first two years. Now in their supreme test, they failed to meet the moment. On the other side a Catholic quartet—O'Rourke, Carroll, Kelly, Trobriand—had played notable roles in preventing the Confederate *en echelon* attack from winning the day, and perhaps the war.

CRITICAL DECISIONS

As the sun buried itself behind South Mountain, James Longstreet realized better than anyone that it was futile to reorganize and renew the assaults on the morrow, even had his men the energy and will to do it. They had made gains during the four hours of fighting, but the main Union line remained intact. Longstreet knew too that the fighting that day had been among the most severe of the war, although he did not know the extent of the casualties. (The Union losses, in wounded and killed, were greater.) Lee was more positive about what his troops had accomplished, judging it a partial success, with footholds gained at the base of Culp's Hill and in the Peach Orchard. Whether that gave promise of final success on the morrow seemed highly questionable.

Lee's confidence would have grown had he been privy to the conference that George Meade had held with his generals that very evening. Meade polled his corps generals, even as the sounds of battle could still be heard from Culp's Hill, whether they preferred to remain at Gettysburg, or retreat just south of the Mason-Dixon Line in Maryland, to mount a new defense line. Meade's top generals, to a man, voted to stay where they were. "Have it your way, gentlemen," Meade responded to their choice, "but Gettysburg is no place to fight a battle."[45]

The First Virginia, which had been serving as a rear guard for the army, had spent much of the previous day marching some twenty-five miles from the Chambersburg area to within four miles of Gettysburg. At 3 a.m. on July 3 the regiment was in line to advance to the battlefield. John Dooley remembered General Lee himself greeting them as they filed into Seminary Ridge and having a discussion with their division commander, George Pickett. As they marched along the ridge to take their position in the Confederate line, Lee rode beside Pickett at the head of the column. Dooley recalled that "the

Genl's face does not look as bright as tho' he were certain of success."[46] That might have been simple projection on Dooley's part, knowing, as a memoirist, the outcome of the day whose beginning he was describing. But Lee's countenance may have reflected his frustration that he had been forced to scuttle his battle plan for that day, because Pickett's division had not been where it was supposed to be. Lee had intended a simultaneous predawn attack on both Union flanks, with Pickett's division spearheading the one on the Union left. What Lee did not know was that Longstreet had instructed Pickett to keep his troops west of Gettysburg until he received further orders. Unable to execute his plan, Lee switched to a frontal attack on the Union center, with Pickett's division at the forefront.[47] It would come to the left of the Peach Orchard and focus on the copse that had been the site of the last fighting on Cemetery Hill the previous day. Lee intended to unleash an immense, sustained bombardment to disable the artillery along the Union center, after which he would send a sea of troops forward over the mile of open ground to overwhelm the hub of the Union defense. Once the troops of the initial charge breached the Union lines, a second wave of 10,000 would exploit the breakthrough and roll up the Union line both north and south. When Lee finished his explanation of the attack plan, Longstreet commented, with all the conviction he could muster: "I have been in pretty much all kinds of skirmishes, from those of two or three soldiers up to those of an army corps, and I think I can safely say there never was a body of fifteen thousand men who could make that attack successfully." Lee was not moved.[48]

As with the planned assault on the Union center, the renewal of Ewell's assault of Culp's Hill before daybreak was a frontal one against a well-established foe in a strong position. For over six hours the Confederates sent brigade after brigade up the hill, only to suffer devastating losses, before being forced to retreat. The Second Maryland Battalion, in its second assault within hours, was among the first units engaged. Many made it to the Union breastworks, only to be cut down, too many mortally. Estimates of the battalion's losses vary from 144 to 192. Whatever the scale of casualties, the losses at Culp's Hill virtually destroyed the Second Maryland Battalion as an effective force. For the Louisiana Brigade, there was also little, if any, rest during the postmidnight hours of July 3. At 4 a.m. the brigade fell in line to renew their attempt to take Culp's Hill. For the next several hours they fought to replicate their partial success of the previous evening, but by midday, they had nothing to show for it except for a ruined forest and many more casualties than they could afford.[49]

ROMANTIC WAR'S LAST HURRAH

Along the nearly half-mile section of Cemetery Ridge where Lee intended his attack to terminate, Meade had some 5,500 men and seventy-seven guns. The Union artillery commander, Henry Hunt, surmising the Confederate plan, ordered his gunners to reply to the Confederate bombardment sparingly to preserve sufficient shot and canister.[50] At 1:07 p.m., Alexander gave the signal for the bombardment of the Union lines to begin. John Dooley, at the epicenter of the bombardment, remembered that the earth itself seemed unsteady "beneath this furious cannonading." Positioned immediately to the rear of a battery, the First Virginia was the recipient of many of the federal missiles. Dooley was in conversation with the soldier lying beside him when the latter suddenly went silent. To Dooley's horror, the man had been fatally struck.[51]

Throughout the artillery exchange, Longstreet paced on his horse back and forth in front of the line of Confederate infantry. When Alexander observed perhaps two batteries of Union guns being withdrawn from the area around the copse, he took it, wrongly, to be the result of the damage the Confederate artillery had inflicted. He urged Pickett to start. Pickett looked to Longstreet for confirmation. Longstreet could only nod. The assaulting force moved out.[52]

The Confederates marched as though it were just another grand review. Union defenders on Cemetery Ridge would never forget what a sublime spectacle their tight columns created. There was even a band to lend its stimulus to patriotic valor. Nineteenth-century romantic warfare had its last hurrah— brief as it proved to be—on that sweltering July afternoon. The First Virginia was part of Kemper's brigade on the right of Pickett's division. It set out from the woods of Seminary Ridge across the open fields to the Emmitsburg Road where they had to scale the fence and execute an oblique left that took them past the Codori barn toward the copse. From Little Round Top to the north end of Cemetery Ridge, scores of artillery pieces were primed to rain down lethal metal upon closed ranks of infantry in open fields. All too soon, they did. Dooley remembered "the work of death" from the "black heavy monsters from their lofty mountain sites . . . belch[ing] forth their flame & smoke and storms of shot & shell upon our advancing line." As they advanced, the artillery created more and more gaps in their lines, which had to be addressed and reformed. Some of the most destructive shelling came from a regular army unit, Battery D, atop Little Round Top. It was the misfortune of the advancing Confederate brigades that two of the guns of Battery D were being sighted by Sgts. Samuel Peeples and Timothy Grady, Irishman known for their marksmanship.[53]

Lieutenant Dooley's rank suddenly changed when the company's captain, James Hallinan, was mortally wounded. Dooley, now a brevet captain, ordered the company into a double-quick when they came within a hundred yards of their target. Thirty yards from a Union battery, Dooley was struck in both thighs by a rifle volley and left behind by the surviving members of the regiment who made it to the wall.[54]

It took less than twenty minutes for the Confederate brigades to march from Seminary Ridge to the ground east of the Emmitsburg Road.[55] As Armistead's brigade approached the Angle, the only Union infantry left was the outnumbered Sixty-Ninth Pennsylvania, composed mostly of Irish. Spotting the opportunity, Armistead urged his men forward. Col. Dennis O'Kane of the Sixty-Ninth ordered that, if any man wavered from his position, the man next to him should shoot him. Reaching back to the lore of Bunker Hill, O'Kane instructed them not to fire until they saw "the white of their eyes." They did just that, doing terrible carnage in an instant. The last working battery at the Angle fired a point-blank charge from their two functioning guns right into the advancing rebels, barely twenty yards away; then the gunners scrambled to the rear.

George Armistead, who by some miracle had survived all of it, rushed to the wall and the still smoking guns. Vaulting the wall, Armistead and some 150 survivors of the Fifty-Third Virginia were inside the Angle. They tried to commandeer the guns, but there was no ammunition to fire. Hand-to-hand combat with the Sixty-Ninth Pennsylvania ensued. Meanwhile the Seventy-Second Pennsylvania had reformed and, from eighty to ninety yards behind the Angle, began firing volleys at the Confederates. One hit Armistead.[56] Elements of Pickett's division continued to fight at the wall. Colonel O'Kane was felled with a fatal wound. The Sixty-Ninth Pennsylvania, engaged for a second day, took the brunt of Union casualties at the wall, losing half its force.[57] But there were no Confederate reinforcements to exploit the opening they had established. Worse, Union reinforcements did arrive, including the Nineteenth Massachusetts under the command of Col. Arthur Devereux, who had seen in reserve what was happening at the Angle and secured Hancock's permission to take his regiment to assist.[58] Of the 10,000 intended Confederate reinforcements, two brigades got misdirected and never came close to the troops they were to support. Longstreet himself held back two other brigades when he determined that the assault had failed.[59] In less than one hour Pickett had lost two-thirds of his effectives.[60] Of the 135 members of the First Virginia that set out from Seminary Ridge, only 35 returned unharmed.

John Dooley lay helpless on the battlefield as the last phase of the failed Confederate charge played itself out. "I knew no bones were broken for I felt no acute pain, but still a kind of fear came over me lest I should bleed to death." Eventually taken to a field hospital, Dooley spent the Fourth exposed to the light but constant rain, and observing some of the human wreckage of the three days' fighting: a fellow officer, with a leg crudely amputated above the knee (Dooley gave him his oil-cloth to wrap around the stump); another with a fractured jaw was starving from his inability to swallow; still another with a gaping hole in his skull shuffled around like an automaton. Five days went by before Dooley was moved into a tent, where his thigh wounds were finally dressed. Two days later, he had a visit from the Jesuit chaplain, Joseph O'Hagan, who had taught Dooley at Georgetown. The priest bore clean clothing and a bottle of wine for his old student. O'Hagan instructed Dooley not to go anywhere. The chaplain intended to transfer him to General Sickles's headquarters, where, Dooley assumed, he would secure a parole. But when O'Hagan returned the following day, Dooley was gone, having agreed with his tentmates that they would all stick together, wherever that might prove to be. Dooley and his companions were on their way by boxcar to Baltimore and the federal prison at Fort McHenry.[61]

RETREAT AND ESCAPE

It rained throughout the Fourth, with both armies eyeing each other. The next day Lee ordered a general retreat toward the Potomac, some forty miles to the south. The Army of Northern Virginia, with a train of wagons carrying provisions and the wounded that stretched over twenty miles, made its cumbersome way through narrow passes of the Blue Ridge over ankle-deep mud roads. One cohort of the Confederate force that was smaller on the retreat than it had been in the invasion was comprised of thousands of slaves employed as teamsters and body servants. Ned Haines had accompanied John Dooley on the Gettysburg campaign, just as he had during the Maryland one nine months earlier. Dooley noted in his memoirs that Haines had assisted him and his company mates in erecting a temporary shelter during a rainstorm in Virginia on their way north. It was Dooley's last mention of Haines. When Dooley failed to return to Seminary Ridge with the remnants of the First Virginia, Haines, at some point during the retreat, may have seized the chance to liberate himself. Nine months earlier, a woman in Hagerstown had tried to persuade Haines, on an errand for Dooley, to "accept his freedom." Haines had ignored her, in part, as he explained to Dooley, because, "if you gets wounded or anything happens to you, who going to take care about you."[62] Dooley was now wounded, but he was beyond Haines's ability to care for him. It seems likely that the Dooley family servant, no longer with anyone to care for, decided that freedom was something worth his risking. As Edgeworth Bird, another Georgetown alumnus, and regimental quartermaster in the Army of Northern Virginia, wrote his wife four days after the battle, "a great many Negroes have gone to the Yankees."[63]

The Massachusetts Ninth had made its way through Emmitsburg and Sharpsburg to Williamsport, where, on July 12, they found what remained of the Army of Northern Virginia behind hastily constructed breastworks just north of the Potomac. The regiment entrenched as part of the line surrounding the Confederates. Two days later they awoke to discover that the rebels had slipped across the Potomac back into Virginia. Among the thousands of the Confederate wounded whom ambulances bore from Gettysburg was Paul Jones Semmes. On July 9, Semmes wrote his wife from Martinsburg: "Severely wounded. Main danger over. Stay at home. Will write." Semmes died the next day.[64]

CONSCRIPTION AND RIOTS

As the Army of Northern Virginia made its perilous retreat, civil war erupted in the North's largest city, New York, over the draft. The Union states having failed to raise sufficient troops through enlistments or conscription, Congress in March of 1863 had nationalized conscription for most males between the ages of eighteen and forty-five. The law provided for the appointment of a provost marshal general and state provost marshals who were empowered to arrest all those resisting the draft in any form, including those advising draftees to desert.[65] This gave the national government an unprecedented reach into local communities not only to co-ordinate enrollments but to monitor any resistance to conscription. In republican ideology, volunteer militias, composed of citizen soldiers, were the bedrock of defense for a republic. Nothing infringed more on individual freedom as well as promoted corruption and inequity than a federal draft.[66]

From the fall of 1862, Catholics had been prominent participants in the violent resistance to conscription which arose in the Northeast and Northwest. Nationalizing conscription galvanized broader and more violent resistance, including the rise of militias to resist the enforcement of the draft. In the new demography of resistance, the larger the Catholic presence in a particular area, the more active was resistance to the draft.[67] Various tactics were deployed to sabotage conscription, from blocking a train filled with draftees to burning down draft offices.

When the Congress enacted a national draft in1863, Democrats had new evidence of the despotic drift of Republicans. John McKeon, a former congressman, gave a speech at the Democratic Union Association in New York City in early March in which he deplored "the sovereignty of the States [being] swallowed up in an immense consolidated government which was undoing the Founders' intention to have the states as the protectors of the life, liberty, and property of citizens."[68]

The temporary magnet of nationalism, which seemed to hold out full acceptance as citizens and relief from jobless poverty, had drawn the New York Irish to enlist. The sickening carnage into which Irish Catholics marched on fields like Antietam and Fredericksburg soon brought war-loathing. When conscription replaced recruiting, loathing turned to anger at the inequity in the system that allowed the rich to buy their way out for $300.[69] Sentiment against the draft had been rising for months. Editors John Mullaly and James McMaster had called for violent resistance to any attempt to conduct the draft in the city. The first day of the drawing of names on Saturday, July 11, at the provost marshal's office at Third Avenue and Forty-Seventh Street proceeded without incident. When the drafting resumed on Monday, July 13, the Irish firemen of Black Joke Engine Co. No. 33 led a crowd to the provost's office. The firemen, angry that several of their members had had their names drawn the previous Saturday, stormed the draft office, routed the police providing security, and wrecked the premises.

Elated by their success, the crowd pushed on to other targets. A former policeman in the crowd recognized Superintendent Kennedy in civilian dress. The mob seized Kennedy, beat him within an inch of his life, then dragged him through the mud, like the working-class version of tar-and-feathering.[70] They then turned to the campus of Columbia College at Forty-Ninth Street to burn the home of President Charles King, a prominent Republican. With some cheers for Jeff Davis, the crowd began to set fire to King's residence, only to be dissuaded by two Catholic priests. Another roving gang threatened to wreck the *Tribune*'s offices, but the two-hundred-strong police squadron defending the offices thwarted their intention. The Colored Orphan Asylum at Fifth Ave. and Forty-Third Street had nearly 240 Black children, all under twelve years of age. Shortly after the mob reached it, the asylum was in flames, which leveled it. Many of New York's several thousand Black residents fled the city.

Overnight rain brought a temporary respite. But Tuesday saw the crowds back on the streets, as the burning and looting and killings of Blacks mounted. The rioters lynched Blacks from lampposts. They dragged them out of their homes to beat them to death. This was racism in its most barbaric form. Although the composition of the rioters changed over the course of the rioting, as unskilled Irish laborers increasingly replaced the skilled workers who were prominent in Monday's initial uprising, the rioters' targets remained constant: the police, for enforcing the draft, and African Americans, for causing the war and the emancipation policy that had arisen out of it. Even an Irish war hero, Thomas Francis Meagher, became a target of the mob for his support of the Lincoln administration. It was Meagher's good fortune not to have been at home. The rioters settled for slashing his portrait.

By the late afternoon of Tuesday, rioters were barricading themselves within an enclave that ran from the East River along Fourteenth Street to First Avenue and down to Eleventh. Within that zone, stores and Black residences came under attack. Charles and Marie Daly hunkered down behind locked doors and extinguished lights, fearful that a Black tenement house in the neighborhood might attract rioters, or, worse yet, that they might seek out the judge to force his verbal support.[71] Catholic priests were working the streets under assault, utilizing the respect that they commanded among the Irish to be peacemakers. None perhaps enjoyed the popularity of Walter Quarters, of St. Lawrence's Church in Yorkville, who was instrumental in getting the rioters in his neighborhood to cease their rampage, in exchange for a suspension of the draft as well as other relief measures. By the time the troops finally restored order on Friday, close to 120 persons had died, most of them Irish, of the 30,000 persons estimated to have participated in the riots.[72]

There was a near-universal fear that the rioting which had consumed New York City would spread across the North. Indeed, violent protests followed in Connecticut, New Hampshire, Vermont, upstate New York (Troy), and Ohio. As Jennifer Weber notes, "Violent resistance to the draft became so common that July that the nation seemed to be on the brink of revolution behind the lines."[73] In other cities in the Northeast, Catholic priests took to the streets to preserve the peace as much as possible by counseling their people to refrain from violence and return to their homes. Nowhere more so than in Boston, where the Irish comprised a smaller portion of the city's population (something more than a quarter) than they did in New York, but, like their New York cousins, dominated the rioting against the draft. Unlike New York, where the clerical peacekeeping was left to the initiative of individual parish priests, in Boston, Chancellor James Healy had directed that the clergy serve as virtual street wardens in the Irish neighborhoods for a week following the initial violence.[74] That comprehensive response may have saved the Boston Black community (about 2,200) from the pogrom that the Blacks in New York had endured.

†

1863

The War in the West

Martyrs to justice, freedom, and good government.

—CLAUDE PASCHAL MAISTRE
AT FUNERAL OF ANDRÉ CAILLOUX,
NEW ORLEANS, JULY 29, 1863

PORT HUDSON

The First Louisiana Native Guards were finally ordered to the front lines in late March of 1863. André Cailloux, despite Nathaniel Banks's purge campaign against Black officers, had managed to keep his position as captain of Company E. The First and Third Native Guards joined Banks's 30,000-man army which was besieging the crucial Confederate bastion at Port Hudson, commanding the Mississippi River from its eighty-foot-high bluff. Despite their lack of military training and without reconnaissance or artillery support, the two Black Creole regiments were chosen by Banks to lead the assault from the far right of the Union line to the rear of the town. Cailloux led his men in skirmish formation through the tangled underbrush of the dense woods that bounded Telegraph Road. When they encountered a flooded ditch, Cailloux was the first into the water, only to be killed instantly by a shell that struck his head. At nearly the same moment, another shell struck the sergeant accompanying him with the regimental banner, shattering his skull as well as the banner and pole. The deadly Confederate artillery barrage broke the First Louisiana assault. That was but the first of many such failures. The day ended with the Union's nearly 2,000 casualties being tenfold what the Confederate garrison suffered.

The following day, a four-hour truce allowed Union burial parties to retrieve the wounded and slain from the field. They chose to ignore the bodies of the Native Guards. For more than a month Cailloux and his fellow Guards lay exposed to all the elements of nature, from sun to rain to vultures and other predators. When the Confederate garrison finally surrendered in July and the bodies of the Afro-Creoles were recovered, Cailloux could only be identified by a ring he had worn. His body was brought back to New Orleans, where his valor at Port Hudson had already made him a hero in the Black community. His corpse having lain in the wilderness of Port Hudson for exactly forty days, Cailloux, for many Blacks, became a Christ figure. Claude Paschal Maistre officiated at the funeral. In his fiery eulogy, the priest called on others to follow in Cailloux's footsteps, à la Christ, to become "martyrs to the cause of justice, freedom, and good government." Then followed the solemn procession to the cemetery, which seemed to encapsulate the institutional world of Black Catholic New Orleans, with more than thirty Black organizations and societies (fraternal, mutual aid, burial) accompanying Cailloux's widow, who rode in a carriage with her four children. For the next month the American flag flew at half-mast in New Orleans in honor of the fallen Cailloux.[1]

THE VICKSBURG CAMPAIGN

After being stymied in his attempts to assault Vicksburg from the north, Ulysses S. Grant determined, despite Cump Sherman's objection, to transport his army by land and river past the heavy guns on the town's bluffs. With minimal loss of ships and men, Grant's army landed on the east bank of the Mississippi some thirty miles below Vicksburg and headed east to Jackson, the state capital. Two weeks later the corps of Sherman and McPherson easily overcame the 6,000-man Confederate garrison at the capital. Sherman promptly ordered all the war-supplying facilities in Jackson burned, which ended in the destruction of much residential property as well.[2] Then he directed his corps west to Vicksburg. Meanwhile, halfway between Jackson and Vicksburg, Union forces had badly defeated Pemberton's opposing army at Champion Hill.[3] Pemberton had retreated within the Vicksburg lines. Grant's forces soon surrounded them.

Grant had no intention of letting the Confederates rest behind their fortifications, even if they constituted the most formidable bastion in the Confederacy: a nine-mile-long network of redans, lunettes, and redoubts. Ringing the fortifications were deep moat-like ravines into which had been positioned felled timber. It was a citadel that dared any army to be foolish enough to challenge it. On May 19, Grant chose Sherman's corps, just arrived from Jackson, to lead the assault to break the Confederate outer defense at the Stockade

Redan, the series of *V*-shaped walls that fortified the northeastern boundary of Vicksburg. It proved a disaster. Sherman's corps never got close to the Confederate lines. Charlie Ewing and the Thirteenth US Infantry were in the thick of the attack. Charlie himself took up the regimental staff after two bearers had been hit; he no sooner had raised it when a barrage of Confederate bullets tore the staff from him, but only one of his fingers grasping the pole was struck.[4]

Grant persisted, renewing an all-out attack in the same sector three days later. This time Sherman chose another foster brother, Hugh Ewing, to lead the assault, over more daunting ground than Charlie had faced on the nineteenth. To breach the Confederate line, the Thirtieth Ohio had to negotiate a trench-like depression fronting the enemy's breastworks. Ewing could not order his men to make such a high-risk charge. To bridge the wide depression, he had portable ladders constructed from the wood of a nearby house which they razed after Hugh persuaded its occupant, Grant himself, to relinquish for the greater good. Under an artillery cover, Ewing led 150 volunteers with ladders toward the breastworks at double-quick pace. When they reached the ditch, they discovered that their homemade ladders, even at twenty-two feet, were too short to span the depression. They took what cover they could in the area they had done everything to avoid—the ditch. For hours they were trapped in their hole, unable to advance or retreat. At one point Ewing had his headquarters' flag planted near the Confederate parapet in the hope of luring the enemy out of their breastworks to seize the Union emblem. The ploy drew out a good number of the defenders, fatally, as it proved for them, but the Union team got no closer to breaching their target. Incredibly they passed the entire day in their exposed position, pushing away the lit shells that Confederates rolled down into the ditch and crouching to avoid the relentless fire from three Confederate regiments. As darkness set in, the order came for the few survivors, including Ewing, to retreat. Convinced of the futility of frontal assaults, Grant settled for a siege, enveloping the town with a fifteen-mile line, and 250 cannon and mortars daily raining an "iron storm" upon Vicksburg, which forced many of the residents to seek shelter in caves.

The Catholic church was the only church in Vicksburg that remained open during the siege. Its pastor, Charles Heuzé, continued to say daily Mass. After Mass he would brave the shells to bring the sacraments to those in the hospitals as well as the rifle pits. One Confederate officer, a Presbyterian, told his wife how deeply the priest had impressed him by constantly putting himself in harm's way: "The Catholic religion may and perhaps does place too much of the hope of heaven of its believers in *Works*—but I tell you that I would rather see Works of charity . . . and courage that is required to go among the sick and wounded, and there attend them as if they were brothers—than all the boast of that faith that is unseen."[5]

John Bannon divided his days between the trenches and the hospital. The eight Sisters of Charity stationed in the town ministered with him in the hospital and the various makeshift infirmaries that had been set up in their convent and private houses throughout Vicksburg. Situated on one of Vicksburg's highest hills, the hospital was a very convenient target for federal artillery. On one occasion, a shell burst between the chaplain and two doctors, one of several times that Bannon narrowly escaped death from shelling.[6] Of at least equal danger was disease, in particular dysentery, typhoid fever, and pneumonia. Being trapped in trenches and parapets, exposed to all of the elements, made for perfect conditions in which diseases flourished. Diarrhea made an invalid of Bannon for two weeks in early June. When he was back on his feet, the impending denouement of Vicksburg made a great many Catholic soldiers seek Bannon's ministry. In the siege's final days, the priest heard more confessions, offered more prayers, distributed more Communions than at any similar period of his priesthood.[7]

On June 25, two thousand pounds of gun powder exploded under the Third Louisiana Redan, at the center of the Confederate defense line. As the immediate fortifications were sent skyward, Union troops poured into the vacuum. The Missouri Brigade was called forward to plug the gap. Bannon, more than a mile south when the explosion occurred, mounted his horse to gallop to the scene, across the ridges, in full view of the federal attackers. By at least one account, hundreds of soldiers on both sides cheered and waved hats in recognition of this extraordinary act of courage and devotion.[8] Three days later, Bannon had begun to celebrate Mass at St. Paul's when a shell tore through the length of the church, several feet above the crowded pews, and came within inches of hitting Bannon at the raised altar. It exploded just after passing Bannon. Flying plaster and bricks left a cloud of choking dust and smoke throughout the church. People immediately scrambled to leave. Bannon somehow managed to talk them back into their pews, and the Mass proceeded. After its conclusion, Bannon delivered a short sermon, an improvised one that urged them to use this reminder of the utter contingency of life to prepare themselves, at all times, for death.[9]

In early June the Ninetieth Illinois was ordered to evacuate their camp in Memphis to reinforce Sherman's corps in the siege of Vicksburg. Transported down the Mississippi and Yazoo rivers, as they made their approach to the town, they had a spectacular view of Admiral David Dixon Porter's mortars shelling the town, day and night, one mortar every five minutes. They had barely arrived at the siege lines when they were ordered to march twenty miles east as a safeguard against any possible relief effort by Joe Johnston's army.[10] By month's end, they were expecting Johnston to attack at any time. Fortunately, for the Ninetieth and the other units, Johnston did not, having decided that he lacked the numbers to save Pendleton. Pendleton accordingly surrendered on July 4. Among those in Pendleton's army who surrendered was the artillery commander Lt. Col. Daniel Beltzhoover, former professor of mathematics at Mount St. Mary's College.[11]

When the news of Vicksburg's fall finally reached Lancaster, Ellen Sherman poured out to her husband her immense relief, having "begun to dread the final struggle as likely to prove fatal to either you or Boyle [Hugh] or Charley."[12] They had survived yet another campaign. In New Orleans, Col. Thomas Cahill was ecstatic over the "glorious news" of Vicksburg's surrender and Port Hudson's capture. A week before, they had been fearing that Richard Taylor's army could well retake New Orleans, given the small garrison to resist a force reputed to number 20,000. "Things began to look bad," Cahill confessed to his wife. Now "All is well and Glorious with us."[13]

A WORLD UNRAVELED

With telegraphic connections cut, the fate of Vicksburg was still unknown in Natchez, days after the surrender. Bishop William Henry Elder, on July 9, had started for Jackson, more than a hundred miles to the northeast, but had gotten only about halfway when his carriage was forced, by Confederate orders, to turn back. Not until July 12 did he learn definitively that Vicksburg had surrendered. On the fourteenth he started once again by carriage for the capital. This time he reached Chrystal Springs, some twenty miles from Jackson, only to discover the road had washed out, just beyond that town. The bishop managed to rent a horse to continue his journey.[14] Not until July 20 did Elder mange to reach Jackson. "The sight is indeed saddening," he wrote in his diary.

> Perhaps one fourth of the town is in ashes. — Some entire blocks & many single houses. All the stores are broken open & sacked. . . . Some of the people of Jackson are still in the woods where they took refuge during the bombardment. Many have gone away. — Strong Southerners toward Alabama—others to Vicksburg & Memphis &c. . . . Many probably most of the people are living on rations from the Federal Army. . . . There is nothing in

town to eat: all the neighborhood is desolated: — from a distance nothing can be brought. There are no teams & no roads—no bridges. The policy seems to make Jackson untenable, for soldiers or civilians.[15]

Among the burned-out buildings was the Catholic chapel, ransacked of its artifacts, including its chalice. Elder had sought out General Hugh Ewing's quarters as a safe place to leave his buggy and horse. Ewing was most accommodating. He promised that the sisters' convent in Vicksburg would not be disturbed. Invited to have dinner with the general, the bishop declined. "When our poor flock is in such distress I thought it would be unfeeling. I had rather share their fare." He also passed on the opportunity to say Mass in the Senate chamber. "Tho' I have not said Mass for a week—yet I did not like to say it there in the present circumstances."[16]

Bishop Elder's trek to Vicksburg was a journey through a countryside devastated by hard war. At least a quarter of Jackson had been reduced to ashes, including the Catholic chapel. Some plantations were in absolute ruin: mansion and outbuildings burned, livestock snatched, Blacks taking their permanent leave. The bishop came upon a few estates where the slaver and family had fled, with the former enslaved virtually in charge, even selling cattle and other goods to federal soldiers who would rather buy than plunder. At one plantation the slaver, wife, and children were all that remained, taking shelter in one of the miserable slave cabins, subsisting on rations from the federal army.[17] Elder at last got to Vicksburg on August 2. He was particularly distressed at the condition of the African Americans he encountered in the town: "The Negroes are dying in the streets of Vicksburg." He thought the US Army was willing to feed them, but distribution was an organizational problem they had not yet solved. A Catholic medical doctor on Grant's staff told Elder that the major problem was psychological—"depression of spirits." Elder asked him and several other federal officers what the government policy was for treating the now formerly enslaved. All he got for his queries were regrets that there was no policy, but also the fatalistic belief that "the race will die out like that of the Indians. They throw the blame on the South," the bishop wrote.[18]

When the federals finally occupied Natchez in July of 1863, thousands of runaways flocked into the city seeking food and shelter. To impose some order, the army built a stockade, bordering the Mississippi, below the city's bluff. With no provision for sewerage or potable water, nor protection from the weather, and exposed to mosquitoes and sand flies, the stockade inhabitants were soon overwhelmed by the many diseases that flourish in such conditions: smallpox, scarlet fever, measles, dysentery. Death galloped through the makeshift place, taking as many as twenty runaways a day. Bishop Elder immediately responded to the crisis at the stockade. He and his priests were a constant presence, ministering in every way they could. Elder himself, in the autumn of 1863, baptized more than 500. Providing material care was a more delicate matter, inasmuch as the runaways were the legal property of locals, many of whom were Catholic. The bishop did make some appeals to north-erners for assistance, including John Purcell of Cincinnati, but little material aid arrived.[19] Not until 1864 was a private residence converted into a smallpox hospital, mostly for Blacks. Elder continued his extraordinary ministry to the Blacks, including wounded and ill federal soldiers.[20]

For the Confederates, the news from Gettysburg and Vicksburg was a double shock to the national psyche such as they had never experienced. In Montgomery White Sulphur Springs, in the remotest part of Virginia, Anna Lynch wrote her bishop brother, Patrick, in mid-July: "I hope very much that Charleston will not meet with the unfortunate fate of Vicksburg but since our late reversals, I would not be surprised at anything."[21] Even Patrick Lynch found himself shaken at the turn of events. "Where are we drifting?" Lynch wrote to John McGill two weeks after the twin disasters, "To subjugation? Things really look dark."[22] Bishop Lynch's sister, Mother Baptista, told him: "We are storming heaven for deliverance from the evils of war, famine & pes-tilence, & to obtain a speedy & honorable peace."[23] With Union forces closing in by land and sea, there were no longer any sanctuaries in the South, even in upcountry Carolina. All in all, the long summer of 1863 produced a growing resignation in more and more white southerners to the bitter reality that the Union forces would prevail; the question was not if a particular portion of the Confederacy would fall to the Yankees, but when.[24]

The outbreak of war had stirred a prodigious number of military-eligible white southern males to enlist. Two and a half years of war, in which the scale of mortal violence had relentlessly risen, had forced the Confederacy to in-crease the pool of the draft-eligible by extending the age span to include those between seventeen and forty-five and eliminating virtually all exemptions. The widened draft included John Lynch's son, the seventeen-year-old Conlaw. At its upper reach, the forty-three-year-old Francis Lynch had to plead the importance of his shoe business to the war economy to escape. As the mili-tary situation grew more critical, the Confederate government asserted itself more and more into everyday life: impressment of slaves, property, and crops to meet war's needs; an income tax; government-issued passes to control civilian traffic. Worsening military prospects spelled disaster for Confederate currency and bonds. The Lynches scrambled, like other entrepreneurs in the region, to find the most secure form of investment—property, cotton, other staples—to protect assets. Cotton shipped to Nassau; a plantation acquired outside of Columbia: all became means of coping with a fluid economy marked by runaway inflation.

CHICKAMAUGA

If William Rosecrans had an uncanny ability to defy death, he could not do so with disease. Following his morale-building victory at Stones River, Rosecrans had contracted lung fever in Murfreesboro. Battling illness, and waiting to have the manpower to contest Braxton Bragg, Rosecrans extended his army's hibernation well into spring and beyond. Not until June 23 did Rosecrans set his army in motion.[25] His reputation and standing among his men had never been higher. As his chaplain friend Paul Cooney described him: "Prudence the best part of valour" is a virtue that he possesses to a high degree—consummate judgment also united [to] unflinching courage—all of which qualities make him the *first* of our Generals and decidedly the most popular. His men and officers almost worship him. . . . 'Old Rosey' is the joy of his army and the perfect model of the 'Christian hero.'"[26] He was a soldier's general, unpretentious, accessible, indefatigably energetic. His supreme self-confidence infected his troops, which his repeated success only strengthened.[27] Yet such self-assuredness, added to a palpable air of rectitude, bred resentment in others, particularly in high places. Throughout the war, Rosecrans paid dearly for it.

In June, Washington ordered Rosecrans to head south to prevent Braxton Bragg from joining up with, or at least reinforcing, the Confederate garrison at Vicksburg. The Chattanooga campaign began brilliantly for Rosecrans. On June 23, he set in motion his 60,000-man Army of the Cumberland to engage Braxton Braggs' 45,000-man Army of Tennessee at Shelbyville. Bragg expected Rosecrans to approach him by way of the main roads. Rosecrans feinted in that direction but sent a corps to his left along a secondary one which took it around Bragg's right. Bragg retreated to establish a new line at Tullahoma. Again, Rosecrans turned the Confederate right; again Bragg retreated, this time to Chattanooga. Through his precise maneuvering the commander of the Army of the Cumberland, in less than two weeks, had forced the Confederates to abandon Middle Tennessee, an area vital to their long-term success.

Rosecrans's remarkable feat barely attracted any notice in the North, occurring simultaneously with the epic victory at Gettysburg and the surrender of Vicksburg. Once again, events had conspired to overshadow Rosecrans's achievements. Still, the future seemed to have no limits for the Army of the Cumberland. As James Connolly wrote his wife on July 5, 1863, "with Rosecrans to lead we think we can go anywhere in the confederacy."[28] Two months later, on September 10, Rosecrans, in a third flanking move, forced Bragg out of Chattanooga. Marie Daly was ecstatic: "Chattanooga is taken without a blow by Rosecrans! Good generalship!"[29]

In Columbia, South Carolina, John Lynch wrote his brother Patrick: "there has been quite a number of soldiers passing through today for Tennessee." The rumor was that Confederate officials were planning to spring a trap on Rosecrans "to rout or capture" his army. "I hope so!"[30] John Lynch's source was accurate. Rosecrans had sought from Washington reinforcements for his Chattanooga campaign. They were denied. Perhaps, if Union intelligence had been better, Stanton and Halleck would have known that James Longstreet's corps, nearly 30,000 men, had traveled some eight hundred miles by six rail lines, from Virginia to Georgia, as part of a major augmentation of Bragg's Army of Tennessee. As it was, Rosecrans knew little about the enemy force that he marched his army south to confront. Perhaps worse still was his ignorance of the terrain over which any fighting would occur. The dense woods rendered signaling virtually useless. The upshot was that Rosecrans's defenses were all too vulnerable to Bragg's now superior numbers, some 72,000 versus 57,000.

In the predawn of September 19, the accidental confrontation of Confederate and Union reconnoiters set in motion a battle that raged through the day. Bragg hurled division upon division against the Union left but failed to turn it in the Wilderness-like landscape. On the morning of September 20, Rosecrans heard Mass before dawn. A heavy fog hung over the field as day broke. When the Confederates renewed the battle in midmorning, a combination of faulty intelligence and personal pique opened another huge gap in the Union line. Rosecrans, misinformed about the deployment of Union units, ordered Thomas J. Wood to relocate his division. Wood knew that withdrawing his division would recreate an enormous gap in their line but was so angered by the order that he followed it to the letter. Five divisions under James Longstreet poured into the gap, forcing the right side of the Union defense line back a mile. Rosecrans, thinking his entire line had collapsed, returned to Chattanooga midafternoon to ensure that Union forces would hold that vital center. On Snodgrass Hill, George Thomas had his surviving troops drawn up in a semicircle, the last force standing between the rebels and Chattanooga.

James Longstreet arrived to oversee the final step to complete victory. To an artillery officer, Longstreet promised all the captured cannon he could locate. What Longstreet did not know was that there was a half-mile gap in this last Union line, between Kelly Field and Horseshoe Ridge. This was densely wooded terrain, made all the more opaque by the smoke of gunpowder, which drew a curtain over any landscape more than a hundred or so yards distant. That lack of visibility had greatly limited the extent of the reconnaissance that Longstreet had duly ordered as soon as he arrived. Longstreet met with Bragg and asked for reinforcements to complete this final sweep, but Bragg claimed he had no fresh troops to spare. Jealousy may well have been at play. Still, it was Longstreet's battle to manage. At just before 4 p.m. he ordered the federal position on Snodgrass Hill to be taken, but the assaults failed to do so. Calling in his last reserves, Longstreet oversaw a series of attacks which, finally as night fell, forced the Union forces to retreat. Rounds of Confederate cheers echoed across the battlefield to mark the triumphant day.[31]

It had not come cheaply for the Army of Tennessee. Longstreet's corps accounted for nearly half of the Confederates' 18,000 casualties. The pyrrhic victory erroneously convinced Bragg that his army was in no condition to take Chattanooga. The Union casualties were equally devastating. Despite Longstreet's insistence that the Confederates attack before Rosecrans had time to establish his defensive line, Bragg demurred. The Confederates set up a siege line from Lookout Mountain to Missionary Ridge.

On October 19, Rosecrans was relieved as commander of the Army of the Cumberland, the Republican victory in Ohio's elections having removed any political reason for retaining him. The enemies that Rosecrans had made within the military and the administration finally had found, in Chickamauga, the occasion to settle scores. His standing among Catholics on the home front may have fallen dramatically since he had become such a defender of the Emancipation Proclamation, but there was still much shock and anger among Catholics that their leading general had been removed, seemingly in an arbitrary manner. Sr. Anthony O'Connell wrote Archbishop Purcell: "Our hearts are broken on account of our dear General [Rosecrans]. We feel like orphans, truly. I have no words to express my indignation at his removal."[32] The *New York Times* gave him high marks: "No history of the rebellion will be written in which his name will not occupy a leading place. . . . There is but one living military man who has accomplished more, and that is Grant."[33]

From besieged Chattanooga, James Connolly gave vent to his anger: "The scoundrels! How can men be so depraved? General Rosecrans was my *beau ideal* of a leader. . . . He was the light and life of this army."[34]

CHATTANOOGA

In late October, Cump Sherman had taken U. S. Grant's position as commander of the Army of the Tennessee, when Grant was placed in charge of all the federal western forces. Sherman's first order was to transport his 17,000 men to Chattanooga, where he joined the 55,000-man federal force in the besieged city in mid-November. Although the Confederates held the vital high ground of Lookout Mountain and Missionary Ridge, dissension raged among the major officers of the Army of Tennessee, largely because of Braxton Bragg's martinet behavior. James Longstreet wrote the secretary of war that "nothing but the hand of God can save us or help us as long as we have our present commander."[35] In early October, President Davis had journeyed from Richmond to Chattanooga as God's surrogate, but the best he could do was to transfer some of the chief complainers, including Longstreet, whom he dispatched in early November with his 15,000 troops to recapture Knoxville. It hardly improved the Confederate odds of completing the siege of Chattanooga successfully, reducing them essentially to a defensive force, one which had to rely on foraging for its food because of Lucius B. Northrop's decision to concentrate the bulk of his commissary resources on the Army of Northern Virginia.[36]

In late November, Grant struck. On the twenty-fourth, under the cover of an early morning fog, he sent three divisions under Joe Hooker scrambling up the crags and boulders of Lookout Mountain against the outmanned left wing of the Confederate defenders. The surprise attack quickly routed the Confederates, who abandoned this left pillar of their siege. That same day, Sherman had struck, with his Army of the Tennessee, the Confederate right flank on Missionary Ridge, which they succeeded in overrunning, only to discover that a rocky ravine separated them from the main Confederate line. The next morning, Sherman ordered an attack across the ravine. The Illinois Ninetieth, part of Loomis's brigade in Hugh Ewing's division, crossed an open field at double-quick pace to attack the Confederate defenses on Tunnell Hill on the left end of Missionary Ridge. The open ground proved all too auspicious for enemy fire. When the brigade encountered a livestock corral which they had to surmount, the fire proved even deadlier for those who found themselves trapped in the corral. Colonel Timothy O'Meara of the Ninetieth, waving his cap in one hand and musket in the other, urged his regiment forward. A Confederate sniper, targeting the crimson sash which O'Meara insisted on wearing, delivered a fatal shot. With their colonel mortally wounded, and all their top officers *hors de combat,* at 4:30 p.m. a company captain, Patrick O'Marah, in the face of the counterattack from Cleburne's division, ordered the Ninetieth to retreat.[37] For its efforts, Loomis's brigade had lost nearly a third of the 1,200 who had started the day, including a disproportionate number of officers. The next morning Ewing rode over the battlefield: "I . . . found Captain [Daniel] O'Connor . . . of the [Chicago] Irish Legion, kneeling upright on one knee, sword in hand, frozen [like] a statue. His men lay dead behind him, in line, well dressed, at their regular intervals of five paces."[38]

With Sherman stalled, and Hooker late due to blocked roads and a wrecked bridge, Grant turned to George Thomas in the center of the Union line to make a limited assault on the virtually impregnable series of rifle and artillery pits that dominated the steep hillside, merely to preoccupy Bragg from directing reinforcements to his flanks.[39] Thomas sent four divisions of some 23,000 men in a two-mile-wide charge up the steep, rugged side of the ridge. This was a much larger assault force than Pickett's at Gettysburg, but seemingly one even more doomed, given the much more difficult terrain and the more formidable Confederate fortifications. James Connolly's regiment was among the sixty Thomas sent forward. The prospect of storming the "rifle pits . . . and at least 40 cannon" some 600 yards up a rocky hillside seemed beyond foolhardy, all the more so when "the batteries on top of the Ridge, open all at once." But the fearsome barrage proved harmless as shells screamed over their heads to land far behind the Union attackers. The waves of Union assaulters poured over the first two lines of rifle pits, before the steepness of the ridge's top forced them to crawl the final 150 feet to the summit and the third line of pits, where thousands of Confederates had regathered to make a final stand. After some brief but fierce "close fighting," Bragg's last troops were scrambling down the ridge's eastern slope, as Thomas's regiments followed in pursuit. "The plain unvarnished facts of the storming of Mission Ridge," Connolly wrote his wife, "are more like romance to me now than any I have ever read in Dumas, Scott or Cooper."[40] Connolly and his fellow assaulters, in their desperate straits, had set in motion the most unlikely human tsunami that miraculously carried them to the very top of Missionary Ridge.[41] Fortunately for the attackers, faulty Confederate positioning along the ridge had obscured the sight lines of infantry and artillery in picking up the ascenders. That and the psychological advantage created by the audacious federal attack served to unnerve the Confederate defenders and to produce the stunning result that outdid the romance novels which had so ill-prepared them for the deadly reality of war.[42] Once in a blue moon, tales of romantic warfare proved prophetic.

KNOXVILLE

In early November, James Longstreet had led the First Corps northeastward to seize Knoxville, a critical base of supply in the eastern part of the state, where Unionist sentiment was strongest. At Loudon, some twenty miles below Knoxville, an advanced guard of Ambrose Burnside's army delayed Longstreet's corps for two days, before it retreated to Knoxville. When the Confederates finally reached the city, Longstreet discovered that the Union forces arrayed on the mile-high plateau on which Knoxville sat above the Holston River were much better prepared to withstand a siege than Rosecrans's had been at Chattanooga. When Braxton Bragg sent word that he wanted an assault made on the city as soon as possible, Longstreet ordered an attack on Fort Sanders, situated on a two-hundred-foot hill on the northwestern edge of the city. Rain and fog delayed the assault by a day. On November 29, Longstreet sent two columns against the 450-man garrison at Fort Sanders. In order to take the federals by surprise, there would be no prior artillery bombardment (as originally planned). Longstreet's artillery commander, Porter Alexander, judged the strategy "crazy enough to have come out of Bedlam."[43] But Longstreet insisted, "Our only safety is in making the assault upon the enemy's positions tomorrow."[44] A division commander urged Longstreet to at least allow the storming party to carry ladders to negotiate the ditches. Longstreet read this as a sign of doubt about success: "If we go in with the idea that we shall fail," he wrote, "we will be sure to do so. But no men who are determined to succeed can fail." On that note, all discussion about the assault ended.

Just before midnight, the operation began with two brigades seizing the federal rifle pits outside the fort, but not before the subdued federals fired a warning shot to their fellow soldiers behind the walls. Four hours later, when a cannon fired, three brigades set out in columns for the fort. The front one got tripped up on telegraph wires strung between tree stumps. When the attackers managed to mount the wire trap, they found the walls of the fort so iced over that they were virtually unscalable. Men got on their fours to provide a boost for comrades to mount the walls while others threw lighted artillery shells to provide some semblance of cover. It was a perfect recipe for failure and, after a half hour under fire, they withdrew. The "crazy" assault had cost the First Corps 800 casualties. The federal count was a dozen.[45]

As Longstreet prepared to lead his corps back to Chattanooga, he received a message from Braxton Bragg, confirming his army's retreat from Chattanooga. Perhaps not surprisingly, the commander of the Army of Tennessee gave Longstreet the option of rejoining him or returning to Virginia. It is quite likely that Bragg knew exactly (or at least was hoping) which one Longstreet would take. In a conference with his principal officers, Longstreet made clear his preference to return east. When Lafayette McLaws questioned whether they could, in good faith, abandon the loyal Confederates in the heavily Unionist section of Tennessee, it was decided that the corps would remain in East Tennessee but much closer to the Virginia border. In a piercing cold downpour the increasingly shoeless corps, now numbering some 19,000, began its march.

Grant subsequently ordered Sherman to assume command of the federal force besieged at Knoxville by Longstreet. Fifteen miles from his destination, Sherman learned that the Confederates had abandoned their siege. He sent his Army of the Tennessee to winter in northern Alabama while he headed home to Lancaster to spend the first family Christmas without their beloved Willie.[46] In August 1863, Ellen Sherman and her three youngest children had joined Cump in Vicksburg for a brief family reunion and tour of the battlefield. When Ellen was preparing to return to Ohio, her second-youngest son, Willie, contracted a fatal case of typhoid fever. Ellen took Willie home to Lancaster to bury him in the family plot. Children's sudden death from fevers were all too common in mid-nineteenth-century America. The abrupt loss of Willie, however, plunged Ellen Sherman into a depression from which she never fully recovered. She increasingly shut out the world, including her husband's military undertakings and his status within the Union military command, which had previously been fierce concerns.[47] It marked the beginning of the hollowing out of the remarkable bond that their marriage had forged, despite Cump's failure to embrace the faith that Ellen had so badly wanted to center their wedded lives.

†

CHAPTER 13

Defining a Nation amid an Unending War

*If the Yankees try long enough and hard enough,
and spend lives enough, of course
they can take Charleston. But we will fight hard.*

—PATRICK LYNCH, JULY 23, 1863

CHARLESTON

P. G. T. Beauregard had returned to Charleston in September of 1862 to take charge of the city's defenses against the expected naval assault. The general immediately put to work his excellent engineering skills. (He had finished second in his class at West Point, having mastered its engineering-oriented curriculum.) Beauregard secured heavier, rifled cannon with the range to reach attacking ships, planted torpedoes at the entrance to the harbor, and commissioned the construction of swift boats with torpedoes on poles projecting from their prows to repel any invading ships.[1] In early April the Union fleet blockading Charleston began its campaign to capture the city. Nine ironclads attempted to close on Forts Moultrie and Sumter to a proximity where their turreted guns would render the forts indefensible. The deep draught of the lead monitor, however, as well as the fear of torpedoes and mines kept the craft far enough from the pair of forts to do fatal damage. Meanwhile, Confederate artillery from the forts as well as from batteries on Morris and Sullivan islands disabled several of the ironclads. After two hours, the attackers gave up and retreated.[2] The repulse of the ironclads greatly boosted Confederate morale and revived Beauregard's heroic status in the South.

Three months later, on July 10, General Quincy Adams Gillmore surprised the Confederate defenders on Morris Island, the barrier isle closest to Fort Sumter, by landing a 3,000-man force on its eastern end. Within hours the force had control of the island, except for Fort Wagner, about a half-mile from Fort Sumter. Beauregard determined that Wagner could not be given up until he had strengthened his inner defenses, particularly on James and Sullivan islands, to neutralize any artillery fire from Morris. The fate of Charleston, for the moment, rested with the Confederate behemoth holding the last ground on the island. On July 11 and July 18, the federals attempted to storm Wagner. At midday on the eighteenth, federal artillery from shore and sea began a bombardment of the fort, which lasted until early evening. Then a force of 6,000, led by the Black Fifty-Fourth Massachusetts, tried in vain to gain the parapets of the fort, with 1,500 casualties for their heroic efforts.[3] Among the Union dead was the colonel of the Fifty-Fourth, Robert Shaw, a Fordham College alumnus. Captain William H. Ryan, of the Charleston Battalion, was among the Confederate fatalities at Battery Wagner on Morris Island. There was citywide mourning at his funeral.

"As I write this fine Sunday evening," Patrick Lynch wrote John McGill, "I hear the cannon, one every three minutes. I fear before a week is over the enemy will have all Morris Island. Then will commence the struggle in earnest—they to put up batteries to destroy Fort Sumter, we to prevent them from putting up such works. . . . If the Yankees try long enough and hard enough, and spend lives enough, of course they can take Charleston. But we will fight hard."[4]

On the late evening of August 21, an unsigned note, purportedly from General Gillmore, was delivered to General Beauregard's headquarters in Charleston. It demanded that, unless the Confederates abandoned Sumter as well as Morris Island, a bombardment of the city would begin imminently. Confederate officials dismissed it as a prank. Three hours later, the first shells fell on Charleston from the fleet as well as from the eastern end of Morris Island.[5] The first bombardment of a major Confederate city began with cannon that could hit targets over five miles distant. The federal shelling continued day and (sometimes) night for over a week before settling into periodic firing. On Morris Island, artillery relentlessly fired away at Wagner and sappers got within a hundred yards of the fort by the beginning of September. On September 6, Beauregard reluctantly abandoned Morris. Sumter had become, in T. Harry Williams's description, "an infantry outpost," with rebuilt ramparts and repaired walls.[6] Still, the federals were unable to seize the harbor—and the city.

Over the next eighteen months, all the lower portion of Charleston became an intermittent battlefield, including the area around St. Mary's Church, where Patrick Lynch had relocated his residence after the fire. The church and its graveyard were repeatedly struck. One shell landed in the backyard of the bishop's house. "The continued bombardment has no military purpose," Lynch wrote a European benefactor, "for it leaves our fortifications and defensive works intact; it can only have as its purpose to destroy houses needlessly, to harass and exterminate women, children and non-combatants."[7] In September the Sisters of Mercy moved their motherhouse and orphanage to Sumter in the upcountry. Virtually all Lower Charleston became a wasteland of collapsed and burnt-out structures. Nature, in the form of tall grass amid the rubble, slowly reclaimed the oldest part of one of the oldest cities in North America.[8]

A DYING INSTITUTION AND
A CALL FOR PEACE

In the border states, slavery was rapidly crumbing amid the vicissitudes of war. Madge Preston, in Baltimore County, was experiencing more and more difficulty in controlling her three slaves. In mid-August she noticed money missing from her purse and concluded that only her house servant, Lizzie, could have been responsible. When she threatened to jail Lizzie if she failed to return the money, Lizzie and her husband, Jim, ran off. Madge claimed to be relieved that they had done so. In her diary she wrote: "I care not if we never see them again. Their ingratitude is so shameful."[9]

In November of 1863, Augustin Verot persuaded the other bishops of the Confederacy to declare a novena for a peace that would bring independence to the South. In his own pastoral announcing the observance, Verot defended the justice of the South's war. In not being faithful to the Constitution, the northern states themselves broke the Union. Thus, when the Confederate States of America were formed, the Union had already been virtually dissolved. That itself vindicated the South's struggle for its independence.[10] Patrick Lynch, who had become the southern hierarchy's chief apologist for the Confederacy, had a message in his own pastoral that went beyond sectional polemics. In the letter, which the bishop issued in November, he wrote that they were in God's hands. "However just in its origin any special war may be, however necessary for the protection of important rights unjustly assailed, it is unavoidably attended by many evils and much suffering." Only God could rescue them from the deluge of iron that was day-by-day leveling the city which had launched their war for independence. The cumulative physical and spiritual evils that war unleashed had reduced them to begging God to save them from themselves by bringing about the peace which He alone could give. All they could do was to own their sins and amend their lives. Only prayer and penance could attain the peace that more than two and a half years of war had failed to deliver.[11] Only that inner peace could sustain them in a world dominated by war.

MOSTLY QUIET
ALONG THE RAPPAHANNOCK

Near Rapidan Station, the Twenty-Eighth Massachusetts was doing picket duty, about three miles removed from the Confederate pickets on the other side of the river. On September 25, Peter Welsh informed his wife that there was a good chance they would be moving in the coming days, probably to attack the Confederate line on either flank since the rebels' position on the hills south of the Rapidan was "very strong." He thought the Army of the Potomac's movements very much depended on "Rosecrans' battle with Bragg in Georgia."[12] They had not yet heard about the dismaying outcome along Chickamauga Creek. When news of Rosecrans's defeat in Georgia did reach the Army of the Potomac, it produced a good amount of schadenfreude. "There are many here," Patrick Guiney wrote his wife, "who are secretly glad that Rosey got a Whipping, as these western fellows were in the habit of taunting the Army of the Potomac with want of success if not cowardice—while they were brave and successful. The truth is we have always been fighting the best and bravest troops in the south—our Western friends have been dealing with poor ignorant undisciplined troops."[13]

Patrick Guiney had at last managed to obtain modern Springfield rifles to replace the muskets the Massachusetts Ninth had been using since their induction. The Ninth was part of the general maneuvering that Meade and Lee engaged in during the fall, but little actual fighting ensued. In late October, Meade's jockeying for position brought the Massachusetts regiment to Manassas, where they slept one night on the site of two landmark battles. "The sight of the unburied skeletons was horrible," Guiney wrote his wife. "The air seemed heavy with the odor of death."[14] Ten days later the Ninth was still moving "about from place to place and for what particular purpose or uses is incomprehensible to all but prophets and Brigadiers!" Guiney thought. "One would think that Meade's object had some relation immediate or remote to the solution of the perpetual motion problem—or perhaps he fears his Army might become attached to *Localities* and . . . jeopardize their love for the *whole* United States of America." Guiney thought that highly unlikely, given the expansionist sentiment that the colonel found yearning to bubble up to dominate public opinion once more. "Our affections embrace not only the United States—but Mexico and several other small places on the Continent!" He thought there were more wars in the country's immediate future.[15]

In early November, the Fifth and Sixth corps of the Army of the Potomac were sent to challenge the Confederates defending Rappahannock Station. Hays's 900-man Louisiana Brigade was in rifle pits on the north side of the Rappahannock River at a crossing for the Orange & Alexandria Railroad, some nine miles west-northeast of Culpeper Court House. When a large Union force suddenly materialized opposite it and began shelling their position, Lee determined that it was inconsequential and sent no additional troops as reinforcements. Suddenly two Union brigades launched an assault from a tunnel on the right of the pits and quickly overwhelmed the Confederate breastworks, which sent Hays's troops pell-mell into the river. Hays himself attempted to surrender, but his horse bolted across a nearby pontoon bridge. A fusillade of bullets wounded the horse; Hays arrived on the southern shore unscathed. Few in the brigade shared Hays's fate. Some drowned. Others were shot in the water. Three-quarters of the brigade were captured. The fiasco at Rappahannock Station left the Louisiana Sixth Regiment reduced to the size of a company. The Army of Northern Virginia had lost one of its best brigades.[16]

A CIVIL SERMON

FOR THE AGES

On November 18, Abraham Lincoln boarded a train for Gettysburg. The president had been invited to give some "closing remarks" at the dedication of the cemetery for the soldiers, known and unknown, who had died four months earlier during the epic three-day battle that Union and Confederate armies had fought around the town. The featured speaker was a Harvard professor, Edward Everett, perhaps the divided country's most renowned orator. On a particularly warm Indian-summer day that seemed to replicate the stifling July weather that had infested Gettysburg during the battle, Everett did not disappoint. Over the course of two hours, he delivered a classical oration that recreated in his incomparably eloquent manner the circumstances that had brought two great armies to this place and the series of violent collisions that occurred on these fields and hills as the Union forces beat back Confederate attacks that grew larger and more desperate by the day. This epic battle, Everett declared, was the culmination of the "monstrous conspiracy against the American Union," a rebellion of privileged slavers who inflamed the masses of the South to join in their violent quest for an independence which would rend the glorious Union that the American people had made. For Everett, that people were a clearly limited cohort, "a substantial community of origin, language, belief, and law (the four great ties that hold the societies of men together)." The quartet of race, ethnicity, religion, and culture constituted the marrow of American nationality.[17]

Finally, it was time for the president's brief afterword. Lincoln moved to the front of the sun-bathed platform erected for the occasion on the crest of Cemetery Hill. With a panoramic view of South Mountain in the distance, and immediately before him the still-hazy fields over which the bloodiest action of the war had taken place, Lincoln laid no claim to being able to add to the honor already paid to the dead by Everett. By their very struggling over this ground, Lincoln noted, the "brave men, living and dead," had already consecrated it far beyond his "poor power to add or detract." Rather he called his listeners to dedicate themselves to the cause for which "they gave the last measure of devotion," no matter how wittingly. In his stunningly few words (272), the president went on to lay bare the magnitude of that cause, and, in so doing, summed up the meaning and mission of the United States as no one before or since has done. In those few minutes, he shattered the boundaries by which Everett had traditionally defined the American core. As Garry Wills has demonstrated, Lincoln, in the address, made the equality proclaimed in the Declaration of Independence the litmus test of any authentic republican polity.[18]

This nation, Lincoln reminded, was something new under the sun; a nation which had been born out of the quest for freedom; a nation whose citizens are defined not by religion, nor race, nor ethnicity, nor gender, nor political affiliation but by a set of ideals, the most fundamental of which is the equality of all members of this society, which equality undergirds their right to full participation in government. Such participation is the bedrock of democracy, a word never mentioned in either of our foundational documents: the Declaration of Independence or the Constitution. It was left to Lincoln to define the democratic nature of our government. Building from the "we the people" phrase that initiates the Constitution's preamble, Lincoln deduced that that democratic source of the Constitution which frames our government also determines its character as one "of the people, by the people, for the people." The people, Lincoln inferred, were all those who, by birth or naturalization, become part of a society committed to living by that set of ideals laid down by the Founders. He was challenging his listeners, and the entire divided nation, to dedicate their own lives to this "unfinished work" of realizing the democratic ideal in all its potential for freedom and equality. In doing so he was immeasurably raising the stakes of the war.

If Lincoln had implicitly changed the nature of the war by his executive order of January 1, 1863, freeing all enslaved persons within the unconquered territory of the Confederacy, that change had been motivated by military necessity, as Lincoln readily admitted. It was only at Gettysburg, nearly a year later, that Lincoln offered the higher explanation for his bold action. His brief but compelling remarks on that fateful field of battle put the proclamation regarding emancipation in its deepest historical and intellectual context. The Emancipation Proclamation was but an instrument in the fulfillment of the promise of the American republic. Antietam had given him the credibility to declare, in effect, that in America freedom is a person's natural state, no matter his color. As he had told Congress in his annual message of December 1862, "In *giving* freedom to the slave, we *assure* freedom to the free." The Emancipation Proclamation, borne of the "victory" at Antietam, was a stone in the monument to democracy that the American nation strove to become, a government of the people, by the people, for the people. As Lincoln told Congress, "in this war: We shall nobly save, or meanly lose, the last, best hope of earth." In freeing the slaves, we were honoring Jefferson's axiom that all men were created equal. The parameters of that freedom and equality were still in flux as the nation struggled to comprehend their full dimensions.[19]

The decisive victory at Gettysburg provided the opportunity, at the dedication of the cemetery holding the bodies of those who had fallen there, for Lincoln to extend the meaning of the hallowed words in the nation's Declaration of Independence. In America, not only were people to be free; they were equal under the law. They all possessed the same civil rights, even those who were slaves or had been slaves; even those who had been in this land before the first ships came; even those who had been part of Mexico before the settlement of the last war made them citizens; even those who came from a continent half a world away from Europe; even those whom misread scripture and millennium-old bigotry condemned to be internal outcasts; even those who professed a deeply suspect religion, whose loyalty was often in question because of their unique allegiance to a religious head who also ruled a country; even women. It was a quantum leap in the search for the true American that predated the republic. Lincoln was systematically tearing down all the old boundaries which separated Americans. He was calling them to live up to the country's motto: "e pluribus unum." At its core this was the fundamental identity—this unity amid diversity—that the war was revealing to Lincoln and to those who cared deeply about the nation.

In his nation-shaping words, the president reiterated that they were fighting to preserve the Union, but the Union to which these dead had given "the last measure of devotion" was founded on principles which every generation must make its own as these principles develop and mature in an ever-changing world. In that light, the preservation of the Union became not a conservative mission, but a very progressive one, committed to moving country and people ever more closely toward the ideal society to which those two foundational documents point us. The freeing of more than four million slaves was a huge step in that direction. Emancipation was the logical consequence of the broader understanding of "all men are created equal" that Lincoln was calling all Americans to make their own.

CATHOLICS
AND THE ADDRESS

Immediately after the president's remarks, Edward Everett told Lincoln that in two minutes the president had captured the occasion in a way that he, the famed orator, had failed to do in two hours. Everett's was an exceptional response. In the words of Harry Stout, "What American memory has since elevated to the status of national scripture evoked hardly a ripple in the national consciousness of 1863."[20] To Catholics, Gettysburg was many things, but hardly a vindication of Lincoln's emancipation policy. Madge Preston noted in her diary that "this is an important day in Gettysburg. . . . Lincoln (and many of the grandees of the Federal party) is expected to be there." Preston wondered whether the Copperheads would seize upon the dedication to make a disturbance,[21] as some part of her no doubt hoped. Marie Daly saw Gettysburg as the proving ground for valor and courage. Both North and South had redeemed themselves on the hills around the town. The battle, to Daly, was the culmination of the purgative effect of two years of war upon the mutual hatred and contempt that the sections had been cultivating toward each other over the past forty years. The brave soldiers who had fought and died there in unprecedented numbers had put the burden on Lincoln to restore the Union by a general amnesty and the annulment of his Emancipation Proclamation. That was believed to be the only way to honor the survivors and especially the fallen.[22] James Gordon Bennett, a month before the battle, had challenged Lincoln's basic premise in his address when Bennett wrote that to assert that a Black man "is equal to a Celt, a Saxon, or a Teuton or any other division of the great Caucasian race" was a blasphemy against "the handiwork of God."[23] A year after Lincoln's remarks, Patrick Lynch would argue in his pamphlet that any attempt to raise up Blacks to equality with whites would trigger the antagonism between the races that comes from upsetting the subordination of Black to white that nature had decreed. The resulting war would be a horror of "rapine, murders, tortures," which would only ensure the extinction of the Black race.[24]

Two weeks after Lincoln had addressed his republic-changing remarks at the dedication of the cemetery at Gettysburg, the president released his third State of the Union message to Congress. It could have been read as Lincoln's exegesis on his Gettysburg Address. In his report, Lincoln noted that "the policy of emancipation . . . gave to the future a new aspect, about which hope and fear and doubt contended in uncertain conflict." The president reported that two previously Confederate states, Louisiana and Tennessee, had been brought back into the Union, with its leaders recognizing emancipation as government policy. Moreover, two of the four border states, Maryland and Missouri, had begun discussions on the best means to end slavery in those states. Responding to critics of his proclamation, who warned that it would inevitably inspire insurrection and worse, Lincoln happily pointed out that, as they approached the first anniversary of its promulgation, there had been no servile insurrection or widespread violence on plantations.

Insurrection and violence may not have come in the wake of the Emancipation Proclamation, but to Southern Catholics, its evil consequences could not have been more evident. "The St. Mary's *Gazette* gives a dismal account of things," John Abell Morgan recorded in his diary in late October of 1863. "The negroes are making tracks for happier, forsooth! Places."[25] When John Purcell issued a statement in late January of 1864 in which he implied that Pope Pius IX supported abolition, the bishops of his province, led by Martin Spalding, boycotted the provincial council that Purcell had called for that spring.[26]

Opinion among northern Catholics all too often echoed that of their southern counterparts. The *Philadelphia Catholic Herald and Visitor,* under the title "The Hope of a Nation," pointed out the physical toll that the military superiority of the North was inflicting upon the South. It implored the rebels to rejoin the Union, if only to suppress the abolitionist crusade. The war, it owned, had once been necessary to put down rebellion. That had all changed with Lincoln's proclamation. That had proven that the real rebels were the abolitionists who were willing to subvert the Constitution to free the slaves. With the Emancipation Proclamation, now nearly a year old, having set slavery on a course of extinction, the *Herald* persisted in seeing emancipation as a threat to the Constitution on the same level as the rebellion itself.[27]

The *Metropolitan Record* of New York saw the war as a waste of lives and treasure in the futile attempt of "this coalition of War Democrats and Abolitionists" to subjugate the South. In the "unholy war" that was entering its fourth year, the editors had "no doubt whatever that she will make even a more powerful resistance than she has yet made against the further advance of the Northern armies." No matter how cruel the means the North adopted in prosecuting the war, the bitter truth was that the South could never be conquered either by the sword or starvation.[28] Only the *Pittsburgh Catholic* expressed confidence that God's justice would be done as the war played out. "[T]he great war," it wrote at the start of 1864, "which is taxing all our energies, has progressed, not as fast as the more ardent hoped for, but still steadily towards victory for the Federal cause." It presciently advised its Catholic readers to consider the president's Emancipation Proclamation not as an assault on the Constitution but rather as something "of great importance" in shaping "the future of the country." The work of the statesman "who is to follow the soldier in the task of re-constructing the Union, will be far more difficult than anything that will have been accomplished by the latter." That Reconstruction, it implied, would involve the implementation of Lincoln's proclamation, an implementation that would surely engender fiercer resistance than any the federal commanders had encountered from their southern counterparts.[29]

THE STRUGGLE FOR
BLACK EQUALITY

The Afro-Creole community in New Orleans became a leading pressure group for Black rights. Frustrated by the failure of occupying federal officials to reform the local political structure to include the franchise for freeborn men of color, a thousand property-owning Afro-Creoles petitioned President Lincoln that he influence the Congress to extend the right to vote to the *gens de couleur* in Louisiana. Republican congressmen persuaded the petitioners to broaden their cause to all males of African descent, especially those who were proving their claim to the vote by their military service. In mid-March 1864, they presented their petition to the president. Lincoln suggested to the governor of Louisiana that some people of color be allowed to vote, a recommendation that the governor forwarded to the constitutional convention that was then forming. Nothing came of it besides the convention's putting into the constitution language that made it possible for the legislature to extend, in the future, the franchise to Blacks in certain circumstances. It was vagueness promoting inaction.

Claude Paschal Maistre was emerging as a leading spokesman for the Afro-Creole community. Meanwhile Archbishop John Odin was navigating his way between Rome and the occupying forces. He appreciated General Nathaniel Banks's consideration for the needs of Catholics, those natives of the city as well as those in the occupying army. Odin assured the *Freeman's Journal* that Banks treated local Catholics better than he did any other denomination in the city. The commander dispensed Catholic churches from reading Lincoln's Thanksgiving proclamation in July 1863. (Odin had persuaded him that such readings were contrary to church tradition.) Conversely, military authorities chose to overlook the Forty Hours Devotions that local Catholic churches held on the very day that President Jefferson Davis had called for prayers to that effect.[30] Of course, this all had to do with the white Catholics of the city. Banks had also forced Maistre to vacate the church that Odin had interdicted for the priest's refusal to discontinue his ministry. Despite Banks's enforcement of the archbishop's order, the priest continued his political activism. At the state constitutional convention of April 6, 1864, Maistre hailed Lincoln as "this noble pioneer of liberty, this other Christ," who had redeemed millions of slaves by his proclamation.[31]

There was at least one New Orleans priest who attempted to disrupt the cozy relationship that Banks had established with Odin. Benedict Poyet bluntly informed Banks that Odin and the vast majority of his priests were disloyal, accusing the archbishop of being "the very fountain of clerical secessionism in Louisiana." Any priest who dared dissent became a target for expulsion from ministry. Poyet moved that the military require the Catholic churches to pray publicly for President Lincoln, as well as to conduct funerals for those killed in federal service. In addition, he recommended that authorities should close the Catholic schools, which were mainly "nests of rebels," in addition to reinstating clergy, with recompense, who had been removed from ministry. Poyet's intervention only served to tighten the relationship between the federal commander and the Catholic prelate.[32]

The Native Guards, following their lead role in the Port Huron assault, were largely relegated to guard duty once more. Such assignments, plus the continuing discrimination in compensation, purging of officers, and neglect of soldiers' families, especially those of soldiers killed in action, led to galloping demoralization and desertions. By the end of 1863, over two-thirds of Cailloux's Company E had abandoned the First Louisiana.[33] It was particularly ironic that Black soldiers in the Western Theater were being confined to guard duty while those in the East were rapidly being incorporated into the frontline operations of the Army of the Potomac.

Earlier in the new year, William Rosecrans had finally secured a new posting, now as head of the Department of Missouri. Catholics initially welcomed his return to duty, but predictably Missourians did not take well to an abolitionist general who seemed determined to suppress any dissent. Banning John Mullaly's *Metropolitan Record* and requiring loyalty oaths whenever religious leaders, including bishops, convened, ruffled many Catholic feathers. Martin Spalding of Louisville regarded the oath requirement as virtually an indictment of Catholics' loyalty.[34]

CHAPTER 14

1864

Roads to Atlanta and Richmond

The City is in turmoil. The Yankees are coming.
—HENRI GARIDEL, MAY 6, 1864

THE OVERLAND CAMPAIGN

In the late winter of 1864, President Lincoln appointed Ulysses S. Grant general-in-chief. It represented a new attempt to centralize command in a general who could effectively coordinate the prosecution of the war. Grant wasted no time in devising a comprehensive plan that would have five armies simultaneously initiate a spring offensive against Confederate forces in both the East and the West, with the goal of converging upon Richmond. The Union forces intended to take full advantage of their ever-growing numerical superiority by attacking the Confederates on multiple fronts, depriving them of the possibility of shifting their military resources to shore up an army in a particular theater, as they had done in the past.[1] With any good fortune, this grandest of all campaigns should bring victory, at last, before another winter set in.

That Grant established his headquarters in Virginia with the Army of the Potomac showed the top priority that the Lincoln administration had given to the Army of the Potomac's latest drive on Richmond. The Confederate government was clearly concerned about the threat to Richmond that the upcoming campaign represented. "There is much talk right now," Henri Garidel recorded in his diary, from his perch in the Ordnance Department in late April, "of moving the government offices to a new location in the Confederate States because of the expected battles that will soon erupt near Richmond." Garidel was expecting a major battle on the Rapidan to begin within the week.[2]

On May 4, as a regiment in Griffin's Division, the Massachusetts Ninth crossed the Rapidan at Germanna Ford and bivouacked near the Orange Turnpike. Little did it know that units of the Army of Northern Virginia were encamped just two miles south. When, the next day, the Army of the Potomac resumed its march south, it encountered the rebels on the turnpike. The fighting developed in the tangled scrub brush that dominated the terrain. The Ninth's division was in reserve during the initial Union attack. Then the division was ordered forward through the nigh-impenetrable underbrush, with the Ninth holding down the left flank. No sooner had Patrick Guiney ordered his regiment to charge when the Confederate defenders let loose a volley which crashed into the regiment. Guiney's charge ended as soon as it began. The Ninth's colonel had been struck in the left eye.[3] In ten minutes of fighting, the regiment suffered 150 casualties, including a dozen of its officers. As the decimated unit staggered to the rear, the brigade commander, who had not observed the losses they had endured, ordered the Ninth's Lieutenant Colonel Hanley to renew the attack. Hanley replied that they had just done that and had come out. "Well, take 'em in again," the lieutenant colonel ordered. Hanley was about to do just that when a division staff officer who had seen what had happened to the Ninth countermanded the order. The Ninth Massachusetts survived to be part of the Overland Campaign for the next five weeks. Patrick Guiney's war was over.[4]

The two armies' chance encounter had caught Lee with Longstreet's corps, encamped five miles west of Gordonsville, still more than a day's march from the Wilderness. Nonetheless, with the 40,000 men available to him, Lee, thanks in good part to the dense foliage, managed to hold 70,000 troops of the Army of the Potomac at bay, although the Union left had gained considerable enough ground against the Confederates on May 5 to lead Grant to order an all-out dawn attack on the following day. That attack had instant success in driving the Confederates back about a mile. Then Longstreet's corps finally arrived in midmorning to stem the federal advance. Utilizing an old rail line, now buried amid the underbrush, Longstreet sent four brigades along this path to flank the Union left. Around noon the brigades suddenly emerged from the thickets to enfilade the federal troops and drive them back three-quarters of a mile. In the fog of war, made infinitely worse by the terrain of this battle, friendly fire became almost too predictable.[5] Francis Dawson was riding with James Longstreet. He remembered that some of the corps's troops were raising a cheer for their commander when a sudden volley brought down several of those on horseback, including Longstreet, who was struck in the shoulder. As aides laid Longstreet by the side of the Orange Plank Road, Dawson, thinking Longstreet mortally wounded, rode frantically in search of a surgeon. At a field hospital, he found one to bring back to treat the fallen general.[6] Longstreet, like Jackson almost a year to the day in nearly the same place, was seriously wounded at a moment when the fortunes of the Confederacy in the East seemed at a pivotal point. In Jackson's battle, the fighting resumed on the next morning and Lee's army realized a major victory two days later. Now, the loss of Longstreet effectively ended the Confederate counterattack. By the time the Confederates were able to renew the assault, the federals had reinforced their lines sufficiently to repel it. On the Confederate left, Ewell's corps attacked late in the day with initial success but ultimately failed to produce any breakthrough.

The third day of the Battle of the Wilderness amounted to isolated skirmishing.[7] The Louisiana Brigade had been involved in the fighting on the Confederate left both on the fifth and the sixth, particularly in the afternoon of the fifth. As the biographer of the Louisiana Sixth writes, "It had been a day of fighting unlike any seen before by the veterans of either army. They had spent it shooting at unseen enemies and being shot at from the leafy thickets in return; men and whole regiments lost their sense of direction in the brushy growth and wandered aimlessly into enemy lines and were captured . . . in an environment straight out of a bad dream."[8] St. Clair Mulholland of the Irish Brigade insisted that the undergrowth was so dense that regimental commanders could not see half their own line, much less survey the field.[9] At the end of the three days' combat, the brigade had suffered 254 casualties, or a third of its strength.

Egidius Smulders, the Jesuit chaplain for a Louisiana regiment, personally witnessed wild dogs devouring those slain. Smulders later learned that one horror of the Chancellorsville battlefield had been reenacted a year later: hundreds of the wounded, mostly Union, had been caught in the path of fires that swept across wide tracts of the Wilderness, including field hospitals. Smulders and others began searching the woods for survivors on May 7. They found scores of Union soldiers badly burned. Those whose burns seemed to hold out some hope of survival were removed for treatment. Others considered "goners" were simply given the minimal kindness of not dying alone.[10] When, on the following day, James Sheeran headed south in the wake of Ewell's corps, the woods still seemed to be on fire. Wherever one looked, "the whole country" was "one dense column of smoke." Bodies, "burned to a crisp," were still lying "among the logs where they fell."[11]

AROUND RICHMOND

In Richmond, Henri Garidel rose at 5 a.m. on May 5 to prepare to attend Mass on the Feast of the Ascension, a holy day of obligation for Catholics. The city was bracing for battle, not only west of Fredericksburg but much closer to home, on the upper Peninsula. "The city is in turmoil," Garidel wrote in his diary on May 6. "The Yankees are approaching. They are coming up the James River with forty transports, gunboats and monitors. They are nearing Drewry's Bluff. Our forces are getting ready to engage them there." After breakfast Garidel went to his office, where he soon received a dispatch from General Lee announcing that "So far we have had the upper hand, having repulsed the enemy in many places." Garidel himself, now a member of the sharpshooters of the local militia, kept awaiting word to head for Drewry's Bluff, to confront Benjamin Butler's force, reported to be between 30,000 and 40,000. The Confederates had fewer than 10,000 troops of any sort to defend the fifty-mile area from Richmond to Petersburg that Butler was directly threatening.[12] Finally on the morning of Saturday, May 7, Garidel and some other militia headed in a boat down the James for Drewry's Bluff. As they got closer, they could hear the cannon fire. "My heart was beating fast," Garidel wrote. But when they reached their destination, there was no fighting in sight. That was occurring some five to six miles farther down river. Having no way of reaching the front lines, the contingent of Richmond militia awaited several hours before returning to the capital.

By May 8, positive reports, both from Fredericksburg and the Peninsula, had buoyed Garidel's spirits. When the alarm sounded that Sunday morning, his response was "Big deal!" He knew now that it was far away and, better still, "they . . . are being beaten on every front." He ended up attending two Masses that day, including the High Mass at the Cathedral, despite the intolerable heat.[13] Monday brought no relief from the heat nor the alarms that continued to sound throughout the city. Worse, Garidel was ill. Still, if summoned, he intended to head back to the Peninsula with the militia.[14] By Tuesday, the clerk felt overwhelmed by the contradictory rumors swirling about the city. "The fact," he noted, "is that we are being attacked on all sides. I don't know how all this will end. The Yankees have a formidable army."[15]

At the beginning of March 1864, P. G. T. Beauregard's wife, Caroline, after a long illness, died in New Orleans. Beauregard's own health was poor, which led him to apply for a leave from his Charleston command. Instead, authorities reassigned him to head up the military district of North Carolina and southern Virginia. On May 6, Benjamin Butler brought his army up the James River and settled the major portion in the Bermuda Hundred, between the James and Appomattox rivers. Beauregard was then directed to concentrate as much a force as he could muster to the defense of Drewry's Bluff, which was the key impediment to any Union attack on Richmond from its southern approach.

Beauregard, typically, was thinking in far broader terms than the war planners in Richmond. He proposed that Lee send him 10,000 troops so that Beauregard would have the numbers to attack Butler on two fronts and corner him on the James River, where his army could be taken out of the war. Meanwhile, Lee would have retreated the forty miles or so to the Richmond defenses. Beauregard would then move north from the James to attack Grant's left flank while Lee assaulted Grant's front. The pincer move, the Little Napoleon felt sure, would mark the end of the Army of the Potomac, thus opening the road to Washington and peace. It says much about Beauregard's continuing high standing in public circles that President Davis himself felt bound to tell the general in person why they had found his plan to be impractical. Davis urged him to deal with Butler with the forces he had available. The subsequent plan involved Beauregard attacking Butler's forces frontally while Whiting attacked his rear.

On the sixteenth, Henri Garidel was on guard duty at 5 a.m., when the fighting began. Early reports were that Beauregard was not only repelling the invaders but separating them from their gunboats, which were a major source of protection as well as their escape. "We are prepared to confront them," Garidel wrote, if only to reassure himself. Then the sounds of battle began to recede. Beauregard had initiated the frontal attack, but Whiting failed to carry out the assault behind the Union lines. Butler escaped destruction, but he was essentially boxed in on the Bermuda Hundred and no longer a threat either to Petersburg or Richmond.[16] The next day, Garidel took a boat down the James to Drewry's Bluff. The river voyagers found themselves in the crossfire as Confederate gunners opened fire on Union gunboats trying to rescue Butler's troops. They returned to Richmond with a boatload of prisoners.[17]

SPOTSYLVANIA COURTHOUSE

Shortly after General Ulysses Grant had arrived in Virginia, several of the officers of the Massachusetts Ninth were at a welcoming ceremony for the new general-in-chief. During some perfunctory remarks by Grant, someone in the audience asked him what he thought of the Army of the Potomac. He replied, "It's a good army, but it has never been fought long enough!"[18] In the aftermath of the Battle of the Wilderness, it quickly became evident what Grant intended to do to correct that shortcoming. Constant engagement was to be the new plan to end the war. Despite the severe losses he had suffered in the Wilderness, Grant executed a crab-like move, flanking Lee's right, and pushed southward. The greatly surprised Lee desperately force-marched his army ten miles south to reform their lines before Grant arrived. The Wilderness became but the first site of a shifting battlefield with virtually constant fighting that aptly came to be known as the Overland Campaign. Not only would the late spring fighting from Fredericksburg to Petersburg mark the introduction of quotidian warfare to the seasonal campaign, but it would also bring casualties of a previously unknown scale to both armies.

Grant, highly confident in the North's enormous manpower advantage, was willing to lose any number of battles, so long as he continued to force Lee ever closer to Richmond. Five miles south of the Wilderness, the two armies now faced each other at the crossroads at Spotsylvania Court House. Overnight, Lee had constructed the most formidable network of breastworks that the Union Army had ever encountered. That did little to deter Grant from maintaining his offensive. After failing to flank the Confederate left, Grant, on the afternoon of May 10, ordered a five-division assault on the left-center of the Confederate defenses, which the Union general assumed Lee had weakened to meet the Union threat to his left. Grant quickly learned that his assumption was wrong, as James Sheeran witnessed from behind the Confederate bulwarks. "About 10 [a.m.] heavy cannonading on our centre and continues till 2½ when it became more intense or rapid; at 3½ a heavy volley of musketry, indicating a charge on our breastworks. The enemy is repulsed with great loss."[19] Behind the Union lines, William Corby saw "our men fell in every direction." He and his fellow chaplains had all they could do to comfort or minister to the fallen.[20]

Grant then opted to exploit an anomaly in the center of the Confederate line, a salient that projected approximately a half-mile in the shape of a mule shoe. A Union attack of twelve regiments in four staggered columns skirted the outer Confederate abatis and overran the trenches to threaten a decisive breakthrough. Once again, as had happened numerous times in past battles, an army division meant to provide crucial support for the lead units failed to show, allowing Confederates to push the federal attackers beyond the apex of the mule shoe.

On May 12, in Baltimore, Jesuit seminarian John Abell Morgan wrote that "the battles of the past week have been terrible; the accounts of them make one's blood run cold."[21] If it were possible, Morgan's blood should have frozen if he could have gotten an honest account of what happened that very day some hundred miles south at Spotsylvania Court House. It was an unprecedented level of interminable, savage fighting that defied any attempt to capture its awfulness in words. The near success of the Union regiments at the mule shoe on the tenth told Grant that an assault large enough and long enough held the promise of producing the decisive victory that could at last bring the Army of Northern Virginia to its knees and effectively end the war in the East. That promise took on a greater prospect of becoming reality when Lee, thinking that Grant's next move would be an attack on the Confederate left, removed twenty-two guns from the salient to meet the anticipated threat. Subsequent intelligence reports of an imminent renewal of the Union's assault on the salient forced Lee to recall the batteries. That was shortly after midnight. By 4:30 a.m. they were still in transit to the mule shoe when 20,000 screaming troops of Hancock's Second Corps stormed the Confederate bulwark, broke through to the base of the salient, and soon were in possession of the itinerant artillery, as well as of 4,000 Confederate defenders. Colonel Monahan ordered the Louisiana Brigade to slide 150 yards to the left; that put them on a small hill perpendicular to the attackers. From that vantage point, the brigade managed to hang on.[22] A Confederate counterattack gradually drove the Second Corps back to the mule shoe's toe, where a primordial hand-to-hand warfare raged over the next fourteen hours, oblivious of the rain which was flooding the trenches or of the rising stacks of corpses in the mud behind the Confederate bulwarks. Grant threw in the Sixth Corps to support the Second. He had the Fifth and Ninth corps attack both Confederate flanks. Nothing broke the rebels. Never in the war had such desperate fighting persisted for so long in one place. It was as though both parties sensed that the fate of their nations depended on the outcome. The fighting had descended, in some mad spiral, into a brutal violence that took the lives of so many at the toe of the mule shoe. Many more it permanently maimed, physically and/or mentally. In the end, Lee put in new breastworks at the base of the salient to straighten the Confederate line. Mercifully, after nearly twenty hours, the carnage came to a halt.

Still, Grant would not abandon his conviction that this battle was the one to decide it all. And so, on May 18, he made one last grand assault on the now collapsed salient. As Chaplain Sheeran wrote of that day: "Grant . . . made a desperate attack all along our lines early this morning. . . . Our men reserved their fire till the enemy were within about fifty yards; then some hundred pieces of artillery opened upon them with grape and canister; and twenty thousand muskets emptied their deadly contents on the advancing foe. The effect of this rapid and destructive fire was much more than any troops in the world could well stand. . . . his men were literally torn in pieces. . . . We took a good many prisoners."[23] Thus ended the longest battle of the war.

This cruel war had never seen the like of Spotsylvania Courthouse. The ferocity of the fighting had intensified from campaign to campaign. At First

Manassas, innocents in war had tested their honor by standing tall in lines of battle to confront the foe. Now elaborate earthworks, designed to maximize the lethality of the weapons occupying them, had changed the calculus of war from the limitation of violence by time-honored rules to mass carnage by any available means. Black-flag warfare appeared to characterize more and more of the fighting. A consequence of the total war that the conflict had become was that there was no longer any place for such humane provisions as truces for the burying of the dead and tending to the wounded trapped as part of the detritus on the battlefield. Nature, Sheeran discovered, had fared no better than had humanity in this slaughter pen. "The tops of the trees are literally mowed off by the shot and shell of the enemy's artillery, whilst the branches and bark are swept off by the incessant volleys of musketry; even the tops and leaves of the underbrush are cut away."[24]

Spotsylvania had cost the Army of the Potomac more than 18,000 casualties, nearly double the Confederate loss (10,000). Of the nearly 120,000 troops who had crossed the Rapidan River on May 4, two weeks later 32,000 of them were no longer among the effectives. For the Army of Northern Virginia, the Louisiana Brigade was a virtual fatality of the battle. More than 800 of them were now captives of the federals. Several hundreds more were wounded or dead.

Peter Welsh wrote his wife from the Carver Hospital in Washington on May 15 that he had been "slightly wounded" three days earlier in the fierce fighting around Spotsylvania Courthouse. It was a flesh wound in his left arm, a small price to have paid for being part of "the greatest battle of the war," in which the Second Corps had "licked saucepans out of them." He expected to be transferred to New York for his recovery. Welsh's diagnosis of his flesh wound proved to be as inaccurate as his claim about the outcome at the mule shoe. Surgeons found that the bullet had shattered his forearm. They removed several bone fragments, but within a few days, pyemia, or blood poisoning, set in. Ten days after writing his wife, Peter Welsh died at the age of thirty-two.[25]

COLD HARBOR

Once more Grant turned a tactical defeat into a strategic victory by outflanking Lee and continuing the race to Richmond. On May 26, Grant wrote confidently to Washington, "I may be mistaken, but I feel that our success over Lee's army is already assured."[26] He *was* mistaken. There was more life left in the Army of Northern Virginia than what a series of all-out federal assaults could extinguish. Grant's facile confidence within the week produced unmitigated disaster.

For a third time, Grant sidled his army southward, with Lee paralleling his movement. As had happened three weeks earlier in the Wilderness, the two armies found themselves facing each other in familiar ground, the Gaines Mills area over which the second of the Seven Days Battle had been fought. Once again Union forces were at the gates of the Confederate capital, in the very place where they had suffered their worst defeat during the Peninsula Campaign. At a misnamed crossroads, some nine miles northeast of Richmond, Grant and Meade yet again attempted to open the door to the Confederate capital through the massive assault of troops. At Cold Harbor, on the first two days of June, attempts to turn an enemy flank failed first for the federals, then for the Confederates. On June 3, George Meade ordered a general attack by all five Union corps, beginning at 4:30 a.m., to be made along the entire six-mile line of battle. Within the Confederate lines, in Breckinridge's portion, Capt. William F. Dement's First Maryland Battery was preparing to receive whatever the federals had in store. They had purposely refrained from responding to a nighttime bombardment by the federal artillery in order to conserve their shells and canister for the morrow. Behind the First Maryland Battery lay 400 of their fellow Marylanders, members of the Second Maryland Battalion. Behind them was Joe Finegan's Florida brigade of Mahone's division.

The federals began their advance, piecemeal, around 4:30 a.m.[27] The Seventh New York Heavy Artillery, their 1,600 members pressed into service as infantry, were among the lead units in the assault. Fred Mather of the Seventh had somehow overslept the call to move forward. He rushed forward to the edge of the woods where he found his company. Apologizing to his captain, James Kenney, he fell in with the rest of the company just as they resumed their advance at the south end of the attacking line.[28] A sunken farm lane, over which the Confederates had constructed breastworks, hid Confederate troops from sight. Then a sudden volley announced John Breckinridge's brigade. Mather had a shell burst near his head, a fragment breaking the scabbard of his sword, another striking his hip. He pressed on, as comrades fell around him. They breached the Confederate line. Captain James Kennedy commandeered one of the rebel guns and swiveled it in the direction of the retreating rebels. Before he could load it, the Confederates had taken position in their second line of defense (there were three) and fired their own artillery toward the attackers. Kenney gave the command to resume the charge, but the Rebels were upon them before any further advance could occur. The Seventh New York beat a swift retreat.[29]

Behind the New York Seventh, Col. Richard Byrnes was killed as he led his Irish Brigade in attempting to exploit the breach the Seventh had made. David Birney's division, for an unexplained reason, never moved to provide critical support. Farther north, Col. John F. McMahon's 164th New York managed to penetrate the Confederate breastworks briefly. James McMahon grabbed the flag from a fallen color-bearer and carried it into the labyrinth of Confederate fortifications, where he defiantly planted it, only to be shot down moments later.[30] With McMahon fatally struck, the breach was quickly closed.[31] At Cold Harbor the 164th New York lost 127 men in the assault, including its colonel and 6 other officers.[32]

It was Fredericksburg revisited. Meade, in command but all too aware of Grant's presence, instructed Winfield Scott Hancock to renew his corps's effort to carry the enemy's works, "if it seems practicable." Hancock was sure that the only result of further assaults were more casualties. Despite Hancock's opinion, Meade still wanted to press the general offensive.[33] It took Ulysses Grant's direct command to bring the attacks to an end.[34] The grand charge at Cold Harbor had all too quickly turned into a federal nightmare as Union regiments charged into the convoluted breastworks that gave their defenders optimal angles from which the Confederate infantry and artillery could fire their weapons. Seven thousand federals had fallen within the first twenty minutes. The day had been the disaster one could expect from attacking intricately formidable defenses without detailed reconnaissance, without specific objectives, without a well-defined plan.

For the next four days, the two armies stared at each other across fields that contained the fallen, many of whom were still alive. Among Kershaw's division, Capt. Edward S. McCarthy of the Richmond Howitzers finally could take no more of the pleas of a wounded federal lying in their front. He asked for one volunteer to go with him to bring the Yank off the field to safety. Sergeant T. D. Moncure joined him. They managed to bring in the soldier, only to discover he had died as they were transporting him. Shortly afterward, Porter Alexander called for a spotter to help them adjust the tilt of their howitzers to function as mortars. McCarthy stood atop the works to gauge the arc and destination of the shells. Before he could complete his observations, a sharpshooter picked him off.[35] On the afternoon of June 7, a formal truce at last allowed the two armies to recover their dead and wounded still on the field between them. Martin McMahon retrieved his brother's bullet-riddled body.[36]

PETERSBURG

Having failed, three times, to maneuver his army between Richmond and the Army of Northern Virginia, Ulysses Grant decided to slip south, across the James River, to seize Petersburg, a vital rail link to Richmond, before Lee could get his army in position to prevent it. During the night of June 12, the vast majority of the Army of the Potomac stole south more than twenty miles to cross two rivers, the Chickahominy and the James, by pontoon bridge and boat, to march due east to Petersburg. For once it was the Confederates who awoke to discover that the Yanks were no longer facing them. Worse still, the Confederate command had no idea where Grant was heading.

On June 7, Beauregard warned Confederate officials that Grant very likely would shift his base below the James River. Two days later, he specifically predicted that the Army of the Potomac was likely to operate from the Bermuda Hundred, where it could move against either Petersburg or Richmond. Beauregard's alert proved to be eerily prescient. That very day a joint infantry-cavalry force struck the Petersburg defenses. Lee deemed it a diversion. Beauregard saw it as the precursor to a much larger offensive.[37] By the evening of the fourteenth there were nearly 50,000 Union troops east of Petersburg. William F. "Baldy" Smith's Eighteenth Corps, with perhaps 18,000 men, attacked Petersburg on the fifteenth of June. Beauregard had fewer than a third of that number to defend the town. Throughout the day Beauregard, from his headquarters north of Petersburg, directed the defense against the measured, uncoordinated attacks on the Confederate fortifications.[38] The hastily assembled defense force of Confederate troops and home guard, much of it composed of men from St. Joseph's Parish in Petersburg, managed to hold off the initial Union attacks. By evening, with reinforcements, Beauregard had 14,000 to confront the federals.

On the sixteenth, the Army of the Potomac, now with 60,000 troops, renewed its assault on Petersburg, with a bombardment of the town. To give the illusion of having a greater force than he did, at intervals Beauregard counterattacked. That boldness caused the federals to be cautious in utilizing the superior numbers that they had.[39] Well before dawn on the seventeenth, the attacks renewed and continued until late the following evening. Beauregard, realizing his lines were at the breaking point, marked out an inner and shorter line to which he had his troops relocate when fighting finally ceased at 11 p.m. Beauregard had campfires lit at the original line, and pickets thrown forward, to provide the cover for the defenders to retreat to the new line he had staked out earlier that day.[40]

Late that night, about ten, Beauregard's wire that the growing federal pressure was forcing him to abandon his position in favor of shorter lines provided Lee with the final proof that Petersburg had become the new vital center in the struggle to preserve the Confederacy. When Meade, on June 18, ordered 70,000 troops to move against the outer fortifications, they found only abandoned trenches. As Beauregard escorted Lee on an inspection tour of the new breastworks, the Creole proposed retaking the offensive by attacking Grant's flank before it was fully established. Lee put down the idea by responding that the past seven weeks of constant fighting had left his army in no condition to consider such a move.[41]

It turned out that the Army of the Potomac was perhaps in even worse condition. It, after all, had been the attacker during this unprecedented month and a half of relentless assaults against virtually impregnable fortifications. Cold Harbor had been the horrific capstone of too many frontal attacks that had left an army suffering from post-traumatic shock syndrome. Thus, when George Meade sent out orders for corps to attack the inner defenses at Petersburg, there was little compliance and much resistance in varying forms.[42] What half-hearted assaults did take place were easily repelled. Meade and Grant finally reluctantly called for entrenchments. Siege warfare had replaced frontal assaults as the key to victory.

In late June, Henri Garidel wrote: "I do not know how all this will end. . . . we are surrounded and communications with the South are cut off."[43] The dizzying pace of development that marked the Overland Campaign had severely disoriented Garidel. What he did recognize was that the federals had finally managed to achieve what the Confederates had been vainly trying to effect over the past three years, to maneuver their foes into such a position that they could be incapacitated, like a block of wood in a vise, with the vise ever tightening its grip to the point that the block could no longer offer any resistance and simply implode.

Petersburg may have marked the beginning of the end for the Confederates, but for P. G. T. Beauregard it had been perhaps his finest hour, or rather days. In defending the town for so long against ever-lengthening odds, he had given Lee the chance to oppose Grant at the new place the Union commander had chosen to be his springboard to final victory. Beauregard, more than anyone else, had forced Grant to resort to a siege operation, dependent on far distant military and political developments to shape its likelihood of success.[44]

The Overland Campaign had been the war's deadliest. The Union's losses exceeded 50,000, the Confederates' 30,000. Those figures represented 45 percent of the Army of the Potomac and 40 percent of the Army of Northern Virginia, respectively. For the federal wounded, Washington became their place for rehabilitation. A young Georgetown student remembered the wounded being brought in on the river steamers by the "thousands every day," with "long lines of ambulances carrying the wounded men from the steamboats to the various hospitals."[45] Bernardine Wiget, who had been serving for the past three years as a chaplain to the many military hospitals that the war had generated in the capital, was still overwhelmed by the latest campaign's harvest of suffering: "So many thousands of men wounded! It scarcely can be believed."[46]

THE ATLANTA CAMPAIGN

In the West, William Tecumseh Sherman's Atlanta campaign, in at least one respect, echoed the pattern of Grant's in the East: one step sideways, and two steps forward. What Sherman's campaign lacked that Grant's had in spades were the head-on battles that proved so costly in eastern Virginia. The army that set out for Atlanta, nearly 120 miles away, in May of 1864, was a veteran army populated by those who had enlisted during the first two years of the conflict, many of whom had reenlisted for the duration. These were volunteers whose experience in war had made them the equivalent of the regular soldiers that Sherman prized.[47] In his way stood Joe Johnston's Army of Tennessee. Despite heavy losses in the summer and fall of 1863 and their (latest) expulsion from Tennessee, the Confederate Army under Joseph Johnston retained high spirits. Johnston's commissary officer, Benedict Joseph Semmes, thought he had "never seen the army in such splendid fighting trim, or in such determined and confident spirits." Semmes attributed the resolve to the Union's shift in their war goals, "when Lincoln issued his Proclamation calling on the negroes to rise upon their masters."[48]

Cump Sherman's first objective was Resaca, a crucial rail link to Atlanta some thirty-five miles south of Chattanooga. The Confederates had established their defensive line at Rocky Face Ridge, some twenty miles above Resaca. Sherman planned to slip several corps around the Confederate left flank by going through Snake Creek Gap to gain Johnston's rear and force his withdrawal. Then, with the main body of the army in pursuit of the Confederates, the flankers would be in position to enfilade the rebels. "I've got Joe Johnston dead!" a confident Sherman reported.[49] Unfortunately, McPherson's corps had moved through the gap more deliberately than Sherman had expected. When his corps reached Resaca, McPherson found Leonidas Polk awaiting him. Even though his force greatly outnumbered Polk's, McPherson pulled back, allowing Johnston to retreat unimpeded to establish a new line of defense at Resaca.[50] Johnston's now enlarged force of 65,000 was within the week forced to retreat again when Sherman, once more, flanked his left. Within two weeks Sherman had gained his first objective without significant loss. He was duplicating Rosecrans's success in Tennessee.

Johnston, south of Resaca, now sent Hardee's corps, with most of the cavalry and wagon trains, to Kingston, to give the impression that his whole army was retreating and lure Sherman into a trap. That might have worked except for the chance arrival of Union cavalry on the Confederate right, which severely complicated any Confederate attack on a pursuing federal army. Hardee pleaded in vain for Johnston to go through with the attack, but the ever-prudent Johnston thought otherwise and renewed his reluctant withdrawal to establish a new line at Allatoona Pass. In three weeks, Sherman had advanced fifty miles toward Atlanta. Johnston had barely set his defenses at the pass when he learned that Sherman was flanking his left yet again. The Confederates abandoned their strongest line of defense to retreat to Dallas, just twenty-five miles northwest of Atlanta. On May 25, at New Hope crossroads, Sherman thought he had isolated a small portion of Johnston's army and struck. It proved to be terrible intelligence for which Sherman paid dearly, with tenfold the casualties which Johnston suffered.[51] Two days later, Sherman tried yet another flanking move at Pickett's Mill which turned out as badly as New Hope for the Army of the Tennessee.

Despite the setbacks, Sherman's army had cleared the Chattahoochee River, the last major body of water above Atlanta, while keeping open his long rail supply line from Chattanooga. The Ninetieth Illinois spent much of its time guarding the rails. "The weather is delightful for campaigning," James Connolly informed his wife, "and I am quite sure we will be in Atlanta by the middle of June, and we are all strongly in hope of celebrating the 4th of July at the 'last ditch' of the rebellion."[52] Meanwhile, Johnston had pulled back a few miles to form a semicircular defense around Kennesaw Mountain, a position even more formidable than the one he had reluctantly abandoned at Allatoona Pass. When Hood, defying orders, typically initiated a frontal attack on the Union left, his corps suffered severely for his rashness. Sherman, fearing that a stalemate might allow Johnston to transfer troops east in support of Lee, and sensitive to his own army's displeasure with his continual maneuverings that avoided conflict (particularly since persistent rain had rendered the roads hardly conducive for maneuvering), decided to attack the Confederates' eight-mile line that he considered overextended. On the morning of June 27, he ordered simultaneous assaults, one on the left center of the Confederate line at Pigeon Hill, the lowest of the three peaks defining the seven-hundred-foot Kennesaw Mountain; the second, a mile to the right. At 8 a.m., two hundred federal guns began a fifteen-minute bombardment. Then came the assaults, which failed miserably. In less than an hour, Sherman lost 2,500 men. When he asked George Thomas whether another assault was feasible, Thomas replied, with at least psychological accuracy: "one or two more such assaults would use up this army."[53]

Sherman reverted to flanking, which forced Johnston to withdraw his army across Peachtree Creek to the outer defenses of Atlanta. That retreat was the last straw for Richmond, which replaced Joe Johnston with John Bell Hood on June 17. Hood wasted no time in taking the offensive. His assault of June 20 failed, a defeat he blamed, with some justification, on William Hardee's slowness in executing Hood's plan of attack. Two days later, Hood tried another tack, this time dispatching Hardee on a Jackson-like flanking move of more than fifteen miles through a heavily wooded area. About noon they emerged from the woods to surprise the Seventeenth Corps, anchoring the left end of the Union line. The battle raged for six hours, with the Sixteenth Corps, including the Illinois Ninetieth, swept up in it. When the Sixteenth was forced to retreat, some of the Irish Legion became captives, including its flag bearer. General McPherson was killed. John A. Logan took command of the Army of the Tennessee, racing along the front of the embattled Union line, cheering on his men. Sherman himself directed the artillery to position themselves in front of Union forces. That tactic, plus John Logan's rallying of the two corps, saved the day, at least in that sector of what became known as the Battle of Atlanta.[54] In the thick of it were the heavily Catholic Thirty-Fifth Indiana Volunteers, whose major, John P. Duffy, was killed in action. Since the beginning of the campaign, the Thirty-Fifth had had a third of its men killed or wounded. Its chaplain, Peter Paul Cooney, CSC, wrote his brother on the twenty-fifth of June that they had had "two terrible battles" but that "we expect to have possession of Atlanta in three or four days."[55]

Two days later there was a third Confederate attempt to break the Union lines at Ezra Church. Once again, the Confederates failed, with terrible losses. Having lost in less than a week more men than Johnston had in ten weeks, Hood had no choice but to hunker down behind the trenches ringing Atlanta. Instead of the federals taking possession of the city, a full-scale siege began, mirroring the one that Grant had established at Petersburg a few weeks before. The *Atlanta Intelligencer* predicted that "Sherman will suffer the greatest defeat any Yankee General has suffered during the war."[56] Nature would accomplish what Johnston and Hood had failed to do: destroy the Yankee army.

A MATTER OF RESOLVE

After three years of war, the outcome was still very much in question. Even with the two major armies of the Union at the gates of Richmond and Atlanta, Confederate resolve remained high. Some might have even argued, as the summer wore on and the casualties mounted, that southern resolve was a good deal higher than northern. As Patrick Lynch had discerned, the South merely had to survive. The North had to continue to win battles and territory, as well as to inflict suffering and destruction of a sufficient order to break the South's will. And, perhaps even more importantly, the Lincoln administration had to retain the popular support to prosecute the war, no matter how long it dragged on, no matter how many casualties it produced. As the major armies settled into sieges in the two major theaters of the war, the North's ability to do that remained an open question.

$\dagger$

CHAPTER 15

Catholic Agents and the
International Dimensions of the War

*Your sympathies have been with us of the south, but
your Government have aided the Yankees. Your neutrality is a farce.*

—ROSE O'NEAL GREENHOW, JULY 1864

REVERSING THE REPUBLICAN TIDE

To survive as a new nation, the Confederacy needed to establish itself within the international order, securing the recognition of foreign powers, if not formal alliances with them. Fortuitously for the Confederacy, European monarchies, particularly Catholic ones, saw the Civil War as an unexpected opportunity to reverse the republican tide which had transformed the Americas since the American Revolution. It reanimated Catholic Europe's designs of remaking the Western World in its image. To a Confederacy whose society celebrated a hierarchical order founded upon slavery, such an antidemocratic movement was a powerful ally in the making.[1]

Spain, as the only remaining European power to have slave colonies in the Americas (in Cuba and Puerto Rico), seemed a natural diplomatic partner. Madrid's *El Pensamiento Español* in September 1862 took satisfaction in what the grim results of America's Civil War were revealing about "the model republic of what *were* the United States . . . [a country] populated by the dregs of all the nations of the world." This was what came of "a society constituted without God."[2]

Spain for years had feared, with good reason, that the United States would seize the Dominican Republic, its former colony, as a springboard for seizing Cuba. To prevent that, the Spanish military commander in Havana had been plotting with the Dominican Republic president, Pedro Santana, to rescind his country's sovereignty to Spain. When the Spanish government failed to act, in March 1861, Santana staged a phony plebiscite to approve a reacquisition of the island by Spain. As planned, two waiting Spanish warships offshore secured the capital. All this was news to the Spanish prime minister, Leopoldo O'Donnell, who feared US retaliation for the takeover. His ambassador in Washington, Gabriel García Tassara, quickly assured him, "The Union is in agony, our mission is not to delay its death for a moment."[3]

Fifteen years earlier, the United States had used Mexico's international financial arrears as a convenient opportunity to expand its territory. Now, it was France's turn. In October, Spanish, French, and British diplomats gathered in London to form the Tripartite Alliance to pressure Mexico into meeting its international obligations. In December 1861, 6,000 Spanish troops landed at Veracruz. A month later, the British and French added over 3,000 more. Louis Napoleon III, meanwhile, was developing his "Grand Design for the Americas," which envisioned a new French American empire, with Mexico as its hub.[4] Louis saw the Civil War providing the opportunity for France to reestablish itself in the Americas by having the Confederacy serve as a buffer between the United States and a French-protected Mexican monarchy. In January 1858, a faction of the Mexican military had revolted against the republican government of Benito Juárez in reaction to that government's reforms which had secularized education and confiscated church property. That "Reform War" lasted for three years before the Juárez forces prevailed, incurring a deep international debt in the process. When the Juárez government announced, in July of 1861, that it was suspending payment on those debts for two years, it provided the pretext for intervention, particularly with the United States preoccupied with its own Civil War.

When the British and Spanish realized the ulterior design of the French, the two nations withdrew their troops. Undeterred, the French headed toward Mexico City. On May 5, 1862, Mexican forces defeated the French. That defeat merely delayed the French conquest for a year. Napoleon III quintupled the French troop level to more than 30,000. In June of 1863, Mexico City fell to the French. A month later, a French-selected assembly of cooperative clergy and landowners declared Mexico a monarchy and sent a delegation to Austria to offer the crown to Emperor Franz Joseph's younger brother, Maximilian.[5] Maximilian agreed to accept the throne, but only with the consent of the Mexican people. The French occupiers forced village elders to stage a sham plebiscite that petitioned Maximilian to be their ruler. Maximilian and his wife, Charlotte, the daughter of King Leopold of Belgium, on their way to their new kingdom, stopped in Rome for Pope Pius IX's blessing in the spring of 1864. At the same time Matías Romero, the ambassador to the United States of the ousted Juárez government, persuaded the US Congress to declare that the United States would never "acknowledge any monarchical government, erected on the ruins of any republican government in America, under the auspices of any European power."[6]

These incursions of European powers into the Americas not only fed the European ideological debate about what was at stake in the American Civil War but deeply affected the positions that major European powers took regarding intervention or mediation in that war. The missions of American agents representing both the United States and the Confederacy took place against this ever-shifting backdrop and perforce were caught up in the struggle to shape public opinion in Europe about what was happening on the other side of the Atlantic.

JOHN HUGHES GETS
HIS GOVERNMENT MISSION

In October 1861, Archbishop John Hughes traveled to Washington from New York to meet with Secretary of State William Seward at Seward's request. Fifteen years earlier, Hughes had received a similar request from another secretary of state, James Buchanan, who was seeking his assistance in securing Catholic chaplains for the war with Mexico. Now, fifteen years later, his friend, former New York governor William Seward, called Hughes to Washington, as a possible participant in a diplomatic mission to Europe to present the United States' case for prosecuting the war.[7] Hughes at first declined the invitation, but Seward persuaded him to accept by playing to Hughes's responsibility as a loyal citizen. Hughes's charge was to act as an assistant to the US minister in Paris, William Dayton, in using his Catholic connections to discern the "dispositions of the French government" regarding the war. The archbishop was specifically instructed to seek an interview with the French emperor, Louis Napoleon.[8] Hughes welcomed the extraordinary opportunity to demonstrate the falsity of accusations that Catholics were "disloyal citizens, unworthy of the equal privileges which the laws of the country extend to all its inhabitants."[9]

When Hughes finally reached France, the archbishop tried in vain to get a meeting with Napoleon through official channels. Desperate, Hughes wrote a personal note to the emperor. The *Trent* affair was then threatening to become a *casus belli* between Great Britain and the United States. Whether that crisis affected the archbishop's request for an interview or not, Louis Napoleon agreed to meet with him. At the meeting with the emperor and the Empress Eugénie, Hughes pleaded with Louis Napoleon to offer his services as a mediator in the conflict. The emperor demurred that it was useless for him to attempt to settle something where both sides considered their honor to be at stake. The archbishop tried to win over the Spanish-born empress by warning her that the Confederacy was planning to dump its excess slaves onto Cuba. He urged the emperor to free France of its dependence on the South for its cotton by cultivating it in Algeria.[10] Hughes left the hour-plus meeting, knowing no more than he did before about what course of action, if any, France would pursue regarding the Confederacy.[11]

In the second week of January, John Hughes, ever seeking to expand his footprint upon affairs domestic or international, suggested to Seward that he make him a roving ambassador without portfolio, which would enable him to enlist the major European powers into a common mediation of the crisis over the *Trent*. Seward diplomatically replied that such a wide-ranging mission was not needed at present.[12] In early February 1862, John Hughes moved on from Paris to Rome, where he spent the next four months, making his decennial report, promoting the Lincoln administration's policies, and informing any Spanish prelates he could find that their government should have nothing to do with a power which was aiming to annex Cuba.[13] Conveniently forgotten was the recent Ostend Manifesto, which had declared the United States' intention to annex Cuba. Nonetheless, by May, Hughes had little optimism about winning the war for public opinion in Europe as a whole: "There are no friends of the United States on this side of the Atlantic."[14]

Hughes became ill during that summer of 1862, which prevented him from extending his mission to Spain. Instead, the archbishop turned to the bishop of Pittsburgh, Michael Domenec, a native Spaniard who was then in Rome. Horatio Perry, the US legate in Madrid, arranged for the bishop to meet with Fernando Calderón Collantes, the Spanish foreign minister. After several such meetings between the bishop and minister, Perry reported that Domenec's strong commitment to the Union, as well as his influence as a native Spaniard, "have been of much service here." Perry obviously felt that Domenec had played a significant role in assuring that Spain would remain neutral regarding the American conflict.[15]

When John Hughes reported to Seward, a year later, the results of his transatlantic undertaking, he uncharacteristically admitted that "I am not certain that any word, or act, or influence of mine has had the slightest effect in preventing either England or France from plunging into the unhappy divisions that have threatened the Union." All he could take comfort in was that "so far that peace [among the nations] has not been disturbed."[16] Bishop John Timon of Buffalo, for one, was not happy that Hughes had made himself an agent of the federal government. When he took his complaint to Francis Kenrick, after Hughes's return, Kenrick, despite his apolitical bent, responded that Hughes had every right "to give his services to the Government in support of the Union."[17]

Bishop Joseph Fitzpatrick of Boston made a trip to Europe in the spring of 1862, apparently at the initiative of the State Department, to present the federal government's case to the Catholic governments of Europe, particularly Belgium. The US consul in that country, Henry Sanford, reported to Secretary William Seward that he was strengthening "our cause" by his efforts.[18]

THE CONFEDERACY AND
THE WAR FOR EUROPEAN OPINION

Henri Mercier, the French minister to the United States, had made a visit to the Confederate capital in April of 1862, expecting to find a government resigned to its demise, given its dire military position as McClellan's grand army worked its seemingly unstoppable way up the Peninsula toward Richmond. To his utter surprise, the Confederate congress had just passed a sweeping conscription law. When Mercier returned to Washington, he told his British counterpart that the South showed every sign of continuing its struggle for independence indefinitely. It was time, Mercier proposed, to shelve their joint policy of neutrality and formally recognize the Confederacy.[19] Back in Richmond, Stephen Mallory had little hope that Mercier's proposal would go anywhere: "Recognition by France & England would help us but there are causes at work which must prevent this measure until it shall be no longer an object of great importance to us." The embargo on shipping cotton to Great Britain, moreover, would, to Mallory's mind, simply provide the British with a greater determination to grow its own cotton in India and Egypt. In the end, Great Britain would emerge with a vertical monopoly on the production of cotton products.[20]

At the beginning of 1862, the Confederate secretary of state, Judah Benjamin, had dispatched Henry Hotze, a Swiss, Jesuit-schooled journalist to open an office in London where he could conduct a systematic campaign to shape public opinion in Great Britain and France. Hotze had persuaded Benjamin that the Confederacy had to open a second front in the war, not on the battlefield but in the public square of European opinion. The multi-lingual Hotze had in mind the formation of a network of propagandists who would present the Confederacy's case through the popular media. In London, Hotze began to publish *Index: A Weekly Journal of Politics, Literature and News*. The journal quickly gained the reputation of being the European semiofficial voice of the Confederacy.

As summer came to a close in 1862, the Confederacy's military success as well as economic distress in Britain's textile industry increased the pressure for European intervention. On September 17, the very day in which Lee's Maryland Campaign came to its bloody end, John Russell informed Palmerston that "the time is come for offering mediation to the United States Government, with a view to the recognition of the independence of the Confederates." Palmerston preferred to wait to see the outcome of the Confederate invasion of Maryland. If Lee was again victorious, there should be an offer of mediation to both sides. If only the Confederate government was willing to accept, then Great Britain would recognize their independence. Russell told the British ambassador to France to alert the French government about joining the British in the overture.[21]

When Antietam ended the Confederate incursion, European governments regarded the subsequent Emancipation Proclamation as a desperate ploy of the Lincoln administration. In October the French formally proposed that the British join them in intervening in the war. Finally, in November, the British cabinet voted against intervention. In the end, the military and political risks in intervening outweighed any economic pressure.[22] The Emancipation Proclamation may not have directly affected British policy, but it seriously changed public opinion. According to Orestes Brownson, President Lincoln had told him that "the only consideration that weighed with" him in issuing the proclamation was to assure that Europe would not intervene in the war.[23] That was hardly the only or even the major reason for Lincoln's action, but there is little doubt that the proclamation became a major factor in deterring European intervention, especially in Great Britain.

By the second year of the war, Judah Benjamin saw France as the Confederacy's best hope for intervention. Napoleon, unlike Great Britain's officials, seemed unconcerned about the slavery question and more immune from public opinion on the matter. French *haute société* seemed, in general, to be more welcoming toward Confederates than their British counterpart.[24] John Slidell and his wife, Marie Mathilde Deslonde, a wealthy Creole heiress, made their way into Paris's highest circles, including the imperial court. Both the imperial couple and the Slidells came to have symbiotic interests in the success of Maximilian's empire and that of the Confederacy. In the summer of 1862, Slidell forwarded a proposal from Judah Benjamin to Louis Napoleon that the Confederacy would assist France in establishing a monarchy in Mexico and provide France with 100,000 bales of cotton, if France would provide a naval escort for Confederate ships bringing products to southern ports. When the emperor raised concerns about the repercussions that would come from this overt recognition of the Confederacy, Slidell pleaded the need to stop the endless war causing so much destruction and death. The emperor, it turned out, would not bite on Benjamin's attempted bribery.[25] Garibaldi's military success in the south of Italy had raised new threats to the pope's survival as a temporal power and forced the emperor to drop any consideration of Confederate recognition. As Slidell complained: "The tide which was setting in so strongly toward our recognition . . . was turned by the frantic folly of Garibaldi in Italy."[26]

ROSE O'NEAL GREENHOW

When Confederate officials, in the late winter of 1863, saw the need to increase their presence in Great Britain and France to press for intervention, Jefferson Davis naturally thought of Rose O'Neal Greenhow. Here was a woman who, for decades, as one of the doyennes of Washington society, had honed her skills in diplomatic polemics as an indispensable hostess and guest. She was fluent in French. Why not commission her to recreate, for the sociopolitical elite of London and Paris, the role she had played so deftly in the Democratic administrations of the 1850s? To say that being a foreign agent was not part of women's sphere was to ignore the sphere-crashing that had characterized Rose Greenhow her entire adult life.

In early August, Rose Greenhow, with her daughter, sailed out of Wilmington on the aptly named blockade runner *Phantom.* Over the next year, Greenhow split her time between London and Paris. An American journalist in Paris marveled at her ability to influence powerful people. "I was rather astonished and not a little amused at the power Mrs. Greenhow seemed to exercise over some people. . . . She had them in fact all at her feet."[27] In England, Greenhow secured Charles Dickens's publisher to release *My Imprisonment and the First Year of Abolition Rule at Washington,* the memoir she had written during her fifteen months in Richmond. Beginning in December, Rose Greenhow moved to Paris. She quickly sized up the Confederate mission to France as a total failure. John Slidell cared more about Parisian social life than Confederate diplomacy. Mason's French was so deficient as to make him useless. She advised recalling Slidell and sending Mason back to London. She herself, by much persistence, finally secured an interview with the emperor and his wife. He impressed her with his depth of knowledge about the war. When she raised with Louis Napoleon the need to recognize the Confederacy, he replied: "I wish to God I could. But I cannot do it without England." Like so many others, Greenhow came away from the interview convinced that the South had a future ally in France. That expectation was short-lived. Two weeks later, she learned that the emperor had refused to stop the British from interdicting at Liverpool the French-built rams that were to be put in Confederate service.[28]

Greenhow also pondered how she might move the Vatican to intervene. She became a daily Mass attendee at Westminster Cathedral and met several times with Cardinal Nicholas Wiseman about her papal hopes. Wiseman told her he sympathized with her intentions but feared being accused of meddling in politics, should he become a public advocate of recognition. He urged her to go to Rome to plead her case personally.[29]

The success of Greenhow's book had increased her popularity in the upper circles of British society, which bolstered her determination to persuade top government officials that their actions needed to match their rhetoric. To Gladstone she wrote in late July of 1864: "Your sympathies have been with us of the south, but your Government have aided the Yankees. Your neutrality is a farce." Gladstone could only point out that recognition of the Confederacy would merely anger the North. Palmerston had not even the grace to rebut her frequent pleas for intervention when she accosted him at gatherings; he simply changed the subject.

The House of Commons held a debate to consider recognition on June 30, 1863, but its chief promoter withdrew his motion before any vote could be taken. With the twin disasters of Gettysburg and Vicksburg devastating Confederate prospects, British intervention was a dead issue, or so it seemed. In the spring of 1864 talk of British intervention renewed when the Palmerston government invited a pro-Confederate member of Parliament to discuss a possible resolution on mediation of the American war. Henry Hotze thought there was a general movement in the government toward such a resolution. Reports from America about Lee's repeated repulses of Grant's attempts to break through to Richmond only intensified hopes that at last Europe would act to save the Confederacy. Rose Greenhow recorded in her diary that the news was "excellent," referring to the bloodbath that the Army of the Potomac had taken at Cold Harbor.[30] Confederate bonds, which had lost over 60 percent of their value by the end of 1863, now, in the summer of 1864, regained most of it, as European investors were bullish on McClellan's election and the peace movement in general.[31]

Deciding that her mission had run its course, Greenhow boarded the blockade runner *Condor* in Glasgow on August 10. A month later, she arrived in Halifax, where the ship underwent repairs for three weeks before heading for Wilmington. When they approached the North Carolina coast, the wild sea allowed the ship to evade the first line of the federal blockade. As they neared the New Inlet to Cape Fear River, another batch of patrolling vessels awaited them. In the middle of the night one gave chase, while firing at the fleeing *Condor*. In its flight the blockade runner struck a sandbank a few hundred yards offshore from Fort Fisher, whose guns afforded some protection for the stranded vessel until the rising tide would free it. Rose, carrying dispatches from Mason and Hotze for Richmond, beside £2,000 in gold, feared being taken captive. She and a fellow passenger begged the captain to put down a rowboat for them. Two sailors offered to row them ashore. As they neared the beach, a wave flipped the boat over. Rose Greenhow drowned within yards of the shore, apparently the victim of the weight of the gold and heavy chain that secured her pouch.[32]

At Wilmington's St. Thomas the Apostle Church, James Corcoran said the funeral Mass on October 2, with Greenhow's flag-draped coffin at the head of the nave, and the pews filled with representatives of the Confederate government and military.[33] When Mary Chesnut learned of Rose's tragic ending, she eulogized her in a way she could not bring herself to do two years earlier when she dismissed Greenhow as an opportunist who had been for sale all her life. "She was a great woman spoiled by education—or the want of it. She has left few less prudent women behind her—and many less devoted to our cause. 'She loved much,' and ought she not to be forgiven? May God have mercy upon her and upon her orphan child."[34]

COUNTERING UNION RECRUITMENT
IN IRELAND

By the summer of 1863 the Confederate government had become deeply concerned about Union recruitment in Ireland. The US Congress had enacted legislation which guaranteed American citizenship for any immigrant who served in Union forces for one year. The British consul in New York was estimating that more than 150 Irishmen were being enlisted into the Union Army for every arrival of a British ship at Castle Garden. The British Home Office calculated that the cumulative numbers probably totaled more than 10,000. Emigration from Ireland to the northern states more than doubled in 1863 from the previous year (from 24,000 to 56,000). That sharp spike only increased Confederate convictions that Union recruiting in Ireland was mainly responsible.

John Bannon, following the fall of Vicksburg, had taken himself to Richmond, where he happened to celebrate a Mass that Stephen Mallory attended. That led to an invitation from President Davis to undertake a secret mission to Ireland in order to stem the Union recruiting campaign there.[35] As a former Confederate chaplain, Bannon was well positioned to point out the horrific casualties the Irish had taken at Antietam and Fredericksburg, not to mention the off-putting likelihood that they would find themselves fighting against other Irishmen wearing gray. Then too he could instruct on how much better the Irish fared in the South rather than in the Know-Nothing North and use the desecration of Catholic places of worship in the South by Union troops as evidence of the anti-Catholic bias that pervaded the North.[36]

Two months later, the priest, now in Dublin, wrote Benjamin that emigration was heavy, even heavier than previously reported. Its major cause, however, was not Union enticements to enlist but poor harvests, a traditional push factor for immigrants.[37] Taking up his role as propagandist, Bannon wrote letters to journals, justifying the Confederacy's cause and distributed clippings from the *Richmond Whig* and the *Freeman's Journal* to a broad number of newspapers across Ireland. When he came to realize that few of the Irish read newspapers, he put together a circular letter that could be posted in boarding houses, churches, and other public places throughout Ireland for communal dissemination. Fifteen hundred copies of his first letter were distributed through Confederate agents in Ireland. Two copies of a second circular in January 1864 were distributed to every priest in Ireland. The circular once more pointed out the dangers of emigration as well as the Confederacy's quest for a peaceful settlement through the mediation of the pope. Then Bannon composed a long exposition of the war's issues, in which he defended the rebellion of the southern states as a new American Revolution in which a wronged minority was seeking independence. He depicted the Confederacy as this precapitalist state which valued religion and treated Catholics justly, unlike the North where working Catholics found themselves lowered to a status worse than slaves. Slowly Bannon sensed opinion shifting in the Confederacy's favor. He quoted one Irish peasant who claimed: "We who were all praying for the North at the opening of the war, would now willingly fight for the South if we could get there."[38] Indeed Bannon himself felt sure that, if Confederate recruiters could compete with the Union in attracting enlistees, four-fifths would choose the South.[39]

Confederate agents besides Bannon thought his campaign had changed the tide of public opinion in Ireland. Henry Hotze reported that the number of Irishmen emigrating to fight for the Union dropped by two-thirds from

December 1863 to May 1864.[40] That month a new Confederate agent, Bishop Patrick Lynch of Charleston, arrived in Ireland. Bannon had recommended that the Confederacy enlist a bishop to represent the nation in Rome. The government had heeded his advice and secured Lynch as a special commissioner to the Papal States.

THE VATICAN AND THE WAR

In the early years of the war, the Holy See, facing an attack on its own Papal States by Italian nationalists, tended to identify with the federal government's resistance to rebellion. No thought was given to acknowledging the South's independence by creating a separate ecclesiastical structure for dioceses located in the region. Since 1847 the United States and the Holy See had had diplomatic relations. When, in June of 1861, John P. Stockton, the US legate in Rome, sought to gain the Vatican's support for the Lincoln administration's efforts to put down the rebellion of the seceded states, the Vatican secretary of state, Leonardo Antonelli, diplomatically remarked that the Papacy "supported law and order everywhere."[41] When John Hughes arrived in Rome in early 1862, he found a widespread belief that the Union would be preserved, a belief that Louis B. Binsse, the papal consul in New York, was strengthening with the accounts of Union success that he was forwarding. By the time a new American legate, Alexander Randal, was in place later that year, the Vatican was renewing its interest in establishing a permanent diplomatic mission in Washington. Roman officials, including the pope, made clear to Randal that his country had their sympathy.

Despite his long involvement with the Catholic community, Secretary of State William Seward did not fully appreciate the role the Vatican could play in influencing opinion, particularly among American Catholics at a time when Catholic support for the war was badly declining in the North.[42] Confederate success in the summer and fall of 1862 led Rome to recalibrate its American position. It seemed increasingly clear to Vatican officials that a negotiated settlement was the only feasible path toward ending the war. That sentiment occasioned Pius IX's letter to the archbishops of the largest sees in North and South respectively, John Hughes of New York and John Mary Odin of New Orleans. When the new American minister, Richard Blatchford, had his first audience with the pope in mid-November 1862, Pius suggested that Blatchford recommend to his government a settlement negotiated through a mediator who had no geopolitical interest at stake. Cardinal Antonelli provided more substance to the papal proposal by telling Blatchford that both sides should have the willingness to compromise on secondary matters in order to achieve the principal goal of reunification.[43] Given that the Lincoln administration had just radically expanded the war's goals by threatening to emancipate the Confederacy's slaves if the states in secession did not return to the Union by January 1, treating abolition as a secondary matter had become a nonstarter for the federal government.

Into the spring of 1863 the Holy See continued to harbor hopes of mediating the conflict. It took a congressional resolution declaring that the government would be party to no foreign mediation toward a peace agreement to convince Rome that Washington would settle for nothing short of total victory. That, to the officials of the Holy See, meant a war whose length God alone could know and whose scale of destruction and casualties seemed to expand to ever more horrific dimensions, becoming ever less compatible with the standards which defined a just war. As the war grew steadily "harder," with moral boundaries having less and less influence in shaping strategy and tactics, the more the Roman press, particularly *L'Osservatore Romano,* saw the North failing to meet the criteria justifying its prosecution of the war.[44]

Ironically the Emancipation Proclamation proved to be the tipping point in turning the Holy See against the Lincoln administration. A likely major influence on this change of opinion was the then bishop of Louisville, Martin Spalding, whose long report to curial officials on the causes and consequences of the war had an immediate impact in shaping the Holy See's thinking about the conflict. Its publication by the semiofficial *L'Osservatore Romano* was one clear indication of Church officials' desire to promulgate Spalding's interpretation of Lincoln's proclamation. But it raised no alarms among American officials in either Rome or Washington.

THE VATICAN AS CHANNEL
TO CONFEDERATE INDEPENDENCE

By 1863 Confederate diplomatic strategy began to focus more on the Vatican as a possible channel toward a negotiated peace and independence. When John Slidell learned that the pope had offered to mediate negotiations between the United States and the Confederacy, he proposed that Judah Benjamin send a mission to the Vatican. Slidell had learned from friends in Rome that the pope's secretary of state, Cardinal Giacomo Antonelli, was predisposed toward the South and could be willing to lend the Church's influence to the peace movement that was gaining momentum in the North. Benjamin instructed Slidell to do all he could to advertise in Catholic countries the vandalism and sacrilege that Union troops were committing against Catholic property in the areas they were occupying.[45]

In September 1863, John Bannon had reinforced Slidell's proposition by recommending to Jefferson Davis and Judah Benjamin that they make a diplomatic approach to the pope about securing the Vatican's recognition. Davis accordingly prepared a letter of gratitude to Pius for his enjoining Archbishops Hughes and Odin to jointly seek a peaceful settlement of the war. Bannon carried the letter to London, where it made its way to the Confederate commissioner in Belgium, Ambrose Dudley Mann, whom Davis had designated as an envoy to the Papal States.[46] When Mann subsequently presented the letter to the pope, Pio Nono stated that the Lincoln government "had endeavored to create an impression abroad that they were fighting for the abolition of slavery, and that it might perhaps be judicious in us to consent to gradual emancipation." Mann responded that the disposition of slavery was a matter for the states to decide, not the US federal government, and, if indeed African slavery were an evil, there was a power which in its own good time would doubtless remove that evil "in a more gentle manner than that of causing the earth to be deluged with blood for its sudden overthrow." Ignoring this comment on God's inscrutable Providence as the best hope for eliminating evil, the pontiff promised a letter to President Davis. Three weeks later he delivered it to Mann, which the envoy proceeded to treat as nothing less than the pope's *de facto* recognition of the Confederacy.[47] Judah Benjamin had no illusion about the significance of the pope's careful response but intended to exploit it for all its propaganda value, both at home and abroad, particularly with American Catholics, North and South.

A CONFEDERATE
BISHOP COMMISSIONER

"April 5. At 7:30 [p.m.] went to church. We said the rosary and heard a sermon by Bishop Lynch from Petersburg [sic]." Little did this New Orleans exile, Ordnance Department clerk Henri Garidel, realize that the bishop was in Richmond to get final instructions from Secretary of State Benjamin regarding his impending European mission to promote the Confederacy among the Catholic powers there, especially the Papal States. The pope's letter had confirmed Richmond's intention to send a commissioner to reside in Rome. Benjamin approached Patrick Lynch as the Confederate government's top preference for the mission.[48] Given Lynch's command of languages, his acquaintances in high places within the Vatican, and his episcopal status, he was an obvious choice.

The day after Lynch had preached in Richmond, he took the train to Wilmington, where he arranged passage on a blockade runner, the *Minnie*, with such primitive accommodations that the bishop thought they should have paid *him* the $200 in gold that the transatlantic trip cost. The *Minnie* successfully eluded the ships patrolling the entrance to Wilmington, then outraced a federal patroller in the open sea, and endured a gale that had the craft rolling "horribly," giving "shower baths" to Lynch from the ocean spray. Finally, the *Minnie* reached Bermuda, the first of several ports that Lynch visited on his way to Europe.[49]

Although John Hughes had been in his grave for three months, Patrick Lynch found himself still in his shadow as he reprised the role the New York prelate had performed two and a half years earlier: cultivating the favor of the Holy See and the Catholic powers of Europe, now for the Confederacy rather than the Union. Lynch carried a commission as a special representative of the Confederate government to the Papal States. His actual charge from Secretary of State Judah Benjamin had a broader reach than the pope's temporal domain. He was to be a good-will ambassador to not only the Papal States, but also to other Catholic powers in Europe who proved accessible. If such interchange led to discussions about formal recognition of the Confederacy, so much the better.

As a blockade runner and a defiant survivor of several months of Union shelling in Charleston, Lynch found himself something of a celebrity in Paris. The papal nuncio provided introductions to the very top officials. Meetings with the French foreign minister and Napoleon Bonaparte III revealed that the French had already sought, in vain, to have Great Britain and Russia join with them in intervening in the Americans' war to impose a peace. The emperor himself hoped that a decisive victory by Confederate forces in the current season of campaigning would provide the opportunity for France at last to recognize the Confederacy as an independent nation.[50] With this psychological tailwind, Lynch headed for Rome.

Meetings there with the papal secretary of state and the pope proved less encouraging. Cardinal Antonelli freely shared with Bishop Lynch his reading of French and British policy regarding the Confederacy but, crafty diplomat that he was, kept papal intentions well concealed. The pope did admit to Lynch that "it is most clear that you are two nations," and offered to serve as a mediator toward a peace settlement, should the North ever agree to such a resolution of the war, which the pope thought would require a miracle to bring about. The Emancipation Proclamation he regarded as a rash act sure to produce much evil, but no one, he warned, should expect the pontiff to do anything that might seem to legitimize slavery in the Confederacy.[51]

The pontiff's desire to avoid any action that might seem to sanction the South's peculiar institution served as a fresh incentive for Bishop Lynch to do something he had been considering doing ever since Paris. The key to securing recognition from European powers, he had concluded, lay in changing the negative image of slavery that dominated popular opinion. "If we could smooth down their prejudices on the subject of slavery, our task would be easy," Lynch had reported to Benjamin following his meetings with French officials. There was a compelling need for a defense of slavery which demonstrated its essential Christian character as the ideal environment for Africans. Such a domestic institution, far from rendering a nation illegitimate, rather should make it particularly worthy of recognition by the Christian nations of the world.

Lynch spent the remainder of the summer and early fall composing his apologia on slavery and preparing for its publication in Italian, French, and German. This business took him to northern Italy, Austria, and Bavaria, where friends like the Princess Wittgenstein gained him entry to government officials, with whom he promoted Confederate interests.[52] The first edition of the treatise came out in Italian in the late fall. Entitled "A Few Words on the Domestic Slavery in the Confederate States of America" under the generic byline of "A Catholic Clergyman," the pamphlet examined slavery under five main aspects: (1) the savage conditions the enslaved had known in their free days in Africa compared with the civilized ones they enjoyed under slavery; (2) the historical forcing of slavery upon the southern states; (3) the loyalty that slaves had displayed during the war by rejecting the opportunities for freedom; (4) the prohibitive economic costs that emancipation would entail; and (5) the evils that would befall ex-slaves either as freedmen in America or colonizers in Africa. Rather than the "statement of facts" that the bishop promised his readers, the paper was a model of propaganda, through which he wove selective facts, racist suppositions, fanciful history, and wishful thinking to compose his highly positive profile of southern slavery. Conversely, should Lincoln's proclamation somehow become reality for the millions of Africans in bondage in the Confederacy, race war, Lynch suggested, would be inevitable, ending in re-enslavement or even extinction for the recently emancipated.[53]

"I presume it will find its way into the press," the bishop advised Benjamin about the paper. He had good reason to expect that it would, given the promulgation that Spalding's letter had received in Rome a year earlier. When the Rome-based Jesuit journal, *La Civiltà Cattolica,* pronounced Lynch's pamphlet the work of someone "impartial, superbly well-informed," and of "broad and just views," the bishop had to have been optimistic about its power to change opinion in the highest places in Catholic Europe, including the Vatican. Little did he know how the Roman curia, in its Byzantine manner, had already rendered his pamphlet a dead letter. Apparently under the influence of Isaac Hecker, Louis B. Binsse, the Papal States' consul in New York, had been prodding Propaganda Fide to publicly condemn slavery as an institution, in the wake of Lincoln's making its abolition a war goal.[54] The congregation finally did take up the question nearly two years after Lincoln's proclamation by examining the 1861 pastoral of Natchitoches, Louisiana, bishop, Auguste Martin, which had extolled slavery as a divine ordination. In the subsequent review, the Dominican Martin Gatti ruled that Bishop Martin's defense of slavery was untenable. Not even the blessing of Christianity could justify the "iniquity" which slavery entailed. His report explicitly condemned chattel slavery as well as slave trading. The pope thereupon condemned the pastoral but ordered the whole matter to be kept secret in order to give Martin the chance to retract his pastoral. Martin's subsequent retraction prevented any promulgation of Rome's ruling on slavery.[55]

And so, the church officially remained mute on the question of slavery, even as the United States prepared to abolish it in its Constitution. In January of 1865, as Bishop Lynch was still making arrangements to have his pamphlet published in France and Germany, the US Congress passed the Thirteenth Amendment, which brought the Constitution into accord with the reality that the course of the war and massive Black abandonment of the plantations and other venues of bondage had shaped. No longer did the fundamental law of the land sanction slavery. The United States had joined most of the rest of the developed world in legally renouncing forced labor as a means of production.

CHAPTER 16

Sherman, Ewing, and Sheridan
Save Lincoln

[Slavery] simmered, and burned into the very vitals of the nation,
until . . . it raised up armies to fight against our Republic.
—PATRICK GUINEY, OCTOBER 1864

THE ALABAMA ROLLS NO MORE

On January 11, 1863, the CSS *Alabama,* commanded by Raphael Semmes,
lured the gunboat USS *Hatteras,* which was part of the Union blockade of Galveston, into giving chase of what the *Hatteras* took to be a blockade runner.
After a twenty-mile chase, the *Alabama,* when challenged to identify itself,
claimed a new identity, that of a British ship. When the *Hatteras* lowered
a boat to investigate the three-masted, 230-foot vessel, Semmes promptly
shouted: "This is the Confederate States Steamer *Alabama.*" Instantly the six
guns of the *Alabama* opened fire. Within fifteen minutes the *Hatteras* began
to sink. The *Alabama* picked up its survivors and released them in Jamaica
nine days later.[1] Over the next six months, the *Alabama* would claim thirty-
three more conquests. By June of 1863, Confederacy raiders, including the
Alabama, Sumter, Florida, and *Georgia,* had destroyed approximately two
hundred Union merchant ships. So vulnerable had US shipping become to
the Confederate raiders that US merchants were forced into selling more than
a third of their ships to neutrals to avoid further attacks.[2]

By the late spring of 1864 the *Alabama,* in the twenty-two months since
its launching in June of 1862, had terrorized US shipping from Europe to East
Asia by capturing or destroying sixty-five US ships, costing the northern maritime trade more than $5 million in losses. The vessel was more than showing
the battle fatigue and wear of the demands that Semmes had put upon it. In
June, Semmes brought the ship to its homeport of Cherbourg, France, for
some desperately needed repairs. Nonetheless, when the USS *Kearsarge* ap-

peared outside of the harbor in pursuit of the *Alabama,* Semmes felt honor bound to give battle, even though his ship was in no shape to do so. At a mile's distance, the two ships exchanged broadsides. The *Kearsarge,* with its hidden chain armor and more powerful guns, soon had much the better of it, scoring several direct hits on the Alabama while having but one shell strike it, which failed to explode. Less than an hour after the first shells were exchanged, the *Alabama* was rapidly taking on water. Nine of the crew lay dead; more than a score were wounded. Rescue boats from the *Kearsarge* and French craft (which had come out to watch the battle) saved most of the surviving crew members, including Captain Semmes. The survivors were taken to Southampton for a heroes' welcome in a port town where Confederate sympathy ran high.[3] The *Alabama*'s demise foreshadowed the battlefield disasters to afflict the Confederacy in the late summer and early fall in Georgia, Missouri, and Virginia that sealed Lincoln's reelection.

FROM DISSENT TO CONSPIRACY

On May 4, 1861, the Catholic editor of the *New York Tablet* had predicted that God would use the occasion of a civil war to make Americans into a true nation by having the "pestilent heresy" of state sovereignty "perish in the flames."[4] For a growing number of Americans, especially Catholics, such concentration of power in the national government was antithetical to the republican ideology that diffused sovereignty. The Democratic Party became the champions of laissez faire government at the national level, while defending the priority of state sovereignty in a federal republic.[5] From the war's outset, there was considerable opposition to the Lincoln administration's assertion of power in its prosecution of the war. The Baltimore riot which followed the attack on Fort Sumter was a precursor of the violence that such dissent could produce. Eventually, the suppression of dissent, including imprisonment, together with the making of emancipation a war goal, provided for a significant minority in the North a rationalization for conspiring with the Confederacy in overthrowing the federal government or at least in replacing it with an administration which would make peace on the South's terms.[6] In this resistance, Catholics, from the beginning, played a prominent role, whether in the courts, the press, local politics, or in the streets.[7]

In late May of 1861, military authorities had arrested John Merryman, a Baltimore County farmer, on suspicion of burning railroad bridges to prevent federal troops from getting to Washington. Immediately, friends of Merryman petitioned for a writ of habeas corpus from Chief Justice Roger Taney, who promptly issued it. At a subsequent hearing, military officials explained they were merely carrying out the orders of the Lincoln administration. Taney reminded them that the military had no right to arrest any civilian unless authorized by the courts, while pointing out that only Congress had the constitutional authority to suspend the writ. For Lincoln to usurp Congress's power was to put the country on the road to despotism. Nonetheless, Taney admitted, the court simply lacked the power to undo the president's order.[8] Military arrests multiplied, especially in the border states, where pro-Confederate sentiment was so strong. In Maryland half of the arrests took place in St. Mary's and Charles counties, the traditional heartland of Catholic Maryland.[9]

As the war wore on and the government became more active in suppressing extreme opposition against the prosecution of the war, Democrats accused Republicans of waging a "reign of terror" against dissenters. Whether it was making military arrests, imposing loyalty oaths and conscription, shutting down newspapers: all this seemed an assault on the Constitution and the civil liberties supposedly at the heart of our republic. Particularly in the border states, loyalty oaths became essential means for combatting Confederate sympathizers and dissenters who occupied crucial positions as clergy, government workers, or educators.[10] In Missouri, Archbishop Peter Richard Kenrick instructed his clergy that they were not to take the oath. "We cannot permit the Civil Power," Kenrick explained, "to interfere with us in any manner in our duties, or to prescribe the conditions on which we may perform them."[11]

Ministers of all faiths wrestled with the response they should make with orders or more subtle forms of pressure to manifest their loyalty to local authority, whether it be by displaying a flag (outside or in the house of worship), oath-taking, or reciting prayers. This last form of allegiance affirmation—recited prayers—became a particular challenge for Confederate ministers of religious denominations with formal liturgies who found themselves in occupied territory. Catholics, with their proslavery record and suspect loyalty even in the most tranquil times, became natural targets for local Union military commanders.

The most significant Catholic prayer case involved Bishop William Henry Elder of Natchez, Mississippi, whose defiance of federal authorities gained national attention. In the spring of 1864, the area commander, General James Tuttle, learning that the Catholic churches were not regularly reciting a prayer for the president, issued an order that they do so. Elder appealed to Washington.[12] "This is ... a question ... that involves the religious liberties of the thousands of Catholic Soldiers," Elder wrote, "& the millions of Catholics

... who are subject to the laws & government of the United States." The secretary of war, Edwin Stanton, subsequently admonished Tuttle for interfering in "ecclesiastical matters" in which he had no authority.[13]

Then, in late June, a new district military commander, Bernard Farrar, issued a new order that all churches that had a "prescribed form of prayer for the President of the United States" should recite it whenever "it is required by the rubrics." Again, Elder took his case to the Lincoln administration. Appealing to reason, scripture, and the spirit of the US Constitution, Elder argued that religious worship, including prayer, should be the exclusive province of "Religious Authorities," not civil ones. Prayer could not be forced for any political purpose, including shows of allegiance. Agreeing to let the government dictate public prayer, Elder argued, would encourage further demands for promoting its policies.[14] When the bishop took his letter to Farrar's quarters, he discovered a new commanding officer in his place, Mason Brayman, who informed Elder that "military orders are to be obeyed, not discussed." Brayman gave Elder a choice: he could either read the prayer and thereby prove his loyalty or refuse to do so and thereby admit his treason. Two days later, Elder mailed off the letter to Secretary Stanton. In late July, Brayman, tired of Elder's intransigence, charged the bishop with being "in rebellion against the United States" and ordered the bishop expelled beyond Union lines. Since Washington had become involved, the general reduced Elder's punishment to ritual banishment to Vidalia, just across the Mississippi River in Louisiana. As though reenacting a biblical event, the bishop passed in his carriage through long lines of white-robed women and girls who had gathered on the sides of the river road, some on their knees and all in tears, to see their prelate into exile.[15]

A few weeks later, General Brayman, apparently under orders from Stanton, informed Elder that he could return home. Apparently channeling the secretary of war, Brayman wrote that "all solemn appeals to the *Supreme Being,* not proceeding from honest hearts, and willing minds, are necessarily offensive to *Him,* and subversive of sound morality."[16] Forcing religious behavior to assure conformity only served to undermine the state by creating untrustworthy citizens. Bishop Elder slipped back into town, but once at the cathedral, bells rang and people rushed to greet their prelate who had prevailed over the occupiers. The Confederacy may have been slowly dying, but their bishop had been vindicated in his insistence that a state-ordered prayer was a clear violation of the religious liberty that was at the core of American freedoms and a mockery of the separation of church and state that the Constitution affirmed.

By the summer of 1864, the relentless campaigning that had distinguished the latest season of the war had produced staggering casualty rates, soaring debts that threatened bankruptcy, and stalemates before Richmond and Atlanta. To a growing number of people in the North, it seemed a relentless waste of lives. Democrats postponed their convention in Chicago for eight weeks, in the hope that by late August a worsening military situation would boost their election chances even more. The *Boston Pilot* concluded in late June, "It begins to look to many folks in the North, that the Confederacy perhaps can never really be beaten, that the attempts to win might after all be too heavy a load to carry, and that perhaps it is time to agree to a peace without victory."[17]

"When Lincoln," the *Catholic Mirror* commented in July of 1864, "turned the war from one whose only goal was saving the Union to one that also sought to free the slaves, he struck the match."[18] By 1864 the slogan "The Union as it was" became code talk for the undoing of the Emancipation Proclamation as well as the prevention of any amendment to the Constitution that would abolish slavery. To preserve the Constitution, so its proponents argued, the federal government needed to reach a peace agreement with the Confederacy that would restore the Union with slavery intact.[19] That was the clear intention of the Peace Democrats, who, by the summer of 1864, were on the brink of taking over the party.[20]

Stephen E. Towne contends that a portion of the Democratic Party utilized an existing secret political organization, the Knights of the Golden Circle, or initiated new ones, such as the American Order of Knights and the Sons of Liberty, to undermine the prosecution of the war: "As the war wore on, the conspirators became increasingly ambitious in their aims, evolving from mutual-protection groups to groups aiding deserters and draft dodgers to plotting the release of Confederate prisoners of war *en masse* and raising insurrection in the North."[21] Antiwar activity increasingly involved collaboration with Confederates. So-called Peace Democrats were anything but pacifists. They were all too willing to use violent means not only to resist recruitment and the draft, but even to overthrow the US government. Catholics, including James McMaster, Charles Walsh, Charles E. Dunn, and Emile Longuemare, held prominent positions in the societies and were intimately involved in advancing their goals. At the same time, a Catholic, General William Rosecrans, played a major role in undermining the conspiracies that these societies were plotting against the country.

In January 1864, Rosecrans took over as commander of the Department of the Missouri. With his military reputation tarnished by Chickamauga, Rosecrans was keen to restore his name. He and his provost marshal, Col. John P.

Sanderson, launched an intensive investigation of suspect individuals and organizations active in St. Louis. Two figures who materialized quickly as prime suspects of disloyalty were Charles L. Hunt and Charles E. Dunn, the Belgian counsel in St. Louis. Both held high positions in the secret society of the Order of American Knights. Rosecrans and Sanderson came to believe that Hunt and Dunn were at the center of a vast conspiracy to launch insurrection throughout the old Northwest region. Rosecrans put together an extensive detective force to ferret out antiwar operations throughout an area that encompassed not merely Missouri but Indiana, Illinois, and Ohio. One of Sanderson's agents, staked out at a hotel in Windsor, Ontario, in April of 1864, reported extensive traffic to a room registered to "A. James," who, as Union intelligence determined, was James A. McMaster, reputedly the New York State supreme commander of the Order of the American Knights.[22]

In June, Rosecrans briefed Lincoln's secretary, John Hay, for several hours about the regional uprising from Kentucky to Illinois that the Order of the American Knights was planning for July 4, while the Democratic Convention was taking place in Chicago. Later, Rosecrans informed Lincoln that the conspiracy extended to the East Coast and had more support from the Confederates than had originally been known. The plotters felt that they had the sufficient means to "overthrow the existing national Government & the dismemberment of this nation."[23] Despite Rosecrans's warnings, the administration did nothing, perhaps lulled by the Democrats' postponement of their convention to late August. Then in mid-July a spate of arsons, first of six steamboats loaded with army supplies at St. Louis, then of a major Louisville warehouse full of equipment and supplies for military hospitals, stirred new fears of an imminent uprising. A wave of arrests ensued, including that of Dunn and John Richard Barret, a St. Louis College graduate and former Democratic congressman known to be active in antiwar activities.[24] Several of them, including Dunn, confessed they had received weapons and other aid from the Confederates.[25]

THE CONFEDERACY AND ITS
COPPERHEAD ALLIES

In 1863 the Confederate government had formed a secret service, which had appropriated $900,000 to agents in Canada seeking, among other things, to provoke, if not cooperate with, the separatist inclinations of the peace forces, particularly in the Northwest. One such agent was George P. Kane, the former police marshal in Baltimore, who, in the late summer of 1963, planned a series of attacks on Lakes Erie and Michigan, to paralyze shipping, burn the towns of Erie and Buffalo, and liberate the Confederate prisoners held at Johnson's Island.[26] The one part of Kane's plan that was attempted, the liberation of the prisoners, failed when an informant enabled Union officials to arrest the Confederate agent who was to lead the operation.[27]

When, in early March of 1864, Confederates killed one of the commanders of a Union cavalry raid on Richmond, they found on his corpse orders to liberate Union captives in the city, then to proceed to put the Confederate capital to the torch and to kill as many Confederate officials as possible, including Jefferson Davis. Federal officials flatly denied that any such orders had been given to those carrying out the mission. Confederate authorities publicly accepted the denials, but their subsequent actions indicated that the traditional guardrails for conducting warfare no longer held.[28] Two weeks after the explosive papers were found on Ulrich Dahlgren's corpse, the Confederate secretary of war directed Thomas Henry Hines, a twenty-five-year-old former member of the Knights of the Golden Circle, to proceed to Canada to organize Confederates who might have escaped there from federal prisons, for "any hostile actions against the United States" which Hines considered appropriate.[29] By summer Hines was put in charge of coordinating the July uprising of Copperheads in conjunction with the Democratic convention in Chicago. The plan envisioned the release of Confederate prisoners from local camps to muster a military force of some 50,000 who would "liberate Illinois, Indiana, and Ohio." When the Democrats postponed their convention until late August, the plan was rescheduled for that week as well. As August entered its last week, Hines headed from Toronto for Chicago with a hundred men. He quickly sensed that the commitment to the plot by the Copperhead leaders was disturbingly weak. Charles Walsh, the supposed brigadier general of the Sons of Liberty militia in Illinois (as well as the Democratic political boss of Cook County), reported that somehow the orders for the Copperhead units in Indiana and Ohio to strike on the appointed day had failed to be sent. When Hines asked them to provide several hundred men to cut the wires and disable the bridges in Chicago to create chaos, they produced a mere twenty-five. Hines concluded that the military wings of the Sons of Liberty and Order of American Knights had little reality outside of the aspirations of their leaders.[30]

ATLANTA

For five weeks in the summer of 1864, Cump Sherman indiscriminately bombarded Atlanta with more than 100,000 projectiles, setting off fires and killing or wounding dozens of civilians.[31] Attempting to make Confederate supplies a more elusive target of Sherman's siege guns, Benedict Joseph Semmes, the quartermaster for the Army of Tennessee, stored them in freight cars which could be moved as the direction of the federal bombardment dictated. As the summer wore on, the shelling increased. By late August, Semmes informed his wife, "the [artillery] fire was so hot at my quarters that I had to get up and vacate to another point a hundred yards distant, but after a while I returned, the shells being as thick there as my quarters."[32] As Sherman extended his lines for ten miles around Atlanta, Hood responded by sending William Hardee with two corps to reopen the Macon & Western railroad south of Atlanta at Jonesboro.[33] Once again, Hood's aggressive tactics brought disaster, with Hardee's 2,500 casualties more than twelve times the Union's. One of the mortal casualties of the Battle of Jonesboro was the Benedictine, Emmeran Bliemel, chaplain of the Tennessee Tenth, the sole Catholic chaplain to die in service.

With his lifeline severed, Hood pulled his troops out of the city on September 1. Joseph Benedict Semmes managed to salvage some of his stores. As he retreated south with what remained of the Army of Tennessee, Semmes, for one, tried to put the best face on Atlanta's capture. "The fall of Atlanta," he told his wife, "will prolong the war another year," implying that the Confederacy would still somehow prevail, that this devastating loss would simply delay the inevitable Union defeat.[34] James Connolly of the 123rd Illinois saw it quite differently. "The long agony is over," he wrote his wife, "and Atlanta is ours! This army is frantic with exultation, and the rebel army is scattered over the country."[35]

With Atlanta's fall, the Confederates had lost their second most important city: a key rail hub that contained foundries, weapons and munition factories, and supply depots. What they had lost psychologically was even worse. When Sherman entered Atlanta the next day, he knew that he had just assured Lincoln's reelection. He also knew that he himself had finally achieved national prominence.[36] As Charles Francis Adams noted from the trenches of Petersburg, "Unquestionably it is *the* campaign of the war." Even Henry Halleck was effusive about Sherman's accomplishment. In his congratulations to Sherman, Halleck deemed his campaign "the most brilliant of the war."[37]

Once in Atlanta, Sherman moved swiftly to stamp out any possible civilian resistance. He ordered all the city's 3,500 remaining civilians to be evacuated. Here was banishment on the grandest scale, terror that would resonate across the Confederacy. As he had in Jackson, he ordered the burning of all war-related facilities, with instructions to the provost guard to shoot anyone burning any other properties. But as would happen in towns in the next year, issuing orders did not guarantee compliance by those in the ranks, especially when liquored up. As Connolly recorded on November 15: "Drunken soldiers on foot and on horseback raced up and down the streets while the buildings on either side were solid sheets of flame. . . . The night, for miles around as bright as mid-day; the city of Atlanta was one mass of flame."[38] The unsurprising result was the torching of many private dwellings and businesses. In all, perhaps 40 percent of the city burned. Atlanta was just the culmination in Georgia of Sherman's strategy of punitive burnings which he had first instituted in Memphis two years earlier. Burning became the routine way of avoiding the cumbersome task of actual occupation of a conquered Confederate town or city. Sherman did not give explicit orders, but he expected it to happen. Indeed, he made clear that the South deserved no better. He intended his army to be an avenging one which brought fearsome retribution to the region for the terrible war the South had started.

MISSOURI CAMPAIGN

For the Confederacy, Sterling Price's invasion of Missouri in September of 1864 was a ray of hope that the South's fortunes could be reversed. Price led his army of 12,000 troops, and an irregular group of several hundred guerrillas, whose specific mission was to take revenge for Rosecrans's General Order No. 11. That order had been Rosecrans's attempt to undermine guerrilla activity which had gotten increasingly worse as the war approached its fourth year. As Price's army headed north, the guerrillas sowed terror through southern Missouri, by raping Black females and murdering military invalids. Rosecrans accordingly dispatched Tom Ewing to investigate. Ewing went unaccompanied to Fort Davidson at Pilot Knob, some eighty-six miles south of St. Louis. The fort had a garrison of 800.

When Price learned that Ewing was at the fort, he abandoned his plans to move on St. Louis and instead put the fort under siege. When Price positioned his eighteen cannons atop Shepherd's Mountain, which gave them an excellent command of the fort, Lt. David Murphy's garrison artillery made quick work of the Confederate guns. Even with his artillery no longer a factor, Price decided to have 7,000 of his force charge the fort in waves. Five times Price sent troops forward to gain the fort, only to be turned back. Hundreds of Confederates fell. When some of the defenders ran out of ammunition, they turned to rocks to repel their attackers. A couple hundred of the Union defenders were casualties; Price lost more than a thousand. That night, around

3 a.m., the Union garrison stole out of the fort, their wagon wheels padded to absorb the sound. They were ten miles west of Fort Davidson before Price realized that the federals had slipped away. They continued westward, in a driving rain, collecting people, Black and white, who might be the guerrillas' next victims. The Confederates eventually caught up to them, but Murphy's field guns kept them at bay. In less than forty hours they had covered sixty-six miles, most of that time with Confederates pressing their rear. Finally reaching Leasburg, they decided to make their last stand, if help did not reach them.

Having sent a messenger on to St. Louis for help, Ewing directed the construction of a breastworks, composed of boxcars and railroad ties. For hours, Ewing's 500 kept repelling the Confederate probes. When their attackers demanded their surrender, they broke into "The Battle Cry of Freedom." Finally, a Union relief column forced the Confederates to withdraw. Pilot Knob and Leasburg had weakened Price's army to the point that they had done all the fighting they intended to do. Confederate military operations, either regular or guerrilla, largely ceased in the Western Theater.[39]

A NEW HERO EMERGES
IN THE VALLEY

At July's beginning, Jubal Early had led his corps down the Valley to invade Maryland for the third straight summer. After extorting kings' ransoms from officials in Hagerstown and Frederick, Early's army had gotten to Washington's outskirts, only to determine that federal reinforcements had made any capture of the capital less than a remote possibility. By the third week of July, Jubal Early was back in Virginia, where, on July 23, he defeated a federal force at Kernstown, in which Col. James Mulligan, leading the Illinois Twenty-Third, was among the Union fatalities. Six days later, Early sent cavalry brigades into Maryland and Pennsylvania, to Cumberland and Chambersburg respectively, where they were to demand ransoms of $500,000 to spare the towns. In Cumberland the Confederate troopers were prevented by local militia from carrying out their mission. At Chambersburg, when town officials failed to come up with the half-million-dollar ransom fee, the Confederate contingent proceeded to burn the town. They left a business section in ruins and hundreds of the townspeople homeless.[40] The shocking arson outraged the northern public and led Ulysses Grant to consolidate all the Union forces in the Valley under Philip Sheridan.

The bantam Sheridan (perhaps five foot five inches in height), was the thirty-three-year-old son of pre-famine Irish immigrants, who had settled in

Somerset, Ohio. The Sheridans were parishioners at St. Joseph's Church in Somerset, to which the Ewing family often traveled from nearby Lancaster to attend Sunday Mass. In 1848, the Ewings were instrumental in securing an appointment to West Point for Phil Sheridan. During the first year of the war, Sheridan was confined to desk jobs in Missouri. Then, through Cump Sherman's recommendation, Sheridan became a brigade commander of cavalry. His battlefield success under General William Rosecrans led to his promotion to division commander of cavalry by the fall of 1862. From Stones River to Missionary Ridge, he continued to distinguish himself as an indefatigable leader under the most extreme pressure. By the spring of 1864 he was put in charge of the cavalry corps of the Army of the Potomac. In appointing him to lead the new Army of the Valley, Grant instructed him to "Follow [Early] to the death," and eliminate the Shenandoah Valley as a breadbasket for the Confederacy.[41]

Sheridan's new army combined nearly 50,000 infantry and cavalry, a force three times larger than the troops Jubal Early commanded. Despite his numerical advantage, Sheridan was initially cautious about engaging Early, knowing that another Union defeat could have a ruinous effect upon Lincoln's reelection prospects. Reading Sheridan's caution as timidity, Early became all the bolder, despite his army's exhaustion from having marched more than 800 miles and fought seventeen battles in less than two months. The Louisiana Sixth could count on no more than fifty effectives. Nearly four times that number were missing. Some were stragglers, but the vast majority seem to have been deserters. Early may have still been committed to prosecuting the war as best he could, but lots of his men were not. The limits of human endurance and the lure of home were leading more and more of Early's corps to walk away from the war. When Richmond recalled one of Early's divisions, his situation became bleaker.

Days later, Early paid the price for his underrating of Sheridan at the Third Battle of Winchester on September 19, in which Sheridan executed a joint cavalry-infantry attack which quickly routed Early's outnumbered, underequipped army.[42] Early lost nearly a quarter of his 15,000 men, 2,000 of them as Union captives. Three days later at Fisher's Hill, twenty miles below Winchester, Early entrenched on the jagged ridge to dare Sheridan to attack. George Crook, commanding the Eighth Corps, proposed leading his corps on a nighttime skirting of the Confederate right through dense woods and ravines to flank Early's left and rear. Sheridan approved. The next day, September 22, as two Union corps feinted a frontal attack, Crook's corps struck from the left and rear of the Confederates. The result was an even more thorough routing, with Early's army fleeing up the Valley some sixty miles to save themselves.[43] In the wake of the second victory in four days, Grant wired Sheridan: "Keep on and your work will cause the fall of Richmond."[44]

In mid-October, Phil Sheridan departed for Washington to consult officials. His army was camped at Cedar Creek, fifteen miles south of Winchester. Amid a predawn fog on October 19, 9,000 Confederates suddenly struck Sheridan's left. Within a couple of hours two of Sheridan's corps, some 20,000 troops, were reeling in panic toward the Potomac. Once again, a Confederate army was its own worst enemy. Savoring the spoils of victory in the Union camp, the Confederates allowed Sheridan's army the chance, not only to survive but to counterattack. Sheridan, who had arrived back in Winchester the previous evening, reached the battlefield in midmorning. Waving his hat wildly and exhorting his panicking troops to stand and fight, Phil Sheridan effected one of the most dramatic transformations of a battlefield during the war. In a devastating counterattack, the Union troops gained the decisive victory that drove the Confederates nearly thirty miles below Winchester. The casualties for Sheridan's army were twice those of Early's, but that seemed a price well worth paying. Early's corps had been eliminated as an effective force.[45] If there had been any residual doubt about Lincoln's reelection, after Sherman's taking of Atlanta and Tom Ewing's repulse of Price in Missouri, Phil Sheridan's overwhelming victory at Cedar Creek dissipated it entirely. Three Catholic generals from St. Joseph's Parish in eastern Ohio had been the catalysts of the decisive turn that the war took as summer turned to fall.

"PERSONAL SECURITY AND PROPERTY, THE CORINTHIAN PILLARS OF CONSTITUTIONAL LIBERTY"

Ten days after the fall of Atlanta on September 1, 1864, the *Pilot* still judged the state of the country to be bleak: "our currency deranged; the necessaries of life at such fabulous figures, that starvation almost impends over the heads of the masses; the good will of Europe gone; our foreign credit far less than that of the Confederates; and above all, . . . an agrarian sentimental policy which seeks to exalt a degraded, inferior race into equality with the white race, and to tear down personal security and property, the Corinthian pillars of Constitutional liberty."[46] Three and a half years into the war, nearly two years after Lincoln first announced the Emancipation Proclamation, and with an amendment before the Congress that would abolish slavery outright, the *Pilot* maintained that such steps toward abolition represented grave threats to our "Constitutional liberty," inasmuch as the respect for property rights, even where the property was human, was simply crucial toward maintaining the security and independence of the white race for whom this republic existed. Nothing guaranteed white supremacy like the chattel slavery which kept an inferior race in bondage *in perpetuum*. This was what the paper for the Archdiocese of Boston, the city that was the nerve center of the abolitionist movement, stated without censure, four months before the passage of the Thirteenth Amendment by the Congress.

The *Pilot* spoke for most Catholic papers and for millions of Catholics. Still, the war had changed the thinking of some Catholics, as the Sherman/Ewing families well illustrate. Cump Sherman, who regarded slavery as the natural state for Blacks, whom he considered to be inferior beings, came to be the outlier in the family which had adopted him. Sherman's foster father, Thomas Ewing, during his long service in the federal government, had championed antislavery legislation and colonization, as well as opposing the spread of slavery in the territories.[47] Cump's foster brother, Hugh Ewing, underwent a sea change in his views on slavery in the course of his war experience. Hugh came to recognize the essential immorality of slavery, and to deplore those in the church who vigorously defended it. When Hugh was stationed in western Virginia, he, with the help of his father, began transferring runaway slaves to Ohio. He wrote his wife, Henrietta, of an old southern Maryland slave-owning family: "slavery . . . is shattering the whole continent in its horrible struggles. Now, I say, in the name of Almighty God who abhors it let it die and disturb the world no more." If he had to give up his own life to achieve abolition, Hugh was ready to do so. Such conviction eventually made an abolitionist, if a reluctant one, of Henrietta. It also persuaded his father-in-law, back in southern Maryland, to transform his own bonded labor force from slaves to wage-earning workers.[48] Cump's own wife, Ellen, had become an abolitionist, indeed an advocate of hard war, partially as an instrument of emancipation.[49]

THE ELECTION AS
PLEBISCITE

For the Republican Party the election became "a national plebiscite on the war and the future of slavery in America." Slavery, the party's platform charged, was an institution fundamentally hostile to the principles upon which this republic had been founded. The two could not continue to coexist.[50] On September 1, New York Democrats launched the McClellan campaign with a rally at City Hall. Judge Charles Daly assured the throng that, under a President McClellan, peace could finally be negotiated with an exhausted South that would include the preservation of slavery. Democrats, he went on, unlike their political rivals, fully recognized that the federal government had no right, under the Constitution, to interfere with any domestic institution, including the South's peculiar one.[51] The judge became an elector for McClellan in New York State.[52]

The *Catholic Telegraph* predictably backed Lincoln, as did Orestes Brownson, after his initial choice, Frémont, dropped his challenge to the incumbent.[53] For most Catholics, McClellan was the only choice, the only hope for restoring the Union in accord with the Constitution.[54] The *Metropolitan Record* made no attempt to hide its antiwar position. The paper urged voters to choose not only McClellan, but Democrats all down the ballot. Once Democrats regained control of the national and state governments across the North, they could simply effect a cease-fire by refusing to supply any further men or funding for the war.[55]

By the end of October, deep frustration overtook many Catholics as they realized the inevitability of Lincoln's reelection. In its last edition before the election, the *Catholic Mirror* fatalistically contended that the divisive question of abolition had destroyed the brotherhood which had created the American Republic. Lincoln and the abolitionists might prevail in the election and in the war, but they had done so at the cost of the Republic itself.[56] For Marie Daly the times were "so out of joint," the country gone so mad that she could scarcely bring herself to keep her diary.[57] On election eve, Daly could only bring herself to write: "all good citizens must wish it over."[58]

In New York City, James McMaster was still working in tandem with Confederate agents to force a peace settlement, by whatever means it would take.[59] Three years earlier the editor of the *Freeman's Journal* had been imprisoned for assaulting a US marshal who had come to arrest him for his intemperate criticism of the Lincoln administration. Prison proved to be a radicalizing experience for McMaster, who remained a month at Fort Lafayette in New York Harbor, before taking an oath of allegiance under protest. Upon his return to the *Journal*, the editor excoriated Lincoln's war as "the most unholy and destructive" one in which the country had ever engaged."[60] By February of 1863, McMaster was calling for an armistice, even if putting it into place should require a violent overthrow of the current government.[61]

Charles Martin, the Baltimorean working as a Confederate operative in Toronto, was sent in the fall of 1864 to New York City to lead the operation there. McMaster informed Martin that, on election day, some 20,000 armed men were ready to set fires in buildings across the city to create the chaos needed for the insurgents to take control of the government buildings in the city and to release the Confederate prisoners being held at Fort Lafayette. McMaster indicated that "the city authorities were our friends." Once the city had been subdued, a convention would be held in the city, at which delegates from New York, New Jersey, and the New England states would form a Northeast Confederacy. Then, the evening before the election, James McMaster informed Martin that the arrival of 10,000 federal troops in the city had forced a postponement of the uprising.

MCCLELLAN'S

CATHOLIC ENCLAVE

Despite a persistent rain that fell across much of the North on Election Day, nearly 74 percent of eligible voters turned out, a remarkable testament to the breadth of civic engagement in nineteenth-century America, but far below the 81.2 percent of the electorate who had turned out four years earlier. The Democratic defeat was a thorough one, not only at the presidential level but the congressional one as well. All the Democratic gains made in the fall of 1862 were now wiped out, as Democrats lost thirty-eight seats.[62] In the twenty-five states that participated in the election, Lincoln won nearly 55 percent of the votes cast. One cohort that the president failed to carry was the Catholic one. In New York City, McClellan doubled Lincoln's total vote.[63] In some heavily Irish areas of Manhattan, McClellan took 90 percent of the vote.[64] In Maryland, where 2 percent of the electorate had supported Lincoln in 1860, now 55 percent did. But not in southern Maryland, where the president got but 14 percent. Indeed, McClellan carried a majority of Maryland counties, many of which were in Confederate-leaning, Catholic-rich areas in southern Maryland and the Eastern Shore.[65]

The evening before November 25, the new date set for the Copperhead uprising in New York, James McMaster wrote Charles Martin, "We have decided to withdraw from any further connection with the proposed revolution." The editor declared that their "revolution . . . was foredoomed to failure."[66] Martin proceeded on his own to deploy Greek fire in the rooms which Confederate agents had rented in six New York hotels in lower Manhattan. The closed rooms proved an effective deterrent against any spread of the fire. No one died. The day after the fire, more than a score of Copperheads were arrested, including James McMaster. Martin and company managed to get back to Toronto, but the plot that had started as a grand plan to establish a new Confederacy in the Northeast ended as farce.[67]

THE FALL OF
SAVANNAH

As part of the Union troops that stormed Fort McAllister outside of Savannah on December 13, the Irish Legion had to navigate the ditch in front of the fort. They could see clearly the stakes planted at the bottom of the moat. What they could not see is whether they were torpedoes. When the order came to charge, all thought of torpedoes disappeared in the rush. Within fifteen minutes the bastion was in Union hands. Twenty-four of the attackers were dead. The "stakes" had indeed been torpedoes.[68]

P. G. T. Beauregard, still vague about Cump Sherman's actual itinerary (he thought Augusta was one of his targets on the way to the sea), had made contingency plans for evacuating the garrisons at the key Georgia cities, including Savannah. At his provisional headquarters in Charleston, Beauregard received word from Hardee that Sherman was approaching the city. Beauregard immediately headed, by rail and wagon, for Savannah, some forty-five miles to the south. Upon his arrival, on December 16, Beauregard took charge of the immediate withdrawal of the 10,000-man garrison.[69] The Savannah City Council, including Catholic members Christopher Casey, John O'Byrne, and John Villalonga, formally surrendered the city to Sherman days later.[70]

Cump Sherman had vehemently resisted having Black soldiers in the ranks of his army. As he had told his wife nearly two years earlier, "I would prefer to have this a white man's war."[71] On the March through Georgia, a growing mass of African Americans flocked behind his army. By the time Sherman approached Savannah, there were more than 10,000 of them. At Ebenezer Creek, a tributary of the Savannah River, Union engineers had built a pontoon bridge for the XX Corps to cross the creek. Once the troops were over, Brig. Gen. Jefferson C. Davis ordered the engineers to disassemble the bridge, leaving thousands of Blacks on the west side of the body of water. Scores subsequently died from drowning or at the hands of Confederate cavalry.[72] Once Sherman reached Savannah, at the insistence of Secretary of War Stanton, he begrudgingly integrated Black soldiers into his army but limited their service to the kind of menial labor which Blacks had routinely provided for the Confederates. To Sherman's Black regiments would fall the daunting task of constructing the roads upon which the army would make its way northward. The general's attitude toward Black soldiers set the example for the whites in his army, resulting in harassment and riots that produced several deaths and many injuries.

At Stanton's prodding, Sherman also agreed to meet with twenty prominent freedmen of Savannah, mostly Methodist and Baptist preachers. The Special Field Order No. 15 that followed the meeting almost surely originated with Stanton, although issued over Sherman's name. The order established a system of redistributing land seized from slavers in the amount of forty acres to each Black male adult. How ironic that this order encompassing the most revolutionary measure regarding the economic status of the former slaves should have borne the name of William Tecumseh Sherman, who had so opposed abolition, and even more any measure to promote Black economic independence.

CHAPTER 17

Final Campaigns

From the Carolinas to Appomattox

General Sherman dismounted and entered the Churchyard where
the Mother Superior . . . came forward to meet him. . . . "Ah, Sister these
are times in which to practice Christian fortitude and patience."
"You have made them thus to us, General," she replied.

—ANNALS OF THE URSULINE COMMUNITY
IN COLUMBIA, SC, FEBRUARY 1865

PROSPECTS FOR THE
CONFEDERACY

As 1865 opened, Bishop John McGill of Richmond petitioned Abraham Lincoln for permission to pass through the Union lines in order to sail from a
northern port for Rome, to fulfil his episcopal duty of making a personal
report to the pope every ten years. As he wrote President Lincoln in January,
he had applied for this permission two years earlier, but had been refused.
This time McGill secured the permission.[1] By the late winter of 1865, unlike
the spring of 1863 or even of 1864, the war's end was clearly in sight. No Confederate bishop in Rome was going to change that reality in the slightest.
No more than any released prisoners would change the battlefield calculus.
General Grant had authorized the release of most of the prisoners precisely
because he realized that the Confederacy was beyond any redemption that
the freed captives could bring for its collapsing armies. Among the Confederates transiting Baltimore was John Dooley, released from Johnson's Island.
As Dooley and his seven hundred ex–prison mates marched from the train
depot to the wharf where a steamer awaited to transport them to Virginia,
they spontaneously began shouting, as though to compensate for the silence
of the streets, a stark contrast to the supportive crowds that had gathered
early in the war to greet Confederate prisoners.[2]

In Richmond, Stephen Mallory had given Raphael Semmes command of the James River Fleet, which consisted of three ironclads and five wooden ships, bottled up at Drewry's Bluff. Visits with President Davis and General Lee left Semmes with the impressions that the president was losing touch with reality and that the general knew all too well the dire state of the Confederacy but could do nothing to change it.[3] In late January, Mallory, sharing the belief among Confederate officials that breaking Grant's siege was their only hope of survival, sent Semmes with his naval squadron down the James River to disperse the federal fleet at City Point and destroy Grant's giant depot, the lifeline of the Union troops manning the trenches from Richmond to Petersburg. That desperate effort predictably proved a futile one as the ships were easily repulsed before they could reach their target.[4]

On February 3, aboard the steamer *River Queen* at Hampton Roads, Confederate representatives had proposed to President Lincoln that an armistice be declared, during which a convention of all the states could be called to work out a peace settlement. Lincoln dashed that prospect with his response that the only option for the Confederacy was surrender. If the seceded states returned to the Union, Lincoln promised generous pardons for those who had rebelled and possible compensation for slaveowners. Slavery as well as the rebellion itself, Lincoln informed them, was doomed.[5] When the Confederate representatives reported back to the Davis administration the terms Lincoln had proposed, Davis and most of his government immediately rejected them. Stephen Mallory, for one, thought it a great mistake. "It should have been peace," he later wrote. "I . . . knew that we could hold out no longer than Grant chose to permit us & that we ought to make peace upon the best terms we could obtain."[6]

The frustration over the unsuccessful conference was hardly confined to some Confederates. During the last week of February, James Longstreet received a note from Edward O. C. Ord, now commanding the Army of the James. Ord asked for a meeting with Longstreet, whom he knew from their days together, beginning at West Point. The meeting was purportedly about pickets engaging in bartering, but when the pair subsequently met, it became clear that Ord had a more important topic in mind: a peace settlement. Ord explained that the recent meeting between President Lincoln and Confederate representatives at Hampton Roads on February 3 had shown that "the politicians of the North were afraid to touch the question of peace, and there was no way to open the subject except through officers of the armies."[7] Ord obviously was not happy about Lincoln's refusal to consider any other terms for peace short of the rebelling states' returning to the Union and submitting to Lincoln's Emancipation Proclamation.[8] Ord claimed to be speaking for other senior officers, including Grant, who felt "the war had gone on long enough; that we should come together as former comrades and friends and talk a little."[9] It was as though a time machine had transported the combatants back to the Peninsula of 1862, and George McClellan was still commanding the Army of the Potomac. But Ord's proposal went further than anything McClellan had contemplated as he had moved toward Richmond nearly three years earlier. Ord proposed that there should be a mutual decision to suspend hostilities. Then Grant and Lee should meet. And not only the top general in each army. Ord wanted Grant's wife, Lucy, and Longstreet's wife, Louise, to exchange visits, accompanied by military escorts. Through this mix of extended conversations, Ord envisioned the emergence of terms of negotiation "honorable to both sides."[10] Longstreet took the proposal to Lee and Secretary of War Breckinridge, who supported Ord's proposal. A second meeting with Ord on February 28 ended with Longstreet agreeing to have Lee write to Grant proposing that they meet with the intention of developing positions which could be submitted to a military convention for arbitration. The alumni of West Point would get to determine the fate of the divided country. In the event, Grant put a quick end to the fantasy by telling Lee that only the president of the United States had the authority to agree to such a convention.[11]

SHERMAN
IN THE CAROLINAS

On New Year's Eve, Cump Sherman had received a letter from the US Army chief of staff, Henry Halleck, in which Halleck praised him for his remarkable march through Georgia but warned him that "a certain class . . . says that you have manifested an almost criminal dislike of the negro, and that you are not willing to carry out the wishes of the government in regard to him." Although there was no evidence that Sherman had been behind General Davis's dismantling of the bridge earlier that month that stranded frantic Blacks attempting to follow the army to freedom, blame for the tragedy nonetheless fell on him. Such accusations little disturbed Sherman, who was absorbed with the planning of his next leg of the odyssey that had brought him over 370 miles from Chattanooga to Savannah.

Ulysses Grant initially urged Sherman to transport his army by ship to Virginia, where his troops could combine with Grant's to defeat the last significant rebel army standing between them and the end of the war. Sherman thought otherwise. He proposed that his army continue the scorched-earth march that it had just made through Georgia, only this time the Carolinas would be its pathway of plunder and destruction. The ultimate objective—joining forces with the Army of the Potomac to end the conflict—remained the same. The means of getting to Virginia, over land rather than by sea, would enable Sherman to continue the punitive measures his army had been executing since Atlanta to destroy the will of the southern people to resist federal authority any longer. Grant had serious doubts about the feasibility of such another extensive march, given the horrendous condition of the roads in the Carolinas in full winter. In the end, Grant went along. What the Army of the Tennessee had accomplished over the past months had earned Sherman the benefit of any doubts.

When Sherman's grand army started out of Savannah toward Charleston in January, it confirmed the fear of most Carolinians. Charleston, after all, was widely regarded as the heart of the rebellion. But that initial move proved a feint. The main body of Sherman's troops headed for the upcountry. Columbia, as the site of the first ordinance of secession, was to be the major target of the retribution that the federals intended to visit upon the state that had started the whirlwind of events that had produced the war. For Sherman, subduing Columbia was more than a matter of vengeance. "I suspect," he wrote Ulysses Grant, "that Jeff. Davis will move heaven and earth to catch me, for . . . Richmond is not more vital to his cause than Columbia and the heart of South Carolina."[12]

Constructing roads through the swampy low country for the army of vindication proved an immense task, involving the felling of trees to provide a foundation for the corduroy roads that often required several tiers of logs to provide a sustainable pathway. Sherman was fortunate to have as his chief engineer General John Newton, who had been with him since Chattanooga, and as his labor force the Black soldiers who had been forced upon him. To the stunned consternation of the Confederate authorities, who were sure that the flooded rivers, swamps, and impassable winter roads would bog down Sherman's army as no opposing Confederates had been able to do, Sherman's troops made their way north at a remarkable pace, thanks to Newton and his Black road layers.

BURNING OF COLUMBIA

Meanwhile, Beauregard plotted a defense against Sherman's anticipated invasion of South Carolina. In keeping with President Davis's policy of comprehensive protection, Beauregard laid out a line of over a hundred miles, from

Augusta to Charleston, for the available thirty-three thousand Confederate troops to defend. It was a design for failure, but, given the circumstances, Beauregard hardly had other options. When Sherman subsequently concentrated his sixty-thousand army on the taking of the South Carolina capital, Beauregard, who had come to the city to take personal charge of its defense, reluctantly ordered the small defense force to withdraw. Columbia was at Sherman's mercy, which proved not a good thing at all.[13]

As the XV Corps marched into the city, they sang: "Hail, Columbia, happy land. If I don't burn you, I'll be damned."[14] Shortly after the Union Army occupied the city on the morning of February 17, a federal major, a Catholic, rode up to the Ursuline convent. He warned the nuns that "Columbia is a doomed city," and offered his assistance in helping them seek safety. Mother Baptista Lynch sent a note by him to General Sherman. Somehow, she knew that the general had a child at the Ursuline academy in Brown County, Ohio. She informed the general that she herself had taught at that academy and was seeking his personal protection of the Ursuline institution in Columbia. As Sherman remembered the incident, he instructed his brother-in-law, Col. Thomas Ewing, to assure the nun that he did not intend to destroy any private property in Columbia. The Catholic major returned to the convent and academy with a special guard: seven Protestants whom the Catholic officer assured the nuns would be the best protection they could possibly have.[15]

Two years before, Columbians had vowed to burn their city rather than have the Yankees occupy it. When the Yankees finally came, burn it did, originating, as vowed, in pyrrhic defiance, and carried to its apocalyptic consequences by random terror. Bluecoats, left to their drunken, revengeful devices by superiors taking their cue from General Sherman's contentment to let the Columbians experience the horrors of hard war and thus hasten its end, spread the blaze until it threatened to consume the city itself. As the inferno neared convent and academy, the Ursulines' guard disappeared, soon to be replaced by soldiers torching and plundering the building. Nuns and students, with what possessions they could frantically carry with them, huddled in the graveyard of the parish church two blocks away. At three a.m. they watched the fire topple the cupola of the convent, completing its destruction. By the morning the Ursuline complex was part of at least a third of the city that lay in ruins.[16]

When Columbia burned upon Sherman's entrance into the city, it was the last straw that doomed Beauregard's last active command. Richmond, still not appreciating the terrible efficiency of Sherman's innovative means of sustaining an invasion over unprecedented distances at startling speeds by living off the land, effectively put the blame on Beauregard for the stunning success that Sherman continued to enjoy on the latest leg of his march across Georgia and the Carolinas. After four months heading the Military Division of the West, Beauregard was superseded by Joe Johnston on Washington's Birthday. Compounding the hurt, Davis kept Beauregard in the Western Theater, now once again Joe Johnston's subordinate.[17]

ON TO NORTH CAROLINA

Sherman's army burned and looted its way north to the border, although on a smaller scale than in the capital. At Cheraw, which they reached on March 4, the day of Lincoln's second inauguration, Sherman, not wanting a replication of Columbia, stationed guards "everywhere," according to Lieutenant White of the Illinois Ninetieth. Nonetheless, there was destruction, including that of the shoe factory of Francis Lynch. His North Carolina tanyard also fell victim to the scorched-earth policy of the conquering federals. The pastor of St. Peter's Church in Cheraw had $500 in gold on his person, as a bargaining chip should he be taken prisoner, as he feared he would. Soldiers did not arrest him but took the gold, as well as his watch.[18] The troops' widespread lethal path took them to Bishop Lynch's upcountry Malta Plantation as well. Bummers among Sherman's advance cavalry ransacked and burned the mansion. When the plantation overseer, Claudian Northrop, refused their demand for money and valuables, they hanged him, as his wife looked on in horror.[19] Her sister's mansion had also been torched, leaving her homeless. With no shelter available, the sister and a friend set out for the only place they could think of as a refuge, St. Joseph's Academy in Emmitsburg, Maryland, where she and the friend's mother had studied. So they proceeded, presumably in a wagon, with their three children, two of whom were but months old, and, more than a month later, arrived on a Sunday morning at the convent's academy, where they shared the nightmares from which they had fled in South Carolina.[20]

The Connecticut Ninth, now on garrison duty in Savannah, participated in the celebration of St. Patrick's Day, a tradition of long standing in the city. The Ninth marched along with the Jasper Greens in honoring the patron saint of Ireland, proving that devotion to homeland conquered all, at least on the seventeenth of March.[21] The same celebration of reconciliation took place in Charleston, where the local members of the St. Patrick's Benevolent Society paraded along with Irish of the occupying federal army.[22]

On March 19 at Bentonville, North Carolina, Joe Johnston, once again in command of what remained of the Army of Tennessee, made a last-ditch attempt to stop Cump Sherman's juggernaut by attacking one wing of his dispersed army with his skeletal force of 17,000. After initial success, Johnston's attack was blunted as the federals dug in, awaiting reinforcements. When the battle resumed on March 21, the XX Corps drove in the Confederates' right wing, but Sherman chose to let Johnston withdraw, rather than pursuing his broken force which had suffered more than twice the casualties (3,500 to 1,500) during the three days of combat. As he had at Atlanta and Savannah, Sherman refused to engage in an all-out battle against a foe on his last legs.[23]

SENSING THE END

John Dooley arrived home in the first week of March. He encountered a besieged Richmond in a shrinking Confederacy. His family and friends were even more despondent than he was about their country's fate. By St. Patrick's Day, food had become too expensive for the average citizen to acquire: Flour at $1,200 a barrel, Eggs $24 for a dozen, pork $18 a pound, butter $25 a pound.[24] As the Confederate Army in the Richmond-Petersburg trenches shrank daily from desertions, disease, and the random hits of sharpshooters and mortars, a pervasive gloom spread across the South. Despite the siege having reduced the Confederacy to a virtual city-state, the government, in desperation, turned to traditional staples of morale-boosting by holding mass meetings and military reviews, as though such citizen participation and parades would revitalize a people, against all odds, to somehow find the will and means to defeat an enemy on the brink of a final conquest. On March 21, Dooley managed to make his way to the surreal spectacle of Pickett's Division staging a grand review south of the capital against the backdrop of the catastrophe that was gathering.

Six thousand troops, in battle formation, with Generals Longstreet, Pickett, and Breckinridge reviewing, paraded before a fair representation of Richmond's polite society, mostly women, with the occasional male escort. A steady rain that became heavy at times did not diminish the excitement of the spectators, forced as it might have been. Dooley was able to visit with members of the First Virginia, whom he had not seen since his capture at Gettysburg, some twenty-one months ago. They informed him that they expected to change their base of operations very soon. Robert E. Lee was planning to shift the theater west and south of the Valley in a desperate gambit to create a viable military force out of the remnants of the two major armies of the Confederacy: the Army of Northern Virginia and the Army of Tennessee.

At the Treasury Department, Margaret Loughborough and what she deemed the "cream of Richmond society" now comprised the largely female staff.[25] Her supervisor had secretly instructed her in November of 1864 to prepare for a sudden evacuation of the capital. It was, she wrote in her diary, "a sad, sad winter. . . . the women who had made Richmond gay, Senators, Cabinet Ministers wives, had left the City." Through her mother-in-law in Washington, she managed to secure a pass from the Lincoln administration. Finally in March, wearing shoes her husband had forced a sutler to sell him for $250 in soon-to-be worthless Confederate money, she left City Point on a large flatboat, to the sound of rockets firing over the siege lines. Reaching Baltimore, she went to Archbishop Martin Spalding's residence to deliver a copy of Bishop John McGill's book, *Our Faith, the Victory.* The archbishop asked her "how can the poor South succeed, they have nothing, here, this Army has everything." The ever-defiant Loughborough wishfully responded that the Confederate soldiers just fought more fiercely, the hungrier they got.[26]

Our Faith, the Victory: Or a Comprehensive View of the Principal Doctrines of the Christian Religion was, as its subtitle stated, a catechetical volume for the church in the South. But its title revealed the bishop's resignation to the imminent collapse of the Confederacy to which he had so totally committed himself and the resources of his diocese. To Confederate Catholics facing the incalculable loss that defeat brings, McGill was offering them the consolation of their faith as the prize, the triumph that no army could deny them, the victory that endured. But the bishop was also offering a jeremiad for his imperiled country. The collapse of the Confederacy, he wrote, was very likely God's judgment for the evils that government had failed to address. None was worse than the utter disregard for the marriage rights of the enslaved, by allowing slavers total autonomy in separating families by sales and other abuses. Bishop McGill concluded: "It would appear that, by the present convulsions, his providence is preparing for them at least a recognition of these rights as [belonging to] immortal beings."[27] By very different paths, John McGill and John Purcell had arrived at the same conclusion, although the Richmond bishop may not have owned it: that in the emancipation of the slaves, God's justice was being done.

On March 27, John Dooley noted in his diary: "Genl Lee announces that he assaulted two of the enemies lines—took 600 prisoners and the artillery which he spiked *not being able* to hold his position but bringing back to his own lines the prisoners and *light field* pieces captured. Genl Lee never lies."[28] Lee indeed was not lying. Nor was he reporting the whole story with its grim repercussions for the Confederacy. With desertions spiking, morale sinking by the day, and the threat of a Union assault growing with spring's arrival, Lee had made a desperate attempt to break the siege by having a third of his effectives assault Fort Stedman, a Union redoubt just east of Petersburg, on March 25. In the predawn the Louisiana Brigade, shrunken as it was to barely four hundred men, was chosen to lead Gordon's corps by posing as deserters or otherwise disarming the pickets. By daylight Gordon's attackers held a half-mile of the federal trenches, including several hundred captives, seventeen cannon and mortars. But the Confederates could not successfully expand their breach, and a Union counterattack regained the lost portion by 7 a.m. The Confederates lost about a quarter of their assault force, about five thousand men, most of them taken captive. In an army which had been hemorrhaging men for months, that was a loss it could ill afford.

John Dooley had learned from the captain of his former company that the First Virginia would soon be relocated to the Lynchburg area. Dooley, being a parolee, was not permitted to rejoin his units until his parole expired, in early April. So, on March 30, Dooley and a fellow parolee headed by train to Lynchburg, supposedly to visit a former prison mate, but likely to be in position to link up with their regiments when the army relocated westward.[29]

THE BEGINNING OF
THE END

As John Dooley headed to Lynchburg, Phil Sheridan was finalizing plans for his infantry-cavalry attack on Five Forks, a critical juncture at the extreme right of the Confederate line southwest of Petersburg. On March 31, he struck. Robert E. Lee countered with George Pickett's two divisions. Pickett, having but one-fourth the troops that Sheridan sent against them, nonetheless drove Warren's Fifth Corps back in disorder in a persistent rain before reinforcements stopped the Confederate momentum and regained much of the lost ground. When morning passed into afternoon the next day with no renewal of the Union offensive, some in the Confederate line took the lack of action to be an April Fool's joke. By 4 p.m. they knew better, as Sheridan sent cavalry and the Fifth Corps to seize the White Oak Road, which served as a main link for the Army of Northern Virginia. Sheridan himself was front and center of the troopers who cleared the Confederate bulwarks and, in short order, secured the area. About 2,500 Confederates surrendered. Some 650 were killed and wounded. The Confederate line had been broken. Grant that evening called for a general assault the next morning all along the siege line, from Richmond to Five Forks.[30]

This time there was no false lull before the storm. At 10 p.m., an hour after Grant's order, the Union artillery began to boom on the Petersburg portion of the siege line. For the next five hours, it continued. Then at 4:30 a.m. on April 2 came the all-out attack that Lee had long feared. Grant had more than 120,000 men to send against the skeletal force that Lee could muster. Success came more quickly in some places than others; in a few, not at all. The Second Maryland Battalion, at the far right of the Confederate line, found it a hopeless task to adequately fill the extensive portion it had been assigned with the 250 defenders it had available. They made a desperate resistance to the Union assault, but finally were overwhelmed with perhaps half surrendering while the remainder fled to join the general retreat.[31]

By the day's end, the Confederates all along the forty miles of lines had been driven into their inner fortifications. Lee had no choice but to evacuate the lines and head west in the hope of linking up with Joe Johnston's army. The order was given to move out quietly during the night of April 2–3.[32] The Louisiana Tigers were among those troops serving as a rear guard, while the army began its retreat toward Amelia Courthouse.[33]

In Richmond, the Daughters of Charity were preparing for their chaplain, Hippolyte Gache, to celebrate Mass in their hospital chapel when there was suddenly a deafening explosion that broke windows in the hospital and nearby buildings. Gache advised that it was best for him to distribute Communion to them immediately and then consume the remaining hosts himself. More explosions followed as priest and sisters hurriedly made their Communions and prepared for they knew not what.[34] The Confederate government was abandoning its capital and blowing up anything it deemed of value to the federal troops who would soon be occupying the city. When Gache made his way out to investigate, he encountered a firestorm which, "meeting with no resistance was rapidly spreading; the ominous murmur of the advancing flames, broken at intervals by the crashing of walls and roofs; the thick, choking billows of black smoke." Residents or looters frantically carried whatever they could manage from imperiled homes and businesses. "Everywhere there was grim silence, drawn faces and a sense of hopelessness and horror. . . . Then, like phantoms against the background of the burning city, the sudden appearance of the first Yankee cavalry scouts: they came galloping sword in hand and pistol in belt giving the impression, as they looked neither to the left nor to the right, that they were even more frightened than frightening."[35]

Jim Dooley was at home on Broad Street when he learned that the commercial district was burning. He raced to his father's hat shop to retrieve papers from the office above the shop. He was still in the process of collecting the papers when a mob began pounding on the door. Dooley managed to escape out the back entrance before the mob broke in to loot the establishment.

Both shop and plant were among the victims of the fire which destroyed some nine hundred businesses in the eighteen blocks of the old city which it ravaged.[36]

On Sunday, April 2, Henri Garidel had been at St. Peter's on Grace Street for the 10:30 Mass. When Mass finally ended around 12:30 p.m., Garidel went to his office to oversee some final packing. He had barely returned to his boardinghouse when news came that General Lee had ordered that the government evacuate the city as soon as possible.[37] Garidel raced down to the War Department only to find that there were not sufficient wagons to carry all the government personnel, along with the archives. Garidel had to wait until the next morning to take the 6 o'clock train from the city. When he reached there on Monday, April 3, his coworker had not yet shown, so Garidel decided to wait for him and catch the next train. Before the 7 a.m. train could depart, the announcement came that Yankee troops had entered the city. There would be no more train departures. Garidel made his way home, amid the windblown fire that had reduced the commercial sector of the city to ashes. "I have never seen such a disaster," was all Garidel could write in his diary.[38] The next morning, Garidel heard cannons firing a salute nearby. Outside, he saw a carriage drawn by four horses, carrying President Lincoln, with a cavalry escort, and followed "by the entire Negro population of Richmond. . . . their cheers were filling the air. I have never seen such an outpouring." Garidel went to Capitol Square, thinking that Lincoln would be there eventually, but so many Blacks were thronging the area that "I couldn't stand it. I went home, heartbroken."[39]

In the District of Columbia, at the Loughborough estate, Margaret Loughborough awoke on Monday morning, April 3, to the firing of cannon from adjacent Fort Reno as well as more distant forts. She awoke her sister-in-law to see if she knew what it meant. "Oh! Some Yankee lie," was the response. "When they want the North to think they are doing something, they pretend a victory." Not until they were at breakfast did they learn from a neighbor, a Confederate sympathizer, that Petersburg had fallen and that the Confederate government had evacuated Richmond. "We were miserable," Margaret remembered. Still, they could not bring themselves to trust the news, no matter what the papers were reporting.[40]

In Baltimore, John Abell Morgan wrote, "Much importance is attached to the downfall of Richmond. . . . In my judgment the war is by no means over as yet, though the next 30 days will show us what space of time will be required to end the struggle. There have been rejoicings and such like all this evening."[41] Three days later he noted: "This is a day of jubilee. All are requested to put out flags and to illuminate. Tonight the sight is grand from the roof of our house. Many persons did not illuminate."[42] Resistance to displaying celebratory signs of victory was particularly strong in the Mount Vernon Square area, in which Loyola College was located. That same day, April 3, William and Madge Preston made their way into Baltimore from their farm in Baltimore County. All the sights and sounds of celebration greeted them: from bells incessantly ringing, to the Stars and Stripes flying from seemingly every building, drums beating, newsboys shouting: "Richmond was taken!" "We are all sad enough tonight," Madge wrote in her diary, "knowing the terrible amount of suffering there is in the South at this time!"[43] Their inner selves had long known what the inevitable outcome of the suffocating siege of Petersburg and Richmond would be. Still, knowing it was bound to happen made it no less easy to accept when it finally did. Three days later the Prestons ventured out on Baltimore Street to see how fully the city's residents were participating in the official celebration of Richmond's fall. "We came to the conclusion," Madge wrote, "it was a very meager affair, and very little enthusiasm evidenced by the people."[44] They were likely seeing what they very much wanted to see.

At the Baltimore Carmelite Convent on Biddle Street, Mother Antonia Lynch tried, as gently as she could, to convey the grim tidings to her brother, Patrick, still in Europe. "Our friends in this city are at the present time making collections to relieve the sufferers in Charleston and Savannah but this prospect of a speedy subjugation of the South has made such a shock upon the money market that many merchants will not be able to meet their bills so they cannot be very liberal in their contributions. . . . I am afraid I am saying too much."[45]

"THE REBELLION IS ENDED"

In mid-March, the US Army called Joseph O'Hagan back to the field. He arrived by steamer on the Peninsula just as Grant finally broke through Lee's ever-thinning lines to take Petersburg and Richmond. Two times previously— from Sharpsburg and Gettysburg, Lee had successfully preserved his army from disaster by a rapid retreat into more hospitable territory. But 1865 was far different from 1862 or even 1863. For one, the army involved in the forced march was in far worse shape than in those previous years. Compounding matters were the 140 or more miles that this army needed to cover over mud roads to the hoped-for safety of a rendezvous in Danville with Joe Johnston's army, more than triple the distance they had had to traverse in Pennsylvania to reach the Potomac. Most important of all, Grant was no McClellan or Meade. The days in which the Army of the Potomac had, at best, pursued retreating Confederates with deliberation and caution were over. George Meade was still of that mind, once it was discovered that Lee's army had slipped out of their trenches on the night of April 3. Phil Sheridan characteristically wanted to complete the disabling of the storied Army of Northern Virginia by having the cavalry race ahead and cut off any escape route. As the Union forces pursued the retreating Confederates to Amelia Court House, 35 miles west of Richmond, Grant, overriding Meade, authorized Sheridan to get ahead of the enemy. With his cavalry, along with three infantry corps, Sheridan blocked the route to Danville, which forced Lee to head toward Lynchburg. On April 6, Sheridan's forces surrounded Ewell's corps, east of Farmville, some 45 miles east of Richmond, and attacked. After a futile attempt to break through, some 6,000 Confederates surrendered. Total Confederate losses surpassed 8,000. Among the Union mortal casualties was Gen. Thomas A. Smyth, who had commanded the Irish Brigade since the start of the Overland Campaign.[46]

By the time the Army of Northern Virginia reached the vicinity of Appomattox Court House, it had shrunk to fewer than 30,000 troops, far less than half the number of their pursuers. The Louisiana brigade, now reduced to fewer than 180 men, was part of John Gordon's attempt to break through the Union encirclement and provide a corridor of escape to the mountains. The Tigers, despite the great odds, had improbably opened a gap in the Union line when the order came to disengage. They soon learned the dismaying news (to most of them) that Lee had surrendered.[47]

One of the last casualties of the war was Colonel Matthew Murphy, the commander of the Irish Legion.[48] Among the surrendering Maryland Confederates were the Georgetown alumni Joseph Stonestreet and Francis X. Ward, whose reputed death during the Baltimore riot had inspired "Maryland My Maryland." William Dorsey's First Maryland Cavalry was having no part of any surrender ceremony. It managed to break through the Union encirclement and rode to the southwest to find other Confederate units and continue the struggle. Only an order from Brig. Gen. Thomas T. Munford forced the remnant of the Maryland Battalion to disband, with the encomium: "You, who struck the first blow in Baltimore and the last in Virginia, have done all that could be asked of you. Had the rest of our officers and men adhered to our cause with the same devotion, today we would have been free from the Yankees. May the God of battles bless you!"[49] Theodore J. Dimitry of Louisiana, whose brother, Alexander, had been killed during Early's Maryland campaign, deserted rather than surrender and made his way to Danville, where he became a member of the bodyguard of Jefferson Davis as the president kept moving his skeletal government southward in search of phantom armies that would save his dying republic.

That same Palm Sunday that marked the unofficial demise of the Army of Northern Virginia, Henri Garidel had attended the High Mass at the cathedral. The new sociopolitical order was all too evident, with five federal soldiers in the pew immediately in front of Garidel's, "praying great gusto." That evening he had just gotten into bed around 10 when cannon throughout Richmond began a hundred-gun salute in honor of Lee's surrender. The other overwhelming sound was the "shout of joy of the Negroes," which, to Garidel's ear, made "Richmond tremble as much as the cannon." Garidel had not the heart to rise from his bed. "I lay there," he wrote, "prey to very despairing thoughts."[50] When he awoke the next morning, the cannon were still booming. Garidel left the house "to see if anyone was going to arrest me." No one did. But it hardly improved his state of mind. He was particularly upset at the locals, particularly those of the business and industrial classes who had so quickly shifted their loyalty to protect their economic interests. That he still had no idea what lay in store for the Confederate bureaucracy, of which he was a part, only intensified his hostility toward these incipient scalawags. Three days later, Charles Dimitry brought him a copy of the loyalty oaths they would require former Confederate employees to sign. "They are horrifying and much worse than the ones they used at the beginning of the war.... I don't know what is going to become of me."[51] Nonetheless, by Holy Saturday, Garidel had arranged with Bishop McGill about securing a pass to return to Louisiana. That Easter Sunday, Garidel attended two Masses. At the High Mass at 10 a.m., the bishop was celebrant, with Fathers O'Hagan and McMullan assisting. Father Darius Hubert preached on the Resurrection. The representation of clergy could have been a tableau of the reunification of the nation, on the feast day of ultimate renewal.[52]

In New York, Marie Daly, having long since made her separate peace with Lincoln's reelection, followed the rapidly developing events in Virginia with growing excitement. "Richmond is ours!" she recorded on April 5. "The streets are brilliant with flags. On Saturday when the news came, there was an impromptu meeting in Wall Street. All business adjourned, a few speeches, and then the multitude sang the Doxology and the 100th Psalm in Wall Street, the seat of the money-changers; it was a good augury. When I got the extra containing the great news, the tears rushed to my eyes, my heart to my throat. I could not speak. A few days more, and God be praised, it would seem as though this great trouble will be past." Then, on Palm Sunday, as midnight neared, the Dalys heard a newsboy shouting "extra" in the street. When Charles Daly opened the door, the cry "Surrender of Lee's army," greeted him. "Glory be to God on high," Marie wrote, "the rebellion is ended!"[53]

†

CHAPTER 18

Assassination and War's End

Our Chief Magistrate, one so universally loved,
the chosen one of the people, the idol of the nation.
—MICHAEL DOMENEC, APRIL 22, 1865

A HOLY SATURDAY SHOCK

On April 12, Charles Daly had taken the train from New York to Washington on behalf of the American Geographical Society, whose president he had become in the previous year. Two days later, on Friday, April 14, he had dinner with notable political and diplomatic figures, including Senator Charles Sumner and the British and French ambassadors. The dinner ended at a late hour. Daly returned to his hotel. The next morning he headed for the president's house, bearing a card signed by President Lincoln authorizing a meeting with Charles Daly at an appointed hour. "The shock was very great," he wrote his wife immediately afterwards about hearing that the president had been assassinated. "All were paralyzed."[1]

THE MAKING
OF AN ASSASSINATION

In the spring of 1861, William Russell had picked up a rumor that an armed band of some five hundred men were gathering to swoop across the Potomac, kidnap the president, and spirit him back to Virginia. Three and a half years later such a plot developed with far fewer participants but far graver consequences. As the stakes continued to rise over the course of the conflict, both sides underwent a radicalization about the means employed to secure victory. By the spring of 1865 even the assassination of Abraham Lincoln seemed on the table.[2] As Edward Steers notes, to Jefferson Davis and Confederate leaders, Lincoln, by his provoking of slave insurrection through his Emancipation

Proclamation, had put himself beyond the pale of the norms that governed warfare.[3] Although there is considerable evidence that Confederate officials were involved in the plot to kidnap Lincoln, nothing links them directly to his assassination. Catholics, on the other hand, played crucial roles in both, greatly exacerbating charges of disloyalty which Catholic dissent had stirred over the past four years.

John Wilkes Booth, twenty-four, was the youngest member of a Maryland family of renowned actors. When Booth's family friend and theater backer George Kane was imprisoned without trial, it made very personal to John Wilkes the Lincoln administration's repression of dissent in Maryland. Then Lincoln's Emancipation Proclamation seemed especially to unhinge Booth. Still Booth remained very active on the stage, appearing in productions across the North, well into 1864. In August of 1864, at Barnum's Hotel, a Baltimore hotspot for Confederate intrigue, Booth laid out his embryonic plans to boyhood acquaintances Samuel Arnold and Michael O'Laughlen, both veterans of the First Maryland Regiment (CSA). O'Laughlen, like Booth, was a member of the Knights of the Golden Circle.[4] Booth intended to kidnap Lincoln on his way to a place Lincoln frequented, the Soldier's Home on Seventh Street. Once the president was safely delivered into the hands of Confederate authorities, he could be used as a bargaining chip for the release of Confederate prisoners. In October, Booth traveled by train to Montreal, to contact Kane, now a Confederate agent based in Canada. Kane, as it happened, was away when Booth arrived in Montreal, but Kane's roommate, fellow Baltimorean and a blockade runner, Patrick Charles Martin, took Booth under his wing. Martin agreed to take Booth's wardrobe with him on his next run South and to deliver it to Richmond.[5] Martin did more for Booth than take his wardrobe under his care. The blockade runner apparently provided substantial funds to the actor.[6] He also gave Booth a letter of introduction to two Marylanders, both Charles County doctors in southern Maryland: William Queen and Samuel Mudd.[7]

Booth, for his kidnapping project, secured the assistance of the main operatives in the Confederate underground network in Charles County in southern Maryland. His abettors were members of the Catholic community or close relations to it.[8] The Queens, the Mudds, the Harbins, and the Coxes were staunch supporters of the Confederacy.[9] All four families were slavers.[10]

William Queen, seventy-five, had spent a decade at Georgetown College, first as a student, then as a seminarian, before having to leave the Jesuits and take up the practice of medicine in order to support his widowed mother.[11] Samuel Mudd, thirty-one, also was a Georgetown alumnus and a doctor.[12] Mudd's farm became part of the Confederate mail line that ran from Virginia across the Potomac to Charles County, and from there to Washington.[13] Heading the rebel espionage system in the region was Thomas Henry Harbin, a thirty-year-old farmer. Thomas Jones, Harbin's brother-in-law, and Samuel Cox, Jones's foster brother, were two other major Confederate agents.

In mid-November 1864, John Wilkes Booth unexpectedly showed up at the Queen household in upper Charles County, with his letter from Charles Martin. The following morning Queen's son-in-law drove Booth to nearby St. Mary's Church, where Thompson introduced him to Samuel Mudd. A month later, Booth was back in Charles County, where he met with Mudd for a second time at St. Mary's. From Mass, Mudd took Booth to the Bryantown Hotel, where they met with Harbin for an extended discussion about Booth's plan.[14] The following week, Mudd traveled to Washington to meet with Booth, who introduced him to John Surratt.[15] John Surratt was the younger son of a widow, Mary Surratt, forty-two, a convert to Catholicism, who had a farm in Prince Georges County, on which was an inn and tavern, which also served as a post office.[16]

Once the war began, the Surratt tavern, scarcely ten miles below the District of Columbia, served as a major link in the Confederate mail system and a safe house for Confederate agents.[17] The younger son, John Jr., had been at a minor seminary, St. Charles College, outside of Baltimore. In the summer of 1862, the seventeen-year-old John Jr. decided to terminate his studies for the priesthood. A month later, his father died of a massive stroke. John Jr. assumed his father's position as postmaster and assisted in running the family tavern and general store.[18] He also soon became a regular mail courier for the Confederacy. Federal authorities became increasingly suspicious of the Surratts' involvement in subversive activity. In November 1863, John Surratt was arrested for transmitting Confederate mail. He was released a few days later, but his disloyal behavior cost him the postmaster's position.[19]

In the fall of 1864, Mary Surratt moved her family to their four-story townhouse on H Street in Washington and took in several boarders, including Louis Weichmann, who shared a third-floor room with John Surratt, a former classmate at St. Charles College. Weichmann, twenty-two, in January 1864 had secured a position in the War Department as a clerk for Col. William Hoffman, the commissary general of prisoners.[20]

THE PLOT EVOLVES

Beginning in January 1865, just a week or so after Mudd had introduced John Surratt to John Wilkes Booth, the Surratt boarding house at 541 H Street became the main meeting place for the plotters, who now included Booth, Surratt, David Herold, George Atzerodt, Arnold, and O'Laughlen.[21] With John Surratt away so frequently on Confederate business, his mother became more and more part of the scheme. In early February of 1865 Lewis Powell, twenty-one, showed up there. For the past year Powell had been a member of Mosby's Rangers, engaging in guerrilla activity in northern Virginia. In January, he had presented himself as a Confederate refugee in Alexandria, Virginia, where he had "swallowed the eagle" by taking an oath of allegiance. He had subsequently traveled to Baltimore to the boardinghouse of the Branson family on Eutaw Street. The Branson daughter, Maggie, had been a nurse at the West Buildings Hospital in Baltimore, where Powell had been brought as a Confederate prisoner after being wounded at Gettysburg. Branson had apparently helped him to escape and hide out at her family's home before he headed to Virginia to join Mosby. From the Branson boardinghouse Powell made contact with David Preston Parr, whose china shop served as a station in the Confederate mail route. Parr put Powell in touch with John Surratt, who subsequently provided Powell with $300, presumably from Booth.[22]

On March 4, Surratt, Powell, Herold, Atzerodt, and Booth attended Lincoln's second inauguration. By this point, dozens of other persons were aware of the plot, if they were not directly involved in it. It is also next to impossible not to conclude that the Confederate secret service was collaborating with the plot, if not directing it. Given the Confederate government's involvement in other conspiracies afoot in the Northwest and in New York City during the summer and fall of 1864, and given that Surratt, Mudd, and Harbin were Confederate agents, it seems likely that top Confederate officials were apprised of what was happening at 541 H Street.

When Booth learned that Lincoln had stopped frequenting the Soldier's Home, he proposed to his team his plan to kidnap the president from his box at Ford's Theatre. Samuel Arnold found it madness to imagine they could handcuff the president, lower him from his box onto the stage in a crowded theater, and manage to carry him out of the city unchallenged. Two days later, on St. Patrick's Day, Booth came up with an alternate scheme. He learned that Lincoln was scheduled to make a visit to convalescing soldiers at the Campbell Hospital on the northern edge of the District.[23] As they awaited Lincoln's arrival, Booth heard from hospital personnel that the president had changed his plans. The would-be abduction team returned to Washington; their months of planning seemingly wasted. The team went their several ways.

On Tuesday, April 11, Booth and Powell went to the White House, where Lincoln happened to respond to the crowd's insistence that he speak to them about the end of the war. What the president had to say infuriated Booth, as Lincoln mulled over the possibility of giving the vote to certain Blacks. Not only had Lincoln ruined southern whites by stripping them of their most valuable property, not only had he made soldiers of so many of those he had freed, but now he was threatening to make them as politically privileged as any white man. It "snapped," as Booth's biographer observes, "the last line holding Booth to the ground."[24] Booth ordered Powell to shoot the president, who was well within range. Powell refused to take the risk. Booth came away, telling Powell that was the last speech Lincoln would ever make.[25]

Meanwhile Louis Weichmann had begun to reach out to persons in and out of authority about his growing concerns about what was going on at the boardinghouse. First was his supervisor at the War Department, Major Daniel Gleason. Gleason's initial impression was that Weichmann was overreacting. He told his clerk to continue to monitor the situation. At the same time, Weichmann had written one of his former professors at St. Charles College, in which he expressed his uneasiness about certain things he was witnessing. The priest sought some more specific information. That letter never reached Weichmann. Instead, it was later found in Booth's trunk.[26] The most likely explanation is that Mary Surratt intercepted the letter when it arrived at her house while Weichmann was at work at the War Department.[27]

In the late morning of April 14, Booth learned that President Lincoln and General Grant were to be at Ford's Theater that evening. Suddenly, this seemed the moment to strike. Booth hastily assembled the members of the kidnapping team who were still in town. Booth mapped out a triple assassination that would throw the entire government into chaos. Powell and Herold would secure entry into Secretary of State Seward's residence and kill him. Atzerodt would do the same to Vice President Andrew Johnson at his suite in the Kirkwood Hotel on Twelfth and Pennsylvania. Booth himself would gain entry to the presidential box at Ford's and dispatch Lincoln.

Booth then notified Mary Surratt to alert John Lloyd, who was running the Surratt tavern, to have the weapons ready for him to pick up later that night.[28] Later that afternoon, Surratt had Weichmann drive her to the family tavern, where she delivered a package to John Lloyd, who was running the place in her absence.[29] Around 4 a.m. on Saturday, Booth and Herold arrived at Samuel Mudd's house. Mudd set Booth's fractured leg. That evening, the pair headed for Samuel Cox's house. In the predawn of Easter, Booth and Herold were led to Thomas Jones, Cox's foster brother, who secreted them in the woods below his house for nearly a week before they crossed the Potomac in a rowboat on April 21.[30] Booth and Herold made their way to a farm in Virginia, where Thomas Harbin had his headquarters. Harbin fed the fugitives and arranged for a guide to take them the next part of their projected journey westward toward hoped-for sanctuary.[31]

The secretary of war, Edwin Stanton, quickly took charge of the pursuit of the assassins and those who had aided them. Provost marshal Major James O'Beirne coordinated the detectives and troopers who were searching for the assassins.[32] Lt. Edward Doherty led the group of troopers who, on April 26, finally corralled Booth and Herold in a barn about twenty miles southeast of Spotsylvania Courthouse.[33]

CATHOLIC OPINION
ON THE ASSASSINATION

In Baltimore County, the news of Lincoln's assassination along with that of his secretary of state and his son made Easter "a pleasant and happy one" for Madge Preston. In this darkest hour for the Confederacy, the death of the tyrant and his chief assistant proved to her that God was still in His heaven and the mills of justice continued to grind. "There seems to be a wonderful excitement in the city and elsewhere," she wrote in her diary Easter Sunday, but feared that, in the end, the killings would "lead to great troubles and misery." Her husband returned from the city to report that the assassination had brought the hitherto suppressed Confederate sympathy back to the surface once more.[34] "People have to be careful of their remarks," he thought. But once Madge herself was in Baltimore, with black crepe seemingly everywhere, "the somber appearance of the city, the tolling of the bells and the firing of the minute guns—all inspired a feeling of sadness." The rituals of public mourning sobered even this staunch Confederate; gradually the gravity of the monstrous deed sank in. By Wednesday, April 19, the assassination had become for her a "dreadful crime."[35]

At the Baltimore Carmel, Mother Antonia Lynch, who had earlier advised her Confederate agent brother that she could not see him returning in the wake of the Confederacy's collapse, now simply hoped that, with the nation in turmoil over an assassinated president, "you will wait until all dangers are over."[36] To John Abel Morgan at nearby Loyola College, Booth's perverted act of patriotism only worsened the situation for the moribund Confederacy and its sympathizers. As for Booth's accomplices, Morgan expected that they would "pay dearly for their part in the nefarious deed." Any hopes that Booth's audacious mass murder attempt would revive southern resolve were wildly misplaced.[37]

James Sheeran heard the news of Lincoln's death as he was heading by boat from Richmond to Baltimore. To Sheeran, all the blood of the war was on the dead president's hands. "He is summoned before his God," the priest wrote with satisfaction in his diary. When he reached Baltimore, all the outpourings of grief soon forced him to Philadelphia, where he hoped to find fewer demonstrations of Yankee patriotism. It was not to be. Even the churches had flags flying from spires—"political flag poles" as Sheeran dubbed them—and black crepe marking the doors. That Catholic churches, in particular, could so honor a man who had "desecrated the day of our Lord's crucifixion so far as to attend the theatre" was more than Sheeran could stomach.[38]

Victor Klausmeyer, of the War Department, was one of the few Catholics to mourn the assassinated head of state as "our beloved President Lincoln." Klausmeyer had no sympathy for those who were attacked by crowds for taking pleasure in the president's fate. No republic, he felt, could tolerate "traitors who rejoice at the assassination of the first citizen of the republic, the best of the patriots."[39] It annoyed Marie Daly greatly that ministers on Easter Sunday glorified Lincoln as a second Christ, "sacrificed on Good Friday." To her, "they gave Our Lord only the second place in his own house." And yet, despite herself, she had to recognize how, in Lincoln, God had showed anew how He "makes use of the foolish things of this world to confound the wise . . . to bring to naught those who are mighty." Daly had to admit that Lincoln had grown in wisdom and self-knowledge in guiding the nation through the devouring trials which had defined his presidency; and to acknowledge that the terrible testing he had endured over the past four years had shaped him to at last be an authentic leader in making the restored country truly the United States.[40]

Raphael Semmes had been at Greensboro preparing to link up the remnant of his former sailors with Joseph Johnston's troops when he learned of Lincoln's assassination. "It seemed like a just retribution," Semmes wrote, "for all the destruction and ruin he had wrought upon twelve millions of people. . . . He had made a war of rapine and lust against eleven sovereign states. . . . As a Christian, it is my duty to say, 'Lord have mercy upon his soul!' but the devil will surely take care of his memory."[41] In much of the former Confederacy, Lincoln in his death became the object of all the hatred that four years of war of the worst kind had bred.

Stephen Mallory had just reached Charlotte, together with the residual Confederate cabinet, when they received a dispatch that Lincoln had been assassinated. The secretary found it beyond belief that such a thing could happen in America. In conversing with President Davis, Mallory found that the itinerant president considered it a likely "canard" but added "that in revolutionary times events no less startling were constantly occurring." Mallory then expressed to Davis his "deep regret" at the news, if true, given "Mr. Lincoln's moderation, his sense of justice, & my apprehension that the South would be accused of instigating his death." According to Mallory, Davis agreed.[42]

At Spring Hill College, outside of Mobile, thousands of federal troops were occupying the campus when word came of Lincoln's assassination. The president of the college entered the study hall to inform the students that President Lincoln had been assassinated. He tried to impress upon them what a despicable murder this was as well as the danger they would court with the federal soldiers throughout campus should they betray any sympathy with the assassin. One student who heard the president's announcement felt that his warning was well needed since, for the past four years, they had regularly sung songs such as "Here's to old Abe, may he soon be in his grave." A thousand miles away, at Georgetown College, black crepe draped over the porches of the campus buildings as well as the front gate. On one of the towers of the main building the Stars and Stripes flew at half-mast. Georgetown, within sight of the president's house, might have ignored the celebration of the war's end; it could not flout the murder of the reunited nation's president.

For the Catholic press there was suddenly a need to, if not praise Lincoln, at least condemn those who had brought about his death. James McMaster termed the assassination an act of "frenzied madness." The *Freeman's Journal* editor wanted a speedy trial and execution of the assassins "without fanfare." Nor should there be any "sentimental rhetoric" regarding Lincoln. The country, he claimed with no elaboration, was simply too "demoralized."[43] John Mullaly, in the *Metropolitan Record,* found the assassination "a terrible tragedy . . . a horrid dream." He urged his readers to pay the slain president "the respect to which he was entitled," while leaving final judgments on him to history.[44] The *Pilot* in an awkward editorial grudgingly acknowledged "the great work to which [the president] gave himself—the salvation of his country."[45] The unprecedented atrocity of a presidential assassination ("a day destined to be forever memorable in the annals of infamy") seems to have jolted the *Catholic Mirror* into a recognition of what Lincoln had accomplished for the nation. "Mr. Lincoln had raised himself 'to the height of the great argument,' and evinced the spirit of a true statesman; the riddle of the future weal or woe of the country was being wisely unraveled, with the promise of great beneficial results, by the departed President. . . . Truly an appalling calamity has befallen us."[46]

Michael Domenec, the bishop of Pittsburgh, chose to see in the slain Lincoln "Our Chief Magistrate, one so universally loved, the chosen one of the people, the idol of the nation."[47] At St. Patrick's Cathedral in New York, Archbishop John McCloskey told the congregation at the Easter Sunday High Mass that he felt, in justice, the need to give voice to his own feelings and, he hoped, to theirs, in sharing with the "nation's grief and sorrow . . . [at the] almost irreparable loss" that the entire nation had just endured in the assassination of the president. He beseeched the Catholic community "to leave nothing undone to show your devotion, your attachment, and your fidelity to the institutions of your country in this great crisis, this trying hour." The archbishop's prayer was that Lincoln's horrific death might be the terrible means through which love might finally overcome hate and reconcile those who had been enemies over the past four years. "Let us pledge ourselves, one to the other," he concluded, "that we will move and act together in unity and in perpetual and Divine peace."[48]

In Baltimore, Martin Spalding, still fearful of stirring the embers of nativism which had more than seared him in Kentucky, was quick to circulate his archdiocese's official response to the assassination. "A deed of blood has been perpetrated," it began, "which has caused every heart to shudder. . . . Words fail us in expressing detestation for a deed so atrocious—hitherto, happily unparalleled in our history. Silence is, perhaps, the best and most appropriate expression for a sorrow too great for utterance."[49] Silence may have been the "most appropriate expression," but it also spared him the need to cast any judgment on the fallen president.

The next morning, General James Hardie, a parishioner at St. Patrick's in Washington, was shocked to discover no signs of mourning adorning the facade of the church when he arrived for Easter Mass. He tried, to no avail, to persuade the pastor to address the oversight by displaying some black crepe or other appropriate symbol of mourning. Hardie returned home to write Archbishop Spalding. "I *earnestly advise,* as a measure of prudence," he wrote, "that you authorize immediately the display of crepe as mourning on all Catholic edifices for religious or benevolent, or educational purposes. If not done, we are in danger of disorder, destruction of property, riot and perhaps bloodshed. It will lead to a bitter feeling against the Catholic faith, & its professors, which we will all feel the consequences of."[50] Spalding managed to get out the specific directive to all of his clergy, who got the message.[51] When, on Wednesday, April 19, the body of the slain president was borne from the White House to the Capitol, where it lay in state, the Catholic pastors of the area churches were all in the procession. Thomas Francis Meagher served as part of the honor guard for Lincoln's lying in state at the Capitol.

By the time that President Andrew Johnson, a month later, called for a day of national humiliation and prayer on the month's commemoration of the assassination, several Catholics, including the Surratts and Samuel Mudd, had been indicted as accomplices of Booth in the assassination. John Abel Morgan, as one who knew Mary Surratt through Bernardine Wiget, was dismayed to learn that she "had a part in the conspiracy. Her character up to this time," he wrote, "has been good."[52] Spalding felt obliged to issue a new circular, "since there was a malicious tendency to place the blame for the president's assassination on the Catholics themselves."[53] The archbishop instructed his priests that badges of mourning were to be displayed at the front of all church-related buildings, the bells of all the churches were to ring for half an hour at the appointed time, and a High Mass to be sung in all the churches throughout the archdiocese.[54]

TRIAL AND JUDGMENT

In the rush to bring the conspirators to justice, David Herold, Samuel Arnold, Michael O'Laughlen, George Atzerodt, Lewis Powell, Mary Surratt, Samuel Mudd, Edman Spangler, Louis Weichmann, Honora Fitzpatrick (a boarder at the Surratts), and Anna Surratt were all imprisoned. Weichmann, Anna Surratt, and Fitzpatrick were eventually released. Weichmann agreed to be a witness for the prosecution.[55]

On May 10 the trial of the accused began before a military tribunal, the District of Columbia still being under martial law. They were charged with conspiracy to assassinate the president. Thomas Ewing Jr. was among the lawyers for the defense.[56] According to law, all those involved with a conspiracy were held responsible for its ultimate outcome, in this case the murder of a president. Unless they had made some significant effort to prevent the conspiracy from taking place, the law considered them responsible.[57] By that standard, Samuel Mudd came perilously close to being condemned to the sentence of hanging that Herold, Atzerodt, Powell, and Surratt received. Five of the nine judges voted Mudd guilty. Six votes were needed to convict. Mudd, along with Arnold and O'Laughlen, was sentenced to a life sentence in the Dry Tortugas off the Atlantic coast of Florida. Mary Surratt was convicted, but five of the nine justices recommended that President Johnson grant her clemency, in view of her age and gender.[58]

Mary Surratt, like Rose Greenhow, maintained an arrogant face to her captors, either as a desperate cover for her grave situation or as a reflection of her confidence in escaping the law she had come to despise during the war.[59] At the trial several priests, including Bernardine Wiget, were put on the stand as character witnesses for Surratt. As the testimony mounted against her, Mary's health seemed to deteriorate by the day. She became increasingly frail, needing assistance in standing and walking. By the end of the trial, she was too ill to even be present in the courtroom.

A local priest, Jacob Walter, applied to General Hardie for a pass to visit Mary Surratt in order to hear her confession and otherwise minister to her in whatever way he could. At some point, Hardie ascertained that Walter was proclaiming Surratt to be innocent. Hardie subsequently implored the priest not to agitate the matter "when circumspection and prudence were especially called for." Proclaiming her innocence would only intensify the anti-Catholic animus that Lincoln's assassination had reawakened, given the Catholic involvement in the conspiracy.[60]

Mary Surratt became the first woman ever executed by the federal government. It stunned the nation. Death on a gallows, for the assassination of a president, was definitely not part of "woman's sphere." The false accusation that Edwin Stanton had callously refused to allow priests of her faith access to her in her final days only spiked public sympathy toward her.[61] The military court which condemned her to the gallows had recommended clemency. The head of the court, Brig. Gen. Joseph Holt, had personally carried that recommendation to President Johnson. Johnson flatly refused to take it under consideration, on the ground that "there was no class in the South more violent in the expression and practice of treasonable sentiments than the rebel women."[62] The reputation that southern women had acquired through their open defiance of federal occupiers in New Orleans and other areas of the South now cost Mary Surratt her life.

At 2 a.m. of July 7, hours before the assassination quartet were scheduled to be executed, Surratt's lawyers obtained a writ of habeas corpus, only to have President Johnson suspend it eight hours later. Anna Surratt, Mary's twenty-two-year-old daughter, frantically attempted to petition Johnson in person on her mother's behalf but was turned away at the door of the White House. Advocates of Mary Surratt had lobbied Stephen Douglas's Catholic widow to intervene, but she also proved unable to change Johnson's mind.[63] Thousands gathered outside the prison to be near the extraordinary event about to take place. General Winfield Scott Hancock, knowing the rumors that efforts might be made to rescue Surratt, had hundreds of soldiers and batteries of artillery guarding the prison. Accompanied by Bernardine Wiget and Jacob Walter in heat approaching 100 degrees, Mary Surratt was hanged, along with the three others involved in the assassination, at the Washington Arsenal.[64]

A CATHOLIC TESTAMENT

In a book that the Catholic historian John Gilmary Shea edited on the assassination of Lincoln and the tributes to the slain president that followed it, Shea seemed to direct his own remarks about Lincoln to his fellow Catholics who had so disdained him. Despite his humble background, Shea wrote, Lincoln was no common man. Although many had regarded the election of someone they considered unqualified for the high office as a sign of the decline of American democracy, Lincoln, to Shea, was the providential man for the crucial hour that the nation faced. His greatness lay in his recognition that slavery, an institution fundamentally unjust and incompatible with democracy, was the root cause of the war. And the greatest achievement of Lincoln, Shea asserted, was his issuance of the Emancipation Proclamation. "To some it was unconstitutional, to others unwise, as unable to reach the class in question; but its effect was immense, as we now see." Lincoln himself, Shea noted, had told the crowd gathered at Independence Hall in Philadelphia, as he headed to Washington to assume office early in 1861, that he would not shrink from doing what he felt duty bound to do in order to preserve the republic, even though "assassination were his fate."

By the election of 1864, Shea contended, the public at large had come to recognize how much Lincoln had grown in office to become the president the nation could not afford to replace. Men felt loosened from party shackles, and many inwardly resolved, against all former political bias, to cast their votes for Mr. Lincoln. One is tempted to see Shea projecting his own change of opinion regarding Lincoln onto the Democrats in general, or his fellow Catholics in particular. The political reality was that Catholics had been among the least likely Democrats to vote for Lincoln, in 1864, as they had been in 1860.[65] Their feelings about his assassination were mixed at best, the legacy of their overall opposition to the president's policies, at the foremost of which was emancipation.

DEATH OF IMPERIAL DREAMS
IN LATIN AMERICA

In the Caribbean, Spanish dreams of imperial revival died hard in the jungles of the Dominican Republic during the spring and summer of 1865. In April,

Queen Isabella II, under the pressure of a treasury-draining war, growing unrest in Cuba, and a US Navy freed from its blockade duties, called off the recolonization project that the US Civil War had provided the occasion for launching. In Cuba, the imperial overreach in the Caribbean had awakened a republican independence movement. That movement failed to gain independence, but it did mark the beginning of the end of slavery on the island. Even in Brazil, emancipation in the United States forced the government to start its own slow path to freedom for its bonded population over the next quarter-century.[66]

The Union victory also doomed the Maximilian monarchy. Maximilian, through his representatives, made several attempts to gain Washington's acceptance of his rule. His minister, Matías Romero, getting no response to his overtures from Andrew Johnson, appealed to the general of the army, Ulysses Grant. The upshot was a warning from Grant to Johnson about the threat to the United States that a monarchial government on its continent constituted. What had alarmed Grant was the report that ex-Confederates were concentrating around "New Virginia," a colony in the Mexican state of Sonora, where Maximilian was allowing slave labor to work the mines in order to attract ex-Confederates. Grant feared that the Maximilian regime would provide a sanctuary for tens of thousands of Confederate veterans who could take control of northern Mexico, in collaboration with French forces there. The general-in-chief ordered Philip Sheridan to take fifty thousand troops to the border to thwart any possible invasion. Sheridan was also instructed to aid, as much as he could, Juárez's troops, which they did by leaving large stores of arms and munitions on the Rio Grande bank at night.[67]

The childless Maximilian tried to preserve his lineage by adopting the infant grandson of Mexico's first emperor, Agustín de Iturbide, whose life a Mexican firing squad had ended in 1824. One of his sons had married a Washington woman, Alice Green. Their son, also named Agustín, had been born in Mexico City in 1863. The parents agreed to have Agustín adopted by Maximilian in exchange for a sizable pension. Then in January of 1866, because of growing tensions with Prussia, Napoleon III announced the withdrawal of French troops from Mexico. Maximilian at first was inclined to abandon Mexico as well, but his empress, Charlotte, was not about to surrender her throne. Instead, she undertook a mission to the Catholic powers in Europe to gain the assistance that France was no longer supplying. In Rome, she suffered a breakdown after failing to get support from Pope Pius IX. Maximilian quickly fell into the hands of Juárez's forces, who charged him with treason. Despite pleas from diverse voices around the world, including Victor Hugo and Garibaldi, Juárez reluctantly agreed to Maximilian's execution on June 19, 1867.[68]

STRANDED IN EUROPE

With the collapse of the Confederacy, Patrick Lynch was not only a man without a country, but, as a Confederate commissioner, formally a traitor liable to imprisonment or even worse, should he attempt to return to the now re-United States. The bishop's only recourse was to put himself at the mercy of federal officials by petitioning for a formal pardon. The petition was a disingenuous recasting of his war experience as that simply of a man of the cloth whose spiritual motivations transcended partisan actions. He had undertaken his mission, he explained, in the hope of convincing some "friendly disinterested voice" in Europe who would be able to persuade both sides to agree to a peaceful settlement.[69] Patrick Lynch's wartime ministry to combatants of both sides was exemplary. It was hardly the sum of his involvement in the war. Forgotten was the *Te Deum* in his cathedral following the attack on Fort Sumter; the blessing of battle flags; the confident championing of the cause of the South in his exchange with John Hughes; the assuring prediction of ultimate Confederate victory to a pro-southern audience in Halifax, Nova Scotia; the extensive apologia for slavery, aggressively distributed throughout Europe to sway continental thinking to the side of the Confederacy about the main *casus belli;* and, most of all, the lobbying for the Confederacy with European officials. The truth was that Patrick Lynch had played a far larger part in the war than he had ever dreamt he might. Now he feared paying the price of that involvement.

When it became known that Patrick Lynch was seeking a pardon from the Johnson administration, Edward Purcell wrote in the *Catholic Telegraph* that, "for his absolution from his higher crime of prostituting his sacred office and dignity, and attempting to drag down the church to the infamous purposes of the Southern slave breeders, he will have to appeal to a higher Judge, incorruptible, who tempers justice with mercy."[70] Some within the Johnson administration indeed thought the bishop deserved some punishment for his treasonous actions. Martin Spalding, the archbishop of Baltimore whom Lynch asked to present his petition, made sure that did not happen. Spalding, despite a distinct aversion to any ecclesiastical lobbying of government, was nonetheless well positioned to serve as an intercessor. The attorney general of the United States, James Speed, under whose office such appeals immediately fell, was an old friend from Spalding's native city, Louisville. Through the efforts of Speed and others organized by Spalding, President Johnson in July issued the pardon.[71] Three months later Patrick Lynch took the oath of allegiance to the United States in Paris.[72]

CATHOLICS AND
THE SEARCH FOR MEANING

For Catholics, the war, in hindsight, took on a providential character. Northern Catholics were confident that the nation, in reflecting upon the war, would see the true meaning and value of the church. No Catholic reflected more on the meaning of the war than did Orestes Brownson. That introspection was perhaps intensified by the extraordinary personal loss that Brownson had suffered during the war. Three of his sons served, or tried to serve, in the Army of the Potomac. Henry Brownson was seriously wounded at Chancellorsville. In June of 1864, a stagecoach accident killed William Brownson on his way to enlist. Two months later, his son Ned Brownson was killed in action at Reams Station. Despite his losses, Brownson looked on the war as a "most brilliant victory" for civilization and democracy. The war had taught the American people that insurrection had no place in a democracy. For Brownson himself, the war had been a triumph of moderate democracy, and a rejection of the extremes of individualistic and consolidated democracy. To the American people all the credit belonged. By an "unerring instinct, they had moved quietly on with an elemental force, in spite of a timid and hesitating administration . . . until" the Union was restored. In that triumph, Catholics had contributed "their full share." To Brownson, their faith enabled Catholics to best understand what was at stake in the war. His was a radical romanticizing of the popular commitment to prosecuting the war. Ignored in the rosy picture that Brownson drew of pervasive patriotism was the widespread opposition to that war in the North, particularly within the Catholic community.

Brownson saw the Civil War as an intellectual coming of age for the United States. The ongoing challenge for the American people was to continue this reflective process, to collectively examine more closely their history and their destiny in the light of their foundational documents and experience. That examination, Brownson contended, would reveal the corporeal nature of the nation: one body with many interdependent members, ideally working together for the common good. That examination would show how the nation had evolved from a simple to a more complex structure of centralized government, complemented by the state governments.[73] The war had been an important step in that evolution. To those who considered government a necessary evil, Brownson contended that "it is a great good."[74] Government enables the nation to function as it is meant to do, to progressively fulfill the promises that the republic's foundational documents make to its citizens.

In the *American Republic,* Brownson made his case to society at large that, by their contributions to the winning of the war, Catholics had earned the right to "be treated as . . . in all respects, on a footing of equality with any other class of American citizens." As equals, Catholics should be full participants in the national discourse about how best to reintegrate the southern people into the Union with justice and compassion so as to win the peace as well.[75] Any such national conversation, of course, had to take up the question of what place the emancipated slaves were to have in the new world that the war had birthed. The wartime experience of most white Catholics, either North or South, did not bode well for their good-faith participation in any such process.

†

CHAPTER 19

The Failure of
Self-Reconstruction

*Set them free, let them claim an equality with the whites, let them
come into competition or be felt as an obstacle in the way of the whites,
and this antagonism of races at once springs into active power.*
—PATRICK LYNCH, 1864

CATHOLICS AND
A POST-SLAVERY WORLD

In the closing pages of his history of the 116th Pennsylvania Regiment, Medal of Honor winner General St. Clair Mulholland recounted the homeward march of the regiment from Appomattox. At Manchester, just south of Richmond, they came upon the remains of an auction block. Systematically the men of the 116th cut it up into small pieces, which they proceeded to burn. "It seemed like a burnt offering on the altar of Liberty," Mulholland noted. "No man, no matter what his color, would ever again be bought or sold in all the land."[1] Mulholland, as William Kurtz has shown, was the major figure in shaping the memory of the Catholic contribution to the northern war effort.[2] The tragedy is that this noble gesture of the 116th was not symbolic of the Irish contribution to the abolition of slavery. With notable exceptions, the Irish had set their boats against the currents which brought down slavery. And no current did they oppose with as much primal determination as they did the one that the Emancipation Proclamation embodied. Catholics, by and large, North and South, continued to regard abolition as an unmitigated evil. Not that their opinion set them apart from their fellow white citizens, among most of whom a rampant racism prevailed. But a certain atavistic clinging to slavery as a God-ordained field for the display of Catholic paternalism was a mindset, if not peculiar to Catholics, at least one for which they had a special proclivity.

Martin Spalding's two-sphere model of society nurtured that proclivity in Catholic thought. It promoted an intellectual inertia which rendered it difficult to pursue any institutional reform, and unthinkable to contribute to any revolutionary change such as the Emancipation Proclamation initiated. Confining the Church strictly to the spiritual realm meant that government and the political sphere did not fall under the Church's moral judgment. All that the Church could teach about slavery involved the mutual fulfilment of obligations. In the absence of any definitive judgment from Rome, Catholic opinion makers, even in a post-emancipation world, still tended to regard slavery as the ideal arrangement for a biracial society.[3]

A month after Appomattox, an anonymous letter to the *Catholic Mirror* sought retroactively to defend the American Catholic community's failure to be part of the crusade that abolished slavery through the Emancipation Proclamation and the Thirteenth Amendment. The writer insisted: "Catholics . . . were very willing to see slavery removed from the land provided the thing were done 'decently and in order,' but they did not care to join in with a . . . politico-religious party, which made slavery a sin, *per se,* that was to be abolished immediately and unreservedly."[4] For the writer, there was serious concern that the formerly enslaved could not cope with the freedom they now enjoyed. There was no consideration about what might be done, by government or individuals, to enable them to cope, much less to prosper, in the new world the war had made. Sadly, the vast majority of the American Catholic community continued to harbor that mindset as the nation set out to confront its greatest challenge to any proper restoring of the Union: how to reconstruct the South, with justice and equity for all its members.

In his proslavery pamphlet, Bishop Patrick Lynch had warned that any general emancipation, with or without compensation, would be disastrous, and to no party more so than those whom it was intended to benefit, the very enslaved themselves: "Set them free, let them claim an equality with the whites, let them come into competition or be felt as an obstacle in the way of the whites, and this antagonism of races at once springs into active power. . . . There would be a war of cruelty, of rapine, murder, tortures and countless horrors . . . where the infuriated whites, from superior numbers and superior intelligence, would conquer." Bishop Lynch made no mention of who might be the instigator of such a race war. Given the innate antagonism between the two races, conflict of the most savage kind was inevitable, as was its outcome. Lynch's apocalyptic prediction was intended as a deterrent against any universal abolition in the South, as part of a last-ditch effort to preserve the peculiar institution. The arc of history, however, was too far in its justice-seeking orbit for any special pleading to affect, even one delivered in three languages. In the very month that Lynch's French edition of *A Few Words* was published, the US Congress passed the Thirteenth Amendment, banning slavery everywhere in the country. Two months later it established the Freedmen's Bureau, to assist the formerly bonded in their passage from slavery to freedom. The Thirteen Amendment and the Freedmen's Bureau represented the first steps in the Reconstruction of the South.

Pierre-Jean De Smet, SJ, was sure that the South was ready to accept the war's outcome. "The majority of the Southerners ask nothing but a fair chance and the means of lifting themselves up once more. A true policy must tend to assure a solid peace and durable prosperity."[5] It was as though the four-million-plus former slaves had no stake in the South's future, much less any say in the matter. For someone who had dedicated his life to the promotion of the well-being of one of the nation's abused minorities, De Smet was uncharacteristically blind to that of an even more abused one. Ironically, Stephen Mallory had a much more enlightened, if self-interested, opinion about the state of the freed people in the South. Writing to the US secretary of state Seward from his Boston jail cell in September 1865, Mallory, in quest of a pardon, boldly acknowledged: "Slavery is abolished & can never, & should never, under any pretences, be reestablished. . . . It is now the duty of every Southern man to do all in his power to harmonize the country fraternally upon this basis." God, in his mysterious providence, had "decreed" that Black Americans, now freed, were to be, potentially, full participants in American society. Mallory owned that Blacks' advancement would depend on the opportunities they had to merit the franchise, but color could no longer be used to bar persons from voting. The challenge was to "make haste slowly."[6] It was a bold statement to make about Black rights in the South, even if it remained vague about what, if any, opportunity should be provided the freedmen to enable them to qualify for the franchise or the other rights associated with citizenship. Worse, it assumed that fitness tests applied exclusively to Blacks.

WHAT CATHOLICS EXPECTED

To the extent that they thought about it at all, most Catholics regarded Reconstruction as something that should enable the South to recover from the war as quickly as possible. The *Catholic Mirror,* in late May of 1865, had editorialized that "magnanimity in the hour of triumph is the characteristic of a great mind." Conversely, the editor continued, "there is no policy more short-sighted than that of vindictiveness."[7] Hadn't Lincoln pointed that way in his Second Inaugural when he talked about binding up the nation's wounds? Catholics wanted Reconstruction to proceed along the lines that they thought Lincoln intended to pursue, had he lived.

In a book published months after the war's end, Anthony Keiley based his assessment of Black inferiority on a broad-brush erasure of their history. "For at least forty centuries they have held undisputed possession of a continent. . . . In all these teeming centuries *they* have stood still. They have written no book, painted no picture, carved no statue, built no temple, established no laws, launched no ships, developed no language, achieved no invention." The status of the Black was as settled as God and Nature could make it. It was tragic folly to attempt to change what had been set in stone. If emancipation had been forced upon the South by the national government, white southerners should at least be the ones to determine the boundaries of the freedom it had conferred. One thing was certain: any steps toward civil and political equality were out of the question.[8]

A voice very much in the minority among the Catholic press regarding the treatment of the conquered South, as it had been on the question of slavery, was the *Catholic Telegraph* of Cincinnati. At the beginning of May 1865, the paper declared that it was not "advocating vengeance in any sense of the word." What it did want was "even-handed justice." That meant that those who had led the rebellion—Jefferson Davis, his cabinet, Robert E. Lee, and the other principal generals—should be tried for treason. "Crimes should be punished," the editor concluded. Treason, of course, was a capital crime that carried the death penalty.[9]

At the beginning of 1866, the *Pittsburgh Catholic* itself confessed that, although it had preferred that slavery could have been ended in a peaceful manner, as the church had led the way in ending it when "slavery was the rule" in the ancient world, still "the termination of such a capital evil must be a source of joy to every friend of humanity." In that termination, "the sunny South," it wrote, had paid a great price, to which "the untilled fields and ruined homesteads" throughout the region were stark witnesses. "Our Southern brethren have been humbled, and made acquainted with sorrow enough to atone for their fault; let it be ours now to soothe them, and make them reconciled to their lot." What the Pittsburgh *Catholic* really regretted was that President Lincoln had been unable to carry out his wish to colonize the freed slaves in Central America, and so "rid this country once and forever of what had been all along a disturbing element in our social status." That the *Catholic*'s focus was almost exclusively on the woes of southern whites in war's aftermath spoke loudly about its priorities.[10]

For Orestes Brownson, Reconstruction involved the completion of the conquest of the South, now at the intellectual and moral levels, rather than at the physical. By their rebellion the seceding states had forfeited or at least suspended their individual sovereignty. But, in a typical contradictory twist, Brownson contended that any just Reconstruction had to fully involve those who had seceded, including their leadership. To impose a political and social revolution upon the class in the South who had made the rebellion would simply ensure the permanent rebellion of the South.[11] In effect, Brownson concluded that self-reconstruction was the only proper path toward the full restoration of the Union. As for Black suffrage, that was a matter for the states, not the national government, to decide. But Brownson tipped his hand by contending that extending the franchise to Blacks in any southern state would be premature. They were simply not ready for it. Their former enslavers would, in one way or another, simply co-opt it. Far better for Reconstruction to limit itself to securing for the freedmen their basic civil rights.

RELIEF FOR A WASTELAND

The Catholic Church in the South bore its full share of the war's devastation. When Bishop John McGill in May of 1865 was able, for the first time since the war began, to make a visitation of his entire diocese, he was shocked at the devastation he found in the Shenandoah Valley, over whose control the Confederate and Union armies had fought for four years. The "Southern Correspondent" for the *Catholic Mirror* reported that "the ravages of war" had left the Catholic population, along with its neighbors, in "great distress." Churches, like those in Bath and Winchester, had been destroyed. Nearly all parishes faced huge debts, which the now impoverished congregations were in no position to address. Their only hope was in the generosity of their erstwhile enemy, "the people of the North."[12] The Diocese of Natchez experienced similar destruction or lasting disruption from the fighting around Jackson, Vicksburg, and Natchez. So too in Alabama and Louisiana. "Our people here have been financially ruined by the war and by the emancipation of their slaves," Mother Hyacinth Le Conniat reported from upper Louisiana to her parents in France in September of 1865. The war had forced her congregation to close its schools at Alexandria and Isle Brevelle. Still, she took heart in the belief that emancipation would actually free the people from the weight of an institution that corrupted character to the extent that it had been difficult, if not impossible, to be good Catholics. "This was really a source of evil in this country." Perhaps now, with no more slaves to do the work for them, they would appreciate life more, including its spiritual dimension, and value education.[13]

No diocese suffered more damage than did the Diocese of Charleston. As though the war's destruction had not been enough for Charleston to bear, the devastating fire of December 1861 had, in an hour, destroyed the heart of the institutional Church in Charleston: the cathedral, the bishop's residence, the seminary, the orphanage, the newspaper's offices, the poor girls' home. Then came the second assault on the city, not from nature but the federal fleet which had bombarded the city sporadically for more than fifteen months, severely damaging three of the four Catholic churches in Charleston, as well as the convent of the Sisters of Mercy. In Columbia, the convent and academy of the Ursulines was burned to the ground. The monies Bishop Lynch had been amassing for a hospital and a boy's college he had largely invested in now worthless Confederate bonds. All told, Lynch calculated the diocesan losses at nearly a third of a million dollars. He wrote Bishop Augustin Verot of Savannah in January 1866, shortly after he returned from Europe: "I am like Marius amid the ruins of Carthage." Almost all that he and his two predecessors had built over the past forty-five years lay in ruin.[14] If money was to be found to begin the work of Reconstruction for the diocese, it would come mainly from the North. Fortunately, Lynch had many episcopal friends in the region, including the prelate of the richest diocese in the country, John McCloskey of New York. When the Charleston bishop had stayed at the archbishop's residence prior to returning to Charleston in December 1865, McCloskey invited Lynch to conduct a collection in the New York cathedral for the needs of his diocese.[15] That was the beginning of a fifteen-year relief campaign to which the Catholics of New York and many other dioceses across the Northeast and Midwest responded. Patrick Lynch became such a regular visitor to New York City that Archbishop McCloskey kept a room for him in his residence.

Catholics in New York and Baltimore especially played prominent roles in organizing the fairs and other fundraisers for southern relief in the immediate postwar years. Mary Mildred Hammond Sullivan, wife of a New York judge, Algernon Sydney Sullivan, whom the Lincoln administration had imprisoned for pro-Confederate activities, organized the New York Ladies' Southern Relief Society.[16] Catholics in the Baltimore region, such as Jane Howard, Mary Norris, and Juliana Martha White Scott, were prominent members of the

Ladies Southern Relief Association. Howard, wife of former gubernatorial candidate for the States' Rights Party, was its president. Juliana Scott was the wife of T. Parkin Scott. In the spring the association organized a fair to raise relief funds. In eleven days in April 1866 the fair raised over $100,000, considerably more than the $86,000 which the Sanitary Fair in Baltimore had raised two years earlier.[17]

COPING WITH DEFEAT

The consequences of defeat spared virtually no one in the South, including the Catholic elite. The Dooleys, the most prominent Catholic family in Richmond before the war, struggled to regain their economic footing. John Dooley Sr. managed to sell some of the real estate he had purchased during the war as a hedge against inflation to get cash to renew his burned-out business. By mid-June of 1865 he was advertising that he was again in business with "a large lot of hats of the newest and most fashionable styles and qualities." Shortly afterwards he received a pardon from President Johnson. That cleared the way for Dooley's election to the board of directors of the Farmers' National Bank of Richmond in September. About the same time, his son James obtained a license to practice law with a Richmond firm. In the unprecedented hard times that that defeat exacerbated, John Dooley found the public had little money to spend on hats or other menswear. Over the next two years, changing locations and lowering prices brought no significant change in sales.[18] In late February of 1868, the fifty-six-year-old Dooley died of a massive heart attack. Members of the First Virginia, of the Ambulance Committee, and much of Catholic Richmond made up the funeral procession which accompanied Dooley's body from the family home on Broad Street to St. Peter's Church. One Dooley family member not among the mourners was John Jr., who, in the fall of 1865, had entered the novitiate of the Society of Jesus in Frederick, having decided that he was called to serve a higher cause than the one for which he had risked life and limb on the battlefields and prisons for nearly three years.

In South Carolina, John Lynch succinctly summed up the state of his medical practice in Columbia as well as that of southern society: "Practice free, times hard, money very scarce, and getting scarcer."[19] The war had virtually wiped out the banking infrastructure of the South. In South Carolina, as elsewhere in the former Confederacy, the lack of local banks from which individuals could borrow money forced southerners to do their banking in the North, as the colonial status of the antebellum South now expanded to include banking. With his shoemaking plant in ruins and his Black labor force liberated, Francis Lynch suddenly faced an impoverished future. He filed a claim to the US government for a $20,000 reimbursement for the losses his tannery and shoemaking plant had suffered at the hands of Sherman's invaders. Meanwhile he took on forty freedmen to work his cotton plantation. He called upon his bishop brother for a loan to enable him to put in a crop and harvest it but discovered that, for once, Patrick was unable to come to his rescue.[20]

Francis's success in replacing his former slaves with other Blacks was not shared by other members of the Lynch family. His parents had lost all the Blacks who had served their household and worked in Conlaw Lynch's shop. At the bishop's estate, Valle Crucis, which had become the new home for the Ursuline Academy, the plantation's Blacks, having ascertained that they would not be getting any of the land, abandoned their quarters in mid-January to go to work for a nearby planter. Even when some of them returned to work for wages, there was no certainty about how long they would stay. "Everything starts anew now," Baptista wrote Patrick. "There is no binding engagement of any kind."[21]

From Texas, Mary Lynch Spann wrote her brother, Patrick Lynch, that her husband was adjusting to the new order of labor by adapting a sharecrop system for his former slaves. "So far," she told Patrick, "he is well satisfied with their dispositions for work which I hope will continue."[22] Nearly a year later, Mary Spann's confidence had weakened. As she observed, people—both Blacks and whites—were warily struggling to gain their footing, as this *novum saeculum* shook itself out. "There is little in our country to work with just now—people seem to be very unsettled in all quarters, the merchants it is said have overreached themselves, planters are generally discouraged from the past year's experience & fearing worse for the next—very many are renting out their lands perfectly disgusted with trying to work the negroes."[23]

STIRRINGS OF RECONSTRUCTION

Of the two Confederate states, Tennessee and Louisiana, which the Lincoln administration attempted to reconstruct, beginning in 1863, Louisiana had a heavy Catholic presence, including French Creoles, the descendants of Cajun transplants from Nova Scotia, Irish immigrants, and Afro-Creoles. In the antebellum era, the 11,000 overwhelmingly Catholic free people of color occupied a middle ground in New Orleans society between the 119,000 whites and 14,000 slaves. They enjoyed certain civil rights, including traveling without restriction, testifying in court, and having their own educational and benevolent institutions. Seizing the opportunity that the movement to reconstruct the state afforded, they began to lobby for a state constitution which would enfranchise them. In March of 1864, they sent two representatives, Arnold Bertonneau and Jean Baptiste Roudanez, to petition President Lincoln for the suffrage. Lincoln subsequently wrote Michael Hahn, the provisional governor, to suggest that the constitutional convention allow "some of the colored people, the very intelligent, and especially those who have fought gallantly in our ranks," to vote.

As for equal accommodations, when the Afro-Creole paper *L'Union* began to advocate for the ending of segregation on public transportation, death threats forced the editor, Paul Trévigne, to shut down the paper in July 1864. Within the fortnight, Louis C. Roudanez, the biracial son of a French merchant and an Afro-Creole, started a replacement paper, the *New Orleans Tribune,* with Trévigne as editor. It soon became a daily, with a second editor, the Belgian Jean C. Houzeau. The *Tribune* quickly acquired a reputation that reached Europe for bringing a progressive Catholic perspective in the service of the advancement of Blacks, whether freeborn or recently freed.[24]

At the opening session of the constitutional convention held in New Orleans in the spring of 1864, some of the delegates had no intention of honoring the president by having its new constitution abolish slavery. Conservative white Catholics, such as Edmund Abel, a Kentucky-born lawyer, fiercely opposed emancipation. Abel contended that, "of all systems of labor, slavery is the most perfect, humane, and satisfactory that has ever been devised; and a slave under a good master is the most happy thing in the world."[25] The convention, despite conservative opposition, adopted abolition as a war expedient. Securing more rights for the freedmen than legal freedom proved elusive. Joseph Gorlinski, a Polish immigrant, introduced a motion that would allow the legislature to extend the right to vote "to such persons, citizens of the US," who had demonstrated their capacity for participation in the affairs of government by military service, taxation, or intellectual fitness. Another delegate, John Sullivan, a night watchman at the US Custom House, objected that "that's a nigger resolution." Nonetheless, it became part of the new constitution, only to have the Free State government that was consequently formed in the fall of 1864 restrict the franchise to those who had possessed it before the war.[26]

During his tour of the South at the close of the war, Whitelaw Reid interviewed an Afro-Creole in New Orleans who told him: "Our future is indissolubly bound up with that of the negro race in this country. . . . We have no rights which we can reckon safe while the same are denied to the field-hands on the sugar plantations."[27] Frustrated by the regressive action of the Free State legislature, the Afro-Creole leadership had concluded that congressional enactment of universal Black enfranchisement was their only hope for effecting a thoroughgoing Reconstruction.[28] There were simply not enough free-born Blacks and white Republicans to form a viable coalition for winning elections and governing in Louisiana. The *New Orleans Tribune* led the way in this shift.[29] Their lobbying helped persuade Congress not to recognize the Free State government.[30]

Claude Paschal Maistre's church provided an independent space for Black Catholics to organize for political or social purposes. Maistre himself was actively engaged in promoting civil and political equality for Blacks, including the formation of the Equal Rights League in January of 1865.[31] Sadly there were too few Maistres among the white clergy, while the lack of a Black Catholic clergy in the South deprived the Black Catholic community of the indigenous leadership from which Protestant communities greatly benefited.

THE FREEDMEN'S BUREAU

Emancipation wiped out the South's greatest asset, its 4.5 million slaves. Without an enslaved labor force to work it, southern land in 1865 was now worth but a fourth of its value five years earlier. Much of it was in government hands. At the beginning of that year, Sherman's Special Field Order No. 15 formally set aside the Sea Islands and a thirty-mile-wide swath of the low country south of Charleston. By June 1865, some 40,000 freedmen occupied forty-acre tracts of land. Was that to be the pattern for the property of all those who had participated in or supported the Confederacy? The Thirteenth Amendment enabled the Congress to enforce and ensure Black freedom. What form and scope such enforcement should take the amendment did not delineate.

The establishment in March 1865 of the Bureau of Refugees, Freedmen, and Abandoned Lands was the first embodiment of that power the amendment provided Congress, but like its empowering clause, the bureau's powers were general, if not vague. The Freedmen's Bureau bill charged the agency to provide relief and management of abandoned lands, including their use by freedmen. As Randall Miller notes, "the act carried an implied promise of government aid to Blacks and Unionists in staking new lives as independent farmers in a reconstructed South." The bureau became the main government channel for the distribution of food, clothing, and fuel to the destitute, whether Black or white. In South Carolina the Ursulines were among the grateful beneficiaries of the bureau's biracial relief program. But effective as the bureau was as a distributor of relief, it failed miserably as a provider of land for the people who most needed it.

With a major responsibility of the bureau being the distribution of abandoned lands to former slaves, it was understandable that the bureau was placed under the secretary of war and staffed by military. Its head was the former commander of the Eleventh Corps, General O. O. Howard. Howard began his tenure with the noble intention of using the considerable resources of the bureau to provide "protection, land, and schools, as far and as fast" as he possibly could. His actions in support of that goal fell scandalously short, undone in part by Howard's evangelistic bent and a ruinous tendency to overestimate his ability to appeal to people's better angels. At the very outset of the bureau's life, Cump Sherman had warned Howard not to expect it to be part of any "New Revolution" to remake the South. Any such effort, Sherman assured him, would only lead to a new civil war in which the North might find that the West had switched sides.[32]

The vague language of the bill creating the bureau had fed the hope, especially among the freed people, that the Freedmen's Bureau represented the institutionalization of Sherman's promise of "Forty acres and a mule" in his Circular 15.[33] The bureau controlled about 800,000 acres of farmland. In July 1865, Howard, through Circular 13, ordered the bureau's land in 40-acre lots to be leased to heads of families for a three-year term, during which time the renters would have the right to purchase the land. The circular stipulated that not even a presidential pardon would entitle a former owner to reclaim land now possessed by the bureau. That directive remained in force barely a month before President Andrew Johnson quickly doused any expectations raised by Howard's circular by appropriating to himself the power to determine what became of the land held by the government.[34] To Andrew Johnson, the goal of the Freedmen's Bureau was not to enable economic independence for the former slaves but to ensure that they would continue to be a docile labor force. The vast bulk of the bureau's lands reverted to owners pardoned by the president. The upshot of Andrew Johnson's restoration of land to its prewar owners was that only about two thousand freedmen in the coastal areas of South Carolina and Georgia received the land which Cump Sherman had promised them in 1865.[35]

With land redistribution no longer in his power, Howard was reduced to appealing to white planters to treat Black workers decently, as the good Christians that the planters presumably were.[36] Howard urged Blacks to take their appeal to Congress, to secure economic justice from that Republican-controlled body. Meanwhile he adopted the policy of having the bureau personnel serve as mediators between planters and Black workers in drawing up labor contracts. In Maryland, the bureau managed the 3,000 acres of abandoned farms in St. Mary's County which provided shelter and wages for the five hundred freedmen who worked them. Edward O'Brien, the bureau's assistant commissioner for Maryland, saw the farms providing "a means of subsistence by procuring for [the former slaves] good homes at fair wages ... the legitimate fruits of their labor."[37] As Richard Paul Fuke observes, "the bureau came to think in terms of an early restoration of the agrarian *status-quo ante bellum* with a well-treated but still restricted labor force taking the place of slaves." By 1870 only about a tenth of Maryland's tidewater Blacks owned land. In the counties of southern Maryland, the percentage was 4.5. And most of that Black ownership predated the war. For the vast majority of Maryland's rural Black population, emancipation did not lead to the economic independence that landowning promised.[38]

Gradually Blacks secured some minimal autonomy and escape from the gang labor that had prevailed before the war by agreeing to a sharecrop system, in which they worked a specific sector of the planter's land in return for a share of that crop. But that system in turn led to a certain economic slavery, notably through the incurring of debts against future crops that eventually led to extensive debt peonage throughout the South.

PRESIDENTIAL RECONSTRUCTION

Andrew Johnson was an accidental president. When he had been chosen as a Democratic running mate to Lincoln on the unity ticket of 1864, no one had the remotest expectation that Johnson would ever find himself president. Like Lincoln, Johnson was a self-educated man who had bootstrapped his way to political office from humble beginnings. There the comparison ended. Eric Foner aptly summed up Johnson as "a self-absorbed, lonely man" in whom "stubbornness, intolerance of differing views, and an inability to compromise" reigned.[39] It was a mindset that spelled disaster for the nation as it tried to bind up its wounds and become once more a united country. The president started out, in the anguish surrounding Lincoln's assassination, by promising to make treason odious and leading the emancipated slaves, Moses-like, into the promised land that Lincoln had pointed to at Gettysburg. But Johnson was too much a Democrat to believe in utilizing the powers of the central government to make that happen. Nor, as a white southerner, did he have any interest in helping Blacks toward economic and political equality.

Johnson, like most Americans, could not envision a biracial South in which Blacks were an integral part of society. "White men alone," he once said, "must manage the South." Like so many whites, Johnson thought emigration was the best prospect for Blacks.[40]

At the end of May 1865, Johnson made public his plan of Reconstruction, which essentially was to be carried out by white southerners themselves. To make that possible, the president conferred a blanket pardon upon all Confederates pledging their loyalty to the United States, whose property was valued at less than $20,000. All that property, except for slaves, was to be restored to them, even if it had been seized by the government. All the remaining Confederates would have to apply individually to the president for pardons. That led to the hope that Johnson intended to redistribute planters' lands to their former slaves, but Johnson's lavish use of individual pardons quickly belied his early rhetoric about making treason odious. By 1866 Johnson had individually pardoned over seven thousand Confederates who had not qualified for amnesty under his May proclamation.

The president chose provisional governors for the southern states and called for the eligible voters of each ex-Confederate state to select delegates for a convention to draw up constitutions which ratified the Thirteenth Amendment and renounced Confederate debts. For the governor of South Carolina, Andrew Johnson chose a friend of Patrick Lynch, Benjamin Franklin Perry.[41] Catholics such as Ellison Keitt, Thomas K. Ryan, P. J. Coogan, and Franz Melchers were all elected members of the South Carolina constitutional convention.[42] That fall elections were held for governors, state legislatures, and representatives to Congress. The upshot was that Unionists generally came to power in the upper South; former Confederates in the deep South.[43]

When the state legislatures assembled across the South, the paramount issue that arose was the need to control the newly freed agrarian labor force. The mechanism adapted was the Black Codes, which on the surface legalized Black rights to acquire and own property, to marry, to make contracts, to sue, and to give court testimony in cases involving other Blacks. But the codes also set the boundaries in the making of contracts. In Louisiana and Texas, a law mandated that all able family members labor in the field, regardless of gender. In many states laws defined vagrancy so broadly as to subject to forced labor those deemed "idle" or misspending their income. Apprenticeship laws bound Black orphans or children of parents found unable to support them to forced labor without pay. The codes involved many not-so-subtle means of re-subduing a supposedly free labor force under planter control. Others curtailed the antebellum hunting, fishing, and grazing traditions, which both

Blacks and whites had enjoyed, in an effort to maximize plantation labor. Militias were reestablished to enforce "order" in the new post-slavery world. The panic that insurrection tales stirred in late 1865 was of a continuum with the scaremongering that ever ran beneath the surface of the antebellum South. The Black Codes and the other repressive legislation that Johnson's governments in the South passed were, in part, a consequence of such fears.

CATHOLIC SUPPORT
FOR JOHNSON

Dan T. Carter, in his volume on Presidential Reconstruction, concluded that, "By the winter of 1865 and 1866, most white southerners were willing to stake everything on the president's political success."[44] Even in the North, there was initial overwhelming support. Within the Catholic community, support for Johnson's conciliatory plan was nigh universal. The *Catholic Mirror* noted that, in the face of cries for "confiscation and vengeance in every form," Andrew Johnson was displaying a "defiant rectitude and the elevated spirit of magnanimity" which the nation very much needed in its president. The *Mirror* found Johnson's policy to be both "conciliatory and truly statesman-like. . . . The great heart of the nation is with the President."[45]

If Andrew Johnson had had a kitchen cabinet, Thomas Ewing would have been a major figure in it. Ewing's opposition to any sort of civil or political equality for Blacks was a key source of the president's obstruction of Congressional Reconstruction. Ewing was a delegate to the National Union Convention in August 1866. His foster son, Cump Sherman, shared Ewing's sentiments. To Sherman, only the southern whites could restore their states to their rightful place in the Union. Sherman's implausible explanation to President Johnson that he considered his order to provide land to ex-slaves to be a temporary war measure gave the president the rationale to return the land to its original owners.

One of the strongest supporters of Johnson's Reconstruction policy was James Gordon Bennett. Bennett was a sponsor of a mass meeting on Washington's Birthday at Cooper Union, at which William Seward defended Johnson's veto of the bill to extend the Freedmen's Bureau.[46] The Civil Rights Bill of March 1866 exposed the bottom line of the *Herald*'s opposition to Congressional Reconstruction. Its headline said it all: "Is This a White Man's government for white men? The Civil Rights bill says that it is not." It required no parsing to determine how the *Herald* understood Lincoln's reference to the republican experiment in America being a "Government of the people, by the people, and for the people." For Bennett and the *Herald,* the only people who counted were white.

A letter to the editor of the *Philadelphia Herald* in late January 1866 contended that, despite President Johnson having done everything possible to satisfy Congress, the "Radicals . . . throw every obstacle in the way of a speedy solution of the problem, hoping and working to gain a little more for self even though *their* gain be their *country's* ruin. . . . The longer the South is kept practically from the Union, the more will sectional jealousies flourish, and the sooner will this new seed of trouble ripen into a terrible harvest of revolution and bloodshed." The path to peace was a simple one, the letter writer insisted: "Every guarantee needful should be demanded from the States, and cheerfully will a spirit of conversion be met by a corresponding spirit of acquiescence."[47]

The picture depicted in this letter, of a vindictive federal government intent on punishing the states of the former Confederacy by refusing to sanction self-reconstructed state governments, ignored the troubling evidence that was driving the congressional resistance to Johnson's policy. The states under Reconstruction had given far too many signs of refusing to accept the basic outcome of the war: that the former persons held in bondage were free and entitled to the basic rights guaranteed by the US Constitution. The passage of Black Codes and other repressive legislation were alarming indicators that southern whites were attempting to impose some form of social control on the liberated Blacks short of that which slavery ideally provided. The correspondent, ignoring these critical developments, simply cast the situation as one in which southerners (read "white southerners") were fully ready to accept whatever reasonable demands the national government made in order to regain control of their state governments. But the federal government, in his fearmongering reading, refused to be reasonable, blocking any reconciliation between the former foes, indeed assuring that sectional tensions would rise again, with terrible consequences likely. What was missing from this vantage point was the recognition that Reconstruction represented the first test of the boundaries of the "new freedom" that the war had birthed.[48]

The dominance of prominent ex-Confederates in the congressional delegations that the reconstructed states sent to Washington in the fall of 1865 was a visual expression of southern defiance of any attempt to remake southern society. When the Thirty-Ninth Congress assembled in Washington in

December of 1865, the clerk of the House failed to include the names of the newly elected congressmen from the former Confederate states. A similar omission occurred in the Senate. That same opening day of the Congress's session, the two houses established a Joint Committee on Reconstruction. It was the Republicans' way of declaring that the president's program of Reconstruction had been unconstitutional, in treating the former Confederate states as though they had never left the Union. It also confirmed that, in the eyes of the Congress, the southern states had failed, by the establishment of Black Codes and their other ill-treatment of the freed people, to accept the outcome of the war, with its abolition of slavery.[49]

In Richmond, John McGill told Roman officials that the "radical members [of the US Congress] . . . are seemingly throwing every obstacle they can in the way of a restoration of the Southern States." Their vindictive behavior, the bishop wrote, was engendering "bitterness between the two races here." Already violent clashes between the races had occurred in Virginia. McGill dreaded that "terrible events" lay ahead.[50] The *Freeman's Journal* found Congress's refusal to seat the southern congressmen to be indefensible, claiming, misleadingly, that the ex-Confederate states had accepted all the conditions that the president had imposed upon them to qualify for national office. More ominously, James McMaster warned that the legislative rebuff would only hasten the coming war between white southerners and armed ex-slaves who were increasingly preying upon white victims. The *Journal* was laying the ground for propaganda that would dominate the southern portrayal of Congressional Reconstruction.[51]

The passage of Black Codes and reports of violence against the freedmen aroused concern about self-reconstruction in Republican circles that spread far beyond those considered "radicals." Regarding the Black Codes as legal attempts to reestablish slavery, the US Senate, in January 1866, extended the lifespan of the Freedmen's Bureau indefinitely throughout the South, including the border states, with agents to be assigned to every county in which Blacks resided. The Senate also called for the government to acquire land from planters and resell it to the freedmen. It also provided federal protection for their civil rights, by requiring that cases involving such rights be adjudicated before federal courts, not state ones. President Johnson, who could not believe that the issue of Black rights could lead Republicans to oppose his entire program, successfully vetoed the bill in February 1866.

The *Freeman's Journal* applauded the president's effort to undermine the Congress's "corrupt" machinations to usurp the Reconstruction of the South: "We consider it a duty of all good men to support the president in this exigency." The stakes, McMaster inferred, could not be higher.[52] The *Catholic Mirror* framed the veto as a necessary response to the radical "revolutionary spirit" of the "central congressional directory." If the radicals, in turn, attempted to impeach the president, they would only assure his reelection. But the paper thought impeachment unlikely, since "the people's heart is with him. . . . The country is steadily gravitating towards its constitutional sphere."[53] As for the Freedmen's Bureau, the *Mirror* questioned the need for military tribunals to protect Blacks when civil courts were functioning. It suggested that the military courts were discriminating in favor of freedmen against their former masters. "Are the rights of the negro held in more respect by the Government than are those of our refined, intelligent, and gallant brethren and fellow-citizens of the South?" To the *Mirror,* the Freedmen's Bureau and Congressional Reconstruction in general were reduced to "sentimental politics," a utopian adventure that wreaked havoc with traditional southern society. In this perspective, the status quo took on a validation that experience was presumed to confirm. By such a rationale, reform became unthinkable since the "is" defined the "ought."

In a landmark move, Congress passed a Civil Rights Bill which recognized African Americans as citizens with the right to own or rent property, as well as to make contracts and to have access to courts. That bill also authorized the Freedmen's Bureau to conduct military trials where conditions of rebellion existed, thus having the bureau serve as the legal protector of Black civil rights.[54] The *Catholic Mirror* judged the law to endow "the negro race with special privileges . . . against the white race," and to widen "still further the gulf which separates race from race, the African from the Caucasian, the civilized, far-seeing and powerful representative of the moral and intellectual properties, from the sluggish, dependent and semi-barbarous race which New England philanthropy has lately made free." The Congress had revealed its flagrant disregard for the Constitution to accommodate the former slaves. It was nothing short of legislative dictatorship.[55]

To no one's surprise, in an attempt to discredit any claim that the federal government had the authority to protect Black rights anywhere, President Johnson duly vetoed this bill in March of 1866. Such a claim, Johnson insisted, stood in violation of the very experience of the American people. Worse, Johnson wrote that the bill discriminated against the white race in favor of the Black. It was a clear appeal to the racism that infected whites throughout the country. That bias drove the insistence on local control against any mandates from the central government. Johnson justified his veto of the Civil Rights Act partly because it put the South on the slippery slope to miscegenation in mandating the "perfect equality of the white and colored races." He also maintained that, by declaring Blacks to be citizens and guaranteeing their rights, the bill discriminated "against foreigners, and in favor of the negro." Furthermore, the bill made "racial distinctions operate in favor the colored and against the white race."[56] Despite the outcry from the Catholic community, Congress, for the first time in its history, overrode a presidential veto of a major piece of legislation.[57]

CONTENDING FOR THE
MANTLE OF RECONSTRUCTION

Congress's thwarting of Johnson's obstruction led to a presidential proclamation, at March's end, which declared that, since the formerly Confederate states had demonstrated by their legislation and other actions that they had accepted the results of the war, including the abolition of slavery, and since military occupation is incompatible with "the individual rights of the citizen, ... the insurrection which heretofore existed" in those states "is at an end." Johnson was asserting that the states of the former Confederacy had reconstructed themselves. It was a proclamation that was contradicted by mounting evidence of white resistance to the new order that the war and the Thirteenth Amendment had supposedly brought to the region.[58]

At the end of April, the Joint Committee on Reconstruction reported an amendment to the Constitution. It recognized that "all persons born or naturalized in the United States" are citizens, regardless of their race or previous condition of servitude. As such, they possessed the full rights to "life, liberty, and property," upon which no state could infringe. The amendment disenfranchised all those who had violated their oath to the Constitution, as officeholders or members of the military, by taking part in a rebellion against the United States. But to the extent that any state denied the right to vote to any other citizen twenty-one or older, to that same extent would the representation of that state be reduced in the Congress. As Eric Foner notes, the amendment represented a national guarantee of equality before the law.[59] What Lincoln had rhetorically framed as the standard of nationality at Gettysburg, the Fourteenth Amendment now made the law of the land. It also extended the protection of the rights enumerated in the first ten amendments from state infringement as well as from that of the federal government.

At the Maryland constitutional convention in 1864, which abolished slavery, Richard Edelen, a Catholic delegate, had warned that freeing the slaves would unleash an untethered Black labor force which would undercut wages and force white retaliation.[60] Black veterans of the Union Army, particularly those in border states, became prime targets of recalcitrant whites who viewed them as emblematic of the disrupted socioeconomic order. In February 1866, at Chaptico in St. Mary's County, Maryland, a band of ex-Confederates attacked two Black veterans. One of the accused assailants, Edward O'Brien, was notorious for targeting Blacks for harm, particularly ex-soldiers, who were seen as a special threat to the white community.[61] Even worse a threat was the establishment of Black militias. Militias had long been a means of promoting the status of ethnic groups. The Irish had been particularly active in forming them, both for the prestige as well as for the training they offered for future service in Ireland's fight for independence. Black militias became a symbol of equality, which the white community would not tolerate. Similar to what happened to the Irish in antebellum New England, public pressure forced Baltimore's mayor to ban Black militias from any public marching. Baltimore police seized their weapons as a threat to public order.[62]

MEMPHIS AND NEW ORLEANS

The tinderbox that the policies of self-reconstruction had made of most of the South exploded in two cities during the spring and summer of 1866, in Memphis in May, and then in New Orleans in July. Perhaps in no other southern city during Presidential Reconstruction were the Irish in such control as they were in Memphis, where they held the mayor's office, had 56 percent of the seats on the city council, and dominated its fire (86 percent) and police (90 percent) departments. When a group of Black soldiers were mustered out of Fort Pickering outside of the city at the beginning of May in 1866, they encountered some Memphis police, whom they taunted by raising three cheers for "Old Abe Lincoln, the Great Emancipator." The Irish responded by insulting the dead president, which led to a scuffle and the arrest of two Blacks. The military commander, with no troops to deploy, requested that the mayor organize a posse, effectively authorizing vigilante action, largely by members of the police and fire departments. A vigilante force subsequently invaded a Black neighborhood in the south side of town and proceeded, for three days, to wreak terror by burning, pillaging, raping, and other forms of violence. By the time federal troops arrived on the third day of mayhem, four churches, twelve schools, and nearly ninety houses had been burned. Forty-eight persons were dead, all but two of them Black.[63]

Under Governor James Madison Wells, conservatives pushing reactionary policies had come to power in Louisiana. Mayor Hugh Kennedy of New Orleans was outspoken in his opposition to the Thirteenth Amendment. Whites waged a defiant campaign of terror, murdering Unionists, both Black and white, throughout much of the upriver portions of the state. Wells, trying to rein in the recalcitrant whites, appealed to Andrew Johnson for support. Johnson gave Wells the ultimatum to hold the municipal elections the Democratic legislature was demanding, or he would order the local military commander, Phil Sheridan, to do so. Wells, accordingly, let the elections occur, which predictably consolidated Democratic power in the city. One of the new administration's first acts was to staff the Police Department with a mixture of Confederate veterans and/or former Know-Nothing mercenaries who had used violence to intimidate voters in antebellum elections.[64]

Desperate, some Free State Unionists, with Wells's cooperation, announced that they would reconvene the constitutional convention of 1864, in an attempt to nullify the conservatives' power grab. Opponents sent a representative to Washington to warn President Johnson that a splinter group from the constitutional convention was determined to reconvene that body in order to enfranchise Blacks and disfranchise former Confederates. Despite a warning from the head of the Freedmen's Bureau in Louisiana that the local government was obstinately resisting any meaningful Reconstruction, Johnson assured the convention's delegate that the federal government would not interfere in Louisiana's local affairs.[65]

Although they had not been invited to be part of the original convention, Black leaders in New Orleans organized a march to the convention hall to lend their visible support. On the morning that the convention was to open, the whole metropolitan police force fanned out to points near the hall where the convention was to take place. John Burke, a former police chief, recognized the potential for a violent racial clash at the convention site. When he reported his concerns to Governor Wells, the governor assured him that he was making too much of what he had seen. The meeting of the delegates was a preliminary one devoted to organization which should be over in less than an hour. Moreover, he had the word of the delegates that, should the police arrest them for meeting illegally, they would offer no resistance. What the governor did not know was that the police, concealing their identifying badges, had no intention of enforcing the law.

Shortly after noon, a procession of at least a hundred Blacks, mostly Union Army veterans, began marching up Burgundy Street toward the convention. At some point in the march the city's fire bell sounded, the signal for the police to descend on the hall. Whites began to attack the marchers, who quickly disbanded to seek refuge. Many found it in the convention hall, where they joined the delegates and observers. Outside of the hall, police and others began firing pistols indiscriminately through the windows. Finally, with guns still firing, they stormed the hall. When police were moving into the hall, shooting indiscriminately as they came, J. D. O'Connell went forward with both hands outstretched, a white handkerchief in one, to talk with the officer in charge. "I implore your men to cease firing," he called out. "These people do not wish to fight, and have nothing to fight with." O'Connell and the officer in charge shook hands. Then police came in and formed a line across one end of the hall. "Now, boys, we have got them," the officer yelled, "give it to them!" They opened fire.[66]

Those inside began to resist with what weapons they had while continuing, to no avail, to appeal for a cease-fire. Police began firing from upper floors of surrounding buildings into the hall. O'Connell managed somehow to escape out the front door. As the frenzy continued, more and more civilians were swept up in a high tide of fury. Mary Ann Larkin, an Irish prostitute, her hair flying and clothes disheveled by her pursuit, chased several Black men as they fled. "Kill the black sons of bitches, kill the black sons of bitches," she cried. She finally caught up with one who had been clubbed by a bystander. She attacked the felled Black with the tip of a sword cane, slashing him in the face and chest and arm, before she continued her pursuit of other terrified Blacks.[67] Two policemen escorted a wounded Black man down Common Street. A third officer crossed the street and held his pistol six inches from the man's head. He fired once, and the man fell to the banquette. Officer Scully, one of Adams's "extras," guarded his prisoner until they reached Gravier. Taking a step back, Scully drew his revolver and shot the man, hitting him in the neck. Scully left the wounded man lying where he was.[68]

Back in the hall, police systematically completed their deadly work. Whites, in general, were allowed to surrender. Blacks were not. Although the evidence indicated that top officials were not involved, this mass murder still amounted to state terrorism. On the part of municipal personnel there was a widespread, if implicit, commitment to inflict such horrific violence on the convention delegates and especially on their Black supporters, so as to crush the will and spirit of those pursuing social justice through reform of the Constitution. It was a terrible reprise of New York City's riot three years to the month earlier, this one instigated and largely executed by the police themselves, with the preordained end of wiping out at its root the movement toward Black equality.[69]

There was never an authentic count of the dead, virtually all of them connected to the convention. One policeman died, of sunstroke. Another victim of the riot was the *New Orleans Tribune,* whose staff fled their building, fearing to be the next target of the mob. Their presses survived, thanks to a company of the Eighty-First US Colored Infantry, who guarded the building. But the rioters succeeded in shutting down the paper indefinitely. Abell and his associates had succeeded in preventing a reopening of the convention, but it was a pyrrhic victory, one that played a large role in upending Presidential Reconstruction and forcing Congress to assume control.

Phil Sheridan, whose department of the army had responsibility for Louisiana, returned to New Orleans the evening following the massacre and immediately set about securing justice to those who had been assaulted and murdered.[70] He found that Mayor John Monroe and other officials had been guilty of behavior "so unnecessary and atrocious as to compel one to say it was murder."[71] Sheridan promptly removed the mayor, the attorney general, and Judge Edmund Abell. The last had defiantly refused to permit trials for any police accused of being party to the massacre.

Sheridan, concerned about the integrity of the upcoming election, took upon himself the oversight of registration. He dispatched troops to upriver parishes to protect registrars enrolling new voters. In his broad interpretation of the disfranchisement language of the Reconstruction Acts to include those who had held any public office or did any military service in the Confederate, Sheridan prevented the registration of about half of the white electorate. Sheridan also persuaded the local transit company to desegregate their cars. Sheridan was not such a believer in social equality; he clearly considered Blacks to be inferior. He knew, however, the importance of preserving the morale of his Black soldiers who deeply resented being forced to ride in separate cars. Resentment, he feared, might translate into another violent clash that would kill additional scores of people.[72]

Believing he had the duty of removing from office all those who were undermining or obstructing the Reconstruction policies that the US Congress was making the law of the land, Sheridan in the summer of 1867 undertook a mass purging of obstructive officials, including the governors of Louisiana and Texas, the New Orleans mayor and most of the city councilmen, as well as many upstate officials. That was too much for President Johnson, who transferred Sheridan as commander of the Fifth Military District in mid-August to Missouri, with that district's commander, Winfield Scott Hancock, replacing Sheridan in Louisiana.[73]

Philip Sheridan did not allow prejudice to subvert his constitutional duty to execute the law. In doing that, "Little Phil" Sheridan stands out in this era as a giant among his military peers.[74] Sadly, his successor, Winfield Scott

Hancock, quickly undid much of which Sheridan had achieved. When Hancock's own successor tried to use his force to protect republican government, Cump Sherman reined him in. Sherman, whose military strategy in marching through Georgia and the Carolinas had been to break the will of the people, now found himself much more in line with the will of the southern resisters to Reconstruction than with that of either southern Blacks or their white allies.[75]

REFERENDUM

With his Reconstruction policy in mortal danger in the wake of the massacres in Memphis and New Orleans, Andrew Johnson attempted to create a new political party, a coalition of Conservative Republicans and Democrats, which he labeled the National Union Party. When the jerry-built party held its convention in Philadelphia in August 1866, it failed to impress James McMaster. The editor wondered what kind of "Constitutional Union Party," one could expect from an amalgamation of "Black Republicans and Southern Know-Nothings." McMaster had turned on Johnson for not doing enough to ensure that the southern states had regained their constitutional rights of representation.[76] As Johnson's self-reconstruction program collapsed, the *Journal*'s rhetoric descended to the rawest racism. "In his best condition," the editor evaluated the freedman, "he is a docile creature. . . . Where they are in appreciable numbers, the admission of any class of them to the elective franchise, is a fearful proposition. The real danger of it is less at the present than it may be in another generation—unless legislation will take the severe line of securing their elimination from the population."[77]

By September 1866, the *Catholic Mirror* was blaming congressional radicals for the failure of Johnson's program. Their campaign to destroy Johnson politically was infecting public opinion with its "daily" indoctrination "in Jacobinical principles," including assassination. In this crisis, it was incumbent upon the people to avert a second civil war by turning out in overwhelming force for the fall elections. The radicals already had the blood of a million Americans on their hands as well as "three or four millions of treasure, and misery in nearly every form in which it visits fallen humanity." Only a political revolution at the ballot box could prevent a second national catastrophe.[78] Meanwhile the *Catholic Telegraph* saw in the biracial composition of the Republican convention in Philadelphia a hopeful sign that racial harmony could indeed become a reality in the country.[79] "It will take a long time to reconcile the two races even when the will of both is favorably inclined, and hence the welfare of the country, for the sake of peace and good order, demands from all a cordial cooperation in the governing policy."[80] That reference was to the legislative, not the executive branch.

The October 1866 elections became a referendum on the Fourteenth Amendment. Johnson's National Union Party carried the Catholic vote decisively enough, but the electoral results were disastrous to Johnson's hope of forging a new political coalition. The Republican landslide gave them a veto-proof majority in both houses of Congress. Even James Gordon Bennett's *Herald* pleaded with Johnson to heed "the voice of the people."[81] Johnson refused to budge in his position, perhaps boosted by the rejection of the Fourteenth Amendment by all the southern legislatures. That defiance proved disastrous for self-reconstruction, as the vast majority of the Republican Congress realized that the South could only be properly reconstituted by ensuring that southern Blacks exercised their franchise and were part of biracial governments in the region. The Union League became the chief mechanism for their political mobilization.

In March 1867 the Republican Congress effectively took unto itself the responsibility for remaking the South by organizing the states of the former Confederacy into five military districts. Andrew Johnson (as had Abraham Lincoln, for the purpose of avoiding the need to treat the Confederacy as a belligerent nation) had never recognized that the seceding states had left the Union. Congressional Republicans had no reason to share that view. To their mind, the repressive legislation and flagrant violence that had marked self-reconstruction showed all too well the continuing refusal of white southerners to accept the war's results. Clearly, they needed to be under military commanders whom the Congress directed to oversee the calling of conventions to establish governments which could satisfy the stipulations that the Congress set down for their states' readmission into the Union.

The *Catholic Mirror* had written in December 1865 that evangelization of the largely unchurched Black community was essential to the integration of the freed people into American society. "Without religion," it asserted, "society is a sham, and measures of the wisest statesmanship but delusion. . . . We know that [the freedman] is unfitted by habits, education, or a previous appreciation of the civilizing arts of freedom, to discharge the duties of the citizen." Only the Church had the wherewithal to prepare the freedman for citizenship.[82]

Although he had been a staunch supporter of the Confederacy, John Abell Morgan took a position on Black suffrage even more progressive than the *Mirror*'s. Morgan wrote in his diary in October of 1865 that "Negro suffrage is on the wane, and many prominent men have declared against it. I think they should have the right of suffrage, attended, however, with an educational qualification." Some critics of Black suffrage, Morgan noted, claimed Blacks lacked "sufficient sense: if this infers that those who vote have all a great amount of wisdom, I would object most heartily." Morgan observed that some were predicting a "total revolution of our ideas concerning Africans." He was sure that, if Catholic principles ever came to govern public opinion, "a wonderful change would be effected."[83] His enlightened stance on race may well have come, in large part, from his interactions with the Oblate Sisters of Providence at their convent on nearby Biddle Street, where he often took part in liturgies and other events. Seeing and engaging with Black religious women leading vowed lives could be highly instructive about racial potential.

CHAPTER 20

The Remaking of the South

The Negro freedmen and the worthless white
With equal intellects have equal rights.
And these combining with designing knaves
Must vote for Generals mute or quondam slaves
. . . For those same laws that set the Negro free
Reduced his master to his slavery.

—JOHN DOOLEY, 1870

CONGRESS AS THE
NEW THREAT TO LIBERTY

With Lincoln dead, Congress, to many, if not most Catholics, had become the great threat to civic liberty, even before it assumed control of Reconstruction. By the spring of 1866, the *Catholic Mirror* decried the "mad crusade" of the Congress to impose oligarchic rule, in place of the monarchial power that Lincoln had pursued during his reign. "[T]hey have no right by political legerdemain to evade the spirit of our laws and override every barrier between conservatism and despotism, between liberty and a worse than Spartan slavery."[1] In the process a vindictive North was destroying the traditional order which anchored southern society.[2] When, a year later, Congress militarized Reconstruction by dividing the former Confederate states into military districts, it confirmed the *Mirror*'s worst fears.

CATHOLIC REPUBLICANS

In that revolutionary work, Catholics played a minor but significant role, both in shaping the new political order and in enforcing it. In the spring of 1869, two priests of the New York Archdiocese, Thomas Farrell and Sylvester Malone, made a trip through the South to promote Reconstruction among their fellow Catholics. When they reached Richmond, they quickly drew the ire of Bishop McGill. McGill reported to Archbishop McCloskey that the pair, throughout their tour, had consistently given scandal by their "negrophily" in supporting Republican governments in the former Confederacy. Worse were their critical comments about episcopal authority, including the infallibility attributed to the bishop of Rome. Regarding the pope, they had even denounced the sending of contributions to Rome, for the defense of the Papal States, on the ground that the Italians were justly pursuing Risorgimento, or Reconstruction in the Italian mode. To McGill this was political and ecclesiastical "meddling" of the worst kind.[3]

A few of the Irish became semipermanent carpetbaggers. Patrick Ford, a famine immigrant, had attended Bernardine Wiget's parochial school in the North End of Boston before apprenticing as a printer for William Lloyd Garrison's *Liberator*. As a member of the Massachusetts Ninth, Ford survived the war, including the ill-fated charge up Marye's Heights. In 1865 he began a five-year stint as a reporter for the *Charleston Gazette* before heading to New York, where he founded the *Irish World,* which became Irish America's leading journal, with a circulation which reached fifty thousand. In an early editorial, Ford asked: "Who and what are the American People? This people are not one. In blood, in religion, in traditions, in social and domestic habits, they are many. Leaving out the aborigines, the veritable Americans ... there are the Anglo-Americans, the Franco-Americans the Irish-Americans, the Spanish-Americans, the German-Americans, and the African-Americans." It was a vision of cultural pluralism which Lincoln had pointed to in his Gettysburg Address and which Congressional Reconstruction was endeavoring to implement in the South, even as Ford penned his editorial.[4]

A more politically involved Catholic carpetbagger was Felix Brannigan, who, after serving as an officer in a Black regiment, secured a law degree at Columbian College in Washington. In 1871 he became the assistant US attorney in Jackson, Mississippi, where his responsibilities included the prosecution of Klansmen. In 1873, he became the attorney for that district.

Charles Dennis O'Keefe moved to South Carolina in 1869, considerably after Congress had seized control of the restructuring of the South. In Fort Mills, O'Keefe joined his uncle, who was a local magistrate in the Republican administration. The younger O'Keefe quickly secured a position as a state tax collector. He also became president of the local Union League, organizing Black males in the area. That involvement caught the attention of the Ku Klux Klan, who assaulted O'Keefe at the Fort Mills railroad station. O'Keefe barely escaped, only to have his life again threatened shortly thereafter. He took to the woods and eventually managed to cross the state line to reach Charlotte. Scarcely had he checked into a hotel when he was told by a local Republican that his life was no safer in inland North Carolina than in upcountry South Carolina. That unnerved him enough to head home to New York.[5]

James Longstreet was probably the most prominent former Confederate to cast his lot with Congressional Reconstruction. Living in New Orleans, by the summer of 1867, Longstreet realized that Reconstruction under a Republican Congress meant the full political integration of Blacks in southern society. Rather than to oppose the inevitable, it was incumbent on white leaders to do their best to influence, if not control, the newly enfranchised. In a letter to the *New Orleans Times,* Longstreet advised his fellow whites to acknowledge that, as a conquered people, they had a duty to accept the terms set down by the victor. He reminded them that, by their surrender at Appomattox Courthouse, they had ceded any right to secede or to determine the political status of Blacks. "These issues," he declared, "expired upon the fields last occupied by the Confederate armies. There they should have been buried." As for the political future of his former comrades in arms, Longstreet advised that the quickest way to regain their place within the governance of the nation was to obey the laws the Congress had enacted. Only by such conduct could the region hope to regain civilian rule.[6] Later that month, in a second letter, Longstreet doubled down on his opinion. "It is therefore our duty," Longstreet concluded, "to abandon ideas that are obsolete and conform to the requirements of law."[7] James Longstreet was, in peace as in war, a realist.

The former hero of the Confederacy quickly paid a heavy economic and social price as his business failed and his family was ostracized in New Orleans. Shortly afterwards, Longstreet formally cast his lot with the Republicans. In 1869, President Grant appointed his old friend and former foe surveyor of customs for the port of New Orleans. That only deepened the antipathy of most southern whites to Longstreet, which intensified when Longstreet agreed to lead the Louisiana state militia for a Republican administration.

Besides Longstreet, a few other notable white southern Catholics became partners in Reconstruction's brave experiment to create a New South in which the races shared political power, social space, and economic opportunity. Thomas J. Coghlan of Sumter, South Carolina, whose foundry had been an important supplier of the Army of Northern Virginia, decided to cast his lot with the Republican Party in the state, even though most of its members were Black. Thanks to Black support, Coughlan was elected sheriff of Sumter County. Coghlan's fellow Irish immigrant, G. W. Reardon, became the Republican clerk of court in Sumter. They remained loyal Republicans throughout the rise and fall of Reconstruction. The most prominent Irish Republican in South Carolina was P. J. Coogan, a Charleston merchant who remained a Unionist after war broke out. Coogan in 1864 escaped to the Bahamas to avoid arrest. He returned in 1865 to become an unlikely delegate to the 1865 constitutional convention. Elected to the South Carolina legislature, Coogan quickly became one of the few members to oppose the Black Codes and the sole one to support citizenship for Blacks. Somehow, he survived politically, perhaps because he was a very active member of the local circle of the Fenian Brotherhood.[8] Whatever the reason for Coogan's continuing survival, he was very much an anomaly as a southern Irish supporter of Congressional Reconstruction.

The most notable Black Catholic Republican in South Carolina was James Spencer, a free-born whose mother was a member of Charleston's Catholic émigré community from Saint-Domingue. Spencer was a delegate to the South Carolina General Assembly from 1870 to 1876, while serving as chief clerk of the South Carolina Land Commission.[9]

The New Orleans massacre brought home to Governor Wells and the Republican leadership in Louisiana that their only recourse was full Black enfranchisement and racial parity in officeholding. In practice that opened the doors to the *gens de couleur.* At the convention called to organize a new government, they comprised about 85 percent of the Black delegates, who held a slight majority of the convention's members.[10] Businessmen were prominent among them, as were veterans. No fewer than fourteen of the Seventy-Third Regiment held leadership roles at some point during Reconstruction.[11] The constitution they helped frame pledged officeholders to respect the political and civil equality of all men and abolished the Black Codes.[12]

IMPLEMENTING
CONGRESSIONAL RECONSTRUCTION

The *Catholic Mirror* in its August 10, 1867, edition carried a rare letter of support for Congressional Reconstruction. That the editor published it may well have been due to the status of the writer, one of the most prominent Catholic generals the war had produced: William Rosecrans. The retired general urged southerners who were about to choose candidates to state conventions to "cast your lot with the Union men of this nation." Yes, he owned, they "opposed and fought you." He was now pleading with them to "trust them. . . . You are our brethren. . . . there should be no wavering in our support of the present general policy of Congress. . . . No representative ought to be elected to Congress on platforms of open or covert opposition to measures wherein finality is more important than detail."[13] To complete the work of emancipation, Rosecrans was urging, Congressional Reconstruction, including Black enfranchisement, had to succeed.

Blacks were a majority in three southern states (Louisiana, Mississippi, and South Carolina) and a near one in three others (Alabama, Florida, and Georgia). Under Congressional Reconstruction, which disenfranchised former federal military or civil officers who had served the Confederacy, more Blacks than whites (750,000 to 635,000) gained the franchise, with a resultant Black majority in five of the ten states under military rule (Alabama, Florida, Louisiana, Mississippi, and South Carolina).[14] The southern Republicans carried the elections in the fall of 1867 to choose delegates for state constitutional conventions. Thanks to the Union League mobilization, Black turnout was prodigious, ranging from 70 to 90 percent in the ten states.[15] In Black-majority South Carolina, Blacks unsurprisingly won a majority of the seats in the legislature, but the results were still a shock to the white community. John Lynch could not quite get his head around the reality that Beverly Nash, a former slave who had been a porter at a local hotel, was now a state senator. "What would *Solon* think if he were living?" John asked his son about one of their former slaves.[16]

The Louisiana convention that assembled in New Orleans in November 1867 was the first major elective body in southern history to have a Black majority.[17] A majority of that majority were Afro-Creole Catholics. The constitution that the delegates drew up enfranchised all adult males in the states, except those who had been part of the rebellion, and established a bill of rights for Blacks, including integrated public education and access to public accommodations. The constitution pledged officeholders to respect the political and civil equality of all men and abolished the Black Codes.[18] For the first time in the state's history, every parish (county) by law had to have a public school. In the system that emerged, integrated schooling was limited to New Orleans, in districts (about a third of the total) where *gens de couleur* controlled the school board. Worse than the failure to integrate the system outside of New Orleans was the failure to provide, in many upstate parishes where white carpetbaggers held power, any schools for Blacks.[19] The new constitution subsequently was approved by a majority Black electorate, thanks to commanding General Philip Sheridan. who had refused to allow nearly half the whites who had tried to register to do so, because of their involvement with the Confederacy.[20]

Unfortunately, Black divisions enabled white outsiders to dominate the initial government elected under the new order. A major victim was the *New Orleans Tribune,* which backed the mixed-race, French-born Francis E. Dumas for governor. Dumas, as a former planter and large slaveholder, understandably received scant support from freedmen. The upshot was the election by a narrow margin of a carpetbagger, Henry C. Warmoth. The *Tribune* paid for its support of Dumas, by losing its state and federal printing contracts. Editor Houzeau resigned to resettle in Jamaica. It marked the end of the *Tribune* in its fourth year of publication.[21]

In this biracial government that the new constitution established, Blacks never constituted anything significantly beyond a third of Louisiana's House membership; in its Senate, no more than a fifth. Catholics seem to have consistently made up at least a half of the Black members of the House; in the Senate, the proportion was considerably less, with that proportion dropping over the course of Reconstruction.[22] Throughout Congressional Reconstruction, much of the Black leadership in Louisiana's state government came from the Afro-Creole community. Of 210 Black office holders in Louisiana during Congressional Reconstruction, at least 62 were Catholic.[23] Unlike the caricature that critics of "Black Reconstruction" circulated about illiterate barbarians, the vast majority of these Afro-Creoles were literate, with many possessing an education much above average.

Black legislators in Louisiana played lead roles in enacting legislation that established public welfare institutions (hospitals, asylums, schools for the deaf, and so forth) on an unprecedented scale. They were much less successful in reforming the tax structure to target corporations, especially the railroads, to provide the revenue to support these new government operations. The governmental debt that accumulated from these new expenditures only intensified the resistance to any new taxes. The Black legislators' efforts to improve sanitation as well as to regulate the drug and gun markets also failed. Their biggest accomplishment was the passing of civil rights legislation, including the 1875 act that prohibited the leasing of convicts from the state penitentiary. Representative Victor Rochon was responsible for a law that ended the restriction of the incorporation of Roman Catholic church property to whites.[24] They also tried, with little success, to ensure that all militias in the state would be ones "established by law."[25] Black members worked to protect agrarian workers, particularly from economic or punitive retaliation for engaging in political activity. They also tried to gain marriage rights for people of color, including the legitimization of children born in slavery, and the legalization of interracial marriages.

COMBATING RECONSTRUCTION IN
LOUISIANA AND VIRGINIA

"Affairs look very gloomy in New Orleans," John Mary Odin wrote to his fellow archbishop, Martin Spalding, in March 1868. "There is a real distress in the country." Odin was referring to the crop failures of the past two seasons, but he went on to reveal what was making "affairs" so "gloomy." "The political aspect of affairs seems to create a real uneasiness in the minds of our best men." He was particularly upset that General Grant was so continually overruling Winfield Scott Hancock, the commanding general of the region, "in his best measures for the welfare of Louisiana." Hancock, unlike Sheridan, had little interest in ensuring the success of Congressional Reconstruction. "We are afraid to lose him," Odin admitted.[26]

Charles Gayarré, at the height of Congressional Reconstruction, remarked that he knew not a single white who would not emigrate from Louisiana if given the means to do so. "They would rather accept any other despotism" rather than "Negro government. . . . A military dictator would be far preferable to them; they would go anywhere to escape the ignominy to which they were at present subjected."[27] In an effort to weaken the political power of white resisters, the Republicans redistricted the state. They created eight new parishes, including one that diluted the heavy white majority in New Orleans by combining Orleans and Jefferson parishes, including its police forces, under the direct authority of Governor Henry Clay Warmoth. The racially mixed Metropolitan police (Blacks comprised about a third of its members) became effectively the Republican government's military arm. The legislature also created the Returning Board to oversee elections and the violence that was disrupting them.[28] Warmoth was also trying to enlarge the Republican coalition by persuading whites, particularly those of foreign origin in New Orleans, to join the party. In this effort, he had much more success with the Germans than the Irish, who, as the *New Orleans Tribune* observed in 1869, "have for the most part sided with the Democratic party against us."[29] The worst was yet to come.

As soon as General John Schofield had told Virginia residents that the state was now under military rule, the *Catholic Mirror*'s "Homophonus" assured that "our people will take no steps tending to obstruct the operation of the Congressional Ultimatum." The congressional acts which had consigned to the military the oversight of Reconstruction, according to him, was a "usurpation of power on the part of Congress at war with the spirit and letter of the Constitution of the United States." Still, it was clear to him that "resistance to tyranny would be futile."[30] By April the correspondent was lamenting that "the South is now passing through the fiery ordeal of an experiment never before attempted under any government professing the slightest regard for popular rights, or any respect for the opinions of mankind. . . . We have acquiesced in the emancipation of our slaves. What other country, in ancient or modern times, has been forced to admit that class as a body, or even as individuals, to a full participation of social and political rights?" The Blacks' congenital inferiority, the correspondent concluded, required the supervision and control of their betters to ensure their well-being. Reconstruction represented a denial of this fundamental reality, indeed a deluded attempt to invert the natural order.[31] By the fall he was lamenting that "there is no justice for the South until the great masses of the North rise in their majesty and might, and hurl from power the miscreants who have so long abused it."[32] A month later, the correspondent hinted at the paramilitary action for which the crisis had forced them to prepare. "We have our Vigilance Committees in every precinct. . . . We know the worst, and are not only well prepared, but vigilant. . . . When the hour of action comes, the white assassins will first be cared for; the negroes will then be easily brought to their senses."[33] "The race of Crassus is not yet extinct," the classically trained correspondent assured his readers, in reference to the Roman commander who had brutally put down Spartacus's slave uprising.[34]

THE PRESIDENTIAL CAMPAIGN OF 1868

The Democratic platform that year declared the Reconstruction laws "a flagrant usurpation of power" that was "unconstitutional, revolutionary, and void."[35] The *Catholic Mirror*, reflecting the spirit behind that platform, vowed at the beginning of August that "Negro Supremacy will . . . never become an accomplished fact in our own or any other government. . . . The poor people of the South, former office-holders and all the others, are subjected to day to a political vassalage, which painfully reminds us of the tribulations of Ireland and Poland." This vassalage, to the editor, was even more intolerable inasmuch as the liege in Ireland was an Englishman. However hated he may be, there was no question but that he was the Irishman's superior, at least by social status and power. What was particularly galling about Black rule (as the editor mischaracterized the Republican governments in the South) was that this was rule by "a class considered inferior by Southern whites generally."[36]

In the late summer of 1868, William Rosecrans became the emissary of Governor Horatio Seymour, then the Democratic candidate for president, to explain to a group of former Confederate officials and officers vacationing at White Sulphur Springs in West Virginia, the Democratic candidate's policy toward the South. In a letter to Robert E. Lee, one of those vacationers, Rosecrans, conveying Seymour's sentiments, acknowledged that the extreme insistence on "State Rights" had led to the break-up of the Union and war. But out of the four years of violence that followed had come a drift toward a consolidation that was threatening the Union by its own extremism. Reconstruction, according to Seymour, had produced a "semi-anarchy" which had hurt the economy nationally, and was impairing "the law and order" to which he knew all Americans, North and South, aspired. Seymour assured these quondam southern leaders that he did not share the belief of Republicans that the only path to reconstructing the South lay through putting power in the hands of "uneducated, landless freedmen" and a few white opportunists eager to exploit the Blacks for their own venal ends.

As a spokesman for the veterans of the Union Army, Rosecrans was prepared to tell these former leaders of the Confederacy that their onetime foes, indeed the "people of the North and West," were of the firm opinion that those who had led the Confederacy during the war should be the ones leading the South back into the peace and prosperity it deserved. He was there to ascertain whether these men gathered at White Sulphur Springs were of the same mind.

Rosecrans's overture was at root an appeal to the South's military and political elite to support, as far as legally possible, the Democratic candidate for president, on the implicit promise that Seymour alone could restore peace to the South by bringing into power in the states currently under military rule those who had led the Confederacy's struggle for independence. It was also an implicit appeal to the Union military. Those who had won the war now had the burden to win the peace by putting into the presidency a Democrat who would undo the revolution to which the Congressional Republicans were subjecting the South.[37] It was a revelation of how limited had been Rosecrans's commitment to abolition.

In his response, Lee claimed, "At present the negroes have neither the intelligence or other qualifications which are necessary to make them safe depositories of political power. . . . The great want of the South is . . . for the re-establishment . . . of that which has justly been regarded as the birth right of every American—the right of self-government." Lee's letter bore thirty-two signatures, including that of P. G. T. Beauregard. It depicted a South in which as "Americans" they accepted the war's outcome regarding slavery and secession. They were ready to do right by the freedmen, this alien body which history had placed in their midst.[38] It was an airy assessment that ignored entirely the widespread, determined resistance that southern whites, including Catholics, were mounting against the Republican attempt to revolutionize their region.

Two months earlier, there were presumably many Catholics among the bloc of German Democrats who gathered at Dueringer's Park in Richmond to protest military occupation and Black rule. The group passed a resolution which declared: "We are proud to be of German descent and we reject with indignation . . . to be placed on equal political and social footing with the Negroes just extracted from the mire of slavery. We consider it as sacrificing the nation, to force the white population of the South under the rule of a half-civilized and inferior race."[39] If anything, outrage over Radical Reconstruction ran even deeper among the southern Irish, to whom it was a reprise of the British occupation of Ireland and the ongoing attempt to force-feed reform down the throats of the Irish people. Abram Ryan, the priest-poet whom Bishop Augustin Verot had made editor of his diocesan paper, in his columns attacked this crusade to promote Black equality, which the priest saw as an alien "fungus" destined to die out in the South.[40]

Harry Northrop, a young priest stationed at New Bern, North Carolina, wrote his friend James Gibbons in September of 1868: "The political sky down here looks very dark. We have had one or two petty disturbances, which people look on as the precursors to more serious ones. The election of Grant will result, if we must believe the professions of our friends here, in a general stampede & desertion of the town to carpetbaggers & scallawags. I am afraid our little church will suffer from the secession."[41] The disturbances were real, both in coastal North Carolina and throughout the South, but they were not the work of carpetbaggers, scalawags, and their Black allies. By 1868 the Ku Klux Klan had launched a reign of terror against Republican leaders, both Black and white, in nearly every southern state. The terror ranged from economic pressure to assassination. In Louisiana, white paramilitary groups, like the Knights of the White Camelia, mushroomed, particularly in the Black-majority Red River Valley region in north-central Louisiana. Murders of local Republicans, both Black and white, became a near-daily occurrence. By mid-August, officials estimated that at least three hundred persons had been killed over the past two months. When Governor Warmoth appealed to the district military commander, Lovell H. Rousseau, for weapons for his under-armed Metropolitan Police force, the general had no weapons for him but only the urgent recommendation that the governor encourage Blacks to sit out the election to avert violence.[42] In October, violence crested in a series of massacres of Black Republicans. In the upriver parishes, at least two hundred Blacks died in the month leading up to the November election.[43]

STIRRINGS OF REDEMPTION

Ulysses Grant captured the presidency in an Electoral College landslide, 214 to 80. It represented a remarkable turnaround for a party whose candidate eight years earlier had not even been on the ballot in ten of the southern states. It seemed a vindication of Congressional Reconstruction, with the former general of the army winning all the states except Georgia, Kentucky, Louisiana, Maryland, New Jersey, New York, and Oregon. The popular vote, however, was much closer, with Grant winning just 53 percent of it. In all likelihood, a majority of white votes went to Horatio Seymour. That Seymour had carried two border states and two states in the Deep South meant that the forces of redemption were already very much in play. Violence and other forms of intimidation had been lethally effective in suppressing sufficiently the Black vote in Georgia and Louisiana to enable Seymour to carry both states.[44] The terror in Louisiana cut the Republican vote to half of what it had been in the previous spring elections. Carole Emberton notes that the tragedy of Reconstruction was that Republicans largely underestimated the warlike nature of the democratic revolution they were attempting. They put too much faith in the political opportunities they were creating, particularly for those emancipated by the war, and not enough in the brute force that the occupying military could bring to bear upon those bent on overturning the revolution. It is no coincidence, she avers, that the two states in which Reconstruction had its longest life span—Louisiana and South Carolina—were those in which Republicans most utilized military force, although they failed to exert it sufficiently in the former state in 1868.[45] To P. G. T. Beauregard, defeating the Republican candidate in Louisiana was scant consolation. "I had supposed," the former Confederate general wrote Bishop Patrick Lynch, "that the elections . . . would have restored us to our constitutional position in the Union— but I fear that we have four years more of patient suffering in store for us."[46]

CONGRESSIONAL RECONSTRUCTION
UNDER GRANT

With the former commander of all US forces now president of the United States, the Reconstruction of the South under military rule seemed complete. A year after Grant assumed office, Congress enacted its third amendment to the Constitution in five years. The Fifteenth Amendment granted all male citizens of the United States the right to vote. No government, federal or state, could deny that right "on account of race, color, or previous condition of servitude." The federal government had now altered the Constitution to assert its power to abolish slavery, to set the standards for citizenship, and to extend the franchise to all those males holding citizenship. This constitutional revolution which the Congress had carried out since the waning months of the war was, to many proponents of states' rights and limited government, the fulfillment of their worst fears. Along with the division of the former Confederate states into military districts, the amendments were providing the legal infrastructure for centralized rule.

Reconstruction, Gerald Fogarty observes, ushered in a "Catholic moment" in Virginia politics as Catholics like Anthony Keiley and James Dooley became leaders in the opposition to the congressional turn that Reconstruction had taken. In May of 1865, Keiley had co-founded the *Petersburg News,* but federal authorities had quickly suppressed it and briefly jailed Keiley for its criticism of the secretary of war, Edwin Stanton. Undeterred, Keiley founded two other papers in Virginia. Then in the summer of 1866 the governor appointed him to fill out a term in the House of Delegates. In the meantime, he became editor of the *Richmond Examiner.* When Military Reconstruction dissolved the Virginia legislature, Keiley became a key player in the Conservative Party. The Hibernian Democratic Club, which Keiley established, became the medium for many Catholics' participation in the Conservative Party. In June of 1868, this bloc of the party met at the Odd Fellows Hall to protest the proposed constitution.[47] Patrick Moore, the former commander of the First Virginia, as well as James Dooley and John Higgins were prominent participants. Dooley urged the assembled party members to make the concerted efforts needed "to defeat the miserable production of twenty-four negroes, scarcely able to read their own printed work, fourteen renegade Virginians, fit associates for them, and twenty-seven scalawags, carpet-baggers, and miserable political adventurers from the North."[48] Among the resolutions they passed was one that condemned the Radical Republicans for their anti-immigration policy and for nominating a former Know-Nothing, Schuyler Colfax, as their vice presidential candidate.

But it was clear that white supremacy, not anti-nativism, was at the heart of their opposition. The members resolved that, "in the national struggle for the re-establishment of the lost authority of the Constitution, and in the local struggle for the maintenance of the political supremacy of the white race as a constituent portion of the people of Virginia," Richmond citizens of Irish birth or descent "will vindicate their respect for the organic law, and their fealty to their own color by every method left them by the power and malice of their enemies." Richmond's Irish called on "the Irish of America to witness the single purpose of Radicalism in the South—to plunder the whites and use the Blacks to aid them in the plundering."[49]

Among the critics of Ulysses Grant's handling of Reconstruction was his former top ally during the war, Cump Sherman. What particularly bothered Sherman were the president's attempts to enforce Black rights in the South and to let stand white disfranchisement.[50] Sherman, now having succeeded Grant as US general-in-chief, was in a critical position to undermine those administrative efforts. One of Sherman's first moves as commanding general was to reduce the nation's military force by half, to twenty-eight thousand. The reductions had a radical impact on the federal government's military footprint in the South. In Louisiana, Sherman left a mere seven hundred soldiers as a shield and enforcer for the state Republican government. Most of the army posts in upriver Louisiana parishes, the very area where vigilante violence was most concentrated, closed. To offset the vacuum of government enforcement, Governor Warmoth formed a statewide militia of four regiments, one composed of freedmen or *gens de couleur*. To attract the enlistment of Confederate veterans, Governor Warmoth appointed as commander James Longstreet. Longstreet succeeded in attracting enough Confederate veterans to comprise about half the militia. Unfortunately, they were mostly from the New Orleans area, as was three-quarters of the militia itself. In effect, it became a military supplement to the Metropolitan Police, with little reach beyond New Orleans.[51] Nonetheless, Longstreet was determined to make his biracial militia a dependable protective force for the Reconstruction government. Every militia member had to take an oath to "accept the civil and political equality of all men and . . . not . . . to deprive any person . . . on account of race, color, or previous condition of any political or civil right . . . enjoyed by any other class of men."[52] Despite Longstreet's efforts, the Louisiana Militia tended to be underpaid, ill-supplied with arms and other equipment, including uniforms, and lacked secure armories.[53]

Typically, Augustin Verot made very public his opinion of Congressional Reconstruction. In a pastoral letter issued in November of 1868, the bishop judged Reconstruction to be a matter of "wicked men and unprincipled demagogues, abusing [the freedmen's] simplicity, their ignorance and credulity [by promising] them rich spoils coming either from the Government or from the estates of their former masters, and have thus made them dupes of their own malice and crafty rapacity."[54] Verot endorsed the opinion that prevailed even in a Republican-controlled federal government: that the government had no responsibility to provide land, whether public or private property, either as recompense for their past services and/or to provide a means to earn a decent living. Given his self-help convictions, Verot dismissed government welfare in the form of food or other supplies as tools for promoting dependency and sustaining false hopes about land distribution among a childlike people.

THE LYNCHES AND REPUBLICAN RULE
IN SOUTH CAROLINA

The mass poverty that was the South's legacy from the war had reduced even the formerly wealthy to seeking relief. As Baptista Lynch reported to her bishop brother about the state of the Carolina upcountry in 1868: "everybody is [so] poor, & willing now to beg that the shame has worn away from even the most respectable."[55] For the Ursulines, Valle Crucis, their new location three miles outside of Columbia, had forced them to become a boarding institution only. But even the limited accommodations at Valle Crucis proved impossible to fill. Enrollment fell precipitously, with parents unable to afford the tuition. Of the few who could, most found it difficult to keep up the payments. Failure in their attempts to secure compensation from the federal government forced the Ursulines to resort to all manner of fundraising from fairs to lectures to circulars sent to all the women's religious communities in the United States. Still their most reliable supporter continued to be their longest-standing patron: Bishop Lynch. By 1870, much of the greatly reduced enrollment in the Ursuline Academy consisted of Lynch children, their tuition and board paid by their great-uncle Patrick.

Francis Lynch was experiencing the worst that mono-staple agriculture could produce. As his wife, Henrietta, told her brother-in-law bishop, "he has had trial after trial, Job's trials, since Sherman's entry into Cheraw."[56] Having lost his shoemaking business to Sherman's avengers, Francis had turned to planting for his economic recovery, only to discover how stacked against him were the forces at play in southern agriculture. Lacking the money to pay wages, Francis had to share the revenue from the sale of his crop with his workers, which left him with barely enough to pay for his fertilizer and other planting necessities. Compounding that shortfall were his wartime debts, which no peace settlement could forgive. In desperation Francis sought to stave off the debt collectors by selling part of his plantation to New York investors. Financing his ambitious enterprises had always been a complicated matter for Francis Lynch. The war's outcome had complicated them much more so, especially with the loss of Francis's most valuable financial asset, his human property. By 1870, selling land had become key to Francis's financial recovery. To find buyers of land or other comparable commodities, southern sellers had no choice but to look north or abroad. The South lacked the capital to acquire such properties.[57] What the Yankees failed to take by war, they now had the sole financial wherewithal to force southerners like Francis Lynch to sell to them at their price. "This is the winter of our disappointment," Francis told Patrick in January of 1868.[58] Gradually the downward spiral of Francis's fortunes humbled him to the point that the once self-confident entrepreneur became overwhelmed by feelings that destiny was no longer his servant but his merciless persecutor.

It fell to his wife, Henrietta, to bring to Patrick Lynch's attention that Francis's family had sunk to a level which they could hardly have imagined themselves inhabiting before the war. They had been brought to depend on their brother bishop to pay their children's tuition, a dependence they thought long behind them. Like the poor folks of the hills, their children now often went shoeless. Henrietta was forced to beg Patrick for ten dollars, simply to put food on the table. Francis himself was so out of sorts as to convince Henrietta that suicide had become a distinct possibility for him.

Before the war, John Lynch had faced the challenge of building up one's practice to the point that it could keep a family in comfort. Now, no matter how many patients one could claim, if they had not the wherewithal to pay for his services, numbers ceased to matter. To compound John's financial shortfall, there was the taxation imposed by the Reconstruction government. Whereas before the war, the planter class bore the brunt of the minimal taxation southern governments imposed, now the considerable tax burden fell broadly across society, the consequence of much more activist postbellum governments. Suddenly the state took on a myriad of enterprises ranging from education to infrastructure to welfare that greatly drove up the budgets funded mainly through property taxes. John Lynch's inability to pay his taxes in full put his greatest financial asset—his house—at risk. In desperation he tried to raise funds by selling a patent he had obtained, as well as a copper mine of dubious value which he owned.

John informed Patrick, "I do not know how I am to get on. . . . I have plenty owing to me, but the money is not in the country."[59] John, like Francis, was increasingly dependent on Patrick to avoid the financial ruin threatening him from his real estate investments. But it was the support John received from a most unlikely source that promised relief and even recovery from his financial woes. Republican governor Robert K. Scott not only cosigned the loans that John was forced to take, but Scott also was apparently responsible for the appointment, in September 1871, to the university's medical faculty, a prize John had been long seeking.[60] For the Lynch brothers, at least John and Francis, financial needs dictated political allegiance. The Lynches were resigned to working with whoever held authority in the state, in order to protect and advance their financial interests. Their own economic well-being had become very much dependent on the Republican government's success, even if its legislative membership had a Black majority. Consider them passive scalawags.

In February 1869 the South Carolina legislature passed the most extensive civil rights law in the nation. The law mandated that all places of public accommodation and any business licensed by municipal, state, or federal authority treat everyone equitably.[61] That law proved extremely hard to enforce, but it reflected the extent of the commitment of the Black majority legislature to integrate society. That commitment extended even to higher education. The new constitution of the state declared that all universities within the state should be "free and open to all the children and youths of the State, without regard to race and color." Later in 1869, a biracial board of trustees formally adopted that policy for the University of South Carolina. Still, for four years, no Blacks applied to enroll. Finally, in 1873 the mixed-race secretary of state, Henry E. Hayne, enrolled in the medical department of an institution that had historically been an aristocratic preserve. That enrollment touched off a boycott by both students and faculty. "The Radical University," as South Carolina whites came to call the groundbreaking institution, struggled to fill its rolls, poaching students from Howard University and having Black legislators enroll nominally to swell the ranks. The college department eventually enrolled some whites, but the student population remained over 90 percent Black.[62]

Despite the white community's treatment of the university as an institutional pariah, John Lynch accepted an appointment to the faculty of the medical college. Here, at last, was his chance for the guaranteed income which could rescue him from the financial peril threatening to engulf him. Unfortunately, the legislature had failed to appropriate the funding for faculty salaries. John Lynch was an unpaid professor, a status that only worsened the impact for him of the financial depression in 1873 that struck South Carolina, along with the country. When his horse died, John could not replace him. So, he became a doctor without means of transportation beyond his own feet, about the worst situation for a physician whose practice was already suffering from the inability of so many people to afford a doctor.

John Lynch's financial woes were subsequently compounded by a lawsuit brought against him and his family, including his brothers, by the family of a former student at the Ursuline Academy. John Lynch in September 1861 had, as the legal guardian of the student, been entrusted with the funds the student was due to inherit when she turned twenty-one. Thirteen years later, the student's family claimed that Lynch had invested those funds principally in Confederate bonds, which were now worthless.[63] A court determined, in 1874, that, of the $12,000 which had been entrusted to Lynch as guardian, he owed $3,867, including interest.[64] Not only did he have that obligation hanging over him, but a mortgage he had taken out on his mine was soon to come due. Such economic straits made John Lynch even more dependent on the Republican government's not merely surviving but flourishing to the degree that it could meet its financial obligations, including those to the university faculty. "I hope the financial condition of S[outh] C[arolina] will be better after the election," he wrote his brother in 1874. He was supporting Chamberlain, "although a R[epublican] & Carpetbagger," because of his belief that Chamberlain would restore integrity to government and with it "confidence restored . . . and capital flowing into the state to develop its manufacturing and mineral resources," including Lynch's mine.[65] Chamberlain became governor, but the court did not give John Lynch the additional time to repay to the student's estate the remaining monies with which he had been entrusted.[66]

John Lynch found himself on the same psychological brink that his brother Francis had already experienced. "It seems to me the times cannot get much darker," he wrote his bishop brother. "Even the University is a failure this year." The college had six students enrolled, all sons of faculty members. The medical school had two, both of whom withdrew when the Black secretary of state, Henry Hayne, enrolled himself. "So we have as yet in the med school, a class of one coloured individual for four professors and the demonstrator to work on. I hardly think the legislature will make an appropriation of nine thousand dollars a year to teach even the sect[retary] of state to practice medicine. What an awkward position I am in." Financial need kept him within the orbit of the reform government. Still, he was willing to become a social pariah in the white community. In violence-prone South Carolina, the willingness to be labeled a "scalawag" counted as heroic, no matter the financial motivations involved in the decision.[67]

CHAPTER 21

Reconstructions in West and North

[Capital is] the despotic ruler and the worker is its slave.
This being the case, I say, leave the poor workers alone. There being
little danger that they do injustice to the tyrannical employer.

—MARTIN SPALDING, 1866

A SEA CHANGE IN SOVEREIGNTY

The postwar era saw a sea change in the hierarchy of sovereignty in America. In the South the central government asserted its sovereignty over that of the individual states in attempting to "reconstruct" society, an effort that fueled an increasingly violent white backlash. In the West the federal government ended its recognition of the indigenous nations as sovereign peoples by assigning them to reservations where they were expected to desist from their nomadic ways and adopt the agrarian life that remained the ideal realization of the American dream. In the North, capital increasingly turned to government to suppress labor's attempts to organize. Amid these shifting forces of sovereignty, the constant victor remained the avaricious capitalists who increasingly controlled government at both the national and state levels to promote and protect their interests.[1]

A PERENNIAL CHALLENGE

As Paul Prucha has noted, the perennial federal challenge was the maintenance of just and peaceful relations with the Indian tribes while facilitating the movement of settler society westward. Inevitably the former too often fell victim to the latter.[2] Relentless expansion time and again rendered peace treaties meaningless. The most effective buffer between the tribes and westward-heading migrants was the US Army. To maximize the ability of the army to serve as a shield, the Bureau of Indian Affairs had been established within the War Department. The federal government erected a line of forts during the antebellum period, as though to demarcate a boundary between two nations. But no number of forts could halt the inexorable westward march. Too often the military served not as a buffer but as an agent of expansion, with the indigenous peoples paying the price for that progress, usually by forced treaties that involved the surrender of land and removal westward to greatly inferior terrain.

In June 1867, three months after Congress took control of Reconstruction, it created the US Indian Peace Commission, composed of three military officers and four civilians. Two of the three officers were Catholics: W. T. Sherman and William S. Harney. Six months later the commission issued a report, which was a jeremiad against the government's handling of its Indian relations. Intrusions of settlers upon their lands had historically caused the Indians to take to the warpath, only to be defeated by the United States deploying means that were uniformly unjust. Expansion, the commission fatalistically claimed, was providentially inevitable. It called for a two-state solution, by which tracts would be set apart for reservations which would be multi-tribal. To manage them, the commission called for the creation of a Department of Indian Affairs independent of the military. Unsurprisingly, none of the military minority favored the proposal.[3]

The following year a series of treaties with the northern tribes carried out the commission's recommendations by creating a homestead program for these Native Americans by assigning 160 acres of arable land to individuals who qualified for them. It was Jefferson's dream of a yeoman nation applied to a large portion of its indigenous people. The difficulty was that the land was suitable not for agriculture but for grazing. Unrest quickly developed among the Cheyenne, Arapahos, and Sioux. In the end, homesteading failed to become the way of life on the reservations.[4]

THE CATHOLIC BUREAU FOR
INDIAN MISSIONS

Since the earliest days of the Republic, Christianization as a civilizer of Amerindian tribes had been an assumption underlying government policy. In pursuing that goal, the federal government had subsidized denominations' missionary work, including education. When the Grant administration announced its intention of delegating the management of the reservations to religious groups, the Catholic Church expected, on the basis of its established missions among the indigenous peoples, to be assigned approximately half of the projected eighty agencies. When the all-Protestant board announced the awards, Catholics received only seven agencies (in the state of Washington, and the territories of Oregon, Montana, and Dakota), responsible for fewer than 18,000 of the approximately 240,000 tribal members. The remainder went to Protestant denominations ranging from the Baptists to the Reformed Dutch, with the Methodists receiving the most.[5]

Pierre-Jean De Smet complained that Catholic bodies received far too few reservations to manage (four of forty-three), given that about a third of Native Americans were Catholic.[6] He found a powerful ally in his friend Ellen Sherman, who used her church and state connections to lobby for Catholic Indian missions to receive more equitable funding and resources from the federal government. Baltimore Archbishop James Roosevelt Bayley authorized Ellen's brother, Charles Ewing, to represent the Catholic Church's missions in Washington.[7] In December, Ewing petitioned that forty tribes with which the church had had evangelizing success be put under Catholic auspices. Ewing argued that, if the point of putting the tribes under religious supervision was to advance the goal of Christianizing them, it would undermine that goal by failing to reward the church whose missionaries had been successful in achieving that end. Despite Ewing's intense lobbying, the allotment remained basically unchanged.

In 1874 the American episcopacy created the Catholic Bureau for Indian Missions, with Charles Ewing as its head. The following year, at the suggestion of Jean-Baptiste Brouillet, a missionary in the Pacific Northwest who was a major player in the institutionalization of Catholic outreach to the Amerindians, the Ladies' Catholic Indian Missionary Association of Washington, DC, was inaugurated with Madeleine Vinton Dahlgren, Admiral Dahlgren's wife, as president. Hugh Ewing's wife, Henrietta, as well as his sister, Ellen, became prominent members. The bureau, beginning in 1877, published *Annals of the Catholic Indian Missions,* a compilation of missionaries' letters and reports, to stir interest in and financial support for the missions. Ellen Sherman was particularly active in making appeals for this apostolate by articles published in the *Catholic World, the Catholic Mirror,* and other journals. Their fundraising brought meager results, in part because of opposition to the bureau's cooperation with the federal government, led by James McMaster and the *Freeman's Journal.* The bureau never achieved its goal of receiving what it considered a fair share of the agencies. In 1881 the government declared that all religious denominations should have access to reservations, a policy change to which denominations complied to varying extents. The bureau did manage to increase nearly sixfold the number of Catholic boarding schools, from three to seventeen.

A vital change in the federal government's Indian policy came about in virtual secrecy. A clause buried in the Indian Appropriation Act of March 1871 stated that hitherto no Indian tribe within the borders of the United States would be recognized as an independent nation with which the US government could make a treaty.[8] That provided the legal sanction for the longstanding goal of segregating tribes onto reservations where they could be educated to assimilate into American society through the destruction of their traditional way of life.[9]

SHERMAN AND SHERIDAN AS AGENTS OF MANIFEST DESTINY

In the postwar period, critical forces were promoting the aggressive confinement of the tribes within reservations, ranging from emigrants to the railroads to the army contractors seeking to profit from military campaigns. Attacks by indigenous Americans on migrants for trespassing on their territory served as the pretext for removing the Native Americans in order to protect the trespassers. The advent of four transcontinental railroad lines in the immediate postwar decades gave the Army an unprecedented mobility advantage in its campaigns against the tribes. The other development that fatally crippled the Native Americans was the destruction of the buffalo. Both proved crucial in eliminating the Indians as obstacles to American expansion.

In late June of 1865 William Tecumseh Sherman had been appointed commander of the vast Military Division of the Mississippi, which included all the country from the Mississippi River to the Rocky Mountains. In that position he oversaw the construction of the transcontinental railway poised to provide the coast-to-coast interconnection that Manifest Destiny ideology had promoted since the 1840s. As commander, Sherman was also responsible for the pacification of the Native Americans who stood in the way of the white settlement of the West. Sherman grasped that interlacing the region with rails would not only foster settlement but eventually fatally disrupt the nomadic lifestyle of the tribes. There were some 270,000 Indians in the West, divided into over one hundred different tribes. Of that number about 100,000 were still trying to hold back the ocean that was the white race's advance. Against them were the 25,000 soldiers posted in the trans-Mississippi region. To eliminate the tribes as a formidable obstacle to expansion, the elimination of the bison, the main food source for the Amerindians, was an absolute necessity.

In late December 1866, a war party of Sioux massacred a cavalry patrol from Fort Kearny under Colonel W. J. Fetterman in retaliation for violence and other abuses that the Sioux had suffered from migrants on the Bozeman Trail. An army investigation into the massacre concluded that it was the inevitable result of vested interests (ranchers, army contractors, army officers, and so forth) goading the military into provocative actions that triggered Indian violence in response. Sherman himself acknowledged that the hostilities started by false rumors were designed to enrich contractors through the supplies they provided for the subsequent fighting. But there were larger factors that spelled doom for the Plains Indians. The construction of the transcontinental railroad put far greater pressure on the federal government to remove the Native Americans who were obstructing the pathways of migration. By 1867 the acting commissioner of Indian affairs had decided that the government needed to use its diplomatic resources to persuade the tribes to move. The commissioner spoke for a minority that was shrinking by the day. Increasingly public opinion was calling for military action against the Sioux for the Fetterman massacre. Sherman accordingly led three punitive expeditions.

Pierre-Jean De Smet, in his final report to the Indian Office, urged that they give "due regard" to the complaints of the Sioux and others. They should take care that the annuities were made available when expected, that the agents of the government needed to deal with them "honestly and kindly." If they did, De Smet was sure that peace would prevail.[10] Government assurances to the Jesuit that the United States would do right by the Native Americans led De Smet to believe that, if the Indians were forced to relocate in reservations, transformation could be the key to the integration of the indigenous people as full citizens in the republic. He envisioned a union of reservations that would form a bloc of states with representation in the Congress.[11]

The commissioner of Indian affairs, Nathaniel G. Taylor, in July 1867 proposed that the government set aside large swaths of territory, both above and below the Platte River, to house the western indigenous Americans. Congress agreed that they should pursue treaties with the tribes to put this plan into action. If diplomacy failed to move them, then General Sherman would be ordered, in effect, to wage total war on them. Over the next year, tribes signed treaties to move to the designated areas, with the government's assurance that whites would not be allowed on their new territory. But the Indians' own movement would be confined to the reservations. No longer would they be able to engage in the annual hunt that had played such a large role in sustaining their way of life. The treaty mode of the relationship between the tribes and the US government had become a farce in which the agents of the United

States gulled the tribal leaders into signing agreements whose implications they little realized.[12]

In the 1868 Fort Laramie Treaty, the United States, in effect, exercised its eminent domain over the Great Plains, while ceding certain tracts of land to the signatory tribes.[13] As Prucha noted, the Fort Laramie Treaty was the culmination of a trend long in the making: the treaty process as a legal rationalization "for accomplishing what U.S. officials wanted to do."[14] The following year, President Grant made no pretense about negotiating a treaty. By an executive order, he simply assigned a tract of territory to the Southern Cheyennes and Arapahos. Two years later, Congress effectively ended the treaty system.[15] No longer was there a pretense that the tribes represented sovereign nations.[16]

In August 1868, Sherman issued Order No. 4, which reorganized the designated reservations as military districts in which commanding officers would have ultimate jurisdiction. Immediately afterward, several hundred Cheyennes, Sioux, and Arapahos went on the warpath. Sherman sent Philip Sheridan on a winter offensive, with the charge to "prosecute the war with vindictive earnestness till they are obliterated or beg for mercy." Sheridan, in sharp contrast to his attitude toward Black Americans, could not bring himself to recognize any rights that the Native Americans had. His relentless winter campaigning against the Indians of the Southern Plains broke the back of their resistance. Particularly in his warfare against the indigenous people, victory itself made right any means used to attain it. Against a people thought to be barbaric, even the most egregious actions were legitimate.[17] So in his Southern Plains campaign in 1874, Sheridan weaponized the buffalo as part of a total war strategy to deprive the Native peoples of the means to continue their struggle as well as to demoralize their resistance to white expansion.[18] Between 1867 and 1874, five million buffalo were slaughtered.[19]

On November 3, 1875, at the White House, President Grant convened a secret policy meeting, which included General Sheridan. The participants understood that there was no stopping the settlers, entrepreneurs, railroads, towns, and "civilization" in general from overrunning the once exclusive domain of the Plains Indians. Manifest Destiny had become such an essential tenet of the American creed as to be beyond moral or legal challenge.[20] The white population in the West had more than doubled in the previous decade, from an estimated 2.3 million, to nearly 5.0 million. Grant ordered Sheridan to be ready to undertake a Northern Plains winter campaign against any tribes which had failed to settle on the reservations.[21] After severe storms quickly terminated the winter campaign, Sheridan prepared to renew it once summer arrived. With nearly 3,000 men in three columns, converging from the west, east, and south, Sheridan intended to strike the Powder River country, where reports had the tribes gathering their warriors. The summer campaign had an ominous start. On June 17 at the Battle of the Rosebud in Wyoming, Cheyenne and Sioux forced the headlong retreat of a 1,100-man unit from Fort Fetterman. Two weeks later came the disaster at the Little Big Horn in Montana, where George Armstrong Custer and 215 troopers of the predominantly Irish Seventh Cavalry had rashly attacked a village which harbored as many as 2,000 warriors. Within the hour, the troopers all lay dead on the hillside of the river.[22]

The massacre of Little Big Horn was the worst defeat the US Army had ever suffered in the nation's century of existence. Unfortunately for the tribes, it proved to be the most pyrrhic of victories. Public opinion about the nation's indigenous peoples turned even more militant. Even the progressive *Nation* magazine called for the "destruction of the Indian race" as retribution for the slaughter in Montana.[23] Sheridan plotted a winter campaign aimed at destroying their means of sustenance and pressing them to the point where surrender or death were the only options.[24] By May 1877, after a particularly devastating winter and assaults against two villages, indigenous resistance on the Northern Plains ceased. The survivors either went onto the reservations or moved northward into Canada.

REJECTING THE NATIONAL MOTTO
ON THE WESTERN PLAINS

By the 1880s the once-nomadic tribes were, by and large, segregated on reservations scattered throughout the West. The dream of Pierre-Jean De Smet for the concentration of the Native Americans in consolidated territory which could become a state or two of the Union never came close to becoming reality. As Michael Fellman concluded about the Indian policy pursued by the Grant administration, the president and his generals, Sherman and Sheridan, "applied their shared ruthlessness, born of their Civil War experiences, against a people all three despised, in the name of Civilization and progress."[25]

If the United States' evolving Indian policy from the 1830s to the 1880s demonstrated anything, it was the clear rejection of the country's motto: *e pluribus unum*. What Paul Prucha said about the Aboriginal people could have been extended to several groups in American society by 1883: that Americans were never ready to accept a pluralistic society which included any folks not considered white. Just as the revival of minstrel shows in the North continued to caricature Blacks in popular culture, so Bill Cody's touring Wild West shows reduced the Indian experience to that same exotic level.[26] Meanwhile the Congress was enacting the first of a series of acts virtually closing the door to Chinese immigrants, who were the major Asian presence in the United States.

WAR'S EXPOSURE OF

THE FREE LABOR THEORY

The Free Labor theory had been an important component of Whig-Republican ideology. The theory posited a social covenant between individual owners and workers in which each party had reciprocal responsibilities. The covenant itself was understood to be a temporary one, with the worker utilizing the experience and skills that his current position gave him to seize the opportunities in a dynamic economy to move upward in the classless society which the theory assumed to be a given in American life. The Civil War fatally exposed the theory's false assumptions. In its creation of so much military demand for a seemingly infinite range of products, from uniforms to petroleum, the war was a godsend for business growth in the North.[27] In putting a premium on volume and speed in supplying the immense armies of the Union on an unprecedented scale, the war acted as a catalyst for big industry and the technology that drove it. Civil War industry prefigured what was to come: large, mechanized factories in which low-skilled workers turned out products for both domestic and foreign markets. For professionals, particularly those in medicine and engineering, as well as the white-collar middle class in general, the war was a positive boon. The federal government was an active partner with private enterprise in expanding the economy and generating wealth. Government contracts, generous land grants, financial legislation and policy, and tax and tariff legislation contributed greatly not only to the Union war effort but to the North's economic expansion.

The Reconstruction era created an even more favorable environment for wealth-making on an enormous scale. New York City became the capital of this consolidating, corporate America, with two-thirds of the country's largest corporations headquartered there. Individuals such as Hugh O'Neill in the department-store business, John Crimmins in construction, and John Roach in shipbuilding constituted a Catholic nouveau riche in the city, while remaining outsiders in the Gilded Age's social hierarchy.[28] Their mansions, in all too close proximity to scandalously overcrowded tenements, were, just as much as those of their social betters, a visual confirmation of the galloping inequality that characterized postwar America.[29]

For labor, within which category most Catholics fell, the war was no bonanza. The "new birth of freedom" that the war was midwifing seemed, if anything, to bring new threats to workers' economic well-being.[30] True, labor shortages resulted in rising wages, but not enough to keep up with inflation. Prices rose nearly 80 percent in the North during the war years, wages less than two-thirds of that figure. The growing reliance on machinery to meet the rising scale of production reduced the labor needed, particularly that of skilled operatives.

GOVERNMENT AS
KEY TO SOCIAL REFORM

In 1876, the centennial year, Patrick Lynch delivered a lecture on "Society and the Poor." Typically, he undertook to examine the question from the perspective of a scientist, intent on impartial observations and deductions. The bishop averred that the inequities in society were the consequence of the inevitable struggle between persons of unequal talents and resolution. Governments could not put an end to the struggle, only provide some relief to the weaker party in the conflict. Looking backward, Patrick Lynch noted that a middling equality had characterized American society in the nation's earlier history. Opportunities existed for the virtuous, hard-working individual to realize some measure of prosperity and independence. But, the bishop admitted, "a change has come over the country." The older quest by the many for a decent living had been replaced by the acquisition of colossal fortunes by the few. Men were deserting honorable work in fields and workshops for "fields of speculation. . . . Capital and labour are being dissociated," he declared. Lynch proceeded to make a persuasive case for the laboring class to have a fair share of the wealth that it helped to produce. Instead of calling for the social reform that would meet the working man's cries, however, the bishop pointed to the necessity of religion in making the social order right. Only a religiously infused education could form the personal character that would produce the virtuous citizens that a healthy republic required. Such an education, of course, could only come from religious schools, ideally Catholic ones.

Beyond the citizen formation that the right kind of education provided, Lynch was reduced to advocating charity as the best hope for reforming society. The bishop noted how well charity had responded to the South's dismal plight at war's end. He was especially proud to have been one of the channels of that Catholic charity. Benevolence bred benevolence, in Lynch's rosy diagnosis of human nature. Missing in his presentation was the greatest beneficiary of the southern people, more so even than the various southern relief societies, the Freedmen's Bureau, that incomparable source of aid to Black and white alike. That, alas, was a government organization. That was official charity. In part, this ignoring of public relief and recovery programs arose from the two-sphere model through which Lynch, like so many of his fellow prelates, viewed the church-state relationship. The church had nothing to say about the state's obligation to provide for the general welfare, about the ways in which it could protect and promote fundamental rights. Bishop Lynch's opinion was constrained by the revelation-based doctrine that grounded it, specifically by Jesus's statement about the inevitable presence of the poor in any society. That comment was elevated to a pronouncement of poverty as a permanent human condition beyond fundamental alteration. The best one could do was to alleviate the suffering and want that poverty entailed. And religion was eminently key to developing the compassionate spirit that issued in works of charity, works that proved to have a chain reaction in imbuing that same urge to give in those who had received. Government charity, "official charity" in Lynch's term, lacking that spirit, inevitably resulted in coldness, abuse, and the dystopia of the workhouse. Private charity, either exercised by religious individuals or religious communities, was the only reliable comforter of the poor.

A few Catholics saw that education and temperance, valuable as they might be in shaping and reforming character, were not enough to overcome the social and economic injustice that undermined the development of a prosperous and virtuous citizenry. Despite his increasing conservatism, Orestes Brownson could, on occasion, rediscover his radical voice from the 1830s which warned that, to achieve social and economic justice, a strong, activist government was an absolute need. In 1866, he wrote: "The men of wealth, the business men, manufacturers and merchants, bankers and brokers, are the men who exert the worst influence on government in every country, for they always strive to use it as an instrument of advancing their own private interests. They act on the beautiful maxim, 'Let government take care of the rich, and the rich will take care of the poor,' instead of the far safer maxim, 'Let government take care of the weak, the strong can take care of themselves.'"[31]

Patrick Guiney and Patrick Ford were two notable Irish Catholic veterans of the US Civil War who championed labor's rights in postwar America. Guiney, despite lingering health problems stemming from his war service, ran for Congress on the Workingman's Party ticket in 1868. In a campaign speech, Guiney recalled that his boyhood experience in a Massachusetts factory had taught him an early lesson about labor's plight in industrial America.

Guiney lost the election to the Republican candidate, who happened to be the president of the Boston & Worcester Railroad.[32] In 1870, Patrick Ford, a Union Army veteran, used his journal, the *Irish World,* the leading shaper of opinion in the Irish American community during the last quarter of the century, to press for political reform as an antidote for the worsening economic situation of workers in America. That concern led to his backing of the Greenback-Labor Party in the latter 1870s. He also became highly critical of Catholic prelates and clergy who identified with the barons of capital who were grinding down the workers in the new industrial order. In the 1880s he went on to promote as channels of economic reform the Irish Land League as well as Henry George's single-tax program.[33]

UNIONIZATION AS EMANCIPATION

Meanwhile, war-shaped industrial development forced the laboring class to look not to "official" or private charity but to themselves to end the tyranny of wage slavery. The consolidation of industry and wartime inflation had caused workers to revive efforts to organize and to strike to improve their condition, only to have the state deploy troops to quell any work stoppages. In St. Louis, in the spring of 1864, artisans, including machinists, blacksmiths, tailors, and shoemakers, combined to strike for collective rights, including higher wages and an elimination of child labor. General William Rosecrans, commanding the Department of the Missouri, ordered the working men of the city to be placed under martial law, effectively serving as an injunction against their strike or any assembling on their part to promote their goals. The general, who had operated an oil refinery in Ohio in the 1850s, had a capitalist's view of labor as being subordinate to free enterprise. In wartime, workers especially had to make their own sacrifices for the country's survival. Rosecrans regarded the unions as "organizations led by bad men," whose "combinations" were undermining "private rights and the military power of the nation." The editor of the St. Louis paper, *Anzeiger,* complained to President Lincoln that Rosecrans's order was in the service of capitalists doing all they could to ensure that non-slave labor would be no freer than the bonded labor they were at war to destroy in the South.[34]

The St. Louis union was a local operation, as were most of the labor associations formed during the war. Strikes to improve their working lives were the inevitable consequence of such combinations. In one month in New York City alone, more than twenty different trade unions struck for higher wages.[35] Inevitably, when workers attempted such strikes to challenge the changes adversely affecting their condition, the Lincoln administration dispatched troops to suppress what was deemed disloyal activity.[36]

Women who replaced male workers who had enlisted or been drafted found themselves even more exploited by employers. In New York City the underpaying and other mistreatment of women workers spurred the creation of the Workingwomen's Protective Union. In March of 1864, Judge Charles Daly chaired the mass meeting at Cooper Union that launched the organization, intended to serve as an employment agency as well as a legal representative to raise wages and improve the working conditions for women. Overall, the WPU seems to have had more success in finding employment for women than in raising their pay or in bettering their work environment.[37] By war's end, wage labor, increasingly performed by an immigrant workforce, seemed to guarantee a permanent proletariat, unschooled in the folkways of republicanism and unable to enjoy the socioeconomic mobility that free-labor ideology had posited as the common American narrative. It raised the specter of a class-ridden society alien to American expectations.[38] It also drove home to labor organizers the need to expand unions to the national level, to better combat the consolidation of industry that the war had set in motion.

THE CATHOLIC HIERARCHY
AND LABOR UNIONS

With Catholics comprising so much of this new industrial class, it was inevitable that the issue of labor organization would come to the attention of the American Catholic hierarchy, especially when unions, in order to protect themselves, imposed oaths upon their members to preserve secrecy. Secret societies, such as the Masons, had already come under the church's ban. It was well known that Rome considered unions to be effectively secret societies, subject to church condemnation. Orestes Brownson, for his part, regarded unions as criminal monopolies in control of labor.

Much more sympathetic to unions was the archbishop of the premier see of the Catholic Church in the United States. In the Second Plenary Council of Baltimore in 1866, Martin Spalding wanted the prelates to go on record as exempting labor unions from the general condemnation of secret societies which the bishops had made during an earlier council in 1846.[39] As the archbishop explained to a Roman inquiry about labor unions, it was impossible to dissuade American Catholics from joining them, since employment was so linked to them (that is, in closed shops). He suggested that reform rather than an outright condemnation was the better path to take. Besides, he dared to inject, capital in all industrial societies is "the *despotic ruler* and the worker is its slave. This being the case, I say, leave the poor workers alone. There being little danger that they do injustice to the tyrannical employer."[40] When, several years later, a secret Irish vigilante group, operating under the umbrella of an Irish fraternal organization, the Ancient Order of the Hibernians, spread lethal terror through the mine country of northeastern Pennsylvania, Spalding's judgment seemed, to many, to be worse than naive.

THE PENNSYLVANIA ANTHRACITE FIELDS
AND THE MOLLY MAGUIRES

Among the most valuable resources of the nation's burgeoning industrial economy was anthracite, which provided coal for the steamships which blockaded the southern coastline as well as fueled the other industries that gave the Union forces such an advantage over their Confederate foes. The war had proved a boon for miners' wages in the coal country in northeastern Pennsylvania. Peacetime brought plunging demand for coal and, with it, collapsing wages and layoffs. The miners formed the Workingmen's Benevolent Association, which proceeded to call a strike against the Philadelphia & Reading Railroad, owned by Franklin Gowen. Arbitrators appointed to settle the issues denied the union membership the right to a closed shop, on the spurious ground that such a practice was "subversive to the best interests of the miners."[41] The strike having failed, Irish American miners turned to the practice long popular in Ireland: a secret vigilante group.

Both sides turned to violence to achieve their ends. For the operatives, it became an ultimate means of suppression, not only of vigilante activity, but of unionization itself. For the miners, it became a desperate instrument to induce bargaining.[42] For Irish miners, the use of violence or its threat was part of the tradition of vigilante groups in their rural homeland. Indigenous resistance groups like the Whiteboys and Mollie Maguires had utilized violence as an effective, if terrorizing, force against landlords who possessed all the levers of power the law recognized.[43] In America they were confronting an even more powerful foe, the mine or factory owners who had behind them all the resources of the state to resist labor's efforts to achieve more equitable conditions in the workplace.

In the fall of 1873 Gowen brought in Allan Pinkerton's National Detective Agency to infiltrate the miners' secret organization to secure evidence of their criminal behavior. Pinkerton assigned that task to an Irish immigrant, James McParlan, the first of four undercover detectives Pinkerton deployed in the area. In late October, McParlan arrived in Pottsville, posing as James McKenna, a tramp with a criminal past. For the next two and a half years McKenna insinuated himself into the company of Mollies along the mining-country line from Mahanoy City to Shenandoah. McParlan joined the Ancient Order of Hibernians, the Irish fraternal organization the Mollies used as a front for their planning and operations. In the late fall of 1874, the miners went on strike. The strike dragged on into June, when Gowen and the other opera-tors decided to reopen the mines. To prevent that, the miners rallied more than six hundred armed men to march on the major mine in the region, the West Shenandoah. McParlan led the march, waving a stick, and carrying two revolvers in his belt. When challenged by twenty-five rifle-bearing railroad security personnel, the marchers temporarily retreated into the woods, only to redirect their route toward Mahanoy City, picking up additional strikers along the seven miles. Approaching Mahanoy, the marchers encountered a solid wall of state militia. That convinced the marchers to disperse. The next day, the mines throughout Schuylkill County reopened.[44]

The following summer the Mollies were reportedly responsible for six re-taliatory murders, including that of a justice of the peace and of a policeman, as well as the killings of four persons involved in mining operations. Over the next two years more than fifty persons, including children and women, were indicted. The Catholic community of the region, including the clergy, was badly split. Bishop James Wood of Philadelphia reissued his pastoral of 1864, in which he had condemned the Fenians, now adding the Ancient Or-der of Hibernians to his anathemas.[45] At Gowen's suggestion, Bishop Wood ordered local priests to take prominent seats in the courtroom where the trials of the Mollies was taking place, to dissuade witnesses from lying, a tactic that seems to have failed.[46] On evidence provided by McParlan, as well as by several Mollies who had turned state's witnesses, prosecutors, most of whom were on the payroll of railroads and mining companies, convinced a jury, from which Irish Catholics had been excluded, to bring guilty verdicts. Twenty Molly Maguires were given lengthy prison terms; twenty others were sentenced to be hanged.[47]

THE LABOR EARTHQUAKE OF 1877

In the first of the social earthquakes that labor uprisings caused in the late nineteenth century, Irish led the railroad strikes in the summer of 1877 that began in Pittsburgh where National Guard troops killed 20 protestors after the strikers burned the Union Depot and engaged in gunfire with the troops.[48]

In Maryland, workers went on strike against the Baltimore & Ohio Railroad, after a pay cut, the second in six months, had reduced their wages to half of what they had been before the 1873 recession. Like wildfire, the strike spread along the line. The president of the B&O, Thomas Garrett, persuaded Catholic Governor John Lee Carroll to mobilize the Baltimore-based Fifth and Sixth regiments of the National Guard. When the 200 soldiers of the Fifth headed out of its armory to march down Howard Street to Camden Station, crowds waiting to challenge them hurled bricks and other missiles which wounded 25 of the soldiers. The uninjured continued their march to the station, only to discover that the rails had been torn up. Meanwhile the Sixth, starting from their armory just east of the harbor, were greeted with a shower of bricks as they exited the building. The Sixth showed less discipline than its sister regiment by firing into the crowd, killing at least 9, wounding 16. The regiment quickly dissolved in the tumult, with many shucking their uniforms to lose themselves among the crowd. At Camden Station, some 15,000 strikers and supporters had trapped the 350 soldiers who had made it to the station. Governor Carroll wired President Rutherford Hayes for relief. Hayes dispatched 2,500 soldiers and marines. The strikers remained at the station, but the violence had undermined the strike, which shook the nation to its core but failed to effect the ends for which the workmen had abandoned their posts.[49] Governor Carroll delivered a laissez-faire coda to labor's uprising. "No political platforms can be of any use to the working man or furnish him with work. In a free country like ours, the relations of capital and labor must always adjust themselves, and are regulated by conditions which politicians cannot control."[50] The Free Labor theory lived on, the overwhelming contradicting evidence notwithstanding.

News of the railroad strikes leapfrogging across the country penetrated even the cloistered walls of the Ursulines in South Carolina. Baptista Lynch's sympathies were clearly with the workers, even though she could not embrace unions and strikes as instruments toward the attainment of justice. "What terrible news from Pittsburg today," Mother Baptista wrote her bishop brother. The violence brought back nightmarish memories of the burning of Columbia. "Awful! . . . One cannot help sympathizing with the laborers when they are defrauded by rich employers. Cannot these RR. Kings be reasoned with? I would think St. Vincent de Paul's society would be the best protection for the defrauded laborer."[51] Her fundamental conservative streak revealed itself in her confidence that charity in the form of the Vincent de Paul Society was the best approach to protecting labor from the oppression that was the consequence of unfettered capitalism.

†

CHAPTER 22

The Making of
the Catholic Ghetto

The afflictions of the Holy Father have made
ultramontanes of all of us here who have any good within.

—JOSEPH KELLER, SJ, DECEMBER 23, 1870

THE SECOND PLENARY COUNCIL
OF BALTIMORE

In June of 1865, Martin Spalding requested that Rome authorize the holding of a second plenary council (the first had been held thirteen years earlier). Among the reasons that Spalding gave for holding a council was that it would provide powerful evidence of the unity of the Catholic Church in America, despite the Civil War the country had just come through; and there was the important matter of meeting the opportunity for evangelization of the more than 4 million formerly enslaved persons. The council opened on October 7, 1866, with 45 prelates and 2 mitered abbots, as well as 120 council officials and theologians processing around the grounds of the Cathedral amid some 40,000 spectators. Martin Spalding had invited Isaac Hecker to address the assembled hierarchy. In his remarks the convert-founder of the Paulists focused on the evangelizing possibilities created by the war record of the Catholic community (its maintenance of unity in the midst of conflict, the patriotic display of Catholic soldiers, the heroic nursing that women religious provided). That record put the church in a far stronger position to bring about the conversion of the United States through an evangelization that inspirited individuals across the reunited country to transform their social and political lives.[1] That evangelization, at least some bishops realized, had to include the Blacks in the United States, particularly the vast majority who had been recently emancipated. By Patrick Lynch's calculation, of the 4 million Blacks in the United States, no more than 150,000 were Catholics.

Developing a Black apostolate, Martin Spalding had informed Rome, was "a golden opportunity, for reaping a harvest of souls, which neglected may not return." Specifically, the archbishop wanted a bishop appointed whose special care would be the spiritual ministry to Blacks. In addition, he wanted separate churches (what would come to be called "national" churches later in the century) for African Americans, African American priests to minister to them, and special missions to evangelize the larger African American society. In his plea, the archbishop pointed out that thousands of Black Catholics had lapsed in the practice of their faith, no longer having a master or mistress to provide for their religious needs. The few Catholic bishops, he went on, who had made zealous attempts to expand the church's reach into the Black community had been frustrated by the lack of priests and money, as well as by white Catholic hostility to such ministry.

If Martin Spalding expected strong support for his plan for Black evangelization at the council, the response he received had to disappoint him greatly. Archbishop John Odin and Bishop John McGill protested that they were doing all they could do for the freed persons in New Orleans and Richmond respectively. Why was Rome pressing them to do more, and thus distract from their major focus on white Catholics who had been so disrupted by the war? Archbishop Peter Kenrick was more adamant: if Rome insisted on a special bishop for Blacks, he would submit his resignation. Only Augustin Verot of Savannah and Richard Whelan of Wheeling supported the proposal for a designated bishop. When McGill suggested that there be annual diocesan collections for the Black apostolate, John McCloskey declared that "in no way was the conscience of the Bishops of the north burdened" by the needs of the Black community. This from the ordinary of the archdiocese where, just over three years before, nominal subjects of his predecessor had waged a pogrom against that city's Blacks. Verot tried to press the council to take some action, but Kenrick's threat to walk out ended the discussion with an agreement that left any response to the initiative of individual dioceses.[2]

Left to their own devices, it should not surprise that it was the Catholic bishops in the former slave states—Augustin Verot, Martin Spalding, Patrick Lynch, William Elder of Natchez, Edward Fitzgerald of Little Rock—who, with John Purcell of Cincinnati, showed the most concern about the need and, indeed, opportunity that emancipation had created for the Church to reach out to the newly emancipated. The South was still home to the vast majority of the African American population. For at least some southern bishops, proximity, if not breeding commitment, seems to have been a powerful conditioner for the concern for Black evangelization that many of the bishops in former slave states displayed through their actions.

Augustin Verot, his biographer observed, "devoted himself to the welfare of the freedmen with a zeal that looked like the excitement of a man convinced that the sudden emancipation of four million men was an undiluted blessing."[3] As Verot had been perhaps the staunchest supporter of Spalding's proposals for the evangelization of Blacks at the council, so he was the bishop who did the most to make it a reality. His outreach began by committing his dioceses (Verot was simultaneously bishop of both Savannah and St. Augustine) to establishing schools for Blacks. As he explained to the Society for the Propagation of the Faith, from whom he was seeking funds in the summer of 1865, "we must make a beginning by establishing schools."[4] To secure teachers, Verot had returned to his native France in June 1865, seeking religious Sisters to undertake schools for the "five or six hundred thousand Negroes without any education or religion." The bishop secured sixty volunteers among the Sisters of St. Joseph at Le Puy. Eventually eight made it to Georgia. In February 1867, Verot established Savannah's first Catholic school for Blacks. The support from the Black community was overwhelming, as students flocked to the school and attended faithfully.[5] In St. Augustine, where Catholics constituted a substantial portion, if not a majority, of the African American community, a biracial Palm Sunday procession of some seven hundred persons in 1868 gave promise of a new order taking shape. By 1876 the Sisters of St. Joseph were operating seven schools for Blacks from Savannah to Key West.[6]

Martin Spalding, in his first year as archbishop of Baltimore, had encouraged the Oblates of Providence to extend their ministries beyond his see city. In laying the cornerstone for a new facility for the sisterhood, Spalding declared to the biracial crowd, "there are no parties in heaven. Irish, German, American, African—I want them all to go to heaven."[7] In 1865 the Oblates established St. Francis Academy for Black girls. A year later they began an orphan asylum to provide a home for children uprooted by emancipation and the migrations that ensued for many freed persons. Spalding, in addition, encouraged the Oblates to extend their outreach to other dioceses. The archdiocese, however, provided little or no financial support for the Oblates' institutions. In 1867, the sisters appealed to the Freedmen's Bureau for assistance. "The continuance of the Free School and Orphan Asylum," they wrote bureau officials, "must depend upon the very precarious collections from our poor race, unless your influence and charity shall come to our assistance."

Their plea brought no federal aid to either academy or orphanage.[8] Race continued to make a difference in securing public assistance, particularly under the Johnson administration.

In Annapolis, the Redemptorists began a parochial school for Blacks in 1866.[9] The order had made the outreach to Black Catholics in the city an important apostolate since they had taken over the parish in 1853. That commitment brought a harvest of Black converts. By 1865, African Americans comprised half the converts that St. Mary's reported for the year.[10] In Cincinnati, John Purcell, who had been the leading proponent for emancipation among the American hierarchy, committed his archdiocese to providing for the now freed people. The Jesuits established St. Ann's Church for Black Catholics, under Francis Weninger, and secured the services of the School Sisters of Notre Dame to conduct an elementary school there. Weninger was also responsible for a group of German Americans creating the Blessed Peter Claver Society, which provided financial assistance to Black Catholics in need.[11]

Mother Mary Teresa Austin Carroll, superioress of the Mercy Sisters in Louisiana, was particularly active in the Black educational apostolate during the Reconstruction era. The Irish-born Carroll had joined the Mercy order in Ireland in 1853. Three years later she was sent to Providence, Rhode Island. She spent the war years in Manchester, New Hampshire, where her sentiments were clearly with the South, whose quest for independence resonated with her own Irish nationalism. In 1869 she was assigned to New Orleans to begin a foundation there. Over the next decade she established a dozen schools for Blacks in Louisiana.[12]

BRINGING THE PARAGUAY REDUCTIONS
TO CAROLINA

In his pamphlet published during the last months of the war, Patrick Lynch had written: "Those who wish to prepare for [the Blacks'] freedom, and would wish to save them from extermination, should prepare homes for them elsewhere, apart from the white race, . . . under the tropics. . . . A government must be provided, suitable to his moral and intellectual character." Given that Blacks were incapable of "Self Government," the bishop proposed that at least some of the freed people "be put under the entire charge of some religious body, like that of the Society of Jesus. The negroes would yield readily to this religious, almost theocratical rule. . . . It is only doing on a larger scale what was done so well in the Indian Missions of California and of Paraguay in the last century."[13]

Barely a month after he had returned from Europe, in January 1866, Lynch had laid out to Martin Spalding his ambitious plan for the emancipated slaves in the Carolinas and Georgia: "There is an Island, some eight miles long, and from half a mile to 3½ miles in width entirely owned by a Catholic friend of mine. I think I could get it on good terms. I would put a religious community on it, and would start a Paraguay village of Catholic negroes which might grow into a community of four or five thousand souls under the fathers."[14] In a lecture delivered in Rome in June of 1867 at a congress of the Society for the Propagation of the Faith, Bishop Lynch fleshed out his plans for the utopian community of Black Catholics he hoped to begin under some religious community on Folly Island. As the Jesuits did with the endangered indigenous peoples of Paraguay in the eighteenth century, so Lynch envisioned their nineteenth-century successors doing with an equally vulnerable group, the recently emancipated slaves. In an area where climate had erected a natural barrier against white intrusion, Lynch planned to carry out a domestic colonization enterprise of offering Catholic freed persons the opportunity to live in a safe environment where education would provide the moral and intellectual means to a virtuous life and the independence that one's own land would secure. This would be a self-sustaining community under the supervision of a religious order of priests which provided for one's changing needs from birth to death, including schools, orphanages, and villages for the care of the aged.[15] As he told his audience, he already had some money in hand for the purchase of the island, but much more would be needed. What he did not mention was that his efforts to find a religious order or congregation to run the colony had, to date, failed. The Jesuits, the Benedictines, the Holy Cross fathers—all lacked the personnel to undertake such an ambitious enterprise. Importantly, Lynch did have the support of the local Freedmen's Bureau commander, General Daniel Sickles, whose wife was Catholic. Sickles had promised to solicit the head of the bureau, General O. O. Howard, to aid the project.

When he returned to Charleston in the late summer of 1867, Bishop Lynch discovered that Andrew Johnson, in response to white complaints about Sickles's favoritism of Blacks, had removed the general from his regional command. That eliminated the possibility of any federal aid. Without religious personnel, or financial support from either the government or private sources, the bishop abandoned the project.[16]

Claude Paschal Maistre continued his ministry at his schismatic Holy Name of Jesus church, which Black Catholics continued to support in large numbers. In 1867 his renegade church recorded nearly one hundred baptisms. Many of his parishioners were Black veterans.[17] Maistre also became a charter member of the faculty of Straight University, a Congregationalist-funded institution for Blacks which opened in February 1870. Given that French-speaking Creole Catholics made up approximately three-quarters of the students, Maistre was a natural fit for the new school. At Straight's first commencement in June of 1870, Maistre was one of three speakers. In his remarks the priest reminded the graduates that the revolution that had extended to Blacks "all the rights that belong to men and to citizens" carried with them corresponding civil duties. Fulfilling them would ensure God's blessing, Maistre told his audience.[18] Two weeks after Straight's commencement, Maistre made his peace with Archbishop Joseph Perché, who had succeeded Odin. The priest repented of any wrongdoing and scandal for which he had been responsible. The following year he shuttered Holy Name, and after duly fulfilling a penitential retreat of some months, became pastor of St. Lawrence, in the remote town of Chacahoula, some sixty miles southeast of New Orleans. There he ended his days in January 1875. Fittingly, Maistre was buried in the cathedral cemetery, in the section set aside for Blacks.[19]

The lack of a Black Catholic clergy certainly contributed to the church's failure to have a more effective outreach to the newly freed Black community. Securing priests to minister to their own ethnic group had always been a priority within a Catholic community becoming ever more ethnically diverse. But racial prejudice deemed the African Americans intellectually and morally unprepared for the training needed to produce a Black clergy. That persistent racism undermined even the most zealous attempts to expand the church's ministry to the Black community. Shortly before his death in 1876, Verot acknowledged that his extraordinary efforts to evangelize the freed people had had little success outside the few cities where he had established schools. One glaring sign of this failure was the changing mission of the Sisters of Saint Joseph who, by the end of the 1870s, were teaching far more white students than Black ones. That inequity would only worsen as the century came to a close.[20] By the turn of the century much of the Black Catholic community that Augustin Verot cherished had evaporated.

Cyprian Davis generously observed in his seminal work on Black Catholics in the United States: "The history of the Catholic church's efforts to evangelize the black people of the US in the period following the Civil War is not a very glorious one. One might note that the ethnic group that she had known the longest in this country, aside from the Indians, longer than any of the more recent immigrant groups in this country, was the group that she treated as stepchildren, the last considered and the first to be jettisoned when funds and personnel were scarce."[21]

FROM EVANGELIZING TO TRIBALIZING

On his way home from the Second Plenary Council in the fall of 1866, Patrick Lynch stopped at Fortress Monroe to pay a visit to the still imprisoned Jefferson Davis. Davis was much taken with Lynch's gesture. The bishop, knowing that Davis, as a student at St. Joseph's College in Bardstown, had once expressed an interest in converting, left with him some Catholic publications in the hope that they might stir some old embers. They did not.[22] The bishop's outreach represented an evangelical lag, a left-over impulse from an earlier era in which much energy and expectation had been focused on the mass conversion of Americans to Roman Catholicism. What had transpired at the council was an indicator of which way the winds were blowing regarding the American Church's relationship with the larger society.

Isaac Hecker, in his address at the council, had predicted that the war had well positioned Catholics for a "second spring" that would lead to America's conversion. But by their legislation and pastoral letter about the council the bishops indicated that any revitalization the Church would experience in the postwar age would come, not from new waves of conversions, but rather from within the community, through the creation of an institutional infrastructure that would meet the complex needs of Catholics from birth to old age—a Paraguay Reductions for American Catholics in general. In their letter the bishops had applauded "the great increase among us of Societies and Associations, especially of those composed of young and middle-aged men. . . . We urge their extension . . . in all the dioceses and parishes of the country."[23] It marked the council's imprimatur for the reconstruction of American Catholicism in which parallel institutions (parochial and industrial schools, seminaries, hospitals, benevolent societies, sodalities, publications, fraternal and learned societies) would be established that made Catholics a people who were socially, culturally, and intellectually apart from the mainstream of American life.

Some of this institutional development was driven by the social consequences of an unprecedentedly large influx of Catholic immigrants; some was the necessary response to the war and subsequent economic recessions. The founding of hospitals and orphanages had begun in the antebellum era, but the war had greatly increased the need for them.[24] So too war widows and the jobless created by economic recession provided unprecedented opportunities for the Society of St. Vincent de Paul and other fraternal societies.

No bishop did more to realize this institutional ghetto than did Martin John Spalding in Baltimore.[25] One of Spalding's most important contributions was the primacy he gave to education in his establishment of parishes for his rapidly expanding see city. In his seven-year tenure in Baltimore, Spalding created a new model for the twenty-four parishes he erected by directing that the initial structure be a temporary chapel that could be converted into a school when a permanent church was built. That committed the archdiocese to the ideal of a Catholic school in every parish. For the orphans and indigent youth generated by the war, Spalding founded St Mary's Industrial School in 1866, under the auspices of the Xaverian Brothers. As the archbishop explained in a circular, there was a pressing need for an institution in which the faith of these Catholic boys would be safeguarded and cultivated, not supplanted by an alien one, as it would be in the existing secular or Protestant protectories.[26] The Sisters of Charity, at Spalding's initiative, opened St. Joseph's House of Industry and St. Rose Technical School, trade schools for girls in Baltimore and Washington respectively. Spalding also brought in the Sisters of the Good Shepherd to establish a home for wayward young women.[27] Three Catholic hospitals began in the Baltimore-Washington area under Spalding. In 1869 he brought in the Little Sisters of the Poor to conduct a home for the indigent aged. In 1872 the archbishop founded the Young Men's Catholic Association to provide "intelligent recreation" and adult education. It featured lectures and an extensive library for the members' use. The following year, the Carroll Institute, with identical purposes, was established in Washington.[28]

To manage these educational and social service enterprises required the recruitment of a veritable army of men and women religious. From 1845 to 1860, the number of women religious in the country had quadrupled, from 1,108 to 4,005. Over the next three decades there was an even more prodigious growth, with more than 32,000 nuns and sisters engaged in ministry by 1890.[29]

In the wake of the council, the temperance movement, which traced its beginnings in the American Catholic community to the 1840s, now revived with temperance societies being formed in various dioceses, beginning in Connecticut in 1869. Five years later, James Roosevelt Bayley, the bishop of Newark, founded the Catholic Total Abstinence Union of America. The Catholic Total Abstinence Union was part of the national consolidation of regional beneficial and reform societies that took place within the Catholic community during the postwar years. Diocesan Irish beneficent societies established before the war to provide relief to the sick and widows joined to create the Irish Catholic Benevolent Union in 1869. By 1876 the Benevolent Union boasted 30,000 members across the country. Similar consolidation of beneficial organizations for Black and German Catholics also took place in this era.

COLONIZATION

Colonization was the ultimate form of ghettoization. From the country's earliest days, Catholics had established colonies in rural enclaves. Associations, such as the Irish Emigrant Society of New York, saw rural environments as more appropriate for Catholics immigrating from rural Germany or Ireland, and certainly more hospitable than the hostile environment Catholics faced in nativistic cities. The antebellum Irish colonies virtually all failed. Catholics were prominent supporters of the colonization of an even more unwelcome ethnic group, emancipated African Americans.

Organized Catholic colonization experienced a hiatus during the Civil War, then revived after Appomattox. John O'Neill founded three Irish colonies in eastern Nebraska during the 1870s.[30] Archbishop John Ireland founded five Irish colonies in Minnesota. In 1879 Ireland founded the Irish Catholic Colonization Association of the United States to expand the colonization that the archbishop had established in Minnesota to other western states. Ireland secured wide backing from the hierarchy, land from the railroads, and funds from eastern donors, but failed to get what he most needed: enough Irish settlers to make the colonies viable. Few workers in the East responded to the invitations to make their future in the West. By the 1880s, Western farmers were beginning to feel the hard times that would worsen for the rest of the century. The West was no longer, if it ever had been, a safety valve for individuals or groups.[31]

PAROCHIAL EDUCATION IN
POSTWAR AMERICA

The "common school," which had been a hot-button issue in the political wars of the 1840s and 1850s resurfaced in the late 1860s to force Americans to confront the most basic questions about public education: what should be its shape, who should control it, and what part, if any, should religion play in it?[32] The compatibility of the Catholic faith and public education revived as an issue during Reconstruction, in part over the federal government's efforts to ensure that education would be one of the civil rights provided to Blacks, whether newly emancipated or not. Indeed, congressional Republicans committed themselves to making public education, a scarce commodity in the antebellum South, a prerequisite for readmission to the Union. Republicans saw education as a propaedeutic for citizenship in any authentic republic which required a literate citizenry to function. Its proponents feared that southern governments might, left to themselves, exclude Blacks from exercising their franchise on the grounds of their illiteracy. Universal public education would be the guardrail against such disfranchisement.

As in the antebellum period, the postwar controversy over public education very much involved Catholics and the institutional church. Catholic authorities continued their attempts to secure public funding for parochial schools. In New York, fears grew of a Catholic plot to take over public education, especially in New York City, where Catholic-dominated school boards set policy in wards where Catholics were in the majority. Catholic critics of public education maintained that the state was usurping a responsibility which primarily rested with family and church.

Catholics saw in the federal concern about education a form of cultural imperialism, an attempt, as Isaac Hecker put it, to achieve "social and religious unification," in effect, amalgamating the diverse peoples of America into what Hecker termed the "New England Evangelical type." Democrats increasingly opposed integrated schools on the racist grounds that they would lead to miscegenation. That focus proved popular in a North which had traditionally practiced segregation.

CATHOLIC PUBLIC SCHOOLS

At the Second Plenary Council, held in Baltimore in 1866, the gathered prelates, in their decrees on education, reiterated the call of the First Plenary Council fourteen years earlier, to have every Catholic parish in the country establish a school where religious and moral formation in the Catholic faith would be at the core of education.[33] Orestes Brownson was a staunch supporter of Catholic education at the elementary level, but he worried about the quality of the instruction at parochial schools. That necessitated funding, something which Catholic prelates had failed over the past several decades to secure from government. In a few cities, local government and church officials had reached an agreement on establishing what amounted to "public" Catholic schools. Parishes would usually provide the buildings and faculty, while the local school board certified and paid the salaries of the parish-selected teachers. Control of the curriculum varied according to the school boards of Savannah, Hartford, New Haven, Poughkeepsie, and other places where agreements were in effect.

An influential critic of such arrangements was James McMaster, editor of the *Freeman's Journal.* McMaster wanted no part of state aid in whatever form. In 1869, he wrote: "The Catholic solution of this muddle about Bible or no Bible in schools is, 'Hands off!': No State taxation or donation for any schools. You look to your children, and we will look to ours. We don't want to be taxed for Protestant, or for godless schools." To McMaster education was the realm of the family assisted by the church, as he ceaselessly preached on the Catholic lecture circuit in the postwar era. He opposed compulsory education, on the ground that the state had no right to control it. In the 1870s James McMaster carried his lobbying efforts to Rome, where he had the invaluable aid of a veteran journalist, Ella B. Edes, a convert like McMaster. They persuaded the officials at the Congregation for the Propagation of the Faith, under whose jurisdiction the Catholic Church in the United States, as a mission country, still fell, to carry out an investigation into the state of the education that Catholic children in this country were receiving. Most of the American bishops the Congregation contacted responded that McMaster was greatly exaggerating the evils he professed to find in public education. Moreover, he was much too optimistic about the ability of Catholic parishes across the country to provide their own schools. To threaten to deny absolution to parents who sent their children to public schools was simply impractical. Despite the bishops' overall response, Ella Edes's influence with Roman officials proved decisive. The Congregation told the American prelates that it deemed US public schools "hostile to Catholicity," and Catholics could not in conscience send their children to them. It charged the American bishops to ensure that Catholics in every parish would have an alternative to public education. The groundwork was laid for the mandate that, nine years later, the Third Plenary Council would issue for every parish in the country to have, within two years, a parochial school for its children.[34]

THE RECONSTRUCTION
OF CATHOLIC HIGHER EDUCATION

Michael David Cohen found in his examination of higher education in the Civil War era that the war created the forces that have shaped modern higher education in America.[35] The Morrill Land-Grant College Act set the standards that have increasingly defined it, with a curriculum which privileges vocational preparation and military training, and diversity (in gender, ethnicity and class) characterizing its student population, as well as a symbiotic relationship between state and school in which the latter assumes a growing role in the public arena. One could argue that the war, for most Catholic colleges, produced the opposite effects. There was a sharp decline in geographical and religious diversity, especially in northern schools which had drawn a large portion of their students from the South. There was a contraction, if not elimination, of the practical alternative (commercial course) to the classical course in most Catholic colleges. And the colleges did not forge a closer relationship with the state nor have more of a public presence in the postbellum era but became less involved with government and the larger society, seeing the state's greater involvement in education as a threat to their autonomy and development.

By war's end, the number of Catholic colleges was remarkably about the same as it had been in 1861. St. Joseph's Bardstown was the one Catholic institution of higher education to close permanently. Meanwhile Boston College, St Mary's College (California), and LaSalle College all began classes in 1863. The fifteen years following the war did not match the decade and a half before the war when bishops and religious congregations had founded more than twoscore of Catholic colleges. Still, some notable institutions began during Reconstruction, including Jesuit colleges in Buffalo, Chicago, Jersey City, Detroit, and Omaha. The Vincentians started St. John's College in New York City in 1870, and the Benedictines established Belmont Abbey in 1876. The Congregation of the Holy Ghost founded Duquesne in Pittsburgh in 1878.

Northern Catholic colleges which before the war had been primarily for boarders, many of whom were southerners, now saw its boarding population shrink, with far fewer students from below the Potomac. For some of these colleges, the loss of their traditional southern market for students forced officials to focus on the local region. By the late 1870s, Catholics from the Northeast were becoming an ever-growing majority. By contrast, Santa Clara in northern California bucked the ghettoization trend that most Catholic colleges exhibited in the postwar period. Half of its students were not Catholic, a reflection of the school's status as the most prestigious of the four private colleges within the state.[36]

In large part the new institutions were colleges for Catholic commuters. Peacetime, as expected, brought a boon in enrollment for many day colleges. Two years after Appomattox, the Jesuits' Xavier College in New York City boasted an enrollment of 330 and the construction of a five-story building to accommodate the growth of the institution. All this demographic change greatly abetted the ghettoization of Catholic higher education.

In 1870 Loyola College reestablished, in response to parental pressure, a commercial course. That change clearly affected the career choices of their alumni. By the late nineteenth century about a third were engaged in business, a statistic few other Catholic colleges could match.[37] Another school in which the commercial course became prominent was Notre Dame. Most of the degrees it awarded to graduates in the 1860s and 1870s were in that area. Loyola's vocational alternative to its traditional classics course was something of an outlier among Jesuit colleges, where the liberal arts remained at the core of the curriculum.

If the liberal arts remained regnant in Catholic colleges, the classics no longer dominated, as the sciences and the humanities beyond Latin and Greek came to have greater prominence in the curriculum. At Notre Dame, in the first academic year of the postwar period, a returning chaplain, Joseph Carrier, was the likely impetus for the establishment of a six-year scientific course which concentrated on mathematics and the natural sciences, including geology, botany, chemistry, and astronomy as well as geography and modern history. In the late 1860s, Notre Dame began courses related to the law and became the first Catholic institution to offer a program in engineering.[38] Like Notre Dame, Georgetown, in the decade following the war, modernized its curriculum by making the sciences a more substantial component as well as giving more emphasis to English literature among the humanities, where the classics had always dominated.

PATRICK HEALY AND
THE CATHOLIC UNIVERSITY

Under the pressure of the proliferation and specialization of knowledge that was taking place in the 1860s and 1870s, a new understanding of the comprehensive role of education at its highest level was emerging, with an unprecedented emphasis on scientific research and training for the professions. At the Second Plenary Council of Baltimore in 1866, under the prodding of Archbishop Martin John Spalding, the prelates had expressed the desire to have "a great college or university—in which . . . all the letters and sciences, both sacred and profane, could be taught!" Orestes Brownson and Isaac Hecker, for two, pleaded the need for the Church in the United States to have "one grand institution" to concentrate "the endowments, the instructors and the pupils . . . to give a much better and higher kind of education" than the motley collection of Catholic colleges could possibly provide in their present state.[39]

Seven years after the council, the sudden death of Georgetown's president, John Early, brought to the helm of the institution someone who shared Brownson and Hecker's vision of a Catholic university for the United States.

Patrick Healy, the illegitimate son of a Georgia Irish planter and his common-law enslaved wife, had entered the Jesuits upon graduating from the College of the Holy Cross in Massachusetts. Superiors had prudently sent him abroad for his priestly formation. At the war's close, he was assigned to the relatively cloistered position of instructing Jesuit seminarians at Georgetown. Then, in 1868, a tragedy brought Patrick Healy into the center of Georgetown College when an Atlantic storm killed the prefect of studies (dean) while he was returning from Europe to America. Healy, as the best qualified member of the faculty, was appointed as his successor. Five years later, upon the sudden death of President Early, Healy, by virtue of his occupying the second-highest office at Georgetown, became the acting head of the college. More than a year later, Rome reluctantly made the appointment official. In such fashion did a man who had legally been a slave become the twenty-eighth president of Georgetown.

Once president, Healy committed to constructing a grand facility which would provide the resources with which to function as a university. For a year and a half, Healy barnstormed the country, trying to raise funds from every wealthy Catholic he could identify. For all his valor, Healy raised less than $60,000, a pittance of the nearly $440,000 that the new building cost. Patrick Healy found monied American Catholics no more willing to invest in education than John Carroll had a century earlier. In 1875 Patrick Healy began preparations for the construction of the grand edifice, 312 feet long and 95 feet wide, that would provide the classrooms, laboratories, administrative offices, and residential rooms for the comprehensive university he was envisioning. The Romanesque-inspired five-story building with a central clock tower scaling some 200 feet, faced east toward the Capitol, the first time in the institution's history that a building on campus faced east toward the city rather than toward the Potomac River. It was a statement in stone of Georgetown's ambition of becoming a major university in the capital city of the United States. The irony was that, as the university was making this dramatic change in its geographic siting, it was becoming an island unto itself, inverting a history in which from its earliest days the institution had been an integral part of the life of the federal government and of the community. The personal relations between Jesuits and officials in the government epitomized this as did the constant interactions between the community and the college. The war changed that profoundly. The faculty and student body continued to be very self-consciously southern. Republican rule, as well as the demographic transformation of the District of Columbia during the conflict (Blacks had tripled their numbers to become nearly one-third of the population) tended to alienate the college from its surrounding society. By 1875 an editorial in the college journal was advocating the retrocession of Georgetown to a "redeemed" Maryland, as a sanctuary from the social engineering of Reconstruction which had found its chief laboratory within the District of Columbia.

HIGHER EDUCATION FOR
CATHOLIC WOMEN

Catholic female academies, concentrated below the Mason-Dixon Line in the antebellum era, were among the war's casualties. In Louisiana, the Sisters of the Cross, which had had four schools with more than two hundred students at the outbreak of the war, by its end counted two academies with barely a score of students between them. The schools of the Religious of the Sacred Heart in the state fared even worse. The Ursulines in Columbia, who had seen their wartime enrollment soar, had been forced to relocate to a rural site with far smaller accommodations, after their academy had become part of the collateral damage inflicted by Cump Sherman's avenging army. A satellite school, which Mother Baptista Lynch established in Tuscaloosa in the fall of 1866 to compensate for their reduced operation in South Carolina, attracted too few students and no new members for the order before the Ursulines reluctantly shut it down in 1880.

Most expansion in Catholic female secondary education took place in the North, where Catholic female academies continued to expand and develop. The most significant development occurred in Baltimore, where in 1863 the School Sisters of Notre Dame had established their first academy, the Collegiate Institute for Young Ladies, which became known as the Institute of Notre Dame. Its formal title, the state charter which the sisters acquired for the school, and regular guest lectures by college professors all indicated an intention by the institute's initial director, Sister Mary Ildephonsa (Louise Wegman), to offer education beyond the traditional secondary level. The very American-oriented curriculum and culture which Sister Ildephonsa created for the school offended many of the more traditional-minded members of her congregation, including her provincial superior, who thought the sisters should restrict their educational apostolate to the parochial schools they had begun across the United States.

In 1870, Ildephonsa and her local superior, Mother Mary Barbara Weinzierl, went over the head of the regional superior to secure permission from the motherhouse in Munich to purchase a large tract of land in Baltimore County, immediately north of the city, as the site of a new boarding school, the Notre

Dame of Maryland Preparatory School and Collegiate Institute for Young Ladies. The large multipurpose, central building echoed the main buildings of the Protestant-affiliated women's colleges that were opening in the postwar decade. On September 23, 1873, Notre Dame began classes on its spacious, lake-ribbed campus. By the end of its first academic year there were more than one hundred boarding students, a significant minority of whom were not Catholics. The curriculum reflected the expanding field of knowledge transforming education in America, including modern languages, science, history, and geography, as well as the traditional offerings of music, drawing, painting, and the domestic arts. Most distinctive were the postsecondary studies offered which led to a "Mistress of English Literature and Liberal Studies" degree. Ildephonsa and her supporters had laid the foundation for the first Catholic women's college that formally opened on the campus two decades later, a landmark toward the goal of educational equality within the Catholic community.[40] In an age in which suffragettes were being told that it was not yet "the women's hour," any advancement had to be considered a significant victory.

PAPAL TEMPORAL POWER

In 1848, Congress had authorized the establishment of a legation in Rome for the Papal States. Three years earlier, in the 1845 edition of *Primacy of the Apostolic See and the Authority of General Councils Vindicated,* Francis Kenrick had observed that "there is no divine guarantee that [the temporal power] will continue." John Hughes had insisted that the pope as the ruler of a political state was "an accident." That was before the uprising in 1848 which forced Pius IX to flee Rome and depend on Catholic powers for his restoration as head of the Papal States two years later. That traumatic event not only changed the pope's thinking about the liberal forces transforming Europe but created a new bond between American Catholics and the supreme pontiff. By 1867, when a Republican-dominated Congress ceased funding the American legation in Rome, partly in response to the Vatican's Confederate leanings during the war, the issue of US recognition of papal sovereignty over the states in central Italy had become an important issue to many American Catholics, who had come to regard the pope's temporal power as touching on the very core of papal authority and independence. At the decade's end, an extraordinary occasion arose for the official Church to declare to the world the nature and extent of that authority and sovereignty.

A VATICAN COUNCIL

In the last year of the American Civil War, Pope Pius IX had first broached his intention to call an ecumenical council, a gathering of the world's Catholic prelates that had last occurred more than two centuries before the establishment of the United States. In late June of 1867 the pope officially announced it. James Corcoran, the American delegate on the planning commission for the council, arrived fifteen months into the planning, but he quickly discerned that ultramontanes, or adherents of a Rome-centric church under an infallible pontiff, were dominating the planning for the council. Some of the proposals concerning civil government utterly rejected "the fundamental principles of our (American & common sense) political doctrines." As for the overshadowing question of papal infallibility, Corcoran could only report that "this definition is a foregone conclusion."[41]

Paradoxically, the growing threat of the loss of the papal temporal realm in the 1860s only increased the movement to concentrate all spiritual authority and power within the church in the bishop of Rome.[42] As Joseph Keller, the American provincial superior of the Jesuits, reported to the superior general in 1870, "the afflictions of the Holy Father have made ultramontanes of all of us here who have any good within."[43] William Henry Elder had considered asking to be excused from the council, but decided to make the voyage "in case there should be manifestations of nationalism. . . . I should not want to lessen by even one voice of thorough Romanism *'Ubi Petrus ibi Ecclesia.'*"[44]

Elder was in the minority among the forty-five American bishops who participated in the council. The large majority opposed any definition on the pragmatic grounds that it would only reanimate the anti-Catholicism which had raged during the 1850s. In a petition which John Purcell drafted, twenty-eight English-speaking prelates warned that, should papal infallibility be defined, it would become a severe handicap for the Church's evangelization efforts in countries where Catholics found themselves in the minority.[45] Of the relatively few Americans who took part in the subsequent debate. Michael Domenec pointed out that previous bishops in the United States (for example, Carroll, England) had openly declared that infallibility was a mark of the Church itself, not its pontiff.[46] Besides, the Pittsburgh bishop went on, to approve the proposition was to jeopardize the progress that the faith had made in America, a growth that was promising to have more Catholics in this young republic than there were in Italy itself. That remark created such an uproar that it led to the session being prematurely terminated.[47] Peter Kenrick was scheduled to follow Domenec. Deprived of the platform, Kenrick published his speech in a pamphlet. The St. Louis prelate did not mince his words: "I boldly declare that the opinion, as set down in the *schema,* is not a doctrine of faith, and that it cannot become such by a definition whatsoever, even of a council. We are custodians of the deposit of faith, not its masters."[48] Kenrick pressed for the council to affirm a more traditional concept of the infallibility of the church and to promote the greater frequency of such councils as the means of exercising that authority. The archbishop was speaking in the conciliar tradition which had shaped the thinking of John Carroll and John England, a tradition that valued the semi-independence of national churches in communion with Rome. In this centrifugal tradition, hierarchical appointments were made not from Rome, but at the local level; councils determined the discipline and missions of the particular national community and managed the finances of that community. Ultimate spiritual authority lay with the pontiff, but doctrine should develop through the councils, with the pope, in collaboration with them, ultimately defining it.[49]

On July 18, after the entire text of the decree *Pastor Aeternus* was read aloud to the episcopal assembly, the roll was called. There were 533 placets, and two non placets, one cast by the Irish American Edward Fitzgerald of Little Rock. The rest of the opposition, including Kenrick and Verot, had managed to absent themselves from the final assembly.[50] The day after the vote, the Franco-Prussian War began, which immediately suspended the council. Two months later Italian troops seized Rome, ending any hope of its resumption, as the pope took refuge in the Vatican.

PROTESTING THE LOSS OF TEMPORAL POWER

Martin Spalding's return to Baltimore from the council in November 1870 became the occasion for a mass protest of the seizure of the Papal States. A parade of Catholic societies led the archbishop from the train station to his Charles Street residence, where 50,000 gathered for speeches. Later that November, 30,000 gathered in Washington to make their own protest.

As a demonstration of the enduring support of Maryland Catholics for the pontiff, Archbishop Spalding organized a three-day celebration of the twenty-fifth anniversary of Pius IX's coronation in 1871. The event, according to the archbishop, drew 100,000 people. "Never has anything like it been seen before in Baltimore," he reported to Rome.[51] In Savannah, a mass meeting at the cathedral produced a statement declaring that "Rome and the Papal Ter-

ritory belong to the Catholic world." Its seizure was a "sacrilegious invasion
. . . a violation of the sacred rights of the whole world."[52]

THE QUEST FOR "HOME RULE"

In late October 1868, the *New York Tribune* carried an article about the revolt of Bishop James Duggan's chief administrators in the Diocese of Chicago
against his absentee, erratic rule. The piece depicted the uprising as a campaign by a liberal cadre to give Catholicism in this country "an American
character." One step toward reaching this goal, the author contended, was to
remove the designation of the American Church as a mission, which placed it
under the jurisdiction of a papal bureaucracy that tended to promote episcopal autocracy in this country. What the author was pressing for was a form of
"home rule" for the American Church, with sufficient independence so that
the indigenous republican forces which shaped American society could penetrate the structure and practices of the Church. In brief, to give democracy
an opportunity to flourish, even within American Catholicism.

Parallel to the international struggle within the church over the forces of
modernity was the emergence in America of a circle of progressive priests
whom the Civil War had spurred to reflect on the implications of the "new
freedom," which Lincoln had proclaimed at Gettysburg. New York Irish
priests Sylvester Malone and Edward McGlynn had been in the city during
the rioting in July 1863, an apocalyptic setting for reflecting on the republican
institutions and values that the war had put to the supreme test. For Malone,
McGlynn, Richard Burtsell, Sebastian Smith, Eugene O'Callaghan, and others, the Civil War was the catalyst that radically committed them to American
democracy and all its implications for the form that Catholicism should take
in America. It was essentially a northern movement, although not without
some southern participants, such as John Moore, who shared the reformers'
concern about Church polity, if not their commitment to Reconstruction.
Richard Burtsell in 1867 summed up the democratic epiphany that the war
crystallized in their thinking: "I once thought rulers ought to take care of the
people: in America I have learned that the people knows how to take care
of itself."[53] From their war experience, Burtsell and his fellow reformers had
witnessed democracy rise successfully to its greatest test. That extraordinary
display of democracy in action had contained lessons for American society
and Catholicism itself which these priests began to enunciate and to endeavor
to put in place. With a few exceptions they became staunch supporters of
Congressional Reconstruction. Above all, they pressed for the rights that

canon law accorded priests in the face of the autocratic governance that increasingly marked episcopal rule throughout the country.[54]

During the council, Spalding continued to receive alarming intelligence of the activities of these priests. Fort Wayne Bishop John Henry Luers wrote Spalding in Rome: "there is a bad spirit among not a small portion of our clergy, and unless a check is put upon it by Rome . . . the Church in the U.S. will suffer." He did caution that the American bishops should realize that they could no longer act arbitrarily, but according to "reason, justice, and Canon law."[55] In May, now Bishop Thomas Becker reported to Spalding from New York that the "liberal party" of that city had become more outspoken and outrageous. Its members not only questioned the doctrines of papal infallibility, the Immaculate Conception, and the Assumption but called the pope a "*swell head* absorbing all the members and causing atrophy in the Apostolic College." They dismissed the devotional culture and practices of the immigrant church, such as the invocation of the saints, the recitation of the rosary, and the veneration of relics. They wanted the liturgy and the sacraments performed in the language of their host society. They were teetering on heresy and a schism, while extolling the public-school systems.[56] A Cleveland priest, Eugene O'Callaghan, who had become a regular contributor to the *Freeman's Journal* under the nom de plume "Jus," attempted to act as the clergy's representative at the council, but to no effect. That spring of 1870, the *Journal* stopped carrying any articles on church reform in the United States. In the wake of the Vatican Council, the clerical movement for making the Church in America more consonant with the values and culture of the society which hosted it gradually went underground for more than a decade. Home rule had begun to return to the South, but it remained an unreachable star for the Catholic community in America.

✝

CHAPTER 23

Redemption

You must fight for the white people now;
the civilization of a thousand years
is not to be swept away.

—JOHN McENERY, JUNE 9, 1874

NEW WAR

Patrick Lynch, in his 1873 report to the Society of the Propagation of the Faith, which was the chief foreign benefactor of his diocese, described the State of South Carolina as remaining an occupied land, eight years after the end of the war: "the civil government is in the hands of the emancipated negroes, who are the vast majority and who even when well intentioned, are ignorant and incapable, and who, in fact, are led by crafty and unscrupulous adventurers, mostly from Northern States, who have come to make their fortunes, out of the wreck of the South."[1] It was the account of Reconstruction that was becoming the prevailing narrative, not only in the South, but, increasingly, in the North as well, stoking the counterrevolutionary forces hell-bent on restoring the old order in former slave states.[2]

From the moment Congress took over the business of Reconstruction, whites in the South waged a war against those trying to build a biracial society in which government was committed to promoting economic and political justice. It was a war utilizing every available weapon—economic pressure, violence, myth—to defeat this revolutionary movement. As Anne Sarah Rubin observes in *A Shattered Nation,* white southerners' perceived mistreatment at the hands of their occupiers and their Black allies reinforced their conviction that their political entitlement had been usurped. A sense of honor violated drove southern whites to resort to whatever means necessary to overturn Reconstruction and regain power.[3]

THE RECLAIMING OF MARYLAND

No state within the Confederate orbit experienced a swifter "redemption" than did Maryland, in large part because the military occupation of the state during the war had been lifted with the coming of peace. There was no federal force to ensure that the reconstruction of the state, epitomized by its new constitution of 1864, would continue in the postwar period. Nor was there a truly radical element within the Republican or Unionist bloc in the state to ensure that Maryland would recognize any Black rights beyond freedom itself, much less employ the power of government to promote or protect those rights. White Marylanders very much continued to identify with the South, particularly in its resistance to any new order that elevated Blacks, either former slaves or free men. When voters, in October 1865, had ratified the state's new constitution, the *Catholic Mirror* claimed that, "had a fair vote of the people of the State been allowed, no one at all acquainted with the political sentiments of the great majority of Marylanders, ever believed that the present Constitution would have been adopted." The editorial included a chart showing that the requirement of an ironclad loyalty oath for all potential voters had shrunk the electorate to a third of its 1860 level. In the heavily Catholic wards, the shrinkage was much greater, to a fifth.[4]

The issue of Black enfranchisement as a gateway to racial interbreeding was a white fear that Democrats exploited to secure support. In the election of 1867 a coalition of conservative Unionists and Democrats, including George Kane, managed to ensure that election officials would look the other way as thousands of disqualified ex-Confederates and their abettors were allowed to vote. The coalition swept to victory, winning all eighteen of Baltimore's seats in the General Assembly. With a ratified Fourteenth Amendment still two years in the future, the party had no recourse to the fifth of the population which was Black to save them.[5] Democrats regained control of the legislature, with sixty of the eighty seats in the assembly. The new assembly authorized changes in the recently adopted constitution to eliminate loyalty oaths and to reinstate disproportionate representation to southern Maryland and the Eastern Shore. Concurrently, white men's clubs sprung up, explicitly calling for "a white man's government for the benefit of white men."[6] In quick order a new convention passed a constitution to replace the one enacted just three years earlier. A subsequent referendum overwhelmingly endorsed the new constitution which restricted the franchise to adult white males and left open the possibility of future compensation to the former owners of emancipated slaves.[7]

Maryland thus became the first of the former slave states to be "redeemed." It was a relatively peaceful redemption, although there was certainly violence and intimidation: burnings of Black schools and harassment of their teachers, even lynchings. Much more employed was legal coercion, by which planters and manufacturers secured court orders to "apprentice" thousands of Black minors to their former enslavers.[8] Unsurprisingly, the state voted overwhelmingly for Horatio Seymour in the 1868 presidential election. Ulysses Grant carried not one county, largely because there was a protest boycott of the election by former Unionists in Baltimore and the northwestern portion of the state.[9] In 1875 John Lee Carroll, the great-grandson of Charles Carroll of Carrollton and a Confederate supporter during the war, became Maryland's Democratic governor in an election which later proved to have been rigged in Carroll's favor.[10] Two years later, in 1877, George Kane was elected mayor of Baltimore.

A RESURGENCE
OF THE DEMOCRATS

In June of 1868, the *Nation* warned that "what was won by the bayonet must not be surrendered at the ballot box."[11] It was a response to the growing success that the Democratic Party, with its racist policies, was having in state elections, both in the North and the South. Over the next six years, Democratic-led conservative forces redeemed all but four of the former Confederate states (Florida, Louisiana, Mississippi, and South Carolina). By 1874, the party was once again a formidable national force.

As Irish Catholics rose in power in New York City and elsewhere in the Northeast, they became an increasingly powerful ally to southern Democrats in the latter's crusade to overturn Reconstruction. At a mass meeting of Democrats in the city in October 1865, one Irish speaker melded economic and racist fear in warning that granting the freedmen anything approaching equality would reduce Whites to "a mixed, degraded caste of laborers."[12] Not by accident did the three Democratic candidates for president between 1868 and 1876 hail from New York. In 1874, Francis Kernan, who had served one term in the House of Representatives during the war, became the first Democrat to be sent to the Senate from New York in nearly a quarter of a century. Kernan became a reliable supporter of white southern interests.

Besides the racism that pervaded white culture throughout the country, there was a constellation of factors imperiling Reconstruction. One was the changing political calculus resulting from the admittance into the Union of new states in the West and Far West. As the Republican Party added these newcomers to its core of states, its dependence on the South to retain its political hegemony steadily declined. Then too Darwinism provided an intellectual cover for racism, as science purported to proscribe any government intervention into a socioeconomic order bound by nature's laws. The intellectual revolution touched off by Charles Darwin on the eve of the war played its role in discrediting a sociopolitical one.

MEMORY AND

THE LOST CAUSE

Anthony Keiley reflected on coming into New York harbor as a captive in the summer of 1864, foreshadowing what became "the Lost Cause" in the South's explication of the war: "In the face of all this wealth, development, material power—all these vast appliances of conquest—I felt a new pride in our beleaguered Confederacy, which has had nothing to oppose to this unexampled affluence of resource except the unconquerable gallantry of her children, and yet has fought this fight against such odds as have never yet stood in the way of freedom, with a calm confidence in the cause, a noble acceptance of sacrifice, and undaunted courage, a patient hope, a chivalric devotion, that fearlessly challenge the comparisons of history."

The Lost Cause, as David W. Blight has best argued, was essentially the mythology that white southerners crafted in the post-Appomattox era to define the meaning of the Civil War and to control its memory. The war, according to Lost Cause shapers, was the tragic attempt of a southern community to secure its independence to protect its unique way of life, an attempt that, despite the heroism and bravery of its legendary military forces, ultimately fell victim to the overwhelming industrial and numerical superiority of the North. The catastrophic result was the triumph of a materialistic, exploitative capitalism over an Arcadian, organic society in which a paternalistic ruling class provided for the weak and vulnerable, both Black and white.[13]

In the shaping and development of the Lost Cause, Catholics, like Keiley, played a significant if not major role in the battle for the collective memory of the war. In 1869, P. G. T. Beauregard became one of the organizers of the Southern Historical Society in New Orleans. Over the years he was a spirited participant in the society's activities, serving on its executive committee and attending its annual conventions. The society's journal became a key channel for spreading the Lost Cause gospel.[14] But it was a priest who became the distinctive shaper and keeper of that sacred history:

Furl that banner for 'tis weary
Round its staff 'tis drooping dreary
Fold it—fold it—it is best
For there's not a man to wave it
And there's not a sword to save it.
And there's not left one to lave it;
In the blood that heroes gave it,
And its foes now scorn to brave it,
Furl it—hide it—let it rest.[15]

So began a poem entitled "The Conquered Banner," published in the *Freeman's Journal* in late June 1865. Its author was Abram Ryan, a twenty-seven-year-old priest of the Diocese of Nashville. "The Conquered Banner," eventually set to music, became an instant favorite in a South numbed by defeat and destruction. It proved to be the primordial expression of the Lost Cause literature that over the next half-century comforted the white people of the region and provided religious meaning for the horrific war experience they had undergone, a veritable sanctification of the cause.

Once Abram Ryan's identity as the author of the poem was revealed a year after its first appearance in print, the priest-poet himself became both a symbol as well as a promoter of the Lost Cause. By 1868 there was an almost singular demand across the South for Ryan to do poetry readings on the Confederacy and its heroes—"The Conquered Banner," "The Sword of Robert Lee," "Cleburne." Through his poetry Ryan drew his readers into the Confederate narrative, to be active players in perpetuating the cause for which the southern heroes had given the last, full measure of their devotion. As southern women, through their memorial associations, gave proper interments in southern soil to those who had been hastily buried on battlefields from Gettysburg to Kennesaw Mountain, Ryan, through his poetry, raised their funeral action to the noble work of providing a fitting resting place for the anonymous Confederate saints who had, Christ-like, "died for me and you."[16]

From Boston to New Orleans, Ryan delivered magnetic speeches that left audiences enthralled, overwhelmed by his "torrent of thought," as one awestruck Boston Jesuit put it after hearing the rebel priest in the heart of New England in 1882.[17] His public persona, a long-haired, cape-shrouded figure in slouch hat, embodied the gothic romanticism that he celebrated in his poetry and oratory. Along with the poetry and lectures, newspapers became, for Ryan, a major instrument in the promulgation of the Lost Cause. The *Banner of the South*, which Bishop Augustin Verot launched in 1868, with Ryan as editor, featured a section entitled "The Lost Cause," which, as Ryan proclaimed in its initial issue, would keep alive "the rights and interests of Native-Land. . . . The armies and government of the Confederacy were but the mortal flesh and blood of an immortal cause. They are gone—it is living. Nor steel, nor lead, could touch its life or take it away."[18]

STATUES, CEMETERIES, AND
THE PRESERVATION OF THE CONFEDERACY

As the first former slave state to be "redeemed," Maryland unsurprisingly became the first southern state to memorialize the "Lost Cause," through the rehabilitation in stone of Roger B. Taney. No sooner had the Democrats regained power in the state than a movement started to honor Taney. As the new Democratic Speaker of the House argued, "The decision in the Dred Scott case was not only just, righteous and right, but endorsed by the State of Maryland to-day." The triumphant Democrats made no bones about the implications of their "redemption" of the state.

The sculptor William Henry Rinehart, a native Marylander, was chosen to execute the monument. The grand ceremony to unveil Rinehart's work on the statehouse grounds took place in December 1872. Despite freezing weather, notables from around the state made the trip to Annapolis for the occasion. The Catholic elite had a prominent place among the dignitaries, including members of the Taney family, and the Washington banker, George W. Riggs. At the close of the ceremony the Navy Band struck up "Maryland, My Maryland," James Ryder Randall's "Marseilles of the Confederacy." A year and a half later, the US Senate made its own nod to redemption by commissioning its own remembrance of Taney in the form of a bust done by noted sculptor Augustus Saint-Gaudens. In redeeming Taney, state and nation had reasserted white supremacy as the standing order once more.[19]

Memorial services quickly became a cathartic occasion for white southern Catholics, as they did for white southerners in general. They became a means for releasing grief while providing hope that a better future lay in store. It was no accident that 70 percent of the Confederate monuments erected in the first two decades following the war were in cemeteries.[20] Catholics across the South quickly took to the annual observance of Decoration Day, to honor the martyrs for the Confederacy.[21] In New Orleans, in 1868, the funeral of Isadore François Turgis became an occasion for hundreds of former Confederate soldiers, including P. G. T. Beauregard, to celebrate the former Jesuit chaplain as an icon of civil religion which the Lost Cause was becoming.

CATHOLICS AND FUSION MOVEMENTS

In Louisiana and South Carolina, a few Catholics were prominent in fusion movements that brought together white Democrats and Black Republicans as a peaceful alternative to redemption. In Louisiana, P. G. T. Beauregard in 1873 headed a Committee of One Hundred that included Louis Roudanez of the *New Orleans Tribune* and other local business and civic leaders. Beauregard averred that "our carpetbaggers must be routed . . . out of the state, or we shall be ruined." But the remedy must not be the terror campaign which the White League was unleashing throughout the state. Instead, the peaceful path to redemption lay in winning Black support by promising them equal civil and political rights, including full access to public accommodation, and even the prospect of owning land.[22] The movement also advocated relief from the heavy taxation that Republican governments had imposed upon businessmen and planters. The platform of the Louisiana Unification Movement had greater appeal in the parishes around New Orleans than it did in the northern ones, where there was little appetite to accept Blacks as equal, much less to enforce laws to ensure that equality in practice.[23] The fusion movement which promised a peaceful redemption quickly died.

A similar fusion movement arose in South Carolina two years later. The Charleston-centered movement included the Catholics James Connor and Francis W. Dawson, the latter now editor of the *Charleston News and Courier.* To Dawson, "straight-outism," or regaining power through unrestricted terror was a bloody path to economic ruin.[24] That movement also went nowhere. Dawson's choice of conciliation over confrontation was one that probably never had a chance of success in a city with the hot-head tradition in which Charleston took pride. Wade Hampton and his Red Shirts, with all the terror and violence they inferred, were the state's future—along with debt peonage, which would bring a terrible stability for the agrarian poor, both Black and white.

ALIGNING FORCES

By 1874 the national government did not have enough soldiers in the South to protect all Republicans, Black or white, or even to ensure the survival of their state governments. In 1872 Congress removed the Fourteenth Amendment's proscriptions against voting and holding office on former Confederate civil and military officials, signs not only of a resurgent democracy but of the weakening Republican commitment to building a new South. Reconstruction fatigue was overcoming the northern public. In September 1873, James Gordon Bennett's *New York Herald* declared that Americans were tired of being "blinded by the flashing of bayonets in our streets, startled by the rumble of Gatlin [*sic*] guns, and the trump, tramp, of the regulars."[25] It was time to let white southerners reclaim their own governance and end the tyranny of Blacks and carpetbaggers propped up by the military.

Eighteen seventy-four proved to be a watershed of the first order in American political history. From a minority with a 110-seat deficit to the Republicans, the Democrats gained a 60-seat majority, to regain control of the House of Representatives after being in the congressional wilderness for a decade and a half. Never had the country experienced such a realigning election. This devastating repudiation of Congressional Reconstruction signaled the end of any hope that Republican governments would long survive in the three states (Mississippi, Louisiana, and South Carolina) in which it still, however shakily, survived.[26]

A sympathetic Supreme Court also proved crucial to the Redeemers' success. In its *Dred Scott* decision, the Taney Court had not only confirmed the right of slavers to take their human property into territories where slavery was not legally recognized but upheld white supremacy in its declaration that Blacks could not be citizens. Despite the loss of its chief justice in 1864, the US Supreme Court continued to manifest its pro-southern bias. In 1866, in the *Ex parte Milligan* case, it jeopardized federal enforcement of civil rights in southern states by ruling that military courts had no jurisdiction over citizens where civil courts were still functioning. Seven years later, the court dealt a mortal blow to the Fourteenth Amendment and the federal government's efforts to enforce it, when it found, in the *Slaughter-House Cases,* that the protection of civil rights fell principally upon the individual states, not the national government. The court disingenuously introduced an arbitrary concept of dual citizenship, divided between state and national, based on the dual sovereignty that defines this nation. Transgressions of civil rights granted by a state, according to the court, were beyond the federal court's jurisdiction. The court's ruling effectively shielded states from federal intervention, thus checking the trend toward centralization of government and greatly expanding the realm in which state sovereignty applied. In 1876 the court, in *United States v. Cruikshank,* dismissed the convictions of those brought to trial for a massacre in Louisiana on the ground that the Fourteenth Amendment protected Blacks from state violation of their civil rights, not that of individuals. In other words, individuals had no need to abide by the three amendments. The two decisions provided a patina of legal justification for private militias to employ whatever means necessary to regain power from a government deemed illegitimate.[27]

MISSISSIPPI

When a massacre of Blacks took place in Vicksburg on July 4, 1874, local Republicans pleaded with Grant for troops to provide adequate protection against further violence and fraud in the August elections. Grant failed to respond, and the Democrats triumphed at the polls. That victory appeared to embolden armed resistance to Republican governments in the states still under Reconstruction. By the summer of 1874 there was an all-out commitment to reestablish white control through violence. Taxpayer Leagues sprang up throughout the South to provide an economic rationale for overthrowing the Republican regimes.

On December 7, Vicksburg was the scene of a second massacre. The desperate governor, Adelbert Ames, called the Republican legislature into a special session. It made a new plea to President Grant for troops. Grant instead ordered the insurgents to disperse and cease disturbing the peace. His order fell on deaf ears. Finally, on Christmas Eve, Grant dispatched Phil Sheridan to take command of the Department of the Gulf, with the charge to investigate the reported disorders in Louisiana and Mississippi and to take whatever action he deemed necessary. On January 4, Sheridan sent troops to Vicksburg, who removed the newly installed Democratic sheriff, A. J. Flanigan. Meanwhile the general of the army, Cump Sherman, sent his own representative to investigate. That officer reported back that the Democrats were really the key to the restoration of democracy in Mississippi. Sherman gave a strong endorsement of the report in forwarding it to the secretary of war, Belknap. At that very time Sheridan was telegraphing the secretary that he regarded the White League as terrorists and wanted authorization to treat them as such. In the end, Grant failed to give Sheridan the go-ahead to deal with the White League.

THE RETURN OF
BLACK FLAG WARFARE

In 1872 Louisiana Democrats nominated for governor John McEnery. McEnery, a lawyer, had commanded the Fourth Louisiana Battalion during the war. During Presidential Reconstruction he had served in the state legislature, where he acquired a reputation as a rabble-rousing, race-baiting promoter of Black Codes and opponent of the constitutional amendments. The gubernatorial election of 1872 ended in a dispute which the Returning Board settled in the Republican candidate's favor. The Democrats continued to claim McEnery as the duly elected governor. The Republican, William Pitt Kellogg, had the backing of the state militia as well as the federal troops. With two governments claiming legitimacy, at the beginning of March 1873 about two hundred members of a Democratic paramilitary group attacked the St. Peter Street arsenal of the state militia in New Orleans. James Longstreet, warned of the attack, easily drove the attackers back to Jackson Square, where he held them at bay. The following day federal troops arrived to arrest the leaders of the paramilitary force.

Governor Kellogg then ordered Longstreet to remove the McEnery legislature from Odd Fellows Hall, where they had set up their rival government. They peacefully abandoned the building, but no prosecutions followed this failed putsch of 1873. That inaction merely emboldened the Democrats to persist in their crusade to end Reconstruction in Louisiana.[28] A disputed sheriff's election in Black-majority Grant County provided an opportunity for the Democrats to assert their military might. Black supporters of the Republican candidate had taken over the courthouse in the county seat, Colfax. They soon found themselves surrounded by the armed white supporters of the Democratic candidate, Columbus Nash. Nash offered safe passage for those who would surrender peacefully. Those within the courthouse refused, knowing that previous guarantees had ended in mass murder. The whites opened fire with their cannon and rifles. Then they set fire to the courthouse, which killed some and forced the surrender of the survivors, who were systematically shot down afterwards. Troops were brought in to make arrests, but the subsequent civil trial, in New Orleans, ended in a mistrial.[29]

The Colfax massacre merely emboldened white insurgents to pursue Black Flag warfare as the surest path to redemption. Regarding their opponents as criminal usurpers, the resurgent Democrats in Louisiana and elsewhere were determined not merely to remove Republicans from office, but to destroy the Republican Party in the South, by whatever means necessary.[30] Across Louisiana sprang up chapters of the White League, a paramilitary group dedicated to using extralegal violence to bring down Republican government and disenfranchise Blacks. Over the next year it recruited between ten thousand and fifteen thousand members, one of whom was Edward Douglass White, a lawyer and Georgetown alumnus. Many of the White League officers were Irish.

A NEW COUP ATTEMPT

The Metropolitan Police of New Orleans had become the chief component of the state militia. The Metropolitans were organized as an army battalion, with infantry, artillery, and cavalry units. Thomas Flanagan, a Union Army veteran and Irish immigrant from Boston, was the infantry regiment's colonel. A biracial force, the Metropolitans counted most of the white militia still loyal to the Republicans. Blacks constituted a growing majority of New Orleans's police, the result of recruiting to counter the rise of the White League.[31] James Longstreet remained the field commander of the state militia and Metropolitan Police, but their ranks counted few other Confederate veterans. Even Longstreet's close friend Col. W. J. Behan had joined the White League. By 1874 militia strength was down to twenty-six companies, thirteen fewer than there had been four years earlier. The militia's shrunken condition was worse than its paper totals disclosed, since the Metropolitan Police, which now made up nearly half of its companies, had not been part of the militia in 1870.[32] Even the *gens de couleur* were waning in their support of Republican rule, as their decline in number of companies from nine to five indicated.

By 1874, with its military strength concentrated in New Orleans, Republican sovereignty was effectively confined to the pale of the Crescent City. As summer set in, John McEnery issued a call to arms: "You must fight for the white people now; the civilization of a thousand years is not to be swept away."[33] By that time the White League, the first to proclaim by its name the goal of reestablishing white supremacy, had spread to more than a third of the state's fifty-seven parishes. The league began a concerted campaign of terror to seize political control of the state. It issued ultimatums for Republican officials to resign or face the consequences. Sometimes even resigning was no guarantee against execution. In August, league members murdered six top officials of Grant Parish, eliminating virtually its entire government. By September, having taken over or paralyzed eight parish governments, the league demanded Governor Kellogg's resignation.[34] It was the race war that Patrick Lynch had predicted, if not in the form he had thought it would take.

In the first week of September, President Grant finally acted against the orgy of terror in Louisiana. He ordered US Marshals and attorneys to prosecute those guilty of the racial violence. When local sheriffs proved unwilling to arrest those indicted, Grant dispatched a regiment to Louisiana. Having been away for the summer, General William Emory, the district military commander, had no sense that Louisiana was on the brink of a full-scale insurrection. Apprised that a cache of arms intended for the White League was due to arrive in New Orleans via steamboat, state authorities made plans to seize them. McEnery and the league were prepared for just such an intervention. McEnery had already sent word to his supporters to gather at the Henry Clay statue at Canal and St. Charles streets at 11 a.m. on Monday, September 14. They intended to use the moment to defeat James Longstreet's militia and seize the statehouse. By midday of the fourteenth there was a crowd consisting of more than five thousand persons at the statue, most without firearms. Meanwhile a delegation was sent to the statehouse to demand Kellogg's resignation. Frank McGloin led a force charged with capturing City Hall on Lafayette Square and cutting the telegraph lines to all the Metropolitan Police precinct stations, to prevent a general alarm. Throughout the city, the White League forces were preparing for street warfare by erecting barricades of streetcars and other bulwarks. Among them was Henri Garidel's son, Joseph.[35] When Kellogg refused to step down, McEnery exhorted the crowd gathered at the Henry Clay statue to overthrow the radical government. The crowd dispersed to retrieve arms and take to the streets.[36]

The few federal soldiers in New Orleans were posted at the Custom House. A trainload of relief troops was delayed, apparently the victim of the rail company conspiring with the Democrats. James Longstreet had under his command about thirty-five hundred militia, including five hundred Metropolitans, with two small cannon and a Gatling gun. When Longstreet and his lieutenants met in the statehouse to decide on a plan of action, they did not know that the league had already seized City Hall and cut the telegraph lines, nor that armed White Leaguers were behind barricades. The commander split his force by race, with the Black militia left to defend the capitol, and the slightly larger white half, including artillery and cavalry, dispatched to the Custom House. The militia, under Longstreet's command, bore the brunt of the subsequent fighting on Canal Street. When the state militia began to waver, Colonel Behan, commanding five companies of White Leaguers, ordered a charge. With a rebel yell they stormed up Canal Street. The Metropolitans quickly fled in all directions. Caught in the crossfire, Longstreet was thrown from his horse, reinjuring the arm that had been struck at the Wilderness. With no opposition, the insurgents seized the huge cache of weapons that the state government had stashed in police stations and ships. The remnants of the militia had taken shelter at the statehouse, but, when facing the imminent threat of shelling, had surrendered, upon the League's promise of amnesty.[37] The Republican government in the largest city of the former Confederacy had been ousted in a *coup d'état* carried out by a military force largely composed of Confederate veterans.

It proved to be a very brief triumph for the would-be redeemers. Grant, no longer able to ignore the challenge, dispatched to New Orleans six regiments of federal troops to restore Kellogg and the Republicans to power. McEnery returned the state government, not to Kellogg, but to the federal military, a clear indication of the inescapable nexus between Republican governance and the US Army.[38] Because the insurgents had surrendered peacefully, there was no punishment for the uprising. Federal forces had once more put down an insurrection in New Orleans, but the statewide network of insurgency remained intact, ready to spring up anew at the next opportunity. In November of 1874, Abram Ryan assured an audience in New Orleans that Catholic theology taught that governments can, by their actions, render themselves illegitimate. When such governments disqualify themselves to rule by their unreasonable policies, "the bullet must reason, the rifle must reason, the cannon must reason."[39]

Governor Kellogg managed to reconstitute the Metropolitan Police, but the militia, including its leadership, was *hors de combat.* James Longstreet, demoralized by the defection to the White League of nearly all his former Confederate colleagues, in early January resigned his commission as commander. Longstreet was not the only victim of demoralization. The Canal Street Battle was the final straw that broke the trust of the Black militia and the community it represented.[40]

SHERIDAN'S SECOND TOUR
IN LOUISIANA

The army's top command was split on the matter of how (or even whether) to continue enforcing any policy of equal rights for Blacks. For several years Cump Sherman had wanted the army to divest itself of its police duties in the South. Phil Sheridan, however, still felt that Black voters were crucial to the survival of Republican government, and that old rebels had no place in government.[41] Following the attempted coup, President Grant sent Phil Sheridan back to New Orleans to ensure that the duly elected Republicans would retain power. All too quickly, Sheridan found himself facing a crisis.

On January 4, 1875, the House of Representatives of Louisiana began its new session. Two immediate matters facing the House were the outcome of five district elections which the Returning Board had left unsettled as well as the selection of a speaker. Colonel Philippe Régis de Trobriand's Thirteenth US Infantry was one of two regiments assigned to provide security. Governor Kellogg had ordered the constables to admit only elected representatives. Somehow dozens of others got in. That set the scene for an audacious power grab by the minority Democrats. In the bedlam that marked the formal opening of the session, the Democrats rammed through the election of one of their own as speaker, with a justice of the peace suddenly appearing from among the spectators to administer the oath, as well as dozens of persons sporting "assistant sergeant-at-arms" badges who were duly appointed by the just sworn-in speaker to maintain "order." The new "speaker" then forced the election of five Democrats to fill the open seats. It was but the latest attempt to overthrow the Reconstruction government, this time by shouting into office a pop-up candidate sanctioned by a deus ex machina judge and security force.[42] When Colonel Trobriand, at the frantic request of Republicans, went to the statehouse, in civilian dress, to restore order, he removed everyone in the assembly hall without credentials, but made no attempt to undo the putsch that the Democrats had engineered. Later, Trobriand conferred with Sheridan, who ordered him to return and ensure that all the representatives were duly certified by the Returning Board as victors in their election. Trobriand, this time in uniform, reentered the hall and ejected the five uncertified representatives. That restored the Republican majority and control of the legislature.[43]

That evening, Sheridan, wanting to root out the Democratic resistance to legal government, appealed to Secretary of War Belknap to allow him to bring to a military trial the "banditti" of the White League so as to foreclose a new campaign of terror in the upcoming elections of 1876. As Sheridan told President Grant later that week, the trail of violence that the resisters to lawful government in Louisiana had left was already a grim one: more than thirty-five hundred dead, mostly Blacks, since 1866.[44] Despite his plea, Belknap refused to authorize such an operation.[45]

For his efforts to preserve the imperiled remnants of Reconstruction, Sheridan generated opposition that rose to death threats. A protest denouncing Sheridan's accusations was signed by the city's civic leaders, including a rabbi, two Protestant bishops, and the Catholic archbishop, Napoléon Joseph Perché. In January of that year, the archbishop, ignoring the obvious violence that the Democratic-related militia were inflicting upon Republican officials and their followers, accused the Republicans of being corrupt, venal politicians whose obsession was to cling to power.[46]

The fierce backlash in Louisiana against the latest use of military force to sustain Reconstruction had stunned the president. He wanted no part in any reinstitution of military government that involved martial law. The coup had failed, but it had succeeded as a ploy to win national support in the North. Resolutions denouncing Sheridan's heavy-handed repression of civilian government poured into Congress from state legislatures from New York to Texas. Responding to the intersectional lobbying, Congress brokered a deal which gave the conservatives/Democrats a sixty-three to forty-seven majority in the House. The reduced Republican presence came at the expense of Black representation, whose numbers shrank from twenty-nine to twenty, down from their high of thirty-eight in 1872, less than three years before. Most of the losses came from parishes where the White League had been most active. Paramilitary terror in the countryside had been the most effective weapon for increasing Democratic political power in the state.[47]

UNDERMINING RECONSTRUCTION
IN SOUTH CAROLINA

South Carolina was the sole ex-Confederate state to have a Black majority in its legislature during the lifespan of Congressional Reconstruction, reflecting the demographics of a state in which nearly 60 percent of the population was Black. That made South Carolina the poster boy for racist depictions of the state government run by corrupt savages who were bleeding citizens by taxes that lined officeholders' pockets and provided services to the idle and worthless poor.[48] James S. Pike, a Republican who had become disillusioned with Reconstruction, published in the *New York Tribune* in 1872 a series of reports about South Carolina in which he depicted a state "prostrate" as a result of the corruption and incompetence of "black barbarism" hell-bent on reaping riches by oppressive taxation.[49] Those reports helped propel Horace Greeley's Liberal Republican presidential campaign in 1872.

South Carolina's success in land reform was seen as the perversion of state authority to make it the channel of the redistribution of property from its rightful white owners to undeserving Blacks. The South Carolina Taxpayers' Association gave public voice to that concern and played a key role in mounting the political opposition to Republican government.[50] Taxes in South Carolina now fell on all property, personal and estate. At a time when poverty was so widespread and cash scarce, taxes were a special threat to one's economic health.[51] Robert Aldrich, Bernard O'Neill, Alexander Melchers, Francis W. Dawson, James Cosgrove, E. W. Wood, and James Claffey were prominent Catholic members of the Taxpayers' Association, which formed in the 1870s. When Governor Chamberlain in 1874 committed his administration to a regimen of retrenchment, the move was hailed by Francis Dawson, now editor of the *Charleston News and Courier*.[52]

No matter to what extent Republican governments in South Carolina tried to conciliate the white minority, Democrats increasingly weaponized racial grievance to reclaim power and limited autonomy.[53] When the Republican government in South Carolina, for self-protection, organized a militia, the subsequent white boycott resulted in an overwhelmingly Black force. When the militia tried to confront the white paramilitary groups terrorizing portions of the state, it was read in the North as the inevitable clash of races to which Confederates like Patrick Lynch had warned that emancipation would lead.

THE RED SHIRT CAMPAIGN

Rutherford B. Hayes, in accepting the Republican nomination for president in the summer of 1876, had pledged to bring to the South "the blessings of honest and capable local self-government."[54] That was as clear a message as Hayes could have sent that, once he became president, he would remove the last vestiges of Reconstruction government from the region. Nonetheless, those bent upon redemption in South Carolina had no intention of depending on Hayes's word. The first indication of the length to which redeemers would go to realize their goal came on July 4 in a Black hamlet close by the Georgia border. Black militia celebrating Independence Day blocked the road where two white farmers were attempting to pass. The following day, when the farmers tried to have the local Black judge order the militiamen arrested for obstructing their passage, the Black head of the militia chastised the Black judge for even hearing the complaint. In response the judge charged the militia commander with contempt of court. Later that day, fighting broke out between the Black militia and a white para-militia. The forty or so Black militia retreated to their shelter. The whites secured a cannon and hundreds of reinforcements in Augusta, just across the Savannah River. The outnumbered, outgunned militia attempted to flee. In their flight, the town's Black marshal fell mortally wounded; twenty-five of his comrades were captured. That evening, five of them were murdered in cold blood. It instantly became the Hamburg Massacre.[55]

Francis Dawson's *Charleston News and Courier* had initially deplored the murder of the Black militiamen after they had surrendered, on the expedient grounds that such behavior would prove detrimental to the Democratic cause. Its editor soon enough discovered how out of step he was with reactionary forces across the state. The first inkling came when readers and advertisers began a boycott of the paper. The next came when Dawson was challenged to a duel for his negative coverage. Obviously, southern honor could not abide any criticism of actions taken, no matter how repulsive they might be, to restore white supremacy.

Terror had shown the way to redemption and would continue to do so through the election. One of the first fruits of the massacre was the permanent flight of hundreds of Blacks from Hamburg. Decrees from President Grant and Governor Chamberlain for Democrats to disband their rifle clubs brought laughter. The Democratic campaign that fall took on the reenactment of the military triumphs of ancient Rome, in which South Carolina's elite women, with red sashes about their waists and red ribbons crowning their heads, led parades dominated by thousands of mounted, red-shirted, torch-bearing, armed men, accompanied by a battery of artillery, and all shouting the rebel yell, in support of the Democratic candidate for governor, Wade Hampton. In Charleston, on streets where, eleven years before, Blacks had paraded in humble celebration of freedom, Wade Hampton's men and women, clad in revolution's color, came now as conquerors.[56]

In the fall an Association of United Irishman was organized to campaign for the Democratic Party "against the rule of outside domination."[57] It was a call to renew the struggle for southern independence that they had been forced to discontinue at Appomattox. Two days later the German community, at Freundschaftsbund Hall in Charleston, made a similar commitment, this one to support the Democrats to protect property, eliminate corruption, and restore economical government.[58]

In Columbia, Mother Baptista Lynch was caught up in the anticipated victory of Wade Hampton, "one of So. C[arolin]a's noblest sons! Grand Preparations," she wrote her brother Patrick, "are being made to give him an ovation in Columbia tomorrow & the *hearts* of our best people & the gentry of the state are in it." She and her community were daily "begging God's blessing on the Cause of honesty, truth, & humanity which he . . . represent[s]." She reminded her brother of the Hamptons' "kind friendship for our Convent for the past 18 years."[59] The convent sent laurels for the street decorations to honor Hampton's anticipated triumph.[60] When Democrats, including Hampton, were declared victorious, Baptista reported that "everybody seems perfectly elated by the result of the elections!" now confident that Redemption would not only rid them of oppressive Republican rule, but open the way to the renewal of the prosperity that had eluded them since the war.[61]

That report proved premature in the extreme. The election's outcome was in dispute, not only in South Carolina, but in Louisiana and Florida as well.

As the centennial year closed, all eyes were on Washington, DC, to see how or if the mounting crisis would be solved.

A BLOODLESS COUP
IN LOUISIANA

In Louisiana, terrorism was less prevalent during the campaigning than it had been two years earlier, if only because the White League already controlled much of the state.[62] The subsequent election, awash in intimidation and fraud, climaxed fittingly with competing Returning Boards submitting contradictory results that left both sides claiming that their candidates for president, governor, and the legislature had prevailed. On January 8, there were twin gubernatorial inaugurations, with the Republican Stephen Packard's taking place behind the closed doors of the French Quarter capitol,[63] while Nicholls's was carried out at St. Patrick's Hall, with an outside crowd of ten thousand thronging Lafayette Square.

With the governorship still in legal limbo, Nicholls aimed to carry out a bloodless coup by creating a functioning shadow government before the Republicans or the federal garrison could react. On the morning of January 9, Nicholls ordered regiments of White League forces to cordon off the statehouse, where Packard's supporters had barricaded themselves, to take over the offices of the Louisiana Supreme Court, and to seize as many of the city police stations as possible. Having named his own supreme court and municipal police force, Nicholls intended to force Washington's recognition, no matter whether Samuel Tilden or Rutherford Hayes succeeded Grant as president.[64] The plan went as smoothly as the conservatives could have imagined, as three thousand White Leaguers by midafternoon occupied the Supreme Court and police precincts peacefully. Nicholls proceeded to appoint five Supreme Court justices and a new Board of Commissioners of the Metropolitan Police. Two of the justices were Catholics, Alcibiades De Blanc and W. B. Egan. Nicholls dispatched his campaign manager, Edward Burke, to Washington as his personal envoy. Once there, Burke lobbied the Democratic caucus to filibuster any decision by the Electoral Commission that Congress had established to adjudicate the disputed results in Florida, Louisiana, and South Carolina. Such a delaying tactic, if carried beyond March 5, would have had the potential of leaving the country without a chief executive who could intervene in Louisiana. Meanwhile the current president, Ulysses S. Grant, refrained from taking any action, no doubt having concluded that Louisiana, like South Carolina, was beyond saving for the Republicans. When Packard appealed to Grant for military assistance to repel the forces of redemption that were sweeping Republicans out of power throughout the state, Grant candidly responded through a secretary that "the President directs me to say that he feels it his duty to state frankly that he does not believe public opinion will longer support the maintenance of State government in LA by the use of the military and that he must concur in this manifest feeling."[65] One cannot imagine the circumstances under which Grant, in the summer of 1864, would have determined that public opinion should decide the outcome of the war, even if that meant a peace settlement.

The inauguration of Governor Nicholls, which took place in St. Patrick's Hall, marked the formal redemption of Louisiana from Radical Republican rule. Ironically Reconstruction ended in the state where it had had its beginning. The city's Irish, who had initially supported Lincoln's plan to reconstruct the region, played an important role in toppling the congressional version of the remaking of the South.[66]

REDEMPTION COMPLETE

In late February, news broke of the Wormley House agreement in Washington in which representatives of Rutherford Hayes agreed to remove federal troops from the three southern states in which they remained in exchange for the Democrats agreeing to accept Hayes's election as president. The news stunned Governor Packard. As he reminded Grant in a telegram, this agreement validated the putsch of the White Leaguers. Grant could only reiterate to the would-be governor that public opinion had turned against any further use of the federal military to sustain Republican governments in the South, and he had to respect that change. Unless overt violence threatened life and property, there would be no federal intervention. Once Hayes officially became president, the new president advised Packard to abdicate and the Republican legislators to try to find a place in the conservative assembly or to go home. On April 19, in their final session, the Packard legislature made a final declaration of theirs being the duly elected assembly of the state, then dispersed.

Five days later, the federal troops withdrew from guarding the statehouse. Later that summer, some of those same troops would be dispatched by the federal government, no longer to protect southern Blacks and their allies, but to safeguard the property of the nation's railroads, the iconic symbol of corporate America, whose advancement had now become the chief concern of the Republican Party. The day after the last US soldiers left New Orleans,

White League militia, in a formal ceremony, occupied the troops' quarters, to the roar of the masses gathered for this historic milestone of redemption.[67]

The Republicans had maintained their hold on the presidency, but only by effectively agreeing to withdraw federal oversight from the last three states of the former Confederacy in which there was still a military occupation. Home rule reigned throughout the South. At the beginning of its second century of independence, the nation, or at least its white majority, was indeed buoyant about its prospects for "prosperity, peace, happiness and glory." Counterrevolutionaries had restored the old order in the South, or at least a passing facsimile. White Catholics were among the chief beneficiaries of the settlement that had ended, or at least put on semipermanent hold, the long struggle for Black rights in the South.

So died the new nation aborning; the revolution turned back until a better day, one that would resume "the unfinished work" of bringing ever closer to fulfillment America's promise for all its people. For most Catholics North and South, home rule inevitably restored the traditional hierarchy, not by reviving slavery, but by instituting new forms of social, economic, and political control—Jim Crow, debt peonage, disenfranchisement—proper for a society composed of unequal races incapable of living together on a level playing field. The Lost Cause became the reigning narrative of the war. The three amendments to the Constitution that the war occasioned effectively went down the national memory hole.

Catholic and American

"A FREE NATION . . . TO BE KEPT . . . UNITED TILL THE END OF TIME"

"It was estimated that fully fifty thousand were present. . . . Officers and men, women and children, came from every quarter. . . . the old field was covered with tents, numbering probably ten thousand." So, the Catholic priest who had immortalized himself by the iconic blessing he had given to Union troops as they sprang into action on the second day at Gettysburg described the gathering in July 1888 for the celebration of the twenty-fifth anniversary of the battle. For William Corby the veterans had come together to remember and honor the "great heroic deeds worthy a nation now so exalted among all the nations of the earth—a free nation handed down to us by our illustrious forefathers to be kept intact and united till the end of time; a nation born of the patriotic, liberty-loving heroes over a century ago and now cemented in the blood of their children's children, never again to be disrupted by political strife or ungovernable passion."[1] Corby clearly regarded Gettysburg as the decisive action in the Civil War's permanent sealing of the Union. Bloodshed itself was the price and justification for a reunited nation, no matter on what terms of inequity that reunion had occurred. The fact that Blacks had no part in this celebration; that slavery, the very cause of the transcendent event they were celebrating went unmentioned amid all the speeches given over the course of the solemn commemoration, said all that needed to be said about who the winners and losers of the war were in the popular mind—about what the war settled.

Abraham Lincoln, for his part, had seen in Gettysburg something that went far beyond reunification, no matter how permanent: a new order that the deaths and suffering of so many on this battlefield and countless others had made possible. Forgotten amid all the remembering at the anniversary, if it had ever really been heard twenty-five years earlier, was Lincoln's radical recasting of the nation's mission as the ongoing fulfillment of the promises of American life that the Founding Fathers articulated at the creation of the Republic. All those brave Irish, along with everyone else, Union and Confederate, who had taken part in that watershed battle and all the other violent encounters during the four seemingly endless years of war, had, Lincoln twice opined, first at Gettysburg, then in his Second Inaugural, been part of a sacrifice of atonement for the nation's original sin, a sin in which all the nation shared. Lincoln said this with the hope that out of the war's cauldron would emerge a nation worth having, in which all were truly free, all equal before the law and in their opportunities to pursue life, liberty, and happiness; a nation which could proudly hail its motto: *e pluribus unum*. Memphis, New Orleans, Colfax, Hamburg were silent, cruel reminders that the work of reconstructing the nation had failed miserably. By 1888, if the nation was truly to be reborn, that rebirth seemed beyond any distant vistas one could imagine.

As Catholics had played a disproportionate role in the winning of the American Revolution, so they had replicated that performance in the turning back of a second revolution which a new civil war had made, one that promised to realize on an unprecedented scale the pursuit of equality which had been a core part of the nation's mission since its inception. Catholics, as a community, had known, for generations, the consequences of being treated inequitably. But when the moment came to be part of a revolution to right the historic imbalance for everyone, most white Catholics could not rise above their tribal interests to treat equality as something more than a zero-sum commodity. At least in spirit, they were with Edward Douglass White in the streets of New Orleans, part of a putsch to complete the nullification of a revolution that would have put the nation on the path to becoming a full democracy.

THE SHIFTING TIDES
OF IMMIGRATION

Beginning in the 1880s, there was a new floodtide of immigrants, now predominantly from Eastern and Southern Europe, but still heavily Catholic. That generated a renewed nativism, driven more by ethnicity than by religion, epitomized by the revival, in 1915, of the Ku Klux Klan, no longer a southern phenomenon but a national force, targeting not only Blacks, but Catholics and Jews as well. The anti-immigration movement culminated with the passage of the National Origins Acts of the 1920s, the final one restricting immigration to approximately 150,000 persons a year. The laws skewed the ethnic distribution to give those from Northwestern Europe a virtual lock on legal immigration.

In 1928 Al Smith became the first Catholic to be nominated for the presidency. Unsurprisingly, he had overwhelming support from his fellow Catholics. Smith, however, lost badly to Herbert Hoover, in part out of anti-Catholic fears that the son of Irish immigrants was a stalking horse for papist designs upon America. One can only imagine to what level those concerns would have risen had Smith's evangelical fearmongers been able to peer a half-century into the future, when more than 175,000 Catholics gathered on the National Mall to attend a Mass celebrated by the pope himself, flanked by crimson-and purple-clad prelates around an altar bordered with American and papal flags against the backdrop of the Capitol.

By 1979 the country had elected its first Catholic president, John Fitzgerald Kennedy. Two years before the 1960 election, Kennedy had published *A Nation of Immigrants,* a manifesto for immigration reform befitting a nation that considered itself an "equal opportunity society."[2] Kennedy did not live to see his goal realized in the Immigration Reform Act of 1965 which, instead of racially skewed quotas, established equitable ones for all nations. Although not the framers' intent, the act produced a radical change in immigration patterns, from one dominated by Europeans to one in which Latin America, Asia, and to a lesser extent, the Middle East, became the leading senders to the United States.

CATHOLICS AND
A NEW CIVIL WAR

With Kennedy's election, Catholics had claimed the Holy Grail of political opportunity, which only a few decades earlier had seemed well beyond their grasp. It was the ultimate symbol of the passage of the Catholic community into the mainstream of American society. Over the next sixty years Catholics became a force in the political establishment far greater than their numbers (a quarter of the population) would suggest, if their dominance of the speakership of the House of Representatives and their majority on the Supreme Court are reliable indicators. At the same time, Catholics experienced the collapse of the parallel world which had made them a people apart over the past century. The civil rights movement, alien (that is, non-white) immigration, and a ruling class perceived to be thoroughly secular suddenly became existential threats to Catholics' traditional cultural and moral exceptionalism. That perception rendered a great many Catholics highly vulnerable to the lure of the merchants of grievance and conspiracy in the Radical Right media-sphere who promoted an epistemic anarchy particularly instrumental in radicalizing their listeners and viewers.

In a remarkable transformation, the Democratic Party had shed its historic identity as a protector of states' rights and white supremacy to become a big-tent party championing diversity and progressive government which culminated in the first African American becoming president. The Republican Party, by contrast, had abandoned its historic roots in the antislavery movement to become, increasingly, a white Christian monolith that alarmingly resorted to ever more undemocratic means to ensure political hegemony: gerrymandering, the filibuster, voter suppression, the termination of the requirement of balanced news reporting by public media, and paramilitias.

As this transformation took place, there was a heavy migration of white Catholics from the Democratic Party to the Republican, particularly after the Supreme Court legalized abortion in 1973. Whether as Democrats or as Republicans, Catholic voters have always been particularly susceptible to the lure of demagogues, particularly those like Charles Coughlin and Joe McCarthy who exploited the anti-communist, anti-socialist animus within the Catholic community. Newer merchants of grievance, like Pat Buchanan and Newt Gingrich, paved the way for Donald Trump's race-fueled demagoguery, particularly against immigrants of a different color and religion. With Trump in the White House, the nation found itself in a new civil war driven by the same racism which rooted the old one. In this latest crisis, a clear majority of the white Catholic community, as in the Civil War era, found itself on the wrong side of history.

To their shame, white Catholics not only strongly supported Donald Trump in 2016 but the vast majority of those Catholics remained loyal to Trump as he waged reckless war on the fundamental norms and institutions of democracy, while hollowing out government, ignoring the climate, infrastructure, and inequality crises, and withdrawing America in every way he could from the international order which this country had led the way in establishing in the post–World War II era. Most scandalous was the cynical engagement in transactional politics of much of the Catholic episcopacy. So long as President Trump appointed antiabortion judges, postured about protecting religious liberty, and promoted parochial school vouchers, the bishops turned a blind eye toward his pathological lying, his escalating abuse of power, and his cruel policies, notably his inhumane separation of refugee families seeking sanctuary from intolerable living conditions in Central America.

Despite a practicing Catholic being the Democratic candidate for president in 2020, once again most white Catholics voted for Donald Trump. Even after the *Mueller Report* had demonstrated the extensive collusion of his campaign team with Russian agents, as well as Trump's repeated attempts to obstruct the investigation into those interactions. Even after the House of Representatives impeached him for attempting to extort a foreign ally into investigating his political rival by withholding vital military aid to that country beleaguered by Russian invaders. Even after Trump refused, for political calculations, to harness the full power of the federal government to combat a deadly pandemic whose costs in economic disruptions and human lives we are still experiencing. For far too many Catholics, Biden's pro-choice position made him an unacceptable alternative to Trump, despite the latter's lethal baggage.

Catholic support for Trump persisted, even after his baseless claims of a stolen election led to the insurrection of January 6, 2021, when thousands of protestors, at the president's planned directive, headed down the mall to the Capitol, their frenzy building under a sea of flags: American, "Trump 2020," Confederate, "Don't Tread on Me." Unlike the Catholic throng which had gathered peacefully in this very heart of the nation more than forty years earlier to demonstrate the compatibility of their faith and their citizenship, this violent mob was bent on counterrevolution, on a new restoration of white supremacy. They ransacked the Capitol, killed a policeman (four others later took their own lives), injured more than 140, and traumatized the congressional community. In the Orwellian world of Trumpism, terror, even insurrection in the service of white, Christian America became the highest form of patriotism.

Within hours of this harrowing assault, a majority of the Republicans in the House of Representatives and eight Republican senators voted to overturn the election results in key states. Out of fear or opportunism or complicity, they remained loyal to a lame-duck president who had just made his final, desperate, seditious attempt to stay in power. Republican-controlled legislatures, under the guise of restoring the integrity of elections, enacted laws intended to suppress the Democratic vote and ensure Republican control of the certification of election outcomes. A major funder of such election "reform" was the Election Transparency Initiative, a collaboration of two Catholic-led organizations, the Susan B. Anthony List and the American Principles Project. Catholic plutocrats, motivated by anti-abortion and economic libertarian convictions, provided the financial means to execute this antidemocratic revolution.[3] Opportunistic Republican Catholics such as Elise Stefanik and Ron DeSantis promoted the Big Lie at the federal and state levels respectively, having calculated that such gaslighting represented their best pathway to uncontested power. They dismissed the bipartisan select committee of the House of Representatives as a "Democrat witch-hunt," in order to ensure that, like the attempts to subvert government in Louisiana in the last years of Reconstruction, there would be no accountability for those most responsible for the storming of the Capitol on January 6.

Through it all, a growing majority of Republican voters, including a large portion of the Catholic community, considered Joe Biden an illegitimate president. For many of these Catholics, this mass delusion was the inevitable consequence of the insistence that abortion law should be determined by the religious beliefs of a minority willing to endorse virtually any means to make that aspiration a reality. As though this were a confessional state in which the official religion gets to determine the laws of the land. Catholics, as much as any group, should realize, from their long history in this country, how much injustice they have suffered from this misperception. Then too there was the long immersion by millions of Catholics in the disinformation-spewing media of the Radical Right which has rendered them impervious to political reality. But the deeper problem was that too many white Catholics have failed to take up Lincoln's challenge to continue the work of fulfilling the ideals that are the marrow of our experiment in democratic governance. They need to read Pope Francis's encyclical *Fratelli tutti,* in which the pontiff teaches that the basis for the inalienable rights that we Americans are so wont to profess is the dignity which God has bestowed on all humans, without exception. A democracy in which all equally participate, Lincoln reminded, is the best assurance that these rights will be honored.

It was Lincoln's great gift to the nation to point us on the path to comprehending the full demographic breadth of our democracy. Too many Catholics refuse to acknowledge, much less to embrace, the full identity of "the people" whom Lincoln saw constituting our polity. Until there is a common commitment to pursuing equality, not just for those who look and speak like ourselves but for all Americans, our democracy will remain imperiled. And the Catholic community will still fall a good deal short of becoming fully American and fully catholic. Never has the Catholic community stood more in need of owning its unvarnished history in this country, to avoid repeating it, this time on a larger scale, with likely fatal consequences for the republic. Openly confronting that history can just possibly reveal the truth which frees us at last to complete the work to which Lincoln called all of us: the making of a nation rooted in equality.

Aftermaths

Pierre Gustave Toutant Beauregard in 1877 became a supervisor of the Lou-isiana State Lottery Company, owned by a New York syndicate. "For over twenty years," Beauregard's biographer wrote, "the lottery company dom-inated the political, economic and social life of . . . the state."[1] Beauregard's name gave the powerful company respectable cover, for which he was paid handsomely. In 1884 he cowrote *The Military Operations of General Beaure-gard,* a two-volume memoir of his war experience. He died in 1893 at the age of seventy-four.

Paul Cooney, CSC, returned to Notre Dame where he rejoined the faculty. Despite chronically poor health, a legacy of his war service, Cooney lived into his eighty-fourth year, dying in 1905.

William Corby, CSC, in the postwar years, twice served as president of Notre Dame (1866–72, 1877–81), during which time he greatly expanded the facili-ties of the university. He died in 1897 at sixty-four.

Charles Daly served as chief justice of the Court of Common Appeals until 1885. He continued to lead the American Geographical Society until his death in 1899 at the age of eighty-two. His wife, **Marie,** had preceded him in death five years earlier.

Francis Dawson became a major advocate of the New South program of di-versifying the southern economy, especially promoting the emergent tobacco and cotton textile industries. Into the 1880s he continued to press for Black rights, including voting, and, through his paper, the *News and Courier,* cam-paigned against dueling and lynching. In 1888 Pope Leo XIII named Dawson a knight of the Order of St. Gregory in recognition of his reform efforts. In that same year Dawson himself was a fatal victim of the region's ancient code of honor, when he accused a local physician of attempting to seduce Dawson's governess, only to have the doctor draw a pistol and kill him.

John Dooley died in 1873 at Georgetown University, a victim of the tuberculosis which he almost certainly contracted during the war. **James Dooley** became one of the prime shapers of the new economy that emerged in the redeemed South. Along with two other lawyers, Joseph Bryan and Thomas M. Logan, Dooley acquired the Richmond and Danville Railroad, which eventually became the core of a holding company under which the trio built railroads in several states. "The Virginians" successfully branched out into the nascent iron and steel industries in Alabama, as well as developing real estate throughout the South and beyond. By his death at the age of eighty-one in 1922, Dooley had likely become the richest Catholic in the former Confederacy.

William Henry Elder, in the yellow fever epidemic which ravaged Natchez in 1878, displayed the heroic outreach to the suffering which had distinguished his tenure as bishop during the war. Elder himself became a victim of the epidemic but survived. Two years later he was named coadjutor bishop of Cincinnati. He formally succeeded John Baptist Purcell as archbishop in 1883, where for the next two decades he led an ambitious expansion of the archdiocese's pastoral and educational facilities until his death at eighty-five in 1904.

Charles Ewing served as Catholic commissioner for Indian missions until his premature death from pneumonia in 1883. Of all the Ewing-Sherman clan, **Hugh Ewing**, despite chronic ailments deriving from his war service, outlived all his siblings, dying at seventy-nine in 1905, after a highly successful career as an author, particularly of historical novels.

Henri Garidel, in 1870, fled New Orleans anew, to become one of the numerous Confederate carpetbaggers seeking a better postwar life in New York City. The creole found work there as a bookkeeper until his death in 1878.

The mixed-race **Healys**, in the postwar era, continued their ascent within the institutional church by successfully identifying as Irish. **James Healy**, as bishop of Portland, Maine, became a staunch member of the ultramontane bloc of the American hierarchy which interpreted Pope Leo XIII's condemnation of "Americanism" in 1899 as a vindication of their position. James died less than a year later. Poor health forced **Patrick Healy**'s resignation as president of Georgetown University in 1882. His last three decades were spent in limited pastoral ministry from Portland to Washington, DC. **Eliza Mary Magdalen Healy** entered the Congregation of Notre Dame in Montreal in 1874. Eight years later she professed her final vows. For nearly forty years she taught in Notre Dame academies across Canada and the United States. In 1903 she was named mother superior and headmistress at Villa Barlow in St. Albans, a position she held until 1918 when she became superior of a Notre Dame school on Long Island. She died the following year at sixty-two.

Isaac Hecker, upon his return from the Vatican Council in the summer of 1870, began to experience the symptoms of leukemia, which ravaged him physically and spiritually for the remainder of his life. His near-invalid condition severely curtailed his extraordinary career as writer, publisher, and evangelist. He died in 1888 at sixty-nine.

In 1882 **Hyacinth Le Conniat** returned from Louisiana to France for the last time—she had made three earlier eastward crossings—to become mistress of novices for her congregation. She died in 1897, at eighty.

Health issues and fear of White League retaliation forced **James Longstreet** to leave Louisiana in 1875 to relocate in Georgia. Two years later, he became a member of the Catholic Church. Beginning in 1880, Longstreet held various offices in Republican administrations, including ambassador to the Ottoman Empire, US marshal, and US railroad commissioner. In 1896 he published his memoirs, *From Manassas to Appomattox*. He died in 1904 at the age of eighty-three.

Margaret Brown Loughborough and her husband, **Henry**, after the war, took up farming in Montgomery County, Maryland, on one of his family's now slaveless estates. Henry became a justice of the peace and was long active in the Maryland Democratic Party. Margaret became a member of the United Daughters of the Confederacy and served as vice president of its Maryland Chapter. She celebrated the centenary of her birth in 1939 before dying in December of that year.

In the post-Reconstruction era the Lynches never regained the status they had known before and during the war. **John Lynch** was one of the victims of the reorganization of the University of South Carolina. Within the year he also lost his position as medical director of the penitentiary. Lynch made increasingly desperate efforts to sell his mine, his sole remaining asset. Financial and physical woes tracked him, Job-like, relentlessly to his death in 1881. Persistent health problems did not deter **Patrick Lynch** from his fundraising tours. By 1882 he had reduced his diocese's debt from $400,000 to $10,000. But death finally claimed him a month shy of his sixty-fifth birthday on February 26, 1882. The Ursulines continued, for at least five decades, to press their claims for a government reimbursement for the burning of their convent and academy, to no avail. Lacking the means to rebuild, they remained at Valle Crucis until 1887 when Patrick Lynch's episcopal successor, Henry Northrop, insisted that they return to Columbia, where their day school was thriving. In mid-July two students and sixteen nuns, including the now invalid mother superior, **Baptista Lynch**, made the trip. Ten days later, she died. She was sixty-three. Ironically, **Francis Lynch**, who seemed, at least psychologically, the most fragile of the siblings, outlived them all, dying at the age of eighty in 1901, having restored his reputation as a respected businessman in Cheraw, if not the wealth he had briefly enjoyed during the war. His wife, Henrietta, had died at fifty-eight in 1888.

John Abell Morgan, SJ, completed his formation for the priesthood at the newly opened Woodstock College outside of Baltimore. In 1892 he returned to Loyola College to become its president, a position he held until 1900. He died six years later at sixty-eight.

Mary Anthony O'Connell, SC, for most of her postwar life, administered St. Joseph's Founding and Maternity Hospital in Cincinnati, which had been established in recognition of the heroic war ministry of O'Connell and her companions. In 1877 O'Connell distinguished herself anew during the yellow fever epidemic which struck the city. She died on her eighty-third birthday in 1897.

Joseph O'Hagan, SJ, became president of Holy Cross College in 1872. Six years later, his declining health led doctors to advise a sea voyage to a warmer climate. Off the coast of Nicaragua, O'Hagan died, at the age of fifty-one, in mid-December of 1878.[2]

In 1866 **Madge and William Preston** sold their Pleasant Plains property and moved full-time to Calvert Street in Baltimore City, a stone's throw from Loyola College, where Madge had easy access to all the religious services at

St. Ignatius Church. In 1878, William finally followed his wife into the Catholic Church. He died two years later. Madge Preston died in 1895.[3]

William Rosecrans resigned from the US Army in 1867. Over the next quarter-century he split his time between private industry (railroads and mining) and government service. In 1868 President Grant made him US minister to Mexico. From 1881 to 1885 he represented California in the US House, then was register of the US Treasury Department. He died at seventy-eight in 1898.

By his death in 1886 **Abram Ryan**'s place in the pantheon of the Lost Cause had been well established through the publication of his poems, as well as the other artifacts (busts, medals, and so forth) that his cult generated. Monuments to Ryan were erected from Loyola College in Los Angeles to Boston College, reminders in stone and glass that the priest-poet's fame, nearly a half-century after his death, extended far beyond the former Confederacy.

James Sheeran, CSSR, at war's end returned to New Orleans, where the redemptorist ministered until 1868. Brief assignments ensued in St. Louis and New York. In 1871 a dispute with his provincial superior led to Sheeran's being dispensed from his vows in 1871. For the next decade Sheeran served as a priest in the Diocese of Newark until his death in 1881 at the age of sixty-three.[4]

In 1884 **Philip Sheridan** succeeded William Tecumseh Sherman as the army's commanding general. Three years later he was named general of the army, joining George Washington, Ulysses S. Grant, and Sherman in holding that title. After suffering a series of heart attacks, Phil Sheridan died in August 1888. He was buried from his parish church of St. Matthew's in Washington. Cardinal James Gibbons of Baltimore preached. Among the mourners at Arlington National Cemetery for his burial was **Cump Sherman**, who was reported to have been the last to depart from Sheridan's grave.[5] Two and a half years later, Sherman was on his own deathbed. Baptized as a boy at the insistence of his foster mother, the man who never identified as Catholic received the last rites of the Church in an unconscious state, at the insistence of his children. His Jesuit son, Tom, conducted the funeral services at Calvary cemetery in St. Louis where he was buried next to **Ellen**, who had predeceased him in late 1888.[6]

James Shields, who had relocated his law practice to Missouri after the war, served in the state legislature until that body elected him to the US Senate in

1879. He died later that year at the age of seventy-three. In 1893 Illinois chose Shields as its representative in Statuary Hall in Congress.

In June of 1869 **Anna Surratt** married William Tonry, who had been at St. Charles College with her brother. Jacob Walter presided at their wedding, before a handful of witnesses. Within the week of their wedding, Tonry was dismissed from his position as a chemist in the US Army Surgeon's Office. The couple moved to Baltimore, where he continued his long career as an analytical chemist. Anna died in 1904.[7] **John Surratt**, after the government's second failure to convict him for his involvement in the assassination, became principal of a Catholic academy in Emmitsburg, Maryland, a hospitable locale for ex-Confederates. Then in the early 1870s he secured a management position in the Old Bay Line, operating steamships from Baltimore to ports in Virginia. He retired in 1915 as the company's treasurer and died within the year in Baltimore.

Louis Weichmann, for his testimony against Mary Surratt, became a pariah within the Catholic community. Through the intercession of Edwin Stanton and Joseph Holt, he secured a clerkship in the Philadelphia Customs Office, where he served for two decades until political pressure forced Weichmann to relocate to Indiana and open a business school. Weichmann died in 1902 at fifty-nine.

Edward Douglass White was a member of the first Louisiana Senate following the state's redemption in 1877. After serving as a state Supreme Court associate justice from 1879 to 1881, White practiced law for a decade before the Louisiana legislature elected him to the US Senate in 1891. In 1894 President Grover Cleveland appointed him to the Supreme Court. Fifteen years later, White became the second Catholic chief justice of the court. He died in 1921. He represents Louisiana in Statuary Hall in the Capitol.

Bernardine Wiget, SJ, was president of Gonzaga College until 1868, when he was sent to Europe to repair his health. Upon his return, he did pastoral ministry in southern Maryland, where he died at sixty-one in 1883.

Boniface Wimmer, OSB, continued to serve as abbot of Saint Vincent's in Latrobe, Pennsylvania, until his death in 1887. In his more than four decades as the head of the Benedictines in the United States, Wimmer founded ten abbeys, four colleges, and 152 parishes across the country.

NOTES

ABBREVIATIONS

AAC	Archives of the Archdiocese of Cincinnati
AAK	Alfred A. Knopf
AANO	Archives of the Archdiocese of New Orleans
AANY	Archives of the Archdiocese of New York
AASMUS	Associated Archives of St. Mary's University and Seminary
ACS	*American Catholic Studies*
ADC	Archives of the Diocese of Charleston
ADNJ	Archives of the Diocese of Natchez Jackson
ADR	Archives of the Diocese of Richmond
ADS	Archives of the Diocese of Savannah
AHR	*American Historical Review*
AM	Archives of Maryland
APF	Archives of Propaganda Fide
ARSI	Archivum Romanum Societatis Jesu
AUSL	Archives of the Ursuline Sisters of Louisville
BP	*Boston Pilot*
BQR	*Brownson's Quarterly Review*
CAUP	Cambridge University Press
CC	*Charleston Courier*
CDA	Charleston Diocesan Archives
CH	*Catholic Herald*
ChM	*Charleston Mercury*
CHR	*Catholic Historical Review*
CM	*Catholic Mirror*
CT	*Catholic Telegraph*
CUAP	Catholic University of America Press
CUP	Cornell University Press
CWH	*Civil War History*
EES	Ellen Ewing Sherman
FJ	*Freeman's Journal*
FUP	Fordham University Press

GUA	Georgetown University Archives
GULBFCSC	Georgetown University Library, Booth Family Center, Special Collections
GUP	Georgetown University Press
HMC	Houghton Mifflin Company
HRS	*Historical Records and Studies*
HUP	Harvard University Press
IN	*Irish News*
ISR	*Irish Studies Review*
JAH	*Journal of American History*
JHUP	Johns Hopkins University Press
JSH	*Journal of Southern History*
KSUP	Kent State University Press
LSUP	Louisiana State University Press
LUP	Loyola University Press
MD	Maryland Province Papers
MHM	*Maryland Historical Magazine*
MHS	Maryland Historical Society
MPA	Maryland Province Archives, Society of Jesus
MPC	Macmillan Publishing Company
MHR	*Missouri Historical Review*
MR	*Metropolitan Record*
NARA	National Archives Records Administration
NYH	*New York Herald*
NYT	*New York Times*
NYTr	*New York Tribune*
NYUP	New York University Press
OR	*Official Records of the Civil War*
OUP	Oxford University Press
PC	*Pittsburgh Catholic*
PH	*Philadelphia Herald*
RACHSP	*Records of the American Catholic Historical Society of Philadelphia*
RH	Random House
S&S	Simon & Schuster
SHC	Southern Historical Collection, University of North Carolina–Chapel Hill Libraries
SUP	Syracuse University Press
UAP	University of Alabama Press
UCP	University of Chicago Press
UIP	University of Illinois Press
UNCP	University of North Carolina Press
UNDA	University of Notre Dame Archives
UNDP	University of Notre Dame Press
UOP	University of Oklahoma Press
UPF	University Press of Florida
UPKS	University Press of Kansas
UPKY	University Press of Kentucky
USCH	*U.S. Catholic Historian*

USCM	U.S. Catholic Miscellany
USCP	University of South Carolina Press
UTP	University of Tennessee Press
UVP	University of Virginia Press
WL	Woodstock Letters
WTS	William Tecumseh (Cump) Sherman
WWN	W. W. Norton & Co.
YUP	Yale University Press

PROLOGUE: ALL SHOULD HAVE AN EQUAL CHANCE

1. Benjamin P. Thomas, *Abraham Lincoln: A Biography* (New York: Modern Library, 1952), 241.

INTRODUCTION

1. See Matthias D. Bergmann, "Being the Other: Catholics, Anglicanism, and Constructs of Britishness in Colonial Maryland, 1689–1763," PhD diss., Washington State University, 2004; John Bossy, *The English Catholic Community, 1570–1850* (OUP, 1976); Joseph J. Casino, "Anti-Popery in Colonial Pennsylvania," *Pennsylvania Magazine of History and Biography* 105 (1981): 279–309; Robert Emmett Curran, *Papist Devils: Catholics in British America, 1574–1783* (CUAP, 2014); Jason K. Duncan, *Citizens or Papists? The Politics of Anti-Catholicism in New York, 1685–1821* (FUP, 2005); James Hennesey, "Catholicism in the English Colonies," in *Encyclopedia of the American Religious Experience: Studies of Traditions and Movements*, ed. Charles H. Lippy and Peter W. Williams, vol. 1: 345–55 (New York: Charles Scribner's Sons, 1988); John D. Krugler, *English and Catholic: The Lords Baltimore in the Seventeenth Century* (JHUP, 2004); Tricia T. Pyne, "The Maryland Catholic Community, 1690–1775: A Study in Culture, Region, and Church," PhD diss., Catholic University of America, 1995.

2. Neither Catholics nor Protestants would have regarded the Roman Catholic Church as one of the denominations of Christianity. Most Protestants would not have recognized Catholicism as a legitimate branch of Christianity. Nonetheless, Protestants were all too aware of Catholicism's metastatic growth in the United States in the late antebellum period. That, in part, may explain the insistence of so many Protestant polemicists that Catholicism was in no way part of the Christian body.

I have cast a wide net in identifying Catholics. It encompasses the cradle-born who grew up to become devout practitioners of the faith (John Dooley, Ellen Baptista Lynch), or simply nominal members (P. G. T. Beauregard), converts who occupied prominent positions, both on the field of battle (William Rosecrans, Joseph Hardee, James Longstreet), as well as the home front (Orestes Brownson, Isaac Hecker); those aspiring to be Catholic but never taking the formal steps to become one (Marie Daly, very much in the Catholic community, if not formally of it); and even William Tecumseh Sherman, who persistently refused to profess the faith that his adoptive family had bestowed upon him. Although baptized and buried as a Catholic, Sherman steadfastly during his adult life declined, despite his wife's relentless efforts, to accept the Church and her teachings. Yet the conferring of its last rites—Extreme Unction, a funeral Mass, and burial in consecrated ground—all constituted an ultimate recognition by the Church that Sherman was a member. In the Catholic community, one might say, but not of it in any sense.

3. See Ella Lonn's two volumes on *Foreigners in the Confederacy* (Gloucester, MA: Peter Smith, 1965) and *Foreigners in the Union Army and Navy* (Westport, CT: Greenwood, 1969); Suzannah

Bruce, *The Harp and the Eagle: Irish American Volunteers and the Union Army, 1861–1865* (OUP, 2006); William Burton, *Melting Pot Soldiers: The Union's Ethnic Regiments* (Ames: Iowa State University Press, 1988); Cyprian Davis, OSB, *The History of Black Catholics in the United States* (New York: Crossroad, 1990); David T. Gleeson, *The Green and the Gray: The Irish in the Confederate States of America* (UNCP, 2013); Craig L. Kautz, "Fodder for Cannon: Immigrant Perceptions of the Civil War," PhD diss., University of Nebraska, 1976; Ryan W. Keating, *Shades of Green: Irish Regiments, American Soldiers, and Local Communities in the Civil War Era* (FUP, 2017); Christian B. Keller, *Chancellorsville, Nativism, and Civil War Memory* (FUP, 2007).

1. THE MEXICAN-AMERICAN WAR AND CATHOLIC LOYALTY

1. *New York Herald Leader,* May 21, 1846.

2. "The Pastoral Letter of 1846," in Peter Guilday, ed., *The National Pastorals of the American Hierarchy, 1792–1919* (Westminster, MD: Newman Press, 1954), 166. Hughes was not the only bishop the government consulted. President Polk also met with Peter Richard Kenrick of St. Louis and Michael Portier of Mobile, two areas highly supportive of the war with a high potential for Catholic volunteering (John McElroy, SJ, "Chaplains for the Mexican War—1846," *WL* 15 (1876): 198).

3. Historians, as well as contemporaries, estimate that Catholics made up from a quarter to almost a half of the regular army. John C. Pinheiro, *Missionaries of Republicanism: A Religious History of the Mexican-American War* (OUP, 2014), 69; Peter Guardino, *The Dead March: A History of the Mexican American War* (HUP, 2017), 37; James M. McCaffrey, *Army of Manifest Destiny: The American Soldier in the Mexican War, 1846–1848* (NYUP, 1992), 29; McElroy, "Chaplains for the Mexican War—1846," *WL* 17 (1888): 2–12.

4. James Buchanan to Hassard, Wheatlands, near Lancaster, November 8, 1864, in Sr. Blanche Marie McEniry, *American Catholics in the War with Mexico* (CUAP, 1937), 155; Robert Emmett Curran, *Shaping American Catholicism: Maryland and New York, 1805–1915* (CUAP, 2012), 129–40.

5. Verhaegen to Johan Roothaan, Worcester, June 5, 1846, Md 8-I-17, ARSI.

6. William Hogan, *High and Low Mass* (New York: Jordan and Wiley, 1847), 55, cited in Russell Shaw, *Dagger John: The Unquiet Life and Times of Archbishop John Hughes of New York* (New York: Paulist, 1977), 219.

7. July 22, 1846, in Pinheiro, *Religious History of the Mexican-American War,* 75.

8. McCaffrey, *The American Soldier in the Mexican War,* 35.

9. Tyler V. Johnson, *Devotion to the Adopted Country: U.S. Immigrant Volunteers in the Mexican War* (Columbia: University of Missouri Press, 2012), 17.

10. L. Paul Thigpen, "Aristocracy of the Heart: Catholic Lay Leadership in Savannah, 1820–1870," PhD diss., Emory University, 1995, 500–503.

11. McElroy, "Chaplains for the Mexican War," *WL* 17: 9.

12. McEniry, *American Catholics in the War with Mexico,* 119.

13. Rey moved "like the spirit of mercy," one doctor remembered on the lethal streets of Monterrey (James Wynne, "Memoir of the Rev. Anthony Rey, S.J." *United States Catholic Magazine* 6 [1847]: 551).

14. Guardino, *History of the Mexican American War,* 138–41.

15. Rey to McElroy, Monterrey, November 10, 1846, in McElroy, "Chaplains for the Mexican War," *WL* 17: 149–50.

16. Rey to McElroy, Monterrey, November 30, 1846, in McElroy, "Chaplains for the Mexican War," *WL* 17: 153–54.

17. McElroy to Rey, *Matamoros,* December 12, 17, 1846, in McElroy, "Chaplains for the Mexican War," *WL* 17: 155–57.

18. McElroy, "Chaplains for the Mexican War," *WL* 16: 226–27; General Zachary Taylor to McElroy, Headquarters, Army of Occupation, Camp at Monterrey, Mexico, April 13, 1847; same to same, June 1, 1847, in McElroy, "Chaplains for the Mexican War," *WL* 17: 162.

19. Guardino, *History of the Mexican American War,* 72–76.

20. *Niles Register* 72, June 19, 1847, 251, cited in McEniry, *American Catholics in the War with Mexico,* 147. The devotion to Our Lady of Guadalupe grew out of her alleged apparitions to a poor Amerindian, Juan Diego, on the outskirts of Mexico City in 1531. When the local bishop demanded proof of Mary's appearance to him, Mary ordered Diego to gather roses, although it was much past their season. Diego brought the roses to the bishop in his cloak, which, when opened, revealed an image which Diego claimed was that of the woman who had appeared to him. This icon of Our Lady of Guadalupe became the symbol of Mary's protection of the Mexican nation as its patroness.

21. McEniry, *American Catholics in the War with Mexico,* 113–14.

22. Guardino, *History of the Mexican American War,* 154–58.

23. Guardino, *History of the Mexican American War,* 197–99; K. Jack Bauer, *The Mexican War: 1846–1848* (MPC, 1974), 265–68.

24. McEniry, *American Catholics in the War with Mexico,* 108.

25. Thirteen percent of regular army soldiers deserted; only 6 percent of the volunteers (McCaffrey, *The American Soldier in the Mexican War,* 110–11; Robert Ryal Miller, *Shamrock and Sword: The Saint Patrick's Battalion in the U.S.-Mexican War* (Norman: University of Oklahoma Press, 1989), 24).

26. Johnson, *U.S. Immigrant Volunteers in the Mexican War,* 14.

27. Pinheiro, *Religious History of the Mexican-American War,* 104.

28. Bauer, *The Mexican War,* 42.

29. Guardino, *History of the Mexican American War,* 250–55.

30. Pinheiro, *Religious History of the Mexican-American War,* 103.

31. Miller, *Saint Patrick's Battalion,* 3.

32. Miller, *Saint Patrick's Battalion,* 158.

33. Mark R. Day, "San Patricio Battalion," in Michael Glazier, *The Encyclopedia of the Irish in America* (UNDP, 1999), 832–33.

34. Bauer, *The Mexican War,* 83.

35. Guardino, *History of the Mexican American War,* 125.

36. Pinheiro, *Religious History of the Mexican-American War,* 107.

37. Guardino, *History of the Mexican American War,* 223.

38. McEniry, *American Catholics in the War with Mexico,* 119.

39. Guardino, *History of the Mexican American War,* 230–31.

40. Bauer, *The Mexican War,* 223.

41. Guardino, *History of the Mexican American War,* 203–10; Amy S. Greenberg, *A Wicked War: Polk, Clay, Lincoln, and the 1846 U.S. Invasion of Mexico* (AAK, 2012), 172.

42. *FJ,* June 24, 1847, cited in William B. Kurtz, "'Let Us Hear No More Nativism': The Catholic Press in the Mexican and Civil Wars," *CWH* 60 (March 2014): 6–31.

43. McEniry, *American Catholics in the War with Mexico*, 16.

44. *FJ*, June 12, 1847, cited in McEniry, *American Catholics in the War with Mexico*, 138.

45. Bauer, *The Mexican War*, 269–79.

46. Miller, *Saint Patrick's Battalion*, 82–83.

47. Miller, *Saint Patrick's Battalion*, 79.

48. Bauer, *The Mexican War*, 297–301.

49. Bauer, *The Mexican War*, 317–21.

50. John M. Belohlavek, *Patriots, Prostitutes, and Spies: Women and the Mexican-American War* (UVP, 2017), 50.

51. Jeffry D. Wert, *General James Longstreet: The Confederacy's Most Controversial Soldier: A Biography* (S&S, 1993), 45.

52. T. Harry Williams, *P. G. T. Beauregard: Napoleon in Gray* (LSUP, 1955), 30–32.

53. Johnson, *U.S. Immigrant Volunteers in the Mexican War*, 57–60.

54. Guardino, *History of the Mexican American War*, 285–88.

55. McEniry, *American Catholics in the War with Mexico*, 79–86.

56. Miller, *Saint Patrick's Battalion*, 107.

57. The Polk administration had seriously considered James Shields for the position, as a Catholic who was fluent in both French and Spanish. In the end Polk chose Jacob L. Martin, secretary of the American legation in Paris (McEniry, *American Catholics in the War with Mexico*, 108).

58. Pinheiro, *Religious History of the Mexican-American War*, 163.

59. January 20, 1848, cited in Isaac McDaniel, "The Impact of the Mexican War on Anti-Catholicism in the United States," PhD diss., University of Notre Dame, 1991, 237.

60. Virginia Trist to Tuckerman, August 23, 1863, Trist Papers, UNC, folder 225, cited in Greenberg, *Polk, Clay, Lincoln, and the 1846 U.S. Invasion of Mexico*, 223.

61. Guardino, *History of the Mexican American War*, 328.

62. David Potter, *The Impending Crisis, 1848–1861* (New York: Harper Colophon Books, 1976), 4.

63. Greenberg, *Polk, Clay, Lincoln, and the 1846 U.S. Invasion of Mexico*, 259.

64. James Hennesey, SJ, *American Catholics: A History of the Roman Catholic Community in the United States* (OUP, 1981), 134–39.

65. Hennesey, *American Catholics*, 137–41.

66. *The Signal*, July 17, 1852, reporting an address by Scott in New York, cited by McEniry, *American Catholics in the War with Mexico*, 126.

67. Shields (1806–1879) had emigrated to the United States as a teenager and became a lawyer in Illinois, but quickly took up public service as a Democratic state legislator, judge, and land commissioner in the Polk administration.

68. Johnson, *U.S. Immigrant Volunteers in the Mexican War*, 8.

69. Pinheiro, *Religious History of the Mexican-American War*, 14.

70. William B. Kurtz, *Excommunicated from the Union: How the Civil War Created a Separate Catholic America* (FUP, 2016), 20.

2. THE REMAKING OF THE CATHOLIC COMMUNITY AND NATIVIST BACKLASH

1. John J. Killoren, SJ, *"Come Blackrobe": De Smet and the Indian Tragedy* (UOP, 1994), 3–15.

2. Tyler Anbinder, *Nativism and Slavery: The Northern Know-Nothings and the Politics of the 1850s* (OUP, 1992), 9. New York City had had a Catholic population of 80,000 in 1840 when

the city's population was 300,000. By 1860, Catholics composed about 300,000 of the city's 816,000 total population (Ira Rosenwaike, *Population History of New York City* [SUP, 2011], 63).

3. Lonn, *Foreigners in the Union Army,* 3–13; Lonn, *Foreigners in the Confederacy,* 3–31; Earl F. Niehaus, *The Irish in New Orleans: 1800–1860* (LSUP, 1965), 23.

4. Cian T. McMahon, *The Global Dimensions of Irish Identity: Race, Nation, and the Popular Press, 1840–1880* (UNCP, 2015), 79.

5. In New York City, there were more than 200,000 foreign-born Irish among the population of 805,000. That did not include Brooklyn, where 56,710 of that city's 266,661 were Irish born.

6. Hasia Diner, "'The Most Irish City in the Union': The Era of the Great Migration, 1844–1877," in Ronald H. Bayor and Timothy Meagher, eds., *The New York Irish* (JHUP, 1996), 90.

7. Dennis Clark, *The Irish in Philadelphia: Ten Generations of Urban Experience* (Philadelphia: Temple University Press, 1973), 90–91.

8. Kerby A. Miller, *Emigrants and Exiles: Ireland and the Irish Exodus to North America* (OUP, 1985), 296–97.

9. Most of the city's neighborhoods lacked sewers. Waste from privies seeped into the wells which were the main water supply for the immigrant poor (Adrian Cook, *The Armies of the Streets: The New York City Draft Riots of 1863* [UPKY, 1974], 14).

10. Glazier, *Encyclopedia of the Irish in America,* 542.

11. Jeff Strickland, *Unequal Freedoms: Ethnicity, Race, and White Supremacy in Civil War Charleston* (UPF, 2015), 38.

12. Edward M. Shoemaker, "Strangers and Citizens: The Irish Immigrant Community in Savannah, 1837–1861," PhD. diss., Emory University, 1990, 145.

13. Jean Baker, *Ambivalent Americans: The Know-Nothing Party in Maryland* (JHUP, 1977), 17.

14. Sherry H. Olsen, *Baltimore: The Building of an American City* (JHUP, 1980), 118–19.

15. Anbinder, *Nativism and Slavery,* 8–10.

16. Anbinder, *Nativism and Slavery,* 9.

17. Stanley Nadel, *Little Germany: Ethnicity, Religion, and Class in New York City, 1845–80* (UIP, 1990), 92; Edward K. Spann, *Gotham at War: New York City, 1860–1865* (Wilmington, DE: SR Books, 2002), 110.

18. Joseph Michael White, "Religion and Community: Cincinnati Germans, 1840–1870," PhD diss., University of Notre Dame, 1980, 214.

19. Barbara Misner, SCSC, *"Highly Respectable and Accomplished Ladies": Catholic Women Religious in America, 1790–1850* (New York: Garland Publishing, 1988).

20. John D. Sauter, *The American College of Louvain, 1857–1898* (Louvain: Publications Universitaires de Louvain, 1959), 10.

21. John T. McGreevy, *American Jesuits and the World: How an Embattled Religious Order Made Modern Catholicism Global* (Princeton, NJ: Princeton University Press, 2016), 1–12.

22. Patrick W. Carey, *The Roman Catholics* (Westport, CT: Greenwood Press, 1993), 35.

23. As Andrew H. M. Stern notes, "In a region struggling to establish schools, Protestants welcomed Catholic assistance. . . . women religious filled the vast territory between Maryland and Louisiana with schools (*Southern Crucifix, Southern Cross: Catholic-Protestant Relations in the Old South* [UAP, 2012], 71–78).

24. *New York Observer,* May 10, 1852, cited in Thomas W. Spalding, *The Premier See: A History of the Archdiocese of Baltimore, 1789–1989* (JHUP, 1989), 155; John P. Marschall, CSV, "Francis Patrick Kenrick, 1851–1863: The Baltimore Years," PhD diss., Catholic University of America, 1965, 84.

25. APF, *Lettere e Decreti della Sacra Congregazione e Biglietti di Monsignore Segretaria,* vol. 343, pars I [1853], ff. 315v–317r.

26. Anbinder, *Nativism and Slavery,* xiii.

27. David A. Gerber, *The Making of an American Pluralism: Buffalo, New York, 1825–60* (UIP, 1989). 294–95.

28. White, "Religion and Community," 349.

29. Hughes to Bedini, New York, July 2, 1854, AANY, A-6, in James F. Connelly, *The Visit of Archbishop Gaetano Bedini to the United States of America, 1853–1854* (Rome: Pontificia Universitas Gregoriana, 1960), 154.

30. Anbinder, *Nativism and Slavery,* 43.

31. Michael Holt, *The Rise and Fall of the American Whig Party: Jacksonian Politics and the Onset of the Civil War* (OUP, 1999), 846.

32. Baker, *Ambivalent Americans,* xi, 3.

33. J. W. Taylor to Hamilton Fish, November 11, 1854, Hamilton Fish Papers, LC, in William E. Gienapp, "Nativism and the Creation of a Republican Majority in the North before the Civil War," *JAH* 72 (December 1985): 532.

34. Anbinder, *Nativism and Slavery,* 24.

35. White, "Religion and Community," 293; 305–6.

36. Fortin, *Faith and Action: A History of the Archdiocese of Cincinnati* (Columbus: Ohio State University Press, 2002) 113–15.

37. Eric B. Brumfield, "Nativist Upsurge: Kentucky's Know-Noting party of the 1850s," PhD diss., University of Kentucky, 2016, 61–62.

38. Nicholas Varga, *Baltimore's Loyola, Loyola's Baltimore 1851–1986* (*MHR,* 1990), 12; Douglas Bowers, "Ideology and Political Parties in Maryland, 1851–1856," *MHR* 64 (Fall 1969): 202–4.

39. Baker, *Ambivalent Americans,* 23.

40. Enoch Lowe of Frederick (Spalding, *Premier See,* 135).

41. Baker, *Ambitious Americans,* 76–80.

42. Baker, *Ambivalent Americans,* 2.

43. Kenrick to Tobias Kirby, September 19, 1854, Archives of the Irish College (Rome), #1470, cited in Marschall, "Francis Patrick Kenrick," 220.

44. Baptista Lynch to Patrick Lynch, Brownsville, OH, April 15, 1854, 9 B1 CDA.

45. Clyde F. Crews, *An American Holy Land: A History of the Archdiocese of Louisville* (Wilmington, DE: M. Glazier, 1987), 127.

46. Bridget Ford, *Bonds of Union: Religion, Race, and Politics in a Civil War Borderland* (UNCP, 2016), 26.

47. November 28, 1854, *Life, Letters, and Travels of Father Pierre-Jean De Smet* (New York: Harper, 1905), cited in Timothy Egan, *The Immortal Irishman: The Irish Revolutionary Who Became an American Hero* (Boston: Houghton Mifflin Harcourt, 2016), 142.

48. *The Bible in Schools Argument of Richard H. Dana, Jr., Esq., and Opinion of the Supreme Court of Maine, in the Cases of Laurence Donahoe vs. Richards and al., and Bridget Donahoe . . .* (Boston, 1855), in John T. McGreevy, *Catholicism and American Freedom: A History* (WWN, 2003), 51–52.

49. McGreevy, *American Jesuits and the World,* 26–55; Curran, *Shaping American Catholicism,* 140–41.

50. Kristen Layne Anderson, *Abolitionizing Missouri: German Immigrants and Racial Ideology in Nineteenth-Century America* (LSUP, 2016), 72, 103.

51. Crews, *History of the Archdiocese of Louisville*, 142–43.

52. Thomas W. Spalding, *Martin John Spalding: American Churchman* (CUAP, 1973), 70–71.

53. Wallace S. Hutcheon Jr., "The Louisville Riots of August, 1855," *Register of the Kentucky Historical Society* 69 (1971): 150–72.

54. UNDA, Cincinnati papers, Spalding to Purcell, Louisville, September 6, 1855, cited in Spalding, *Martin John Spalding*, 72.

55. Frank Towers, *The Urban South and the Coming of the Civil War* (UVP, 2004), 137–38.

56. *CM*, October 18, 1856; William J. Evitts, *A Matter of Allegiances: Maryland from 1850 to 1861* (JHUP, 1974), 97–98.

57. Towers, *Urban South*, 120.

58. J. Thomas Scharf, *Chronicles of Baltimore, Being a Complete History of "Baltimore Town" and Baltimore City, from the Earliest Period to the Present Time* (Baltimore: Turnbull Brothers, 1874), 560–63.

59. *CM*, October 22, 1860.

60. Marius M. Carriere Jr., "Anti-Catholicism, Nativism, and Louisiana Politics in the 1850s," *Louisiana History* 35 (Autumn 1994): 467–68.

61. David Grimsted, *American Mobbing, 1828–1861: Toward Civil War* (OUP, 1998), 239.

62. Roger Baudier, *The Catholic Church in Louisiana* (New Orleans, 1939), 380.

63. Carriere, "Anti-Catholicism," 473.

64. *Orleanian*, November 14, 1856, cited in Niehaus, *The Irish in New Orleans*, 92.

65. Towers, *Urban South*, 145.

66. Anbinder, *Nativism and Slavery*, 162–63.

67. Anbinder, *Nativism and Slavery*, 170–71.

68. Dana to Carey, November 27, 1856, Carey Papers, Historical Society of Pennsylvania, cited in Anbinder, *Nativism and Slavery*, 278.

69. Holt, *Rise and Fall of the American Whig Party*, 957.

3. THE SLAVERY CRISIS AND THE TANEY COURT

1. David Goldfield, *America Aflame: How the Civil War Created a Nation* (New York: Bloomsbury Press, 2011), 100.

2. Holt, *Rise and Fall of the American Whig Party*, 412–13.

3. William T. Sherman, *Memoirs of General William T. Sherman* (New York: Appleton & Co., 1875), vol. 1: 103–4.

4. Lowe to Fillmore, September 15, 1851, Governor and Council Letterbook, 1845–1854, 253–55, Maryland Hall of Records, in Thomas Slaughter, *Bloody Dawn: The Christiana Riot and Racial Violence in the Antebellum North* (OUP, 1991), 104n24. Lowe, whose mother, Adelaide Vincendiere Lowe, was a refugee from Saint-Domingue in 1793, had grown up on a plantation, l'Hermitage, outside of Frederick, that counted ninety slaves.

5. Slaughter, *Christiana Riot and Racial Violence*, 133.

6. Slaughter, *Christiana Riot and Racial Violence*, 137, 182.

7. Potter, *Impending Crisis*, 140.

8. Robert Emmett Curran, *For Church and Confederacy: The Lynches of South Carolina* (USCP, 2019), 128–29.

9. Immigrant clergy, who mostly experienced slavery in the upper South, were wont to consider the condition of American slaves to be better than that of European serfs.

10. Marschall, "Francis Patrick Kenrick," 338.

11. Gaetano Bedini, "Report," in Connelly, *Visit of Archbishop Gaetano Bedini to the United States*, 238.

12. Marschall, "Francis Patrick Kenrick," 343–44.

13. Marschall, "Francis Patrick Kenrick," 341.

14. Francis Kenrick, *Theologiae Moralis (Mechlin:* H. Dessain, 1861), vol. 1: 255–58.

15. Antoine Blanc, February 2, 1852, Pastoral Letters Collection, AANO.

16. Corcoran, *USCM*, December 31, 1859.

17. Davis, *History of Black Catholics in the United States*, 80.

18. Davis, *History of Black Catholics in the United States*, 94–97.

19. Davis, *History of Black Catholics in the United States*, 87–88.

20. Marschall, "Francis Patrick Kenrick," 338.

21. Stephen J. Ochs, *A Black Patriot and a White Priest: André Cailloux and Claude Paschal Maistre in Civil War New Orleans* (LSUP, 2000), 52–60.

22. Shannen Dee Williams, "Forgotten Habits, Lost Vocations: Black Nuns, Contested Memories, and the Nineteenth Century Struggle to Desegregate U.S. Catholic Religious Life," *Journal of African American History* 101 (Summer 2016): 230, 238–39.

23. See James M. O'Toole, *Passing for White: Race, Religion, and the Healy Family, 1820–1920* (Amherst: University of Massachusetts Press, 2002).

24. Michael Todd Landis, *Northern Men with Southern Loyalties: The Democratic Party and the Sectional Crisis* (CUP, 2014), 4–5.

25. Potter, *Impending Crisis*, 173–75.

26. Landis, *Northern Men with Southern Loyalties*, 158.

27. Ann Blackman, *Wild Rose: The True Story of a Civil War Spy* (RH, 2006), x–xii, 7–8.

28. Taney to J. Mason Campbell, October 2, 1856, cited in Don Fehrenbacher, *The Dred Scot Case: Its Significance in American Law and Politics* (OUP, 1978), 557.

29. Fehrenbacher, *Dred Scot Case*, 377.

30. Austin Allen, *Origins of the Dred Scott Case: Jacksonian Jurisprudence and the Supreme Court, 1837–1857* (UGP, 2006).

31. John H. Van Evrie, *The Dred Scott Decision* (New York, 1859), iii, cited in Fehrenbacher, *Dred Scot Case*, 429.

32. *Sun,* May 19, 1857, cited in Martha S. Jones, "Confronting Dred Scott: Seeing Citizenship from Baltimore," in Charles W. Mitchell and Jean H. Baker, eds., *The Civil War in Maryland Reconsidered* (LSUP, 2021), 65. Ironically, another Maryland Catholic jurist, John Carroll LeGrand, chief justice of the Court of Appeals, challenged the reach of Taney's decision by ruling in 1858 that Blacks, while not full citizens, possessed certain rights associated with citizenship, including the right to sue in court (Jones, "Confronting Dred Scott," 69–76).

33. Costello, Harpers Ferry to Fr. Harrington, All Hallows, February 11, 1860. Copy in ADR.

34. Mary Lynn Bayliss, *The Dooleys of Richmond: An Irish Immigrant Family in the Old and New South* (UVP, 2017), 37.

35. Bayliss, *Dooleys of Richmond*, 37.

36. *Sun,* November 28, 1859, cited in Potter, *Impending Crisis*, 384.

37. Landis, *Northern Men with Southern Loyalties*, 217.

38. Evitts, *Matter of Allegiances*, 126.

39. *CM,* October 29, 1859.

40. "At Home and Abroad," *PC*, October 29, 1859.

41. *BP*, November 19, December 3, 1859; January 7, 1860, cited in Thomas H. O'Connor, *Civil War Boston: Home Front and Battlefield* (Boston: Northwestern University Press, 1997), 36–37.

42. *FJ*, October 22, 1859.

43. *NYH*, November 19, 1858, cited in Douglas Fermer, *James Gordon Bennett and the New York Herald: A Study of Editorial Opinion in the Civil War Era, 1854–1867* (New York: St. Martin's Press, 1986), 22.

44. "The Trouble at Harpers Ferry," *NYH*, November 5, 1859.

4. THE ELECTION THAT RENT A NATION

1. Douglas R. Egerton, *Year of Meteors: Stephen Douglas, Abraham Lincoln, and the Election That Brought on the Civil War* (New York: Bloomsbury Press, 2010), 8–10.

2. James Shields, an Illinoisan, had been best man at their wedding (Egerton, *Year of Meteors*, 3).

3. Charles W. Mitchell, "Maryland's Presidential Election of 1860," *MHM*, Fall 2014, 311.

4. Tyler Anbinder, *Five Points: The 19th-Century New York City Neighborhood That Invented Tap Dance, Stole Elections, and Became the World's Most Notorious Slum* (New York: Free Press, 2001), 235–36.

5. Landis, *Northern Men with Southern Loyalties*, 238.

6. *NYH*, October 28, 1860, cited in Fermer, *James Gordon Bennett*, 127–54.

7. *NYH* November 10, 1859; May 3, 5, 8, 1860, cited in James L. Crouthamel, *James Gordon Bennett and the Rise of the Popular Press* (SUP, 1989), 111.

8. *IN*, September 22, 1860, 89–90.

9. Ernest A. McKay, *The Civil War and New York City* (SUP, 1990), 22.

10. Anbinder, *Five Points*, 307.

11. James Sigurd Lapham, "The German-Americans of New York City, 1860–1890," PhD diss., St. John's University, 1977, 192–94.

12. Walter D. Kamphoefner, "German Americans and Civil War Politics: A Reconsideration of the Ethnocultural Thesis," *CWH*, September 1991, 242–43.

13. Evitts, *Matter of Allegiances*, 145–53.

14. Thomas Scharf, *History of Maryland from the Earliest Period to the Present Day* (Baltimore: John B. Piet, 1879), vol. 3: 360

15. "It Has Come At Last," *USCM*, November 10, 1860.

16. David C. R. Heisser and Stephen J. White Sr., *Patrick N. Lynch, 1817–1882: Third Catholic Bishop of Charleston* (USCP, 2015), 75.

17. *USCM*, December 22, 1860, UNDA.

18. Elder to Kenrick, undated fragment, 29 D12, AASMUS, cited in James J. Pillar, OMI, *The Catholic Church in Mississippi, 1837–1865* (New Orleans: Hauser Press, 1964), 161.

19. Elder was particularly offended by "the contempt with which [the North] treated the old man we all venerated so much," referring to fellow Marylander Taney, who claimed the same part of Maryland as his ancestral home as did Elder (Elder to McCloskey, Natchez, June 23, 1863, in Elder Letter Book, #8, 435, ADNJ, cited in Pillar, *Catholic Church in Mississippi*, 163.

20. Elder to Duggan, March 5, 1861, Elder Letter Book #6, 96, ADNJ, cited in Pillar, *Catholic Church in Mississippi*, 163.

21. Printed in *Catholic Telegraph* (Cincinnati), February 16, 1861, cited in Oscar Hugh Lipscomb, "The Administration of John Quinlan, Second Bishop of Mobile, 1859–1883," *RACHSP* 77 (March–December 1967): 99.

22. Joseph Durkin, SJ, *Stephen R. Mallory, Confederate Navy Chief* (UNCP, 1954), 122–23.

23. Thomas Parkin Scott, *The Crisis (Baltimore: Kelly, Hedian and Piet,* 1860), 5–7.

24. Timothy R. Snyder, "'The Susquehanna Shall Run Red with Blood': The Secession Movement in Maryland," *MHM* 108 (Fall 2013): 38–39.

25. Spalding, *Martin John Spalding,* 28.

26. Spalding to Purcell, Louisville, February 27, 1861, II-5-a, AAC, UNDA, cited in Carl C. Creason, "'The whole world seems to be getting out of joint': The Catholic Response to the Start of the Civil War in the Border South," *USCH* 35 (Summer 2017): 33.

27. Cited in Judith C. Wimmer, "American Catholic Interpretations of the Civil War," PhD diss., Drew University, 1980, 100.

28. Murphy to Roothaan, September 6, 1851, ARSI, in Gilbert J. Garraghan, SJ, *The Jesuits of the Middle United States* (New York: America Press, 1938), vol. 2: 154.

29. Murphy to Beckx, March 24, ARSI, in Garraghan, *Jesuits of the Middle United States* 2: 154.

30. McGreevy, *American Jesuits and the World,* 90.

31. *FJ,* February 2, 1861, cited in Benjamin J. Blied, *Catholics and the Civil War* (Milwaukee: self-published, 1945), 53.

32. Fortin, *History of the Archdiocese of Cincinnati,* 141.

33. *Irish-American,* December 15, 1860.

34. McKay, *Civil War and New York City,* 32.

35. Burton, *Melting Pot Soldiers,* 23.

36. *Irish-American,* February 16, 1861, cited in Anbinder, *Five Points,* 307.

37. McKay, *Civil War and New York City,* 40.

38. Marie Daly, January 31, 1861, in Harold Earl Hammond, ed., *Diary of a Union Lady: 1861–1865* (Lincoln: University of Nebraska Press, 2000), 5.

39. Wood to Lynch, January 25, 1861, cited in Edward Dennis Lofton, "Reverend Doctor James A. Corcoran and the *United States Catholic Miscellany* Concerning the Question of Slavery and the Confederacy," *RACHSP* (1982), 952.

40. Young to Kenrick, March 1861, 32–0-18, AASMUS, quoted in Wimmer, "American Catholic Interpretations of the Civil War," 182n124.

41. "What the Rebellion Teaches," *BQR,* July 1862, *Works of Orestes Brownson* 17: 287, cited in Wimmer, "American Catholic Interpretations of the Civil War," 172–73.

42. *Life, Letters and Travels of Father Pierre Jean De Smet* 4: 1441, cited in Garraghan, *Jesuits of the Middle United States* 2: 152–53.

43. Joseph R. Frese, SJ, "The Catholic Press and Secession, 1860–1861," *HRS* 45 (1957): 82–84.

44. *CH,* October 20, 1860; *CH,* November 17, 1860; Joseph George Jr., "Philadelphia's *Catholic Herald:* The Civil War Years," *Pennsylvania Magazine of History and Biography* 103 (April 1879): 196–202.

45. Crouthamel, *James Gordon Bennett,* 79.

46. Sr. Mary Augustine Kwitchen, OSF, *James Alphonsus McMaster* (CUAP, 1949), 116–17.

47. Kurtz, *Excommunicated from the Union,* 33.

48. *CT,* February 2, 1861.

49. *CT,* March 2, 1861.

50. *CT,* March 23, 1861.

51. *La Propagateur,* January 26, 1861, cited in Pillar, *Catholic Church in Mississippi,* 184.

52. David C. Keehn, *Knights of the Golden Circle: Secret Empire, Southern Secession, Civil War* (LSUP, 2013), 50–53.

53. Keehn, *Knights of the Golden Circle,* 84–86.

54. Keehn, *Knights of the Golden Circle,* 99.

55. Nathaniel Cheairs Hughes Jr. and Thomas Clayton Ware, *Theodore O'Hara: Poet-Soldier of the Old South* (UTP, 1998), 3–108.

56. Hughes and Ware, *Theodore O'Hara,* 105–9.

57. Michael J. Kline, *The Baltimore Plot: The First Conspiracy to Assassinate Abraham Lincoln* (Yardley, PA: Westholme Publishing, 2008), 113, 342–47.

58. Kane had written a letter to the mayor of Washington, declining any assistance. There was no need for an armed escort for the president, he insisted. "The Day for mobs and riots has passed, never to return" (Kline, *Baltimore Plot,* 174).

59. Williams, *P. G. T. Beauregard,* 49–50.

5. WAR FEVER

1. Lynch to Francis Kenrick, February 9, 1861, 30 M17, Kenrick Papers, AASMUS.

2. William C. Davis, *"A Government of Our Own": The Making of the Confederacy* (New York: Free Press, 1994), 307.

3. Nineteen out of 83 (box 6, Lynch Papers, CDA).

4. Williams, *P. G. T. Beauregard,* 61; Davis, *"A Government of our Own,"* 311–14.

5. Kenneth J. Heineman, *Civil War Dynasty: The Ewing Family of Ohio* (NYUP, 2013), 111–12.

6. Linton Album, 1861, 57, Jesuit Missouri Province Archives, cited in Killoren, *De Smet and the Indian Tragedy,* 232.

7. Spann, *Gotham at War,* 15–16.

8. Leonard R. Riforgiato, "Bishop Timon, Buffalo, and the Civil War," *CHR,* January 1987, 72.

9. Cecilia Murphy, "A Reevaluation of the Episcopacy of Michael Domenec, 1860–1877, Second Bishop of Pittsburgh and Only Bishop of Allegheny," PhD diss., St. Louis University, 1974, 61–62.

10. Domenec to Kenrick, AASMUS, 19-C-2. April 1861, cited in Murphy, "A Reevaluation of the Episcopacy of Michael Domenec," 64.

11. Quoted in Sr. Mary Agnes McCann, *Archbishop Purcell and the Archdiocese of Cincinnati: A Study Based on Original Sources* (CUAP, 1918), 78, cited in David J. Endres, "Rectifying the Fatal Contrast: Archbishop John Purcell and the Slavery Controversy among Catholics in the Civil War," *Ohio Valley History* 2 (Fall 2002): 28.

12. Blied, *Catholics and the Civil War,* 131.

13. *PC,* April 20, 1861.

14. *Tablet,* May 4, 1861, cited in Blied, *Catholics and the Civil War,* 79.

15. Keating, *Shades of Green,* 2, 11.

16. McMahon, *Global Dimensions of Irish Identity.* 125.

17. William T. Minor to Justin Hodge, August 245, 1855, reprinted in Thomas Hamilton Murray, *History of the Ninth Regiment, Connecticut Volunteer Infantry* (New Haven, CT: Price, Lee and Adkins Co., 1903), 10–15, cited in Keating, *Shades of Green,* 45; Matthew Hart to Thomas Cahill, August 26, 1862, cited in Keating, *Shades of Green,* 161.

18. Burton, *Melting Pot Soldiers,* 132–33.

19. Thomas H. O'Connor, *Boston Catholics: A History of the Church and Its People* (Boston: Northeastern University Press, 1998), 109.

20. Kautz, "Fodder for Cannon," 145; Burton, *Melting Pot Soldiers*, 11; William Burton, "'Title Deed to America': Union Ethnic Regiments in the Civil War," *Proceedings of the American Philosophical Society* 124 (December 17, 1980): 460.

21. Keating, *Shades of Green*, 75.

22. Kautz, "Fodder for Cannon," 80.

23. German Catholics were the second-most underrepresented group.

24. Burton, *Melting Pot Soldiers*, 110.

25. Spann, *Gotham at War*, 111.

26. Pillar, *Catholic Church in Mississippi*, 178.

27. Blied, *Catholics and the Civil War*, 65.

28. McGill Papers, UNDA.

29. Patrick Foley, *Missionary Bishop: Jean-Marie Odin in Galveston and New Orleans* (College Station: Texas A&M U. Press, 2014), 145–46.

30. Lofton, "Reverend Doctor James A. Corcoran and the *United States Catholic Miscellany*," 89–98.

31. Baptista Lynch to Patrick Lynch, June 4, 1862, 14 H11, CDA.

32. Lipscomb, "Administration of John Quinlan," 42.

33. Gleeson, *The Green and the Gray*, 7.

34. David T. Gleeson, "'To Live and Die [for] Dixie': Irish Civilians and the Confederate States of America," *IRS* 18 (2010): 142.

35. Kraszewski, *Catholic Confederates*, 10–30.

36. *IN* (New York), May 11, 1861, cited in Gleeson, "Irish Rebels," 124n22.

37. Jones, "Confronting Dred Scott," xii, 8.

38. Gleeson, *The Green and the Gray*, 54.

39. Patriotism as a form of maintaining or improving one's societal status plus pressure from the white majority may have been at work here (Ochs, *A Black Patriot and a White Priest*, 69).

40. Ochs, *A Black Patriot and a White Priest*, 68–69.

41. William M. Freehling, *The South vs. The South: How Anti-Confederate Southerners Shaped the Course of the Civil War* (OUP, 2001), 61–64.

42. Martin Spalding to Benedict Spalding, Louisville, April 26, 1861, 37 E19, AASMUS.

43. Kline, *Baltimore Plot*, 349.

44. George William Brown, *Baltimore and the Nineteenth of April, 1861: A Study of the War* (Baltimore: N. Murray, 1887), 168.

45. "War in Baltimore," *CM*, April 20, 1861.

46. Kevin Conley Ruffner, *Maryland's Blue & Gray: A Border State's Union and Confederate Junior Officer Corps* (LSUP, 1997), 35.

47. Jonathan W. White, ed., "Forty-Seven Eyewitness Accounts of the Pratt Street Riot and Its Aftermath," *MHM* 106 (Spring 2011): 771–77.

48. Matthew A. Crenson found that more than half of those who can be identified held nonmanual occupations and owned more real and personal property than average Baltimoreans. Most were merchants or clerks. Evidence points to Custom House clerks being particularly involved (Crenson, *Baltimore: A Political History* [JHUP, 2017], 241).

49. Tracy Matthew Melton, "The Lost Lives of George Konig Sr. & Jr., A Father-Son Tale of Old Fell's Point," *MHM* 101 (2006): 347–48.

50. Towers, *Urban South*, 170.

51. Frank Towers, "'A Vociferous Army of Howling Wolves': Baltimore's Civil War Riot of April 19, 1861," *Maryland Historian* 23 (1992): 21.

52. Klein, *Baltimore Plot*, 352.

53. Kenrick to Spalding, May 4, 1861, 34K 51, AASMUS.

54. Robert J. Brugger, *Maryland: A Middle Temperament, 1634–1980* (JHUP, 1988), 280.

55. Ruffner, *Maryland's Blue & Gray*, 215.

56. Jack T. Hutchinson, "Number of Men Maryland Supplied to the Union and Confederate Armies," *MHM* 63 (1968): 442–43.

57. An even greater disparity is found in the applications for bounties that the Baltimore City Council authorized mothers or wives of enlisted men in Union service to make. Of 1,325 applications, only 235 came from the relatives of Irish soldiers, less than a fifth of those filed (Bounty Applications, Baltimore City Archives).

58. The Irish accounted for 44 percent; the Germans 56 percent.

59. Statistics based on figures in *History and Roster of Maryland Volunteers, War of 1861–65*, part 1, vols. 366 and 367; *History and Roster of Maryland Volunteers, War of 1861–65*, part 2, vol. 371: *The Maryland Line in the Confederate Army, 1861–1865*, AM.

60. William A. Tidwell, with James O. Hall and David Winfred Gaddy, *Come Retribution: The Confederate Secret Service and the Assassination of Lincoln* (New York: Barnes & Noble, 1999), 58–61.

61. Ruffner, *Maryland's Blue & Gray*, 53.

62. George Anderson, ed., "The Civil War Diary of John Abell Morgan, S.J.: A Jesuit Scholastic of the Maryland Province," *RACHSP* 101 (Fall 1990): October 20, 1862, 51n48; Ruffner, *Maryland's Blue & Gray*, 75.

63. Ruffner, *Maryland's Blue & Gray*, 45.

64. Ruffner, *Maryland's Blue & Gray*, 258

65. Ruffner, *Maryland's Blue & Gray*, 336–38.

66. Martin Spalding to Benedict Spalding, April 26, 1862, 37 E19, AASMUS.

67. Lowell H. Harrison, *The Civil War in Kentucky* (UPK, 2009), 7–9.

68. Spalding, *Martin John Spalding*, 132.

69. James W. Finck, *Divided Loyalties: Kentucky's Struggle for Armed Neutrality in the Civil War* (El Dorado Hills, CA: Savas Beatie, 2012), 50–51.

70. Aaron Astor, *Rebels on the Border: Civil War, Emancipation, and the Reconstruction of Kentucky and Missouri* (LSUP, 2012), 41–69.

71. Anne E. Marshall, *Creating a Confederate Kentucky: The Lost Cause and Civil War Memory in a Border State* (UNCP, 2010), 2.

72. Kent T. Dollar et al., eds., *Sister States, Enemy States: The Civil War in Kentucky and Tennessee* (UPK, 2009), 4.

73. An estimated 77,000 enslaved Kentucky workers were sold or taken to the Deep South during the antebellum period. By 1860 there were still over 275,000 slaves in the state (Dollar et al., eds., *Sister States*, 4, 17).

74. Marshall, *Creating a Confederate Kentucky*, 12–13.

75. Astor, *Rebels on the Border*, 24–25.

76. C. Walker Gollar, "Catholic Slaves and Slaveholders in Kentucky," *CHR* 84 (January 1998): 44–47.

77. Astor, *Rebels on the Border*, 129–30.

78. William Barnaby Faherty, *Exile in Erin: A Confederate Chaplain's Story: The Life of Fr. John B. Bannon* (Missouri Historical Society, 2002), 32.

79. Louis Gerteis, *Civil War Saint Louis* (Lawrence: University of Kansas Press, 2001), 98–114; Adam Arenson, *The Great Heart of the Republic: St. Louis and the Cultural Civil War* (HUP, 2011), 116–18.

80. Murphy to Beckx, St. Louis, April 24, 1861, ARSI, in Garraghan, *Jesuits of the Middle United States* 2: 155.

81. Faherty, *Exile in Erin*, 55.

82. Gleeson, *The Green and the Gray*, 59.

83. Walter D. Kamphoefner, "German-Americans and Civil War Politics: A Reconsideration of the Ethnocultural Thesis," *CWH* 37 (September 1991): 236.

84. Kamphoefner, "German-Americans and Civil War Politics," 246.

85. Anderson, ed., "The Civil War Diary of John Abell Morgan," 110.

86. Patrick Lynch to John Hughes, Charleston, August 4, 1861, printed in *New York Daily Tribune,* Thursday, September 5, 1861.

87. "Lecture on St. Patrick to Catholic Library Association," March 17, 1861, in Lawrence Kehoe, ed., *Complete Works of the Most Rev. John Hughes, D.D., Archbishop of New York* (New York: Lawrence Kehoe, 1866), 157.

6. FIRST SEASON OF WAR

1. Durkin, *Stephen R. Mallory,* 136–55.

2. Warren F. Spencer, *Raphael Semmes: The Philosophical Mariner* (UAP, 1997), 5.

3. Spencer, *Raphael Semmes,* 110–11.

4. Spencer, *Raphael Semmes,* 112–36.

5. Terry L. Jones, *Lee's Tigers: The Louisiana Infantry in the Army of Northern Virginia* (LSUP, 1987), 46–48.

6. Edward Longacre, *The Early Morning of War: Bull Run, 1861* (UOP, 2014), 94–103.

7. Kathryn W. Lerch. "Prosecuting Citizens, Rebels & Spies: The 8th New York Heavy Artillery in Maryland, 1862–1864," *MHM* 94 (1999): 134.

8. Benjamin F. Cooling, "Defending Washington During the Civil War," *Columbia Historical Society,* 1971–72, 317.

9. Rose Greenhow, *My Imprisonment and the First Year of Abolition Rule at Washington* (London: Richard Bentley, 1863), 49–50.

10. Edwin C. Fishel, *The Secret War for the Union: The Untold Story of Military Intelligence in the Civil War* (HMC, 1996), 59.

11. Fishel, *Secret War for the Union,* 61–64.

12. WTS to EES, July 28, 1861, Sherman Family Papers, UNDA.

13. Longacre, *Early Morning of War,* 196–202.

14. Kelly J. O'Grady, *Clear the Confederate Way! The Irish in the Army of Northern Virginia* (Fredericksburg [VA]: Savas Publishing Co., 2000), 55.

15. Jones, *Lee's Tigers,* 49–53.

16. Longacre, *Early Morning of War,* 358–60.

17. Longacre, *Early Morning of War,* 385.

18. Thomas Francis Meagher, *The Last Days of the 69th in Virginia* (New York, 1862), 13.

19. Ruffner, *Maryland's Blue & Gray,* 92–93.

20. Captain Charles C. Edelin of the Maryland First captured a federal flag in the climactic fighting. It may well have been that of the Sixty-Ninth (Ruffner, *Maryland's Blue & Gray*, 93).

21. Longacre, *Early Morning of War*, 378–438; Bruce, *The Harp and the Eagle*, 77.

22. Patrick Daniel O'Flaherty, SJ, "The History of the 69th Regiment of the New York State Militia, 1852–1861," PhD diss., FUP, 1963, 290.

23. WTS to wife, July 28, 1861, Sherman Family Papers, UNDA.

24. Robert O'Connell, *Fierce Patriot: The Tangled Lives of William Tecumseh Sherman* (RH, 2014), 78.

25. James Lee McDonough, *William Tecumseh Sherman* (New York: WWN, 2016), 267.

26. Longacre, *Early Morning of War*, 465–71.

27. Killoren, *De Smet and the Indian Tragedy*, 233.

28. J. Fairfax McLaughlin, *College Days at Georgetown, and other Papers* (Philadelphia, 1899), 187.

29. Garesché to Early, July 22, 1861, book 1, folder 1, Early Papers, GUA.

30. Williams, *P. G. T. Beauregard*, 92–98.

31. Williams, *P. G. T. Beauregard*, 97.

32. Blackman, *Wild Rose*, 44.

33. Daly, July 22, 1861, in Hammond, ed., *Diary of a Union Lady*, 39.

34. "Recollections of Sister Rose Noyland, Richmond General Hospital," in Betty Ann McNeil, ed., *Balm of Hope: Charity Afire Impels Sisters of Charity in Civil War Nursing* (Chicago: De Paul University Press, 2015), 61–63.

35. Blackman, *Wild Rose*, 45.

36. Amanda Foreman, *A World on Fire: Britain's Decisive Role in the American Civil War* (New York: RH, 2010), 134.

37. As one historian who has studied her career as a spy summed up her performance before the military commission: she "made treason seem a civil right. Her hauteur never lapsed" (Fishel, *Secret War for the Union*, 68).

38. Greenhow, *My Imprisonment*, 322.

39. Foreman, *Britain's Decisive Role in the American Civil War*, 263.

40. Fishel, *Secret War for the Union*, 75–76.

41. Kurtz, *Excommunicated from the Union*, 80–81.

42. Heineman, *Civil War Dynasty*, 142.

43. Williams, *P. G. T. Beauregard*, 100–101.

44. Williams, *P. G. T. Beauregard*, 110.

45. Kurtz, *Excommunicated from the Union*, 60.

46. *Daily Tribune*, September 5, 1861.

47. John F. Marszalek, *Sherman: A Soldier's Passion for Order* (New York: Free Press, 1993), 157.

48. Heineman, *Civil War Dynasty*, 132–33.

49. James Gibbons, "My Memories," *Dublin Review* 160 (April 1917): 165.

50. Hicks to Banks, October 26, 1861, *Secret Correspondence Illustrating the Condition of Affairs in Maryland*, in Charles Branch Clark, "Politics in Maryland During the Civil War," *MHM* 37 (December 1942): 390–91.

51. Jean Baker, *The Politics of Continuity: Maryland Political Parties from 1858 to 1870* (JHUP, 1964), 69–74.

52. Fermer, *James Gordon Bennett*, 46–47.

53. Foreman, *Britain's Decisive Role in the American Civil War,* 175–95; Heineman, *Civil War Dynasty,* 3. Judge Charles Daley, as well as Thomas Ewing, played a role in persuading the Lincoln administration that the law governing the case gave them no option but to release Mason and Slidell. Marie Daly claimed that Seward's public statement employed the very words that her husband reported he had used in his meeting with the secretary (Daly, March 22, 1862, in Hammond, ed., *Diary of a Union Lady,* 113).

54. Francis Lynch to Patrick Lynch, Cheraw, December 14, 1861, 14 D3, CDA.

55. Baptista Lynch to Patrick Lynch, Ursuline Convent, December 14, 1861, 14 D4, CDA.

56. W. Scott Poole, *South Carolina's Civil War: A Narrative* (Macon, GA: Mercer University Press, 2005), 49.

57. *Charleston Mercury,* December 25, 1861; *Charleston Courier,* December 31, 1861.

7. GRAND CAMPAIGNS

1. Daly, January 29, 1862, in Hammond, ed., *Diary of a Union Lady,* 99.

2. Roy P. Basler, ed. *The Collected Works of Lincoln* (New Brunswick, NJ: Rutgers University Press, 1953), 5:49.

3. James M. McPherson, *Crossroads of Freedom: Antietam* (OUP, 2002), 17–22.

4. Daly, March 3, 1862, in Hammond, ed., *Diary of a Union Lady,* 110–11.

5. Williams, *P. G. T. Beauregard,* 122–24.

6. Stanley J. Guerin, ed. and trans., *The Shiloh Diary of Edmond Enoul Livaudais* (New Orleans: Archdiocese of New Orleans, 1992), 31; Turgis to Odin, Grand Junction, Tennessee, April 16, 1862, AANO, UNDA, cited in Michael Pasquier, *Fathers on the Frontier: French Missionaries and the Roman Catholic Priesthood in the United States, 1789–1870* (OUP, 2010), 192.

7. Marszalek, *Sherman,* 177–79.

8. Guerin, ed., *Shiloh Diary of Edmond Enoul Livaudais,* 31; James M. McPherson, *Battle Cry of Freedom: The Civil War Era* (OUP, 1988), 409.

9. Williams, *P. G. T. Beauregard,* 141–43.

10. James Lee McDonough, *Shiloh—in Hell before Night* (UTP, 1977), 168–95.

11. Kehoe, ed., *Complete Works of the Most Rev. John Hughes,* 115.

12. Williams, *P. G. T. Beauregard,* 144–46.

13. Guerin, ed., *Shiloh Diary of Edmond Enoul Livaudais,* 33.

14. Judith Metz, SC, ed. *The Sisters of Charity of Cincinnati in the Civil War: The Love of Christ Urges Us* (Cincinnati: Sisters of Charity, 2012), 27–28.

15. Metz, ed., *Sisters of Charity,* 26.

16. Williams, *P. G. T. Beauregard,* 182.

17. McDonough, *Shiloh,* 322–23.

18. Williams, *P. G. T. Beauregard,* 152–54.

19. Thomas Cahill to Margaret Cahill, onboard Steamer "Matanzas," April 29, 1862, in Ryan W. Keating, ed. *"The Greatest Trial I Ever Had": The Civil War Letters of Margaret and Thomas Cahill* (UGP, 2017), 74–77.

20. Foreman, *Britain's Decisive Role in the American Civil War,* 248; Gleeson, "To Live and Die [for] Dixie," 148.

21. Cahill to wife, New Orleans, May 4, 1862, in Keating, *Civil War Letters of Margaret and Thomas Cahill,* 81–82; Keating, *Shades of Green,* 101.

22. Cahill to wife, onboard Steamer McClellan, Mississippi River, June 1, 1862, in Keating, *Civil War Letters of Margaret and Thomas Cahill*, 87.

23. Ochs, *A Black Patriot and a White Priest*, 107.

24. Baptista Lynch to Patrick Lynch, June 4, 1862, 14 H11, CDA.

25. Ochs, *A Black Patriot and a White Priest*, 74–78, 89–90.

26. Ochs, *A Black Patriot and a White Priest*, 91–94.

27. Approximately one hundred Blacks served as commissioned officers for the Union. About two-thirds of them were in the Native Guard regiments (Ochs, *A Black Patriot and a White Priest*, 207–8).

28. Ochs, *A Black Patriot and a White Priest*, 116–24.

29. Mallory to Capt. Buchanan, February 24, March 7, 1862, *OR*, ser. 1, vol. 6: 776–77, 780–88; Durkin, *Stephen R. Mallory*, 196–97.

30. McPherson, *Battle Cry of Freedom*, 375–77.

31. Guiney to Jennie Guiney, Camp Winfield Scott, May 1, 1862, in Christian Samito, ed., *Commanding Boston's Irish Ninth: The Civil War Letters of Colonel Patrick R. Guiney, Ninth Massachusetts Volunteer Infantry* (FUP, 1998), 98–99.

32., Peter Tissot, SJ, "A Year with the Army of the Potomac," ed. Thomas Gaffney Taffel, *HRS* 3 (1908): 68.

33. Tissot, "A Year with the Army of the Potomac," 70.

34. Dale Cyrus Wheary, "James and Sallie Dooley of Maymont," Archives of the Maymont Foundation, Richmond, Va.

35. Stephen R. Mallory Diary, May 13, 1862, SHC.

36. Stephen Sears, *To the Gates of Richmond* (New York: Ticknor & Fields, 1992), 87.

37. Tissot, "A Year with the Army of the Potomac," 71–72.

38. Baptista Lynch to Patrick Lynch, Ursuline Convent, Columbia, SC, May 26, 1862, 14 H6, CDA.

39. Fishel, *Secret War for the Union*, 178–79.

40. Ruffner, *Maryland's Blue & Gray*, 105.

41. Jones, *Lee's Tigers*, 74.

42. Jones, *Lee's Tigers*, 27–32.

43. Richard R. Duncan, *Beleaguered Winchester: A Virginia Community at War, 1861–1865* (LSUP, 2007), 98.

44. Murray to mother, June 28, 1862, in Ruffner, *Maryland's Blue & Gray*, 107.

45. Baptista Lynch to Patrick Lynch, Ursuline Convent, Columbia, SC, June 4, 1862, 14 H11, CDA.

46. McPherson, *Battle Cry of Freedom*, 457–60.

47. James P. Gannon, *Irish Rebels: Confederate Tigers: The 6th Louisiana Volunteers, 1861–1865* (Mason City, IA: Savas Publishing Co., 1998), 51–61.

48. Sears, *To the Gates of Richmond*, 156–63.

49. Sears, *To the Gates of Richmond*, 195–206.

50. Francis W. Dawson, *Reminiscences of Confederate Service, 1861–1865*, ed. Bell I. Wiley (LSUP, 1980), 50.

51. Gannon. *Irish Rebels*, 79–84/

52. Sears, *To the Gates of Richmond*, 222–29.

53. Sears, *To the Gates of Richmond*, 240.

54. Sears, *To the Gates of Richmond*, 241; Glenn David Brasher, *The Peninsula Campaign and the Necessity of Emancipation: African Americans and the Fight for Freedom* (UNCP, 2012), 186.

55. Samito, ed., *Civil War Letters of Colonel Patrick R. Guiney*, 115.

56. Christian G. Samito, "Thomas F. Meagher, Patrick R. Guiney, and the Meaning of the Civil War for Irish America," in Lorien Foote and Kanisorn Wongsrichanalai, eds., *So Conceived and So Dedicated: Intellectual Life in the Civil War–Era North* (FUP, 2015), 193.

57. Robert K. Krick, *Civil War Weather in Virginia* (UAP, 2007), 60–61.

58. Sears, *To the Gates of Richmond*, 293–307; Wert, *General James Longstreet*, 144.

59. Wert, *General James Longstreet*, 146–49.

60. Jones, *Lee's Tigers*, 110.

61. Egan, *Immortal Irishman*, 212.

62. Daniel G. MacNamara, *The History of the Ninth Regiment Massachusetts Volunteer Infantry* (Boston: E. B. Stillings, 1899), 158–59.

63. Jones, *Lee's Tigers*, 110.

64. Sears, *To the Gates of Richmond*, 343.

65. Mallory to Milton, July 4, 1862, cited in Durkin, *Stephen R. Mallory*, 222.

66. Wert, *General James Longstreet*, 151.

8. SLAVERY AND THE SHIFTING GOALS OF THE WAR

1. Brasher, *Peninsula Campaign*, 69.

2. John J. Hennessy, *Return to Bull Run: The Campaign and Battle of Second Manassas* (New York: S&S, 1993), 14–15.

3. Entry for August 8, 1862, in Patrick Hayes, ed., *The Civil War Diary of Father James Sheeran, Confederate Chaplain and Redemptorist* (CUAP, 2016), 15.

4. Entry for August 9, 1862, Hayes, ed., *Civil War Diary of Father James Sheeran*, 16–19.

5. Gache to Carrière, Richmond, August 20, 1862, in Cornelius M. Buckley, SJ, ed. and trans., *A Frenchman, A Chaplain, a Rebel: The War Letters of Pere Louis-Hippolyte Gache, S.J.* (LUP, 1981), 130–33.

6. David Newson Lott, ed., *The Presidents Speak: The Inaugural Addresses of the American Presidents, from Washington to Clinton* (New York: Henry Holt and Co., 1994), 138–45; Richard Striner, "Lincoln's Threat to the Supreme Court," *New York Times*, Disunion Series, March 3, 2011, opinionator.blogs.nytimes.com/2011/03/03/lincoln-address-the-nation/.

7. *Congressional Quarterly*, 37th Congress, 1st Session, 222–23; 258–62, cited in McPherson, *Battle Cry of Freedom*, 312.

8. Mary Mitchell, *Divided Town* (Barre, MA: Barre Publishers, 1968), 60–61.

9. Paul Finkelman, "From Union to Freedom," *New York Times*, Disunion Series, October 5, 2012, opinionator.blogs.nytimes.com/2012//10/05/.

10. Entry for December 7, 1861, in Keating, *Civil War Letters of Margaret and Thomas Cahill*, 29.

11. Entry for January 7, 1862, in Keating, *Civil War Letters of Margaret and Thomas Cahill*, 38.

12. William C. Harris, *Lincoln and the Border States: Preserving the Union* (UPK, 2011), 159–89.

13. Brasher, *Peninsula Campaign*, 203.

14. Charles Sumner, *The Works of Charles Sumner* (Boston: Lee & Shepard, 1872), vol. 6: 215, cited in Stephen W. Sears, *Landscape Turned Red: The Battle of Antietam* (New York: Popular Library, 1985), 46.

15. McGreevy, *Catholicism and American Freedom,* 48–56.

16. Patrick Lynch to John Hughes, Charleston, August 4, 1861, in *New York Daily Tribune,* September 5, 1861, 6.

17. Patrick W. Carey, "Orestes Brownson and the Civil War," *USCH* 31 (Winter 2013): 5.

18. "Slavery and the War," *BQR* (August 1861), in *Works of Orestes Brownson* 17: 144–78.

19. Brown to Sumner, October 23, 1861, UNDA, cited in Wimmer, "American Catholic Interpretations of the Civil War," 176n101.

20. *BQR,* October 1861, cited in Frese, "Catholic Press and Secession," 88.

21. *MR,* October 12, 1861, cited in Carey, "Orestes Brownson and the Civil War," 10–11.

22. *BQR,* January 1862, cited in Carey, "Orestes Brownson and Civil War," 12.

23. H. Marshall, *Brownson and the American Republic* (CUAP, 1971), 189.

24. Joseph George Jr., "'A Catholic Family Newspaper' Views the Lincoln Administration: John Mullally's Copperhead Weekly," *CWH* 24 (June 1978): 118–19.

25. *CM,* April 19, 1862.

26. *BP,* March 22, 1862.

27. *BP,* November 29, 1861.

28. *FJ,* May 24, 1862.

29. *NYH,* July 11, 1862; July 21, 1862.

30. *PC,* July 26, 1862.

31. Kurtz, *Excommunicated from the Union,* 98–99.

32. Endres, "Rectifying the Fatal Contrast," 26.

33. For text of pastoral, see *PC,* September 20, 1862; Wimmer, "American Catholic Interpretations of the Civil War," 156–57.

34. Fortin, *History of the Archdiocese of Cincinnati,* 143.

35. *New York Daily Tribune,* July 5, 1862.

36. *CM,* July 5, 1862.

37. Michael Fellman, *Citizen Sherman: A Life of William Tecumseh Sherman* (RH, 1995), 74.

38. EES to WTS, August 4, 1864, Sherman Family Papers, UNDA.

39. EES to WTS, April 23, 1862, Sherman Family Papers, UNDA.

40. Mallory to his wife, August 31, 1862, cited in Durkin, *Stephen R. Mallory,* 248.

41. Hennessy, *Return to Bull Run,* 188.

42. Hennessy, *Return to Bull Run,* 259.

43. Hennessy, *Return to Bull Run,* 268–303.

44. Jones, *Louisiana Infantry,* 124.

45. Robert Emmett Curran, *John Dooley's Civil War* (UTP, 2012), 30–31.

46. Daniel G. MacNamara, *History of the Ninth Regiment Massachusetts Volunteer Infantry* (Boston: F. B. Stillings & Co., 1899), 195.

47. September 1, 1862, in Hayes, ed., *Civil War Diary of Father James Sheeran,* 49–50.

48. George Barton, *Angels of the Battlefield: A History of the Labors of the Catholic Sisterhoods in the Late Civil War,* 2nd ed. (Philadelphia, 1898), 110.

49. D[enis] A. Mahony, *The Prisoner of State* (New York, 1863), 222–23.

50. As it happened, Cox's division was not part of the Army of Virginia which was engaging the Army of Northern Virginia around the initial major battle site (EES to WTS, Lancaster, August 30, 1862, Sherman Family Papers, UNDA).

51. Michael V. Gannon, *Rebel Bishop: The Life and Era of Augustus Verot* (Milwaukee: Bruce, 1964), 71.

9. THE WAR COMES TO THE CATHOLIC HEARTLAND

1. Virginia Walcott Beauchamp, ed., *A Private War: Letters and Diaries of Madge Preston, 1862–1867* (New Brunswick, NJ: Rutgers University Press, 1987), 3.

2. "The Invasion of Maryland," in *Battles and Leaders of the Civil War* (New York, 1887), vol. 2: 663.

3. Richard Slotkin, *The Long Road to Antietam: How the Civil War Became a Revolution* (WWN, 2012), 178–80.

4. Daly, September 11, 1862, in Hammond, ed., *Diary of a Union Lady,* 170.

5. Entry for September 10, 1862, in Curran, *Dooley's Civil War,* 36.

6. Mary M. Melina and Edward F. X. McSweeny, *Story of the Mountain: Mount St. Mary's College and Seminary* (Emmitsburg, MD: Weekly Chronicle, 1911), n.p.

7. Heineman, *Civil War Dynasty,* 160.

8. D. Scott Hartwig, *To Antietam Creek: The Maryland Campaign of September 1862* (JHUP, 2013), 373–74.

9. William Corby, CSC, *Memoirs of Chaplain Life: Three Years with the Irish Brigade in the Army of the Potomac* (FUP, 1992), 112.

10. Hartwig, *To Antietam Creek,* 44–77.

11. Hartwig, *To Antietam Creek,* 483.

12. Hartwig, *To Antietam Creek,* 632–33.

13. Gannon, *Irish Rebels,* 131–32.

14. Gannon, *Irish Rebels,* 139.

15. Terry Jones, "The Dead of Antietam," opinionator.blogs.nytimes.com/2012/09/24/the-dead-of Antietam/.

16. Joseph L Harsh, *Taken at the Flood: Robert E. Lee & Confederate Strategy in the Maryland Campaign of 1862* (KSUP, 1999), 368–95.

17. Egan, *Immortal Irishman,* 224–25.

18. *OR,* ser. 1, vol. 19, chap. 31, pt. 1: 298.

19. Bruce, *The Harp and the Eagle,* 119.

20. McPherson, *Crossroads of Freedom,* 125–26.

21. McPherson, *Crossroads of Freedom,* 130.

22. Heineman, *Civil War Dynasty,* 163–64.

23. Curran, *Dooley's Civil War,* 47–49.

24. Samito, *Commanding Boston's Irish Ninth,* 136–37.

25. Harsh, *Robert E. Lee & Confederate Strategy,* 425.

26. Wert, *General James Longstreet,* 199–200.

27. McNeil, ed., *Balm of Hope,* 73–74.

28. *Herald,* October 1, October 6, 1862, cited in McPherson, *Crossroads of Freedom,* 138.

29. Heineman, *Civil War Dynasty,* 165.

30. James Lee McDonough, *War in Kentucky: From Shiloh to Perryville* (UTP, 1994), 149–50, 198.

31. Baptista Lynch to Patrick Lynch, Columbia, September 14, 1862, 14 M7, CDA.

32. Astor, *Rebels on the Border,* 90.

33. Spalding Journal, September 22, 1862, AASMUS.

34. Spalding Journal, September 29, 1862, AASMUS.

35. Kenneth W. Noe, *Perryville: This Grand Havoc of Battle* (UPKY, 2001), 80–83.

36. Cooney to brother, Louisville, October 2, 1862, in Thomas McAvoy, ed., "The War Letters of Father Peter Paul Cooney of the Congregation of Holy Cross," *RACHSP* 44 (1933): 69.

37. John Ellis to his mother, October 2, 1862; Wood to his wife, September 26, 1862, in Wood Papers, Alabama Dept. of Archives and History, Montgomery, in Noe, *Perryville*, 100–101. The Catholics in the area mainly had origins in slaveholding southern Maryland; the Protestants tended to trace their roots back to Pennsylvania and the nonslaveholding portions of western Virginia.

38. McPherson, *Battle Cry of Freedom*, 522–23.

39. William B. Kurtz, "'The Perfect Model of a Christian Hero,': The Faith, Anti-Slaveryism, and Post-War Legacy of William S. Rosecrans," *USCH* 31 (Winter 2013): 82; William M. Lamers, *The Edge of Glory: A Biography of General William S. Rosecrans, U.S.A.* (New York: Harcourt, 1962), 94–129.

40. Phillip Thomas Tucker, *The Confederacy's Fighting Chaplain: Father John B. Bannon* (UAP, 1992), 94–95.

41. Lamers, *Biography of General William S. Rosecrans*, 153.

42. Lamers, *Biography of General William S. Rosecrans*, 169.

43. Lamers, *Biography of General William S. Rosecrans*, 175–77.

44. Harrison, *Civil War*, 42–51.

45. Noe, *Perryville*, 139.

46. Noe, *Perryville*, 215.

47. Noe, *Perryville*, 232–33.

48. Noe, *Perryville*, 267–69.

49. Noe, *Perryville*, 343.

50. Archives of the Sisters of St. Dominic, St. Catherine, KY, cited in Sr. Mary Denis Maher, *To Bind Up the Wounds: Catholic Sister Nurses in the U.S. Civil War* (New York: Greenwood Press, 1989), 76.

51. *OR*, vol. 16, pt. 1: 1088, cited in McDonough, *War in Kentucky*, 308.

10. EMANCIPATION

1. Bruce, *The Harp and the Eagle*, 137.

2. Albion P. Man Jr., "The Irish in New York in the Early 1860s," *Irish Historical Studies* 7 (September 1950): 98.

3. *FJ*, October 4, 1862.

4. *BP*, October 4, 1862.

5. *Irish-American*, November 8, 1862; January 17, 1863, cited in Edward K. Spann, "Union Green: The Irish Community and the Civil War," in Bayor and Meagher, eds., *New York Irish*, 203.

6. Frank L. Klement, *The Copperheads in the Middle West* (UCP, 1960), 44.

7. *Daily Patriot*, August 23, 1862, in Keating, *Shades of Green*, 75–76.

8. *Herald*, December 10, 1862, in Keating, *Shades of Green*, 151n32.

9. Patrick Steward and Bryan McGovern, *The Fenians: Irish Rebellion in the North Atlantic World, 1858–1876* (UTP, 2013), 52.

10. Hammond, ed., *Diary of a Union Lady*, 196.

11. George C. Rable, *Fredericksburg! Fredericksburg!* (UNCP, 2002), 134–39.

12. Rable, *Fredericksburg*, 150.

13. O'Hagan to Wiget, November 30, 1862, in *WL* 15 (1886): 111–12.

14. Corby, *Memoirs of Chaplain Life*, 131.

15. St. Clair Mulholland, *The Story of the 116th Regiment Pennsylvania Volunteers in the War of the Rebellion: The Record of a Gallant Command* (Philadelphia, 1903), 26–45.

16. Kevin E. O'Brien, ed., *My Life in the Irish Brigade: The Civil War Memoirs of Private William McCarter, 116th Pennsylvania Infantry* (Campbell, CA: Savas, 1996), 172.

17. O'Brien, ed., *My Life in the Irish Brigade*, 175–78.

18. Bruce, *The Harp and the Eagle*, 125–32.

19. Guiney to wife, Near Falmouth, December 18, 1862, in Samito, ed., *Civil War Letters of Colonel Patrick R. Guiney*, 156

20. O'Grady, *Clear the Confederate Way*, 118.

21. O'Hagan to Wiget, near Falmouth, December 18, 1862, in *WL* 15 (1886): 112–13.

22. Lamers, *Biography of General William S. Rosecrans*, 182.

23. Lamers, *Biography of General William S. Rosecrans*, 196.

24. Louis Garesché, *Biography of Lt. Col. Julius P. Garesché* (Philadelphia: J. B. Lippincott, 1887), 436.

25. Lamers, *Biography of General William S. Rosecrans*, 227.

26. Lamers, *Biography of General William S. Rosecrans*, 232–33; Garesché, *Biography of Lt. Col. Julius P. Garesché*, 462.

27. Hughes and Ware, *Theodore O'Hara*, 123–27.

28. Peter Cozzens, "Rosecrans to the Rescue," *NYT*, December 31, 2012, opinionator.blogs .nytimes.com/2012/12/3'/Rosecrans-to-the-rescue/; McPherson, *Battle Cry of Freedom*, 580–82.

29. Lamers, *Biography of General William S. Rosecrans*, 245.

30. Kurtz, "Perfect Model of a Christian Hero," 87.

31. Lamers, *Biography of General William S. Rosecrans*, 258.

32. *Telegraph*, May 6, 1863, cited in Kurtz, "Perfect Model of a Christian Hero," 87.

33. Kevin Thaddeus Brady, "Fenians and the Faithful: Philadelphia's Irish Republican Brotherhood and the Diocese of Philadelphia, 1859–1870," PhD diss., Temple University, 1998, 207–8.

34. Quoted in *L'Union*, April 14, 1863, in Ochs, *A Black Patriot and a White Priest*, 115.

35. Ochs, *A Black Patriot and a White Priest*, 115.

36. T. Parkin Scott, *Authority and Free Will: A Lecture Delivered Before the Catholic Institute of Baltimore*, January 11, 1863 (Baltimore: Kelly, Hedrin and Piet, 1863), 4–7.

37. *Illinois State Register*, January 6, 1863, cited in Klement, *Copperheads in the Middle West*, 48.

38. *Irish-American*, January 10, 1863.

39. *MR*, January 3, 10, 1863, cited in Albion P. Man Jr., "The Church and the New York Draft Riots of 1863," *RACHSP* 62 (1951): 43.

40. William L. Lucey, ed., "The Diary of Joseph B. O'Hagan, S.J., Chaplain of the Excelsior Brigade," *CWH* 6 (December 1960): 408.

41. James B. Swan, *Chicago's Irish Legion: The 90th Illinois Volunteers in the Civil War* (Carbondale: Southern Illinois University Press, 2009) 25–26.

42. Swan, *Chicago's Irish Legion*, 59–63.

43. Peter Welsh to Margaret Welsh, in camp near Falmouth, February 3, 1863; February 8, 1863, in Lawrence F. Kohl and Margaret C. Richards, eds., *Irish Green and Union Blue: The Civil War Letters of Peter Welsh, Color Sergeant 28th Regiment Massachusetts Volunteers* (FUP, 1986), 68–70.

44. Patrick Guiney to Jennie Guiney, Headquarters 2nd Brigade, February 11, 1863, in Samito, ed., *Civil War Letters of Colonel Patrick R. Guiney,* 166.

45. McKay, *Civil War and New York City,* 240.

46. Cited in Steward and McGovern, *Fenians,* 56–57.

47. Aaron Astor, "'I Wanted a Gun': Black Soldiers and White Violence in Civil War and Postwar Kentucky and Missouri," in Paul A. Cimbala and Randall M. Miller, *The Great Task Remaining Before Us: Reconstruction as America's Continuing Civil War* (FUP, 2010), 31–33.

48. Brugger, *Maryland,* 302.

49. Such retribution no doubt played a role in the drastic reduction of Blacks in Kentucky after the war. By 1870 the black population had dropped by a precipitous 65 percent (Astor, "I Wanted a Gun," 40–52).

50. Cimbala and Miller, *Reconstruction as America's Continuing Civil War,* 53.

51. Margaret Loughborough and James H. Johnston, *The Recollections of Margaret Cabell Brown Loughborough: A Southern Woman's Memories of Richmond, VA and Washington, DC in the Civil War* (Lanham, MD: Hamilton Books, 2010), 67.

52. Brownson, "Emancipation," *Works of Orestes Brownson* 17: 206, cited in Louis P. Masur, *Lincoln's Hundred Days: The Emancipation Proclamation and the War for the Union* (Cambridge, MA: HUP, 2012), 54.

53. *National Anti-Slavery Standard,* June 13, 1863, cited in McGreevy, *Catholicism and American Freedom,* 36.

54. McGreevy, *Catholicism and American Freedom,* 36–40.

55. Spalding Journal, February 26, 1862, AASMUS.

56. Spalding Journal, 80, AASMUS.

57. Satish Joseph, "'Long Live the Republic!' Father Edward Purcell and the Slavery Controversy: 1861–1865," *ACS* 116 (2005): 49–53.

58. Spalding Journal, February 13, 1863, AASMUS.

59. Francis Kenrick to Spalding, Baltimore, April 18, 1863, cited in David Spalding, "Martin John Spalding's Dissertation on the American Civil War,'" *CHR* 52 (April 1966): 66; Spalding Journal, April 21, 1863, AASMUS.

60. Kenrick to Spalding, April 18, 1863, 34-L63, AASMUS.

61. Francis Patrick Kenrick to Barnabò, Scr. Rif. A.C., vol. 20, folios. 213r–214v, APF. When asked to issue a statement in support of the federal government's war policies, Kenrick responded: "I desire the prosperity of the whole country on the basis of the General Constitution, without detriment to the reserved rights of the states. This I believe to be loyalty and patriotism" (Kenrick to Henry Major, Baltimore, May 19, 1863, Letterbook II, AASMUS, cited in Marschall, "Francis Patrick Kenrick," 369. For Kenrick, patriotism was taking a position that was consistent with the Constitution. He could not square the Emancipation Proclamation, among other matters, with that standard.

62. Spalding, "Martin John Spalding's Dissertation," 69–84.

63. "The Cause of the War," *PC,* April 18, 1863.

64. *PC,* August 15, 1863.

11. 1863: THE WAR IN THE EAST

1. Fishel, *Secret War for the Union,* 362–83.

2. Stephen W. Sears, *Chancellorsville* (HMC, 1996), 240–47.

3. Sears, *Chancellorsville*, 275.

4. Ernest B. Furgurson, *Chancellorsville 1863: The Souls of the Brave* (AAK, 1992), 186.

5. Furgurson, *Chancellorsville*, 188–89.

6. Furgurson, *Chancellorsville*, 184–85.

7. Sears, *Chancellorsville*, 281.

8. Sears, *Chancellorsville*, 285–95.

9. Sears, *Chancellorsville*, 336.

10. Sears, *Chancellorsville*, 336–42.

11. Furgurson, *Chancellorsville*, 249.

12. Guiney to wife, Headquarters, 9th Massachusetts, May 13, 1863, in Samito, ed., *Civil War Letters of Colonel Patrick R. Guiney*, 190–91.

13. Jones, *Lee's Tigers*, 164–66.

14. Gannon, *Irish Rebels*, 184–202.

15. Sears, *Chancellorsville*, 440–45.

16. Fishel, *Secret War for the Union*, 442–55.

17. Longstreet to Louis Wigfall, May 13, 1863, in Stephen W. Sears, *Gettysburg* (HMC, 2003), 1–7.

18. Sears, *Gettysburg*, 7–17.

19. Kent Masterson Brown, *Retreat from Gettysburg: Lee, Logistics, & the Pennsylvania Campaign* (UNCP, 2005), 26–29.

20. Edwin B. Coddington, *The Gettysburg Campaign: A Study in Command* (New York: Charles Scribner's Sons, 1968), 149–50. According to the Census of 1860, there were 5,622 Blacks residing in the two counties.

21. Sears, *Gettysburg*, 112, 73–74.

22. Coddington, *Gettysburg Campaign*, 186; Sears, *Gettysburg*, 118; Wert, *General James Longstreet*, 255; Allen C. Guelzo, *Gettysburg: The Last Invasion* (AAK, 2013), 113–14.

23. Corby, *Memoirs of Chaplain Life*, 177.

24. Sears, *Gettysburg*, 28–42; Coddington, *Gettysburg Campaign*, 209–20.

25. Sears, *Gettysburg*, 165.

26. Guelzo, *Gettysburg*, 157.

27. Sears, *Gettysburg*, 165, 220–21.

28. Guelzo, *Gettysburg*, 206.

29. Coddington, *Gettysburg Campaign*, 360.

30. Coddington, *Gettysburg Campaign*, 362–63.

31. Coddington, *Gettysburg Campaign*, 374–75.

32. Coddington, *Gettysburg Campaign*, 383–84.

33. Donald M. Fisher, "Born in Ireland, Killed at Gettysburg: The Life, Death, and Legacy of Henry O'Rorke," *CWH* (March 1994): 238.

34. Fisher, "Born in Ireland, Killed at Gettysburg," 237–38; Sears, *Gettysburg*, 163; Coddington, *Gettysburg Campaign*, 396.

35. Corby, *Memoirs of Chaplain Life*, 185.

36. Sears, *Gettysburg*, 291.

37. Coddington, *Gettysburg Campaign*, 405; Sears, *Gettysburg*, 286; Paul Jones Semmes to wife, Martinsburg, VA, July 9, 1863, in Gilder Lehman Collection, www.gilderlehman.org.

38. Sears, *Gettysburg*, 291–92.

39. Peter Welsh to Margaret Welsh, Pleasant Valley [MD], July 17, 1863, in Kohl and Richards, eds., *Irish Green and Union Blue*, 108–10.

40. Ruffner, *Maryland's Blue & Gray*, 181.

41. Gannon, *Irish Rebels*, 197.

42. Guelzo, *Gettysburg*, 342–43.

43. Jones, *Lee's Tigers*, 170.

44. Sears, *Gettysburg*, 305.

45. Guelzo, *Gettysburg*, 356.

46. Entry for July 2–3, 1863, *Dooley's Civil War*, 157.

47. Jeffry D. Wert, *Gettysburg: Day Three* (S&S, 2001), 98–99.

48. Coddington, *Gettysburg Campaign*, 460–63.

49. Jones, *Lee's Tigers*, 175.

50. Coddington, *Gettysburg Campaign*, 479.

51. Curran, *Dooley's Civil War*, 158; Sears, *Gettysburg*, 397, 405; Wert, *Gettysburg*, 173.

52. Wert, *General James Longstreet*, 291–92.

53. Sears, *Gettysburg*, 421.

54. Curran, *Dooley's Civil War*, 162.

55. Guelzo, *Gettysburg*, 415.

56. Sears, *Gettysburg*, 451.

57. Bruce, *The Harp and the Eagle*, 169–72.

58. Sears, *Gettysburg*, 452.

59. Coddington, *Gettysburg Campaign*, 519.

60. Guelzo, *Gettysburg*, 442.

61. Curran, *Dooley's Civil War*, 163–79.

62. Curran, *Dooley's Civil War*, 38, 152.

63. Edgeworth Bird to Sallie Bird, July 7, 1863, in John Rozier, ed., *The Granite Farm Letters: The Civil War Correspondence of Edgeworth & Sallie Bird* (UGP, 1988), 119.

64. Semmes to wife, Martinsburg, July 9, 1863, Gilder Lehman Collection.

65. Grace Palladino, *Another Civil War: Labor, Capital, and the State in the Anthracite Regions of Pennsylvania* (UIP, 1990), 105.

66. Jean Baker, *Affairs of Party: The Political Culture of Northern Democrats in the Mid-Nineteenth Century* (CUP, 1983), 155.

67. Kurtz, *Excommunicated from the Union*, 116.

68. John McKeon, *Peace & Union, war & disunion: speech of Hon. John McKeon delivered before the Democratic Union Association, at their headquarters at no. 932 Broadway, on Tuesday evening, March 3* (New York: Van Evrie, Horton & Co., 1863).

69. Tyler Anbinder concluded from his study of draftees that "immigrants were not more likely than natives to serve in the Army as a result of the draft." Of those drafted in 1863, immigrants comprised a half, but the overwhelming majority of them were substitutes ("Which Poor Man's Fight?" *CWH* 52 [December 2006]: 344–72).

70. Iver Bernstein, *The New York City Draft Riots: Their Significance for American Society and Politics in the Age of the Civil War* (OUP, 1990), 18–19.

71. Entry for July 14, 1863, in Hammond, ed., *Diary of a Union Lady*, 246–48.

72. Cook, *Armies of the Streets*, 198; Man, "The Church and the New York Draft Riots of 1863," 33–34.

73. Jennifer L. Weber, *Copperheads: The Rise and Fall of Lincoln's Opponents in the North* (OUP, 2006), 111.

74. O'Connor, *Boston Catholics*, 110–11

12. 1863: THE WAR IN THE WEST

1. Ochs, *A Black Patriot and a White Priest,* 4.

2. McPherson, *Battle Cry of Freedom,* 629–30.

3. Keating, *Shades of Green,* 109.

4. Heineman, *Civil War Dynasty,* 181.

5. William A. Drenna, Diary of the Defense of Vicksburg from May 30 to July 4, 1863, vol. 2, in Mississippi State Archives, cited in Pillar, *Catholic Church in Mississippi,* 288.

6. Faherty, *Exile in Erin,* 111.

7. Tucker, *Father John B. Bannon,* 146.

8. Tucker, *Father John B. Bannon,* 147–48.

9. Tucker, *Father John B. Bannon,* 149.

10. Swan, *Chicago's Irish Legion,* 64–70.

11. John Miller, "From Professor to Civil War Hero," Emmitsburg Area Historical Society.

12. EES to WTS, Lancaster, July 8, 1863, Sherman Family Papers, UNDA.

13. Cahill to wife, New Orleans, July 10, July 14, 1863, in Keating, *Civil War Letters of Margaret and Thomas Cahill,* 171–72.

14. William Henry Elder, July 16, 1863, Civil War Diary (copy), Woodstock Library, Georgetown University.

15. Elder Diary, July 21, 1863.

16. Elder Diary, July 20, 1863.

17. Elder Diary, July 22, July 28, July 30–31, 1863.

18. Elder Diary, August 4, 1863.

19. Elder to Spalding, Natchez, December 30, 1863, in Elder Letter Book 9: 58, cited in Pillar, *Catholic Church in Mississippi,* 273.

20. Elder Diary, October 2–29, 1863.

21. Anna Lynch to Patrick Lynch, Montgomery Springs, July 14, 1863, 14 T11, CDA.

22. Patrick Lynch to John McGill July 26, 1863, 29 H1, CDA.

23. Baptista Lynch to Patrick Lynch, Columbia, August 23, 1863, 14 W10, CDA.

24. Baptista Lynch to Patrick Lynch, Columbia, August 23, 1863, 14 W10, CDA; same to same, Columbia, September 4, 1863, 14 Y4, CDA.

25. Lamers, *Biography of General William S. Rosecrans,* 245.

26. Cooney to Very Rev. Dear Father [Sorin?], McMinnville, Tennessee, July 17, 1863, in McAvoy, ed., "War Letters of Father Peter Paul Cooney," 164.

27. Lamers, *Biography of General William S. Rosecrans,* 52–55.

28. Connolly to wife, Wartrace, TN, July 5, 1863, cited in Paul M. Angle, ed., *Three Years in the Army of the Cumberland: The Letters and Diary of Major James A. Connolly* (Bloomington: Indiana University Press, 1959), 100.

29. Entry for September 10, 1863, in Hammond, ed., *Diary of a Union Lady,* 253.

30. John Lynch to Patrick Lynch, Columbia, September 18, 1863, 15 A2, CDA.

31. Alexander Mendoza, *Confederate Struggle for Command: General James Longstreet and the First Corps in the West* (College Station: Texas A&M University Press, 2008), 46–48.

32. O'Connell to Purcell, Nashville, November 14, 1863, in Metz, *Sisters of Charity,* 45–46.

33. Lamers, *Biography of General William S. Rosecrans,* 402.

34. Connolly, Chattanooga, November 5, 1863, cited in Angle, ed., *Letters and Diary of Major James A. Connolly,* 135.

35. *OR,* ser. 1, vol. 30, pt. 4: 706.

36. Mendoza, *Confederate Struggle for Command,* 83.

37. Heineman, *Civil War Dynasty,* 204–5; James B. Swan, *Chicago's Irish Legion: The 90th Illinois Volunteers in the Civil War* (Carbondale: Southern Illinois University Press, 2009), 111.

38. Heineman, *Civil War Dynasty,* 206.

39. McPherson, *Battle Cry of Freedom,* 677–80.

40. Angle, ed., *Letters and Diary of Major James A. Connolly,* 156–58.

41. McDonough, *William Tecumseh* Sherman, 442–43.

42. McDonough, *William Tecumseh* Sherman, 443.

43. Gary W. Gallagher, ed., *Fighting For the Confederacy: The Personal Recollections of General Edward Porter Alexander* (UNCP, 1989), 327.

44. Longstreet to Lafayette McLaws, November 28, 1863, McLaws Papers, SHC, cited in Mendoza, *Confederate Struggle for Command,* 132–33.

45. Mendoza, *Confederate Struggle for Command,* 133–34.

46. McDonough, *William Tecumseh* Sherman, 447.

47. Heineman, *Civil War Dynasty,* 202.

13. DEFINING A NATION AMID AN UNENDING WAR

1. Williams, *P. G. T. Beauregard,* 167–68.

2. Williams, *P. G. T. Beauregard,* 176–77.

3. Williams, *P. G. T. Beauregard,* 188–89.

4. Lynch to McGill, Charleston, July 26, 1863, 29H1, CDA.

5. Williams, *P. G. T. Beauregard,* 192; Foreman, *Britain's Decisive Role in the American Civil War,* 513.

6. Williams, *P. G. T. Beauregard,* 196.

7. Lynch to Conseils Centraux de la Société de la Propagation de la Foi, Lyon, June 17, 1864, MPFL, F31, reel M10, AUND, in Heisser and White, *Patrick N. Lynch,* 86.

8. W. Chris Phelps, *The Bombardment of Charleston, 1863–1865* (Gretna, LA: Pelican Publishing Co., 2002).

9. Entry for August 28, 1863, in Beauchamp, ed., *Letters and Diaries of Madge Preston,* 73–74.

10. Gannon, *Life and Era of Augustus Verot,* 73–74, 83.

11. Patrick Lynch, Pastoral Prayers for Peace, Charleston, SC, November 26, 1863, 29Y7, CDA.

12. Peter Welsh to Margaret Welsh, Near Rapidan Station, September 25, 1863, in Kohl and Richards, eds., *Irish Green and Union Blue,* 126.

13. Patrick Guiney to Janet Guiney, Culpepper, September 28, 1863, in Samito, ed., *Civil War Letters of Colonel Patrick R. Guiney,* 223.

14. Patrick Guiney to Janet Guiney, New Baltimore, VA, October 21, 1863, in Samito, ed., *Civil War Letters of Colonel Patrick R. Guiney,* 228.

15. Patrick Guiney to Janet Guiney, Camp near Warrenton Junction, November 1, 1863, in Samito, ed., *Civil War Letters of Colonel Patrick R. Guiney,* 231.

16. Gannon, *Irish Rebels,* 215–16.

17. Edward Everett address at dedication of cemetery on Gettysburg battlefield, November 19, 1863, in Garry Wills, *Lincoln at Gettysburg* (S&S, 1992), 213–47.

18. Wills, *Lincoln at Gettysburg,* 145–46.

19. Rable, *Fredericksburg,* 129–30.

20. Harry S. Stout, *Upon the Altar of the Nation: A Moral History of the Civil War* (New York: Penguin Books, 2006), 269.

21. Entry for Thursday, November 19, 1863, in Beauchamp, ed., *Letters and Diaries of Madge Preston*, 82.

22. Entry for July 12, 1863, in Hammond, ed., *Diary of a Union Lady*, 244–45.

23. *NYH*, June 6, 1863.

24. *A Few Words on the Domestic Slavery in the Confederate States of America. By a Catholic Clergyman* [1864].

25. Entry for October 23, 1863, in Anderson, ed., "The Civil War Diary of John Abell Morgan," 45.

26. Endres, "Rectifying the Fatal Contrast," 30.

27. *PH*, December 2, December 16, 1863.

28. *PC*, February 13, April 30, 1864.

29. *PC*, January 2, 1864.

30. Ochs, *A Black Patriot and a White Priest*, 192.

31. Ochs, *A Black Patriot and a White Priest*, 200.

32. Ochs, *A Black Patriot and a White Priest*, 194.

33. Ochs, *A Black Patriot and a White Priest*, 208–9.

34. Kurtz, "Perfect Model of a Christian Hero," 91.

14. 1864: ROADS TO ATLANTA AND RICHMOND

1. Ernest B. Furgurson, *Not War But Murder: Cold Harbor 1864* (AAK, 2001), 294.

2. Entry for April 20–21, 1864, in Michael Bedout Chesson and Leslie Jean Roberts, eds., *Exile in Richmond: The Confederate Journal of Henri Garidel*, (UVP, 2001), 127–28.

3. Surgeons considered it a mortal wound, but Guiney insisted they operate. He miraculously survived to lead his regiment in parade in Boston five weeks later when the Ninth's three-year term of service expired.

4. Samito, ed., *Civil War Letters of Colonel Patrick R. Guiney*, 240–50.

5. Wert, *General James Longstreet*, 385.

6. Dawson, *Reminiscences of Confederate Service*, 116.

7. McPherson, *Battle Cry of Freedom*, 724–26.

8. Gannon, *Irish Rebels*, 230.

9. Mulholland, *Story of the 116th Regiment Pennsylvania Volunteers*, 186.

10. Jones, *Lee's Tigers*, 200.

11. Entry for May 8, 1864, in Hayes, ed., *Civil War Diary of Father James Sheeran*, 360–61.

12. Entry for May 6, 1864, in Chesson and Roberts, eds., *Confederate Journal of Henri Garidel*, 131.

13. Entry for May 8, 1864, in Chesson and Roberts, eds., *Confederate Journal of Henri Garidel*, 134.

14. Entry for May 9, 1864, in Chesson and Roberts, eds., *Confederate Journal of Henri Garidel*, 134–35.

15. Entry for May 10, 1864, in Chesson and Roberts, eds., *Confederate Journal of Henri Garidel*, 135.

16. Williams, *P. G. T. Beauregard*, 212–20.

17. Entry for May 17, 1864, in Chesson and Roberts, eds., *Confederate Journal of Henri Garidel*, 142.

18. MacNamara, *History of the Ninth Massachusetts*, 364.

19. Entry for May 10, 1864, in Hayes, ed., *Civil War Diary of Father James Sheeran*, 362.

20. Corby, *Memoirs of Chaplain Life*, 234.

21. Entry for May 12, 1864, in Anderson, ed., "The Civil War Diary of John Abell Morgan," 46.

22. Jones, *Lee's Tigers*, 207.

23. Entry for May 18, 1864, in Hayes, ed., *Civil War Diary of Father James Sheeran*, 364–65.

24. Hayes, ed., *Civil War Diary of Father James Sheeran*, 366.

25. Peter Welsh to Margaret Welsh, Washington, May 15, 1864, in Kohl and Richards, eds., *Irish Green and Union Blue*, 156–57.

26. MacNamara, *History of the Ninth Massachusetts*, 399.

27. Furgurson, *Cold Harbor 1864*, 137.

28. Furgurson, *Cold Harbor 1864*, 139–41.

29. Furgurson, *Cold Harbor 1864*, 141.

30. Thomas Shelley, *Fordham: A History of the Jesuit University of New York:1841–2003* (FUP, 2016), 92.

31. McMahon was one of three brothers, all Fordham alumni, who served in the Union forces.

32. Lonn, *Foreigners in the Union Army*, 482.

33. Furgurson, *Cold Harbor 1864*, 157.

34. Furgurson, *Cold Harbor 1864*, 164.

35. Furgurson, *Cold Harbor 1864*, 211.

36. Decades later, Martin received the Congressional Model of Honor for his bravery at Glendale (Shelley, *Fordham*, 92).

37. Williams, *P. G. T. Beauregard*, 226.

38. Williams, *P. G. T. Beauregard*, 228.

39. Williams, *P. G. T. Beauregard*, 230.

40. Williams, *P. G. T. Beauregard*, 231.

41. Williams, *P. G. T. Beauregard*, 232.

42. Foreman, *Britain's Decisive Role in the American Civil War*, 635.

43. Entry for June 24, 1864, in Chesson and Roberts, eds., *Confederate Journal of Henri Garidel*, 168.

44. Williams, *P. G. T. Beauregard*, 237.

45. Longyear Reminiscences, GULBFCSC.

46. Wiget to Beckx, Washington, July 22, 1864, *Md* 10-XXIII-I, ARSI.

47. O'Connell, *Tangled Lives of William Tecumseh Sherman*, 216–24.

48. B. J. Semmes to his sons, Dalton, GA, March 8, 1864, quoted in Anderson Humphries and Curt Guenther, *Semmes America* (Memphis, TN, 1989), 350.

49. McDonough, *William Tecumseh Sherman*, 476.

50. Marszalek, *Sherman*, 266.

51. Marszalek, *Sherman*, 268–69.

52. Connolly to wife, in the woods near Dallas, GA, May 28, 1864, in Angle, ed., *Letters and Diary of Major James A. Connolly*, 214.

53. Sherman, *Memoirs* 2: 531.

54. Swan, *Chicago's Irish Legion*, 151–54.

55. McAvoy, ed., "War Letters of Father Peter Paul Cooney," 227–28.

56. Quoted in O'Connell, *Tangled Lives of William Tecumseh Sherman,* 148.

15. CATHOLIC AGENTS AND THE INTERNATIONAL DIMENSIONS OF THE WAR

1. Don H. Doyle, *The Cause of All Nations: An International History of the American Civil War* (New York: Basic Books, 2015), 21.

2. Cited in Doyle, *International History of the American Civil War,* 85.

3. Kinley J. Brauer, "Gabriel Garcia y Tassara and the American Civil War: A Spanish Perspective, *CWH* 21 (1975): 11–12, cited in Doyle, *International History of the American Civil War,* 95.

4. Doyle, *International History of the American Civil War,* 92.

5. Doyle, *International History of the American Civil War,* 100–101.

6. Doyle, *International History of the American Civil War,* 108.

7. Doyle, *International History of the American Civil War,* 68–69.

8. Hughes to Seward, New York, November 1, 1862, in Kehoe, ed., *Complete Works of the Most Rev. John Hughes,* 540; Charles Patrick Connor, "The American Catholic Political Position at Mid-Century: Archbishop Hughes as a Test Case," PhD diss., Fordham University, 1979, 337–39.

9. Hughes to Barnabò, February 13, 1862, NYAA, cited in Connor, "The American Catholic Political Position at Mid-Century," 359–60.

10. Blied, *Catholics and the Civil War,* 84–85.

11. Doyle, *International History of the American Civil War,* 70.

12. Seward to Hughes, May 10, 1862, Seward MSS, University of Rochester Archives, cited in Connor, "The American Catholic Political Position at Mid-Century," 385.

13. Connor, "The American Catholic Political Position at Mid-Century," 382.

14. Hughes to Seward, May 10, 1862, Seward MSS, University of Rochester Archives, cited in Connor, "The American Catholic Political Position at Mid-Century," 385.

15. Horatio Perry to William Seward, July 21, 1862, NARA, cited in Murphy, "A Reevaluation of the Episcopacy of Michael Domenec," 72.

16. Kehoe, ed., *Complete Works of the Most Rev. John* Hughes, 540.

17. Kenrick to Timon, October 17, 1862, Kenrick Letterbook, AASMUS, in Wimmer, "American Catholic Interpretations of the Civil War," 152.

18. O'Connor, *Boston Catholics,* 108–9.

19. Foreman, *Britain's Decisive Role in the American Civil War,* 248.

20. Entry for June 24, 1862, Mallory Diary, SHC.

21. Foreman, *Britain's Decisive Role in the American Civil War,* 293–95.

22. Foreman, *Britain's Decisive Role in the American Civil War,* 330.

23. Orestes Brownson, *The American Republic* (New York: 1865), 215.

24. Thomas Wiltberger Evans, *Memoirs of Dr. Thomas W. Evans: The Second French Empire,* ed. Edward A. Crane (New York: D. Appleton, 1905), 118–19, cited in Doyle, *International History of the American Civil War,* 160.

25. Doyle, *International History of the American Civil War,* 164–66.

26. Doyle, *International History of the American Civil War,* 186.

27. Bayly Ellen Marks and Mark Norton Schatz, eds., *Between North and South: A Maryland Journalist Views the Civil War: The Narrative of William Wilkins Glenn 1861–1869* (Rutherford, NJ: Fairleigh Dickinson University Press, 1976), 121–22.

28. Foreman, *Britain's Decisive Role in the American Civil War,* 582–83.

29. Blackman, *Wild Rose,* 291.

30. Foreman, *Britain's Decisive Role in the American Civil War,* 620.

31. Doyle, *International History of the American Civil War,* 213–14.

32. Foreman, *Britain's Decisive Role in the American Civil War,* 686.

33. Blackman, *Wild Rose,* 301.

34. Chesnut, November 6, 1864, in C. Vann Woodward, *Mary Chesnut's Civil War* (YUP, 1981), 664.

35. Charles P. Cullop, "An Unequal Duel: Union Recruiting in Ireland, 1863–1864," *CWH* 13 (June 1967): 1–2.

36. Faherty, *Exile in Erin,* 129.

37. Faherty, *Exile in Erin,* 131.

38. Bannon to Benjamin, March 9, 1864, in *Picket Papers,* no. 6, cited in Faherty, *Exile in Erin,*134.

39. Faherty, *Exile in Erin,* 134.

40. Tucker, *Father John B. Bannon,* 177.

41. David J Alvarez, "The Papacy in the Diplomacy of the American Civil War," *CHR* 69 (April 1983): 228–29.

42. Alvarez, "The Papacy in the Diplomacy of the American Civil War," 235–36.

43. Alvarez, "The Papacy in the Diplomacy of the American Civil War," 237–38.

44. Anthony B. Lalli, SX, and Thomas H. O'Connor, "Roman Views on the American Civil War," *CHR* 57 (April 1971): 21–41.

45. Doyle, *International History of the American Civil War,* 205–6.

46. Heisser and White, *Patrick N. Lynch,* 98.

47. Doyle, *International History of the American Civil War,* 206–11.

48. Patrick N. Lynch, Memorandum on Roman Mission, July 13, 1864, Lynch Collection, box "CSA-Vatican," CDA.

49. Patrick Lynch to Baptista Lynch, St. George's, Bermuda, April 15, 1864, AUSL.

50. Patrick Lynch to Judah Benjamin, Paris, June 20, 1864, Patrick Lynch Papers, photostat, CDA.

51. Patrick Lynch to Judah Benjamin, Rome, July 5, 1864, unclassified Lynch Papers, CDA.

52. François zu Sayn-Wittgenstein-Berleburg was of the Catholic German nobility (Heisser and White, *Patrick N. Lynch,* 116).

53. In her 1863 work, *My Imprisonment,* Rose O'Neal Greenhow had written: "Two races— one civilized, the other barbarous— . . . Only by the bonding of the barbaric race in perpetual slavery has the South flourished as a civilization. Destroy that institution and race war will surely ensue, with the sure extermination of the 'barbarians'" (349–52).

54. Binsse to Alessandro Barnabò, New York, September 18, 1863, *Scritture,* 1864–65, vol. 20, folios 213r–214rv, APF; Binsse to Barnabò, New York, January 5, 1864, *Scritture,* 1864–65, vol. 20, folios 503rev–506rv, APF.

55. Gatti, Minerva, November 25, 1864, *Scritture,* 1864–65, vol. 20, folios 1199r–1205v, APF. See Curran, *Shaping American Catholicism,* 106–10.

16. SHERMAN, EWING, AND SHERIDAN SAVE LINCOLN

1. Foreman, *Britain's Decisive Role in the American Civil War,* 374.

2. Spencer, *Raphael Semmes,* 141–57.

3. Foreman, *Britain's Decisive Role in the American Civil War,* 623.

4. *Tablet,* May 4, 1861, cited in George Rable, *Almost Chosen People,* 65.

5. Mark E. Neely Jr., *The Fate of Liberty: Abraham Lincoln and Civil Liberties* (OUP, 1991), 77.

6. Harold Hyman, *A More Perfect Union: The Impact of the Civil War and Reconstruction on the Constitution* (HMC, 1975); Eric Foner, "The Civil War in 'Postracial' America," *Nation,* October 10, 2011, 24.

7. Weber, *Copperheads,* 20.

8. *Ex Parte Milligan* (1861), 148–53, cited in Jonathan A. White, *Abraham Lincoln and Treason in the Civil War: The Trials of John Merryman* (LSUP, 2011), 31–32; Neely, *Abraham Lincoln and Civil Liberties,* 83–89.

9. Neely, *Abraham Lincoln and Civil Liberties,* 16.

10. Thomas S. Barclay, "The Test Oath for Clergy in Missouri," *MHR* 18 (April 1924): 349.

11. Kenrick to Spalding, St. Louis, August 30, 1865, 34M15, AASMUS.

12. Elder Diary, April 12, 1864.

13. Elder Diary, June 25, 1864.

14. Elder to Spalding, Natchez, July 22, 1864, 33T5, AASMUS; *CM,* September 10, 1864.

15. *CM,* August 20, 1864.

16. Special Order of Brig. General. M. Brayman, Natchez, August 23, 1864, in Elder Diary, appendix.

17. *Pilot,* June 25, 1864, cited in O'Connor, *Civil War Boston,* 202.

18. *CM,* July 9, 1864.

19. Spann, *Gotham at War,* 168.

20. Weber, *Copperheads,* 10.

21. Stephen E Towne, *Surveillance and Spies in the Civil War: Exposing Confederate Conspiracies in America's Heartland* (Athens: Ohio University Press, 2015), 5.

22. Towne, *Surveillance and Spies in the Civil War,* 186.

23. Towne, *Surveillance and Spies in the Civil War,* 228.

24. Towne, *Surveillance and Spies in the Civil War,* 243–48.

25. Towne, *Surveillance and Spies in the Civil War,* 248–53.

26. Weber, *Copperheads,* 124–29.

27. Curran, *Dooley's Civil War,* 300.

28. See Tidwell, *Confederate Secret Service,* 18.

29. Thomas Henry Hines, "Autographic Notes on the Northwestern Conspiracy," Canada West, March 14, 1865, Thomas Hanes Papers, box 2, folder 17, Special Collections Research Center, University of Kentucky.

30. James D. Horan, *Confederate Agent: A Discovery in History* (New York: Crown Publishers, 1954), 125–38.

31. Phil Leigh, 'Who Burned Atlanta," *NYT,* November 14, 2014, opinionator.blogs.nytimes.com/2014/11/13/who-burned-atlanta/?

32. B. J. Semmes to Iorantha Semmes, Atlanta, August 21, 1864, in *Semmes America,* 355.

33. McDonough, *William Tecumseh Sherman,* 547.

34. B. J. Semmes to Iorantha Semmes, Barnesville, September 4, 1864, in *Semmes America,* 356.

35. Entry for September 3, 1864, Jonesboro, GA, in Angle, ed., *Letters and Diary of Major James A. Connolly,* 256–57.

36. O'Connell, *Tangled Lives of William Tecumseh Sherman,* 143–44.

37. Henry Halleck to Sherman, September 16, 1864, in *OR*, ser. 1, vol. 38, pt. 5: 856, cited in O'Connell, *Tangled Lives of William Tecumseh Sherman*, 149.

38. Connolly, Tuesday, November 15, in Angle, ed., *Letters and Diary of Major James A. Connolly*, 301–2.

39. Heineman, *Civil War Dynasty*, 232–40.

40. Cooling, "Defending Washington," 211–20. Nearly 560 buildings, including one church, were burned in this heavily German town (Keller, *Chancellorsville*, 300–301).

41. Joseph Wheelan, *Terrible Swift Sword: The Life of General Philip W. Sheridan* (Cambridge, MA: Da Capo Press, 2012), 1–99.

42. Wheelan, *Life of General Philip W. Sheridan*, 112–14.

43. McPherson, *Battle Cry of Freedom*, 777.

44. Grant Papers 12: 192–93, in Wheelan, *Life of General Philip W. Sheridan*, 117.

45. Wheelan, *Life of General Philip W. Sheridan*, 141–54.

46. *Pilot,* September 10, 1864, cited in Bruce, *The Harp and the Eagle*, 223.

47. Heineman, *Civil War Dynasty*, 44–54.

48. Hugh Ewing to Henrietta Ewing, June 25, 2862; August 10, 1862, Hugh Ewing Papers, box 2, Ohio Historical Society, cited in Heineman, *Civil War Dynasty*, 145–46.

49. EES to WTS, Lancaster, April 23, 1862, Sherman Family Papers, UNDA.

50. Doyle, *International History of the American Civil War*, 222.

51. Spann, *Gotham at War*, 170–71.

52. Daly, September 11, 1864, in Hammond, ed., *Diary of a Union Lady*, 302.

53. Kurtz, *Excommunicated from the Union*, 122.

54. O'Connor, *Civil War Boston*, 215.

55. *MR,* October 15, 1864.

56. *MR,* November 5, 1864.

57. Daly, October 30, 1864, in Hammond, ed., *Diary of a Union Lady*, 306.

58. Daly, November 7, 1864, in Hammond, ed., *Diary of a Union Lady*, 311.

59. Kwitchen, *James Alphonsus McMaster*, 141–42.

60. *FJ,* May 17, 1862.

61. *FJ,* February 21, 1863.

62. Joel H. Silbey, *A Respectable Minority: The Democratic Party in the Civil War Era, 1860–1868* (New York: WWN, 1977), 153–57.

63. Spann, *Gotham at War*, 73–75. Thanks to the heavy Catholic presence, a majority of New York Germans voted for McClellan (Lapham, "German-Americans of New York City," 213).

64. McKay, *Civil War and New York City*, 286.

65. Adam Arenson, *The Great Heart of the Republic: St. Louis and the Cultural Civil War* (HUP, 2011), 152.

66. Horan, *Confederate Agent*, 211.

67. Ron Soodalter, "The Plot to Burn New York City," *New York Times*, November 5, 2014, opinionator.Blogs.nytimes.com/nytimes.com/2014/11/05/the-plot-to-burn-new-york-city.

68. Swan, *Chicago's Irish Legion*, 183.

69. Williams, *P. G. T. Beauregard*, 247–48.

70. Thigpen, "Catholic Lay Leadership in Savannah," 637.

71. WTS to EES, April 10, 1863, Sherman Family Papers, UNDA.

72. Connolly, December 18, 1864, in Angle, ed., *Letters and Diary of Major James A. Connolly*, 367.

17. FINAL CAMPAIGNS: FROM THE CAROLINAS TO APPOMATTOX

1. McGill to Spalding, Richmond, February 17, 1865, 35 G14, AASMUS.

2. Curran, *Dooley's Civil War,* 338

3. Spencer, *Raphael Semmes,* 181–82.

4. Durkin, *Stephen R. Mallory,* 336.

5. McPherson, *Battle Cry of Freedom,* 822–24.

6. Mallory Diary, 208.

7. James Longstreet, *From Manassas to Appomattox: Memoirs of the Civil War in America* (New York: Mallard Press, 1991), 583–84.

8. McPherson, *Battle Cry of Freedom,* 822–24.

9. Longstreet, *From Manassas to Appomattox,* 584.

10. Longstreet, *From Manassas to Appomattox,* 584.

11. Longstreet, *From Manassas to Appomattox,* 587.

12. Sherman to Grant, Pocotaligo, SC, January 29, 1865, quoted in *Memoirs* 2: 260.

13. Williams, *P. G. T. Beauregard,* 250–51.

14. Quoted in Swan, *Chicago's Irish Legion,* 204.

15. Annals of the Ursuline Convent, Columbia, SC, February 1865, AUSL.

16. Marion Brunson Lucas, *Sherman and the Burning of Columbia* (USCP, 2000), 165.

17. Williams, *P. G. T. Beauregard,* 251–52.

18. Antonia Lynch to Patrick Lynch, Mt. Carmel, April 9, 15 H11, CDA.

19. Heisser and White, *Patrick N. Lynch,* 128–29; David C. R. Heisser, "Bishop Lynch's People: Slaveholding by a South Carolina Prelate," *South Carolina Historical Magazine* 10 (July 2001): 260.

20. May Preston to Madge Preston, St. Joseph's, March 30, 1865, in Beauchamp, ed., *Letters and Diaries of Madge Preston,* 167–69.

21. Keating, *Shades of Green,* 180–81.

22. Heisser and White, *Patrick N. Lynch,* 131.

23. Marszalek, *Sherman,* 331–32.

24. Chesson and Roberts, eds., *Confederate Journal of Henri Garidel,* 353.

25. Loughborough, *Recollections of Margaret Cabell Brown Loughborough,* 85.

26. Loughborough, *Recollections of Margaret Cabell Brown Loughborough,* 86–89.

27. John McGill, *Our Faith, the Victory: Or a Comprehensive View of the Principal Doctrines of the Christian Religion* (Baltimore: Kelly & Piet, 1865), 429–30.

28. Entry for March 27, 1865, in Curran, *Dooley's Civil War,* 345.

29. Curran, *Dooley's Civil War,* 342–48.

30. Noah Andre Trudeau, *Out of the Storm: The End of the Civil War, April–June 1865* (LSUP, 1994), 22–48.

31. Ruffner, *Maryland's Blue & Gray,* 143.

32. Trudeau, *End of the Civil War,* 49–56.

33. Jones, *Lee's Tigers,* 224.

34. McNeil, ed., *Balm of Hope,* 146–47.

35. Gache to Carrière, Charleston, July 18, 1865, in Buckley, ed., *War Letters of Pere Louis-Hippolyte Gache,* 222.

36. Bayliss, *Dooleys of Richmond,* 77.

37. Chesson and Roberts, eds., *Confederate Journal of Henri Garidel,* 366.

38. Entry for April 3, 1865, in Chesson and Roberts, eds., *Confederate Journal of Henri Garidel*, 367–68.

39. Entry for Tuesday, April 4, 1865, in Chesson and Roberts, eds., *Confederate Journal of Henri Garidel*, 370.

40. Loughborough, *Recollections of Margaret Cabell Brown Loughborough*, 60.

41. Entry for April 3, 1865, in Anderson, ed., "The Civil War Diary of John Abell Morgan," 46.

42. Entry for April 6, 1865, in Anderson, ed., "The Civil War Diary of John Abell Morgan," 47.

43. Entry for April 3, 1865, in Beauchamp, ed., *Letters and Diaries of Madge Preston*, 169.

44. Entry for April 6, 1865, in Beauchamp, ed., *Letters and Diaries of Madge Preston*, 170.

45. Antonia Lynch to Patrick Lynch, April 9, 1865, 15 H11, CDA.

46. Mulholland, *Story of the 116th Regiment Pennsylvania Volunteers*, 342.

47. Jones, *Lee's Tigers*, 225–27; Gannon, *Irish Rebels*, 299.

48. Spann, "Union Green," 209.

49. Ruffner, *Maryland's Blue & Gray*, 210.

50. Entry for April 9, 1865, in Chesson and Roberts, eds., *Confederate Journal of Henri Garidel*, 375.

51. Entry for April 12, 1865, in Chesson and Roberts, eds., *Confederate Journal of Henri Garidel*, 377.

52. Entry for April 16, 1865, in Chesson and Roberts, eds., *Confederate Journal of Henri Garidel*, 379.

53. Hammond, ed., *Diary of a Union Lady*, 349–52.

18. ASSASSINATION AND WAR'S END

1. Daly, April 15, April 19, 1865, in Hammond, ed., *Diary of a Union Lady*, 353–54.

2. Tidwell, *Confederate Secret Service*, 27.

3. Edward Steers Jr., *Blood on the Moon: The Assassination of Abraham Lincoln* (UPK, 2001), 41.

4. Bertram Wyatt-Brown, "Honor and Theater: Booth, the Lincoln Conspirators, and the Maryland Connection," *MHM* 104 (Fall 2009): 312, 320.

5. Terry Alford, *Fortune's Fool: The Life of John Wilkes Booth* (OUP, 2015), 166–81.

6. Edward Steers Jr. *The Trial: The Assassination of President Lincoln and the Trial of the Conspirators* (UPK, 2003), xx.

7. Kline, *Baltimore Plot*, 383–84.

8. Tidwell, *Confederate Secret Service*, 6–7.

9. Steers, *The Lincoln Assassination Encyclopedia* (New York: Harper, 2010), 125.

10. Henry Lowe Mudd, Samuel's father, had a plantation of over seventeen hundred acres worked by nearly ninety enslaved persons. His son owned five slaves (Slave Schedule, Census of 1860, Bryantown, Charles County, MD, 55); William Queen owned nineteen slaves (Slave Schedule, Census of 1860, Allens Fresh, Charles Country, MD, 13).

11. Robert Emmett Curran, *A History of Georgetown University, 1789–1989* (Washington, DC: Georgetown University Press, 2010), vol. 1: 411n78; Steers, *Lincoln Assassination Encyclopedia*, 451–52; Tidwell, *Confederate Secret Service*, 334–35.

12. Curran, *History of Georgetown University* 1: 225; Steers, *Lincoln Assassination Encyclopedia*, 385–90.

13. Alford, *Life of John Wilkes Booth*, 192.

14. Alford, *Life of John Wilkes Booth*, 200; interview of Harbin by George Alfred Townsend, 1885, cited in Tidwell, *Confederate Secret Service*, 337.

15. Steers, *Lincoln Assassination Encyclopedia*, 264–65; Louis Weichmann, *A True History of the Assassination of Abraham Lincoln and of the Conspiracy of 1865*, ed. Floyd E. Risvold (New York: Vintage Books, 1977), 68–69.

16. Kate Clifford Larson, *The Assassin's Accomplice: Mary Surratt and the Plot to Kill Abraham Lincoln* (New York: Basic Books, 2008), 21.

17. Larson, *Assassin's Accomplice*, 11–12.

18. Alfred Isacsson, "John Surratt and the Lincoln Assassination Plot," *MHM* 52 (1957): 317; Weichmann, *True History of the Assassination*, 14.

19. Larson, *Assassin's Accomplice*, 33.

20. Weichmann, *True History of the Assassination*, 14–26.

21. Weichmann, *True History of the Assassination*, 34.

22. Steers, *Assassination of Abraham Lincoln*, 82–84.

23. Alford, *Life of John Wilkes Booth*, 238–39.

24. Alford, *Life of John Wilkes Booth*, 257.

25. Tidwell, *Confederate Secret Service*, 421.

26. Larson, *Assassin's Accomplice*, 70–71.

27. Weichmann was a Baltimore native who grew up in Philadelphia, where there was considerable feeling for secession and the Confederacy, particularly among Catholics. He was destined to do his work as a priest in Richmond. When he left the seminary, he did not return to Philadelphia, but remained in Maryland, then took a position in a Catholic school in the District of Columbia whose pastor was a known Confederate sympathizer. In Washington, he linked up with John Surratt and then seized the opportunity to become a clerk in the bureau of the War Department that dealt with prisoners. This at a time when the Confederacy was pursuing serious plans to liberate its captured soldiers from Union prisons. Then Weichmann accepted John Surratt's invitation to room with him at his family's boardinghouse on H Street, yet claimed to be largely oblivious to what was going on around him. Such circumstantial evidence suggests that Weichmann may well have been aware of, if not involved in, the plot to kidnap Lincoln, long before he, for whatever reason, began expressing his concerns to others.

28. Larson, *Assassin's Accomplice*, 84.

29. Weichmann, *True History of the Assassination*, 170–72.

30. Steers, *Assassination of Abraham Lincoln*, 158.

31. Alford, *Life of John Wilkes Booth*, 289.

32. Tidwell, *Confederate Secret Service*, 468–69.

33. Tidwell, *Confederate Secret Service*, 475–76.

34. Entry for April 16, 1865, in Beauchamp, ed., *Letters and Diaries of Madge Preston*, 174.

35. Entry for April 17–19, 1865, in Beauchamp, ed., *Letters and Diaries of Madge Preston*, 174–75.

36. Antonia Lynch, April 20, 1865, 15 H12, CDA.

37. Entry for April 26, 1865, in Anderson, ed., "The Civil War Diary of John Abell Morgan," 47.

38. Hayes, ed., *Civil War Diary of Father James Sheeran*, 554.

39. Klausmeyer, April 28, 1865, in Kamphoefner, "German-Americans and Civil War Politics," 239–45.

40. Entry for April 19, 1865, in Hammond, ed., *Diary of a Union Lady*, 354–56.

41. Spencer, *Raphael Semmes*, 187.

42. Mallory Diary, April 1865.

43. McMaster, *FJ*, April 22, 1865.

44. George, "A Catholic Family Newspaper," 128.

45. *BP*, April 22, 1865.

46. *CM*, April 22, 1865.

47. *PC*, April 22, 1865.

48. John Gilmary Shea, ed., *The Lincoln Memorial: A Record of the Life, Assassination, and Obsequies of the Martyred President* (New York: Bunce and Huntington, 1865), 100–101.

49. "Circular of the Most Rev. Archbishop of Baltimore on the Assassination," Spalding Papers, AASMUS.

50. Hardie to Spalding, Washington, April 16, 1865, 34D10, ASSMUS.

51. Hardie to Spalding, Washington, April 1865, 34D11, ASSMUS.

52. Entry for May 19, 1865, in Anderson, ed., "The Civil War Diary of John Abell Morgan," 47.

53. Entry for May 16, 1865, Spalding Journal, AASMUS.

54. *CM*, May 20, 1865.

55. Weichmann, *True History of the Assassination*, 229.

56. Mary Clare Mudd, Samuel's younger sister, had been at Georgetown Visitation with Ellen Ewing. It was but one of the relationships between the Mudd and Ewing families encompassing Maryland, the District, and Ohio. Samuel's wife, Sara Francis, reached out to Tom Ewing to defend her husband. Ewing subsequently represented three of the defendants, Samuel Arnold, Ned Spangler, and Mudd.

57. Joan L. Chaconas, "John H. Surratt Jr.," in Steers, *Assassination of President Lincoln and the Trial*, lxiv.

58. Louis Weichmann's testimony proved especially damning in convicting Mary Surratt.

59. Larson, *Assassin's Accomplice*, 116.

60. Hardin to Spalding, Washington, July 22, 1865, 34D14, AASMUS.

61. Larson, *Assassin's Accomplice*, iii–xiv.

62. Larson, *Assassin's Accomplice*, 199.

63. Larson, *Assassin's Accomplice*, 212–13.

64. Larson, *Assassin's Accomplice*, 217–19.

65. Shea, *Lincoln Memorial*, 55–58.

66. Doyle, *International History of the American Civil War*, 236.

67. Wheelan, *Life of General Philip W. Sheridan*, 214–16.

68. Doyle, *International History of the American Civil War*, 236–39.

69. Lynch to William Seward, June 24, 1865, copy, 34 U4, AASMUS.

70. June 8, 1865, cited in Lipscomb, "Administration of John Quinlan," 37.

71. Patrick Lynch to Martin Spalding, Rome, May, 1865, 34U3, AASMUS; Jacob Walter to Martin Spalding, Washington, June 9, 1865, 36K5, AASMUS; same to same, Washington, June 26, 1865, 36K7, AASMUS; Patrick Lynch to Martin Spalding, Lyons, October 7, 1865, 34U7, AASMUS.

72. Heisser, *Patrick N. Lynch*, 139–41.

73. Brownson, *American Republic*, 31–32.

74. Brownson, *American Republic*, 41.

75. Brownson, *American Republic*, 29.

19. THE FAILURE OF SELF-RECONSTRUCTION

1. Mulholland, *Story of the 116th Regiment Pennsylvania Volunteers,* 400.

2. Kurtz, *Excommunicated from the Union,* 146.

3. The first public condemnation of slavery came in Pope Leo XIII's 1890 encyclical, *Catholicae Ecclesiae.*

4. *CM,* May 24, 1865.

5. Quoted in Killoren, *De Smet and the Indian Tragedy,* 235.

6. Mallory to Seward, September 27, 1865, in Mallory Letters, SHC.

7. *CM,* May 27, 1865.

8. A. M. Keiley, *In Vinculis; or The Prisoner of War, Being the Experience of a Rebel in the Federal Pens* (New York: Blelock & Co., 1866), 210–11.

9. *CT,* May 2, 1865, cited in *CM,* August 12, 1865.

10. *PC,* January 6, 1866.

11. Brownson, *American Republic,* 202–3.

12. "Southern Correspondent," *CM,* May 13, 1865.

13. Hyacinth to family, Presentation, September 15, 1865, in Sr. Dorothea Olga McCants, DC, trans. and ed., *They Came to Louisiana: Letters of a Catholic Mission, 1854–1882* (LSUP, 1970), 176–77.

14. Patrick Lynch to [Charles G. Schwartz], Rome, September 1865, unclassified Lynch Papers, CDA.

15. McCloskey to Spalding, New York, January 16, 1866, 35 E7, Spalding Papers, AASMUS.

16. Heisser, *Patrick N. Lynch,* 144.

17. Robert W. Schoeberlein, "Maryland's Women at War," *in* Mitchell and Baker, eds., *The Civil War in Maryland Reconsidered,* 280–84.

18. Bayliss, *Dooleys of Richmond,* 83–86.

19. John Lynch to Patrick Lynch, September 24, 1866, 15 T10, CDA.

20. Francis Lynch to Patrick Lynch, Cheraw, January 7, January 26, 1866, 15 M3, 15 M10, CDA.

21. Baptista Lynch to Patrick Lynch, Valle Crucis near Columbia, SC, January 8, 1866, 15 M4, CDA.

22. Mary Spann to Patrick Lynch, Washington Cty., January 29, 1866, 15 N1, CDA.

23. Mary Spann to Patrick Lynch, Washington Cty., December 14, 1866, 15 W7, CDA.

24. Charles Vincent, *Black Legislators in Louisiana during Reconstruction* (LSUP, 1976), 22–24; Eric Foner, *Reconstruction: America's Unfinished Revolution, 1863–1871* (New York: Harper & Row, 1988), 63–64

25. James G. Hollandsworth, *An Absolute Massacre: The New Orleans Race Riot of July 20* (LSUP, 2001), 21–22.

26. Ochs, *A Black Patriot and a White Priest,* 190; Ted Tunnell, *Crucible of Reconstruction: War, Radicalism, and Race in Louisiana, 1862–1877* (LSUP, 1984), 65.

27. Tunnell, *Crucible of Reconstruction,* 66–67.

28. Tunnell, *Crucible of Reconstruction,* 80.

29. Foner, *Reconstruction,* 62–66.

30. Tunnell, *Crucible of Reconstruction,* 81.

31. Ochs, *A Black Patriot and a White Priest,* 234.

32. William S. McFeely, *Yankee Stepfather: O. O. Howard and the Freedmen* (New York: WWN, 1970), 18.

33. Randall Miller, "The Freedmen's Bureau and Reconstruction: An Overview," in Paul A. Cimbala and Miller, eds., *The Freedmen's Bureau and Reconstruction: Reconsiderations* (FUP, 1999), xxi.

34. The Southern Homestead Act of 1866, which opened up for settlement 46 million acres of public land in five southern states, with freedmen and Union veterans given first claim to 80 acres, benefited relatively few of the former, about 1,000, despite efforts of bureau officials to assist Blacks in taking advantage of the act (Miller, "The Freedmen's Bureau and Reconstruction," xxiv; Michael L. Lanza, "'One of the Most Appreciated Labors of the Bureau': The Freedmen's Bureau and the Southern Homestead Act," in Cimbala and Miller, eds., *Freedmen's Bureau and Reconstruction,* 67–86; McFeely, *Yankee Stepfather,* 114.

35. Foner, *Reconstruction,* 164.

36. McFeely, *Yankee Stepfather,* 140.

37. Richard Paul Fuke, *Imperfect Equality: African Americans and the Confines of White Racial Attitudes in Post-emancipation Maryland* (FUP, 1999), 24.

38. Fuke, *African Americans and the Confines of White Racial Attitudes in Post-emancipation Maryland,* 35, 46–52.

39. Foner, *Reconstruction,* 177.

40. Foner, *Reconstruction,* 180–81.

41. Baptista Lynch to Patrick Lynch, Columbia, July 17, 1865, unclassified Lynch Papers, CDA.

42. Richard C. Madden, *Catholics in South Carolina: A Record* (Lanham, MD: University Press of America, 1985), 116.

43. Foner, *Reconstruction,* 186–93.

44. Dan T. Carter, *When the War Was Over: The Failure of Self-Reconstruction in the South, 1865–1867* (LSUP, 1985), 223.

45. *CM,* October 21, 1865.

46. Crouthamel, *James Gordon Bennett,* 144.

47. *PH,* January 27, 1866.

48. G. Ward Hubbs, "Introduction: An Unfinished War," in Cimbala and Miller, *Reconstruction as America's Continuing Civil War,* 8.

49. Foner, *Reconstruction,* 228–40.

50. McGill to Barnabò, Richmond, n.d., APF, SCAmerCent,21,42r-44rv, cited in Gerald P. Fogarty, SJ, *Commonwealth Catholicism: A History of the Catholic Church in Virginia* (UNDP, 2001), 195.

51. *FJ,* December 30, 1865.

52. *FJ,* March 3, 1866.

53. *CM,* March 3, 1866.

54. McFeely, *Yankee Stepfather,* 271.

55. *CM,* April 14, 1866.

56. David Warren Bowe, *Andrew Johnson and the Negro* (UTP, 1989), 137, cited in Anderson, ed., "The Civil War Diary of John Abell Morgan," 147.

57. Foner, *Reconstruction,* 250–51.

58. Johnson quoted in *CM,* April 7, 1866.

59. Foner, *Reconstruction,* 257.

60. Fuke, *African Americans and the Confines of White Racial Attitudes in Post-emancipation Maryland,* 219–21.

61. Fuke, *African Americans and the Confines of White Racial Attitudes in Post-emancipation Maryland,* 207.

62. Fuke, *African Americans and the Confines of White Racial Attitudes in Post-emancipation Maryland,* 204–5.

63. David T. Gleeson, *Irish in the South: 1815–1877* (UNCP, 2001), 17.

64. Hollandsworth, *New Orleans Race Riot,* 73.

65. Hollandsworth, *New Orleans Race Riot,* 48.

66. Hollandsworth, *New Orleans Race Riot,* 109.

67. Hollandsworth, *New Orleans Race Riot,* 123.

68. Hollandsworth, *New Orleans Race Riot,* 126.

69. Tunnell, *Crucible of Reconstruction,* 104–6.

70. Wheelan, *Life of General Philip W. Sheridan,* 219.

71. Hollandsworth, *New Orleans Race Riot,* 144–45.

72. Joseph G. Dawson III, *Army Generals and Reconstruction: Louisiana, 1862–1877* (LSUP, 1982), 51.

73. Dawson, *Army Generals and Reconstruction,* 56–57.

74. Dawson, *Army Generals and Reconstruction,* 62.

75. Dawson, *Army Generals and Reconstruction,* 103.

76. *FJ,* August 18, August 25, 1866.

77. *FJ,* November 24, 1866.

78. *CM,* September 15, 1866.

79. *CT,* September 12, 1866.

80. *CT,* October 17, 1866.

81. Foner, *Reconstruction,* 268.

82. *CM,* December 2, 1865.

83. Entry for October 21, 1865, in Anderson, ed., "The Civil War Diary of John Abell Morgan," 48.

20. THE REMAKING OF THE SOUTH

1. *CM,* June 9, 1866, 4.

2. *CM,* April 21, 1866.

3. McGill to McCloskey, Richmond, June 14, 1869, cited in Spalding, *Martin John Spalding,* 274n158.

4. McMahon, *Global Dimensions of Irish Identity,* 170–73.

5. Gleeson, *The Green and the Gray,* 194.

6. Wert, *General James Longstreet,* 410–12.

7. *New Orleans Times,* June 8, 1867; Stephen Budiansky, *The Bloody Shirt: Terror After Appomattox* (New York: Viking, 2008), 149–56.

8. Gleeson, *The Green and the Gray,* 195.

9. Suzanne Krebsbach, "James Spencer and the Colored Catholic Congress Movement," *USCH* 35 (Winter 2017): 1–21.

10. Tunnell, *Crucible of Reconstruction,* 112–15.

11. Ochs, *A Black Patriot and a White Priest,* 233.

12. Vincent, *Black Legislators in Louisiana,* 58–66.

13. *CM,* August 10, 1867.

14. Heather Cox Richardson, *The Death of Reconstruction: Race, Labor, and Politics in the Post–Civil War North, 1865–1901* (HUP, 2001), 64.

15. Foner, *Reconstruction,* 314–15.

16. William Beverly Nash (1822–1888) had become a leader in upcountry Carolina in the postwar period. The literate Nash served in the state senate until 1877. He held various offices during that decade, including director of the state penitentiary, where John Lynch was the medical doctor (John Lynch to Conlaw Lynch, Columbia, April 19, 1868, 16 M3, CDA; Eric Foner, *Freedom's Lawmakers: A Directory of Black Officeholders during Reconstruction* (OUP, 1993), 158–59.

17. Tunnell, *Crucible of Reconstruction,* 107.

18. Vincent, *Black Legislators in Louisiana,* 58–66.

19. Tunnell, *Crucible of Reconstruction,* 116–26.

20. Tunnell, *Crucible of Reconstruction,* 134.

21. Foner, *Reconstruction,* 331–32.

22. Vincent, *Black Legislators in Louisiana,* appendix.

23. Foner, *Freedom's Lawmakers,* 242–44.

24. Vincent, *Black Legislators in Louisiana,* 98–111, 161, 176.

25. Vincent, *Black Legislators in Louisiana,* 71–80.

26. Odin to Spalding, New Orleans, March 6, 1868, 35 M8, AASMUS.

27. Quoted in Edward King, *The Great South,* ed. W. Magruder Drake and Robert R. Jones (LSUP, 1972), 32–33.

28. Tunnell, *Crucible of Reconstruction,* 160.

29. *Tribune,* January 29, 1869, cited in Tunnell, *Crucible of Reconstruction,* 163.

30. *CM,* March 23, 1867.

31. *CM,* April 27, 1867.

32. *CM,* November 2, 1867.

33. *CM,* December 7, 1867.

34. *CM,* December 21, 1867.

35. Richardson, *Death of Reconstruction,* 69.

36. *CM,* August 1, 1868.

37. "Letter from General Rosecrans to General Robert E. Lee," White Sulphur Springs, WV, August 26, 1868, *CM,* September 12, 1868.

38. "General Lee's Response," August 26, 1868, *CM,* September 12, 1868.

39. Michael B. Chesson, *Richmond After the War, 1865–1890* (Richmond: Virginia State Library, 1981), 65.

40. Gleeson, *Irish in the South,* 182.

41. Northrop to Gibbons, September 9, 1868, Gibbons Papers, 71 R1, AASMUS.

42. James K. Hogue, *Uncivil War: Five New Orleans Street Battles and the Rise and Fall of Radical Reconstruction* (LSUP, 2011), 67.

43. Tunnell, *Crucible of Reconstruction,* 155–56.

44. Foner, *Reconstruction,* 342–43.

45. "Reconstructing Loyalty: Love, Fear, and Power in the Postwar South," in Cimbala and Miller, *Reconstruction as America's Continuing Civil War,* 173–82.

46. P. G. T. Beauregard to P. N. Lynch, New Orleans, November 9, 1868, 45 N4, CDA.

47. Joseph P. O'Grady, "Anthony M. Keiley (1832–1905): Virginia's Catholic Politician," *CHR,* January 1868, 625–28.

48. Fogarty, *History of the Catholic Church in Virginia,* 204.

49. Fogarty, *History of the Catholic Church in Virginia,* 204.

50. Marszalek, *Sherman,* 425.

51. Hogue, *Uncivil War,* 72, 87.

52. Hogue, *Uncivil War,* 74.

53. Hogue, *Uncivil War,* 76–77.

54. Pastoral Letter, Savannah, November 11, 1868, in Gannon, *Life and Era of Augustus Verot,* 137.

55. Baptista Lynch to Patrick Lynch, Valle Crucis, February 15, 1868, 16 K1, CDA.

56. Henrietta Lynch to Patrick Lynch, Cheraw, January 2, 1868, 16 H1, CDA.

57. Francis Lynch, Cheraw, to Patrick Lynch, January 21, 1871, 17 R3, CDA.

58. Francis Lynch to Patrick Lynch, Cheraw, January 12, 1868, 16 H3, CDA.

59. John Lynch to Patrick Lynch, Columbia, November 2, 1867, 16 D10, CDA.

60. As John admitted to Patrick, Governor Scott had done more for him in adjusting to the new order than anyone else (John Lunch to Patrick Lynch, Columbia, August 31, 1872, 17 Y2, CDA).

61. Strickland, *Unequal Freedoms,* 178.

62. Daniel W Hollis, *University of South Carolina* (USCP, 1951–56), vol. 2: 44–79, cited in Foner, *Reconstruction,* 368.

63. John Lynch to Patrick Lynch, Columbia, July 16, 1874, 18 S1, CDA; same to same, August 15, 1874, 18 S9, CDA.

64. John Lynch, "Statement of the Situation, Sept. 1874," 18 T1, CDA.

65. John Lynch to Patrick Lynch, Columbia, November 2, 1874, 18 W3, CDA.

66. John Lynch to Patrick Lynch, Columbia, December 18, 1874, 18 W11, CDA.

67. John Lynch to Patrick Lynch, Columbia, October 8, 1873, 18 K3, CDA.

21. RECONSTRUCTIONS IN WEST AND NORTH

1. See Emma Teitelman, "The Properties of Capitalism: Industrial Enclosures in the South and the West after the Civil War," *JAH* 106 (March 2020): 879–900.

2. Francis Paul Prucha, *The Great Father: The United States Government and the American Indians* (Lincoln: University of Nebraska Press, 1984), 29–31.

3. Prucha, *United States Government and the American Indians,* 493.

4. Prucha, *United States Government and the American Indians,* 494–95.

5. Peter J. Rahill, *The Catholic Indian Missions and Grant's Peace Policy* (CUAP, 1953), 79–166, 517–18.

6. Killoren, *De Smet and the Indian Tragedy,* 338–40.

7. Heineman, *Civil War Dynasty,* 273.

8. Prucha, *United States Government and the American Indians,* 532.

9. Prucha, *United States Government and the American Indians,* 549–59.

10. Killoren, *De Smet and the Indian Tragedy,* 295.

11. Killoren, *De Smet and the Indian Tragedy,* 305–6.

12. Prucha, *United States Government and the American Indians,* 531.

13. Killoren, *De Smet and the Indian Tragedy,* 313.

14. Prucha, *United States Government and the American Indians,* 531.

15. Killoren, *De Smet and the Indian Tragedy,* 327.

16. Killoren, *De Smet and the Indian Tragedy,* 327.

17. Wheelan, *Life of General Philip W. Sheridan*, 252.

18. Wheelan, *Life of General Philip W. Sheridan*, 2.

19. O'Connell, *Tangled Lives of William Tecumseh Sherman*, 191–93.

20. Wheelan, *Life of General Philip W. Sheridan*, 275.

21. Wheelan, *Life of General Philip W. Sheridan*, 276.

22. Wheelan, *Life of General Philip W. Sheridan*, 276–78; McCaffrey, *The American Soldier in the Mexican War*, 3.

23. Wheelan, *Life of General Philip W. Sheridan*, 279.

24. Wheelan, *Life of General Philip W. Sheridan*, 279.

25. Fellman, *Citizen Sherman*, 260.

26. Goldfield, *How the Civil War Created a Nation*, 454.

27. Goldfield, *How the Civil War Created a Nation*, 306.

28. William E. Devlin, "Shrewd Irishmen: Irish Entrepreneurs and Artisans in New York's Clothing Industry, 1830–1880," in Bayor and Meagher, eds. *New York Irish*, 169–92.

29. Thomas J. Shelley, *The Archdiocese of New York: The Bicentennial History 1808–2008* (Strasbourg: Editions du Signe, 2007), 213.

30. Goldfield, *How the Civil War Created a Nation*, 307.

31. Brownson, *American Republic*, 383.

32. Samito, ed., *Commanding Boston's Irish Ninth*, 252–55.

33. James P. Rodechko, "An Irish-American Journalist and Catholicism: Patrick Ford of the Irish World," *Church History* 39 (December 1970): 527–30.

34. Gerteis, *Civil War St. Louis*, 259.

35. Palladino, *Another Civil War*, 122; Spann, *Gotham at War*, 150.

36. Goldfield, *How the Civil War Created a Nation*, 308.

37. Spann, *Gotham at War*, 154.

38. Clayton Sinyai, *Schools of Democracy: A Political History of the American Labor Movement* (Ithaca, NY: CUP, 2006), 18–21.

39. Spalding, *Martin John Spalding*, 250–51.

40. Spalding, *Martin John Spalding*, 252.

41. Wayne G. Broehl Jr., *The Molly Maguires* (New York: Vintage, 1968), 120.

42. Palladino, *Another Civil War*, 134.

43. Timothy G. Lynch, "'Erin's Hope,' The Fenian Brotherhood of New York City, 1856–1886," PhD diss., City University of New York, 2004, 18; Broehl, *Molly Maguires*, 11–15.

44. Broehl, *Molly Maguires*, 205–7.

45. Broehl, *Molly Maguires*, 247–87.

46. Broehl, *Molly Maguires*, 303.

47. Kevin Kenny, "Molly Maguires," in Glazier, *Encyclopedia of the Irish in America*, 624.

48. Glazier, *Encyclopedia of the Irish in America*, 765.

49. Sherry H. Olson, *Baltimore: The Building of an American City* (JHUP, 1980), 195–96.

50. Olson, *Baltimore*, 197.

51. Baptista Lynch to Patrick Lynch, Valle Crucis, July 24, 1877, 20 A9, CDA.

22. THE MAKING OF THE CATHOLIC GHETTO

1. David O'Brien, *Isaac Hecker: An American Catholic* (Mahwah, NJ: Paulist Press, 1992), 204–8.

2. Thomas Joseph Peterman, *The Cutting Edge: The Life of Andrew Thomas Becker* (Devon, PA, 1982), 70.

3. Gannon, *Life and Era of Augustus Verot*, 117.

4. *Annales* 25 (September 1865): 401–2, in Gannon, *Life and Era of Augustus Verot*, 117.

5. Gannon, *Life and Era of Augustus Verot*, 128–32.

6. Gannon, *Life and Era of Augustus Verot*, 132–33.

7. Spalding, *Martin John Spalding*, 111.

8. Diana Batts Morrow, "'Not only Superior, but a Mother in the true sense of the word': Mary Louisa Noel and the Oblate Sisters of Providence, 1835–1885," *USCH* 35 (Fall 2017): 38–39.

9. Robert L. Worden, "Soldiers of the Cross: Blessed Francis Xavier Seelos and the Catholic Community in Annapolis during the Civil War," unpublished manuscript, 531–32.

10. Worden, "Blessed Francis Xavier Seelos and the Catholic Community in Annapolis," 527–32.

11. Fortin, *History of the Archdiocese of Cincinnati*, 145; Lee J. Bennish, SJ, *Continuity and Change: Xavier University, 1831–1981* (Chicago: Loyola University Press, 1981), 70, 79.

12. Bryan Giemza, "Sisters of Secession: The Unclaimed Legacies of Two Southern American Irish Women," *ISR* 8 (May 2010): 199–211.

13. Curran, *Church and Confederacy*, 327–28.

14. Folly Island, one of the barrier isles off Charleston (Lynch to Spalding, Charleston, January 12, 1866, 34 U8, AASMUS).

15. "The Church in the United States," Miscellaneous Lynch Documents, CDA.

16. Heisser, *Patrick N. Lynch*, 157–61.

17. Baptismal and marriage registers of the church indicate that at least a third of the male parishioners had served in the military during the war (Ochs, *A Black Patriot and a White Priest*, 251).

18. Ochs, *A Black Patriot and a White Priest*, 253.

19. Ochs, *A Black Patriot and a White Priest*, 255–60.

20. Gannon, *Life and Era of Augustus Verot*, 142.

21. Davis, *History of Black Catholics in the United States*, 136.

22. Heisser, *Patrick N. Lynch*, 151.

23. "Pastoral Letter of 1866," in *National Pastorals*, ed. Guilday, 220.

24. "Pastoral Letter of 1852," in *National Pastorals*, ed. Guilday, 187.

25. Spalding, *Martin John Spalding*, 349–51.

26. Printed Circular, Spalding Papers, AASMUS.

27. Spalding, *Premier See*, 195.

28. Spalding, *Premier See*, 219.

29. Barbara J. Howe and Margaret A. Brennan, "The Sisters of St. Joseph in Wheeling, West Virginia, during the Civil War," *USCH* 31 (Winter 2013): 22; Anne M. Butler, *Across God's Frontiers: Catholic Sisters in the American West, 1850–1920* (UNCP, 2012), 1.

30. Steward and McGovern, *Fenians*, 217.

31. James P. Shannon, *Catholic Colonization on the Western Frontier* (YUP, 1957), 265–66; Aaron Abell, *American Catholicism and Social Action: A Search for Social Justice* (UNDP, 1963), 51.

32. Benjamin Justice, "Thomas Nast and the Public School of the 1870s," *History of Education Quarterly* 45 (Summer 2005): 171.

33. Pastoral Letter of 1866, in *National Pastorals*, ed. Guilday, 215.

34. Curran, *Shaping American Catholicism*, 215–19.

35. Michael David Cohen, *Reconstructing the Campus: Higher Education and the American Civil War* (UVP, 2012).

36. Gerald McKevitt, SJ, *The University of Santa Clara: A History, 1851–1977* (Palo Alto, CA: Stanford University Press, 1979), 55–106.

37. Varga, *Baltimore's Loyola*, 65, 79.

38. Thomas E. Blantz, CSC, *The University of Notre Dame: A History* (UNDP, 2020), 94–97.

39. "Shall We Have a Catholic Congress?" *Catholic World* 8 (November 1868): 224–28.

40. Mary David Cameron, SSND, *The College of Notre Dame of Maryland, 1895–1945* (1947); Paul H. Mattingly, *American Academic Cultures: A History of Higher Education* (UCP, 2017), 146; Mary J. Oates, *Pursuing Truth: How Gender Shaped Catholic Education at the College of Notre Dame* (CUP, 2021), 10–24.

41. James Hennesey, SJ, *The First Council of the Vatican: The American Experience* (New York: Herder & Herder, 1963), 10–17.

42. See Sandra Yocum Mize, "Defending Roman Loyalties and Republican Values: The 1848 Italian Revolution in American Catholic Apologetics," *Church History* 60 (December 1991): 480–92.

43. Keller to Peter Beckx, Baltimore, December 23, 1870, *Md* 10 II 14, ARSI.

44. Quoted in Hennesey, *First Council of the Vatican*, 24.

45. Hennesey, *First Council of the Vatican*, 101; Fortin, *History of the Archdiocese of Cincinnati*, 122.

46. Hennesey, *First Council of the Vatican*, 242.

47. Domenec to Tuigg, June 5, 1870, #1295, PDA, cited in Murphy, "A Reevaluation of the Episcopacy of Michael Domenec," 199.

48. Kenrick to Henry Muehlisepen, Rome, March 6, 1870, AAC, cited in Hennesey, *First Council of the Vatican*, 174.

49. Kenrick, *Concio in Concilio Vaticano habenda at non habita* (Naples, 1870, 40), cited in Hennesey, *First Council of the Vatican*, 247–48.

50. Hennesey, *First Council of the Vatican*, 280–81.

51. APF, Congressi 23, folios 1167r–1168v, in Spalding, *Martin John Spalding*, 327–28.

52. Thigpen, "Catholic Lay Leadership in Savannah," 397.

53. Burtsell Diary, vol. 3, January 25, 1867, AANY.

54. See Curran, *Shaping American Catholicism*, 159–80.

55. Luers to Spalding, March 30, 1870, 34-S-11, AASMUS, cited in Spalding, *Martin John Spalding*, 280.

56. Becker to Spalding, New York, June 7, 1870, 33 E6, AASMUS, cited in Peterman, *Life of Andrew Thomas Becker*, 223.

23. REDEMPTION

1. Lynch to Propagation of the Faith, 1873, UNDA microfilm, in Gleeson, *The Green and the Gray*, 199.

2. Michael Perman, *The Road to Redemption: Southern Politics, 1869–1879* (UNCP, 1984), 141.

3. Rubin, *A Shattered Nation: The Rise and Fall of the Confederacy, 1861–1868* (UNCP, 2005), 143–45.

4. *CM*, "The Registry Law," October 28, 1865; Jonathan W. White, "Achieving Emancipation in Maryland," in Mitchell and Baker, eds., *The Civil War in Maryland Reconsidered*, 240–41.

5. Foner, *Reconstruction*, 40–41.

6. Baker, *Politics of Continuity,* 181–82.

7. Richard R. Duncan, "The Era of the Civil War," in Richard Walsh and William Lloyd Fox, eds., *Maryland: A History, 1634–1974* (MHS, 1974), 388–91.

8. Baker, *Politics of Continuity,* 140.

9. Baker, *Politics of Continuity,* 192–93.

10. Crenson, *Baltimore,* 299.

11. *Nation,* June 25, 1868, cited in Silbey, *Democratic Party in the Civil War Era,* 230–31.

12. New York *Tribune,* October 19, 1865, quoted in Spann, *Gotham at War,* 200.

13. David W. Blight, *Race and Reunion: The Civil War in American Memory* (HUP, 2001), esp. chap. 8.

14. Williams, *P. G. T. Beauregard,* 320.

15. Autograph copy in Donald Robert Beagle and Bryan Albin Giemza, *Poet of the Lost Cause: A Life of Father Ryan* (UTP, 2008), 108.

16. "LINES RESPECTFULLY INSCRIBED TO THE LADIES MEMORIAL ASSOCIATION OF FRED-ERICKSBURG, VA.," Virginia Historical Society, cited in Rubin, *Shattered Nation,* 236.

17. Beagle and Giemza, *Poet of the Lost Cause,* 216.

18. *Banner of the South,* March 21, 1868, cited in Beagle and Giemza, *Poet of the Lost Cause,* 139.

19. Corey Brooks, "Sculpting Memories of the Slavery Conflict: Commemorating Roger Taney in Washington, D.C., Annapolis, and Baltimore, 1864–1887," *MHM,* Spring–Summer 2017, 6–35.

20. Gaines M. Foster, *Ghosts of the Confederacy: Defeat, the Lost Cause, and the Emergence of the New South* (LSUP, 1987), 41.

21. Savannah *Daily Morning News,* April 27, 1868, cited in Thigpen, "Catholic Lay Leadership in Savannah," 642.

22. Beauregard to Lee Crandall, June 21, 1873, published in *Alabama State Journal,* July 1, 1873, cited in Perman, *Road to Redemption,* 154.

23. Williams, *P. G. T. Beauregard,* 271.

24. Perman, *Road to Redemption,* 166.

25. Reprinted in the Lafayette *Advertiser* on September 13, 1873, cited in Dawson, *Army Generals and Reconstruction,* 152.

26. Nicholas Lemann, *Redemption: The Last Battle of the Civil War* (New York: Farrar, Straus and Giroux, 2006), 80.

27. Hogue, *Uncivil War,* 124–25.

28. Hogue, *Uncivil War,* 114.

29. Lemann, *Redemption,* 22.

30. Tunnell, *Crucible of Reconstruction,* 6.

31. Hogue, *Uncivil War,* 120–22.

32. Hogue, *Uncivil War,* 122–23.

33. *Daily Picayune,* June 10, 1874, cited in Dawson, *Army Generals and Reconstruction,* 157.

34. Hogue, *Uncivil War,* 128–30.

35. Chesson and Roberts, eds., *Confederate Journal of Henri Garidel,* 28.

36. Hogue, *Uncivil War,* 135.

37. Hogue, *Uncivil War,* 137–38.

38. Hogue, *Uncivil War,* 170–76.

39. *New Orleans Bulletin,* November 19, 1874, in Beagle and Giemza, *Poet of the Lost Cause,* 175.

40. Hogue, *Uncivil War,* 139.

41. Hogue, *Uncivil War,* 181.

42. Hogue, *Uncivil War,* 203–5.

43. Hogue, *Uncivil War,* 148–49; Dawson, *Army Generals and Reconstruction,* 207.

44. Upon having these statistics challenged, Sheridan adjusted the figure to 2,141 (Dawson, *Army Generals and Reconstruction,* 210). Stephen Budiansky estimates that more than 3,000 Blacks and their white allies lost their lives in the terror campaign that white southerners waged during Reconstruction against state governments they deemed as illicit as any government including ex-slaves could be (*Terror After Appomattox,* 7).

45. Wheelan, *Life of General Philip W. Sheridan,* 274–75; Sheridan to Grant, New Orleans, January 10, 1875, cited in Hogue, *Uncivil War,* 1–2.

46. Ochs, *A Black Patriot and a White Priest,* 263.

47. Dawson, *Army Generals and Reconstruction,* 148–57.

48. Richardson, *Death of Reconstruction,* 89–121.

49. Richardson, *Death of Reconstruction,* 10.

50. Richardson, *Death of Reconstruction,* 121.

51. Richardson, *Death of Reconstruction,* 90.

52. Perman, *Road to Redemption,* 145.

53. Perman, *Road to Redemption,* 150–51.

54. Foner, *Reconstruction,* 570.

55. Foner, *Reconstruction,* 570–71.

56. Budiansky, *Terror After Appomattox,* 247.

57. *News and Courier,* October 3, 1876, cited in Strickland, *Unequal Freedoms,* 278–79n162.

58. Strickland, *Unequal Freedoms,* 279.

59. Baptista Lynch to Patrick Lynch, Valle Crucis, November 2, 1876, 19 P8, CDA.

60. Baptista Lynch to Patrick Lynch, Valle Crucis, November 8, 1876, 19 P9, CDA.

61. Baptista Lynch to Patrick Lynch, Valle Crucis, November 17, 1876, 19 R1, CDA.

62. Hogue, *Uncivil War,* 164.

63. Hogue, *Uncivil War,* 166.

64. Hogue, *Uncivil War,* 166.

65. Dawson, *Army Generals and Reconstruction,* 254–55.

66. Gleeson, *Irish in the South,* 185.

67. Hogue, *Uncivil War,* 176.

EPILOGUE: CATHOLIC AND AMERICAN

1. Corby, *Memoirs of Chaplain Life,* 188–89.

2. John Fitzgerald Kennedy, *A Nation of Immigrants* (New York: Harper & Rowe, 1958); Thomas J. Archdeacon, *Becoming American: An Ethnic History* (New York: Free Press, 1983), 207.

3. Christopher White, "Major Catholic Funders Spearhead Voter Suppression Efforts," *National Catholic Reporter,* April 30–May 13, 2021, 1, 8.

AFTERMATHS

1. Williams, *P. G. T. Beauregard,* 292–93.

2. Anthony J. Kuzniewski, *Thy Honored Name: A History of the College of the Holy Cross, 1843–1994* (CUAP, 1999), 132.

3. Beauchamp, ed., *Letters and Diaries of Madge Preston,* 336.

4. Hayes, ed., *Civil War Diary of Father James Sheeran,* 4–5.

5. Wheelan, *Life of General Philip W. Sheridan,* 309.

6. Marszalek, *Sherman,* 492–98.

7. Andrew C. A. Jampolier, *The Last Lincoln Conspirator: John Surratt's Flight from the* Gallows (Annapolis: Naval Institute Press, 2008), 267–71.

INDEX